A Physician's Paraphrase

The New Testament

Robert Earl Bolton, MD

TEACH Services, Inc.
P U B L I S H I N G
www.TEACHServices.com • (800) 367-1844

Copyright © 2014 TEACH Services, Inc.
ISBN-13: 978-1-4796-0457-9 (Paperback)
ISBN-13: 978-1-4796-0458-6 (ePub)
ISBN-13: 978-1-4796-0459-3 (Mobi)
Library of Congress Control Number: 2015936318

Published by

TEACH Services, Inc.
PUBLISHING
www.TEACHServices.com • (800) 367-1844

Table of Contents

The Rest of the Story

Dr. Robert Earl Bolton was leading a Bible discussion group when I visited his class one Sabbath. I heard him read a well-known passage from Paul's letter to Timothy. The verses were familiar, but the wording was fresh and vigorous.

"Doc, I don't recognize the translation. What version is it from?" I asked.

"It's not a common paraphrase," he replied modestly and proceeded with his subject for the morning study.

When the group left, I lingered and asked, "Was that by any chance your own work?" He seemed a little embarrassed that his secret had been guessed. With downcast eyes he confessed in just one word, "Yes."

"Have you done Paul's entire letter to Timothy?" I pressed.

Again the modest one word answer: "Yes."

"Have you done any of Paul's other letters?" I probed.

"Yes," was all he said.

His short answers and unfeigned modesty made me suspect I hadn't yet gotten the rest of the story, so I phrased a question he could not answer in one word. "How much of the New Testament have you done?"

With a sheepish little smile he looked me right in the eye and said, "I cannot tell a lie. I've done it all."

"And the Old Testament?" I asked in wonderment.

Then he told me his story. One day in his quiet study time he was enjoying a passage of Scripture. He mused, "I wonder how the Bible writer would say that if he were writing to me today?" He mulled over each thought in the King James Version then picked up his pen and wrote out what that passage said to him. The adventure became a daily study habit he enjoyed for thirty years! He did not stop with the New Testament but went right on until he had completed all sixty-six books.

His son, Robert, is a computer analyst. He learned of his father's study habit when Dr. Bolton was working through Samuel. Computers and skills were in their infancy a third of a century ago, but with Robert's help and his father's persistence, the monumental task of taking a doctor's handwritten notes and converting them into a digital format was completed.

In the complex world where the primary physician is assailed by the pain of patients with the rapidity of machinegun fire—where medical scientists often disagree, where life threatening illnesses may elude sophisticated diagnostic tests, where loneliness and psychosomatic issues may destroy health, where often the physician must break the worst news to those bearing the most pain, where the best efforts may lead to hostility or litigation, where multiplicity of regulations absorb time from patient care—how does a human being maintain compassion and courage to keep on caring? Dr. Bolton's prescription: "Take a large dose of God's Word every day—more when the pressures increase."

His work is shared here with the prayer that it provides just the medication you need to thrive with whatever challenges you face in your world. This medication has been thoroughly tested in the real world of an active practice. It is intended to become habit forming. All side effects are beneficial. It has helped Dr. Bolton remain vigorous—still learning, teaching, driving, and thriving into his one hundredth year. May it do the same for you is his prayer.

Glenn Aufderhar
Project Manager
June 30, 2014

Benefits From This Book

The book you hold in your hands is no ordinary book. It is medication. Used as prescribed it will extend your life and add joy to your years. That is a promise made by the Creator of all life—the Master Physician who never saw a disease He could not cure, an injury He could not heal, or a sinner He did not love.

Like all prescriptions, it is of no value if not taken as directed. It comes with instructions for proper use and warnings about neglect or misuse. No other medication in the history of mankind has ever been so thoroughly tested and the results replicated and documented.

Rather than overwhelm you with mountains of statistics, let me share my personal story and why I believe it has played a major part in my enjoying life beyond my 100th birthday. To me, life is rich. I'm still happily maintaining my own home, trying new recipes, mowing my own lawn, gardening, and driving across the state alone to visit family and friends.

Genetics do not seem to adequately explain why I've survived. My mother died when she was sixty-nine. I've lived about three decades longer than most of my close relatives. To me, the best explanation is in Hebrews 4:12: "The Word of God is living and powerful, sharper than any surgeon's scalpel ... actually able to read the motives and thoughts." That means to me that if I am willing, the Master Surgeon is able to use His scalpel to excise the cancers of sin to which all mankind is exposed.

May I tell you how that worked for me? Many years ago I was reading a passage of Scripture during my daily devotional time. I had just completed the chapter and was impressed to write it out in my own words. When I finished, I read and reread the chapter! I liked it so well that I wrote out the following chapter. It too was a blessing to me.

From that time onward I received new blessings with every chapter I paraphrased. A few weeks later I finished putting the entire book of John into my own words. It was a blessed event. The Bible came to life. It was like the Holy Spirit was energizing my life, leading to practical applications to my daily needs.

So I continued the practice, and several months later I finished the entire New Testament. God's Word had become more and more precious to me. The next step was to do the Old Testament. It took several years, but I enjoyed it greatly.

What an experience!

It reminded me a bit of Jeremiah's statement, "Thy words were found and I did eat them." Or words that Jesus quoted from Moses, "Man shall not live by bread alone but by every word that comes from the mouth of God."

Maybe that's why society is malnourished and wracked with crime and pain—we as a people are missing key vitamins and trace minerals found only through God's Word.

Many times Jesus and the New Testament writers quote the Old Testament prophets and songwriters. It was a special joy to hunt for the original quotation and read it in context. (I've included those references.) It helped me better understand the whole process of God's effort to communicate His love for every one of us and His plan to save everyone who will take His saving antibiotic.

By now I suspect someone is asking, "But Doc, how should I use this book to get maximum benefit from it?"

You might try one of two methods to see which works best for you. The first we can call the Vitamin Approach. The second I call the LifeStyle Regimen. Both have several things in common. Start with a good dose of prayer. Ask for two things, insight to see what God wants you to know and willingness to do what His Scripture asks.

In the Vitamin Approach read looking for three specific things: Promises that bring courage and hope, principles that form the foundation of a life well-lived, and texts that reveal the source of power. As you find these gems, label them P1 for Promises, P2 for Principles, and P3 for Power. Periodically review those passages you have marked. Choose some to copy onto 3x5 index cards to carry with you to memorize in spare moments or to give you encouragement to meet the challenges you face throughout the day.

The LifeStyle Regimen begins with prayer just like the Vitamin Approach but has the following differences:

1. Its best to be at a table or desk where you can write in a spiral notebook and have access to recognized translations like the New King James Version, New American Standard Bible, Today's New International Version, Holman Christian Study Bible, or New Living Translation.

2. Read a chapter in one of the gospels in this paraphrase then read it in one of the recognized versions.

3. Write out verse by verse in your own words what that text means to you.

4. Do anything the passage suggests like practice healthy habits, forgive, share with the needy, be kind, truthful, honest—do whatever God's Spirit asks you to put into practice that day.

5. Thank Him for your discoveries in Scripture and ask for help to implement His requests until they become a habit.

6. Systematically continue on through the New Testament.

I cannot guarantee that you will live pain free for 110 years. But I can guarantee on the strength of God's Word, and from personal experience, that you will get to know God better "whom to know is life eternal." And I can guarantee that you will live longer and happier than you would have without feeding daily on God's Word.

Yours in His Grace,
Robert Earl Bolton, MD
December 26, 2014
Wenatchee, WA

Introduction

This book is unusual in the world of Christian literature, falling in that neglected niche between a true paraphrase and a personal testimony. It penetrates that unseen veil through which the Holy Spirit guides a busy country physician to write his own prescription to restore his personal energy and tranquility to continue the unending struggle against fatigue, disease, and pain.

Daily for more than thirty years Dr. Bolton took time to digest a passage from the King James Version and ask, "What does that say to me today?" In this volume he lets us look over his shoulder to see the New Testament as a source of coping with today's problems.

The book is laid out in typical chapter and verse style so you can compare his thoughts to your most loved translations.

Warning: All the side effects are positive and hopefully habit forming.

Matthew

Chapter 1

¹First let me record the genealogy of Jesus Christ, for it is important, fulfilling the prophetic writings as it does. You will remember that He is a descendent of both Abraham and David, so let us first trace the line beginning with Abraham.

²Abraham was the father of Isaac, Isaac fathered Jacob, and Jacob was the father of Judah as well as his brothers. ³Judah was father of Perez and Zerah through his daughter-in-law, Tamar. Perez fathered Hezron, and Hezron fathered Ram. ⁴Ram fathered Amminadab, and Amminadab fathered Nahshon, and Nahshon fathered Salmon. ⁵Salmon fathered Boaz through Rahab; Boaz fathered Obed through Ruth, and Obed was the father of Jesse. ⁶Jesse fathered David the king, and David was the father of Solomon through Bathsheba, who had been the wife of Uriah. ⁷Solomon's son was Rehoboam; Rehoboam was father of Abijah, and Abijah was father of Asa. ⁸Asa was father of Jehoshaphat; Jehoshaphat fathered Joram, and Joram fathered Uzziah. ⁹Uzziah's son was Jotham and his son was Ahaz. Ahaz fathered Hezekiah. ¹⁰Hezekiah was father of Manasseh. Manasseh was father of Amon, and Amon fathered Josiah. ¹¹Josiah fathered Jeconiah and his brothers about the time of the Babylonian captivity.

¹²During the captivity in Babylon, Jeconiah fathered Shealtiel, who was the father of Zerubbabel. ¹³Zerubbabel was father of Abiud, and Abiud was father of Eliakim. And Eliakim was father of Azor. ¹⁴Azor was father of Zadoc; Zadoc was father of Akim; Akim was father of Eliud. ¹⁵Eliud was father of Eleazar, and Eleazar was the father of Matthan. Matthan was father of Jacob. ¹⁶Jacob was father of Joseph, who was the husband of Mary, the mother of Jesus, called the Christ.

¹⁷So there were fourteen generations from Abraham to David; then fourteen generations to the Babylonian captivity, and fourteen generations to Christ. ¹⁸The birth of Jesus came about like this: His mother Mary was engaged to be married to Joseph, but before the marriage was consummated, she became pregnant through a miracle of the Holy Spirit. ¹⁹Joseph was a devout person and was shocked to realize that he had been deceived into believing she was a virgin, but he did not want to embarrass her publicly, so he planned to quietly cancel the engagement and the arranged marriage. ²⁰However, in this time of perplexity, he had a dream in which a messenger of the Lord came to him and spoke to him, "Joseph, son of David, do not hesitate to take Mary as your wife. It

is true that she is pregnant, but her pregnancy is the result of a miraculous conception by the Holy Spirit of God. [21]The child she has conceived is a boy, and His name shall be Jesus (Savior) because He will save His people from their sins."

[22]These events were the fulfillment of prophetic messages from God, which are quoted next. [23]"Listen! A virgin will conceive and give birth to a son whose name will be Emmanuel—a name which means GOD WITH US." (God in human form). [24]Joseph awoke and was no longer fearful. They were married as planned, [25]but they had no sexual intercourse until after the Baby was born. Then he followed the instruction of the Lord's messenger and named the baby "Jesus."

Chapter 2

[1]Soon after Jesus was born in Bethlehem, Judea, during the reign of king Herod, some influential, well-educated, trusted counselors from an eastern nation arrived in Jerusalem. [2]They had followed a mysterious star for a long time because they believed the star would lead them to the newborn King of the Jews, according to Balaam's prophecy. Being worshippers of God, they must worship this newborn Son of God and find the place of His birth.

[3]Of course, Herod was soon aware of their visit and its purpose, but he was definitely unhappy about it. [4]So he called together the chief priests and scribes, "My friends, do you have information in any of your writings as to where the Messiah is to be born?"

[5]"Sir, we can help you," they replied. "In Micah's prophecy, we find this passage, [6]'And you, Bethlehem of Judea, are not the least among the towns of Judea because

from you will come a royal governor who will rule over my people Israel.'"

[7]With this information, Herod arranged a meeting with these magi and was able to obtain a definite date on which they first noticed the star. [8]He then planned his strategy for destroying the young prince. First he must locate the baby. He asked the magi if they would be willing to go to Bethlehem and conduct a search for the young king. "And when you find Him, I would greatly appreciate your willingness to come back here and share with me what you found so that I may also go and honor Him by my royal visit."

[9]They listened to the king and were not at all apprehensive about the request. They assured him that they would begin the search at once. [10]As soon as they left Herod's palace, they made their way out of the city, and to their delight they again saw the star that had led them on their long journey. It was directing them toward Bethlehem. Finally it stopped moving at a spot directly over the place where the child was lying.

[11]Mary was surprised, but she invited them in, and to her amazement they unpacked expensive gifts for her baby— gold coins, frankincense, and myrrh— items which Joseph and Mary had never been able to afford. The visitors then bowed their heads in a circle around Jesus and worshipped Him. Needless to say, Mary and Joseph were deeply moved by this display of confidence.

[12]Before leaving Bethlehem, the magi received a warning in a dream that they should not return to King Herod, so they left by a different route. [13]Shortly after their departure, Joseph had an impressive dream in which he heard God saying through a

messenger, "Joseph, get up and do as I say and do it as quickly as possible. You must leave for Egypt, and you must stay there until I give you further instructions, for King Herod will search for Mary's baby, hoping to kill him."

[14]Fortunately, Joseph was a man with complete confidence in God and was also a man of action. He lost no time in awakening Mary, putting some necessary items together, and getting the child ready to travel. Now he could see clearly the providential purpose in the visit of the magi. There was money available and spices that could be sold for more funds as needed. This could sustain them for a long time while they were away from home. Within hours they were on their way to Egypt, a distance of about two hundred miles. [15]In obedience to God, they remained in Egypt until Herod's death. This fulfilled a prophecy of the Messiah found in Hosea 11:10: "Out of Egypt have I called My Son."

[16]Back in Jerusalem, Herod waited and waited for the magi to return with the information he had requested. Surely they could not have discerned the reason for his request, he thought. But as day after day passed it became evident that the magi had outsmarted him. He was furious. He ordered his soldiers to go to Bethlehem and slaughter every male child under two years of age. The bloody mission was carried out in the town and in the surrounding country without mercy, leaving many parents wailing in grief, devastated and angry. [17]A scripture came to mind. Jeremiah had prophesied of such an event (Jeremiah 31:15): [18]"In Rama was heard a voice of sorrow, weeping and anguish. Rachel weeping for her children, unable to be comforted because they are dead."

[19]After Herod's death, the Lord's messenger appeared to Joseph in a dream in Egypt, telling him, [20]"It's time for you to return to the land of Israel, Joseph. Prepare Mary and the Baby for the return trip. There will be no attempts on the child's life, for the one who wanted to kill him is dead." [21]Always obedient, yet still apprehensive, they returned. [22]On reaching his homeland, he learned that Herod's son Archelaus was occupying the throne in Judea. Joseph was afraid to settle there, so God instructed him in another dream to proceed on to Galilee where he had lived before and resume his life in Nazareth. In this way another prophecy of the Messiah's coming was fulfilled. It reads, "He shall be called a Nazarene." (Matthew must have known about this prophecy, but it is not recorded in our Bibles.)

Chapter 3

[1]Years later while Jesus was still living in Nazareth, John the Baptist began preaching in the Judean wilderness. [2]The main emphasis of his message was for the people of Israel to repent of their sinful ways because God's kingdom was approaching and the Messiah would soon appear. [3]His key text was Isaiah 40:3, "Prepare the way of Jehovah, straighten out His road, enlarge His tent."

[4]John was indeed a "different" person. Even his clothing was not your ordinary garb, just a coarse woolen poncho and a leather belt. And his diet! Imagine eating nothing but carob pods and honey as your staple food. [5]So famous did he soon become that virtually all the people of Jerusalem and all of Judea finally came to hear him. [6]They came to confess their sins and to submit to baptism, a symbol of being washed clean and the beginning of a new

life after death and burial. [7]With supernatural insight he could detect hypocrisy in some of those who listened, such as some of the Pharisees and Sadducees. These he challenged with words like this: "You vipers, who has warned you to turn from your evil ways in order to escape the coming judgment? [8]Do not resist the conviction that you should change your ways. You must do so if you are to be eternally saved. [9]Never think that just because you are descendants of Abraham, you 'have it made.' [10]All of you know that if a fruit tree fails to produce fruit an axe is brought and the roots of the tree are cut with decisive blows. The tree then falls and is turned into firewood. Let this realization challenge you, for this same condition will bring about the downfall of this nation if it continues on its present course. [11]I am baptizing with water, and baptism symbolizes repentance and a change of lifestyle, but someone is soon to follow me, a person who is much greater than I, so much greater in fact that I am not worthy to carry his shoes. He will baptize with the Holy Spirit and with fire. You will want to listen to Him, and you must believe Him and His teaching. [12]He will have the power to fan the fire, then to gather the wheat into His storehouse. He will be able to assess character with one-hundred-percent accuracy."

[13]One day John was busy preaching and baptizing when Jesus left His home in Galilee and made His way to the Jordan River to be baptized by John. [14]At first, John tried to protest, "No! Indeed, You should be baptizing me, so why do You want to be baptized by me? Is not baptism a sign of repentance of sin?"

[15]"Yes, I know you are right, but try to think of it this way, John. I must give a perfect example to My people, going through the very steps that they must go through, showing them by My example what is needed." John understood and with awe and trembling baptized Jesus. [16]Coming up out of the river, Jesus paused and looked into the sky where a vision appeared to Him. The Holy Spirit came down from heaven in the shape of a dove and hovered over Him. Just then the voice of God the Father spoke, "Here is my beloved, precious Son, and He is giving me great joy."

Chapter 4

[1]Shortly after His baptism, the Holy Spirit directed Jesus out into the vast wilderness. There was no food for Him, and Satan himself began to put Jesus through a fearful trial. [2]After forty days, He was so weakened that His life was threatened. Right at this crucial moment, the tempter made his presence known. [3]His first statement was an attempt to convince Jesus to doubt the voice He had heard from heaven at His baptism. "If You are God's Son, You have power to create. Let's see You create bread from some of these stones."

[4]But a text of scripture instantly came to Jesus' mind. "The scripture says that human beings cannot survive on material food alone. They must also obey the word of God."

[5]Next the tempter took Jesus to the temple at Jerusalem, to one of its highest pinnacles. [6]"Now jump off, and You will demonstrate Your supposed divinity, for the scripture clearly teaches that God's angels will carry you and protect you so that you will not even bruise your foot on a stone."

[7]But Jesus' response was another familiar text of scripture: "Never put the Lord to a test just to call attention to yourself."

⁸Once more the devil made a heroic attempt to defeat Jesus. He brought Jesus to the summit of a very high mountain, from which all the nations of the earth were miraculously spread out before them in all their splendor and beauty and power. "Look at all the nations down there. ⁹They are all mine, but I am willing to surrender them all to You under one condition. Just bow here and worship me as Your superior."

¹⁰Jesus' answer was immediate and very positive. "Get away from Me, Satan, for the scripture says plainly that only God is worthy of worship and is the only One I must serve." ¹¹The devil was defeated. He was forced to leave at once. Then loyal angels appeared and began to help Jesus with water, food, and courage. ¹²After Jesus left the wilderness, He learned the sad news that John had been arrested and put in prison, so He decided to go into Galilee. ¹³Then instead of going to Nazareth, He moved to Capernaum, a city on the shore of the Sea of Galilee near the border between Naphtali and Zebulon. ¹⁴Isaiah had prophesied of this in chapter 9:1, 2, ¹⁵where they are named as walking in darkness, ¹⁶then being lightened with a great light, "And those who were in the shadow of death are now in the full light of day."

¹⁷As soon as Jesus was in Capernaum, He began to preach this message, "Now is the time to repent for the kingdom of heaven is coming soon." ¹⁸Shortly after this, He was walking along the shore and came across two brothers who were about to put their nets into the lake. They were commercial fishermen, Simon and Andrew by name. ¹⁹He approached them with this simple invitation, "Please come and join Me, and you will become fisher's of human beings." ²⁰Unbelievably, they abandoned their trade right there and went with Him. ²¹A little farther on He encountered two other brothers, James and John, who, with their father Zebedee, were in the process of mending their nets. ²²Jesus called them, and they left their nets, their boat, and their father at once and went with Jesus.

²³Jesus went to every town and village in Galilee, worshipping with the people in their synagogues, teaching them, and announcing the arrival of the kingdom of God. Then He would miraculously heal every sick or disabled person, regardless of the affliction. ²⁴As one might expect, He rapidly achieved widespread fame, even in Syria. All kinds of sick people were brought to Him, those in severe pain, those possessed by evil spirits, and those with mental illness or paralysis. Without hesitation, He healed them all. ²⁵Crowds began to follow Him wherever He went. Residents of Galilee, Decapolis, Judea, and Jerusalem, and those from the region east of the Jordan River, all were among His followers.

Chapter 5

¹With a huge crowd following Him, Jesus led them to a hilly area, stopped, and invited them to sit down on the grass. It seemed certain to the people that He was about to bring them some truths that were very important, and He did not disappoint them. ²As He began to speak, the crowd became silent, and everyone could hear His words plainly. Following are the principles that He emphasized. (His discourse follows without quotation marks.)

³Fortunate indeed are those who recognize their spiritual needs, for they are

the ones who will inherit the kingdom of God. ⁴Fortunate also are those who sorrow over their sins, for they shall realize the comfort of complete forgiveness. ⁵And although it now seems impossible, those who are meek, unassuming, yet strong without being overbearing, assertive, or aggressive, will one day be the owners of the earth. ⁶Fortunate indeed are those who are hungry and thirsty for clean hearts, for true righteousness, because their hunger will be satisfied. They will be given righteousness. ⁷And those who show mercy and pity toward others will find that mercy and pity will be shown to them. ⁸Fortunate are those whose hearts have been cleansed, who are altogether in harmony with God's will, for they will see God face to face. ⁹And those who are peacemakers—what an outstanding blessing they are, for they will be adopted into the family of God.

¹⁰Now hear this! Impossible as it may seem, those who are persecuted for their faith will be happy. It really will work out that way, and God's kingdom will belong to them. ¹¹Really! Those who are "cussed out," reviled, and slandered because of their loyalty to Me are to be envied. ¹²Now I want to tell you this: If such things occur, you should be truly grateful and thankful, for this is an indication that you are in a saving relationship with God, a relationship that will have its reward in heaven. Remember that the prophets of old were persecuted in these ways. And one can only imagine how honored they will be.

¹³Those of you who believe in Me can be compared to salt in the world. For salt enhances the flavor of many foods. But if it is diluted with other substances, it is no longer useful and must be dumped out on the ground and becomes just like ordinary soil that is trampled. ¹⁴You also might be called "the light of the world," and if you are on a high plain that is planned for you, your light will be seen far and wide, just as the lights of a city on the hilltop can be seen for many miles. ¹⁵A candle is never lit and then covered with a basket. Instead, it is placed on a candlestick where it will light up a whole room. ¹⁶Now all of you, being lights, should be visible to all those around you, and your lifestyle should help them to understand the heavenly Father.

¹⁷Now let me clear up a misunderstanding that some of you may have had. My mission is not, and I repeat, NOT to destroy or deemphasize the law or the prophets. Rather, it is to be in complete harmony with them and to uphold them. ¹⁸In fact, friends, believe me, the law will endure longer than earth and heaven shall endure and will finally be recognized in all of its true significance. ¹⁹So remember, anyone who violates even one of these commandments and leads others to do the same will be called least by those in the kingdom of God, but whoever obeys them and teaches others to obey them will be most highly honored in God's kingdom.

²⁰And by the way, genuine righteousness is far above what you observe in the scribes and Pharisees, and yours must greatly exceed theirs. ²¹Let me illustrate: You have read this in Scripture, "You must not murder," and you know that murderers will be in grave danger on judgment day. ²²But let me challenge you with this truth: Whoever will be angry against another human being, with no real cause for anger, will be in danger on judgment day, and whoever hates another human being will be in danger when his case is considered by God's council, and whoever says to

another, "You stupid fool" will be in danger of hell fire.

²³Remember this, when you bring gifts to God's treasury, search your heart and remember if someone has been offended by your words or actions. If there is such a person, ²⁴do not deposit your gift—yet! Go to that person and apologize for the wrong you have done to him and make things right. Then it will be OK to come and present your gift. ²⁵Another thought: If someone accuses you, do not act with hostility to him, but be willing to listen to the evidence and perhaps the evidence will show that you are at fault and the court will sentence you to be jailed. ²⁶You will surely stay there until you have paid off the last penny of the debt.

²⁷And of course, you know the commandment that reads: "You must not commit adultery." ²⁸Let me show you the real implications of the seventh commandment. If you allow yourself to look lustfully at a woman or fantasize a forbidden relationship with her, you are violating the commandment. ²⁹If you have a "roving eye" that leads you into sin, far better to have that eye destroyed and removed from its socket than to have your whole body destroyed in the lake of fire. ³⁰And if one of your hands leads you into sin, far better to have it amputated than to lose out on eternal life and having your whole body cast into the lake of fire.

³¹Written in the law is this statement concerning divorce: "To be divorced there must be a document, duly drawn up and signed." ³²Anyone who divorces his wife for any reason other than infidelity shall be accountable for her adultery, and furthermore a man who marries a woman who is divorced is an adulterer. ³³You also

remember the law regarding oaths. It is this: "You must not swear by My name falsely," ³⁴but I say, swearing lightly such as "by heaven" is wrong, for heaven is God's throne. ³⁵To swear by the earth is also wrong, for it is God's footstool. To swear "by Jerusalem" is no better, for it is God's city, so let us avoid all such swearing completely. ³⁶Even by your own head is out of place, for it is not really yours. God is its creator, and He has jurisdiction over that head and the color of that hair and every cell. ³⁷But let your speech be very simple: Yes, Yes, or No, No. Anything more than this is rooted in evil.

³⁸Perhaps you have read this, "An eye for an eye and a tooth for a tooth." ³⁹But there is a better philosophy, believe Me: Do not fight back. If a man slaps you on the cheek, turn your other cheek to him also. ⁴⁰And if someone sues you and the court awards him your coat, let him have your overcoat also. ⁴¹And if you are ordered to carry a burden for a mile, surprise him and carry it two miles. ⁴²Go ahead and share something with the one who is asking for help, and if he wants to borrow, lend it to him.

⁴³Some of you have heard that the scripture says to love your neighbor and hate your enemy, ⁴⁴but my command is this: Love your enemies, give blessings to those who curse you, do good to those who hate you, and pray for those who treat you hatefully, the very ones who persecute you. ⁴⁵This is what your Father in heaven does, and you will be like Him if you are His children, for He makes the sun shine on both the wicked and the righteous, and produces rain for the evil and the good. ⁴⁶You see, to love those who love you is no big deal, there is no miracle here, for

even the hated publicans do this. [47]If you welcome your fellow countryman and ignore a stranger, you are no different than the publicans. [48]Now to be altogether like your Father in heaven, you will have to be perfect.

Chapter 6

[1]You each have two options: 1) To do good, hoping "for brownie points" with humans, or 2) To do good whether or not it is noticed. It is important to remember that God notices everything you do and that His reward is ample for any good that you have done. [2]When you want to give to a good cause, forget the trumpet, leave it at home (trumpets are for hypocrites who like to blast away out on the street or in the synagogue in order to be noticed). Hypocrites do have a certain sort of reward, of course, but this is all that they will ever receive. [3]Your benevolent deeds should be done so unobtrusively that your left hand will not know what your right hand is doing. [4]Be assured, however, that your heavenly Father is able to see all of those good deeds, and the ultimate reward will be given by God Himself.

[5]Now about praying in public. You should know that these people who love to stand on the street corner or in the synagogue giving long loud prayers are also hypocrites and what you see is all the reward they will ever have. [6]Here is my suggestion for prayer: Let it be done in your own room alone with the door closed. Your heavenly Father is able to see you and hear your prayers, and it just might be that His answer might be in the open where others can see it. [7]Another thing, there is no need to keep repeating over and over any part of your prayer, especially repetition of God's name. He hears everything, so what purpose could there be in such repetition? [8]So let's not be like heathens who utter their prayers, repeating over and over the same words. Remember this, your heavenly Father knows all your needs before you even ask Him to help.

[9]Listen and I will give you an example of the ideal prayer: "Our Father in heaven, even Your name is holy. [10]Please, quickly establish Your kingdom so that this earth will be like heaven. [11]Provide for today the food we need to sustain us. [12]And give us the same forgiving attitude that we desire others to have toward us. [13]And please, guide us away from trials and temptations to do wrong, and when troubles do come, bring deliverance. We recognize that the entire universe is Yours and that You are omnipotent and glorious and that You will be so forever."

[14]Here is something you should know. Your sins will be forgiven as freely as you forgive others who have wronged you. [15]But if you do not forgive others, neither can you be forgiven. [16]Another topic is fasting. If and when you fast, make it a time of private communion with God. Only hypocrites assume a sad, doleful expression when fasting. They do this to impress others, and this is their only benefit. [17]But when you fast, spruce up. Wash up and apply some fragrance. [18]In this way, no one will suspect that you are fasting, but God the Father knows, and your reward will be certain one day.

[19]Next, let Me share with you some ideas regarding material things. You will be happier if your efforts are not directed to accumulating a lot of material possessions. You have noticed, no doubt, that there will always be losses. Moths destroy clothing,

rust destroys iron goods, thieves steal from you, robbers rob you, and thus your efforts may be entirely in vain. [20]If you spend your energy trying to get permanent riches—character, integrity, spirituality, honesty, truthfulness, kindness, helpfulness, joyfulness, and contentment—moths, rust, or thieves cannot affect such treasures and you will be able to carry them with you into heaven. [21]Your treasures will always be where your heart is.

[22]Light is perceived by your eyes, so if your eyes are disciplined to dwell on only good things, your whole body will benefit from this good, [23]but if your eyes are directed to wickedness, your whole body will be affected by that evil. That's how important your eyes are—they monitor the difference between light and darkness.

[24]Now to illustrate another truth. You know, of course, that a slave cannot work for two different owners. He will always prefer one over the other and give his best service to the one he likes the best. In the same way you cannot serve God and material riches at the same time. [25]So choose God above material things. Material riches should always be secondary, and you should never be unduly worried over them, even over necessary items like food, water, clothing, and the like. For life is much more than just food, and the human body is much more than clothing. [26]Notice the birds. They don't plant seeds or harvest crops and store food in a barn, and yet your heavenly Father supplies their food. Now remember this: You are of much greater value than any of them. [27]Can any of you by just thinking about it grow a foot and a half in height? No, your height is God's decision.

[28]Remember not to fret over clothing. Think of the beautiful lilies that you see growing all around you. They don't have to sew or spin yarn or weave cloth. [29]And yet Solomon, at the height of his splendor, had no clothing that compared to the beauty of one of these flowers. [30]Now why did I remind you of the lily? Just this, if God created the plants, even just plain grass, with such meticulous detail when it lasts only just a few brief days, then is cut down, and dried in an oven, wouldn't you conclude that He will be sure that you, too, will be clothed? [31]So let not your major concern be on questions such as, "What shall I eat or what shall I drink or what shall I wear?" [32]Actually, many heathens spend every day wondering over such questions. Remember, your Father in heaven knows that you need all these things.

[33]Here is the bottom line: Center your goals, your attention, and your efforts on the kingdom of God and on God's goodness, and these other things will be supplied. [34]So do not worry about tomorrow, for tomorrow will have its own concerns to attend to.

Chapter 7

[1]You human beings have no business in trying to judge others as to their spiritual status and their motives. All you have as evidence is their behavior, and if you insist on trying to assess motives, you will find that your own motives will be judged by others also. [2]You will yourselves be declared to be against God in one way or another and the standards you try to impose on others will be used against your behavior.

[3]Listen! How foolish of you to try to remove a tiny gnat from someone's eye when you have a two-by-four in your own eye. [4]Would you say to the person, "Come, let me remove that gnat from your eye,"

while you still have the two-by-four in your own eye? ⁵Of course, this is a hypocritical attitude. No, first have the two-by-four removed from your own eye; then your vision might have improved enough to remove the gnat from your brother's eye. ⁶There may be cases in which the attempt to help a sinner would be as useless as trying to share valuable treasures with a dog who, of course, has no appreciation of their value and may respond by biting your hand. Or perhaps comparable to tossing some pearls into a pigpen only to have the pigs trample them into the mud.

⁷When you ask God for blessings, He has promised that you will receive them; when you go forward attempting to enter new territories for God, the doors will open for you. ⁸In fact, everyone who asks receives, and those who search find, and those who knock at doors will find doors opening. ⁹Think of your own lives, you who are fathers, your hungry son comes to you crying, "Dad, I'm hungry, may I have a sandwich?" Will you offer him a stone? ¹⁰If he asks for a fish, will you give him a snake? ¹¹Try to compare your actions to God's actions. You are a sinner; God is good. If you would give only good things to your son, how much more certain it is that God will give only good things to those who ask.

¹²Here is a rule you should always follow: Whatever it is that you want others to do for you, do those very things for them. This sums up what the prophets have written and what is in the law. ¹³It may seem to you that the wide gate ahead of you is the more desirable one to enter, but be on your guard, for in eternal matters that narrow gate, the one you must squeeze through, is the better one to enter. The crowds who choose the wide gate are almost always wrong, and the route that they take usually leads to eventual destruction. ¹⁴Yes, that obscure, narrow entrance with only an occasional traveler entering is the one that will lead to eternal life.

¹⁵And now about prophets, be on your guard against false prophets, for even if they seem benign and gentle, they are actually like hungry wolves. ¹⁶Notice what their teaching leads to, what results are seen in response to their advice? Do people find grapes on thorn bushes or figs on thistles? ¹⁷A good tree can be expected to yield good fruit, and a diseased tree will produce bad fruit. ¹⁸A good tree will not yield bad fruit, neither will a diseased tree yield good fruit. ¹⁹A tree that is not yielding fruit is chopped down, cut into firewood, and burned. ²⁰Just as one makes decisions regarding a tree by its fruit, so one can conclude what type of person he is dealing with by examining the person's actions.

²¹Unfortunately, there are those who call me "Lord, Lord" who will not be in the kingdom of heaven because their actions do not match their words. In the final analysis of one's life, a person's actions indicate his true nature and are a correct indication of his destiny, either in the heavenly Father's kingdom or outside of it. ²²I predict that many will say to Me at the final judgment, "Lord, Lord, haven't we been great? We were prophets in your name. Furthermore, we even cast out demons in your name, and we did a lot of other wonderful deeds in Your name."

²³But alas! I will be forced to say, "You and I are really not friends; we aren't on the same team. Your deeds are selfish and wicked; leave at once!" ²⁴Now of all the

instruction I have given you, be sure to accept it and do it, for if you do it, you will be like a wise man who, when selecting a place to build his house, decided to place it on solid rock. ²⁵Its foundation was so substantial that when violent rains, floods, and hurricanes the house was undamaged, safe and sound because of its foundation. ²⁶On the other hand, those who hear My instruction and ignore it are like the foolish builder who built his house on sand. ²⁷The same rainstorms came, the flood waters rose, the hurricane howled, and his house collapsed with a tremendous crash.

²⁸This ended the messages of Jesus to His listeners that day on the hillside, and they were tremendously impressed. ²⁹His teaching was so convincing, powerful, and reasonable that it contrasted sharply with the teachings of the scribes.

Chapter 8

¹It was after the conclusion of this discourse that a large crowd began to follow Him, obviously deeply impressed by His message. They were convinced, or nearly so, that the long-awaited Messiah was here at last. ²Things began to happen that added evidence that this was indeed true. For instance, a leper made his way to Jesus, knelt down, and said, "Lord, if it is Your will, You can rid me of this leprosy." ³Jesus broke the Jewish rule and touched the leper, after which He said, "It is My will; be cured." Instantly the man was cured. ⁴Then Jesus gave him this instruction, "Don't go to anyone about this healing until you have followed Moses' instruction. Go to the priest and offer a gift so that you will be in perfect compliance with the law. This is important."

⁵In Capernaum a Roman centurion came to Jesus with an urgent request. ⁶"Please, Master, may I have a few seconds of your time? Here is my need. My trusted, loyal, capable slave has suddenly become paralyzed and is in a desperate condition."

⁷Jesus interrupted him, "Certainly, I will come and heal him."

⁸"Oh no, not that," replied the soldier. "I am not worthy to have You enter my home. Would You not rather just say the word right here? I know that will be enough. ⁹You see, this sort of thing happens every day in my work. I am a person who is under a superior, and I do whatever he tells me to do. And I have those under me who obey me. I say to this man, 'Go,' and he goes. I say to this man, 'Do this,' and he does it."

¹⁰When Jesus heard this, He was deeply pleased with the man's faith. Then, turning to his followers, He said, "I have not seen so much faith, even in an Israelite. ¹¹Remember this, you are not entitled to a place in God's kingdom just because you are a descendent of Abraham. There will be those from the east and from the west who will fellowship with Abraham, Isaac, and Jacob. ¹²But alas, the sad truth is that many who should be there, those who have been specially favored by being children of Israel, will be left out in darkness where they will weep and gnash their teeth." ¹³Next He turned to the centurion, "You may now return home, and because of your perfect trust in Me, your request has been granted." The slave recovered completely at that moment.

¹⁴The group then went to Peter's home where they learned that Peter's mother-in-law was in bed with a high fever. ¹⁵Of course, this wasn't a problem. Jesus touched her hand and the fever left her.

She at once got up and began waiting on them. [16]After sundown people began to gather at Peter's home, bringing with them many who were demon-possessed or ill. All it took was a word from Jesus and they were restored to health and freedom from the demons. [17]This was in fulfillment of Isaiah's prophecy of the Messiah: "He carried our infirmities and sicknesses away."

[18]As the crowds increased, Jesus finally led his disciples away and left for the opposite side of the lake. [19]But before leaving, a scribe came up to Jesus and said, "Teacher, I want to follow You and be with You wherever You go."

[20]"Are you sure?" Jesus asked. "Remember that foxes have dens to live in and that birds have nests, but the Son of man does not even have a cot of His own."

[21]Then another follower began, "My Lord, I want to continue with You, but let me wait until my father's death so that I can give him a decent funeral."

[22]"You," said Jesus, "would be better advised to follow Me now and depend on another person to arrange your father's funeral."

[23]Finally Jesus and His disciples boarded a fishing boat and set out for the opposite shore. [24]They had barely started when a violent windstorm began. The waves became so high that they crashed over the boat. The disciples were frightened and decided to awaken Jesus who had fallen asleep. [25]He did not seem to be the least bit afraid. "You dear men, why all the fear? Have you no faith after all you have seen?" [26]He then stood up and shouted to the wind and the sea, ordering them to calm down. Immediately the sea was perfectly calm. [27]As one might expect, this demonstration of supernatural power overwhelmed the disciples. Their thoughts were expressed in words such as these: "Just what sort of a person are we dealing with? This Man can actually command the wind and water to obey Him."

[28]The boat crossed to the eastern shore and landed in the country of the Gadarenes. They were met by two screaming demon-possessed men who had no home but took shelter in the local tombs and caves. They were so frightful in manner that no one dared come near the area. [29]The two men rushed toward Jesus, yelling, "Why have You come here? Have You decided to disturb us, to overcome us before we expected You? Let us go into those pigs over there." [30]Nearby was a large herd of pigs grazing, and when Jesus gave the command, "Go," the demons went, taking over the herd and causing them to go berserk and charge down the steep hillside into the lake, where they drowned. [31]The herdsmen were terrified, naturally, and disappeared as fast as possible, fearing for their lives. Back in town they reported the entire incident, especially the miraculous healing of the demon-possessed men, [32]but the townsfolk organized a mass protest and told Jesus in no uncertain terms to get out of their country or face the consequences.

Chapter 9

[1]With a sorrowful heart, He yielded to their request even though two men had been restored to useful life. Jesus returned to His own town. [2]Shortly thereafter, when Jesus was teaching the people, a man was brought to Him on a stretcher, paralyzed and helpless. Jesus interrupted His discourse, and impressed by the faith of the man and his friends, said to him, "Son,

cheer up, your sins are forgiven."

[3]Some scribes were in the audience, and they saw a point whereby they might accuse Jesus. They thought to themselves, *God alone can forgive sins, so this must be blasphemy.* [4]But Jesus read their minds like a book, and he looked straight at them and asked. "Why are you thinking such thoughts? You are trying to discredit Me before these people, but you are unwilling to speak up. [5]Tell Me, what is more difficult to say, 'Your sins are forgiven' or 'Get up and walk?' [6]I hope to persuade you that this Son of man has the authority to forgive sin." He turned to the paralytic and gave this order, "Get up from your stretcher, stand, and carry your cot home." [7]The patient instantly obeyed, picked up his cot, and set out for home. [8]The amazed onlookers were impressed and praised God who had shared His miraculous power with a human being.

[9]From this place Jesus went to the local tax office where He met the man in charge, Matthew by name. "Matthew, I have come to invite you to join Me in My work." Surprisingly enough, Matthew needed no urging. He resigned from his job right then and there and went with Jesus.

[10]Later Jesus was at a dinner in His honor where a number of other tax collectors were guests, and they were all eating at the same table. [11]When the Pharisees heard about it, they confronted the disciples. "Why does your Master lower Himself by eating with such trash?"

[12]Jesus heard of their complaint and answered the question Himself. "Friends, consider this. Those who are well do not go to the doctor, only those who are sick. [13]You remember, I am sure, the words of Hosea 6:6, 'I prefer mercy above sacrifice.'"

[14]One day some of John's disciples came to Jesus with this question, "Why is it that fasting is a routine practice with us and with our religious leaders but is ignored by You and Your disciples? You are failing to set a proper example."

[15]His reply came in the form of an illustration. "Can the groom's attendants be expected to fast while the bridegroom is with them? Hardly. But after He has gone away, they very likely will resume the practice. [16]And when patching clothes, the tailor will not put a piece of new cloth in as a patch, for it will likely tear the old cloth and make the garment worse off than when he started. [17]Also you know that new wine is never placed in old wineskins because of the real possibility that they might leak, losing the wine. No, new wine must be put into new wineskins."

[18]It was while explaining these things that one of the rulers came to Him, knelt before Him, and sorrowfully implored Jesus to come to his home. "My daughter has just died, but if You will come, Master, and touch her, she can be restored to life." [19]So Jesus went with him, but the crowd so tightly surrounded Him that progress was slow. [20]On the way a woman who had suffered for twelve years with anemia due to menorrhagia managed to get close enough to Jesus to touch the hem of His robe. [21]She thought, *I don't need to have Him even see me or notice me. If I can only touch the hem of His coat.* [22]But Jesus was aware of her all along, so He turned to her and said, "Daughter, cheer up. Your faith is rewarded. You are cured." She was cured from then on.

[23]When Jesus reached the ruler's house, the paid musicians were already there as well as neighbors and friends. It was

bedlam. [24]But an authoritative command from Jesus cleared the courtyard, "Let Me through please; this girl is not dead, just asleep." Of course they laughed at His ignorance. [25]When the way was clear, Jesus went into the home, took the girl by the hand, and restored life to her lifeless body. [26]As one might expect, this event resulted in a lot of publicity for Jesus, near and far.

[27]From this home, Jesus journeyed on and was followed by two blind men who implored Him, "Please, Son of David, have mercy on us."

[28]They followed Him into a house where Jesus faced them and asked, "Do you really believe that I can do this?"

"Yes we do, Lord."

[29]So He touched their eyes saying, "Let it be done in proportion to your faith." [30]Their sight was immediately restored. Jesus then admonished them, "Please do not publicize this, friends." [31]But instead of keeping quiet, they told everyone they saw, adding to his fame in that part of the country.

[32]Going on from there, a demon-possessed man was brought to Jesus. He could not even speak, so complete was the control over him. [33]And like others in such a condition, he was freed from the demon's power by the word of Jesus. Once healed, he began to speak, much to the amazement of the crowd following Jesus. They all seemed to recognize that they were witnesses to God's power, such evidence as had not been seen for centuries. [34]In spite of these impressive events, the Pharisees stubbornly opposed Jesus and concluded that the only way to reduce the interest in Him was to proclaim that the exorcisms were done through the power of Satan rather than through God's power.

[35]But Jesus continued traveling from city to city, village to village, teaching in the synagogues, preaching the good news of God's kingdom, and healing every imaginable sickness and disease. [36]As He taught He was saddened to see so many people who had been left without spiritual leadership, like sheep without a shepherd. [37]He expressed His concern to His disciples, "As you can see, the harvest is really tremendous, but the workers are altogether too few. [38]Please pray that the Lord of the harvest will be able to find many reapers to bring in the harvest."

Chapter 10

[1]Next Jesus gathered His twelve disciples around Him and gave them power to do as He had been doing, casting out demons and healing diseases and sicknesses of all kinds. [2]Here is the roll call of the twelve: Simon Peter, Andrew his brother, James and John the sons of Zebedee, [3]Philip, Bartholomew, Thomas, Matthew the tax collector, [4]James the son of Alphaeus, Lebbaeus who was often called Thaddaeus, Simon the Zealot, and Judas Iscariot who later betrayed Jesus. [5]He sent these twelve out with instructions to wait until ordered to go to the Gentiles or to the Samaritans. [6]For now they were only to go to "the lost sheep in the nation of Israel."

[7]"Everywhere you go, preach that the kingdom of heaven is near. [8]Heal those who are sick, restore lepers to health, raise the dead, cast out demons. You have received much, so share it with others. [9]You will not need to carry money with you, [10]nor will you need credit cards, extra clothing or shoes, or even a walking stick, for those who hear you and are blessed by you will provide for all your real necessities.

[11]"When you enter a town, find out

who the best citizen is and ask for lodging. Stay there until you have finished the tasks assigned you. [12]And be sure to bestow God's blessing on that home where you stay. [13]If it is indeed what you thought it to be, let God's peace be called upon it, but if not, omit this. [14]You will want to know what to do about those who refuse to listen to what you have to share. Just this, leave the town or city, and in a symbolic ceremony shake the dust from your feet. [15]Alas, it will be more likely that Sodom and Gomorrah can be saved than for that city on judgment day. [16]Remember, I am comparing you to sheep in a pack of wolves, so be as wise as snakes, but as harmless as doves.

[17]"Be prepared for anything human beings can devise, for you may be brought before the council, you may be beaten right in the synagogue, [18] or you may be tried before governors and kings because of Me. Consider that an opportunity for you to give your testimony to these people. [19]If you are brought to trial, do not be anxious about what to say because you will be supplied with the right words at the right time. [20]You see, in such circumstances, the Holy Spirit will speak through you. [21]Sadly enough, a person will accuse his own brother, even though it means conviction and the death penalty. A father will accuse his own child; people will rebel against their parents, even to the point of condemning them to death. [22]You, my friends, will find that you will be hated everywhere, but learn to accept it and be constant in your trust, for those who do so will be saved. [23]However, if you find yourselves persecuted, do not feel it your duty to stay and continue to be persecuted, but move on to another place. It is vital to realize that every town in Israel needs the message that you are willing to share with them. I will also come there after your visit because these people need all the help they can get. [24]You, as my disciples, should expect to be treated like your teacher, not any better. [25]Consider yourselves fortunate if you are treated no worse than I am treated. Remember, I have been called Beelzebub, so don't be surprised if you are called even worse names. [26]But don't be afraid of these hecklers. Eventually their motives will be made plain, their hidden agenda will be apparent.

[27]"The things I have told you are to be publicized everywhere, even all those truths that have been taught you in our private conversations. [28]Yes, even those who are able to kill you are not to be feared, because they cannot inflict the second death. Do fear the one who can bring about your eternal death. [29]What is the price of two sparrows? Let's say one farthing. Your Father is aware of that one small life and knows when it dies. [30]And as a matter of fact, He has such an accurate knowledge of everything that He knows how many hairs you have on your head. [31]And you are vastly more valuable than any number of sparrows. In God's sight this is true, so you have no need to be afraid.

[32]"Continue on with your proclamations, your testimony regarding Me, and I promise to keep your name constantly before the Father in heaven. [33]But the corollary is also true. If you shall deny me here on earth, I will be forced to deny you before God. [34]Unfortunately, My coming to earth will not always bring peace, but rather fighting and bloodshed. [35]Actually, a man and his own father will oppose each other, a daughter will oppose her mother and a daughter-in-law will oppose her

mother-in-law. [36]Yes, a person's own family may be his bitterest enemies. [37]But if a person puts family above Me, a father, a mother, a son or daughter, he is not really worthy of Me. [38]And if a person is unwilling to carry a cross, he is not worthy of Me. [39]And the one who considers temporal life to be more important than anything else will lose it, but if he is willing to lose his life for My sake, he will have eternal life.

[40]"Those who receive you are receiving Me and in so doing are receiving the Father who sent Me. [41]Those who receive a prophet and his message will be rewarded the same as the prophet himself, and those who accept the testimony of a righteous man will be rewarded equally as the righteous man. [42]Just the mere act of giving a cup of cool water to a thirsty child is evidence enough that you are My disciple, and I promise you, that your reward will be certain."

Chapter 11

[1]After Jesus completed His instruction to the twelve, He left them to preach alone for a while. [2]While thus teaching, He was visited by two of John's disciples with a very earnest question, [3]"Are You truly the promised Messiah or shall we expect someone else?" John was by this time imprisoned, and Jesus had done nothing to have him released.

[4]In reply, Jesus calmly asked them to return and give an accurate report on just what they saw and heard. [5]"The blind are having their vision restored, the crippled are walking normally again, the lepers are restored to health, the deaf are hearing again, and even the dead are resurrected; also the good news is being published to even the poor people. [6]Those who accept Me for who I am are truly fortunate and will not be offended."

[7]After they had left, Jesus used the opportunity to explain some things to His followers, clearing up some questions about John the Baptist. He first asked, "What did you go out into the wilderness to find? A reed waving in the wind? [8]Or perhaps you went out to find a richly clothed man. No, such people are in the king's palace, rather than out in the desert. [9]Or did you travel out there to see and hear a modern prophet? Indeed you did. John is much more than a prophet. [10]John is a fulfillment of prophecy, as well as being a prophet. Remember Malachi 3:1, 'Look, I am sending my messenger ahead of Me to prepare the way for Me?' Remember also Isaiah 40:3. [11]Let me assure you that of all the people on this planet, there has never been and there never shall be a greater person than John the Baptist. And yet even greater are the ones saved in God's kingdom?

[12]"From the time John began preaching until now, the kingdom of God has been besieged by determined forceful people, demanding and receiving the things that they so much desire. [13]All the Old Testament prophets have been pointing to John's time, and now we are witnessing the fulfillment of those prophecies. [14]And now, if you will accept it, he is the fulfillment of Malachi 4:5—the Elijah.

[15]"Whoever has ears, please use them. [16]Honestly now, what is this present generation coming to? It reminds me of children playing together. [17]One asks the other, 'What's wrong with you? Here we have been playing music and you refuse to dance, we have been sorrowing and crying and you have had no sympathy. We can't

seem to win.' [18]Here was John living an austere life, refusing to feast and drink in his zeal to do God's will and what is said of him? 'He's possessed by a devil.' [19]Now in contrast, here is the Son of man who eats and drinks with people and what is said of Him? 'He is a wino and a glutton!' or 'He even makes friends of tax collectors and other sinners.' However, in the end, wisdom will be vindicated by the results of her deeds."

[20]At this point, He began to bewail the fate of some of the cities that He had visited, where many miracles had been performed and yet where the majority of its people had rejected the message to repent. [21]"Woe to you, Korazin! Woe to you, Bethsaida! For if the wonderful things that were done in you had been done in Tyre and Sidon they would have repented long ago in sackcloth and ashes. [22]Believe me, on judgment day, Tyre and Sidon will have a better chance than you have. [23]And you, Capernaum, you who consider yourselves about ready for heaven, you will actually be found worthy only of hell, for if the marvelous things that were done in you had been done in Sodom, it would still be a thriving city at this time. [24]Yes it will be more hopeful for Sodom on judgment day than for you."

[25]Then Jesus paused and prayed this prayer: "Thank you, Father, Lord of the universe, because You have made these things plain to children, even though supposedly wise and experienced minds don't seem to grasp them. [26]In your wisdom and love, You will always choose the right course to take."

[27]Then speaking again to the people, He said, "The Father has given Me everything and only He knows His Son and only the Son really knows the Father, well, yes, the Son and those who accept Him as a revelation of the Father. [28]Please, come to me all of you who are weary and laden down with trials, and I will give you real rest. [29]Yoke up with Me, learn from Me, for I am not hard to approach, and your soul will indeed find rest. [30]My yoke is easy to carry and My burden is light."

Chapter 12

[1]Then Jesus and His disciples passed through a field of grain on the Sabbath. They were hungry, and the disciples began to pick heads of grain, rub them out to get the kernels, and then eat them. [2]As usual there were observers watching them closely, Pharisees ready to criticize anything they did. "Look, Teacher, Your disciples are breaking the Sabbath."

[3]Jesus replied, "Have you forgotten what David did when he and his men were hungry? [4]He actually went into the sanctuary, ate some of the sacred bread, and gave some to his men. This of course was forbidden. This bread was only for the priests. Even being in the sanctuary was off limits to everyone except the priest. [5]Or have you forgotten that on the Sabbath day the priest worked more than on any other day and yet he is not breaking the Sabbath. [6]In fact, you are in the presence of One who is greater than the temple. [7]And if you understand this scripture properly: 'I will have mercy rather than sacrifice,' you will not condemn innocent persons. [8]The bottom line is this: The Son of man is creator and Lord of the Sabbath day."

[9]From this encounter, He went directly to the synagogue, [10]where there was a man who had total atrophy of one of his hands. [11]The Pharisees challenged Him: "Is it

legitimate Sabbath keeping to heal people on this sacred day?" They thought they would be able to trap Him.

[12]"You men here," He replied, "if you have one sheep and that sheep falls into a pit on the Sabbath, will you lift it out or will you allow it to remain helpless there until the Sabbath is over?" He needed no answer. [13]"You see, a human being is far more valuable than a sheep, and to help one of God's creatures on the Sabbath is fully in harmony with God's law." Now He turned to the patient, "Hold out your hand." The man obeyed and immediately it was restored to normal strength.

[14]Then the Pharisees got together in a council with only one purpose in mind, to come up with a plan to have Jesus executed. [15]But Jesus was already aware of their plans and left the area. A large number of people followed Him, all of who were healed of their diseases. [16]They were advised not to publicize their healing because of the hostility of those in authority. [17]What was being accomplished had been predicted by the prophet Isaiah hundreds of years before which reads as follows, [18]"Look, everyone! Here is My Servant, My Beloved, My Chosen One in whom I am well pleased. I will put My spirit on Him, and He will show what true justice is, not only to My people but to the Gentiles also." Isaiah 42:1–3 [19]"He will not provoke a fight or a riot, neither will He be a rabble-rouser. [20]He will not add to the damage already accomplished on a bruised reed, nor will He put a smoking fire out until He leads to peace through justice.

[21]He will be so utterly fair that Gentiles will come to trust Him."

[22]Just then a cluster of people arrived bringing with them a man possessed by a demon, both blind and dumb. Without a moment's hesitation, Jesus performed a miraculous healing and restored both sight and speech to the sufferer. [23]And needless to say, the onlookers were amazed and began to say among themselves, "This must be the promised Son of David," [24]but the Pharisees differed with them, "This fellow must be casting out devils through Beelzebub the chief devil."

[25]However, Jesus could read their minds and countered with a profound observation: "Any nation which is rent by civil war, half of it fighting the other half, will certainly destroy itself eventually; even a household or a city could not endure divisiveness such as that. [26]And if Satan should cast out Satan, he would be fighting against himself. He is much too smart to do such a thing. His reign would have ended long ago if he had operated like that. [27]Now if I have cast out devils by the power of Beelzebub, think seriously, by whom have your followers cast them out? Let them evaluate your theory. [28]And remember this, if I have cast out devils by the Holy Spirit of God, then the kingdom of God is right here today.

[29]"You see, a strong man is able to protect his home from burglars who are not his equal in strength. In order to get his goods, they would have to tie him up first, which would be impossible. [30]If you are not on My side, you are opposing Me, and if you are not helping Me, you are trying to weaken and destroy Me. [31]Now in view of what is so reasonably true, it is apparent that even though every conceivable sin can be forgiven by God, when a person rejects the work and impressions of the Holy Spirit, he has removed the only influence that leads to repentance; therefore,

his sins remain unforgiven. ³²Yes, you may say anything you want to against Me and yet be forgiven, but if you say the same things against the Holy Spirit, you cannot be forgiven in this world, nor in the world to come.

³³"A tree can be accurately evaluated by the fruit it produces. A diseased tree cannot be expected to produce good fruit. But if the tree is healthy, it will produce good fruit. ³⁴Please, please, you who are speaking wickedness, you truly need divine help for your souls—without this you cannot speak good things. ³⁵A good man with a good heart says good things, while a wicked man will naturally say wicked things. ³⁶It is a fact, friends, that your words will be brought up on judgment day and will be witnesses as to what kind of persons you are. ³⁷And by those words, you will be declared right with God or you will be condemned."

³⁸Then some of the scribes asked Him to give them a miraculous sign to prove that He was who He claimed to be. ³⁹His reply was that a whole generation of people, a generation that was actively unfaithful to God, was looking for some kind of sign but were not willing to accept the evidence of divine miracles. These should be evidence enough for a teachable person. "So there will be only one sign given, and it should be further evidence and that sign will be the sign of the prophet Jonah. ⁴⁰You remember that Jonah was in the whale's belly for three days, don't you? Well, the Son of man will be in the earth for three days. ⁴¹The people of Nineveh will justly pass judgment on this generation because the inhabitants of that wicked city repented when they heard Jonah's message. But here is a case where repentance is not seen even when a person greater than Jonah is preaching.

⁴²"Also you will recall the story of the visit of the queen of Sheba when she wanted to meet Solomon. She had heard of his wisdom and was determined to test it out for herself. However, you are rejecting Someone greater than Solomon. ⁴³Now let us think again about that evil spirit that possessed the man. He finds himself cast out and begins to look for a new victim, but he is unable to find one. What does he do? ⁴⁴He decides to return to the person from whom he had been ejected, and there he finds a place all prepared for him. ⁴⁵This was totally unexpected, so he goes about and finds seven other demons more wicked than he is and tells them of his find. Then all of them repossess the man, and, of course, the poor man's condition is much worse than he was before. This illustrates the condition of this generation."

⁴⁶While Jesus was giving this discourse, His mother and His brothers came and began to press their way through the crowd to see Him. ⁴⁷Someone noticed them and interrupted Him, "Master, Your mother and brothers are here wanting to speak with You."

⁴⁸Jesus answered, "Who are My brothers and who is My mother?" ⁴⁹Then pointing to the crowd, He explained, "Here are the members of My family, ⁵⁰for whoever is willing to obey My Father in heaven is My brother, My sister, and My mother."

Chapter 13

¹Later that day Jesus went to the lakeshore followed as usual by hundreds of people. ²In order to be heard better, he asked for and received permission to get into one of the fishing boats moored there. ³His message

that day was a series of parables that were intended to teach the people vital things they needed to know. "One day a farmer began to sow grain in his field, [4]and as he scattered the seed some fell along the roadway where birds quickly found it and snatched it up. [5]Some of the kernels fell among stones where the soil was shallow, allowing germination to take place rapidly, [6]but with such shallow soil, the young seedlings soon died when the sun became hot during the day. [7]Other seeds fell in a weed patch where they sprouted normally, but the thorny weeds grew much faster than the wheat, eventually crowding out the wheat. [8]Fortunately, most of the seed fell onto good soil, sprouted, grew rapidly, and produced new grain from thirty to a hundred fold. [9]If you have ears, listen and learn."

[10]The disciples were puzzled and asked Him, "Why do you teach in parables? Why not tell them straight out what you are trying to teach them?"

[11]"It is because they have so little chance to learn the facts about the kingdom of God. You have so much advantage over them. They need to think things through, and parables are remembered and contemplated better than straight teaching. [12]The way things actually are in this world is that the rich get richer and the poor get poorer, not just in material things but also in one's ability to understand truth. [13]This is one reason why I use parables. They have ears, but they don't really listen; they have eyes, but they really don't see.

[14]"It is just as the prophet Isaiah wrote (Isaiah 6:9), 'Even though they hear, they don't understand; even though they see, they don't really grasp things' [15]For My people have, as a nation, become calloused, uncaring, bigoted, and opinionated,

unable to see, hear, and understand so that they cannot be converted and healed.' [16]How blessed you are. You have eyes and see; you have ears that hear and are functioning normally. [17]It is a fact that many prophets and righteous people have longed to see the things you are seeing and hear the things you are hearing, but were disappointed.

[18]"So let me explain the parable of the farmer sowing his grain. [19]When a person hears about the kingdom of God but does not comprehend it, then the devil comes along and snatches away the seed that was planted in his mind before it takes root; he is like the roadside. [20]Another person is like the stony ground. He gladly receives the word. It sprouts up quickly and begins to develop. [21]But the days pass, and he cannot endure the persecution that hits him because of his beliefs; then he gives up his hope. [22]Another is like the briar patch. The word begins to grow, but he allows the interest in material things to take first place in his life—getting rich, for instance—so that there is no growth in his relationship with God, and thus no spiritual maturity develops. [23]Finally, we come to the good soil. Here is the person who hears the truth, grasps it, and allows it to develop and grow in his mind. It produces a rich harvest of character development and thus becomes a great blessing to others."

[24]Another parable followed. To illustrate the kingdom of heaven, He told of a farmer who sowed the best seed he could get. [25]But when everyone was sleeping, his enemy crept into his field during the night and scattered weed seeds. He then slipped away before dawn, and no one caught him in his mean trick. [26]Of course, it was not apparent what had taken place until the

wheat began to ripen; then the weeds, which resembled grain until harvest time, were spotted throughout the field. [27]The slaves were the first to be aware of the problem. They went to their owner. "Did you not sow certified seed in this field last spring? How then do you explain the great amount of wild grasses we see out there?"

[28]"This has to be the work of my enemy," he reasoned.

Then his slaves asked, "Do you want us to dig up those weeds?"

[29]"No, let us not attempt to do that for the wheat is not quite mature, and it would uproot much of the grain. [30]Let them all grow together until the harvest begins. We shall save the wheat that way, and then the weeds can be uprooted, bound in bundles, and burned."

[31]Next came the parable of the mustard seed. "God's kingdom is like this very tiny seed. Although it is so small, it grows into a plant much larger than other crops. [32]In fact, as you know, it is one of the largest of the herbs, large enough so that birds can build their nests in it. [33]And let us consider bread making. A very small amount of yeast will permeate a large amount of dough and transform that mass into a large, light spongy substance."

[34]The public crowds were thus instructed, and they learned much regarding the nature of God's kingdom. [35]"And now remember that the psalmist has foretold this very thing you have been hearing (Psalm 49:4 and Psalm 78:2): 'I will speak to them in parables. I will express ideas that have been kept secret all through history.'"

[36]And with that, Jesus finished up his instruction and asked the listeners to return home, after which he went into the house, giving the disciples their chance to ask about those parables beginning with the one about the weeds in the field. [37]Here is His explanation: "The farmer sowing the wheat is the Son of man. [38]The field is the world. The good seed represents those who will be saved in God's kingdom. The weeds are those who reject God and follow the evil one. [39]The enemy that sowed the weed seed is the devil. The harvest is the end of the world, and the reapers are the angels. [40]And just as the weeds were pulled, bundled, and burned, so will be the fate of the wicked at the end of the world.

[41]"The Son of man will send his messengers, the angels, into the world to separate from his kingdom everyone who is offensive and wicked. [42]They shall wail and gnash their teeth in anguish, then die, and be consumed in the fire. [43]But the righteous, saved ones, shall glow with radiance like the sun in God's kingdom. If you hear, take heed and remember."

[44]Another parable followed: "The kingdom of God is like a treasure chest buried in a field, completely hidden from view. A worker discovers it and quickly covers it again, goes home, and sells everything he owns in order to raise the money needed to purchase that field."

[45]And yet another parable: "A retailer searches for the finest pearls available. [46]One day he finds a pearl so precious that he is willing to sell everything else to purchase that one pearl."

[47]And finally this one: "God's kingdom is like a fishing net in the lake. It catches all sorts of fish, [48]and when it is filled to capacity, it is taken ashore where the catch is sorted. The edible fish are saved and the inedible ones discarded for fertilizer. [49]It will be like this at the end of the world. The

angels will be sent to separate the wicked from the righteous, [50]and the wicked shall be dumped into a furnace fire. There will be weeping and gnashing of teeth. [51]Are you able to understand these things?" Jesus asked them.

"Yes, Lord."

[52]"Alright, if you understand, you will be a person who is a scribe, an authority about the kingdom of God who in some ways resembles a wealthy merchant who owns a great many valuable objects, some antiques and some brand new."

[53]After this discourse by parables, Jesus left the area [54]and returned to his hometown where he taught the people in the synagogue. Here too, the listeners were deeply impressed and commented among themselves: "How does He get so much wisdom, and where does all that power come from? [55]Isn't this the son of the carpenter? Isn't this Mary's son? Are not His brothers named James, Joses, Simon, and Judas? [56]Are not His sisters all here in our community?"

[57]They wouldn't believe their common neighbor was anything special. His remark was, "A prophet is honored everywhere except in his own country and in his own family." [58]He performed very few miracles there because of their unbelief.

Chapter 14

[1]It was about this time that Herod the tetrarch heard of Jesus' fame. [2]He asked his advisors, "Do you suppose that this is John the Baptist who has been miraculously resurrected? Just such a person is likely to be able to perform miracles."

[3]Herod had ordered John arrested because John had publicly criticized him for taking his brother Philip's wife, Herodias, and was living with her. [5]He wanted to have John executed at once but was afraid that such a course would alienate him entirely from the people who were convinced that John was a prophet. [6]However, one day at Herod's birthday party Herodias' daughter came out and danced as part of the entertainment. She was an accomplished performer, and Herod was so favorably impressed [7]that he called her over and vowed that he would give her anything she asked for. [8]She already knew what to ask for because her mother had coached her ahead of time. "Give me the head of John the Baptist on a platter," she quickly replied. [9]Herod was stunned, but he knew that he must fulfill his promise in order to save face. [10]The order was given to one of the guards who was standing near, and John was beheaded in the prison. [11]Shortly after, a large platter was brought to the party with the bloody trophy on it, and the girl turned it over to her mother.

[12]John's disciples heard about his execution and came to claim his body for burial. Then they located Jesus and informed Him of the tragic event. [13]Upon hearing the sad news, Jesus left for an uninhabited place and was followed by a large group of people from the nearby cities. [14]This large following caused Jesus a lot of joy, but also some sorrow as He saw so many with sickness and disabilities. He lost no time in healing every one of them.

[15]By late afternoon, the disciples became concerned for the people because they had gone without food for most of the day. They approached their Master. "There is no food here. May we send them away? Perhaps in the nearby villages they may be able to find food."

¹⁶"No," Jesus replied, "you give them some food."

¹⁷"But Master, all we have been able to find for ourselves is only five small rolls and two small fish."

¹⁸"Bring them to Me, please." This was done. ¹⁹"Now, everyone, please be seated in the grass," He instructed. When everyone was quiet, He took those five little rolls and the two fish, looked up into the sky, and pronounced a blessing on them. Then He broke them into smaller portions and handed these to the disciples who went into the crowd of people and passed out the food. ²⁰Every person in that whole place received food, and it was more than enough for their needs. The food that was left over after all had eaten was collected and filled twelve baskets! ²¹The number of those who ate there that day was five thousand men, besides women and children.

²²Everyone wanted Jesus to become king, but Jesus made the disciples get in the boat and head home. Then He sent the people away, and He went up into the hills to pray. ²³He spent the evening alone in prayer until darkness descended. ²⁴The night was windy, and the boat in which the disciples were travelling was tossed about dangerously, making no progress toward shore. ²⁵During the late hours of the night, Jesus returned to the lake and began walking on the water toward the boat. ²⁶As he approached it, the disciples could see a form on the water and were terrified, thinking that this was some spirit being. A cry of fear went up from them all. ²⁷But Jesus quickly calmed them as He shouted out, "Don't be afraid; it is I. Cheer up!"

²⁸Peter suddenly came up with an idea. "Lord, if that is really You, ask me to come and meet You on the water."

²⁹"OK, come," was the reply. So Peter climbed out of the boat and began to walk on the water toward Jesus. ³⁰But he began to fear for his life out there on the rough waves and took his eyes off of Jesus. Immediately he began to sink, and in his terror cried out, "Lord, save me!" ³¹Jesus was right at his side in an instant, and he reached out, took his hand, and lifted him to the surface, dripping wet and chagrined. Together they walked back to the boat, and Jesus asked only one question, "Why did you doubt?"

³²As they were climbing aboard, the wind suddenly subsided, and the disciples, awestricken, surrounded Jesus with this confession, "Master, you have to be the Son of God." ³⁴The boat landed at Gennesaret. ³⁵The people there had learned a little about Jesus and that He was in their vicinity. Quickly they began transporting sick and crippled people to Jesus. ³⁶They begged Him to let the sick just touch the hem of His robe, because all who touched Him were healed of all diseases.

Chapter 15

¹At Jerusalem a delegation of scribes and Pharisees was appointed to find Jesus and question Him. ²Their first question was, "Why do Your disciples violate the ceremonial regulations that have been followed for generations, such as the washing of hands before eating?"

³In reply, Jesus began with a question of His own. "Why is it that you allow tradition and custom to permit you to violate the Ten Commandments? ⁴Here is what I am referring to: You know that the fifth commandment reads, 'Honor your father and mother.' Anyone who breaks this commandment is subject to the death penalty.

⁵However, your present practice allows a person to retain material blessings for his own use by saying that a certain asset is 'given to God.' This effectively relieves you of the responsibility to help your aging parents who are in need. ⁶This seems to be fully legitimate in your minds, but frankly, it shows that tradition is followed rather than God's moral law.

⁷"Now I must speak very plainly. You are hypocrites, just as Isaiah predicted in Isaiah 29:13: ⁸'This nation is very vocal about their loyalty to Me. Their lips say all the right things, but deep inside, they are far from Me. ⁹Their worship of Me is entirely futile, for they teach as truth many things that are entirely human tradition.'"

¹⁰Jesus then called out to the multitude to listen, then He enlarged on this topic, which had been introduced by the scribes and Pharisees. ¹¹"Please, understand that what you eat, even with soiled hands, is not what makes you unclean in God's eyes, even though it is a good idea to wash before eating. But what really defiles one is what comes out of the mouth, and I speak of your words and conversation."

¹²After this clarification, His disciples confided in Him: "Were you aware, Master, that the Pharisees took offense at what you just told them?"

¹³"Any plant that My Father has not planted will eventually be uprooted," He replied. ¹⁴"It is better not to engage them in disputes, for they are blind and yet are trying to lead other people who are also blind, and the result will be that both will fall into the ditch."

¹⁵It still perplexed Peter who was trying to understand just what Jesus meant by these illustrations. "Could you explain Yourself a bit more clearly, please?"

¹⁶"Don't you understand yet, Peter? ¹⁷Don't you see that whatever enters the mouth proceeds through the GI tract and is expelled? ¹⁸But the mouth expresses things that are part of the real person, and these things truly defile a person. ¹⁹From the real person come evil ideas such as murder, adultery, abnormal sexual practices, theft, lying, and blasphemy. ²⁰These are true sources of defilement, but just failing to wash your hands before eating does not defile anyone."

²¹Shortly after this incident, Jesus started on a trip toward Tyre and Sidon. ²²Not long after reaching the boundary of this foreign nation, He encountered a Canaanite woman who boldly approached him and began to beg Him: "Please, have mercy, O Lord, Son of David, my daughter is hopelessly tormented by an evil spirit."

²³Jesus listened, but her entreaties did not seem to make the least impression on Him. He ignored her completely, much to the satisfaction of the disciples, who were vocal about their feelings. "Please tell her to 'get lost,'" they said. "She is bothering us."

²⁴They felt even more smug when Jesus added this, "My mission is only to the lost sheep of the nation of Israel."

²⁵But still she continued to beg, "Lord, please help me."

²⁶And once again the disciples were pleased to hear Him say, "It wouldn't really be right to take the children's food and feed it to the dogs."

²⁷"I hear You, Lord, and yet dogs always eat the crumbs that fall from their master's table, do they not?"

²⁸Imagine how the disciples felt when Jesus commended this heathen woman. "You have genuine, effective faith, woman.

And your request will be granted as of now." Her daughter was freed at that very moment. [29]Jesus left that place promptly, willing to perform just that one miracle in order to teach the disciples a lesson about the value of just one soul, even a Gentile.

After returning to Galilee, He climbed to a nice spot on the hillside, sat down, and waited for the crowds to gather again. [30]Before long an immense crowd had gathered around Him, and in their midst were people with every conceivable ailment and disorder—the lame, the aphasics, and the blind—all came to Jesus with the hope of being healed. Not one was turned away. Imagine the tumult of joy that day. [31]The effect was the same on all present: a combination of amazement, gratitude, and thankfulness to the God of Israel who had furnished the creative power to restore such hopeless victims. [32]When the last patient had been healed, they heard Jesus say, "I have pity on all these people. They have been away from home for three days now and have run out of food. They will be exhausted unless they can find something to eat."

[33]The disciples must have already forgotten the miracle of the five thousand, for they expressed perplexity in trying to solve the problem. "Where can we go to find enough food for all these people in the wilderness?"

[34]"Well, how much food can you come up with?" Jesus asked.

"Seven loaves of bread and a few fishes is all we can find."

[35]"Spread the word for them to sit on the ground." [36]Once this was done, he took the seven loaves and those few fish, offered a prayer of thanksgiving and blessing, broke the food into pieces, and gave it to the disciples to distribute to the people. [37]Everyone ate and had enough, and the leftovers amounted to seven basketfuls of food. [38]About four thousand men, besides women and children, were fed that day.

[39]Now it was back to the boat with directions to proceed to Magadan.

Chapter 16

[1]It was at Magadan that the Pharisees and Sadducees got together (for a change) and agreed to question Jesus. Their first request was that He would produce a miraculous sign in the sky. [2]"In the evening," He began, "you study the sky for an indication of what the weather will be like. When you see a red sky in the evening, you conclude that there will be fair weather. [3]But if you see a red sky in the morning, you prepare for rainy weather because of the same red color. Now if you are wise enough to interpret the weather by such signs, can you not interpret the signs you see now in these very times? [4]It is a wicked and unfaithful generation that we are dealing with. Everybody is looking for some significant 'sign' to give them guidance, but no such sign as you might expect will ever be given to you. There will be one sign, however, and it relates to Jonah and his experience."

[5]He left them to ponder just what He might be thinking of by a sign of the prophet Jonah. The disciples and Jesus were again on the other side of the lake, and they had forgotten to bring any bread with them. [6]And Jesus' first words were about bread. "I want you to be on your guard about the leaven of the Pharisees and Sadducees."

[7]His disciples immediately thought, *Is He saying this because we forgot to bring bread?*

[8]But Jesus read their minds and answered the unspoken concerns. "Come now and exercise more faith. [9]You surely remember the five loaves and the five thousand that ate, with twelve basketfuls of leftovers. [10]Or the seven loaves and the four thousand who were fed, with several basketfuls of leftovers. [11]I wonder why it is difficult to comprehend and interpret the meaning of that statement. It had nothing to do with food but with the teaching and influence of the scribes and the Pharisees." [12]Then His disciples began to grasp the meaning of His words. "Beware of their doctrines for they are not always truthful."

[13]One time on a journey to Caesarea Philippi, Jesus asked them this question, "Just who do most of the people think I am?"

[14]Someone answered, "Well, there is little agreement among the people about this. Some think that you must be John the Baptist, some say Elijah, others say Jeremiah, or one of the other prophets."

[15]"Now, the sixty-four dollar question. Who do YOU think I am?"

[16]Peter's answer was immediate and positive, "You are the anointed One, the Messiah, the Christ, the Son of the living God."

[17]"Simon, son of Jonah, you are truly blessed," He answered, "for no human being was able to convince you of the truth you have just uttered. Only My heavenly Father is able to bring about such a miracle. [18]And let Me add this: You are just Peter, just a human being, but I am ready and willing to build my church on the rock-solid truth you have spoken: this faith in Me as God's Son. Against My church all the forces of evil will be unable to triumph. [19]Moreover, I am giving to you,

My followers, the wonderful keys to the kingdom of heaven, keys that will open to you a rewarding life even in a sinful world, then everlasting life where there will be no sin. Whatever you decide on earth that is in harmony with My word will be precisely the same as what is decided in heaven."

[20]Then He urged them not to publicize the fact that He was Jesus the Messiah, NOT YET. [21]From this time onward, He began to open before them His future, how He was destined to go to Jerusalem, be put through a fearful ordeal by the chief priests and scribes, and finally be executed and come back to life on the third day. [22]In disbelief Peter seized Him and shook Him as if to shake some sense into Him. "Lord, let this fate never be mentioned again, never!"

[23]But Jesus calmly turned his back on Peter and addressed Satan, "Get out of here, Satan, you are trying to turn Me away from My mission and from My disciple. You only express things that appeal to the world, not the things of God."

[24]Next, addressing all the disciples, He gave this instruction, "If anyone wants to follow Me, let him abandon his own interests, even to the point of carrying his own cross and do as I will do. [25]Because whoever clings to life, preferring life rather than staying with Me, shall eventually be lost, and whoever is willing to lose his life for My sake will find everlasting life. [26]Let me ask you. Just suppose you are able to plan your business so well that you are able to own the entire world, but you lose out on eternal life. Would it be worth it? Or putting it another way, Is there anything you would not give up in order to have everlasting life? [27]Be aware of this: I shall return to the earth in the splendor of My

Father with His angels and that is when I shall give rewards that are appropriate. Every person on earth will receive exactly what is due him. ²⁸And there are some of you right here now who will not die until after you obtain a glimpse of my coming kingdom."

Chapter 17

¹Only six days after that prediction, Jesus took Peter, James, and John aside and invited them to go with Him to the summit of a nearby mountain. ²As soon as they reached the summit, Jesus became radiant with glorious light—about like the brightness of the sun—even His clothing was brilliantly white. ³There were two men talking to Him. It became apparent that one of them was Moses and the other Elijah. ⁴The three disciples were awestricken, but Peter was the only one who could speak any words. "Lord, I'm glad we are here. What would you think if we built three simple shelters: one for you, one for Moses, and one for Elijah?"

⁵Even while he was speaking, a bright cloud enveloped them all, and from the cloud a mighty voice thundered, "This is My beloved Son. He fully pleases Me. Please, listen to Him and take heed." ⁶The disciples were understandably terrified and fell flat to the ground in fear.

⁷But Jesus came, gently touched them and said, "Don't be afraid." ⁸When they finally had the courage to look up, there was no one present except Jesus. ⁹The momentous experience was over, and the four of them began to descend the mountain. Jesus instructed them not to say a word about this experience until after His resurrection. ¹⁰Then one of them asked, "What do the scribes have in mind when

they say that Elijah must appear first. Is this what they are talking about?"

¹¹"Well, it's like this," He replied. "Elijah will indeed come in order to bring restoration. ¹²In fact, Elijah has already come, and they treated him just as they wanted to. They rejected him and then executed him. I will be treated the same way." ¹³Now the disciples understood. He was speaking about John the Baptist.

¹⁴The four of them joined the other disciples at the base of the mountain where there was a large crowd assembled. Among these was an anxious man who came up to Jesus, knelt before Him, and begged Him ¹⁵to have pity and do something about his son. "He is insane, Lord, and often he seems to be actually grabbed and thrown into fire, or even water. ¹⁶I brought him here to Your disciples, but they could not do anything for him."

¹⁷This did not perplex Jesus in the least. He went right to the root of the trouble at once. "You and your generation are weak in faith and in trust, high on selfishness and rebellion. Bring the boy to Me." ¹⁸When the lad was brought, Jesus publicly challenged the devil who left the boy and never returned, leaving him a perfectly normal young fellow.

¹⁹As soon as possible, the nine disciples drew Jesus aside and urged Him to reveal the reason why they had failed to help the boy. ²⁰"You want to know? Well, it was because of unbelief. The truth is that just a tiny speck of faith represented by this tiny mustard seed is powerful enough to move a mountain from where it is to that spot over there. In fact, no good thing will be impossible. ²¹But this particular case demands not only faith but an earnestness great enough to fast and pray."

²²Once again while still in Galilee, Jesus spoke of the future, knowing that they had not been listening carefully when He brought up the subject before. "I am going to be betrayed and given over to My enemies, ²³and they will kill Me, but I will rise to life again on the third day." Solemn thoughtfulness came over the disciples, but nothing more was said at the time.

²⁴After returning to Capernaum, the tax collector for the temple found Peter and asked him, "Does your Master pay the temple tax?"

"Oh, indeed He does," Peter responded.

²⁵But before Peter could ask Jesus about the matter, Jesus asked him a question, "What do you think, Simon? Do kings collect taxes from their own children or from other subjects?"

²⁶"Only from others," was his answer.

"Then," said Jesus, "the children are exempt, right? ²⁷However, we do not wish to offend them, so here is what we will do. Go to the lake, put in a baited hook, and the first fish to take the bait will have a coin in its mouth. Take that coin and go pay the tax for us, please."

Chapter 18
¹It was still only a short time after the transfiguration that the disciples asked Jesus, "Would You be willing to tell us who will be the greatest in God's kingdom?"

²In His answer, Jesus used a visual aid, calling to His side a nearby child. ³"Truthfully, I tell you this, unless you make a definite about-face and become like this child, you will never see the kingdom of heaven. ⁴But everyone who is willing to humble himself as this child will be great in the kingdom of God. ⁵Furthermore, if anyone accepts a child of Mine, one who claims My name, that person is accepting Me. ⁶And alas, if someone offends, troubles, or abuses one of these children who believes in Me, it would be better for him if a millstone were tied to his neck and he was dumped into the ocean. ⁷The world is full of woe because of such abuse, and you can expect such things, but how fearful will be the fate of him who commits such abuse.

⁸"Look at it this way. If your hand or your foot threatens your eternal life, it is better to have it amputated than to be eternally lost and perish in the lake of fire. ⁹In the same way, if your eye threatens your spirituality, it would be better to have it enucleated than to have two eyes and be eternally lost. ¹⁰Never underestimate one of these children, for in heaven, their guardian angels are always in communion with My Father. ¹¹And don't forget that the Son of man has come to this earth to rescue and save the lost.

¹²"Let me ask you a question. If a sheep rancher has one hundred sheep and even one gets lost, will he not leave those ninety-nine and go out into the mountains to hunt for that one lost sheep? ¹³And when he finds it, you may be sure that his joy over finding the lost one is greater than the joy over the ninety-nine who stayed in the pasture where they belong. ¹⁴It is something like that with God and lost people. It is never acceptable in His sight to have even one of these children lost.

¹⁵"And how about this situation? Let's say that one of your brothers or neighbors has injured you in some way. Here is what to do. First, go to him personally and tell him how badly hurt you feel over what he has done to you. If he is willing to listen and confess, be thankful for he will be

your friend and make things right. [16]Now if he is unwilling to accept what you have to say, you have another option. Take with you two or three witnesses who will help him to realize you have been truthful. [17]In case he rejects the evidence against him at that time, then you have the right and the responsibility to bring the matter to the church. Your next option? Let's hope he will listen meekly to your appeal in the presence of the church, but if he still refuses to listen and do something about it, do not abandon him, but treat him as you would treat the heathen or a traitor, and how would that be? You still want to win him over to God's side.

[18]"Truly I tell you, anything you bind here on earth will be just the same way in heaven. And whatever you release here will be the same in heaven. [19]One more assurance. If even two of you get together and ask for any of God's blessings, My Father will answer your prayer and carry out your request. [20]And if two or three of you assemble in My name, I am always with them."

[21]Here, Peter wanted to ask a question. "Master, I have a question that has perplexed me for a long time. May I ask about it?"

"Yes, of course," Jesus replied.

"Master, if another person sins against me, how many times am I obliged to forgive him? Would it be seven times?"

[22]"Try to accept my answer, Peter. The correct answer would be seventy times seven! [23]And speaking of forgiveness, learn a bit about the kingdom of heaven from this story. A certain king was going over his accounts when he came across the shocking fact that one of his trusted advisors owed him three million dollars. [24]The man was summoned, but when questioned, it was discovered that he was bankrupt and totally unable to pay the debt. [25]So the king signed an order to have him, his wife, and his children sold as slaves, and all his possessions sold as well, all of which was only a drop in the bucket. [26]The poor fellow knelt before the king, begging for mercy, 'Please, please, give me time, and I will pay it all back.' [27]The king was touched by the predicament the fellow was in, and with a sudden outburst of generosity, he cancelled the order and forgave the debt.

[28]"But now notice what happened. This very man who had just been forgiven a three-million-dollar debt went and found a fellow servant who owed him one hundred dollars. What do you think he did? He seized the man by the throat and demanded, 'Pay me what you owe me!' [29]The fellow servant fell to his knees and begged, 'Please, please, have mercy. Give me time, and I will pay you what I owe.' [30]The plea fell on deaf ears, and quickly he was arrested and jailed until he paid the full amount.

[31]"However, that was not the end of the matter because his fellow workers saw the confrontation and were indignant over the harshness shown to the debtor, so they reported it to the king. [32]It took but a short time for the king to summon the unforgiving man into his presence. 'You are a wicked person, if I ever saw one. I just forgave you an enormous debt in response to your earnest plea, [33]and what did you do? You went right out and demonstrated not the least trace of compassion toward a fellow worker who owes you only a tiny debt. Don't you think you should have shown him the same kindness that I showed you?' [34]After explaining his indignation, the king then called the guards and ordered the fellow imprisoned

until his huge debt was settled. [35]This story clearly shows what sort of sinners will be forgiven by My Father—only those who are forgiving of their fellow men."

Chapter 19

[1]Next, Jesus left Galilee and went to Judea. [2]Again a large number of people surrounded Him, many of whom were healed by His marvelous power over disease. [3]As usual there were Pharisees in the crowd looking for evidence of some misdemeanor or crime. They first confronted Him with another sticky question. "Is it legal to divorce one's wife for each and every reason that our law now recognizes?"

[4]In His answer He asked them a question as to whether they had read the book of Genesis recently in which marriage was first mentioned. Here the Creator is presented as the inventor of sexuality, male and female human beings. [5]His words were as follows: "It is the way that you were designed that upon maturity a man should become independent of his father and mother and instead should be united to his wife, thus forming a single unit. [6]After this union has been established, it should never be dissolved, but they should stay together always. Now if God Himself designed them this way and intended for them to remain together, let us not think that human beings should come up with a plan to separate them."

[7]But the enemies of Jesus, in a triumphant attitude, retorted, "Oh, Oh, You have forgotten that Moses states that divorce is OK."

[8]"No, I have not forgotten that statement, and it was a fact that divorce was allowed in society because God knew the perversity of the human heart, that selfishness and wickedness would be the lot of humanity. However, that was not God's original plan. [9]Let us try to understand the true significance of marriage. If a man divorces his wife and marries another woman, unless the divorce is the result of unfaithfulness on the part of his first wife, he is committing adultery. Furthermore, the man who marries the divorcee also commits adultery."

[10]The disciples later questioned Him, bringing up the idea that it's never good to marry in view of the serious faults of the human race. [11]But Jesus assured them that when God gives them grace, which is promised, they need not fail while following the original plan. [12]"Yes, there are some who will not marry for they are eunuchs, born with this deficiency. Others were transformed into eunuchs by injury or by surgery and others have chosen to remain celibate because of their complete dedication to God's service in proclamation of His kingdom, which demands their whole life. So try to understand these things in their true setting."

[13]Then some little children were brought to Him by parents who were hoping that He would put His hands on them in blessing and prayer. This annoyed the disciples who tried to discourage those parents from such unnecessary (they thought) rituals, but He gently corrected them. [14]"Always allow the children to come to Me; in fact, encourage more to come for the kingdom of heaven will be occupied by people who have the simple trust that these children have." [15]Having said this He placed His hands on them and blessed them before moving on.

[16]After that an adult came with this question, "Good Master, what good thing

need I do to have assurance of eternal life?"

[17]"Why are you calling Me good?" Jesus asked. "As you know, the only person who is good is God Himself, and to be given eternal life, one must be willing to keep God's commandments."

[18]"Which ones, Master?"

"The Ten Commandments," Jesus responded. [19]"Don't commit adultery, honor father and mother, don't murder, don't lie, don't steal, and love your neighbor as yourself."

[20]The young fellow asked, "Anything else?"

[21]"Yes, there is," was the answer from Jesus. "If you want to be completely mature in God's sight, go home, sell all your material goods, and give to the poor, then you will have a real heavenly investment. Then come and join Me in My work."

[22]He became very solemn and then turned away. (He was very rich). [23]Now speaking to His disciples, Jesus explained, "I am telling it like it is; it is extremely difficult for a rich person to enter God's kingdom. [24]Here is an illustration to make My point: it is harder for a rich man to enter God's kingdom than for a camel to go through the eye of a needle."

[25]The disciples were stunned. "Who then can expect to be saved?" they asked.

[26]Jesus looked at them kindly and yet seriously, then answered, "Humanly speaking, this is of course impossible. But with God anything is possible and can be expected to be done."

[27]In a serious mood, Peter then asked, "Look at us here, Lord. We are twelve men who have given up our livelihood and everything else we value in this world in order to be with You. What can we expect?"

[28]The answer Jesus gave reassured them all. "Truthfully, I say to you, you men who are with Me today will, when I am enthroned in the universe and return to establish the new earth, be given positions as judges over the inhabitants of the earth. [29]And everyone who has been willing to place his own interests secondary to Me and the truth, his home, his wife, his children, father, mother, and property, will be enriched ten thousand percent in addition to receiving everlasting life. [30]But alas, many who seem to be first now will be last then, while those who seem to be last now will be first then."

Chapter 20

[1]"Let me illustrate God's kingdom this way: 'A farmer who owned a vineyard went out early in the morning to hire farm laborers. [2]He found several and agreed to pay them the going rate, so they went to work. [3]"However, he could see that he still did not have enough workers, so about 9:00 a.m. he went looking for more. Sure enough there were several in the town square doing nothing. [4]"'Would you like a job?' he asked, and they responded affirmatively. 'OK, come and work for me, and I will pay you what is right,' he continued, so they went to work.

[5]"The same took place again, about noon; then again at 3:00 p.m. [6]Once more, at about 5:00 p.m. he went into town and found some more idle ones and asked them, 'Why are you not working?' [7]'Simple, sir, no one has hired us.' 'Well I am offering you a job right now and will pay you a fair wage.' [8]At the end of the working day, the owner called the vineyard manager and gave him these instructions, 'Begin with the last ones hired and give all of them a full day's wages.'

⁹"The ones hired at 5:00 p.m. were pleasantly surprised when they received a full day's pay. ¹⁰But when those hired in the morning received only a full day's pay, they were disappointed. ¹¹They went to the owner with a complaint. 'Look, sir, why have you paid us the same as these who have worked only one hour? We worked all through the hot day. ¹²This just is not fair, and we are about to see our attorney.'

¹³"'Of course you are free to see your attorney,' he replied, 'but you won't have a leg to stand on. For when I hired you, I promised to pay you a full day's wage, and you agreed and went to work. ¹⁴Take your money and go home. It just happens that I want to pay all of you the same. ¹⁵Are you trying to say I am an evil person. It is my money, and I can do with it whatever I choose. In fact, I am rather generous? Look how I rewarded those who helped in the rush to close the harvest.'

¹⁶"Do you get the message? Some of those who come last will be first in God's kingdom. And another thing, many of those who are called to eternal life will not choose to accept it."

¹⁷The time had come that Jesus must go up to Jerusalem. He and His disciples traveled together, but many more were also on their way. At an appropriate time, Jesus drew His disciples aside and confided in them once again: ¹⁸"As you know, we are on our way to Jerusalem. Sadly enough this is the place where I will be betrayed and delivered to the chief priests and scribes who will condemn Me to death, ¹⁹after which I shall be turned over to the Romans who will scourge and crucify Me. But on the third day I will rise from death."

²⁰It was not long after this that the mother of James and John brought them to Jesus with a request. ²¹He knew that she wanted to ask a favor, so He invited her to make it known. She hesitated a bit, knowing that her request would sound a bit selfish, but then took a deep breath and began: "Would it be possible for You to appoint my two sons as next-in-command when You are made ruler?"

²²His answer was given at once. "Madam, you are asking something that has been long misunderstood by everyone." Then He turned to James and John, "Are you two able to drink the cup that I shall drink and be baptized with the same baptism that I receive?"

"Of course we are, Master," they cheerfully answered.

²³"I hesitate to inform you, but both of you will drink from the same cup from which I will drink and will pass through the same baptism which I will experience, but the privilege you are requesting is one that I cannot promise, for My Father will make all such appointments."

²⁴As one might expect, the other disciples were indignant over the bold request made on behalf of James and John. ²⁵So Jesus called them all together in an attempt to help them understand more clearly His mission, the character of the Father, and their own condition. "You are aware, I am sure, that in this world, the kings and kingly families are the ones who dictate life for their subjects and that these authority figures are considered the great ones. ²⁶But let me tell you how things will be with you. Any of you who wants to be the greatest will be the one who serves the others, the one who actually ministers to their needs. ²⁷Yes, the very greatest will be a servant to others. ²⁸This will demonstrate that you are like Me, for I came to this world, not to be

waited on, but to serve others and even to give My life as a ransom for all who will accept Me."

²⁹As they proceeded on their way, they were accompanied by a large crowd. ³⁰Then two blind men who had been sitting by the road approached Jesus. As He came nearer, they called out to Him, "Please, take pity on us Lord, Son of David." ³¹Some of the people with Jesus became annoyed at their noisy yelling and tried to quiet them down, but they cried louder and louder, "Please, please, have pity on us Lord, Son of David."

³²Jesus stopped, then spoke to them, "Just what is it that you want Me to do for you?"

³³"Lord, we want to be able to see!" ³⁴So Jesus touched their eyes, and instantly their vision was restored, and they joined the group who were following Jesus.

Chapter 21

¹The throng was now approaching Jerusalem and had reached Bethphage when Jesus sent two of his disciples on ahead with these instructions: ²"Go into the village, and when you get there, you will find a donkey tied up with her colt. Untie them and lead them back here to Me. ³If anyone asks you what you are up to, just tell them that the Lord needs them and a consent will be given." ⁴This little experience fulfilled the prophecy of Zechariah 9:9, which says, ⁵"Inform the daughter of Zion that her King is coming, a meek King, but a King nonetheless. He will be riding on an unbroken colt of a donkey."

⁶So they followed His directions exactly as He had told them. ⁷They brought the donkey and the colt to Jesus, tossed some of their own clothing on the colt, and Jesus rode toward town. ⁸Recognizing the significance of the occasion, the people began to lay their clothing on the road, while others cut branches from the trees and put these on the road where Jesus was to pass. ⁹Ahead of Him and behind Him a chant began to be heard: "Hosanna to the Son of David. Blessed is He who is coming in the name of the Lord. Hosanna, Hosanna!" ¹⁰Upon reaching Jerusalem, the people in the city became very excited about what was happening. People asked each other, "Who is this, anyway?" ¹¹The answer was, "This is Jesus the prophet from Nazareth in Galilee."

¹²The procession went right to the temple, and when Jesus entered it, He drove out the merchants who sold sheep, cattle, and doves; then he overturned the tables of the currency exchangers. ¹³His explanation was freely given, "It is written: 'My house shall be called a house of prayer, but you have turned it into a den of thieves.'" ¹⁴When the merchants and money changers were gone, the blind and the lame were invited in, and Jesus healed them.

¹⁵Scribes and Pharisees were watching, of course, and they took note of all that occurred, the amazing healings, the children singing "Hosanna to the Son of David," and this angered them greatly. ¹⁶They confronted Jesus, "Do you hear what these people are saying?"

"Yes, I hear them. Perhaps you have never read Psalm 8 where it has been foretold, 'Out of the mouth of babies and nursing children, you have heard perfect praise.'"

¹⁷That evening Jesus left the city for Bethany where He stayed at Lazarus' home. ¹⁸The next morning He was hungry as He made His way to the city, for He had eaten no breakfast. ¹⁹They passed

a fig tree that had leafed out and gave the impression that it might have fruit on it. However, a search proved that no fruit was present. "May you never bear another fig" was the fate pronounced on it by Jesus, and within a brief moment the whole tree withered and died before their eyes. [20]The disciples were shocked and commented on the speedy death of the tree. [21]"Let me add a thought," Jesus said. "You may believe Me when I say that if you have complete faith and do not doubt you will be able to do what I did to the fig tree. You will also be able to say to this mountain, 'move over and fall into the ocean,' and it will obey you. [22]Everything you ask in a prayer of faith shall be done for you."

[23]Once again in the temple, Jesus was teaching the people. The chief priests and the elders had also come, and one of them suddenly interrupted Him, inquiring, "Just who gave You the right to teach here?"

[24]"I shall answer that question if you will answer one of My questions: [25]'Regarding John the Baptist and his life: was it directed by God or was it just a human effort?'"

They held a quick caucus and realized that they were in trouble. "If we say that it was from God, He will ask why we did not believe in Him. [26]But if we say it was all human work, we will lose credibility with the people for John is considered a prophet by a large percentage of our nation." [27]So they broke up their huddle, and the spokesman admitted, "We are not able to answer that question one way or the other."

"Then I shall not reveal to you My source of authority," Jesus answered. [28]He then asked them to comment on a hypothetical question. "A man has two sons. He asks the first one to go work in the vineyard. [29]The son sneered, 'No way,' but his conscience bothered him, and he repented and went to work with his father. [30]The second son, when given the same request replied, 'I'm on my way, Dad,' but he didn't go. [31]Which of these sons actually obeyed his father?"

They were compelled to answer, "The first."

Jesus then stunned them with this statement, "Please think this through, for the tax collectors and prostitutes are more likely to enter the kingdom of heaven than you are. [32]For John was sent by God for a special work, a very righteous mission, but you leaders would not believe him. But the tax collectors and prostitutes believed him and repented; then even after you saw the change in their lives, you would not repent and confess that he was telling the truth. [3]

[3]"Listen to another parable. Once upon a time there was a successful farmer who planted a large vineyard, then planted a hedge around the vineyard and built a winepress and a tower on the property. He then leased the whole operation to some renters, for he was going to a distant country on other business. [34]At the time for the harvest, he sent representatives to collect the rent from the renters. [35]But those scoundrels grabbed them, beat one of them up unmercifully, killed another, and stoned a third one, almost fatally. [36]The owner was furious and sent more men, but they were treated in a similar fashion. [37]Finally in desperation he dispatched his son, thinking that they would listen to a person with that kind of authority. [38]But when the son appeared, they conspired among themselves and reasoned this way: 'Hey, here is the heir to the vineyard. Let's kill him and take the vineyard ourselves.'

³⁹So they captured him and killed him. ⁴⁰Now when the owner returns, what do you think he will do to these criminals?"

⁴¹Quickly came the response, "He will try them all for murder, then lease the vineyard to new renters who will deal honestly with him."

⁴²"Another scripture comes to mind: 'The stone that was rejected by the builders is now the chief cornerstone. This is the Lord's doing and it amazes us.' ⁴³So let me say that the kingdom of God must be and will be placed in other hands, other people, who will actually bear the fruit desired. ⁴⁴And about the stone, if a person falls on it in his utter helplessness, he will surely be a subdued person, but if the stone falls on a person it will grind him into small fragments."

⁴⁵These metaphors were easily understood by the Pharisees and priests; they knew He was talking about them. ⁴⁶They would have had Him arrested on the spot, but they were afraid of the people because the vast majority considered Him a prophet.

Chapter 22

¹So Jesus went on giving them more parables. ²"One time there was a king whose son was soon to be married and a great banquet was planned. A long guest list had to be prepared, and at the proper time, ³messengers were sent out to all of the invitees with this message: 'The wedding feast is ready; time to come to the banquet.' Imagine the king's consternation when he learned that those who had been invited had declined the invitation. ⁴More messengers were sent with a more urgent plea. 'The feast is ready, the oxen are killed, the fat calves prepared, and everything else is ready. Please come!'

⁵But surprisingly enough, they treated the invitation as a big joke and proceeded to go right on with their own interests: farm, merchandise, or whatever. ⁶A few were actually violent in their treatment of the messengers, shamefully brutalizing some of them and actually killing a few. ⁷As one might expect, the king was really upset and sent armed troops to destroy the criminals and to torch their city.

⁸"Next the king gave new instructions to his messengers, 'Look, the ones I originally invited are not deserving of my kindness, so the wedding and the feast will have to be on hold. ⁹Now go to the streets, the alleys, and to rural areas, and keep on inviting until there are enough to fill the banquet hall.' ¹⁰So they went and began inviting any and everyone they found, bad and good, until there were enough.

¹¹"When the guests had been seated, the king came in and began greeting them, but one of the men had refused to put on the special robe that had been offered him at the door, thinking that this was really unimportant. ¹²'My friend, would you please explain why you do not have on the robe offered to you?' The fellow couldn't answer a word. ¹³'Soldiers, take this gentleman out of the banquet hall, handcuff him and hobble him, and take him out of the palace into the darkness of night, even if he cries and gnashes his teeth.'

¹⁴"Let us learn from this. Although a large number were invited, very few were finally admitted into the hall. Even so, there is an invitation from God to everyone on planet earth, but a relative few will be saved in God's kingdom."

¹⁵Once again the Pharisees got together in another attempt to trap Jesus so that He could be arrested. ¹⁶Their next plot was one

that seemed to have promise of success. Some diplomatic fellows along with some Herodians came to Jesus with a flattering statement, "Master, we recognize You to be a true preacher of God's word, not influenced by any human being regardless of their standing and reputation. [17]Please, give us Your honest opinion regarding a problem we face. Is it or is it not proper for God's people to pay taxes to the emperor?"

[18]At once Jesus could see through their scheme. "You hypocrites, you are pretending to want information when your real purpose is to trick Me into saying something you can use against Me. [19]Bring me a coin please." Someone handed Him a coin. [20]"Whose picture is on this coin and whose words are found on it?"

[21]They answer, "Caesar's."

So Jesus replied, "OK, then pay to Caesar what is his and to God what is His." [22]They were defeated. His answer displayed His wisdom, so they left Him.

[23]But that very day some Sadducees came, and not believing in any resurrection, they wanted to trap Him with a question. [24]"Teacher, in Deuteronomy 25:5 we have instruction that if a man dies childless his widow must marry his brother and that their first child shall be considered the descendant of the deceased. [25]Now we have a problem with this instruction. You see, there was a family with seven brothers. The oldest married, but died having no children, so his widow dutifully was given in marriage to the brother. [26]Unfortunately, this man died also, and he had no children. So the woman was given to the third brother who also died childless. This went on until all seven had married the woman and none of them had any children. [27]And of course, eventually the woman herself

died. [28]My question is that when resurrection day comes whose wife will she be for she was married to seven different men, all legitimately?"

[29]"Friends," Jesus replied, "your perplexity is brought about by two things. First, you don't know the scriptures well enough, and second, you cannot comprehend the power of God. In the resurrection, they will be like angels. (They excel in strength, Psalm 103:10, and they 'stand by' human beings, Zechariah 3:5.) [30]At the resurrection, men will not marry and women will not be given in marriage. However, they will all excel in strength and they all will 'stand by' in helpfulness. [31]And let me add another thought about the resurrection. You probably remember what God said in Exodus 3:6 and 3:16: He proclaimed Himself to be the God of Abraham, Isaac, and Jacob. These were all dead at the time. [32]God would not proclaim Himself to be the God of the dead and leave them lifeless. No, He is the God of life and living, and yes, there will be a resurrection."

[33]A large number of people heard this explanation and were deeply impressed by His teaching. [34]The word got around that the Sadducees had been defeated in their confrontation. This delighted the Pharisees, so they held a little caucus and returned to Jesus with more questions. [35]Their leading lawyer challenged Him with this question: "Teacher, which of the Ten Commandments is the most important one of all? [36]Perhaps there is an even greater one somewhere in the scripture."

[37]"The greatest of all commandments is this one," Jesus answered. "You will love the Lord your God with all your heart, soul, and mind. [38]Yes, this is the greatest and most important commandment of all.

[39]The next in importance is this one: You will love your neighbor just as you love yourself. [40]The entire scripture, including the Ten Commandments, is based on these two." [41]Then he asked them a question. [42]"What do you believe about the Messiah? Whose descendant is He?"

They answered, "David's."

[43]But the next question baffled them. "Then why does David, speaking by inspiration, call him 'Lord?' [44]As in Psalm 110:1: 'Jehovah said to my Lord, "sit here at my right hand while I bring your enemies into subjection to you."' [45]How could David call one of his descendants 'Lord' unless that descendant was really greater than David himself?"

[46]The point was made. They dared not ask Him any more questions.

Chapter 23

[1]Once again Jesus began instructing His disciples and all who were following Him. His message was as follows: [2]"You people have your spiritual leaders, scribes and Pharisees, who, in a way, occupy the position that Moses occupied. [3]So when they instruct you, listen and act upon the instruction, but do not use them as role models, for they may tell you the right things, but they don't always practice what they preach. [4]They are perfectly willing to tie wagon loads on other people, but as for themselves, they would not carry a load easily moved by one finger.

[5]"They do everything just to be admired, such as making special amulets to wear or making extra-wide hems on their robes. [6]They love the best positions at feast time, the best pews in the synagogues, [7]the satisfaction that comes from being addressed as 'Rabbi this, Rabbi that.'

[8]No, let's not be called 'Rabbi.' You have only one authoritative teacher—Christ the Messiah. And you are all brothers and sisters. [9]And don't look up to human beings, calling them 'Father,' for you have only one real father, the heavenly Father. [10]And avoid calling another person 'Master,' for you have only one master—Christ.

[11]"The very greatest person among you is the one who serves others. [12]If one of you aspires to be 'top man,' he will likely be put down, and if a person is genuinely humble, that person will wind up with true honor. [13]You Pharisees, woe be unto you, and you scribes, woe be unto you, for you are trying to take the responsibility of deciding who will be saved, leading them astray as a result. You will not enter God's kingdom yourselves, and you are turning some away who are on the right road to His kingdom. [14]Another reason for concern, real concern, listen, you hypocrites! You repossess homes belonging to widows. Then piously mouth long, eloquent prayers. It is because of such behavior as this that you will receive condemnation.

[15]"Now more woes to you, scribes and Pharisees, you hypocrites! You go to tremendous lengths to make one proselyte, and once he is a believer, your influence turns him into a worse child of death than you yourselves are. [16]Yes, woe to you, blind guides who say one thing and do another, like this little rule: To swear by the temple is perfectly OK, but to swear by the gold that is in the temple, well that is terrible. [17]Are you so blind that you are unable to see that gold is holy only as it is dedicated to the service of the temple?

[18]"Another inconsistency: If one swears by the altar, there is no fault, but if one swears by the gift on the altar, he is a great

sinner. [19]Is it not a bit ridiculous to make a big difference between the gift and the altar that makes that gift a sacred object? [20]The fact is that if one swears by the altar, the oath must also include the gift on the altar. [21]And if one swears by the temple, one also swears by the One who dwells in that temple. [22]If you swear by heaven, you would be swearing by God's throne and by God Himself.

[23]"Again, woe be upon you, scribes and Pharisees—hypocrites indeed—because even though you are very exacting about the paying of tithe on such things as mint leaves, anise, and cumin, you are neglecting much more important things such as justice, mercy, and faith. These are the things you should have centered your attention on while continuing to be faithful tithers. [24]You are guides, to be sure, but truthfully you are blind ones. You are concerned about small matters such as gnats in the drinking water, which you carefully strain out, while you swallow a camel.

[25]"Woe be upon you, scribes and Pharisees—hypocrites indeed—for you clean, scour, and polish the outer side of the cup and saucer while at the same time the inside is covered with leftover residue (extortion and greed). [26]Take My advice; if you are this blind, scour out the inside of the cup and saucer, then the outside will be easy. [27]You remind me of a beautiful sarcophagus, brilliantly white, while within it are rotting corpses and bones. [28]This is the way you are. Outwardly you seem to be righteous people while in your hearts you harbor wickedness.

[29]"Woe be unto you, scribes and Pharisees—hypocrites—because you build beautiful tombs to memorialize the prophets [30]while proclaiming loudly that had you lived at the time of these heroes you would never have treated them as shabbily as your ancestors did, [31]but you are in truth proud of those ancestors [32]and are outdoing them, continuing in the very wickedness of those days.

[33]"Serpents! A whole generation of vipers! I declare that as things are now you cannot escape the condemnation to eternal death. [34]I have sent prophets, wise men, and scribes, and will continue to send them, but you will scourge them right in your synagogues and will harass them from one city to another. [35]Your actions will be such that it can be truthfully said that you are responsible for the deaths of righteous people from Abel right on through history, including the death of Zacharias the son of Berakiah who was assassinated right in the temple precincts between the porch and the altar. [36]It is absolutely true that this generation is responsible and will necessarily receive appropriate consequences.

[37]"Oh Jerusalem, Jerusalem! You who have killed the prophets and stoned those who have been sent to help you! How often would I have gathered your children together for protection as a hen gathers her chicks under her wings, but you have refused, and finally, it is too late! [38]Your beautiful temple is without meaning from now on. It will never be visited by God's presence again. [39]The next time you see Me you will be forced to admit, 'Blessed is the One who is coming in the name of the Lord.'"

Chapter 24

[1]At last Jesus slowly turned away from the temple and sadly left it, never to return. His disciples followed along, silent and thoughtful, but finally some called His

attention to the temple and the solid way it had been constructed and its beauty, attempting to understand Jesus' words. [2]He did not disappoint them. "Honestly, friends, look again at these buildings. They might appear to be so strong as to stand here forever. But alas, they won't. Some day there will not be one stone left on another."

[3]Upon reaching the Mount of Olives, the disciples urged Him to share with them the full impact of the events He had predicted. "Tell us please when all this will take place and give us clues as to what we can expect before You return at the end of the world."

[4]His first words were, "Be on your guard so that you will not be deceived, [5]because there will be many who will come and claim to be Christ. This claim will be believed by great numbers of people. [6]Another thing to keep in mind, wars and more wars will be fought. They will result in unbelievable pain, loss, poverty, and sorrow and will be one of the things that will result in a great longing for the end, but be patient through it all and do not give up your faith. [7]One nation after another will go to war against its neighbor, one kingdom against another kingdom, plus famines, epidemics, and earthquakes will take place in many different regions. [8]Of course, these will be the source of terrible sorrow, which will be prevalent all through history.

[9]"Furthermore, you will be arrested and persecuted, some of you will be executed, and many will be hated by people in every nation because you profess My name. [10]It distresses Me to tell you this, but many will lose faith and will betray others and even hate their former brethren. [11]Beware of false prophets who will

present deceptive ideas very effectively. [12]Sin will get worse and worse. Fewer and fewer people will have love for each other, [13]but you who hold to your faith to the very end will be saved. [14]And here's the encouraging news: the good news about God's kingdom will be preached throughout the entire world and then the end will come.

[15]"Remember this, when you see the fulfillment of Daniel 9:27, the 'abomination that destroys' enter the sanctuary (whoever reads please, understand), [16]then it will be time for you believers who live in Judea to escape to the mountains. [17]If you happen to be on the roof napping, don't waste time to go back into the house to save any possessions, [18]and if you are in the field working, don't try to grab more clothing than you happen to have on at the time, [19]and for those women who are pregnant, it will be a difficult time and for those who have nursing babies, it will be very difficult. [20]But it is proper to pray that your escape will not be in the wintertime, nor on the Sabbath day.

[21]"These times I am telling you about will be filled with greater trouble than the world has ever seen or will ever see. [22]Fortunately, that time of trouble will be shortened or else all human life might be wiped out, but for the sake of you believers, that time will be cut short. [23]So once again, be warned. If you hear of anyone saying, 'Here is Christ' or 'there is Christ,' don't believe a word of it. [24]For many false Christs and false prophets will be abroad, some of them even performing miracles in their attempts to deceive even you believers. [25]But you are properly warned ahead of time, [26]so if anyone says, 'He is out in the desert,' don't waste time going out there, for you would run the risk of being deceived,

or perhaps they might proclaim, 'He is in a séance over here.' Don't believe it.

[27]"Let me tell you how the Son of man will return. You know how the whole sky is lightened from the eastern horizon to the west by flashes of lightning. That illustrates the brilliance of My return. [28]And as vultures gather over a carcass, so multitudes will gather about Him at His return.

[29]"Now a few more details: In that time of trouble, but after the persecutions have subsided, there will be an unexplained dark day, the sun will be dimmed that day and the moon that night will scarcely produce any light. After that phenomenon, there will be a shower of meteors, the like of which has never been witnessed and after that a mysterious shaking of the heavenly objects, [30]and finally the appearance of the Son of man in the sky. This will result in unbelievable mourning and sorrow among earth's people, as they see Him returning with unlimited power and splendor, for they have rejected Him. [31]He will then sound out a blast of music over the earth, like a trumpet tone, which will gather up those who have received Him, people from every part of the earth. [32]You are wondering when this will take place. [33]And here is a clue. Just as a fig tree begins to grow new leaf buds in the spring and you know that summer is on the way, so you will know by these signs that I have given you, that it is near, perhaps right at the door. [34]The generation now living will see the fulfillment of some of the events I have foretold and the generation of those who see the last of these signs will see the final fulfillment of my predictions.

[35]"Even though the heavens and the earth should disappear, My words cannot fail. [36]But no one knows and no one will know the exact time for My return. Not even the angels of heaven have been told. Only My Father knows, and He has told no other being yet. [37]But this world will resemble to some degree the world at the time of Noah. [38]People were living their lives rather normally, eating and drinking, marrying and being given in marriage, right up until the very day that Noah boarded the ark. [39]They were totally unaware that disaster was coming until the flood began, and then it was too late. This very same condition will prevail just prior to My return.

[40]"Unfortunately, not all will choose salvation. Let us imagine two working together in a field. One of these may be taken away, the other saved. [41]Or imagine two women working at the mill. One may be taken away, the other saved. [42]You simply must be watchful, for you will not know the time of My return. [43]In your society, one would expect the home owner to be on guard if he knew the very time when a burglar would arrive so that he could prevent loss. [44]But you must be ready at all times because the Son of man will return at a time when you sincerely think He will not.

[45]"Who is the wise steward who has full authority over the owner's estate, even to manage the food of the slaves and the work of the other employees? I'll tell you. [46]It is the one who is always doing his job and doing it well until the owner returns. [47]Truthfully, I tell you, this is the very reason he was given authority over the entire estate. [48]But just imagine what would have happened to a person who had been entrusted with management and then through selfishness and irresponsibility, began to reason, [49]'Oh, let's not worry,

the owner won't be back for a while, so he will never know. Let's just have a good time.' Then he puts on a big drinking party, becomes violent, and even assaults other employees and slaves. [50]"You may rightly conclude that the owner will return at some unexpected moment and quickly discern what has happened. [51]Then he will fire the steward, leaving him with no job and a ruined reputation. Weeping and gnashing of teeth will follow.

Chapter 25

[1]"The kingdom of heaven can be illustrated by the story of the ten virgins who lit their lamps and went out to meet the bridegroom. [2]Five of these were wise in planning for the event, while five were not so wise. [3]The poor planners failed to take extra oil for their lamps, [4]while the wise ones took a reserve supply of oil, just in case. [5]The bridegroom was unexpectedly delayed, and the girls were all getting drowsy, so they found some mats and plopped down to rest. Soon they were all asleep. [6]About midnight someone shouted, 'Hey, he's coming, go out there and meet him.' [7]So they got up, trimmed their lamps, and were ready to go. [8]The foolish girls learned that their lamps were out of oil, or nearly so. [9]"May we borrow some of your oil,' they asked the wiser ones. 'No, unfortunately, there would not be enough for all of us. You had best go to the store and buy some for yourselves.' [10]Off they went, but by the time they had located a clerk who would open the store and sell them the oil, the bridegroom arrived, and those who were ready entered the wedding chapel, shutting the door behind them. [11]When the tardy ones got there, they pounded on the door, asking to be let in. [12]But he turned them down, 'Honestly, I don't know you.'"

[13]"Let this be a warning for you believers, for you will not know when I am about to arrive, so always be ready!"

[14]"And now another illustration. A man leaves home for an extended trip abroad and places his assets in the hands of his dependable staff. He left cash with three of his best managers. Then he left. [15]To one he entrusted five talents, to another two talents, and to another one. [16]The man who received the five talents quickly invested the money in a paying enterprise, and by the time the owner returned, his investment had doubled in value. [17]The man to whom had been entrusted two talents also made a successful investment, and his investment doubled in value as well. [18]But the person with the one talent did not put the money to use. He carefully boxed up the money, dug a hole, and buried it in the ground. [19]After an extended period of time, the owner returned and called them in, one by one, to hear their reports.

[20]"First was the man to whom had been give five talents. 'Sir, your five talents were invested, and they earned five more talents, and here they are.'

[21]"The owner was visibly pleased. 'You must have used good judgment in dealing with these five talents. I am going to ask you to assume greater responsibilities. Enjoy life with me.'

[22]"Next came the man with the two talents. 'Sir, your two talents were invested, and the investment doubled in value while you were away.'

[23]"The owner showed equal pleasure with this person's performance. 'You must have made a wise choice. You are to be commended for your good judgment and diligence in this rather small responsibility.

I would like to give you new assignments involving greater responsibilities. Enjoy life with me.'

[24]"Finally the third man gave his report. 'Sir,' he began, 'I was aware that you are a demanding person and that everything you own seems to turn into money, and I was afraid to invest your money lest I lose it and be disgraced, [25]so I just hid your money in the ground for safe-keeping and here it is. I am giving it back to you.'

[26]"'You stupid idiot!' the owner shot back. 'Knowing me as well as you do, why would you do such a thing? If you had died in my absence, no one would have known where the money had been hidden. The very least you should have done would have been to [27]put the money in the bank where it could have been drawing interest. [28]Give that talent to the man who has ten, for he is a more valuable helper than you.'

[29]"Every person who receives and puts to use the blessings I give shall have more and more blessings, but if he does not treasure them and use them, they will be taken from him. [30]The unwise person will lose out on eternal life in the end, and there will be weeping and gnashing of teeth.

[31]"When the Son of man returns to this earth in the splendor of heaven, escorted by the angelic host, He will be seated on His throne, a glorious one indeed. [32]Before Him on the earth will be the entire population of the world. As He approaches, He begins to separate them into just two groups, as a shepherd separates sheep from the goats. [33]Let's say the shepherd puts the sheep on his right, the goats on his left. [34]The coming King will place some on His right and some on His left, then He will announce their eternal destiny. He speaks first to those on His right, 'Come, you are

to be happy indeed. My Father has acquitted you, and you are to be citizens of His eternal realm, which He has planned since the earth was created. [35]This is no arbitrary decision on His part. You have demonstrated that you have been willing to be changed from selfish people to unselfish ones, helpful, caring, and self-denying.'

"'Here is what He has been able to accomplish in you: When you saw Me hungry, you fed Me. When you saw Me thirsty, you gave Me water. When you saw Me a stranger, you invited Me in. [36]When I was without clothing, you supplied Me with needed garments. When I was sick, you took care of Me. When I was put in prison as a criminal, you came to see Me and to encourage Me.'

[37]"These people were astonished as He recounted how they had helped Him. 'My Lord, when did we ever see You hungry and feed You? When did we ever see You thirsty and give You cool water? [38]When were You ever a stranger and we invited You in? When were You without clothing and when did we supply any? When were You sick and needed our care? When were You in prison needing encouragement? We just don't understand.'

[40]"Their King will reply in a way that they can understand, 'Let the truth now be told. In treating even one of My earthly brothers or sisters this way, you have done it to Me!'

[41]"But now the sad part: The King will then turn to those on His left and utter these awful words, 'Leave My presence! You are condemned to eternal death. Your bodies will be consumed by the fire that has been produced to deal with the devil and his angels. [42]For I was hungry and you refused to feed Me. I was thirsty, and you failed to

give Me so much as a drink of water. ⁴³I was a stranger, and you did not invite Me in. I was naked, and you failed to provide Me any clothing. I was sick and I was in prison, and you did nothing to help Me.'

⁴⁴"With astonishment they will ask, 'When did we ever see You hungry, thirsty, a stranger, naked, or in prison and fail to help You?'

⁴⁵"He will explain. 'When you failed to do these things to one of the least important ones around you, this was failing to help Me!'"

⁴⁶"These will be sent into final eternal annihilation while those who did right will go into life eternal."

Chapter 26

¹When He had finished, He talked to His disciples about the events that would take place within the next few days. ²"You know already that in two days our nation will be celebrating Passover. Please, be prepared to see the Son of man betrayed and crucified." ³It was at about this very moment that the high priest Caiaphas assembled the chief priests, the scribes, and the elders for a meeting at his palace. ⁴The express purpose of the meeting was to devise a plan whereby they might capture, condemn, and execute Jesus, ⁵but they were a bit reluctant to do anything on the feast day, knowing that an uproar would be the result.

⁶Out in Bethany there was a man by the name of Simon. He was known widely as Simon the leper, even though Jesus had already cured his leprosy. It was at Simon's house that a dinner was given for Jesus and His followers. ⁷Into Simon's house came a woman, uninvited and unannounced. She went right into the dining room and opened an alabaster box of pure nard and

began to anoint Jesus' head. ⁸The disciples thought among themselves that this was an outrageous waste of valuable hard-earned money. ⁹*Would it not be far better to sell this valuable ointment at its market value and use the proceeds to help the poor?*

¹⁰Of course, Jesus was aware of their thoughts, so he explained it to them like this: "Please don't give her a hard time, for she has accomplished a valuable service. ¹¹There will always be plenty of opportunities to help the poor, and of course, you should help them, ¹²but you will not always have Me. Unknown to her, she has anointed my body for burial, ¹³and it is an actual fact that the whole world will learn of her kind act, and it will be part of the gospel story."

¹⁴One of Jesus' disciples, known as Judas Iscariot, at this point made a fateful decision. He left the group and went to the chief priests with a proposition. ¹⁵"How much will you give me, if I deliver Jesus to you?" They finally agreed to give Judas thirty silver coins. ¹⁶From that moment on, he was working on a plan to betray Jesus into their control.

¹⁷On the first day of the feast of unleavened bread, Jesus' disciples asked Him, "Where would you like to celebrate the Passover meal? We would like to get things ready for it."

¹⁸His reply was this: "As you enter the city, you will see a man, and you will know he is the right person when you see him. Ask him to allow you to use a room where the Master would be welcome to eat the Passover meal with His disciples. He will understand."

¹⁹Things turned out just as Jesus had predicted, so they went ahead with the preparations. ²⁰By sunset everything was

ready, and Jesus with the disciples sat down at the table. [21]His voice was sad as He began, "You will find this hard to believe, but one of you is planning to betray Me."

[22]Shocked, the disciples began to ask, "Lord, is it I? Lord, is it I?"

[23]All He would answer was this: "It is one who shares this dish with Me. [24]The Son of man will go through His part in this event as it is written of Him, but woe be to the person by whom He is betrayed. Far better would it be for him if he had never been born."

[25]Finally Judas asked Him, "Is it I?"

The answer, "You said it." [26]While at the table, Jesus took a piece of unleavened bread, and as they watched, He asked a blessing on the bread, then began breaking it into smaller fragments, passing a portion of it to each of the disciples with this instruction, "Take this, eat it, each one of you. It is symbolic of my broken body." [27]Then He took a cup, uttered a prayer of thanks for it, passed it around with the instruction to drink a little of it. [28]"This symbolizes My blood, the blood of the new covenant, which is to be shed for everyone to make possible the forgiveness of sin. [29]I should like to add one thing. This is the last time I will drink any grape juice until I drink it, fresh and pure, in My Father's kingdom with you."

[30]The meal finished, and He led them out of the room, singing a hymn as they went toward the Mount of Olives. [31]On the way, He began to unfold before them the events of the immediate future. "All of you will be ashamed to be associated with Me tonight as is predicted in Zechariah 13:7, 'Smite the shepherd and scatter the sheep,' [32]But remember, I will rise again, and I will meet you in Galilee."

[33]As usual, Peter was the first to respond. "No matter how many others are ashamed to be with You, I shall never, never be ashamed to be with You!"

[34]Quietly, Jesus stunned him with this prophecy, "It is absolutely true, Peter, that some time during this night, before the rooster crows, you will deny three times that you even know Me!"

[35]"Impossible!" Peter assured Him, "I might die with you, but to deny you? IMPOSSIBLE, UNTHINKABLE!" The others gave Him the same assurance.

[36]When the little group had reached a garden called Gethsemane (the name means "oil press"), Jesus spoke, "Please, all of you stay here except for Peter, James, and John. I am going on a little farther to pray." [37]So the four of them went a little farther into the grove. He began to feel dreadfully sorrowful as if there were no hope. [38]"Please, I cannot explain this, but My very being is so terribly depressed that I fear I cannot go on living. Wait and be watchful."

[39]He went a little farther, then fell to the ground, and in agony poured out His heart to God, "Oh Father, Father, I plead with You. Take this bitter cup from Me! But no, don't do it unless it is Your will." [40]After some time, He returned to the three, but they were all asleep. "Couldn't you stay awake for even an hour?" He asked Peter. [41]"To overcome temptation, you will need to watch and pray. I know your intentions are good, but the human flesh is weak."

[42]In deep disappointment, He left them again for more agonizing prayer to God. "Oh My Father, if this bitter cup will not leave My lips unless I drink it, Your will be done." [43]Once again He returned to the disciples, but again they had fallen asleep.

[44]Then back into the grove, He repeated the same anguished prayer. [45]When He returned to His disciples, He invited them, "Go ahead and sleep on—but now it is time for My betrayal to My enemies. [46]Let's go, friends, My betrayer is nearly here."

[47]Then the sound of a shouting mob was heard, and to the astonishment of the disciples, Judas, their friend and admired colleague, was in the lead, bringing with him a posse of priests and guards, all armed with clubs and swords. They could see at once that Jesus was trapped and His doom was certain. [48]Judas had told his men, "I'll do this, I will walk right up to Him and kiss Him. You will know which one to arrest by this sign, and whatever you do, hold Him securely, for He may escape from you yet." [49]The plan was followed to the letter. Judas walked up to Jesus, saying, "It is good to see You," then he kissed Him.

[50]Jesus spoke kindly to Judas even though He knew the significance of the kiss. "Friend, why have you done this?" Then the mob surrounded Him, seized Him forcefully, and led Him toward the city with no resistance on His part. [51]However, one of the disciples decided to take the matter into his own hands, so he pulled a sword out of its sheath, swung it at one of the high priest's servants as he was leaving the garden, and cut off the man's ear.

[52]Jesus turned to him and said, "Put your sword away, for those who depend on the sword will die by the sword. [53]Don't you realize that I could call My Father for protection and that instead of human protectors He would send Me ten thousand angels? [54]However, the scripture will be fulfilled as you will see." [55]Then speaking to the mob He asked, "Have you come out here to catch a thief with swords and clubs?

I am amazed. I was in the temple day after day teaching, and you didn't lift a finger, [56]but as in so many other experiences, this one also fulfilled prophecy."

By this time every one of His disciples abandoned Him and took off. [57]Into the city the mob took Jesus and delivered Him to the palace of the high priest even though it was illegal to try a person during the hours of darkness. The chief rulers and elders were already there waiting for Jesus to be brought in. [58]At quite a distance Peter had followed the mob and reached the palace. He entered, intending to see what the outcome would be. The place was full of people, and wanting to be as inconspicuous as possible, he mingled with the employees. [59]The chief priests and elders had searched for witnesses to testify against Jesus, [60]and had finally found two who were willing to perjure themselves in presenting evidence that could condemn Jesus to death. [61]They both testified that they had heard Jesus boast that He would be able to destroy the temple and rebuild it again in three days.

[62]After hearing this testimony, the high priest stood up and faced Jesus. "Do you have anything to say in Your defense? You have heard this testimony, I believe." [63]But Jesus declined to answer such an absurd charge. Then the high priest called on Jesus to answer a question under a judicial oath, God being His witness. "Are You the anointed Son of God?"

[64]"I am, just as you have said, and one day you will see this human Son of God sitting on God's right hand, the position of authority, returning in the clouds."

[65]The high priest then tore his robe in utter outrage and scorn. "This is nothing less than blasphemy. What do you gentlemen say? We surely do not need any other

witnesses." ⁶⁶The answer was, "He deserves to die."

⁶⁷Then Jesus was subjected to demeaning abuse. They spat on Him. They slapped Him and then asked, "Who was it who slapped you, Christ? You should be able to name us all."

⁶⁹During this time Peter was in an outer room of the palace, when a young girl confronted him. "You were with this Jesus of Galilee, were you not?"

⁷⁰Loudly Peter denied it before all who heard. "I don't know what you are trying to say."

⁷¹He went out to the porch where another person spotted him and said to all who were near, "This character was one of those with Jesus of Nazareth." ⁷²Once again he denied having any relationship with Jesus, this time using a common oath.

⁷³Later on others who had been milling around came up to Peter and accused him, "You surely are one of that group of followers because your accent gives you away. Now be honest."

⁷⁴At this he began to curse and swear with a series of expletives too awful to record, ending in a flat denial, "I do not know this Man." Immediately after the third denial, a nearby rooster crowed. ⁷⁵Suddenly Peter remembered the prediction that Jesus had made that evening, "Before the rooster crows you will deny three times that you know Me." Crushed and sorrowful, he left the palace, weeping and sobbing uncontrollably as he made his way out of the city.

Chapter 27

¹After daybreak the chief priests and elders got together and began devising a strategy that would successfully destroy Jesus. ²First, they tied his hands securely, then led him to the mansion where the Roman governor Pontius Pilate lived. ³It was about this time that Judas, His betrayer, began to realize that Jesus had been condemned and might actually be executed. Trembling with fear, he brought the thirty silver coins back to the chief priests and elders with his confession. ⁴"I have committed a terrible wrong, gentlemen, when I betrayed an innocent man." Their cynical reply? "That's your problem, not ours."

⁵Judas then publicly threw the silver coins to the temple floor, bolted from the building in despair, left the city, and hanged himself. ⁶The priests gathered up the coins, but were forbidden by tradition to put it into the treasury because it was a payment for an execution. ⁷So they held a quick meeting and settled on a plan. They would purchase a plot of ground from a potter, which could then be used as a burial ground for strangers. ⁸That field has been known as "the field of blood" ever since. ⁹Remember Zechariah's prophecy (Zechariah 11:12)? ¹³Here is the fulfillment, "They accepted the thirty pieces of silver, the selling price of a slave, ¹⁰and with the money bought the potter's field as the Lord had predicted."

¹¹So Jesus stood before the governor. The first question Pilate asked Him was this, "Are you actually claiming to be the King of the Jews?"

To which Jesus responded, "It is true."

¹²Then the chief priests and rulers brought their accusations, but He refused to answer any of their questions. ¹³Pilate could not understand why He refused to answer them and questioned Him, "Don't you realize the seriousness of these accusations?" ¹⁴But again Jesus made no reply,

and Pilate was filled with admiration for His fortitude and self-restraint. ¹⁵An idea came to Pilate. It had been customary for several years to appease the Jews by releasing a political prisoner at the time of the Passover feast. The choice of whom to release was up to the Jews. ¹⁶In prison at that time was a well-known troublemaker and rabble rouser named Barabbas, a real scoundrel. ¹⁷So Pilate asked which one they wanted released, Barabbas or Jesus, called the Christ. ¹⁸(He sensed that it was jealousy that led them to bring Jesus to him.)

¹⁹Just then a messenger came to Pilate and delivered an urgent message from his wife, which read, "Please have no part in the prosecution of that good person, for I have had a dreadful dream about His very case."

²⁰But the crowd was being influenced by the priests and elders to release Barabbas and execute Jesus. ²¹The governor then asked them, "Have you made your decision, Christ or Barabbas?"

A great shout went up, "Barabbas."

²²"Then what shall I do with Jesus, called Christ?"

"He should be crucified," was the answer."

²³"Why, why? What crime has He committed?"

There was no answer, except a louder shout, "He should be crucified."

²⁴No amount of reasoning seemed capable of changing their minds. It seemed that a full-blown riot was about to begin, so Pilate had water brought, and before the crowd, he washed his hands, saying as he did, "I am innocent in the death of this Man as you well know."

²⁵A spokesman replied, "Yes, we understand. We and our children are ready to accept the responsibility, so don't feel guilty."

²⁶Barabbas was then unshackled, and Pilate ordered the soldiers to flog Jesus, after which he turned Him over to the soldiers for crucifixion. ²⁷They took Him into the inner recesses of the palace. Here they stripped off His clothes, then placed an old scarlet robe on Him. ²⁸They next fashioned a "crown" of thorns and placed it on His head. ²⁹A reed was then placed in his hand and the soldiers filed by Him one by one, kneeling as they passed and shouting, "Hail, King of the Jews." ³⁰In order to insult Him further, they took turns spitting in His face, then grabbed the reed and began to strike the crown of thorns. ³¹When their seemingly insatiable appetite for torture was satisfied, they removed the red robe and put His own clothing back on Him and led Him out of the city to crucify Him.

³²On the way, the procession met a man from Cyrene, named Simon, on his way into town. Simon was commanded to carry Jesus' cross, for they could see that Jesus was not going to make it to the place of execution. ³³Reaching a place known as Golgotha (or Calvary, the place of a skull), ³⁴they offered Him a drink of vinegar and gall, but He refused to drink it. ³⁵So they went ahead with the crucifixion, removing His clothing and casting lots to see who would get each garment. (This was a fulfillment of Psalm 22:18.) ³⁶Then, satisfied with their cruel chore, they sat down and watched Him for a while.

³⁷A placard had been prepared and was then placed on the cross over His head naming His crime: "This is the King of the Jews." ³⁸At the time of Jesus' crucifixion, two others suffered a similar fate. They were both thieves, and their crosses were placed, one on each side of Jesus. ³⁹Onlookers came by

and taunted Jesus, "Oh, so You are the One who could destroy the temple and rebuild it in three days? [40]You have claimed to be the Son of God. If You really are, prove it by coming down from the cross!"

[41]Not only casual onlookers, but the chief priests, the elders, and the scribes hurled insulting words at Him such as, [42]"He claims to have saved others, but He can't even save Himself. If He is so great, claiming to be the King of Israel, He should come down from the cross now and we would believe in Him. [43]He claimed God would deliver Him, let God do it now. After all, He claimed to be the Son of God."

[44]The two thieves also directed similar taunts at Him. [45]At about noon, an unexplained darkness swept over the land, bringing consternation and fear to everyone. [46]Then about three hours later Jesus cried out in despair, "Eli, Eli, Lama Sabachthani," or as we would say, "My God, My God, why did You forsake Me?" [47]Some misunderstood His words and thought He was calling out for Elijah. [48]One person thought to help Jesus, so he offered a sponge tied to a reed and soaked in vinegar. [49]Others suggested, "Let us wait and see if Elijah comes to help Him."

[50]Then Jesus cried out loudly and abruptly died. [51]Just at that time there was an earthquake, several large boulders split apart, and in the temple the great veil separating the Most Holy Place from the Holy Place was torn apart by unseen forces, starting at the top! [52]A number of graves opened up, and saints were resurrected. [53]These were seen in the city of Jerusalem by a number of people after Jesus' resurrection. [54]The earthquake, the darkness, and the amazing behavior of Jesus through the terrible ordeal had a profound effect on the centurion and on others who were there at the time. The centurion was heard exclaiming, "It has to be true just as He claimed. He was the Son of God."

[55]Among those who stayed there through the awful scene were a large number of women from Galilee who had supplied food and had helped Jesus in other ways. [56]Mary Magdalene was one, the mother of James and Joseph was another, the mother of James and John was still another. [57]Time passed and a wealthy man from Arimathea, Joseph by name, a believer in Jesus, came to the scene. [58]He confidently went to Pilate and requested permission to bury the body of Jesus. Permission was given and an order sent to the centurion to release the body. [59]Joseph then removed Jesus from the cross, wrapped His body in linen cloth, [60]and carried Him to a nearby tomb that he owned, one that had only recently been excavated. The body was placed in the tomb, and a huge stone was rolled in its groove over the mouth of the tomb. [61]Watching the burial were Mary Magdalene and the other Mary. [62]This was the day called preparation and the Sabbath was soon to begin.

Some time during the Sabbath the chief priests and elders met with Pilate. [63]They had great concern on their minds, and said, "Sir, this great deceiver predicted that He would rise to life on the third day. [64]Would you please do everything possible to protect that tomb from those who might try to come and remove His body, then claim that His prediction has been fulfilled, for if they could pull this off, they would have a great deal more power to deceive than they already have."

[65]Pilate's only response was to remind them that there was already a guard on duty

who would see to it that nothing like that could happen. ⁶⁶So they left and were satisfied that no one could break through the guard, roll that stone, and remove the body.

Chapter 28

¹The Sabbath had passed, and the first day of the week was beginning, but darkness still prevailed. Hour after hour went by, but as daylight began to be noticeable, Mary Magdalene and the other Mary headed to the tomb. ²Suddenly the earth trembled under their feet, but it was no ordinary earthquake. No, it was produced by a mighty angel who had come down from heaven, rolled the huge stone from the mouth of the tomb, and sat on it. ³His face was a brilliant white, like lightning, and his robe white as fresh snow. ⁴The guards were terrified and fell to the ground as if dead.

⁵Then the angel addressed the two women who had just arrived, "Please, don't be afraid. I happen to know that you have come to look for Jesus who was crucified on Friday. ⁶Well, He is no longer here. He has been brought back to life just as He promised. You might want to come in and see where His body was. ⁷Then you will want to go at once and tell His disciples that He has been raised from the dead and will fulfill His appointment with them in Galilee. You can count on seeing Him there."

⁸In a strange mix of fear and joy, they left the gravesite and sped as fast as possible to notify the disciples. ⁹But on the way, Jesus suddenly appeared to them. "Joy to you," He exclaimed. They both fell at His feet in adoration and worship. ¹⁰"Now don't be afraid." He continued, "Go ahead and tell My friends that they can count on seeing Me at the appointed place. I promise to be there."

¹¹There were others who were on their way into the city also. They had a disturbing message for the chief priests. These men had been the guards over Jesus' tomb and were now fearful for their lives, but they had decided to go straight to the chief priests with their story rather than to wait for others to tell them. They had been alert, diligent, and watchful while on duty. ¹²The priests and elders were quickly assembled, and the whole story came out. It took but a short time for the priests and elders to find a solution to their dilemma. ¹³A handsome bribe was offered to the soldiers if they would only report that they had fallen asleep on guard and that during that time the disciples of Jesus had come and had taken His body away. (How would they know what had happened if they had been asleep?) ¹⁴Furthermore, they assured the guards that if this story should get to the governor, he too could be appeased by more money. ¹⁵The offer was too tempting to resist. They accepted the bribe and no punishment ever was given them, and it is accepted as fact even to this day.

¹⁶Now back to the eleven disciples. They all left for Galilee to keep the appointment with Jesus. ¹⁷When they finally saw Him, they worshipped Him, but there were a few who would not accept their word. ¹⁸Jesus' words to them were challenging, "I have been given complete authority over everything on earth and in heaven. ¹⁹I want you to go into all the world and teach people everywhere, inviting them to be My disciples. They should be baptized in the name of the Father, the Son, and the Holy Spirit. ²⁰They must be taught to follow everything I have taught you, and be certain of this promise: I will always be with you, even to the very end of the world."

Mark

Chapter 1

¹Let's start at the beginning in telling the good news of Jesus Christ who is the Son of God. ²I refer you first to Isaiah 40:3 and Malachi 3:1 for prophecies: "I send my messenger ahead of you to prepare your way. ³The voice of one who proclaims a message in the wilderness, 'Get ready for the Lord, let His coming be announced and the people be made ready for Him.'" ⁴These prophecies met their fulfillment in the preaching of John the Baptist. He preached, then baptized those who repented of their sins, and indeed it was in the wilderness. ⁵So great was John's impact on Judea and Jerusalem that the majority of the whole nation was convicted of their sins and went out to be baptized in the Jordan River.

⁶John was a very humble, plain person who dressed in inexpensive clothing. For example, he wore a camel's hair shirt and a leather skirt. His food, too, was simple: locust pods and wild honey. ⁷The burden of his message was not only to call sinners to repentance but to foretell the coming of a greater one than himself. "Soon, friends, a person is coming who is so much greater than I, that I am not even worthy to remove His sandals. ⁸Now I have been baptizing you in water, but He will baptize you in the Holy Spirit."

⁹It was while John was preaching and baptizing at the Jordan River that Jesus of Nazareth arrived and asked to be baptized. John, of course, was willing. ¹⁰As Jesus was coming up out of the water, He looked up and saw the sky above Him seem to split open and a form resembling a dove coming down toward Him. That form was the Holy Spirit, and it hovered over Him. ¹¹At that very moment, a voice from the sky was heard declaring this: "You are My beloved, precious Son. I am well pleased with You." ¹²As soon as Jesus was baptized, the Holy Spirit compelled him to withdraw from the crowd and find solitude in the wilderness. ¹³He stayed there forty days while Satan tempted Him. Heavenly angels were sent to strengthen Him through the ordeal.

¹⁴But John was arrested by the civil authorities and imprisoned—a story in itself—and presently Jesus returned from the wilderness and began preaching in Galilee about God's kingdom and the wonderful news ¹⁵that this divine kingdom was finally being set up, and with that good news came the plea, "Repent, believe the good news, and turn from your sins."

¹⁶While Jesus was walking along the shore of the Sea of Galilee, He came upon two brothers, Simon and Andrew, who were about to put their nets into the

water and spend the night fishing. [17]"Men," Jesus said to them, "if you will come with Me, I will give you the ability to 'fish' and catch people." [18]Believe it or not, they both decided to do just that. They pulled in their nets, tied up the boat, and went with Jesus.

[19]Not far from there, they encountered two more brothers, James and John, sons of a man named Zebedee, who were mending their nets. [20]Jesus gave them the very same invitation, and they responded as quickly, leaving the boat, their father and his employees, and joining Jesus, Simon, and Andrew.

[21]From there they entered Capernaum, and when the Sabbath arrived, they attended the services and Jesus began to teach. [22]It was soon apparent to the listeners that here was no ordinary teacher like the scribes. He was clearly not in the same category. [23]Here is what happened: A man controlled by a demon was present and began to yell, [24]"Let us alone, Jesus of Nazareth. Get away from here. I know You are here to destroy us. Besides, I happen to know that You are God's holy one."

[25]Jesus kindly but firmly ordered: "Stop at once; no more from you! Come out of that man!" [26]The demon screamed, injured the man, and then released his victim. [27]You can imagine what affect this had in the synagogue. Everyone talked at once. The general idea was, "What authority He has! What supernatural power! For even demons are forced to obey Him." [28]The word spread like wildfire and Jesus was quickly famous in Galilee. [29]But back to the synagogue. The meeting broke up and Jesus, Simon, Andrew, James, and John were invited to Simon's home.

[30]Unfortunately, Simon's mother-in-law was having a chill and fever (likely malaria) and was very ill. So they told Jesus about her condition. [31]He checked her briefly, took her hand, and lifted her up without so much as one word. The fever subsided instantly, and she was perfectly well and began waiting on the guests. [32]That evening after sundown others were brought to Jesus with various health problems as well as demon possession, [33]so many that it seemed as if the whole city was there surrounding the house. [34]He healed all those who had ailments; He cast out demons, not permitting the demons to speak, for He knew they recognized who He was and that should they speak at all they might say something that could have cast doubt in people's minds regarding his mission.

[35]The following morning He awoke before daybreak, left the house, and found a secluded spot where He could spend time in prayer. [36]But after some time had passed, Peter, Andrew, James, and John went looking for Him. [37]When they discovered His prayer spot, they informed Him that everyone was looking for Him, convinced that He was the awaited Messiah.

[38]"Fine," He replied, "now let us go to the next town and then to others because My mission includes them all." [39]So that was the pattern: go to all the towns in Galilee, meet with the people in their synagogues, cast out demons, and heal the sick. [40]At one place a man with Hansen's disease (leprosy) came right up to Him, knelt down, and pled with Him, "If You will only choose to do so, You can make me clean from this disease." [41]Jesus broke all the rules in His pity for the sufferer by actually reaching out and touching him as He said, "I so choose. Be clean." [42]At that very moment, the leprosy disappeared,

and he was healed!

[43]Jesus then sent him away with this sound advice: [44]"Do not tell anyone of this before you present yourself to the priest and fulfill the Mosaic law." This was in order to make certain that even the priests were aware that an actual miracle had been performed, before they developed a prejudice against Jesus. [45]Sadly enough, the healed man disregarded the advice and told everyone he met of his healing. This produced a virtual boycott by many municipal authorities, forcing Jesus to avoid cities and spend time in remote, rural areas. However, even there people flocked to Him in large numbers.

Chapter 2

[1]Finally, Jesus returned to Capernaum, and the word got around that He was at Simon's home again. [2]People began to gather in such numbers that the house could not hold them all. Still more came and surrounded the entrance and even beyond. Many of these were now in good health as the result of the previous session of healing, and they wanted to hear the message that He had for them. So He taught them. [3]But there was a case of one man who had been disabled by a stroke, and he was helplessly paralyzed. Four of his friends carried him on a stretcher to where Jesus was teaching. [4]There was no way they could get to Jesus through the crowd of listeners, so they went to the stairway leading to the roof, carried him up to the roof, and removed enough of the roofing to allow the stretcher to be lowered through the opening and placed right in front of Jesus. [5]Jesus stopped His discourse, impressed by the trust shown by the man and his friends, then looked him squarely

in the eye and said, "Son, your sins are forgiven." This may have seemed to many listeners as irrelevant as well as blasphemous. [6]In fact, there were some scribes in the crowd who wanted to speak up about this, [7]knowing that only God can forgive sins. [8]But Jesus accurately read their thoughts and addressed his next words directly to them. "Why not think these things through, gentlemen?" He asked. [9]"Which would be easier to say? 'Your sins are forgiven' or 'get up off your stretcher and walk?'" [10]In order for you to be informed fully that this Son of humanity has the authority to forgive sin, watch this carefully."

[11]Then He turned to the patient lying on the stretcher and said to him, "Get up from your stretcher and walk. Then return home." [12]Immediately he got up from the stretcher, picked it up, and walked out through the crowd, heading for home. Astonishment, awe, and silence followed, and soon after that praises to God were heard. Many expressed it like this: "I have never seen anything to equal what I have seen today."

[13]From Capernaum, Jesus went to the shore of the sea, followed by a mass of interested people wanting to hear more of His teaching. [14]On the way, He went by the office of a tax collector named Levi. Jesus went right up to him and invited him, "Please come and be with Me." And surprisingly enough, Levi went with Him. [15]Not long after this, Levi invited Jesus and the other disciples to a meal at his home. It was a large event with a number of other revenue agents present, as well as several friends of other occupations. [16]As usual, Jesus was being closely observed by the scribes and Pharisees, not for the purpose of learning but to obtain evidence that

they could use against Him when needed. Here was an ideal opportunity.

"Why does He associate with tax collectors and sinners?" they asked among themselves.

[17]However, Jesus knew their questionings and proceeded to tell a parable to illustrate why He did such things. "You know, friends, that people in good health do not need a physician, only those who are ill. I did not come to help righteous people but sinners who need repentance."

[18]They threw another question at Jesus. "Why is it that the disciples of John practice regular fasting, as do the Pharisees, but Your disciples never seem to fast?"

[19]He responded, "Would you expect the friends of a bridegroom to fast while the wedding feast was in progress? As long as the groom is present, they will never fast. [20]But after he leaves then they will resume fasting. [21]You will never see a person sew a new patch onto an old garment, for it is much stronger than the old cloth and will only tear the old cloth and make the rent worse. [22]Neither will you ever see anyone putting new wine into old wineskins, for the old one is more likely to burst and waste all the wine. No, new wine must be put into new wineskins."

[23]One Sabbath Jesus and the disciples were walking through a field of grain, and the disciples were picking off heads of grain, rubbing them in their hands, and eating the kernels. [24]Some Pharisees watched them and complained to Jesus, "Why do you permit Your disciples to break the Sabbath like this?"

[25]Now Jesus referred them to David. "Have you never read what David and his men did when they were hungry? They went right into the sanctuary and actually ate some of the shewbread, which was intended for only the priests. [26]Always remember this: the Sabbath was made for mankind's benefit. Mankind was not created for the benefit of the Sabbath. [27]And one more thing: this Son of man is Lord of the Sabbath."

Chapter 3

[1]On another Sabbath Jesus and the disciples were in the synagogue, and in this congregation was a man whose hand was atrophied. [2]Sure enough, there were those present who attended only to see if Jesus would heal on the Sabbath, so they could have evidence against Him and eventually condemn Him. [3]He went right to the man and said, "Stand up please." Now He faced the spies and asked this question, [4]"Is it within the law to do good deeds on the Sabbath or wicked deeds? Is it legal to save life or to kill?" The spies were silent. They would not respond. [5]He then glared at them with exasperation in His heart, knowing the real motives of the spies and their hardheartedness.

Next He gave a calm command to the man, "Hold out your hand." The patient obeyed. That atrophic hand was instantly restored to normal, and all who were there could see that a miracle had been performed. [6]The Pharisees left and went to the Herodians for counseling. They wanted to come up with some idea as to how they might yet trap Jesus and execute Him.

[7]But Jesus led His disciples to the lake, followed by many from Judea as well as from Galilee, [8]from Tyre and Sidon, and from east of Jordan. It was a vast crowd who had heard of the great things He had done. [9]Approaching the lake, He asked the disciples to obtain the use of a boat. [10]There had

been many healings, and yet others kept coming to be touched, those with various illnesses and those who were demon-possessed. [11]As demons encountered Jesus, they would fall on their faces and cry out, "You are God's Son." [12]His order to them was direct and authoritative, "Do not tell anyone about Me. You understand?"

[13]From there Jesus led His disciples up the hillside. He had chosen these men for a special ministry, [14]and they were to be sacredly ordained to accomplish the work that Jesus had planned for them: [15]preaching, healing, and exorcism. [16]Here is the roll call of His disciples: Simon (Jesus renamed him Peter), [17]James, son of Zebedee, and his brother John (Jesus referred to them as "sons of thunder") [18]Andrew (Peter's brother), Philip, Bartholomew, Matthew, Thomas, James the son of Alphaeus, Thaddaeus, Simon the Zealot, [19]and finally Judas Iscariot, the one who would one day betray Him. After the ordination of these twelve, they returned home.

[20]Crowds of people again surrounded Him, and there was no time even to eat. [21]Some of His family members heard of the situation and went out with the purpose of capturing Him, for they concluded that He must have become psychotic. [22]Also, some scribes had been sent from Jerusalem to size up the situation, and their statement clearly showed their hostility. "He is controlled by Beelzebub; it is through his power that demons are exorcised."

[23]So Jesus called them over and asked them a pointed question, "How can Satan cast out Satan? [24]If a nation is split into two factions, it will not survive. [25]If a household becomes divided, it cannot endure as a family, [26]and if Satan should start fighting against himself, well, he is just too smart to do such a thing. He knows he could not win in the great controversy that way, but will come to an end. [27]No assailant can do much to a strong person unless the strong one is first handcuffed and tied, but after that he could do whatever he wanted to do about the strong man's property. [28]Now friends, let me plead with you. Do not ever resist the Holy Spirit in His attempts to convict you of sin. Continually refusing to repent will finally force the Spirit to leave you. It's like this, each and every sin can be forgiven, but it is the mission of the Holy Spirit to convict of sin and bring sinners to repentance and salvation. [29]Now if one totally rejects the attempts of the Holy Spirit, one will never be forgiven and will be eventually condemned."

[30]He made this point very emphatic so that they would understand that His power to exorcise could not be the work of Satan. [31]It was about this time that Jesus' mother Mary and His brothers came looking for Him. They were on the outskirts of the crowd as He had been speaking. [32]And when He heard the news that His family was waiting, [33]He made a public statement that was significant, "Who is My mother? And who is My brother?" [34]He answered His own questions, gesturing toward those in the crowd. [35]"Look at these here today, mine indeed, [36]for whoever is willing to obey God is a brother, sister, or mother of mine."

Chapter 4

[1]Once again Jesus went to the lake followed by a huge gathering of listeners. On a boat was a convenient place for Him to stand and speak while the people were on the shore nearby. [2]He began by telling them parables so that they could more readily

understand His teaching. [3]"Please, listen carefully," He urged. "A farmer went out to his field to sow seed, [4]and as he scattered the seed, some fell on the path and were quickly picked up by birds. [5]Some of the seed fell in rocky soil where the soil lacked depth. [6]This allowed it to sprout quickly, but the shallow roots could not sustain the young plants, and they quickly dried up. [7]Other seed fell into clumps of thorns, and these young plants were crowded out by the thorns. [8]But other seed fell on good soil, sprouted well, grew rapidly, and produced an abundant harvest, some thirtyfold, some sixtyfold and some a hundredfold. [9]If you have ears, use them well and remember."

[10]After the crowd left, the disciples and a few others asked about the meaning of this parable. [11]"I needed to speak through parables," He responded, "because so few of the people would accept direct instruction. Now you are different. I can teach you directly. [12]Remember Jeremiah's passage, (Jeremiah 5:21) 'Who have eyes but don't see, who have ears but don't hear'? This type of person is resistant and defensive about accepting the truth of conversion and repentance and forgiveness of sin.

[13]"Just to be sure you know the meaning of this parable, I shall explain it. [14]The farmer sowing the seed is the one who teaches God's word. [15]The seed on the path represents the truths that are snatched away by Satan so that the hearers are not affected by them. [16]The seed in the stony soil represents the truths that are accepted with delight, [17]but the hearers are not really, solidly helped because persecution and other matters seem too important and they allow the truth to die in their hearts. [18]The seed among the thorns represents

truths that cannot mature, [19]because of being crowded out by many trivial, earthly interests, such as trials, riches, etc., until spiritual things die out completely. [20]Now for the rich soil. This represents the reception of truth that is studied, cultivated, and nourished. The word of God is able to change their lives and make them productive, of strong character, to help others, some thirty, some sixty, some a hundredfold.

[21]"And just as a candle or any other source of light is placed on a candlestick so that its light will spread widely, so should a person open up his influence to help all those around him to see spiritual truths. [22]Nothing they do will be forgotten by God, even seemingly unimportant, hidden things will one day be publicized. [23]If you have ears, listen carefully to what I have just said. [24]Be very discerning in what you allow yourself to listen to. And when you weigh an item, do so with accurate scales, for this is the only right thing to do. And you yourself will want others to be accurate in weighing out things for you. Also, God will be as accurate with you as you are with others. Then, if you heed what I am telling you, you will keep on learning more and more. [25]Whoever treasures what he has will be able to obtain more, but those who neglect to add to their knowledge and wisdom will eventually lose the small amount they might have ever possessed.

[26]"And here is another illustration of God's kingdom. A farmer first plants his seed, [27]then he goes about his daily tasks. Days and nights pass and gradually the seeds swell, then sprout, and finally emerge from the soil through some process quite unexplainable. [28]This is the way plants grow; gradually but surely the

sprout becomes a stem, the stem produces a head, and the head produces seeds, all with no further work on the part of the farmer. [29]His work commences when the grain is ripe, for then harvest begins."

[30]Trying to further illustrate His teaching, He continued, "How can I illustrate another aspect of the kingdom of God? Perhaps it would be helpful to remind you of some facts. [31]Mustard plants produce very tiny seeds, smaller than almost all other seeds. [32]But small as it may be, that wee little seed grows into a larger shrub than any other garden herb, so large, in fact, that it provides shelter for birds who are able to nest in its large branches."

[33]In these little parables one is able to see how Jesus used stories to teach about the kingdom of God. [34]And this was His way of teaching, telling parables to the large audiences, then explaining them in detail to His disciples.

[35]That evening He said to them, "Let's take a boat to the other side of the lake." [36]The throngs of people finally went home, leaving them free to enter a boat and launch forth, followed by a few other small boats. [37]But a windstorm struck the lake with violent force soon afterward, and the waves began splashing into the boat. [38]Jesus had decided to lie down in the stern of the vessel and had fallen asleep. The disciples became fearful of their safety and went to Him with their concern, "Don't You care about us? Here we are about to lose our lives in this storm and You are sleeping."

[39]Getting up from the little bunk, He gave an order to the elements, "PEACE, BE STILL," and the storm was over—just like that! [40]Now it was His turn to give a gentle rebuke, "Why were you so afraid? Do you not have any faith?"

[41]Needless to say they were awed by the experience and voiced their amazement to each other, "What kind of Man is this? He can give orders to the wind and the waves, and they obey Him at once."

Chapter 5

[1]After the storm their boat landed safely on the shore in the land of the Gadarenes. [2]They were just in the process of leaving the boat when they were confronted by a man who was running wild because he was possessed by a demon. [3]His only shelter was among the tombs of the area, and although some had attempted, none had succeeded in restraining him and incarcerating him. He had even broken chains that had been used to restrain him. [4]He was so strong that on several occasions he was able to break free from both ropes and chains. And the idea of rehabilitation had finally been abandoned. [5]So here he was, running around at all hours of the day and night, sometimes in the hills, sometimes among the tombs, or along the shore, screaming and cutting himself with sharp stones.

[6]Before Jesus had left the boat, the possessed man had seen Him coming and was running toward the group. He reached Jesus, prostrated himself at Jesus' feet, and implored him, "Sir, please tell me. What are You here for? You are Jesus, Son of God. In God's name I plead, do not torture me."

[8]Jesus, with total composure and evident authority, gave orders to the demon, "Come out of that man, you dirty spirit!" [9]Then He demanded, "Tell Me your name."

The demon answered, "My name is 'Legion,' for there are a large number of us here in control of this man. [10]And please do not send us far away." [11]A short distance from there, a herd of swine was feeding. [12]"Please, send us into those hogs, Jesus," the legion requested.

[13]And to this Jesus agreed. The demons went into the hogs at once, causing the poor animals to run frantically as the man had been doing, and shortly they charged headlong into the lake where the herd of perhaps two thousand drowned. [14]The swine herders were terrified and ran back to the city where they told everyone about the experience. The listeners then came and verified the truth of what they had been told. [15]Here was the man, now in his right mind and clothed. And the herd of pigs was gone, some floating on the surface of the lake. A deep impression was made on their minds, but fear was a real result too. [16]Now they became the bearers of the news about the demoniac, the swine, and of course about Jesus.

[17]However, the majority of the people considered Jesus a threat rather than a blessing, and they urged him to leave the area, which He was willing to do. He never stayed anywhere unless He was asked to stay. [18]So the group headed back to the boat. However, the restored man was loathe to leave Jesus and implored Him to stay or perhaps allow him to follow Jesus as the disciples were. [19]Jesus, though, had a better idea. "I want you to go back home and tell your family and friends how the Lord has taken pity on you and has released you from the terrible affliction through which you were suffering." [20]The grateful man could see the wisdom in this and accepted the advice. He was able to go through the whole area of those ten towns and tell his fabulous story to a vast number of people.

[21]Back on the other side of the lake, Jesus was again surrounded by a large number of people almost as soon as He left the boat. [22]One of the officers of the local synagogue, Jairus by name, came and fell to his knees in front of Jesus, obviously in some crisis. [23]"Jesus, my little daughter is nearly dead. Would it be possible for You to come and place Your hand on her so that she might be restored to life and health? Please say You will."

[24]Jesus started to follow him at once, much to his joy. But a problem arose. The crowd around Jesus slowed His progress almost to a standstill. Jairus was impatient to move faster. [25]Among this throng of people was a woman who had been experiencing metrorrhagia for twelve years. [26]She had been to doctor after doctor, had spent everything she had in order to obtain relief from her anemia, but the medical knowledge at that time was inadequate to solve her problem, and she was still deteriorating and was now so weak that even walking was difficult. [27]She had pressed far enough into the mass of humanity so as to get close to Jesus. [28]She had heard of His miraculous cures, *If only I could just touch His robe,* she thought, *I will be cured.* [29]She reached for His robe and touched it. Instantly her bleeding ceased, and she knew that the miracle had happened. Oh joy!

[30]Jesus was fully aware of her need and her act of faith, yet He turned to the crowd and asked, "Who touched Me?" [31]The disciples thought this to be a rather absurd question. "Lord, there are people all around You, touching You all the time. Why did you ask this question?" [32]He looked straight into her eyes and she knew that He had sensed her need and had performed the miracle. [33]In profound gratitude, she fell at His feet in worship, then told her story. [34]Imagine her joy when she

heard Him say, "My daughter, your faith has made the difference. You are fully healed. Go in peace, and may you continue in good health."

³⁵ As Jesus was speaking to the woman, a messenger pushed his way through the crowd to Jairus with the crushing news, "Sir, your daughter has died. Why bother the Master any longer?"

³⁶Jesus heard the message, to which He responded, "Jairus, believe Me, you have no need to fear." ³⁷Then they went on toward the home of sorrow, where Jesus selected Peter, James, and John to go with Him into the house. ³⁸Already there were paid mourners, weeping and wailing as the custom was in those days. ³⁹Within the home, Jesus asked, "Why is all this weeping going on, all this noise? The girl is not dead, just asleep." (To Him death was no problem). ⁴⁰But those who heard Him speak actually laughed at Him, supposing that He really had never seen a dead person before and was not qualified to make a statement on such matters. He then invited Jairus and his wife along with three of His disciples into the bedroom where the child was lying dead.

⁴¹Walking up to the bedside, He took her hand and in a voice of authority commanded, "Young lady, I am ordering you to get up this minute!" ⁴²There was not a moment of hesitation. She sat up, climbed out of bed, and walked just as might be expected of a twelve year old. The stunned parents and amazed disciples were silent with awe. ⁴³How He expected them to obey His next instruction is not clear, but He definitely told them to keep quiet about this miracle. Then, to the parents, He said, "Get her something to eat, for she is hungry."

Chapter 6

¹From Jairus' home Jesus and His disciples went back to His own neighborhood. ²The next Sabbath found Him in the synagogue again, teaching as usual. Those who heard Him were deeply impressed by His wisdom, especially since they realized He had never gone to school. "How can He be such a powerful teacher?" was the question on every mind. ³"We know that He is the carpenter, son of Mary, brother of James, Joses, Judah, and Simon, and that his sisters are well known." Unfortunately, many did not recognize His true identity and came to wrong conclusions. ⁴"Remember this," Jesus said. "Rarely is a prophet honored in his own hometown or even among the members of his family." ⁵It was because of their unwillingness to face the facts of His true identity that He was unable to do many miracles for them, but even so, He was able to lay His hands on a few people and heal them. ⁶Jesus was amazed at their refusal to believe, and so He moved on to other towns and villages.

⁷About this time, He gathered His disciples around Him and presented to them His plan for their future work. First and very important, He wanted them to gain on-the-job training, teaching, healing, and exorcizing. They would go in pairs so as to encourage each other. ⁸Jesus instructed them, "Travel simply like common people. Don't take food, money, or even an extra change of clothing—just your staff. ⁹Don't dress as religious teachers, giving the impression of wealth or position. ¹⁰When you come to a village or city and are invited to stay in a home, stay in that home until you leave the community. Don't flit like social butterflies from house to house seeking food and entertainment.

[11]Sadly enough, you will not always have success. Not everyone will listen to you, and when this happens, leave and shake off the dust of that place. It will be evidence against them. Solemnly I tell you that on judgment day Sodom and Gomorrah will have a better chance than that city."

[12]So they left and began teaching people everywhere to repent of their sins. [13]They cast out devils; they anointed many who were sick and healed them. [14]It wasn't long before King Herod heard of Jesus with all of this going on. His immediate reaction was to believe that John the Baptist had been resurrected and that these miracles were the result of his reincarnation and his power. [15]But his counselors wondered if it might be Elijah or another of the prophets. [16]"No," said Herod, "it has to be John whom I had beheaded. He must have been resurrected."

[17]John had been put in prison because he had spoken strongly that Herod should not have taken his brother's wife. [18]John had assured Herod that the marriage was illegal as well as immoral. [19]Of course, Herodias was furious about this, and if she had had her way, John would have been executed at once. [20]But Herod had a lot of respect for John, knowing that he was a genuinely good person, so he protected John from Herodias so that he could learn more about John's teaching. [21]But one fateful day—Herod's birthday—the king made a feast for his officials, generals, and other responsible men in the kingdom. [22]For entertainment the daughter of Herodias came in and danced for them. She proved to be immensely popular as a dancer, so much so that Herod called her over and invited her to name anything she wanted and it would be done for her. (He had been

drinking heavily.) [23]"I give you my solemn oath that you can have anything you want, even to half of my kingdom."

[24]The girl went to her mother for advice, "Mother, what shall I request?"

There wasn't a second of hesitation on Herodias' part. "Ask for the head of John the Baptist."

[25]Back to the king she went. "My request is the head of John the Baptist on a platter."

[26]Dismay overwhelmed Herod. What a mistake he had made! But to save face and keep his reputation as one in command, he would not deny the request. [27]Right then an executioner was called, and he went straight to the prison and executed the prophet. [28]The gory trophy was brought in for all to see, carried on a large platter. It was given to the girl who promptly gave it to her mother. [29]John's disciples soon heard of the tragedy and came to get the body for burial.

[30]After some time Jesus' disciples returned from their mission and gave a complete report of their experiences and of their teaching. [31]Discerning their weariness, Jesus invited them to spend some time away from their work, in fellowship, instruction, and relaxation. This would restore their physical and spiritual strength, which had been overworked to the place that they had often been unable to eat regular meals. [32]So down to the lake, into a boat, and off for a vacation cruise at some resort—or so they thought.

[33]But there were those on the shore who were watching the boat and the direction they took. They led a large crowd around the lake on foot to the area where the boat docked. [34]This meant no rest for the weary. Jesus took pity on those people

who reminded Him of sheep without a shepherd, so instead of refusing them, He went right ahead and taught them hour after hour. [35]Toward the end of the day, the disciples whispered to Jesus that it was time to send the people home to obtain food. [36]Surely in some nearby village there would be places where they might find food for their needs. [37]Astonishment struck them when Jesus came up with a different plan. "No, don't send them away. You give them some food."

Doubting what they had just heard, they asked, "Would You want us to spend a little of our meager supply of money so that they could have a dry slice of bread and no sandwich filling?"

[38]Calmly Jesus asked, "Just what do we have here with us?"

The report came back, "Five small rolls of bread and two fishes."

[39]"Alright then, have everyone sit down in groups of fifty and groups of one hundred." [40]This was rapidly done. [41]Then Jesus took the five loaves and the two fishes, looked up toward heaven, thanked God for the food, and asked a blessing on it. Then He broke the food into small fragments and handed these out to the disciples who distributed them to the waiting people. [42]The food supply never seemed to be depleted, and finally everyone there received enough to satisfy their needs. [43]Believe it or not, when the leftover food was collected, there were twelve basketfuls of bread and fish. [44]The crowd was estimated at about five thousand men plus their families.

[45]Once again Jesus began arranging things so that they could have some rest and relaxation. He gently asked the people to return home, then He sent the disciples to the boat and head for Bethsaida. [46]When He was alone, He climbed a little distance into the hills and spent time praying. [47]As the sun went down, He was still alone, and the boat was now far out onto the lake. [48]He could see that the disciples were having to row because the wind was against them, so He went out on the lake, walking on the water toward them. [49]He was about to pass the boat by late in the night, and would have done so, but the disciples spotted Him out on the water and were terrified, supposing this to be some spirit being. [50]They shook with fear, but He was near enough to call to them. "Don't be afraid of Me! It is I. Cheer up!" [51]He climbed into the boat with them and the wind quieted down, much to their astonishment. [52]They were all still wrestling with the reality of what they had witnessed in the feeding of the five thousand. Like the rest of the people, they wanted to crown Jesus king and were bitter because He had refused.

[53]They landed at Gennesaret and anchored there. [54]Here the word got around rapidly that Jesus had arrived. [55]And, as would be expected, the sick and crippled folk began to converge, some on stretchers, to seek help and healing. [56]No matter where He went, it was the same. Those who were too sick to walk were carried to Him, placed in front of Him, or perhaps brought close enough to touch the hem of His robe, and without exception all were healed.

Chapter 7

[1]It is hard to believe, but many religious leaders were unimpressed by the miracles that were being seen so frequently. Instead, a delegation was dispatched from Jerusalem to complain and cause trouble.

²First they noticed that Jesus' disciples did not follow the ritual hand washing required by custom before eating. ³It was a nation-wide requirement that a washing similar to a physician's 'surgical scrub' must be done before eating, not just to remove soil but also to remove ritual defilement. ⁴When they returned from the marketplace, they must wash before eating. Also their pots, pans, cups, tables were considered polluted until this was done.

⁵So the Pharisees and scribes confronted Jesus about it. "Why don't Your disciples follow the rules? They don't wash their hands before eating?"

⁶Jesus answered, "Isaiah has some words that apply to you hypocrites. Listen, 'My people say all the right things, but in their hearts they are way off.' ⁷They are accomplishing nothing by this sort of religion, for it is only human habits and ideas. ⁸Here is an example: You ignore one of the Ten Commandments and yet go through all these ritualistic washings of hands, pots, pans, tables, cups, etc. ⁹You are deliberately ignoring the fifth commandment by your traditions, and I shall be specific. ¹⁰Moses has written it very plainly, 'Honor your father and your mother.' Also, 'Whoever curses his father or mother must be executed.'

¹¹"But here is your scheme: Let's say you have some property or savings of some kind and your parents are old and needy. But instead of honoring your parents by helping them, you declare these holdings as gifts to the temple at your death. ¹²By this ruse you gain a lot of brownie points with the authorities and at the same time retain possessions for your present use rather than helping your parents. ¹³This is in violation of what God would have you

to do and is only one example of how you break God's law by following your own traditions."

¹⁴After pointing out the hypocrisy of the scribes and Pharisees, Jesus gathered the common people around Him and began to give them more instruction. "Listen carefully to what I have to say," He began. ¹⁵"There is no such thing as being defiled ritualistically by taking food into the body, whether by washed hands or by unwashed hands. The only significant defilement comes from the heart of a person. ¹⁶If you have ears to hear, this is the time to listen carefully."

¹⁷When the discourse was over and the disciples and Jesus were at home again, they asked about this matter. ¹⁸"Let Me see if I can help you understand. Food taken into the body is just food and any soiling of the food is just physical. ¹⁹It cannot contaminate the mind, the spiritual entity, but goes through the GI tract and the residue is expelled from the body, resulting in no defilement. ²⁰Now about true defilement, real pollution. The human being is polluted, defiled, in reality by the things originating within. ²¹To name a few: evil thoughts, adultery, deceit, sexual immorality, all kinds of murder, ²²theft, covetousness, rebellion, deceit, lewdness, sexual abuse, blasphemy, pride, and foolishness. ²³All of these have their origin in the human heart and result in true defilement."

²⁴Not long after this discourse, Jesus began an extended trip into the country of Tyre and Sidon, where he was welcomed into a certain home. He had hoped that no one would know of His presence, but as usual the word got out. ²⁵A neighbor woman brought her daughter to Jesus. The girl was demon-possessed, and as the

woman reached Jesus, she bowed toward the ground. 26She was Greek and was from Syrian Phoenicia, but somehow she had learned of Jesus and had the faith that He could help the poor girl. She poured out her heart to Jesus, asking if He would be willing to perform the exorcism. 27The disciples were there, taking in the whole scene, and they heard Jesus respond by saying, "Really, I appreciate your situation, but we must feed children first, rather than give the food to dogs."

28She answered, "Yes, Lord, You are right, the children must be fed first, but when crumbs fall from the table this is legitimate food for the dogs, is it not?"

29"My dear woman, you have a marvelous attitude. And when you return home, you will find that your precious daughter has been freed from the demon that possessed her."

30When she heard this, she ran home as fast as her legs could carry her, and it was true! The girl was perfectly normal, lying calmly on her bed. 31Apparently this was the only purpose Jesus had in going on this long trip, for he soon left and returned to Galilee and the ten towns. 32A typical scene soon took place. A deaf man was brought to Jesus. He had been deaf since childhood, so he had never learned to speak plainly. His family had heard of Jesus and had brought him, pleading for a miracle such as they had heard about.

33Jesus first took the man away from the crowd. Then He put His fingers in the man's ears. Following this symbolic act, He let His patient know that the next thing was to protrude his tongue, and while thus exposed, Jesus spit on the ground, then touched the man's tongue. 34Looking up into the sky, He uttered a sort of sigh, and commanded, "Ephphatha," which meant, "Be opened." 35Instantly the man's ears could hear, and his tongue could form words. 36He started to speak distinctly. For some reason, known only to Jesus, He pled with the family and the patient not to spread this miracle around, but they could not keep quiet and began to tell it everywhere they went. 37People were exuberant with incredible joy. They exclaimed, "He makes the deaf ear hear and the dumb tongue speak!"

Chapter 8

1During the next few weeks, the crowds were huge, and one day they ran out of food. Calling the disciples to Him, He presented the problem. 2"I feel sorry for these people. They have been with us for three days and have not been able to get any food. 3If they try to walk home, they may faint with hunger on the way."

4The disciples had not yet reached the place where they knew that Jesus already had the answer to the problem, so they expressed their dilemma. "How can we ever find enough food here to give even a snack to all of these thousands?"

5"Well, how much food do you have?" They quickly counted seven individualized loaves of bread. (There were also a few small fishes.) 6"Good, have the people all sit down." He then took the bread and the fishes, broke them into small fragments, asked God to bless the food, and gave it to the disciples to distribute to the people. 7It did not take long to carry a small lunch to all who were present, and gratitude was evident throughout the group. 8Everyone present had enough to satisfy their hunger, and when all had finished eating, the disciples gathered up seven basketfuls of leftover food. 9A count of the people was made, and it was found that approximately four thousand were fed that day by the miracle that Jesus had performed. And remember also that this number of four thousand does not count women and children, just men. So Jesus dismissed them, and they started for home.

[10]After they were alone again, Jesus and His disciples entered a boat and sailed for Dalmanutha. [11]It was here that the Pharisees encountered Him and began demanding a miraculous sign from heaven, just to test Him of course. [12]"It seems strange," He said with a sigh, "that this generation should be asking for a 'sign' when they have already seen so many convincing ones. No, I shall not give anymore signs right now." [13]Leaving the Pharisees, He boarded another boat and left for the far shore. [14]It was soon apparent that the disciples had forgotten something very important. There was no food on board except for one loaf of bread.

[15]"Please, my friends, do not be deceived by the 'yeast' of the Pharisees, or by the 'yeast' used by Herod," Jesus began. [16]The disciples thought He must be referring to the fact that they had forgotten to buy bread. [17]Then Jesus showed them again that He could read their minds. "Are you still wrestling with this problem, this lack of bread? [18]Have you already forgotten what you have so recently seen and heard? Think again of what you saw and witnessed when there were five thousand persons present and they were fed by five loaves. How many baskets of leftovers did you gather up?"

"Twelve," they answered.

[19]"And when there were four thousand present and only seven loaves, how many baskets of leftovers?"

"Seven," they correctly answered.

[21]"So do not try to apply My statement about yeast to your failure to bring bread. Think again."

[22]One day at Bethsaida someone brought a blind man to Jesus hoping that He would just touch the man; [23]however, Jesus elected to lead the poor fellow out of the city, where He anointed his eyes with some clay made from fine dust mixed with His own saliva. He then laid His healing hands on the blind man's shoulder and asked him if he could see anything.

[24]"Hey, I can see what looks to me like trees, and they are walking."

[25]Then Jesus placed His hands on the man's eyes and asked him to look up; clear vision was now restored. [26]"By the way," Jesus told him, "it's OK to go home now, but it will be better if you do not go into town."

[27]Later when Jesus and the disciples were on their way to Caesarea Philippi, He began questioning them, "What is it that people believe about Me? Whom do they believe Me to be?"

[28]Their answers were varied. "Some think You are John the Baptist, others think You are Elijah, and still others think You are some other resurrected prophet."

[29]"But you? What is your opinion?"

[30]As might be expected, Peter was the first to respond. "Master, You are the promised Messiah."

[31]"Please do not tell anyone just yet," He urged. Then He began to reveal to them the future, the things that would take place soon. He told them that He would be put through suffering, rejected by the leaders and finally killed, then be restored to life on the third day. [32]They all heard what was said, but Peter began to reject the idea of such a fate. [33]So Jesus faced Peter and

spoke as though He were speaking directly to Satan, "Get out of here, Satan; you don't want to hear the truth about God but only those things about humans."

[34]Another gathering took place, and Jesus began to tell them what it would eventually mean to stay with Him and follow Him through life. "It will mean self-denial and cross-bearing. [35]Whoever will try to avoid this will eventually lose his life, but if you are willing to lose your life for Me and My cause, you will save your life for all eternity. [36]Tell Me which is better, to gain the whole world and lose out on eternal life, or to give your life and be awarded eternal life? [37]Is there any material consideration that you might not be willing to give up in order to have everlasting life? [38]Believe Me, in view of what value there is in My promise to you, anyone who considers my gifts lightly and refuses Me now will be looked on in that same way when I return to earth in glory with all the loyal angels."

Chapter 9

[1]"And speaking of the kingdom of God, friends, there are some of you who hear My voice today who shall be alive and witness a taste of the kingdom of God." [2]Six days later, Jesus invited Peter, James, and John to go on a climb with Him to the summit of a high hill. It was dark by the time they reached the summit, and suddenly Jesus began to be transformed before their very eyes into a brilliant, celestial being. [3]As they watched in astonishment, His clothing turned whiter than snow, far whiter than any laundry could have done. [4]Then two men appeared and began talking with Jesus. By their conversation it became obvious that one was Moses and the other

was Elijah. Moses had died and had been resurrected; Elijah had been translated to heaven without having to die.

[5]By this time the three disciples were overwhelmed with awe, but finally Peter was able to recover his speech enough to comment, "Lord, it is wonderful to be here; shall we make three shelters here, one for you and one for Moses and one for Elijah?"

[6]This idea must have sounded rather inane to Jesus, but he knew Peter well enough to realize that the awe-struck disciple was sincere and always had a lot to say. To tell the truth, the men were terrified. [7]Next a cloud appeared and covered them all and from somewhere above the cloud a thundering voice was heard: "This is My beloved Son, listen to Him." [8]Just as suddenly as the apparition had begun, it ended. Jesus was alone again on the summit, and the frightened men began to calm down.

[9]On the way down from the mountain, Jesus gave orders that nothing should be said about this experience until after His resurrection. [10]They were perplexed again, but didn't have the courage to ask Him what He meant, but amongst themselves they often spoke about what that might mean. [11]But there was a question that they wanted to ask, "Master, what do the scribes have in mind when they say that Elijah will come back?"

[12]He replied, "Yes, Elijah must come first in order to prepare the way and get things ready and in order, then the Son of man will come and be rejected and suffer greatly. [13]You see, 'Elijah' has already come and has met his fate at the hands of wicked people." Now they recognized that he was speaking of John the Baptist. [14]As the four of them reached the valley, they found

the other disciples in the center of a large gathering of people that included some of the scribes. [15]As Jesus approached, people seemed shocked and began surrounding Him. [16]Jesus asked the spokesman of the group what the excitement was all about. Then a man in the group interrupted and told Jesus what was going on.

[17]"Let me explain, Master. I am bringing my son to You. He is possessed by a demon who drags him here and there, [18]bruising him frequently, causing seizures and frothing at the mouth and loss of weight. I brought him to Your disciples and asked them to cast this demon out, but they were unable to do so."

[19]Jesus spoke, "This generation is filled with those who lack faith. How long must I keep on encouraging you to exercise real faith? Please bring your son to Me." [20]The young man was brought, writhing and foaming, falling down and covered with bruises. [21]"Sir, how long has your son been in this condition?" Jesus inquired.

The father responded, "Ever since he was a young child. [22]And often the demon will lead him into the fire, then perhaps into water trying to kill him. Now if You can do anything for us, I would be deeply appreciative."

[23]"It is like this, sir; it will depend on whether or not you can completely trust in Me. Nothing is impossible if this is your level of trust."

[24]The poor man began to weep. "Lord, I do trust You," he implored, "but I need that complete faith that You have mentioned, please."

[25]By this time the crowd was much larger, and Jesus now addressed the demon, "You demon of deafness and dumbness, I am ordering you out of this lad at once. Don't you ever molest him one more time!"

[26]As a last effort the demon hurled the boy to the ground, leaving him apparently lifeless. A murmur spread through the crowd, "Is he dead?" [27]But Jesus took him by the hand and lifted him to his feet. He was perfectly restored to normal. [28]The crowd finally dispersed, amazement evident in every face. Jesus and the disciples started for home. Their first question was this, "Lord, why did this demon refuse to respond to our command? Other demons have always obeyed."

[29]"In cases like this, there is a necessity for prayer and fasting," Jesus told them.

[30]From here He led them through Galilee, all the time trying to impress them with two things. First, that their movements should be as unannounced as possible, [31]and second, but more important advice, that He would be arrested, tried, and condemned to death and that He would be raised from death on the third day. [32]This was too much for their minds to accept, but fear kept them from asking Him more about it.

[33]They reached Peter's house in Capernaum and were made welcome. Then He questioned them frankly about what their discussion was as they were on their journey. [34]They were so embarrassed that they were not willing to share this with Him. The facts had been that they had been discussing who would be the greatest in His kingdom, and they had known all along that this was not a priority to Jesus. [35]Again He demonstrated His supernatural self when He invited them to sit down, then began, "Whoever plans to be the greatest is actually the least of all and will be like a slave to the others." [36]Then He called a little

child, lifted him to His lap and explained, [37]"Whoever accepts one little child in My name, accepts Me, and if he accepts Me, he is not just accepting Me, but also the One who sent Me."

[38]Then John spoke up, "Teacher, guess what we saw? A man casting out devils in Your name, and he isn't one of us favored ones. Boy, did we tell him straight from the shoulder that he shouldn't be doing such things." [39]John's enthusiasm was doubtless tempered greatly by Jesus' reply.

"John, please don't stop such people, for anyone who performs any kind of a miracle in My name cannot easily convince people that I am evil. [40]Besides, there will be only two sides, one side is for Me, the other side against Me. [41]Anyone who shows the slightest kindness, even a drink of water, because you are My follower, will receive a reward one day. [42]But anyone who gives offense to a child or to a young believer could do nothing worse, better for him that a millstone were tied to his neck and that he were dumped into the sea. [43]Here's another illustration. If your right hand should cause you to sin in offending someone, have it amputated and go on to eternal life with only one hand, rather than go to the second death with both hands, where the fire cannot be extinguished, [44]where worms live and where fires are not put out. [45]So also, if one of your feet becomes an agent of offense to another, it would be better to live with a prosthesis than to walk into hell with two feet, into the lake of fire that cannot be put out until everything there is burned up, [46]the place where worms cannot be crushed and the fire continues until its work is done. [47]And if your eye is an organ of offense and sins, better to have it enucleated and enter God's kingdom blind in one eye than to end up in the lake of fire with two good eyes. [48]There the fire cannot be extinguished as it can be here, and there, worms cannot be crushed as they can here.

[49]"Remember this, everyone will be tried with fiery tests, just as every offering is salted with salt. [50]Salt is good, unless it loses its flavor, then it cannot be used. Salt represents peace between you and others."

Chapter 10

[1]From here Jesus went to Judea and then to the area east of the Jordan River, and as usual, large crowds of people followed Him. [2]Some Pharisees joined them and finally cornered Him and asked this question, trying to trap Him: "Is it really legitimate to divorce one's wife?" [3]Rather frequently, when confronted by a question, He asked His own question, and here is His question: "What did Moses say about divorce?"

[4]"Moses allowed a person to obtain a divorce," they responded.

[5]"Yes, that is indeed true," Jesus admitted, "but this is not God's original plan. It is only because of hard hearts that divorces were allowed. [6]Let me quote the original plan. 'At creation, God made male and female, [7]and He intended that a man should leave his father and his mother when he matures and should be joined to his wife for life, [8]and these two should become one unit, a complete unit.' [9]In view of this plan, God has joined them into one unit, and human beings should not separate them."

[10]Back home the disciples asked Him to clarify this matter for them. [11]"Let Me explain what adultery really is. If a man divorces his wife and remarries, he has

committed adultery against his wife. [12]And if a woman divorces her husband and remarries, she has committed adultery against her husband."

[13]On another occasion, some little toddlers were brought to Jesus by parents who hoped that Jesus would put His hands on them and give them a blessing. The disciples complained amongst themselves about what was going on, thinking this would interfere with Jesus' work. [14]Out of the corner of His eye, Jesus detected their complaints and was disappointed to say the least. "Look, friends, I'm serious. Please do not discourage these parents from bringing their children to Me, for the kingdom of heaven will be populated with people like these children. [15]It is a fact that without the attitude of a little child, no one will be a citizen of the kingdom of heaven." [16]Then lifting them, one by one, into His arms He blessed them by placing His hand on their heads.

[17]On His way to another location, they were overtaken by a young runner who came right up to Jesus, knelt in front of Him, and earnestly asked, "Good Master, please tell me what I must do to inherit eternal life."

[18]"Why do you call Me 'good'?" Jesus asked. "You surely know that all human beings are sinners, don't you? And that only God is 'good.' [19]Now I am sure that you know the Ten Commandments—do not commit adultery, murder, steal, lie, cheating, and honor your father and your mother, etc."

[20]"Yes, Teacher, I have endeavored to keep these commandments all my life."

[21]Jesus already loved this young man and answered him like this, "You lack only one important thing. Are you willing to go home, sell whatever you have, and give to the poor? If so, you will have great treasure in heaven. Then come, join me in carrying your cross."

[22]He became silent and thoughtful, then left with his head down. You see, he was a very wealthy person. [23]The disciples were silent for a while, and Jesus looked from one to another. Then He spoke, "Oh how difficult it will be for a wealthy person to enter God's kingdom!" [24]This was a surprising, if not incredible, statement! In the opinion of the disciples, they firmly believed that wealth was a special blessing from God and that it indicated that the wealthy were more pious, more spiritual, and, therefore, more deserving of heaven than the average person. So Jesus began to explain things to them. "Children, the problem is not the actual possession of wealth, but the idea that wealth indicates a special standing with God and the pride that goes with this attitude. [25]A person then so proud of his own righteousness will find it harder to enter the kingdom of God than for a camel to go through the eye of a needle, which is obviously impossible."

[26]The disciples were aghast at this statement and they exclaimed, "Master, then who, pray tell, can be saved?"

[27]"Remember, He answered, "although it is impossible, humanly speaking, anything is possible with God."

[28]Another period of silence prevailed. Then Peter found his voice. "Teacher, what about us who have left our families, our homes, and our livelihood to follow You?"

[29]This comforting assurance was given. "I am not offering you some vain hope, friends. As surely as I live, you here, and anyone who is willing to leave home, brothers, sisters, father, mother, children,

or property, in order to follow Me and help promote the gospel, [30]shall receive one hundred times over what he has invested, even in this life, in the persons of fathers, mothers, children, brothers, sisters he is able to win, plus temporal needs, with only one drawback, He may well encounter persecution, but then—EVERLASTING LIFE! [31]However, many who seem to be first now will be last, while others who seem to be last here will be first then."

[32]The group was on its way to Jerusalem, and as usual Jesus was leading the way. Frankly, the disciples hardly believed that Jesus would ever return to Jerusalem, knowing the animosity, hostility, and purposes of the leadership there. Fear for His safety became their one overpowering emotion. Again He told them what could be expected once they arrived at the capital. [33]"As you know, we are on our way to Jerusalem, where the Son of man will be captured by the chief priests and scribes, then condemned to die, and turned over to the Roman authorities. [34]They will insult Him, scourge Him, spit on Him, and finally execute Him, but on the third day, He will be restored to life, resurrected from death."

[35]Even this direct account of His future, plain as it was, failed to uproot the idea that He was soon to reign as a king, conquer the Romans and the world, and then reward the disciples. James and John's request perfectly illustrated this attitude. "Master, we have a special request and hope that You will give it serious consideration."

[36]"Yes, tell me what you have in mind," He answered.

[37]"Just this, Teacher, in the glorious kingdom You are planning, we want the two highest positions in the government."

[38]"I'm afraid you are not aware of the implications of this request, friends," He replied. "First, there will be a bitter cup to drink, if you know what I mean, plus a type of baptism which will be painful and revolting. Can you accept these with Me?"

[39]Confidently they assured him, "Yes, indeed we can share that cup and that baptism with You."

[40]But Jesus added more. "Yes, truly you will share this cup with Me and this baptism, but the positions you are asking for will not be My choice at all, but will be selected by God the Father."

[41]The other disciples heard this conversation and were irritated. *The very idea! Just who do they think they are?* [42]Gently now, Jesus gathered them all around Him and tried to help them understand the nature of the kingdom of God. "You are all aware, I am sure, that in the Gentile kingdoms the government is an organization built on the idea of the most powerful at the top, then those less influential in lesser positions. [43]But in your case, it will not be like this. Instead, those with the most important positions are the ones who will assist, uplift, and wait on others. [44]And the very greatest will be the one who serves everyone else. [45]I, the Son of man, did not come here to be waited on, but to help, lift up, and wait on others, then to give My life as a ransom for them."

[46]Their journey led through Jericho, and as they were leaving the city, they encountered a blind man named Bartimaeus. Blind people in those times had no source of income, except begging. [47]Somehow he had learned that Jesus was to pass through the city and that He was on his way. He had heard also of the wonderful miracles that had been performed for so many afflicted,

and he determined to ask Him for healing. His hopes soared. He heard the crowd approaching, and although there was a lot of talking, his voice was strong enough to be heard above it all. "Jesus, Son of David, have mercy on me," he cried. [48]Those nearest to him tried to persuade him to keep quiet, but the more they pled, the louder and more insistent was his cry, "Jesus, Son of David, have mercy on me!"

[49]Jesus heard the poor man. He stopped walking and ordered Bartimaeus to be brought to him. Someone took him by the hand, lifted him up, and told him that Jesus wanted to see him. [50]He dropped his coat and came. [51]"What is it that you want Me to do for you?" Jesus asked.

"Lord, only one request. Please—my sight."

[52]"Your faith has made possible the answer to your request," Jesus assured him. His sight was restored to normal at once, and he followed Jesus.

Chapter 11

[1]When the followers of Jesus reached Bethphage and Bethany and the Mount of Olives, Jesus sent two of His disciples ahead into the village. [2]"In the village you will see a colt tied up. Untie him and bring him to Me. [3]If anyone asks you what you are doing, just tell him that the Lord needs the colt and he will tell you that you are welcome to use it as needed."

[4]Once they reached the village, it was exactly as Jesus had foretold. At an intersection of two streets, there was the colt. [5]They began untying it and were asked, "Why are you untying my colt?"

[6]"Jesus needs him," they said. There was no protest from the owner. [7]They brought the colt to Jesus, and before He sat on the animal, people brought their coats, some to put on the little beast and [8]some to place on the trail where the procession would be moving. Then tree branches and smaller twigs were brought to scatter on the trail. [9]Those ahead of Jesus and those who followed sensed the significance of the occasion and began to announce loudly, "Hosanna! May blessings be on the one who is coming in the name of the Lord. [10]May blessings be on the kingdom of our father David and the One coming in his name! Hosanna!"

[11]After entering the city, Jesus went directly to the temple where He carefully, thoughtfully observed everything that took place there. As evening approached they left and returned to Bethany where they spent the night. [12]The next morning they were again on their way to the city when Jesus spotted a fig tree well leafed out. [13]Hoping to teach them a lesson, He went to the tree and looked for figs. There were none. A fig tree with abundant leaves should have had figs on it, but none were there, and it reminded Jesus of a hypocrite. [14]Now speaking directly to the tree, He said, "No one will ever eat fruit from you again!" *How strange*, thought the disciples.

[15]At the temple that morning a lot of buying and selling was going on, and He was deeply offended by the commercialism of the sacred place, to the extent that He physically escorted the merchants out. He then went systematically from one table to another tipping them over, spilling the coins on the floor, and freeing the doves that were there for sale. [16]The containers that remained were removed, and He forbade anyone from bringing them back into the temple. [17]The disciples began to understand His actions when He quoted

this scripture, "My house shall be called a house of prayer for the entire world, but you have turned it into a den of thieves."

[18]The chief priests and scribes observed what was happening and were more and more inflamed over the way He had taken charge, and they were ready to murder Him then and there. But they could not do so for fear of the people who really loved to listen to His messages. [19]That evening Jesus and the disciples again left the city. [20]When morning came and they were again on their way to the city, they passed the place where the fig tree had been cursed the day before. Imagine the shock that the disciples felt when they spotted the fig tree, now completely dried and dead from the ground up.

[21]"Master," Peter exclaimed, "look at that fig tree You cursed yesterday. It is completely dead!"

[22]"Yes, you are right, it does indeed look terrible, but always have faith in God to do the right thing. [23]Let me tell you the actual truth, Peter. Anyone with faith and complete trust in God would be able to say to this mountain, 'Move off into the ocean,' and this would take place. [24]So let Me repeat, whatever you pray for with real trust, that you will receive. [25]Nevertheless, be reminded that when you begin to pray, always have a forgiving spirit toward those who have wronged you, for it is only this type of people who will be forgiven by the Father. [26]If you are harboring resentment toward that wrongdoer, you are not really forgiving him, and need I remind you that you too have wronged others just as you have sinned against your heavenly Father."

[27]In the temple again, they were accosted by the chief priests, scribes, and elders with this question, [28]"Just who gave You the right to teach such things as You are teaching? [29]I am willing to tell you where my authority came from if you will answer one question from Me. 'Who gave John the Baptist the authority to baptize? Was it God or just another human being?'" He asked.

[30]They were eager to hear Him say that His authority was from God so they could testify to His "blasphemy." [31]But they dare not answer His question, for if they admitted that God had given John his authority, He would ask why they refused to believe him. [32]And if they answered that John was only speaking on his own authority, they would be severely criticized by most of the people, because most believed John was a true prophet. [33]In defeat they refused to commit themselves, and Jesus then declined to answer their question.

Chapter 12

[1]Then followed a parable that clearly represented the nation as a whole. "Once upon a time a man cleared some ground and planted a vineyard. He also planted a hedge around it, dug a pit for the wine vat, built a tower, and, when the vines matured, leased it to some tenants. [2]At the season for ripe grapes, he sent a representative to collect the percentage of the crop that was due him so that it could be sold. [3]Those renters turned out to be scoundrels. They captured him, beat him up severely, and drove him out of the vineyard. [4]Another collector was sent, but he was treated no better than the first one. He was stoned, one of the stones striking his head and dangerously injuring him, so he left the vineyard. [5]A third man was sent but those renters actually killed him. Then several more men were sent, some of whom were killed and

others severely beaten. [6]The owner finally resorted to sending his one son, a kind, gracious man, thinking that the renters would treat him well and that the transactions could be completed. How wrong he was! [7]Those reprobates recognized him at once as the son of the owner and plotted against him. 'Let's kill him,' they said. 'Then we can seize the property by force.' [8]Their plot was carried out. The son was murdered, and his body thrown out of the vineyard.

[9]"Now what would be the best way to deal with a situation like this?" Jesus asked. All agreed that those murderers should be tried, condemned, and executed. "Then he should find new tenants for his vineyard."

[10]The implication was clear. The Jewish nation must be replaced. [11]"One more thing," Jesus added. "Do you remember reading this passage of scripture? 'The stone that the builders rejected has turned out to be the chief keystone.' The Lord had a hand in bringing about this wonderful discovery."

[12]Oh how those in power wanted to capture Him now! They realized the significance of the parable as applying to themselves, but so great was His popularity among the people that they dared not do anything at that time. [13]His enemies now got together and planned to send a committee to interview Him, hoping that He would say something which would give them a reason to arrest Him. [14]The first question they used was this, "Is it OK to pay taxes to Rome?" Of course, this was a loaded question. He could be accused whatever answer He gave. In order to flatter Him, they said, "We know that You are so committed to God that human opinions are unnecessary. [15]So what do You say, shall we pay taxes or not? Please give us Your best answer." They reasoned that if He said 'no,' they would report Him to the Roman authorities, and if He said 'yes,' they would accuse him of being disloyal to his own nation. They didn't realize how clear their motives were to Him.

"Why are you trying to trap Me? Do you by chance have a Roman coin with you?" Someone handed Him a Roman penny. "OK, whose picture is on this coin? And whose words are stamped on it?"

"Caesar's," they replied.

[17]"Now I shall tell you the principle that should give you the answer to your question, and here it is. Always give to Caesar that which is due him, and do not forget to give God that which is due Him."

Their plot had totally failed. He had proposed such a reasonable solution that they had no words with which to retaliate. [18]And still He was not free from harassment. Next up to challenge Him were some Sadducees. These leaders were well educated, powerful, and respected, but they denied that anyone would ever be resurrected. (Hadn't they heard of the young man at Nain, Jairus' daughter, or Lazarus of Bethany?)

[19]"Master, we are facing a situation that needs to be clarified. If You will, please, according to long established tradition, if a man dies having no heirs, his brother must marry his widow, and if she has a child by this brother, her firstborn will legally be heir of her first husband. Moses was the author of this plan, as You probably know, and the first child born will belong to the dead man. [20]Now, Master, there was a family of seven sons. The oldest married, but before there were any children, he died. [21]So the second son married the widow,

but alas, he too died before children were born. Then the third brother married her and the same thing occurred. [22]Finally, all seven brothers died after marrying the same woman, and some time later the woman herself died. [23]Our question? In the resurrection, whose wife will she be? For she had been married to all seven during her lifetime."

[24]"Your problem," said Jesus, "is that you do not know the scriptures well enough, nor do you know the power of God. [25]Briefly, the answer to your question is this: When the resurrection occurs, none will find themselves married, but they will resemble the angels of heaven in that respect. [26]Now let us think a little about the dead and the resurrection. Do you remember what God told Moses at the burning bush? 'I am the God of Abraham, Isaac, and Jacob.' [27]He is not just the God of dead folks, but of living beings." Thus, He reasonably implied that Abraham, Isaac, and Jacob will be resurrected.

[28]Having heard these reasonable answers, one of the scribes was so impressed that he sought out and found Jesus later and asked Him which was the most important of all the commandments. [29]"I am glad to share with you the answer to this good question," Jesus replied. "Here it is: 'Hear, Oh Israel, the Lord our God is one Lord, [30]and you should love the Lord your God with all your heart, with your whole being, with all your mind, and with every bit of strength you have.' This is the most important of all commandments. [31]And for your information, here is the next most important commandment: You should love your neighbor to the same degree that you love yourself. No other commandments can equal these two in importance."

[32]The scribe was thoughtful and then replied, "Thank you, Master, for this expression of truth. There is indeed but one God; there can be no other. [33]And to love Him with the whole heart, the whole being, the whole intellect, the whole strength, and to have the very same concern for one's neighbor as for oneself is certainly of more value than any burnt offering or sacrifice."

[34]Jesus commended him with this encouraging statement, "You are very near the kingdom of God." After this, there was no one who had a question for him.

[35]One day as Jesus taught in the temple, He challenge them with His own question. "Our scribes have been teaching that the Messiah will be a descendant of David, [36]but under the influence of the Holy Spirit, David refers to the Messiah in these words: 'Jehovah says to my Lord, Sit on my right hand until I make your enemies your footstool.' [37]Here David calls him 'Lord,' so how can he be a descendant?" This made them think.

[38]Among other issues, his teaching included this: "Beware of the scribes. They seem to enjoy dressing differently just to be noticed, and they enjoy being in the marketplace where people address them with a special title. [39]They demand the places of honor in the synagogue and always hope to be placed in the positions of importance at feasts. [40]And yet these same scribes are prone to manipulate things so that widows are ousted from their homes. They often pray long monotonous prayers to impress listeners, but in the end their condemnation will be certain."

[41]A short time later, Jesus was seated on a bench near the treasury building, watching people as they made their contributions

to the treasury. He noticed first a number of wealthy people come by and place large offerings in the slot, while trying to let others know that these contributions were really large. [42]Then he noticed a widow quietly approaching. She was obviously poor, but she wanted to do her part in sustaining the temple service. She put in two coins, then slipped away hoping no one would notice how little she was giving. [43]However, Jesus called attention to her, saying to His disciples: "Did you see what just took place? This widow put a small offering into the treasury, and yet it was a significant amount for her, even resulting in a sacrifice of her true needs. Now in the sight of God, she put in more than those others. [44]You see, they had plenty of money left, while she gave everything she had."

Chapter 13

[1]As Jesus and the disciples were leaving the temple, one of them commented to Jesus, "Look, Master, at these beautiful buildings. Don't they speak eloquently of Your people Israel?"

[2]The response from Jesus was saddening. "Yes, indeed look at them and remember them, for the time is coming when they will be utterly destroyed. Not one stone will be left on another. The place will be nothing but rubble."

[3]When they reached the Mount of Olives, where they could again see the temple in the distance, Peter, Andrew, James, and John took Him off to one side and suggested, [4]"Would You be willing to tell us when this will take place? At least give us some clues as to when we may expect this to take place."

[5]"First, I want to warn all of you to be alert and on your guard against deception, [6]because a number of men will come along claiming to be Me, and sadly, too many people will fall for this. [7]A great deal of history will pass before all will be fulfilled, such as many wars and reports of distant wars. This will be common. [8]One nation will attack another nation, one kingdom will fight against another; there will be earthquakes of severe magnitude in many different parts of the world. Trouble will be almost constantly a problem for our planet, but what I have told you will be only like the first labor pains of a woman at the time of delivery. [9]What you all will need is to frankly examine your own hearts, for you will be turned over to courts, will receive whippings, and will be tried before kings, tyrants, judges and all because you believe in Me and they need to know about your belief in Me.

[10]"And here is encouragement for you. This gospel of the kingdom must and will be preached in every nation on earth. [11]Now when you are arrested and compelled to tell of your faith, you need not be terrified and wonder what to say. There will be no need to memorize a speech. Only be assured that the Holy Spirit will then give you just the right words at the right time. [12]The time will come when a man will testify against his brother, a father against his son, children against their parents, and this may result in execution because of their faith. [13]You will all be hated by someone because of your faith in Me, but patient endurance will characterize those who stand to the very end. [14]Please do not neglect the prophecy of Daniel. He mentions 'the abomination of desolation' that will come over this sacred place. When this occurs it is the sign for you to get out of this city and flee, then out of Judea. [15]Do

not even take time to take an extra garment or valuables, [16]but run for your life in order to escape in time. [17]It could be disaster for those who are pregnant and for those with nursing babies. [18]And do pray that you will not have to escape in the winter.

[19]"The troubles I am warning you about will be such as never has been seen on this world and will never again be equaled. [20]Unless God shortens those troubles, humanity itself would not survive, but for the sake of you who believe, that persecution will be shortened. [21]So remember, don't listen to anyone who tells you, 'Christ has come, He is over here.' It won't be like that. [22]Nevertheless, false christs will come and false prophets will appear and perform genuine miracles so that if possible the most ardent believers could be deceived. [23]So be on guard. I am warning you ahead of time to protect you.

[24]"Let me continue. In those times and after the persecution has subsided, there will be a notable warning sign. The sun will fail to give light in the day, and the moon will fail at night. Darkness shall prevail over the land, and there will be no adequate explanation of the phenomenon. [25]Another omen. There will be a shower of meteors such as has never been seen before, as if all the stars in the sky were falling. And yet another sign: The heavenly bodies and the forces that control them will become unstable so that actual shaking will be witnessed. [26]After this last sign, the Son of man will be seen coming in clouds with total authority and unbelievable splendor.

[27]"At His coming He will dispatch His angels to rescue those who have chosen Him as their Lord, wherever they might be here on the earth. [28]You all know about fig trees. When those leaves begin to appear, you know that summer is on the way, [29]so, when you witness the things I've been mentioning, you will know that I am near, right at the door. [30]In fact, this generation will not have disappeared before these things will begin to occur. [31]The heaven and the earth might disappear completely, but My word shall be fully fulfilled. [32]An important thing to remember, however, is this. No one will know the exact time of My return until it happens. Even the heavenly angels do not know, and, believe it or not, I myself do not know. The Father knows, of course, but He has not revealed it to Me. [33]Because no one knows, it is of utmost importance to be alert and ready for My return.

[34]"It reminds Me of the home owner who went on an extended trip. Before leaving, all the slaves were given their tasks. The steward was properly instructed, and the gatekeeper was admonished to be ready to open the gate when the owner returned. [35]You are like that gatekeeper. If I return at midnight, dawn, or broad daylight, be alert and ready to open the gate, [36]for you might easily be caught asleep, [36]and this advice applies to everyone. Keep on watching."

Chapter 14

[1]Two days later the Passover and the feast of unleavened bread would begin, and it was during those two days that the chief priests and scribes conspired together how best to develop a case strong enough to convict Jesus and have Him executed. [2]They finally concluded that it might be best to wait until after the feast days, because of His popularity among the people.

[3]Jesus and His disciples had been invited to the home of Simon the leper who

lived in Bethany. They had surrounded the table and were engaged in conversation as they were eating, when a woman quietly came in, unannounced, and began to anoint Jesus' head with pure nard from an alabaster box that she had purchased. [4]Although no one spoke for a time, several were thinking, *Why all this waste of hard-earned money? All this wasted on Jesus. The very idea!* [5]*Just think of how much money might have been realized had this been sold and the money used to help the poor. A whole year's wages!*

Mutterings went on until Jesus spoke up. [6]Gently Jesus tried to show them a different side of the issue. "Please do not give her a hard time. She has done something good. [7]And please remember that as long as the world lasts, there will be poor people that you can and should help, but you will not have Me much longer. [8]She has done what she could, and this was anointing Me for My burial. [9]Let me tell you something. Wherever the gospel is preached, this little story will be told. And she will be remembered."

[10]Shortly after the meal at Simon's house, Judas Iscariot, one of the twelve disciples, left and went secretly to the chief priests for the express purpose of betraying Jesus into their hands. [11]After listening to his idea, they were delighted. They promised him a handsome reward in cash for doing so, and he knew just how it could be done. [12]Passover day came, and Jesus was asked where He wanted to celebrate the feast. [13]He appointed two of them to go into the city and told them they would meet a rare sight—a man carrying a pitcher of water. "Follow him. [14]When he enters a house, go in with him and meet the owner and tell him, 'The Master needs your guest

room so that He can keep the Passover there with His disciples.' [15]He will be expecting this and will show you a large upstairs room suitably furnished. There you should complete the preparations for us."

[16]They went and found things exactly as Jesus had described them, and the plans for the Passover were carried out. [17]Jesus and the twelve assembled there in the evening. [18]While solemnly eating the meal, Jesus shocked them with an unthinkable announcement: "It is a fact that one of you here will betray Me into the hands of My enemies."

[19]They began questioning him, "Lord, is it I? Lord, is it I?"

[20]"It is one of you who is eating with Me right now." Then He added this awful statement regarding the guilty one. [21]"The Son of man will indeed fulfill the prophecy and will be captured, but woe be to the man who betrays Him. It would be far better for him if he had never been born."

[22]As they were eating, He took some of the unleavened bread, broke it in pieces, and gave a morsel of it to each one of the twelve as he said, "Take, eat it, for it represents My broken body." [23]Then He picked up the cup, gave thanks for it, and offered a sip to everyone as He said, [24]"Take this and drink it, for it represents My blood, which will be shed for you. [25]Truly, friends, this is the last time I shall drink this juice with you in this world. Next time it will be with you in the kingdom of God."

[26]The little ceremony closed with the singing of a hymn, following which, they left the room and went out to the Mount of Olives. [27]"Do you remember the prophecy that says, 'I will strike down the shepherd, and the sheep will be scattered?' You will see the fulfillment of that prophecy this night.

In fact, all of you will be offended tonight because of Me. ²⁸But after I rise again, I will meet you in Galilee. I promise."

²⁹Peter spoke in a very confident tone, "You are mistaken. I don't care how many are offended because of You, yet I never will."

³⁰"Oh? Let me tell you the truth. Before the rooster crows in the morning, you will deny three times that you even know Me."

³¹Peter loudly protested, saying that such a thing could not possibly happen. "Lord, if I am called to die for You, I still would never deny You." The others stoutly promised the same loyalty.

³²They came to a place called Gethsemane where Jesus stopped and asked the disciples to wait for Him while He was praying. ³³Peter, James, and John followed Him farther into the garden, however, and were aware that He had become unusually quiet, sorrowful, and depressed. ³⁴He shared his feelings with them and pled with them to pray, for He felt as if He were about to die of sorrow.

³⁵Going a little farther, He fell to the ground and begged His Father to release Him from this ordeal. ³⁶"Father, Papa, please do not compel Me to go through with this—and yet You know what is best regardless of My feelings, so let Your will be done." ³⁷When He made His way back to the disciples, they had gone to sleep. He awakened Peter and asked, "Couldn't you have stayed awake one more hour? I needed you to keep on praying. ³⁸Stay awake and alert and keep praying, for without this you will fall a victim to temptation. Yes, I know you want to do the right thing, but humanity is weak."

³⁹Again He left them and prayed the same agonizing prayer over and over.

⁴⁰Then again He found them asleep, overcome by weariness. They did not seem to know how to help Him. ⁴¹He returned to them the third time, and this time He no longer begged them to stay awake. He had made His decision. "You may now sleep on, for I have committed myself into God's will. I am about to be betrayed into the hands of sinners, and I will not escape. ⁴²Get up, for my betrayer is coming and is almost here."

⁴³It was only moments before Judas Iscariot arrived leading a mob with swords and clubs, all of whom were sent by the priests and scribes to capture Jesus. ⁴⁴Judas had planned the meeting. "Watch me closely; the one I embrace and kiss is the one you want. Then hold Him tightly, for He might yet escape." ⁴⁵He went directly to Jesus and greeted Him. "Greetings, Master." Then he kissed Him. ⁴⁶The mob leaders then seized Jesus and started off with Him. ⁴⁷Now one of the high priest's slaves was with the mob and was moving along with Jesus when a man, intending to protect Jesus, swung his sword at this ruffian, and instead of decapitating him, he just cut off his ear.

⁴⁸"Are you here to arrest Me as a common criminal, armed with swords and clubs?" Jesus asked. ⁴⁹"I was teaching day by day in the temple, and no one hindered Me in any way. However this, what you are now doing is a fulfillment of prophecy."

⁵⁰The disciples began to realize that Jesus was not going to free Himself from the mob, so they all abandoned Him and disappeared. ⁵¹A young man, a believer in Jesus, was clothed only with a sheet of linen when some young punks tried to grab him. ⁵²But they only were able to get the linen cloth, and the young fellow

ran naked from the scene. [53]From the garden they led Jesus to the home of the high priest where were gathered the chief priests, scribes, and elders.

[54]Peter was on the outskirts of the mob; he had been watching everything that had been going on. He was mingling with the high priest's slaves as they entered the palace courtyard, and within the area was a small warming fire where he stood with others. [55]Jesus was then arraigned before the high priest and charged with crimes against the nation, but when witnesses were asked to present evidence of this crime, none could be found. [56]A number of people offered to testify, but as they spoke it became evident that they were all fabricating their stories, for no two of them agreed. [57]One example of this sort of testimony was this. "We heard him say, [58]'Destroy this temple, and I will rebuild it in three days.'"

[59]There was only one person who gave this testimony, and the high priest [60]stood up and challenged Jesus to answer these charges. "Don't You hear what these people are saying?" [61]Jesus made no move to admit or deny these absurd charges. So the high priest continued, "Are You the anointed, the Son of the Blessed One?"

[62]To this question, Jesus was not silent. "I am. One day this Son of man, this human who is now speaking to you, will be seen by you, occupying the throne of power and returning to this earth in the clouds of heaven."

[63]The high priest was enraged. He broke the Levitical code. He actually tore his priestly robe in indignation and shouted out, "We don't need any more testimonies from witnesses. [64]We have heard it from His own lips. He is blaspheming! What is your verdict?" The answer was unanimous, He should be condemned to die. [65]Such was the intensity of hatred that some of the most honored men of the nation had for Jesus that they stooped so low as to spit in His face, to blindfold Him, then hit Him and ask, "Who hit You?" And then the slaves were ordered to do the same thing.

[66]Out in the courtyard, Peter was confronted by one of the female slaves [67]as he stood by the fire keeping warm. She suddenly seemed to recognize him. "I remember you; you were with Jesus of Nazareth! Right?"

[68]He instantly denied it. "I don't even understand what you are saying." He then went out to the porch and a rooster crowed.

[69]Presently another slave girl saw him and began telling those around her, "This fellow was a follower of Jesus." [70]Peter overheard her statements and again vehemently denied it.

Shortly after his second denial several of those standing closer to Peter closed in on him. Their spokesman challenged him, "Look fellow, don't try to deny being one of His followers, for your Galilean accent gives you away at once."

[71]At this Peter lost his cool and began to curse and swear as only a fisherman can. "I absolutely do not know this Man you are talking about!" [72]All at once the rooster crowed again, and Peter remembered Jesus' prediction. "Before the rooster crows twice, you will deny three times that you even know Me." The awful realization was too much for Peter. He left the place and fled, sobbing uncontrollably with remorse.

Chapter 15

[1]When morning dawned and a trial was now legal, the priests, scribes, and elders huddled for a time trying to decide what

to do with Jesus. They decided to turn Him over to the Roman governor, Pilate. [2]His first question was direct and was intended to settle the issue at once. "Are you the king of the Jews?"

Jesus responded, "I am."

[3]Then the chief priests began a tirade against Him, accusing Him of various crimes, but He remained silent during their outbursts. [4]"Have you nothing to say after hearing all these accusations?" Pilate demanded. [5]But Jesus, in a dignified manner, declined to comment. Pilate was amazed at His calmness and realized that these charges were all trumped up and without foundation. [6]Then Pilate had an idea that he thought might resolve his problem, so he proposed it to the priests. "At every Passover I have been willing to release one political prisoner, whichever one you might choose. [7]We have in custody a man named Barabbas who was convicted of murder, which occurred during an attempted coup." [8]Here the listeners began to urge him to continue his practice. [9]"So shall I release 'the King of the Jews' or Barabbas?"

[10]It seemed clear by this time that Jesus had been arrested and referred to Pilate because of jealousy. [11]The chief priests now agreed on one thing. They preferred releasing Barabbas rather than Jesus. [12]"If I release Barabbas, what shall I do about Jesus, who calls Himself the king of the Jews?"

[13]The cry was shouted out in unison, "Crucify Him!"

[14]"Why? What crime has He committed?"

There was no answer except a louder cry, "Crucify Him!"

[15]Pilate caved in. Barabbas was released, and Pilate gave the order to scourge Jesus, then to crucify Him. [16]Soldiers immediately led Him into the praetorium. [17]Here they stripped Him, then put on an old moth-eaten purple robe and ceremoniously "crowned" Him with a wreath of thorns. [18]With ultimate sarcasm they filed by Him, one by one, bowed and saluted Him, and greeted Him, "Hail, King of the Jews." [19]Then with reeds they struck the crown of thorns, spit in His face, and mockingly knelt down as if in reverence. [20]Following this inhumane treatment, they removed the old purple robe, replaced His own clothing, and led Him out to be crucified.

[21]By this time Jesus was so exhausted, dehydrated, and abused that He just could not physically carry the cross, as all such victims have to do. So on an impulse, they arrested a stranger coming into the city who showed interest in the scene. He was ordered to carry Jesus' cross to the place of execution. He was a person named Simon, a resident of Cyrene who was arriving in Jerusalem for the Passover feast. He had two sons, Alexander and Rufus.

[22]The site of the execution was an area known as Golgotha, which means. "The place of the skull." [23]After being nailed to the cross, Jesus was offered wine with dissolved myrrh, but He refused to drink any. [24]His clothing, now lying on the ground nearby, was raffled off to the soldiers. [25]The crucifixion occurred at about 9:00 a.m.

[26]His crime was written down and attached to the cross above His head. It read, "The king of the Jews." [27]Two others were crucified that day, both of which were thieves, and Jesus was placed between them, indicating that He was the worst of the three criminals. [28]Remember Isaiah 53:12, which states, "He was numbered

with the transgressors?" This was the fulfillment of that prophecy. [29]Onlookers
taunted Him over His statement about
destroying the temple and rebuilding it
in three days. [30]"If You are so great, save
Yourself and get down from the cross."
[31]This was similar to the attitude of the
scribes and priests. "He saved others, but
He can't save Himself. [32]Let the anointed
King of Israel come down from the cross,
and we will believe in Him." The two
thieves also gave Him a hard time.

[33]At about noon, darkness descended
over the whole country, silencing most of
the chatter and comments and striking
terror into everyone. It lasted about three
hours at which time, [34]Jesus cried out in
abject despair, "Eloi, Eloi, lama sabattani,"
which translated means, "My God, My
God, why did You forsake Me?"

[35]"Listen," someone said, "He is calling
for Elijah." [36]One sympathetic person, after
hearing this cry, grabbed a sponge, soaked
it with vinegar, and offered it to Him. Then
he said to others there, "Let's see if Elijah
will come and take Him down."

[37]Just a few minutes later, Jesus cried
out again and slumped in death. [38]At that
very moment, over in the temple, the massive veil that separates the two parts of the
sanctuary was torn apart from top to bottom by an unseen force, a supernatural act.
[39]The Roman centurion in charge of the
execution was close by when Jesus died,
and he was heard to exclaim in awe, "It
must be true that this man was indeed the
Son of God." [40]Some distance away, several
women were watching the fearful scene,
among whom were Mary Magdalene, Mary
the mother of James and Joses, and Salome.
[41]These three had been loyal followers while
he was in Galilee, doing what they could

to help Him. Also many other women
had come up to Jerusalem with Him, and
it seemed that they all gravitated together
into a small band to comfort each other.

[42]Leaving the crucifixion scene, a man
made his way rapidly to Pilate with a verbal
request for the custody of Jesus' body. [43]He
had been present throughout the awful
spectacle and was obviously in sympathy
with Jesus rather than with the majority
of the priests and rulers. His standing in
the nation was unquestioned, for he was
none other than Joseph of Arimathea, a
wealthy, devout, God-fearing individual.
[44]Pilate could not believe that Jesus was
already dead, so he summoned a centurion who verified that it was true. [45]The
situation was urgent for this was the day of
preparation and soon the Sabbath would
begin. Fortunately, Pilate was in the mood
to grant the request. [46]Joseph quickly
purchased enough top quality linen with
which to wrap the body, then went to
the cross, where with the help of soldiers
and friends, he removed the corpse and
wrapped it in the linen. Then he took it
to his own unoccupied sepulcher nearby,
a stone tomb of walk-in size with a large
stone disc that rolled across the entrance.
[47]Mary Magdalene and Mary the
mother of Joses had their own plans, so
they watched carefully as Jesus' body was
placed in the tomb. They would bring
spices and embalming herbs, but their
time had run out. This would have to wait
until after the Sabbath.

Chapter 16

[1]The Sabbath finally passed and none of
them slept very well. Their disappointment was intense, thinking of the terrible
injustice meted out to Jesus. But somehow

they knew what had to be done, so very early Sunday morning they approached the tomb to prepare His body for burial. [2]Before sunrise, they were almost to the tomb, but wondered who would be there to roll the huge stone away from the entrance. Plus, it had been sealed with a Roman seal. [3]Imagine their amazement and perplexity when they reached it, only to find [4]that the stone had already been rolled away in its groove. The seal was broken and the entrance was wide open.

[5]Boldly walking into the tomb, they were startled to meet a young man in a long white robe sitting quietly on the right side. Needless to say, they were frightened until he calmed them with these words, [6]"Please, do not be afraid. I happen to know that you are looking for the body of Jesus of Nazareth who was crucified last Friday. As you can see, He is no longer here, for He was resurrected. Right there is where His body had been placed. [7]Now please return to the city and give this message to His disciples and Peter, 'I have left for Galilee just as I had promised you and will meet you at the designated place.'"

[8]They lost no time getting out of that tomb, trembling with a mixture of fear, hope, and joy. [9]Mary Magdalene had the honor of being the first person to see the risen Christ that Sunday morning. She was the one who had been freed from seven different demons. [10]Going to the upper room she found the disciples, still in stunned sorrow, but her good news scarcely had an impact on their mood. [11]For they dismissed her account as mere wishful thinking or a hallucination. [12]Shortly afterward two other followers were on their way home from Jerusalem, about eight miles distant, when Jesus showed up and convinced them of the truth of the resurrection. [13]They trudged right back into the city to break the great news, but the disciples were no more willing to listen to their story than to believe Mary.

[14]But then, one day they were all together eating when Jesus Himself appeared! Now they were ready to listen. First He gently chided them for not believing what Mary and the two others had told them, eyewitnesses as they were and reliable men and women. [15]But having said this, He outlined to them their mission for the rest of their lives. "You are to go into the whole world and tell the good news everywhere. [16]Those who believe what you tell them and are baptized will be saved, while those who refuse to believe face condemnation. [17]People who believe will be given miraculous capabilities, such as the power to cast out demons, to speak in different languages, [18]to encounter poisonous snakes without harm, to have protection from other poisons, and to have power to touch sick folks and heal them."

[19]After fully instructing them, Jesus ascended to heaven where He sits at God's right hand. So off they went and began preaching everywhere, working with the Lord. They demonstrated with powerful evidences that they were teaching truth.

Luke

Chapter 1

[1]Perhaps I may be forgiven for adding one more book to the list of those already available regarding the Christian religion, a faith well-founded and certain. [2]Those who were eyewitnesses have provided us with abundant facts, both from the scripture and from their personal experiences. [3]With this much already available, it may seem redundant to add even more words, yet somehow I feel that my efforts will be worthwhile. So my dear sir, your excellency, Theophilus, let me fortify, reinforce, and strengthen your faith with my account of the events and teachings that you already have in mind.

[4]Let me begin with the reign of King Herod of Judea. [5]During his reign there was a priest by the name of Zacharias, in the course of Abijah, whose wife Elizabeth was also a descendant of Aaron. [6]Both of these were sincere folk who faithfully followed all the Hebrew rites and ordinances and kept God's commandments. [7]Unfortunately, the family had a fertility problem, and by the time our story begins, they were well up in years, and it seemed utterly impossible that they could become parents, and of course you know what a disappointment that can be. [8]But one day Zacharias was at his priestly duty at the temple and was about to burn the incense. [9]Just outside was a crowd of people. [10]Their prayers were ascending to God for the priest and for the nation.

[11]As Zacharias stood before the golden altar, an angel appeared just to the right of the altar in full view. [12]Understandably, Zacharias was terrified, [13]but the angel quickly calmed him by assuring him that he was on a friendly mission. "Do not be afraid for I am your friend and have been sent as a special messenger from God. I have been sent to bring you some wonderful news. You and Elizabeth have been praying many years for a child have you not? Well your prayers are about to be answered. Elizabeth will soon become pregnant and will give birth to a son whose name will be John. [14]His birth will bring great joy to you and to many others who will be blessed by his life. [15]He is to become one of God's great men. He must never drink any fermented beverages, and he will be fully under the influence of the Holy Spirit from the time of conception. [16]His influence will be widespread, and he will turn large numbers of people to the Lord. [17]And now the really important thing: He is God's choice to introduce the Messiah to the world. His message will be similar to that of Elijah whose life brought about a

great revival, a rebirth of love in families, in the tribes, and in the entire nation."

[18]Zacharias was stunned! "This all sounds wonderful, but I'll believe it when the child is born. You may not understand physiology, but at my age I am essentially impotent, and Elizabeth entered menopause years ago."

[19]The angel gently tried to assure him. "You obviously don't know me, Zacharias, but I am Gabriel and my post of duty is in the very presence of God Himself, so I have learned more about you and Elizabeth than you could imagine, and my message to you is indeed the truth and nothing but the truth. [20]Because of your tendency to doubt, I am giving you a supernatural sign. You will be aphasic, unable to speak a word from this moment on until the child is born."

[21]Outside the temple, while this was going on, the watchers were becoming apprehensive, recognizing that something unusual had been taking place. [22]When he finally emerged, they realized that something indeed had happened. He tried to motion with his hands and could not speak. Most of them thought he had experienced a prophetic vision. [23]In spite of his handicap, he was able to complete his tour of duty before returning home. [24]Not long after he returned, Elizabeth actually became pregnant just as the angel Gabriel had predicted. She was so thrilled by this miracle that she isolated herself from her friends for the next five months, [25]while she composed a psalm of praise which follows: I am overwhelmed to realize that God has performed a miracle in me so that never again will anyone be able to look down on me with scorn.

[26]It was during the sixth month of Elizabeth's pregnancy that God sent the angel Gabriel to the town of Nazareth where he was to introduce himself to a young girl, a virgin named Mary. [27]This girl was engaged to marry a man named Joseph, a descendant of David. [28]"Greetings, Mary," he began. "You are highly honored by the Lord. He is with you, and you are blessed above all other women in the world."

[29]Poor Mary was frightened. She could not expect to understand what this was all about, but Gabriel calmed her fears. [30]"Please do not be afraid, Mary. For God really looks on you with utmost favor. [31]And in spite of what you might think or believe right now, you will conceive and give birth to a son whose name will be Jesus, meaning Savior. [32]He will be great indeed and will be called 'son of the Highest' and will become king of Israel, as was his earthly ancestor David. [33]He will be the king, not just for life, but forever. Think of it! His kingdom will be eternal, never ending!"

[34]But Mary was skeptical and asked, "How can you account for what you have just told me. You may not realize that I am a virgin, and virgins never have babies."

[35]So Gabriel quietly explained it this way: "Mary, the Holy Spirit of God, the creator of the universe shall possess your body and cause a miraculous conception to take place. Therefore, the child thus conceived will rightly be called the Son of God. [36]And, Mary, I want to tell you a secret. Your cousin Elizabeth has become pregnant in her old age after a long life of sterility. About three months from now she will give birth to a baby boy. Yes, I even know the gender of her child. [37]So you see, nothing is impossible with God."

[38]Mary, bless her heart, believed the angel and expressed herself in these

words: "Here I am, Lord; I am ready for my assignment with God's help." At that moment the angel disappeared. [39]Mary began at once for a journey to Judea to visit Elizabeth to share the news with her, aware that they both were actors and participants in remarkable miracles. [40]As soon as she walked through the door, the two women embraced each other and wept, overcome by emotion. [41]Just at that moment, as if to emphasize the wonder of it all, Elizabeth's unborn son "jumped up and down" for joy, and Elizabeth was moved by the Holy Spirit and proclaimed, [42]in beautiful language, words that have become classic. "You are blessed above every other woman on this earth, and your Baby is even more blessed. [43]Will someone tell me, please, why I have this unbelievable privilege of greeting the mother of my Lord, God's Messiah. [44]For just as Mary's greeting was heard, my baby jumped up and down for joy. [45]Furthermore, because of her implicit faith in the words of God, every prediction will be fulfilled."

[46]Then it was Mary's turn to become poetic: "My entire being exalts the Lord, [47]and my spirit is rejoicing in God my Savior. [48]For He has overlooked my humble circumstances and has made it possible for 'little me' to be one of earth's most well-known women. [49]Yes, He who is infinite in strength has accomplished a miracle in me. His very name is Holy. [50]His mercy toward those who hold Him in reverence is not measurable and is everlasting. [51]His strong arm is now evident to everyone, but He has not bestowed blessings like these on the proud ones. Far from it; they are humbled and defeated. [52]He has deposed some of earth's greatest and has honored humble ones having placed heavy responsibilities

on them. [53]He has satisfied those who deeply hunger for the best blessings, but many who feel rich have been allowed to remain empty. [54]He has truly helped Israel, His servant, showing again His wonderful mercy, [55]and in fulfillment of the promise made to Abraham and to the other patriarch."

[56]For about three months Mary stayed with Elizabeth; then she returned home. [57]Not long afterward, Elizabeth delivered her son just as Gabriel had promised. [58]The neighbors heard the news and rejoiced with the proud parents. Here was an elderly woman with a newborn baby! [59]When the baby was eight days old, the priest and his helpers came to circumcise and to christen him and register his birth. They assumed his name would be Zacharias after his father. [60]But Elizabeth protested, "No, he must be named John."

[61]"Now listen, Elizabeth. None of your relatives or your husband's relatives have that name."

[62]So they went to Zacharias to find out what to name the child. [63]He motioned for a pen and some writing paper. Then he wrote, "His name is John," much to their surprise. [64]Instantly his aphasia disappeared, and his first words were of praise to God. [65]As could be expected, the whole story spread rapidly through the hill country of Judea, bringing about a deep sense of reverence and awe in all who heard it. [66]Deep in the hearts of everyone was a realization that God had something special in store for the baby who was so obviously blessed by God.

[67]Even Zacharias was filled with the Holy Spirit and was given the gift of prophecy, writing it down like this: [68]"Praise be to Israel's God for He has finally fulfilled

His promise to bring the world's Redeemer through His people Israel. [69]He has raised up a horn (a symbol of power and authority) in David's family as predicted. [70]His holy prophets from the earliest times have written accurately! [71]Now we, members of God's beloved nation will be rescued from our enemies who hate us. [72]At last, our God will fulfill every promise He made to our ancestors, Abraham, Isaac and Jacob, and, of course, to David. [73]Once these promises are fulfilled and we are rescued, there will be no further fear in serving him, no anxiety again, but only perfect trust and confidence. [74]And this blessed experience will endure forever, [75]as He imparts to us His holiness, His righteousness.

[76]"And now my child, I will address some words to you. For your title will be 'prophet of the Highest.' You will be the one who goes along ahead of the Lord to prepare the world to receive Him. [77]Then He will teach us about salvation and how it is the result of the forgiveness of sin. [78]This forgiveness is wholly due to the tender mercy of our God and not to anything we deserve, but due to God's coming to earth in human form. [79]His coming is for a grand, noble purpose: to bring light into the world, spiritual light to us who are in fearful darkness, leading us safely into the way of peace."

[80]The child John grew normally from babyhood, showing profound spirituality as well as intelligence. Most of his adult life was spent in the solitude of the wilderness until God called him to begin preaching.

Chapter 2

[1]Shortly after John's birth, the emperor Augustus Caesar issued a decree that applied to the whole empire. Every resident must be registered for tax purposes. [2]This decree was first implemented while Quirinius was governor of Syria. [3]The registration was to be carried out in the ancestral city of every inhabitant, so Joseph, a law-abiding citizen, must travel from Nazareth to Bethlehem, for he was a descendant of David and David's city was Bethlehem. [4]But he faced a real problem. The deadline for registration was rapidly approaching, [5]and Mary was near term, and they must make the ninety-mile trip before her due date. [6]The hardships of that journey can scarcely be imagined, but they made it to Bethlehem just before Mary went into labor.

[7]At the inn Joseph explained his predicament to the manager but to no avail. There just were no available rooms because of the influx of visitors responding to the emperor's decree. All he could offer was a stable, and into this stable Joseph led the donkey, and just in time, for Mary was in active labor. Not long afterward she delivered her son. She wrapped the Baby in the only available cloth and used the manger as a crib.

[8]In the hills around Bethlehem, there were shepherds tending their flocks. [9]Suddenly an angel confronted them, accompanied by a brilliant light in the sky. They were terrified. [10]But the angel quickly calmed their fears with his lovely voice, "Friends, try not to panic. I know that this is a bit startling, and I'm not surprised that you are so fearful, so let me tell you why I have come. I am bringing you good news, joyful news, the greatest news in earth's history, not just for you but for everyone living on this planet. [11]Today in Bethlehem is a newborn Baby boy, first promised back in the Garden of Eden, a Savior, Messiah,

the Lord. [12]Go to Bethlehem, look for Him in a stable, and you will find this little fellow lying in a manger and wrapped in some soft cloth."

[13]When the angel's message had been given, a large company of heavenly beings began singing such music as the shepherds had never heard in their lifetime with words, melodies, and harmonies that gave praise to God. [14]The lyrics went like this: "Glory be to God, highest glory be given to God, and for this earth, may peace and goodwill come and remain."

[15]As suddenly as they had appeared, the angelic choir ceased and returned to heaven, while the astonished shepherds all agreed that they most go to Bethlehem and find this baby. [16]They searched the town until they found the right stable, and within was the little family, Joseph, Mary, and the little Baby in the manger. Their account of the experience encouraged Joseph and Mary, for they may have easily wondered if God would have permitted His Son to be born in a stable. [17]After telling their experience to Joseph and Mary, the shepherds told everyone they could find the same story. [18]And those who heard it were also filled with wonder and awe. [19]Even Mary was now thoroughly convicted that her child was God's Messiah. [20]As for the shepherds they finally remembered their sheep out in the field and returned to find them all safe. Praises to God continued for the rest of the night.

[21]On the eighth day, according to long-standing custom, the little fellow was circumcised, and His birth registered under the name "Jesus." [22]When Mary had recovered from the birthing process and was again ceremonially pure, she and Joseph went to Jerusalem to dedicate their child to God. [23]This followed the instruction given in Exodus 13:2 and repeated in Numbers 8:16, 17. [24]They followed also the instruction to bring a sacrifice of two doves or pigeons.

[25]Living in Jerusalem at this time was an elderly gentleman named Simeon, a devout person who was earnestly looking for the Messiah to appear and deliver Israel. The Holy Spirit continually encouraged him [26]and had revealed to him that he would not die until after seeing the Messiah. [27]One day he was impressed to go to the temple at the exact time Jesus was brought there for dedication as an eldest son. [28]Simeon sensed that the Holy Spirit was telling him that this was indeed the Messiah, the one so long waited for, hoped for, and prayed for. He begged for the privilege of holding the Baby in his arms as he thanked God for this rare experience. [29]He then uttered a prophetic prayer, perhaps his only prophecy, in these words: "Lord, now You may let me die in peace for You have fulfilled Your promise to me. [30]And these eyes have seen Your promised Savior, [31]the One who will bring salvation to all who live on this earth. [32]Even the Gentiles will be enlightened through His coming to Your covenant people Israel."

[33] Joseph and Mary must have felt both awe and astonishment while this was being witnessed. But Simeon was not yet finished. [34]He then pronounced a blessing on them and followed with a statement directed to Mary, "Your child is destined to witness the fall of many in Israel, then to see them rise up again. He Himself will face bitter opposition. [35]And this violent action will be as a sword being thrust through your heart, as prophecies are fulfilled."

[36]Following Simeon's visit, a prophetess named Anna, daughter of Phanuel,

arrived. She was very old and had been widowed after seven years of marriage and now was about eighty-four years of age. [37]She left the temple only briefly and spent most of her time as a volunteer serving as she was able, day or night. [38]As soon as she entered, her voice began giving thanks to God, then telling all who were nearby about the long expected Redeemer in Jerusalem. [39]When the ceremonies were completed in Jerusalem, the family left for their home, Nazareth, in Galilee. [40]Their child grew normally and developed a strong, loving personality, admired by all and blessed by God.

[41]During those early years of Jesus' life, His parents made the Passover a high priority event, regularly going to Jerusalem and taking Jesus with them. [42]At the age of twelve, Jesus celebrated the Passover for the first time as a man. [43]The days passed swiftly and the family made plans to return home, but in the rush of preparation and the presence of many others from their town who were planning to travel together, it was not noticed that Jesus was not with them as they left. No, He was left in Jerusalem. [44]When evening came they were well on their way and were making camp for the night when it dawned on them that Jesus was not with them. Frantically they began enquiring about Him among the other travellers and friends, but no one had seen Him after leaving the city.

[45]With desperate fear, feelings of guilt and remorse, they returned to Jerusalem to search for Him. [46]Three terrible days followed, and then they found Him in the temple involved in discussions with the highly educated professors, listening to them and asking them questions. [47]It was obvious to all that here was young lad with unusual insight. Those teachers, scholars that they were, were astonished at the understanding He demonstrated regarding the great themes of salvation and the nature of God.

[48]Marvelously relived, Joseph and Mary did not interrupt the discussion until it was over. Then Mary could not suppress her exasperation, "Son, why on earth did you run away like this? You have no idea how we felt, how we have wept and prayed for these three days looking for You."

[49]He seemed sure that they would understand and explained that He had not intended to cause pain and anxiety. "How could you be so surprised? Don't you realize that I am twelve years old and should begin taking interest in My Father's house and in His plans for Me?" [50]Of course they could not understand. He was so young, and God's plan was so poorly understood at that time. [51]With great relief, the family returned home where Jesus continued to be an obedient, faithful son, but you may be certain that Mary remembered His brief statement and prayed daily for better understanding. [52]As for Jesus He developed normally, gaining physical and intellectual maturity as would be expected of any teenager. Moreover, He was well liked by all who knew Him and by God Himself.

Chapter 3

[1]It was in the fifteenth year of the reign of Tiberius Caesar; Pontius Pilate was governor of Judea, and Herod Antipas was tetrarch of Galilee; Philip, brother of Herod, was tetrarch of both Iturea and Traconitis; and Lysanias was tetrarch of Abilene. [2]Annas and Caiaphas were high priests. It was during this time that, out in the wilderness, John, son of Zacharias,

began to proclaim God's message. ³He moved into every inhabited part of the country along the Jordan River, preaching the need of repentance, baptism, and cleansing from sin. ⁴We can now see clearly that He was fulfilling prophecy, the one in Isaiah 40:3–5, which reads as follows: ⁵"The voice of one crying in the wilderness; prepare for the Lord's coming, make His path straight, smooth it out, fill in every pot hole, level off the high spots and redesign the curves into straighter stretches, ⁶the whole human race is to be aware of salvation provided by God."

⁷John was forthright and direct in his presentations to the multitudes that came to listen, then to be baptized. For instance: "You generation of vipers, who has warned you to avoid the coming wrath to our nation?" The implication was that no one had warned them, accounting for their slide into apostasy. ⁸"I call on you to really repent, turn from your sins, and the lifestyle associated with them. You dare not settle down smugly in your present condition, trusting that because you are Abraham's descendants you are guaranteed favor with God. Let me tell you something. God could create children of Abraham from these stones lying here if He so chose. ⁹Let's start at the root of the tree with our axe if the tree is unproductive, then turn it into firewood."

¹⁰When the people heard this, they asked him in fear, "Just what shall we do?"

¹¹"For starters," he replied, "suppose your neighbor is in need of a coat while you have two. Give one of yours to him. If he is hungry and you are well fed, share your food with him."

¹²Among those who came for baptism were tax collectors. Their question was,

"What must we do?"

¹³And his reply, "Stop taxing people more than the law requires in order to pocket the extra money." ¹⁴Roman soldiers came asking the same questions. He told them, "Never use force when it is unnecessary, and second, do not falsely accuse people. Third, live within your means."

¹⁵It is easy to conclude that many of the ones who went to hear John began speculating as to the possibility that he was the promised Messiah. ¹⁶John was aware of some of these ideas and included in his preaching the answer to their speculations, plainly telling every audience, "My dear people, I am baptizing you with water, but soon another will come, much more important than I am, much more powerful, more significant. In fact, I am not even worthy to untie His sandals. He will baptize too, not in water but in the Holy Spirit and with fire. ¹⁷He will carry in His hands a mighty fan and will completely separate the chaff from the grain, the chaff to be totally, utterly annihilated, and the grain to be gathered and preserved in His grain bins." ¹⁸This was typical of the sermons he preached to the listeners.

¹⁹Eventually John was bold enough to rebuke Herod because of his illicit relationship with Herodias, the wife of Herod's brother, Philip. ²⁰There were other wrongs of which Herod was guilty, but the worst of all was to arrest John and put him in prison ²¹Before John's arrest, while he was still preaching and baptizing, Jesus came with others to be baptized. As He was coming up out of the water, He knelt and prayed. ²²At that moment the heavens opened and the Holy Spirit appeared as a dove-shaped blaze of light settling over His head, and a voice from heaven was heard saying, "You

are My beloved Son, in whom I have great pleasure and confidence."

²³Jesus was about thirty years of age and was commonly regarded as the son of Joseph, a direct descent from King David. Let me name his ancestors in order beginning with Joseph his legal father. Joseph, ²⁴Heli, Matthat, Levi, Melki, Jannai, Joseph, ²⁵Mattathias, Amos, Nahum, Esli, Naggai, ²⁶Maath, Mattathias, Semein, Josech, Joda, ²⁷Joanan, Rhesa, Zerubbabel, Salathiel, Neri, ²⁸Melki, Addi, Cosam, Elmadam, Er, ²⁹Joshua, Eliezer, Jorim, Matthat, Levi, ³⁰Simeon, Judah, Joseph, Jonam, Eliakim, ³¹Melea, Menna, Mattatha, Nathan, David, ³²Jesse, Obed, Boaz, Salmon, Nahshon, ³³Amminadab, Aram, Esrom, Phares, Judah, ³⁴Jacob, Isaac, Abraham, Terah, Nahor, ³⁵Serug, Reu, Peleg, Heber, Shelah, ³⁶Cainan, Arphaxad, Shem, Noah, Lamech, ³⁷Methuselah, Enoch, Jared, Mahalaleel, Cainan, ³⁸Enos, Seth, Adam. And Adam was created directly by God Himself.

Chapter 4

¹Jesus was scarcely dry from His baptism when the Holy Spirit took charge of Him and led Him out of civilization into the wilderness. ²There was nothing out there to eat, and for forty days He endured without food, while His adversary the devil prepared to attack Him when He was weak from hunger. ³The devil said to Him, "Look, Jesus, if you are the Son of God— if that's really true, all You will have to do to survive out here is to speak and these stones will become bread. Right?"

⁴Jesus, however, remembered a word of scripture in Deuteronomy 8:3, which reads, "Human beings need more than just bread or any other form of food. They need to obey every word of God."

⁵Another temptation that Jesus faced was when the devil carried Him to the summit of a high mountain from which the whole world and its nations could be seen, promising Him this, ⁶"Everything you see here can be yours. I own it and can do whatever I want with the world. But you can have it all with one stipulation. ⁷Just kneel in worship briefly in front of me, and I will give up my claim to the world. It will all be yours."

⁸Jesus quickly detected that this must be his adversary and ordered, "Get lost, Satan! In my Bible are these words, 'You will worship God and worship only Him' (Deuteronomy 6:13).

⁹A third temptation was this one: The devil took Him to Jerusalem and placed Him on one of the spires of the temple, then challenged Him to believe a scripture that promises, ¹⁰"He will command His angels to protect you. They will lift you up, carry you wherever you go so that you will not even bruise your foot on a stone." ¹¹The devil said, "So if You are God's Son, prove it. Claim this promise and jump off."

¹²Jesus' responded, "Aha, you have forgotten another command found in Deuteronomy 6:16, 'You must never put God to a test, for this is presumption, not faith.'" ¹³After these three fundamental temptations (physical desire, power and authority, and presumption) had been rejected by Jesus, Satan knew he was defeated, at least for a while, and he left Jesus alone.

¹⁴Jesus was still under the control of the Holy Spirit and was directed now to return to Galilee where He soon became the topic of discussion throughout the whole region. ¹⁵He was quickly in demand as a teacher in the synagogues and was respected by

everybody. ¹⁶But at Nazareth where He had been reared, He went into the synagogue on the Sabbath as usual, and stood up, indicating that He had a message for the people. ¹⁷The presiding elder handed Him a scroll containing the book of Isaiah, which He unrolled to the sixty-first chapter and began to read, beginning with the first verse. ¹⁸"The Spirit of the Lord is on Me for He has anointed Me to preach wonderful news to the poor. He has sent Me to heal broken hearts, to announce freedom to those enslaved by sin, to restore vision to those who are blind, to relieve the pain of those who have been bruised, ¹⁹and to proclaim the fulfillment of the Lord's prophecy in the very year predicted."

²⁰After reading this passage of scripture, He took a seat of authority, every eye being centered on Him, ²¹and He boldly claimed that He was the fulfillment of Isaiah's prophecy. ²²As He proceeded to explain the prophecy, they all could testify that this was just what they needed and His words were truthful and kind, but the question that was uppermost in everyone's mind was this, *How can we be sure He is who He claims to be? Is He not Joseph's son, and a carpenter for the last twenty years or so?*

²³He seemed to read their minds perfectly and continued, "You will no doubt remind me of the adage, 'Physician, heal yourself,' in other words, 'You claim to be the fulfillment of prophecy, so let's see you perform a miracle here and now. You have a reputation as a miracle worker in Capernaum, so demonstrate your power in your hometown.' ²⁴Hear me through, dear people. It is truly said that no prophet is accepted in his own country. ²⁵Remember Elijah? There were plenty of widows in Israel during the three and one half years

of famine, ²⁶but none of them, not even one, was blessed by his ministry. Only a foreigner, a widow of Sidon, who lived in Zarephath was blessed. ²⁷And another example, there were plenty of lepers in Israel during Elisha's ministry, but we have no record that he healed any of them. However, he did heal the Syrian Naaman. The reason? His own people would not believe him."

²⁸Alas, instead of searching their own hearts as they should have done, repenting of their sins and unbelief and bigotry, they became angry and turned on Him! ²⁹Mob psychology took over, and He was seized by several men, dragged out of the building, and hurried out of town to a nearby cliff where they intended to hurl Him to His death. ³⁰Try to imagine the dismay of these ruffians when unseen guardian angels wrested Him out of their grasp and protected Him until He was safely out of the area.

³¹Leaving Nazareth, He went down to Capernaum, a prominent city of Galilee, and was there welcomed as a teacher in their synagogue every Sabbath. ³²These people had been exposed to the scripture for years but had never heard anyone compared to Jesus with His warm, friendly personality, His uncanny knowledge of God's word, and His way of applying it to their own lives. ³³To illustrate, one day a man walked into the synagogue who was under the control of a demon. He at once began to interrupt the teacher, yelling at the top of his voice. ³⁴"Hey, just leave us alone, quit bothering us, Jesus of Nazareth. Have You come to do us in? I happen to know just who You are. You are the Holy One sent from God."

³⁵Now, even though the devil was telling the truth about Jesus, the listeners

were not likely to believe it, coming from a person like that, so Jesus confronted him, and with the authority of God, Jesus commanded the demon to leave. "You will, this moment, stop talking and release this man!" The poor victim was thrown to the floor but was not injured; then the demon left. ³⁶The congregation was amazed and began to talk among themselves about what they had just witnessed. The most impressive feature of the whole experience was the instant power in that word of Jesus, a power that could compel a demon to release a human being. ³⁷This was just one of the incidents that spread His fame through that entire region.

³⁸After freeing the man at the synagogue, Jesus went to Simon Peter's house. Peter's mother-in-law had developed a high fever, threatening her life. The family appealed to Jesus in her behalf. ³⁹With little fanfare, but with complete confidence in divine power, Jesus uttered a rebuke to the disease, and she instantly recovered, got out of bed, and began to serve the whole group. ⁴⁰That evening after sunset all the sick ones in town were brought to Jesus, and none left in disappointment, for just a touch was enough to restore them to health. ⁴¹Furthermore, a number of demon-possessed people came and were freed from their tormentors. As had happened earlier, the demons publicly admitted, "You are the anointed Son of God," but Jesus had urged them not to publish their ideas even though they were correct.

⁴²Early the next morning Jesus left the city and went to an uninhabited area, but He was quickly followed, all pleading with Him not to leave them. ⁴³So He kindly told them of the need to preach the good news of God's kingdom to other cities, even to the whole nation, for that was His mission. ⁴⁴So on He went preaching in every synagogue in Galilee.

Chapter 5

¹So great were the crowds that pressed around Him, eager to hear His message, that He was about to be forced into the water of the lake. ²So He persuaded the owner of two fishing boats anchored nearby to allow Him to use them as a speaking platform. They readily agreed for they were washing their nets. ³One of these belonged to Simon, and Jesus persuaded Simon to move out a few yards from the shore while He preached. ⁴When the sermon was completed, He told Simon, "Now if you will launch out into deeper water, you will be able to catch a large number of fish."

⁵"Master, we worked all night with no success," Simon answered. "We are now tired and discouraged. And besides, the night is the time to catch fish. And I can see that You are no fisherman, yet if You say so, we are going." ⁶His obedience was quickly rewarded, for within a few minutes, the net had caught a huge number of fish, so many in fact that the net began to tear in places. ⁷The effect on Simon Peter was profound. He fell on his knees in front of Jesus, "Please, leave me, Lord, for I am a sinner, and You surely want to have nothing more to do with me."

⁸As for the catch of fish, it was so great that Peter called for the other boat to come and help them carry the load, and even then the two boats were so full that they were about ready to sink. ⁹Amazement filled the hearts of all who witnessed this incident. ¹⁰Not only Peter and his crew, but James and John saw the miracle and were

deeply affected. Jesus then spoke to them earnestly, "Do not be afraid, Simon, for one day you will be able to catch human beings."

[11]When they had brought the load ashore, they were convinced to abandon fishing and stay with Jesus from then on.

[12]In a nearby city Jesus encountered a man who was covered with lesions of leprosy. The poor fellow knew that it was illegal to approach a non-leper, but in spite of this he came up and fell on his knees in front of Jesus, worshipping Him and pleading, "Lord, if you are willing, you are able to cure me of this leprosy."

[13]Jesus, not fearing the dreaded disease at all, reached out, touched the man, and said, "I am willing; be healed." The lesions disappeared as they watched, and he was completely normal. [14]He was urged not to say a word to anyone about the healing until he had gone to the priest and made the ceremonial offering required by the law of Moses so that his recovery would be documented and so that no one could claim that Jesus had ignored the Mosaic law. [15]In spite of this it wasn't long before the news had spread far and wide and huge crowds searched out and found Jesus in order to be healed of their own ailments and to hear what He was teaching.

[16]It is important to know that Jesus was human and became weary just as we do, and that He would often remove Himself from the people and find a solitary place for rest and prayer.

[17]One of the most significant instances of healing was done about this time. He was teaching in a home, surrounded by His disciples and many others, including some Pharisees and theologians and other religious lawyers who were there mostly in order to obtain evidence against Him. The crowd consisted of folk from Galilee, Judea, and Jerusalem. The Holy Spirit was present and would have converted them all had they been willing. [18]During His teaching session, a paralyzed man was carried on a stretcher by four people, hoping to get close enough for Jesus to heal the afflicted man. [19]They circled the house and examined every entrance but were turned back by the number of people there. At the suggestion of one of his stretcher bearers, they carried him up to the roof, found a spot directly over the room where Jesus was speaking and began removing enough of the roofing tiles to let him down through the opening right into the presence of Jesus. [20]Although this interrupted the discourse, Jesus was not disturbed in the least. Instead, He centered His attention on the poor fellow. "Son, your sins are forgiven."

[21]The scribes and Pharisees heard this but were not interested in the forgiveness of sins as much as in finding a complaint against Jesus, and here was a perfect opening. [22]Everyone present knew that God is the only One who can forgive sins, and Jesus' bold statement was seized upon at once to charge Him with blasphemy, a human being assuming the prerogatives of God. But before they could prepare an accusation, Jesus had already read their minds and now turned His attention to His critics. [23]"You there, and you too; you are thinking, 'How can this Man forgive sin?' [24]Let me ask you this question, Is it easier to say, 'Your sins are forgiven,' or to say, 'Get up and walk'?" Hearing no answer, He continued, "I shall demonstrate that this Son of man now speaking to you has the authority to forgive sin." With that He turned to the paralyzed man, "I command

you, get to your feet, pick up your stretcher, and go home under your own power!"

²⁵The place was in complete silence. What would happen? Then that paralytic stood up, folded up his cot, and walked out through the amazed crowd of people, heading for home on the run, shouting for joy and praising God. ²⁶The sermon was over. The astonished people praised God, awed at what they had just witnessed. More than one was heard to comment, "We have seen some rare, wonderful things today."

²⁷Soon after this Jesus went to the tax collector's office where he stepped up to the officer in charge, a man by the name of Levi Matthew, and said, "Come and join me, Levi." It took but one little invitation. ²⁸Immediately Levi left his job and followed Jesus. ²⁹One of the first things Levi did was to host a big dinner at his home. Among the guests were a large number of tax agents and other acquaintances, many of whom were secular, worldly people. ³⁰The scribes and Pharisees were quick to notice this and went to Christ's disciples with a question, "Why, pray tell, are you willing to sit at the same table with these tax collectors? Don't you know any better?"

³¹But Jesus spoke up. "It's like this, friends. A person in good health never calls the doctor. Only a sick person will do so. ³²I did not come to this world to help those who have never sinned. No, I came to invite sinners to repent."

³³But then his foes had another critical question, "Why do John's disciples fast regularly like we Pharisees do, but your followers eat and drink?"

³⁴"I will explain this by another illustration," replied Jesus. "At a bridal feast, no one fasts, not one. ³⁵But after the bridegroom leaves they resume their fasting."

Then He gave another illustration to show how difficult it is to change one's mind about things. ³⁶"No one will patch an old garment with a new piece of cloth, for the new cloth, being stronger would tear the old cloth, thus enlarging the hole. ³⁷Likewise, no one will store new wine in an old wineskin for the old wineskin would likely deteriorate and leak before the wine is used and the whole amount would be lost. ³⁸Yes, new wine must be stored in new containers. ³⁹And as a person enjoys old wine better than new, so also is it with new ideas. We seem to cling to the old ones."

Chapter 6

¹On the very next Sabbath, Jesus and His disciples were walking through a field of ripened grain when the disciples began to pick off heads of grain, rub them in their hands and eat the kernels. ²Spying Pharisees confronted them. "Hey, you! Don't you know you are breaking the Sabbath? You are harvesting and threshing."

³Jesus at once came to their defense and spoke directly to these accusers. "You must have never read the scripture telling of David and how he violated the sanctuary rules when he and his soldiers were hungry. ⁴They went into the sanctuary and ate the showbread that was intended only for the priests. ⁵You see, God's rules are intended for the good of mankind, and this applies to the Sabbath. I must also assure you that the Son of man is creator of the Sabbath, and therefore, He has complete authority over the Sabbath, its meaning, its purposes, and the principles of its observance."

⁶On another occasion He was in the synagogue on the Sabbath teaching the people. Among the people was a man

whose right hand was atrophied and useless. [7]Here, too, the Pharisees intently watched everything He did. They were certain He would never allow a serious disability like this one to continue. But would he actually heal the man on the Sabbath? If so they would have an airtight case against Him in court. [8]Jesus was reading their minds all along, a fact that should have persuaded them of His divine nature. He turns and speaks to the patient, "Please come here to me." [9]Every eye eagerly watched the drama unfolding before their eyes. "Is it legitimate to do good on the Sabbath or to do evil, to save life or to kill?" Jesus asked. [10]Then after searching the room in every direction for a response, He paused. Now He looked directly at the crippled man and commanded, "Hold out your useless hand." That hand shot out at once and was instantly restored to normal size, strength, and mobility. [11]Although it is hard to believe, this infuriated the Pharisees so greatly that they got together and plotted how to destroy Jesus!

[12]Jesus was tactful, and as on other such occasions, He withdrew from the public eye for a while to spent the night in prayer. Not for Himself, this time but for those He had come to save. And for those who would soon be called to join Him in forming an organization of believers. [13]The next morning, however, He was back with them and with other believers. It was then that He formally invited them to commit their lives to Him and to the proclamation of the gospel wherever they might be sent, calling them "apostles." [14]Here are the names of those twelve men: Simon (Jesus called him "Peter"); his brother Andrew; James and his brother John; Philip and Bartholomew; [15]Matthew; Thomas; James, son of Alphaeus; Simon generally called "the zealot"; [16]Judas the brother of James; and Judas Iscariot who turned traitor.

[17]Now with all of them together and with a large crowd of people from Judea, Jerusalem, Tyre, and Sidon, who had come to hear Him and be healed, He resumed His ministry. [18]There were also a number of demon-possessed sufferers in the gathering. They too were set free. [19]Everyone there seemed intent on touching Him for as soon as they did so their maladies were miraculously cured. [20]And now that all were comfortable and happy, they were more than eager to listen to what He was about to teach. His first statement was somewhat surprising, "You people out there, you are blessed above others, for you possess the kingdom of heaven. [21]You who are hungry for something better than this life are blessed too, because your hunger will be satisfied. And those of you who are sorrowing because of your failures and your sins, take heart for you will laugh and shout for joy. [22]Those of you who are hated and ostracized, consider yourselves blessed if that hatred and cursing is due to your decision to follow Me. [23]Yes, you should jump up and down for joy, for these trials are evidences that you are rewarded in heaven, just as the prophets of old were mistreated and have a heavenly reward.

[24]"Now you wealthy people, I hate to tell you this, but troubles are coming your way. You may have already enjoyed all the blessings that can come to you. [25]You who are overweight and overfed may find yourselves hungry, not just for food, but for enduring, satisfying hope and assurance. And you who are now laughing will have a cause for mourning and weeping. [26]And this may be hard to accept, but if people

are saying nice things about you, be on guard, for remember that people spoke well of false prophets.

[27]"And please listen to this: Love your enemies, and if there are those who hate you, do something good to them. [28]If there are people who curse you, instead of retaliating, bless them. [29]If someone slaps you on the cheek, let him slap the other cheek also. And if someone steals your raincoat, let him have your coat also. [30]If you are asked to help someone, do it and do not charge him for your help. [31]Here is a marvelous code by which you are to live: Treat others exactly as you would like to have them treat you. [32]Think this one through: If you love only those who love you, can you claim to be any different from the heathen? [33]And if you are kind and generous to only those who have done something good for you, you are really no different from the sinners around you.

[34]"Furthermore, if you are willing to lend only to those who can repay you, with interest, your behavior is just like ordinary sinners. [35]Now hear this: God's love is the ultimate love, and if you truly want a high standard, follow this creed, love your enemies, and be willing to help them. This means even lending to them when you know you will never be repaid. Eventually your reward will be great, for this demonstrates that you are God's children and will inherit everything He has. He is constantly kind to those who never appreciate Him, and to those who actually hate Him. [36]So be tolerant and forgiving just as your heavenly Father is.

[37]"Friends, it is never safe to judge the motives of other people. You simply do not have the authority or the wisdom to do so. Besides, if you are judgmental, that very trait will be the basis for judgment against you. While on the other hand, if you display a forgiving spirit, you, too, will be forgiven. [38]Please believe me when I say that as you give to others you yourself will receive more, not just what you gave, but even more, full measure, tightly packed and overflowing. Others will give you the same generosity that you have demonstrated.

[39]"Have you ever seen a blind person trying to lead another? No, of course not, for they are both doomed to fall into the ditch. [40]It seems obvious that a disciple is never in higher standing than the leader he is following, but remember, everyone who keeps on maturing will become more and more like that master. [41]And think about this: Just why would you or anyone look into another person's eye and find a speck of sawdust while he himself has a plank in his own eye? [42]Think how foolish you would be to say to your brother, "Please let me remove that speck of sawdust from your eye while at the same time this plank is imbedded in your own eye. So the better way would be to first have the plank removed from your eye, and then to offer to remove the speck of sawdust from that other person's eye.

[43]"Here is the way to evaluate a tree. If it produces good fruit, it is a good tree. If it produces defective fruit, it is a poor tree. [44]All trees then are evaluated by the fruit that they produce—the fruit is the bottom line. Good fruit means a good tree. Poor fruit means a worthless tree. Furthermore, you will never see figs growing on a cactus plant or grapes growing on a thorn bush. [45]It is the same with human beings. A Christian does right because he is a Christian, never in order to be one.

A good person is one who acts out in his lifestyle the good that is in his heart, and a wicked person is wicked because he acts out the wickedness in his heart. The words of a person will effectively reveal what the inmost being is.

[46]"Why would anyone want to call me 'Lord, Lord' if he is not willing to follow My teachings? [47]However, if a person comes, listens, and then does something about it, [48]he is like a man building a house. First he digs deep enough to reach solid rock. Here he places the foundation, and that house will withstand violent storms and even floods. The foundation is solid. [49]But in contrast, if you listen to my teachings and ignore them, you are like a man who put his house on surface soil. When a violent storm came and the flood waters rose, the house was doomed, you may be certain."

Chapter 7

[1]This series of lessons was completed, and Jesus returned to Capernaum. [2]As soon as He arrived, some leading citizens came to Him in behalf of a Roman centurion who was very anxious about a dangerously ill slave. It seemed that the poor man might be terminal, but the owner had heard of Jesus and the remarkable healings that had been reported. He was very uncomfortable to go directly to Jesus, choosing rather to ask the elders if they would intercede with Jesus for him. [3]The city fathers had a lot of respect for this centurion in spite of the fact that he represented the hated Roman Empire, and they were glad to help. [4]They presented the request and with it a glowing recommendation of the centurion, hoping that Jesus would be willing to heal the slave. "Believe us," they implored, "This man is an unusual Roman. [5]He actually seems to have a fondness for us Jews, going so far as to donate funds for the building of a new synagogue."

[6]This was just what Jesus loved to do. So they led the way toward the centurion's home, but before reaching it, friends were sent to Jesus and his party with this message. [7]"My Lord, You very likely are unwilling to be defiled by entering my house, and I am completely unworthy to come to you. Would it be possible to just speak the word where You are? For I know that this would be all that is needed in order to heal this slave. [8]It is like my situation. I take orders from my superiors, and I give orders to those under me. I say to a soldier, 'Go,' and he goes; I say to another, 'Come,' and he comes. I say to another, 'Do this,' and he does it. You are able to command disease, aren't You?"

[9]The attitude of this Roman amazed Jesus, so He turned around and spoke to the people with Him. "I have not yet found people in Israel who have so much faith as this Roman!" [10]The centurion's friends got the message, returned, and found that the sick slave was completely recovered.

[11]The next day Jesus and His disciples, along with a large number of followers, went over to a little town called Nain. [12]As they neared the town, they met a funeral procession. The deceased was a man, the only child of a widow, who naturally was devastated by this second bereavement, as were most of the residents of Nain. They were all in the procession showing their love and concern. [13]When the Lord saw the sad woman, He went right up to her and said gently, "You may stop weeping now, my dear woman." [14]Then He touched the coffin. The pallbearers stopped, and Jesus commanded, "Young man, I command

you, rise up!" [15]Instantly the man who had been dead, sat up, and began to talk! Then he was restored to his mother.

[16]This made a tremendous impression on everyone there, and the news spread rapidly throughout the entire region. The general opinion was expressed, "A really great prophet has come to us, and God is really blessing His people." [17]The news spread rapidly to Judea and beyond. [18]The followers of John the Baptist heard about it, and they reported to John all that had happened. [19]John himself was a bit skeptical at this time and determined to find out the truth of the matter. Summoning two of his most loyal followers, he sent them to find Jesus and bring back the answer to his big question. He would wait for the answer. [20]They located Jesus and brought John's question, "Are you really the Messiah or must we wait longer yet?"

[21]Jesus elected to give an indirect reply, but right there many were restored to health from various ailments, many demons were cast out, and many blind received the gift of sight. [22]When John's messengers had witnessed enough miracles to be fully persuaded, completely convinced, Jesus gently urged them to return and to report to John exactly what they had seen. Blind people now had 20/20 vision; crippled, deformed people were walking, jumping, and running without crutches or prosthesis; lepers were completely cured; deaf ones could now hear everything; dead people had been raised to life; and good news had been given to all, especially to the poor. [23]His brief personal message to John was this: All who fully trust Me will be wonderfully happy.

[24]The messengers left, pleased and hopeful. Then Jesus told the crowd about John the Baptist and his mission. "Who did you go out to see in the wilderness? Only a reed blown around in the wind? [25]Did you go out to see a man dressed in the latest expensive style? If so, you went to the wrong place, for such people may be seen only in the palaces of kings, courts and such places. [26]Did you travel out there to see and hear a prophet? I hope so for that is exactly what you heard. [27]Yes, John indeed is a prophet and is the one foretold in Malachi 3:1, 'Look, I am sending My messenger on ahead of Me, and he will prepare the minds of his listeners to receive Me.' [28]And friends, I want to emphasize an important truth, and this is what I believe, of all people who have ever been born on this planet, none are greater than John the Baptist. And that includes all the prophets of old. And yet, great as he is, he is no greater than the person who is saved in God's kingdom."

[29]Those who had been baptized by John were greatly encouraged as they heard this strong affirmation of John. So also were the tax collectors he had helped. They thanked God. [30]But there were some who had rejected John's preaching, including most of the Pharisees and the teachers of the law. They had been rebuked by John because of their lifestyle. [31]The Lord then asked His listeners, "What do you think this generation reminds Me of? I'll tell you. [32]It is like children playing together and calling out to other children, 'Hey what's wrong with you? We have been playing happy music, and you won't dance so we played mournful music and you won't cry?' [33]Yes, this generation is like that. Some rejected John because he was austere, dedicated, and committed, a person who refused to overeat or to drink

any wine. They decided that he must be demon-possessed. ³⁴But now I, the Son of man, come along and they say, 'Look He's a glutton; He eats at every banquet table He can find. He drinks with everyone. Yes, He hangs out with tax collectors and other sinners.' ³⁵Friends, wisdom is admired by all of her children."

³⁶On one occasion there was a Pharisee who invited Jesus to a meal, one of the few Pharisees who was willing to listen to Jesus with an open mind. So Jesus accepted the invitation to this rather ostentatious occasion. ³⁷In this same city was a prostitute who had been rescued by Jesus from her life of sin. She had heard about the upcoming feast. In her immense gratitude, she spent a year's income to purchase an alabaster container filled with pure nard, then she went to the banquet hall. ³⁸After locating Jesus, she knelt at His feet, and as tears of gratitude fell from her eyes, she opened the box of ointment and anointed his feet with the perfume and wiped them with her hair. ³⁹The fragrance of the perfume quickly filled the banquet hall, leading the host to investigate its source. Imagine his dismay when he recognized the girl as a local prostitute. What should he do? *If this Man were a prophet as He claims, He would know that this woman is a terrible sinner and should be shunned completely.*

⁴⁰Then Jesus spoke directly but quietly to Simon, "Brother Simon, may I say a few words to you?"

"Yes, of course, I'm listening."

⁴¹"Once there was a man who had lent money to two different people. One owed him five hundred thousand dollars, the other fifty dollars. ⁴²Neither of them could repay the loan, and this gracious man, knowing their condition, cancelled their debts. Which one will have the greatest esteem for the lender?"

⁴³Simon's reply was honest enough, "I'd think it was the one who had the greatest debt."

"You are absolutely right," replied Jesus. ⁴⁴Now turning toward the woman, he continued, "Simon, here is this young woman. I came to your house at your invitation, but no one offered to wash My feet with water. However, this girl has wept with gratitude, and her tears have washed My feet. Then she wiped them with her hair. ⁴⁵You did not greet me with a kiss, but she has kissed my feet, several times. ⁴⁶You did not anoint My head with oil, but she has anointed My feet with the most expensive ointment known. ⁴⁷It is clear that she loves Me deeply and this is the reason: She has had her many sins forgiven. But the forgiveness of just one or two 'little sins' would not call forth such an expression of love."

⁴⁸Then speaking to the woman, Jesus said, "Yes, your sins are truly forgiven."

⁴⁹As He spoke, several at the table heard the words and began to question in their minds, *Who does He think He is? He is claiming the authority to forgive sins.*

⁵⁰So Jesus continued speaking to the girl. "Your faith is well-founded, and because of it you are saved. You may leave this place with peace in your heart."

Chapter 8

¹Following this experience Jesus and the twelve went through town after town, village after village preaching the good news of God's kingdom. ²In addition to the twelve, several women were in the group, among whom were Mary Magdalene who had been freed from seven demons, ³Joanna the wife of Herod's steward, Cuza,

plus a number of others who helped with food and other necessities. [4]People seemed to be coming from all directions until a very large group was present. Then Jesus began to teach in parables. Here are two that He used.

[5]"A farmer went out into his field to sow seed, scattering it well into the soil he had prepared. However, some seed fell on the roadway, and it was stepped on by passersby or picked up by birds. [6]Other seed fell among stones in rocky areas where the soil was very shallow, and although it sprouted quickly, the scanty soil could not sustain the young seedlings. They dried up and died. [7]Other seeds fell into a thicket of thorn bushes where there was very little sunshine and nourishment. Here too the sprouts died. [8]But most of the seed fell into good soil, sprouted, and grew, producing an excellent harvest with a yield up to one hundred fold." He then added, "If you have ears, listen, and take heed."

[9]The disciples were somewhat perplexed as to the meaning of the parable, and they cornered Him privately and asked about the meaning of the illustration. [10]"You are very fortunate," He replied, "in that you are able to delve deeply into the mysteries of the kingdom of God, but these listeners must grasp truth after hearing but a little here and there. So parables are very useful in helping them learn and remember. [11]My parable is very simple. The Word of God is represented by the seed. [12]The seed on the roadway teaches that the Word of God is often snatched away by Satan, hoping to prevent their joy in learning truth. [13]The seeds among the stones illustrate what happens when those who hear the word actually believe it, but they are shallow-minded ones who fail when temptation and stress occurs. Then they give up their faith. [14]The seed among the thorns illustrates what happens when those who begin living for God become involved in cares, worries, and riches, allowing these things to crowd out a genuine relationship with God and thus produce no growth and development. [15]But the good soil represents the minds of those who hear the word, grasp its meaning and treasure it, feed on it daily, and allow God to give them constant growth so that they develop into happy, fruitful Christians.

[16]"Have you ever seen a person light a candle, then cover it with a kitchen kettle, and put it under a bed? No, of course not. A candle when lit is placed on a candlestick so that those who enter the room will be able to see their way around. [17]You are now being enlightened with sufficient knowledge that up to now has been hidden. [18]So think seriously about your responsibilities, because God will hold a person accountable for the way he deals with truth. If he receives it, more will be given, and if he rejects it, he can be expected to lose what he had."

[19]While Jesus was busy talking, His mother and brothers approached the crowd wanting to have a few words with Him. But they could not get close enough. [20]One of His friends interrupted Him, "Teacher, Your mother and brothers are here and wish to see You."

[21]He replied, "Everyone who hears and obeys the word of God is considered to be My mother, My brothers, and My sisters."

[22]One day Jesus announced to the disciples, "We are going to the other side of the lake in this boat," so they stepped in and began the journey. [23]Jesus was very weary, so He lay down and fell asleep soon

after leaving the shore. And while He slept a violent storm hit the lake. The waves tossed the boat around, and water began to fill it so that they were in real peril. ²⁴The disciples finally decided to awaken Him and let Him know the danger they were in. "Master, our boat is about to sink in this storm."

He stood up and spoke to the wind and the raging water, commanding the storm to stop. At once, the wind ceased and the water quickly became calm. ²⁵His next words were, "Where is your faith?" as if they might still be unconvinced of His divinity.

Their wonderment was expressed to each other, "What sort of Man are we following? He even rules the wind and the water with ease, yes, just a word or two."

²⁶They beached the boat in the country of the Gadarenes across from Galilee. ²⁷As they were getting out of the boat, a mad man rushed at them. He had been demon-possessed for a long time, was stark naked, and lived among the tombs nearby. ²⁸Falling on his knees before Jesus, he shouted out, "Jesus, Son of God, why would You have anything to do with me? I beg of You, do not bother me!" ²⁹Then Jesus commanded the demon to leave. This poor sufferer had often been captured, tied up, and hobbled, but such was his strength that he was able to break the ropes and chains, and the devil had driven him out of town. ³⁰Now as Jesus confronted the demon, He asked, "What is your name?"

"My name is legion." (There were many demons involved.) ³¹The demons recognized their helplessness in the presence of Jesus and now began to beg for mercy. "Please do not send us into oblivion." (They probably knew their ultimate

fate already.) ³²Not far away was a huge hog farm. "Please let us possess those pigs." Their request was granted.

³³As soon as the animals were under the control of the demons, they stampeded and ran down the steep hillside into the lake where they all drowned. ³⁴The terrified herders fled into the nearest town and recounted what had happened, resulting in a great interest in Jesus. ³⁵A big crowd came out to see Him and found the recently freed man, now clothed and in his right mind, sitting at Jesus' feet listening to his Savior. Astonishment filled the crowd. ³⁶Eyewitnesses were there to tell everyone exactly how the exorcism had been performed. ³⁷One would suppose that such an experience would result in a number of invitations for Jesus to heal and teach, but no, most of them urged Him to leave. They were that fearful. And not wanting to force His presence where He was not wanted, He went back to the boat and prepared to return to Galilee.

³⁸Just before leaving, the newly freed man pled to go with Jesus, but Jesus gently denied the request. "That would not be the best thing to do. You will do more good to return home and tell everyone in your own words just what God has done for you." ³⁹Obediently, he went and explained what had happened to all who would listen. ⁴⁰Later on, when Jesus was again in this area the change in attitude was marked. Now people welcomed Jesus gladly and listened to His teaching.

⁴¹Back in Galilee, it was the same pattern. Crowds of people surrounded Jesus. Included in one such group was a leader in the synagogue by the name of Jairus. The poor man poured out his sorrow to Jesus and asked Him to come as soon as possible

to his home. [42]He had a twelve-year-old daughter who was near death and no help had been found for her. Could Jesus come and heal her? Others had been miraculously restored. Yes, indeed, Jesus assured him He would be on His way at once. [43]His progress was very slow, however, because of the throngs of people around Him. On this occasion it was virtually impossible to hurry. Just when they were moving the slowest, an event took place that was never forgotten by those present. Among those who were trying to get closer to Jesus was a woman with severe anemia because of menorrhagia. She had been to several physicians, but no one could help her. Now she was broke and helpless. For twelve years this had been her story, and now she was very weak from loss of blood. [44]Elbowing her way through the mass of humanity, she found herself close enough to reach out and touch the hem of Jesus' robe. Suddenly she knew she was well again. That's all she needed. [45]Hoping not to be noticed, she tried to make her way out of the crowd when Jesus stopped and asked, "Who touched Me?"

A strange question indeed, Peter, always ready to comment, said, "Master, with this many people around You there must have been a score or more who touched You."

[46]"Yes, Peter, there have been many casual touches, just as you have suggested, but someone touched Me with a definite purpose in mind and that purpose was for healing of a long-standing disorder, and she received what she desperately needed."

[47]Now the woman realized that Jesus was aware of everything that had happened, so she fell at His feet and told the whole story to everyone around—her long illness, her attempts to find help, and now her complete recovery. [48]Jesus very kindly spoke to her. "My daughter, your fears are ended, and I am impressed by your faith. Because you believed, you were completely healed. Go now and be at peace."

[49]Before Jesus had finished his little talk to her, a messenger arrived, made his way through the crowd, and spoke to Jairus. "Your daughter has died; there is no point in having Jesus come."

[50]Jesus heard the message and astounded the grieving man with this statement. "If you have faith and are not afraid, your daughter shall be healthy again." [51]When they reached the home, Jesus chose Peter, James, and John, along with the parents of the girl, to be with Him when He entered the house. [52]All those around the home were weeping and wailing, but Jesus said, "Please do not weep any longer, for the girl is only sleeping, not dead." [53]Now they actually sneered, for they knew she was dead. [54]Next came His command, "Everyone out of the house please." Now in the home, Jesus went straight to the dead girl's bed, took her by the hand, and spoke, "My dear girl, arise!" [55]All at once, she began to breathe and then sat up, much to the wonder and joy of the parents, as well as to that of the disciples with them. "Now would someone get her some food? She is hungry," Jesus suggested. [56]The parents were completely stunned by this miracle, but Jesus advised them not to publicize the story.

Chapter 9

[1]Soon after this wonderful experience, Jesus bestowed on His disciples the same miracle-working power that He had demonstrated so that they could perform

acts of healing and exorcism. [2]Now they were to separate into teams of two and go through the whole country while preaching the true facts about God and His kingdom and bringing healing to those who were ailing. [3]His instruction to them was rather brief: "Don't take supplies along, not even a staff, a knapsack, food or money, and only take one coat. [4]When shown hospitality by a family, stay with that family until leaving the town. [5]There will be those who refuse to accept what you wish to share. In such a circumstance it would be proper to engage in a little ceremony as you leave town. Remove the dust from your sandals and leave it with them as a symbol to them that they have been offered a valuable gift but have refused it."

[6]So the six teams left Jesus and started out on their own, preaching the good news and healing wherever they went. [7]The news of Jesus' miracles reached Herod the tetrarch and filled him with consternation. Some of his counselors suggested that perhaps John the Baptist had been raised to life. [8]Others suggested that perhaps Elijah had been returned to earth, or perhaps another of the ancient prophets. [9]Herod reminded them that he was positive that John was dead for he had been beheaded and that this must be someone else. He commanded, "I want to know who He is, and I want to see Him."

[10]With their first tour of duty over, the disciples returned to Jesus and reported to Him their experiences. Jesus sensed their need of rest and recuperation, so He led them into an uninhabited area near Bethsaida. [11]But quickly the news got out, and people began to flock there as they had to other places. None were turned away. Many were healed of their ailments, and all were told of the kingdom of God. [12]Toward the late afternoon the twelve came to Jesus and suggested that He send the people back to their homes for food and rest. [13]But Jesus had another idea. "I want you to feed the people."

"How can we do such a thing? All we have here are five small loaves of bread and two fishes. Unless we go and buy food, there would not be more than a morsel for anyone, and frankly we don't have enough money."

[14]Their perplexity was wholly justified. There must have been five thousand men, besides women and children, yet confidently Jesus asked them to seat the people on the grass in groups of fifty. [15]When all were seated, He took those five small loaves and the two fishes, looked up into heaven, thanked God for them, and pronounced a blessing on them. Then He broke them into smaller pieces for the disciples to distribute to the waiting crowd. [16]This seems hard to believe, but it is true: the thousands of people present all ate until they were satisfied. [17]Then after everyone had eaten, they gathered twelve baskets of leftovers.

[18]One time Jesus was in earnest prayer away from the crowds and only the twelve were with Him. When He finished praying, He asked them, "Just who do people say that I am?"

[19]"Well frankly, they have various ideas. Some say you must be John the Baptist. Others say Elijah or one of the old prophets who has been resurrected."

[20]"OK, then, just who do you think I truly am?" As expected, Peter was the first to answer. "You are the Messiah, the Son of God!" [21]Jesus' response was a bit surprising. He told them very strictly to never tell anyone just yet what He had said regarding

His mission for there was to be much more evidence given.

[22]He went so far as to tell them directly that He would be rejected by the nation's leaders and would eventually be executed but that on the third day would be restored to life. [23]Then He gave them a clue as to the details of His death. "Anyone who wishes to follow Me must reject selfish desires and be willing to carry a cross. [24]In fact, whoever puts his own life first will eventually lose it, and whoever puts his relationship with Me as a number one priority, even though it means being a martyr, will save his life for eternity. [25]Let me ask you this: If you should gain possession of everything in this world but lose your life in the process, have you benefited in the long run? [26]Any person who is ashamed to be known as a Christian will find that I am forced to disown him when I return in glory, the glory of My Father and of the heavenly angels. [27]And speaking of glory, some of you standing here will be given a view of that glory before you die."

[28]About a week later, he invited Peter, James, and John to a midnight prayer session on a nearby mountaintop. [29]While He was praying, His face began to glow with a radiance that had never before been seen by the disciples, even His clothing became a brilliant white, glistening so brightly it was hard to look at. [30]As if this were not impressive enough, two men began talking to Him about His coming ordeal in Jerusalem. The three disciples were able to realize that these men had a knowledge of history that was so detailed that they had to be Moses and Elijah. They realized that Jesus' remark about the kingdom of God a few days earlier was about this experience. [31]Here was a representation of the eternal kingdom, Jesus now glorified, Moses a saved human being who had been resurrected, and Elijah a human being who had never died but had been taken directly to heaven.

[32]Unfortunately, Peter and the two brothers had been sleeping when this began to occur, and they had awakened after the conversation was underway. Now they were fearful enough to retreat from the scene a bit. [33]Nevertheless, Peter proposed that they build a small booth for Jesus, Moses, and Elijah. He hardly knew what to say. [34]While he was still speaking, a fog covered the mountain so that they could no longer see Jesus.

[35]Then a voice was heard that calmed their fears. "This is My beloved Son; pay attention to what He tells you." [36]As soon as the voice had finished its message, Jesus was seen again, but now He was alone. The experience was so powerful that the three disciples were unwilling to attempt to describe it for some time.

[37]The next morning as the four of them descended from the mountaintop they came upon a crowd of people looking for Jesus. [38]Out of the crowd came a man carrying the limp form of his only son. He came right up to Jesus and poured out his heart. "Would you please do something for this son of mine? [39]An evil spirit has been seizing him, injuring him, and causing him to scream in pain. This has been so continuous that he can hardly get any rest. [40]Master, I thought that surely Your disciples could cast out this demon so I brought him to them, but they were unable to help."

[41]Jesus now called out, "Oh you dear people, how long will it be before you are able to have complete faith in Me? I will not be with you much longer. Yes, I will help

your son." ⁴²At that moment the demon grabbed the little fellow and hurled him to the ground, bruising him again. Jesus took command of the situation, ordered the demon out of the boy, and freed him from that wicked spirit. Then he healed the bruises and returned him to the grateful father. ⁴³One could sense the amazement of the crowd as they witnessed the mighty power of God.

Now Jesus began to talk very seriously to the twelve. ⁴⁴"Listen, my dear men, you must realize that things will not always be as they are today. You can sense the favor that we are in at this time, but very soon I will be arrested and My work will stop." ⁴⁵Although the disciples heard what was said, they failed to grasp the reality of Jesus' prediction and were afraid to have Him explain it.

⁴⁶Once again the disciples began engaging in one of their favorite discussions, "Which one of us will be the top man in the new government?" ⁴⁷Jesus had no trouble reading their minds and began to try again to teach them about the future. So he brought a young child over to them, and sat down.

⁴⁸Here is the way He explained things. "If you accept this child, you accept Me, and if you accept Me, you accept the Father who sent Me. Therefore, by accepting a child, you are accepting God. It is the humble, teachable person that will be the greatest in My kingdom."

⁴⁹Next, one of the disciples spoke up. "Master, we encountered a person who was casting out demons in Your name, and we told him in no uncertain language that he was doing wrong because he was not a member of our group." ⁵⁰Jesus answered very kindly, knowing that John was totally

sincere in his belief that no one who was not among the twelve had the authority to heal in Christ's name. "No, friends, when you find anyone doing a good work in My name, do not discourage him. He may be a person who has had a demon driven from him or has been healed himself and then has been converted. His influence is on our side and will be a factor in spreading the good news about our loving God."

⁵¹Apparently John needed more gentle instruction about God's character. A little later as they were on their way to Jerusalem, ⁵²Jesus attempted to find lodging in one of the Samaritan villages. ⁵³But the innkeepers all refused to allow them to reserve any rooms because they were on their way to the Passover at Jerusalem. ⁵⁴James and John blew up when they heard this insult. "Lord, won't you call fire down from heaven as Elijah did to annihilate those soldiers who came to capture him under orders of the king of Samaria? Now here are Samaritans just as wicked as they were. What about it, Lord?"

⁵⁵But Jesus sadly turned to them and showed them how He felt about the idea. "You hardly know how much your ideas differ from those of God. ⁵⁶You see, I did not come to destroy human life but to save it." His solution? "Let's go on to another village."

⁵⁷At one time as they were traveling, a man came up to Jesus and said, "Lord, I want to go with you wherever you might go."

⁵⁸Jesus replied, "You might want to reconsider your plan, friend, for I have nothing material to offer you. Even foxes have holes in which to stay, but I have nothing, not even a bed and pillow."

⁵⁹On another occasion He invited someone to join Him but the man refused

with this excuse, "Yes, Lord, I would be glad to do so but only if You let me stay with my father until he is dead and buried. After that I would gladly accept Your offer."

⁶⁰Jesus suggested that it would be better for him to join now and preach about the kingdom of God. "Let someone else bury your father."

⁶¹Another excuse was this, "Let me first go home and bid my family goodbye, OK?" Even this thought, reasonable as it seems, could have meant that someone was more important to him than Jesus could ever be.

⁶²Jesus emphasized this in His answer. "No one who looks back to the world after following Me is fit for the kingdom of God."

Chapter 10

¹Some time later Jesus sent out seventy helpers to make initial contacts in every town where He had planned His itinerary. They were told to go in pairs in order to encourage each other. ²His instruction began like a parable. "There is a great harvest before us but very few harvesters. So pray that there will be more sent into the fields for the harvest. ³As you go on your way, remember that you will be like lambs surrounded by a wolf pack, totally helpless without divine protection." ⁴He then gave instruction similar to that given to the twelve when they went out in pairs—no money, no knapsack, just sandals.

"And do not stop just to chat. That is not your duty. ⁵When you are invited into a home, your first words should be, 'Let peace be with this home.' ⁶And if in this home there is a person who is willing to receive peace, your peaceful influence will help him, and if there is no such person

there, at least you will be blessed by internal peace. ⁷So, stay in that home, living and eating as they do, for you can be considered a worker who is serving the homeowner and is entitled to wages such as food and shelter. ⁸Yes, wherever you may go, if you are received in a friendly manner, do not demand food differing from what the family eats. ⁹You are there to bring healing to any and all sick ones in that home, then to give them the good news of God's kingdom, news available to all who will listen.

¹⁰"On the other hand, if you enter a city and find that people are hostile and unwilling to listen to you, go out into the street and tell them, ¹¹'We are wiping the dust off of our sandals as a symbol that we have offered truth to you and hope in the kingdom of God but you are refusing it.' ¹²Sodom and Gomorrah will have a better chance on judgment day than that city—¹³alas for you, Korazin, and for you, Bethsaida. Think of the miracles that were performed in your city. ¹⁴If such things had been done in Tyre and Sidon they would have repented in sackcloth and ashes long before this. Yes, in the judgment, Tyre and Sidon will have a better chance, a better standing than you. ¹⁵And you, Capernaum, you self-righteous, boastful, proud city that considers itself a heaven on earth; you will finally be lost in the second death.

¹⁶"My dear men, always remember this: Whoever will listen to you is actually listening to Me, and in listening to Me, they are listening to God the Father. And of course the converse is equally true. Whoever refuses to hear your message is refusing to hear My message and My Father's message."

So they left to complete their assignments. ¹⁷When they returned you should have heard them telling of their experiences. Were they happy? Yes, wonderfully so. "Lord, even demons are forced to obey us when we give orders in Your name."

[18]"Yes, and I remember Satan himself falling from heaven like lightning when I gave him orders. [19]You may not have to use the full power that is available, but when necessary, you will be able to even trample on poisonous snakes and scorpions as well as the ultimate enemy, Satan. Nothing will be able to harm you. [20]However, with all this assurance, your joy should not be based on your ability to command evil angels but rather that your name is written in heaven."

[21]Right then Jesus demonstrated His joy by expressing it in this prayer: "Thank you, Father, Lord of the universe, for having revealed these truths to those who are teachable, even though such profound ideas are not always grasped by those who consider themselves wise. Yes, this is like You, Your wisdom is perfect and Your decisions are always the right ones. [22]Everything—all capabilities and wisdom—I have received from My Father. I recognize Myself as His Son, for He gave Me that realization, something that no human being could have given. And now it is My privilege to let others know who the Father is by My life and words. [23]You are truly blessed because your eyes have witnessed the things that you are seeing day by day, [24]and I assure you that many prophets and kings would have given a fortune to have seen the things that you have seen, to have seen firsthand the things you have witnessed."

[25]On another occasion a lawyer interrupted Him and tried to test Him with this question, "Master, what can I do to inherit eternal life?"

[26]"Well, what do you find as you read the law?"

[27]He knew the law of course and quoted it by memory: "You must love the Lord Jehovah with all your heart, with all your strength, with your whole being, and you must love your neighbor just as you love yourself."

[28]"Your answer is absolutely correct," Jesus replied. "If you fulfill this command, you will have everlasting life."

[29]However, this man still believed that somehow he was lacking something, so he questioned Jesus further. "What I need to know then is just who my neighbor might be."

[30]To answer this question, Jesus told of an episode that had recently taken place involving a priest and a Levite, both of whom were listening in the audience. "One day, not long ago, a man was traveling alone from Jerusalem to Jericho. In a remote area, thugs were waiting for just such an opportunity. They surrounded him, tore off his clothing, robbed him of all his money, and then beat him unmercifully, leaving him bruised and bleeding to death. [31]Soon after this brutal event, a priest came upon the scene and glanced at the injured victim from across the road, then hurried on, hoping to escape a similar fate. [32]A Levite was the next traveller to go by. He went over and sort of sized up the situation but didn't think he could do anything to help so went on his way, watching carefully for the criminals.

[33]"Then a Samaritan came riding along on his donkey. As soon as he spotted the injured man, he quickly began to help. [34]He first used water from his own canteen to wash the injuries. Then he applied ointment and bandaged the abrasions. He

then lifted the wounded fellow onto the saddle and took him to the nearest inn where he paid for a night's lodging. [35]The next morning he went to the innkeeper and said, 'Please keep him until he is able to travel, and when I return I will pay you whatever it costs.'

[36]"Here are three persons facing the very same need. Which one of them, would you say, proved himself to be a neighbor to the needy man?"

[37]The lawyer was in a tight spot. It was plain what the answer must be. But he hated the Samaritans and would not so much as mouth the word but answered. "I suppose it was the one who showed mercy."

"You see my point," said Jesus. "Now be sure that you do as well in such a circumstance."

[38]Jesus was in another town later and met a woman by the name of Martha. She was rather well off financially, and she invited them to stay at her spacious home while they were in the area helping the people. [39]Her sister Mary also lived there and became so fascinated by Jesus' teaching that she wanted to spend all her time learning. [40]Martha wanted to be the best hostess possible and spent her time preparing food for the group and was upset because Mary was doing nothing to help, so she finally shared her frustration with Jesus. "Lord, you probably have not noticed it, but I happen to be the only one around here that is doing any work. Mary has been neglecting her share. I am wondering if a word or two from You might help her to recognize her duty and help out."

[41]Jesus' answer surprised Martha. "Yes, I have noticed what has been going on. Martha, I appreciate more than you realize the wonderful hospitality and diligence you are so faithfully showing. But let me say a word for Mary too. She is making choices that are giving Me true joy. You know her past, of course, and you see the wonderful change that has taken place in her life. She is taking in My teachings as a hungry person feasts on food. This is the best thing that could take place here. [42]It may be possible that we could get along with less elaborate food and that you could then have time to listen as I share the truth from heaven. You will never forget what you learn."

Chapter 11

[1]One day Jesus was praying with His disciples, and when the prayer was ended, one of the disciples suggested that He teach them how to pray. "John taught his disciples such things, and maybe we should have some advice."

[2]"Of course, I would be happy to do so. When you pray say, 'Our Father who is in heaven, may Your name be reverenced by us Your children on earth. May Your kingdom be established soon, and may the world accept Your will for it just as heaven accepts Your will. [3]Day after day we depend on You for our necessary food. Thank you for continuing to supply our physical needs. [4]We are counting on You to forgive our sins as we come to You in repentance, just as we forgive those who have wronged us. Please do not test us more than we are able to endure, but snatch us away from sin.'

[5]Here is another illustration He used to contrast our willingness to give and God's willingness. [6]"You go to a friend's house at midnight and wake him up. You say, 'Unexpected company has arrived, and I have no bread in the house. Will you lend me three loaves of bread?' [7]Well, this neighbor who is thought to be a friend

shouts back, 'Forget it, man. Don't you know that my family and I have retired and the house is locked up. Talk to me in the morning if you must but not at midnight. Have a heart.' [8]It is almost a certainty that if you keep on asking, that after a time he will give up, 'OK, OK. If you just have to have some bread, I'll get you some,' Even though the neighbor does not respond because of friendship, he will because of continued urging.

[9]"Now let me share with you the way God deals with you under similar circumstances. You ask. He gives gladly. You search. He helps you find. You knock, and He opens the door and you are welcomed inside. [10]Yes, everyone who asks God for a good gift will get it. Everyone who looks for God and asks for salvation will find it, and everyone who wants admittance into God's kingdom will be admitted. [11]What about you as a parent. If one of your children asks for some bread, will you give him a stone? [12]If he asks for a fish, would you give him a snake? And if he asks for an egg, would you give him a scorpion? [13]Now if you human beings are always willing to give good things to your children, how much more likely is it that your heavenly Father will give good things to those who ask Him, especially the gift of the Holy Spirit, the most valuable gift of all?"

[14]One time Jesus was confronted with a case of demon possession, a demon that prevented the victim from speaking. When the demon was forced to leave the man, his speech returned and the onlookers marveled. [15]But a few skeptics were in the crowd and suggested that Jesus was directed by Beelzebub to cast out demons. [16]Others demanded a sign from heaven, testing Jesus to see what would happen.

[17]Although the people were unaware of it, Jesus had been reading their minds and knew they were just testing Him. In spite of this He explained things graciously and kindly so that they would never forget.

"Friends, in an earthly nation, a breakdown will occur if there is substantial opposition to the existing regime. Satan knows this and would never let one of his demons cast out another of his demons, for he would be defeating his own purposes. [18]How can he expect his reign to continue under such a plan? This would be the case if I were casting out demons by Beelzebub. [19]And I would like to ask you a question. If I am casting out demons through Beelzebub, by whom do your followers cast them out? If they are not driving them out then perhaps they are in league with Satan and passing judgment on you.

[20]"Now if I am banishing demons by the power of God as I claim to do, it is certain that the kingdom of God is being played out before your very eyes. [21]When you have a palace that is protected by a well-armed strong man, the property is safe, [22]but only until a stronger one attacks him. When he is defeated, his possessions are all taken, even his weapons, the very things he depended on. They are divided up among the conquerors. [23]Just so in my case. If a person is not on My side, he is on the side of Satan. If he does not help others to come to Me, he helps drive them away. [24]And let Me remind you of the persistence of demons. Even if one is cast out, he still does not give up. He will search around until he finds another person to be taken over. And if none other is found, he will very likely reenter his former victim. [25]That person still has the option to keep the door locked or to open up again and

let the demon in, or to actually welcome him back in. [26]And when this happens, the demon will invite seven more demons, all of whom are more wicked than himself, to come in with him so that the victim is now far worse off than he had been before."

[27]The listeners could understand these concepts easily and were really moved. So much so that one woman was led to shout out in the hearing of all, "Blessed be the womb in which You were formed, and the breasts that nourished You as a baby!"

[28]"Much more blessed," He responded, "are the ones who hear God's word and obey it."

[29]The crowds increased in size but many were only seeking political power and financial reward. Those types wanted to be sure Jesus really was the Messiah before they jumped on the bandwagon. To them, Jesus said, "You people in this generation are always looking for a sign. Well here is one for you. Remember Jonah? His experience has great significance. [30]Just as Jonah was a sign to the people of Nineveh, warning them of coming destruction, so I, the Son of man, will be such a warning to this whole generation. [31]Let Me remind you also of the Queen of Sheba. She will be amazed at the great judgment day and will pass judgment on this very nation because she was willing to travel hundreds of miles to hear truth from Solomon, and here is a nation who has in their midst a person greater than Solomon!

[32]"Back to Nineveh, the inhabitants of that wicked city will be justified in passing judgment on this generation because of their willingness to repent when Jonah's message was given, and here is a generation who has in it Someone who is greater than Jonah.

[33]"A lighted candle must be lifted up on a candlestick rather than be put under a basket. [34]Figuratively speaking, one's eyes are like light. They must be the guide to the whole body if the body is to be protected from the darkness around it. But if the eyes are blind or defective, the whole body is left in darkness. [35]So take care of your spiritual lights; protect them from every evil in order to keep the whole body from eternal darkness. [36]If your whole body is glowing with light, with truth, and with righteousness, it will be similar to the glow of a lighted candle, giving truth and help to all around."

[37]While Jesus was presenting His messages to the people, a Pharisee went to Him and invited Him to have a meal with him and his family. The invitation was gladly accepted. [38]Jesus took His place at the table without first going through the ceremonial washing of the hands. This shocked the host, and he lost no time in expressing his concern. [39]So Jesus kindly showed the host how He felt about this matter.

"You, dear friend, are very meticulous to keep all cups and dishes clean on the outside whether or not the inside of the vessel is clean. (In other words, this ceremonial cleaning is worthless because it does not guarantee that the inmost person is cleansed from sin.) [40]You really need to think things through. The same Creator made the outer person as well as the inner, real person. The whole being, the whole personality needs to be cleansed from sin. [41]If you will demonstrate unselfishness, helping the poor as you are able, you will need no ceremonial washing.

[42]"Another thing. I happen to know that you are very faithful in tithing, even to the mint, the dill, and other herbs. But

sometimes you neglect to deal justly and forget about the justice of God. These things are of vital importance. Of course, tithing should not be forgotten. [43]You Pharisees must take warning. You covet prestigious places in the synagogue, and you love those greetings that are heard in the markets, extolling your position. [44]What a shame, Pharisees and scribes! You are like graves that are scarcely noticed on the outside, yet within it is death and decay."

[45]These statements stirred up the ire of a lawyer who had the courage to respond. "Teacher, in Your view we lawyers are on the same level as the scribes and Pharisees, right?"

[46]"Now that you brought it up, the answer is yes. You are always ready to insist that your clients adhere to many regulations and ceremonies that you yourselves never follow. [47]Furthermore you are promoting campaigns to erect imposing monuments to the prophets, and yet you are exhibiting the same bigotry, the rebelliousness against the messages of those prophets, as your ancestors demonstrated when they had those people executed. [48]It is evident by your behavior that you approve of your father's crimes, for you are calling attention to the burial places placed by your ancestors.

[49]"Was not God very wise when He wrote, 'I will send prophets to them and apostles also, but some of them will be persecuted and some will actually be killed'? [50]It is a fact that this generation will be responsible for the death of all the prophets since the beginning of history, [51]beginning with Abel and on through to Zacharias who was murdered between the temple and the altar. [52]You lawyers have been like a dog in a manger. He would not

eat there himself, neither would he allow the cow to come for food. You have refused to be taught yourselves and have urged others to reject the teaching of truth."

[53]Not surprisingly these criticisms, truthful as they were, brought about hateful responses among the Pharisees, scribes, and lawyers. But instead of admitting their guilt, they kept on needling Him, hoping that He would say something, [54]just anything, that would give them some material with which to accuse Him before the Roman government.

Chapter 12

[1]As Jesus made these accusations, more and more people crowded in to listen, many of whom were pleased to hear someone who was not afraid to expose some of the abuses practiced by the spiritual leaders. The throng was so tightly assembled that some were actually stepping on the toes of others. Next, the disciples were given a warning. Using a figure of speech, he told them bluntly to avoid the leaven of the Pharisees, meaning their doctrines, which were pure hypocrisy.

[2]"Some day you will see that they can no longer cover up their real characters, much as they may attempt to do so. [3]You, too, must face the fact that wherever you are you will be widely recognized and if even one person tells something everyone will soon hear about it. [4]However, friends, never be afraid to speak, even if there are enemies who are ready to kill you, for this is all they can do. [5]But let me warn you of someone who has not only the power to kill but to commit you to eternal death. Indeed, you should fear him.

[6]"It is generally true that one can buy five sparrows for two farthings, and yet

even these little creatures are tenderly noticed by our Creator. [7]And more than this, God knows you so minutely that He knows the exact number of hairs on your head. And this shows how much more valuable you are than any number of sparrows. [8]Even more important than physical factors, God is aware of your spiritual condition and shares it with the heavenly angels. [9]Whoever rejects Me here on earth will be rejected by the heavenly beings. [10]And yet, never be discouraged over your past failures, for even your rejection of Me can be forgiven. In fact, every sin known except one can be forgiven. Only one? Yes, and it is the rejection of the Holy Spirit, for the Spirit is the agency that leads men to be on God's side. Final rejection of the Holy Spirit is incurable, for it is this that convicts us and persuades us to come for forgiveness and salvation. [11]The Spirit is also the agency to teach you what to say [12]when you are arrested and brought to trial in churches, civil courts, or before judges."

[13]At that moment a man interrupted, "Jesus, would You kindly speak to my brother and remind him that he should share the inheritance with me?"

[14]"Sir," Jesus answered, "these matters must be settled by your laws and by the judges and established courts. I have not come to settle temporal disputes. If your heart is right and your brother's heart is right, it can be decided because of your love for each other." [15]Then He used this incident to warn against the dangers of selfishness. "Remember, all of you, possessions do not indicate the value of life." [16]Then He told a parable that emphasized His message. "There was a wealthy farmer who knew farming and was a wise manager. He had harvested excellent crops and was running out of storage space for his grain. [17]*Just what would be the best thing for me to do?* he thought to himself. [18]*It seems to me that I will have to tear down my old barns and storage buildings, then rebuild with much larger ones so that I can save all this wealth.*

[19]*"Then I can say to myself, At last I have enough to keep me in luxury for many years. I will just loaf, eat and drink, and have a good time.* [20]But God had other plans. 'You are being terribly unwise. You have no life ahead of you as you have planned, for you will die before morning, so what plans do you have for the distribution of your wealth?' [21]This is the condition of anyone who is thinking only of self and is not rich in God's estimation."

[22]Then, speaking to His disciples, He explained truth in more detail. "I am telling you the honest truth. You will be better off when you have such a trust in God that you will not be anxious about your next meal and what you have to wear the next day. [23]There are much more important things than even food and clothing, even though they have their place in this world, but eternal considerations are of infinite consequence.

[24]"Try to remember the ravens when tempted to worry about your supply of food. They never plant grain, and neither do they harvest any crops whatever. They live only from one meal to the next, and yet your Father in heaven always helps them find enough, and are you not more precious in God's sight than any bird? [25]Can you add a single inch to your height by worrying? Your worrying will have about as much influence on your supply of food as it has on your height. [26]And if

you cannot make a significant difference in minor matters by worrying, why not just trust God for everything?

²⁷"Here's another example: What about those lilies? Their beauty is legendary, and yet they never work or spin yarn or weave cloth or sew clothing together. In spite of this, their beauty surpasses all the rich clothing of Solomon himself. ²⁸If God dresses the simple grass in the meadow, grass that is here today and gone tomorrow, will He not also provide for you? Where is your faith? ²⁹Furthermore, let Me add this, your first concern should be something more important than food and water. But these minor matters tend to keep you anxious. ³⁰You people have a knowledge of God and, therefore, have a great advantage over other nations. They might well fret over their temporal needs, but as for you, your heavenly Father knows all your needs, so learn to trust Him.

³¹"Far more important than anything else is this: Center your attention on God's kingdom and these earthly matters will be cared for. ³²Have no fears, even if you are in the minority, for God is doing everything He can to persuade you to choose eternal life through Him. ³³Better for you if you will sell off what you have and help the poor, for in this way you will actually be more secure, having achieved heavenly riches that do not depreciate, are not accessible to burglars, and are not damaged by moths. ³⁴Your heart, your true self, will be exactly where your treasures are. ³⁵You are advised to be in constant readiness for entering the heavenly kingdom, day and night.

³⁶"Wise stewards who are anticipating the return of their owner from his wedding are always ready for his return so that when he knocks the door will be thrown open for him and his bride. ³⁷How happy they are then! They have been watching and waiting, and now they find that he treats them royally, like a waiter treats a VIP at a banquet. ³⁸The time of his arrival is of no concern, for the end result will be the same, day or night.

³⁹"Here is another illustration. A homeowner is concerned about burglary. He, of course, cannot know just when the fellow might make his entrance, so to protect his property he is always on the alert. ⁴⁰Be like this man. Always be prepared, for I will return at a time you are not expecting Me."

⁴¹Peter had a question, "Lord, are You warning only us here or will You give this same warning to everyone?"

⁴²And here is the answer Jesus gave, "Imagine a wise steward who has authority over everything on the estate, including all servants and slaves. He assigns their jobs and distributes their food at the right time so that all are as ready as he is. ⁴³So when the owner gets home all are just as ready as he is himself. ⁴⁴And what do you think awaits that faithful caring steward? He will become responsible for everything that happens in that house. ⁴⁵But if that man becomes careless, believing that his lord has delayed his coming, he is likely to become despotic in his management, flogging other slaves, both men and women, then getting drunk. ⁴⁶You can be certain that he will be surprised when the owner finally arrives. He is then demoted or fired and treated like an enemy. ⁴⁷Because he knew what the owner needed, and yet failed, he may even expect a flogging. ⁴⁸In case one is sincerely ignorant of the Lord's requirements, he is likely to be punished very lightly, even if he fails. It is just that

a person who has adequate instruction will be responsible for a greater degree of perfection than the one who has limited instruction.

[49]"Friends, My coming to this world should result in a great deal of discussion, but what shall I do if everyone is so deep in squabbling that they will not even hear Me? [50]One thing is certain, I am facing a baptism of fire, and it will be very painful. [51]Do you suppose for a moment that My coming to earth will result in worldwide peace? By no means. No, rather, there will be widespread differences. [52]You will be saddened to learn that there will be in the same household a contest between two on one side and three on the other. [53]A father will oppose his son, and the son will oppose his father. Mother-in-law and daughter-in-law will be at odds over Me and My teachings.

[54]"All of you here today, try to believe in My prophecies. When you see a cloud forming in the west, you are correct in predicting rain. [55]Also, if a south wind is blowing, you are likely correct in predicting warmer weather. [56]If you are that accurate in predicting the weather by studying the sky, it is reasonable that you will be accurate in predicting many future events because of the omens that I have been teaching you. [57]Yes, you can rightly expect to come to correct conclusions. [58]And here is yet another illustration. To help us see ourselves as we really are, think seriously before you take another person to court over some wrong he has done to you, because he may counter sue and likely win if you have ever done any wrong to him. [59]The judge will then send you to prison until you have made full restitution."

Chapter 13

[1]It was about this time that some concerned citizens reported to Jesus about a gruesome thing that had befallen a number of Jews. Pilate had executed them by beheading and then had saved their blood so that he could mix it with his sacrificial blood. What they wanted to know is this: [2]Were these Galileans more wicked than other sinners and, therefore, met a more severe punishment? This was the widely accepted belief at the time that God was in the habit of treating sinners in such a manner.

[3]"I suppose you all may believe this about God, but My answer is positively NO! Every human being on earth deserves eternal death because of sin, and if you are unwilling to repent, all of you will face that fate. [4]And do you remember the tragic death of those eighteen when the tower of Siloam fell on them? Were they worse sinners than others living in Jerusalem at the time? [5]My answer again is NO! I assure you that all are sinners and that all will be punished by eternal death unless they repent."

[6]To illustrate God's willingness to save lost sinners, He told of a gardener who had a fig tree that always disappointed him when no fruit was ever found. [7]The gardener said to the foreman, "Don't you think that we ought to just cut it down?"

[8]The foreman hated to see such drastic methods used just yet. "Please allow me to till the soil around it for another year, then apply a lot of composted manure, [9]then wait for a year or two to see if it makes any difference. If by then it produces fruit, we shall all be happy, and if not, we will reluctantly have to cut it down."

[10]One Sabbath while He was teaching in the synagogue among the worshippers

[11]He noticed a woman who had a severe spinal deformity. She had been in this condition for eighteen years, and the deformity was so severe that she could not stand up straight but was bent over into a stooping position. [12]He called her over and spoke these words: "Woman, your deformity is being corrected as of now." [13]Then He put His hands on her, and she immediately stood up straight and tall, then shouted out her praise to God.

[14]There was at least one in the congregation who took a dim view of the wonderful event. You guessed it, the chief officer of the synagogue. He arose and publicly rebuked Jesus, contending that this had been in violation of the Sabbath commandment. He then addressed the people and continued, "There are six days of the week in which people should work. Let them come on one of the working days if they need healing, not on the holy Sabbath."

[15]"I'm sorry to have to say this," replied Jesus, "but frankly and truthfully, you are a hypocrite. Every Sabbath day without exception you go and untie your donkey and your ox and lead them to the water trough. [16]It is much more important to help a person than it is to help a donkey or an ox. She has been tied up by Satan these eighteen years, and would you honestly refuse to untie her if you had the power, just because it is the Sabbath? Have a heart! She is one of God's special people, a daughter of Abraham." [17]His point was so well made that those who heard him were able to understand God and His character much better. Most of those present rejoiced, but His enemies must have felt somewhat sheepish to say the least.

[18]He then began to try to help them understand the kingdom of God more accurately. "What can I say that will perhaps illustrate it? [19]"Here is one illustration. You all know what a mustard seed looks like—a tiny, insignificant thing. Yet it has the capability to grow into a shrub that is larger than any other garden crop. Large enough for birds to nest in. [20]Let me suggest another illustration. [21]A woman wants to make some bread. She takes just a little yeast, mixes it into the dough, and kneads thoroughly. When that mixture is baked that tiny bit of yeast has transformed the entire pan of dough."

[22]So Jesus went from village to village, city after city, teaching and helping people, then cheering them up with the good news. During all this time He was getting closer and closer to Jerusalem, a significant fact. [23]One day an interested follower asked Him, "Lord, cannot everyone be saved?" It seemed that only a few were believing.

The answer Jesus gave made it clear that the choice is up to the individual. Salvation is indeed available to all. Then He gave this advice: [24]"Do your utmost to find this narrow gate through which you will find salvation. It is always open, but eventually the gate will no longer be kept open because no one else wants to enter it. [25]It is like a home owner who shuts his door at night and bolts it solidly. If you come pounding on his door he will have to tell you, 'I'm sorry, but I don't know you.' You may respond, [26]'But don't you remember me? I had lunch with you that day and listened to you speak in the street of my village.' [27]He is still unable to recognize you and replies, 'No, I am afraid I do not know you. I cannot let you in; your lifestyle demonstrates that you really did not accept my plan for you but continued in your sinful way.'

[28]"Don't be among those weeping, wailing ones who have neglected salvation and finally realize that Abraham, Isaac, and Jacob and all the prophets are admitted. Those left out will be those who choose to reject God's grace. It will be by their own choice that they are lost. [29]The saved ones will be from the north, the south, the east, and the west, and these will be given responsible positions in God's kingdom, [30]but sadly I tell you, many who expect to be there are outside, and many are inside who have surprised their friends and acquaintances."

[31]That very day a delegation of Pharisees came to Him with a message, "Sir, you should know that we have information that Herod wants You executed, so You had better get out of His territory."

[32]His answer to them was like this, "I suggest that you go straight to that 'fox' Herod and tell him that I plan to continue with My mission of healing and casting out demons until it is completed. If it is God's will that I should continue, you will be powerless to stop Me. [33]However, friends, as sure as we are standing here, I am to be captured in Jerusalem, that fateful city where so many prophets have perished; the most dangerous place on earth for God's prophets to be working."

[34]At this point Jesus began sobbing as He cried out, "Oh, Jerusalem, Jerusalem, you who keep on murdering God's messengers, stoning the very ones sent to you from God. Oh! How often I would have sheltered you from danger and eternal loss, as a hen gathers her chicks under her wings, but you have refused! [35]Your beautiful temple is to be totally desolate, useless, and of no significance, for the One symbolized by its services is here and will soon depart, having fulfilled the prophecies concerning Him. You will never see Him again until that awesome day when you will be forced to admit that I am all I have claimed to be—God in human flesh."

Chapter 14

[1]The enemies of Jesus seemed to be everywhere, spying on His every move. It is hard to comprehend the thinking of a mind that could produce so much hate for a person who was doing so much good, but this is Satan's way. Such as the time when He was invited to the home of a leading Pharisee for a Sabbath lunch. [2]A large number of VIPs were present, including one man who was in congestive heart failure. His dependent edema and shortness of breath was so great that he was barely able to be up and walking.

[3]Jesus asked the Pharisees, "Is it within the law to heal on the Sabbath day? I need a straightforward answer." [4]They dared not answer either "yes" or "no." They stared down in sullen silence. Then Jesus went to the suffering man, touched him with miraculous power, and presented him to the gathering in perfect health. [5]He then continued to reason with His enemies as He questioned them, "Is there any of you men who would not go to the rescue of your donkey or your ox which had fallen into a pit on the Sabbath day?" [6]Again they would not answer Him. [7]"My friends, let Me give you some sound advice." (He had noticed how they had been vying for the most honored places at the table.) [8]"When you are invited to a wedding feast, you would be smart to assume that you are not the most honored guest. If you should take that honored spot, it would indeed be humiliating [9]to have the host come and

say, 'Sorry, sir, but over here is your place,' and he leads you to the last place available. [10]Far better to take that place when you arrive, then when the host spots you, he might say, 'Friend, come with me, you are to be seated close to the head of the table.' [11]Ultimately, any person who attempts to exalt himself will be humbled, while the truly meek ones will be honored."

[12]Next Jesus had some thoughts directed to the host. "Would you like to generate the greatest possible joy? If so, try this. The next time you are planning a dinner forget about your relatives or your rich neighbors. They will feel that they have to invite you back, and you will not have the satisfaction of having done a good deed. [13]So instead, invite some poor folks, some cripples, some mentally challenged ones, or some blind ones. These cannot invite you back, and you will have the joy of sharing your blessings. [14]Then at the resurrection day, you will receive an eternal reward."

[15]One of the guests who had been listening carefully to what Jesus had been saying spoke up, "Master, I have been trying to imagine what it will be to eat my first meal in the kingdom of God. What a thrill that will be!"

[16]Jesus followed that remark by telling a parable. "Once upon a time there was a man who planned a huge banquet. The man was wealthy, and money was no consideration, so he was willing to spend whatever was necessary to put on the greatest banquet ever. [17]He sent RSVP invitations to a long list of guests, telling them that he would send his servant when the final preparations had been made. They all accepted. When the time came for the guests to arrive, he sent his servant to everyone who had accepted an invitation, 'It is time for the banquet. Please come.'

[18]"Would you believe it? Each one gave him a different excuse for not being able to attend. One said, 'I'm sorry but I just purchased a farm and really must go and see it.' [19]Another said, 'I just purchased five yoke of oxen and need to go and find out what they can do. Please excuse me.' [20]A third one said, 'I was just married since receiving the invitation, and of course I cannot come.'

[21]"Such were the excuses for not attending, all of which were rather absurd and every excuse was eloquent evidence that the person had not the slightest respect for the host or their initial promise to attend. The servant returned home and related what he had encountered. The wealthy man was angry, and understandably so. [22]He said, 'Now go out into the highways, streets, and alleys and invite the poor, the crippled, the lame, and the blind.' He soon returned with a large number of guests and reported to his master. 'We have more room, sir.' [23]'OK, now go out into the country and invite everyone you can find so my banquet hall may be filled. [24]This much is certain, none of those who were first invited will get a taste of my banquet."

[25]During this time Jesus was followed by a great number of people who were eager to hear Him, but He realized that some of them had selfish purposes in following Him, so He turned around and told them this, [26]"Everyone who really wants to be a disciple of mine must be willing to put his family second: father, mother, wife, children, brothers, sisters; and yes, even his own life must be secondary to his decision to be with Me in My mission. [27]And this includes a willingness to face crucifixion.

²⁸Yes, to be My disciple is costly. If you want to build a tower for your vineyard you will first calculate the cost so that you will know whether you have the necessary funds. ²⁹If this is not done, you might find yourself with a foundation built but no money to complete the project. People would surely look at the incomplete structure and wonder about your intelligence. ³⁰Look at this. He must have been a poor manager.

³¹"Consider also the plight of the king who is considering going to war against a neighboring king. If he has good judgment, he will first evaluate his chances of defeating a foe who has twice the number of troops that he has. ³²If his information indicates certain defeat, he will try to work out some diplomatic settlement rather than risk a disaster. ³³And just as a king before going to battle must commit his whole army to the conflict, so it is with you who follow Me: you must make a complete commitment. ³⁴A little salt is good, but if it is mixed with tasteless substances it is of no value whatsoever. ³⁵No, not even useful as fertilizer."

Chapter 15

¹Jesus and His teachings were becoming so popular that tax collectors and other "sinners" were listening more and more. ²This fact was noted by the Pharisees and scribes who began to complain to their constituents, "You surely cannot believe that He is much of a spiritual leader if He accepts this sort of people."

³But the very next parable He gave illustrated His mission. ⁴"You sheep-breeders, I have a story for you. Suppose there are one hundred sheep in your flock, and one of them turns up missing. Will you not leave the ninety-nine and go out into the wilderness looking for the lost one? You will no doubt search for it as long as it takes to find it. ⁵And when at last you have found it, you will pick it up, place it on your shoulders, and carry it home. ⁶When you reach home, you will gather the household and perhaps even the neighbors together so that they can share your joy in finding the lost one. ⁷Friends, let Me tell you a wonderful reality. In heaven there is more profound joy over one sinner who repents than over ninety-nine sinless beings who never have needed repentance.

⁸"And think of this scenario: A woman has a dowry made up of ten silver coins. She treasures them for their physical worth and even more for their emotional value. But one day she discovers that one of her precious coins is missing. What can she do? She first lights a lamp and searches the whole house thoroughly. Then she gets out her broom and sweeps the whole house and eventually finds that lost coin. ⁹After finding it she is so overjoyed that she calls her neighbors over so that they can share her joy in finding the coin that was lost. ¹⁰As surely as she and her neighbors rejoice, so God's angels rejoice over one sinner who repents.

¹¹"There was a very prosperous farmer who had two grown sons. ¹²One day the younger son came to his father with a request. 'Father, you must be old enough so that you will die soon and of course at your death, your property will be distributed between my brother and me. Wouldn't it be just the same with you if you deeded to me the part of the farm which would become mine and the share of cash that would also become mine?' Whether or not the father thought this

was a good idea, he complied with this son's wishes. [13]The young fellow moved swiftly, sold his portion of the property, and converted it into cash. Then, loaded with money he left home and headed for a distant country where he could enjoy life without Dad seeing his riotous living. Money flowed freely as he associated with others who engaged in his party lifestyle, both men and women, who had abundant reasons to socialize with him and help spend his money. [14]This lifestyle continued until finally his money was gone. And then a drought descended on the whole area. Food became scarce. With no money he really got hungry. He was now in a fearful situation. [15]As much as he hated to do it, he finally started looking for a job, and he soon located a farmer with a large herd of hogs who needed a farmhand. In order to survive, he spent all day feeding the pigs. [16]And even this income was not enough to supply him with the food for survival. Eventually he was forced to eat from the hog trough.

[17]"One day it dawned on him that he would be far better off to return home and work at his father's place as a hired man. At least there would be plenty of food. [18]So he began planning for the long trip on foot. He even thought out the speech he would make when his father met him, 'Dad, you must have known long before I did how wrong I was in what I have done to you. [19]Heaven knows what a fool I have been. But is it possible that I could be taken on as a hired man? I am no longer worthy to be known as your son.'

[20]"With his plans complete, he found an old wine skin for water and saved up a little grain. His clothing was in tatters. He went to the farmer and resigned as hog feeder and left the country. The way was long, tiresome. Hunger and thirst were endured for several days, but he kept at it. At last his father's farm was in view. What a thrill! And coming out to meet him was his dad. Utter joy filled the father's heart as he reached his son, the hobo, and gave him a loving embrace. Father shed some tears and welcomed his son home.

[21]"The young tramp began his prepared speech, 'Father, I have made a terrible mistake. I have wronged both heaven and you, and I certainly do not deserve to be known as your son.'

[22]"Here, the father interrupted him, shouting to his hired men, 'Take this man in the house, give him a bath, put the best clothing on him, the best shoes on his feet, and put a signet on his finger. [23]Then kill that special calf we have been saving for a banquet. Make a great feast. We are going to celebrate, [24]for my son is alive, and I thought he was dead. He was lost and now has been found.'

"So the household began to prepare for a big party. [25]Unfortunately, the story has a sad feature. The older son was in the field working when the younger brother returned, and as he approached the house, he heard music and dancing. [26]Calling a nearby servant, he asked what the big deal was all about. [27]'Oh, you haven't heard? Your brother has returned, and your father is preparing a big celebration. That special calf is already being roasted, and the whole thing is because of your brother's safe return.'

[28]"The older brother could not see how this could make the father so wildly happy. He actually refused to enter the house and join in the merriment, but the father came out to him and urged him to come on in.

²⁹His answer revealed a lack of understanding and a failure to realize the love that a father has for each of his children. 'Look, Dad, all of these years I have served you faithfully. I have worked as hard as you have. I have never given you any trouble, and yet you have never put on a party for me! Not one celebration with my friends. ³⁰But as soon as this traitor comes back home, this good-for-nothing guy who conned you out of your money, then spent it on prostitutes, you throw a big party for him! I just can't see it. It isn't fair!'

³¹"Calmly the father replied to this tirade, 'Son, I think I understand how you feel, but remember that everything we have here is now yours. It was deeded to you and is twice what your younger brother received. So I cannot give him more. He will have to work for a living. But even so, it is appropriate to celebrate his return, for he has had a total change of heart and has learned the hard way. Now he is home again, and it is as if he had been raised from the dead or that he had been lost and now is found.'"

Chapter 16

¹"Let me illustrate another quality of character that My followers need," Jesus began. "They need utmost integrity. There was a wealthy man whose manager was suspected of embezzlement. ²This manager was summoned to account for the evidence that had been found to support the suspicions. He was asked if he could account for the discrepancies, and if there was no way to deny the evidence, he would be terminated. ³He was in a tight spot but crafty enough to come up with an idea that assured him of sympathy among many members of the community. He was in no condition to work as a common laborer and was far to proud to be a beggar, so his idea was this. ⁴'I will make friends among my owner's debtors so that when I am unemployed they will take pity on me. ⁵He invited all the accounts receivable in to his office and asked them about their debts.

"'How much do you owe this firm, sir?' he asked the first man.

⁶"'One hundred measures of oil,' was his answer.

"'Friend I have some good news for you,' the manager reported. 'Your bill is cut in half as of today.'

⁷"'And what is your current balance?' he asked the second man. 'One hundred measures of wheat,' was the answer. 'Your new statement is for only eighty measures of wheat,' the manager reported. ⁸The owner of the firm recognized the talent of his manager, not that he was honest, but that he was shrewd enough and smart enough to assure his future survival. Yes, it often is the case that 'worldly' people are more interested in their future than are those who want to be known as God's people. ⁹So my advice to you listeners is this: by any and all means available, go out and make friends, because some day money and riches will fail you—true friendship will be all there is left for you, and your most important friend is God, who will eventually give you a priceless reward. ¹⁰The importance of even small responsibilities cannot be overestimated, for if you are above reproach in small matters, you can be depended on to be the same in more important matters. Conversely, if you are willing to cheat in small transactions, you will be no better in larger deals.

¹¹"Think this through: If you have not been faithful and trustworthy in financial

dealings, can you expect God to entrust you with eternal riches? [12]How could you expect God to give you eternal wealth if you have been undependable as a manager of his property in this life? [13]You all know that it is impossible for a man to have two bosses. He will always prefer one over the other. It is just that way with God and earthly wealth. Their demands are incompatible with each other."

[14]A number of Pharisees were listening to this discourse and, being grasping and covetous, they tried to "put Him down." [15]He, however, was completely unruffled and attempted to help them see themselves as they really were. "You perhaps, are outwardly very upright people, but remember that God knows your inmost being, your thoughts, your motives. He knows your real self, and often the qualities that are admired by other humans are utterly foreign to God's character and to His will for us human beings. [16]Until the preaching of John the Baptist, all that you had to go by were the writings of Moses and the prophets and the psalms. But now you have a great advantage, for the true nature of God's kingdom and His character has been preached widely. And thousands have been enlightened. [17]But remember that those writings are so important that heaven and earth will vanish before those revelations fail.

[18]"In the 'law' is the command forbidding adultery, a law that is for the benefit of human society. Some of you may have been under a false impression as to what constitutes adultery, so I shall give you a brief definition. Anyone who divorces his wife and remarries commits adultery, and a person who marries that woman who has been divorced also commits adultery.

[19]"Here is another question that may have given you some confusion, the issue of poverty versus prosperity. An allegory may help you to straighten out this issue in your mind. Once upon a time there was a very wealthy man who wore only the finest clothes, ate the most expensive food, lived in a mansion, and enjoyed luxury. [20]The entrance to his estate was guarded by a beautiful gate, and just outside this gate was a beggar by the name of Lazarus who was hungry, in rags, and destitute. He hoped that some crumbs from the wealthy man's table would be dumped out for him to eat. [21]He had skin lesions that attracted dogs who came and licked his sores. A more miserable creature cannot be imagined. [22]Now let's find out the fate of these two men. Lazarus finally died, and, wonder of wonders, he was rewarded with a resurrection into paradise and association with father Abraham. And of course, the rich man died also. He, too, was resurrected in the second resurrection much to his dismay and despair. He had been confident of being in heaven, judging by the many blessings he had enjoyed all his life on earth. But alas, he realized too late that it could not be. His sadness was emphasized by the fact that he was able to look into heaven and see that awful beggar, Lazarus, enjoying a close friendship with Abraham. [24]He called out across the great abyss to Abraham, 'Please, Abraham, I am doomed to die in this fire. Could you possibly send Lazarus to me with his finger dipped in some cool water to quench my thirst while I am dying here?' [25]But Abraham replied, sadly, 'Son, remember your lifetime of prosperity and abundance? You thought all along that God was rewarding your goodness, didn't you? It just wasn't that

way at all. Lazarus, here, had nothing in life whatsoever, yet now, because his heart was right with God, he has everlasting life and joy without end, while you are reaping the end result of selfishness and pride. [26]Furthermore, please remember that in the afterlife there will be no communication between the saved and the lost for the simple reason that the lost will not even exist. Thus, the barrier between the saved and the lost is infinite in magnitude.'

[27]"Yet the rich man went on pleading, 'Then, Abraham, would you be willing to send Lazarus to my five brothers and warn them of their danger [28]so that they will mend their ways and avoid the fate that has overtaken me.'

[29]"But Abraham answered, 'Alas, they have already had ample warning through Moses and the prophets. Surely they will heed that warning, don't you think?'

[30]"'No, Abraham, if someone rises from the dead, it will be much more persuasive. I feel certain that they would listen to Lazarus and repent.'

[31]"'Unfortunately, this is not the case, for the facts are that if a person will not heed the messages of Moses and the prophets, they will not listen to a person who rises from the dead.'"

Chapter 17

[1]The next point that Jesus made with His disciples was that in this world there will be dreadful crimes committed, even against innocent children. Jesus said, "But woe to those who commit such atrocities, [2]for it would be better for them in the long run if a millstone were tied to their necks and they were thrown into the ocean than to perpetrate evil against a little child. [3]Even you, my followers, must be on your guard.

"When a brother has offended you, it is appropriate to tell him that you have been deeply hurt, but you must then forgive him even if he does not apologize. [4]"Even if he offends you seven times in one day, then comes and asks forgiveness every time, you must forgive."

[5]This was almost too much for the disciples, and their plea was, "Lord, please strengthen our faith."

[6]"Yes," the Lord added, "your faith needs growth, and it should be like a mustard seed that is very tiny, but with water and nourishment it will grow. Your faith must keep on strengthening to the place where you can say to this sycamore tree, 'Up, out of here and fall into the lake,' and it will uproot before your eyes and fall into the lake.

[7]"Can you imagine yourselves as landowners with slaves who would say, 'Come in for supper; it's all ready for you'? [8]Far more likely you would say, 'Time to quit in the field, so come in and get my supper for me. After I have eaten you may eat.' [9]Does a landowner thank a slave for doing what he is commanded to do? Decidedly not. [10]It is like that with you. After you have done everything assigned to you, never feel that you deserve thanks for having done your job."

[11]On their way to Jerusalem from Galilee, they were in a Samaritan village when ten lepers approached the group. [12]They were forbidden to touch a non-leper, [13]so they kept their distance but yelled out so that they could be heard, "Jesus, master, have mercy on us."

[14]He looked their way, then gave orders, "Go at once and be examined by the priests." Without hesitation they obeyed and in the process were instantly healed of the leprosy.

¹⁵One of the healed men, when he saw that he had been healed, whirled around and came back to Jesus with words of loud praise to God on his lips. ¹⁶Then he fell on his knees and thanked Him for the miracle of healing. The unusual feature of this is that he was a Samaritan. ¹⁷This was shocking to the disciples. Jesus was happy that the man was so grateful. Even so, He said rather sadly, "There were ten of you, but where are the other nine? ¹⁸It seems a pity that the only one of the ten who returned to give thanks was a foreigner." ¹⁹He then addressed the Samaritan, "You may stand up, friend, and go on your way. You were healed because you had faith in Me."

²⁰The Pharisees were constantly asking questions as to when the kingdom of God would be established, and one day He answered them this way. "The kingdom of God will not come as you expect, for it is not an earthly kingdom with pomp, ceremony, and wealth. ²¹Neither will people shout, 'The kingdom of God is here,' for the kingdom of God is something internal, a change in the person from within to transform the nature, a change that is very real and yet is not forced upon anyone."

²²Later Jesus warned His disciples about their future. "Some day you will remember these times together and will long to be here again as we are now, but it will not be possible, for I will not remain on the earth much longer. ²³People will say, 'Oh, there He is,' or 'Oh here He is,' but do not believe them, ²⁴for My next appearance will be spectacular—like a brilliant flash of lightning—visible from one horizon to the other. No one will miss seeing that great event.

²⁵"Before that event occurs, I will have to go through the sorrow of seeing My own nation reject Me as the fulfillment of the prophecies; ²⁶however, it will be somewhat as it was in Noah's time. ²⁷Everyone was going about life as usual, eating, drinking, marrying wives, being married to husbands, right up until the day Noah and his family went into the ark, just before the flood came and those outside were lost in the rising water. ²⁸And remember the story of Lot. They were eating, drinking, buying, selling, planting, and building. ²⁹And the very day that Lot left Sodom fire descended from heaven and annihilated the city.

³⁰"Just as suddenly and unexpectedly, I will return. ³¹At that time if a person should be on the solarium and his valuables are within the house, he should not take time to retrieve his valuables. And if a person is in the field, do not go back to the house to carry valuables with you. ³²Remember Lot's wife! ³³Whoever puts temporal life above every other consideration will lose it, but if in following Me you lose your life, this will be only a temporary loss for you will have gained eternal life. ³⁴You should know that there will be cases where two people will be in the same bed, one will lose his life, the other will be saved. ³⁵Two may be working at a mill, one of whom will lose his live, the other will be saved. ³⁶There will be two out in the field working together, one of whom will lose his life, the other will be saved."

³⁷The listeners were quick to ask a question, "Lord, where will this happen?"

So He tried to explain, "Where there is a dead carcass, there will be a group of vultures."

Chapter 18

¹One parable He told showed how important it is to persevere in prayer. Never quit praying for the needs that one senses.

²"Once upon a time there was a judge who was not a God-fearing person and neither did he have much in the way of concern for other people. ³One day a local widow came to him with a problem. Someone had wronged her, and she wanted justice imposed on the offender. ⁴He refused to act on this request for a time, but she continued asking repeatedly, finally the judge began to reason things out like this. ⁵'If I do nothing, this widow will keep pestering me about this issue, so I will bring the offending party to face punishment.'

⁶Then the Lord explained, "Did you hear what this atheistic judge said? Even a person like him would help a plaintiff who persists in asking. ⁷How much more likely will God, who loves His creatures with an infinite love, answer the plea of a person who continues to plead for help? ⁸I assure you that God's people will get justice quickly, and yet as kind as God is, do you suppose I will find many who trust in My Father and Me when I return?"

⁹Here is another parable told to illustrate a common human fault: spiritual pride and putting others down. ¹⁰"Let's say that two men go up to the temple at the same time to pray. One is a Pharisee, the other a tax collector. ¹¹The Pharisee stands and prays like this: 'Oh Lord, how thankful I am to be honest, pure, and just, and not like this tax agent next to me. ¹²You know, God, how faithful I am in fasting twice every week and in giving tithes of everything I obtain.'

¹³"The tax agent's prayer is quite different. Listen as he bows his head in humility and contrition, wringing his hands together and crying out in sincerity, 'God, please be merciful to me for I am a guilty sinner.'

¹⁴"Let Me assure you that this tax agent's prayer was answered. He went home forgiven. Remember folks, human beings who attempt to exalt themselves will eventually be humbled, and those who recognize their need will finally be exalted."

¹⁵Then several mothers came, carrying their babies to Jesus, hoping that He would be willing to touch them. They were disappointed when the disciples tried to turn them away. ¹⁶But Jesus called them back, "Please do not prevent these children from coming to Me because the kingdom of God will be inhabited by people like these. ¹⁷Truly I tell you, whoever does not accept the kingdom of God with the same trusting attitude as a child does will not be a citizen of that land."

¹⁸One of the rulers came to Jesus with this inquiry, "Good Master, tell me what I should do to inherit eternal life."

¹⁹"Why are you calling Me 'good'? You should know that there are really no 'good' beings except God Himself. ²⁰And you already know the commandments, which forbid adultery, murder, stealing, and lying, and the one that insists on honoring one's parents."

²¹"You are right, I am well acquainted with the Ten Commandments. In fact, I have kept them all my life."

²²Then Jesus added one more commandment, "All you need now is to sell all that you own and give the proceeds to charity. You will than have a treasure in heaven, for you will be following Me."

²³The ruler's face fell. He was really saddened, for he was a very wealthy man. ²⁴As he turned sorrowfully away, Jesus watched him leave and His own heart was saddened. He expressed it this way to His disciples,

"Friends, it is almost impossible for those who are wealthy to enter the kingdom of God. ²⁵In fact it is easier for a camel to go through the eye of a needle than for a rich man to enter the kingdom of God."

²⁶"Well then, who can be saved?"

²⁷"Remember," He reminded them, "things that are utterly impossible for human beings are possible with God."

²⁸"How about us?" Peter asked. "Do we have a chance? We have abandoned our families, our occupations, in fact, everything in order to follow You."

²⁹"Let Me assure you that anyone who leaves his home, his parents, his brothers, his wife, or his children in order to spread the word about God's kingdom ³⁰shall have a far better life here and now. Then in the new earth, he shall have everlasting life."

³¹Next He addressed the twelve, "We are now going up to Jerusalem where the prophecies will be fulfilled about the Messiah, such as Psalm 22 and Isaiah 53. ³²"The Son of man will be turned over to the Gentiles, He will scoffed at, sneered at, mocked, spit on, ³³scourged, and finally killed. But on the third day, He will rise to life again."

³⁴The poor disciples heard these words, but they just could not understand the meaning of them as applying to Jesus. ³⁵The journey continued, and as they neared Jericho, they saw a blind man sitting by the road begging. ³⁶He had heard a crowd of people approaching and enquired as to who was coming. ³⁷Jesus was so well known that almost everyone was aware of His travels, so he was told, "It is Jesus of Nazareth who is passing through."

³⁸The blind man called out, "Jesus, Son of David, have mercy on me." ³⁹He was told to hush up, but he only cried out louder, "Jesus, Son of David, take pity on me."

⁴⁰Jesus stopped and asked someone to bring the blind beggar to Him. A friendly hand helped him to his feet and led him to Jesus. ⁴¹"What do you want, my friend?" Jesus asked.

"Lord, I want to be able to see!"

⁴²"OK, you may begin seeing as of now. Your faith was placed in Me, and it is rewarded." ⁴³Instantly his sight was restored to 20-20 vision, and he followed along with Jesus and the rest, praising and thanking God for the great miracle.

Chapter 19

¹In Jericho was a man by the name of Zacchaeus. He had become wealthy by working as a tax collector for the Roman government. In fact, he was the chief of the collectors for the whole area. ²Now Jesus was about to enter Jericho, and Zacchaeus was thinking seriously about his life. He had heard enough about Jesus to stimulate a great desire to see Him.

³The man was in a perplexing situation. The crowd was so large that he would never be seen. It would be hard for a normal person, but it was even harder for Zacchaeus because he was a very short man. What could he do? ⁴Then an idea came to him. Along the road ahead was a sycamore tree. He raced to the tree, climbed up into it, and from there watched for Jesus! ⁵Right in the middle of the crowd was the Man he had been longing to see. Imagine his surprise when Jesus stopped, looked up into the tree, and called him by name, "Zacchaeus, my friend, please come down out of the tree. I want to stop at your home for a while today."

⁶*Is this real?* Zacchaeus thought. It was. He came down from the tree, overjoyed

that he could escort Jesus to his home. [7]But a number of people criticized Jesus for this. To think that He was willing to enter the house of such a sinner as this fellow!

[8]"Let me share with you something on my heart," Zacchaeus began after Jesus was seated. "I have been seriously considering my lifestyle and am convinced that I have done a lot of wrongs, so I have decided to give half of my property to help poor people. I also decided to return to those I have defrauded, an amount equal to four times what I took from them."

[9]Jesus responded, "Today I assure you that your repentance has been accepted by our Father in heaven and that salvation is now yours. [10]You see, this is the very reason I have come to this earth. To look for and save those who are lost."

[11]A large number of people believed that this was the time that God's kingdom was about to be established. (Wasn't Jesus on His way to Jerusalem for this purpose?) So Jesus gave them a parable to help them understand things as they really were. [12]"A certain noble inherited a kingdom in a distant land, so he left to accept the crown. [13]Before leaving he called ten of his stewards and gave each of them a mina with instructions to invest it so that when he returned there would be a favorable increase. [14]Unfortunately, for him the citizens of the kingdom he inherited hated him, so he returned home. [15]When he reached home, he called the stewards together for a report on their investments.

[16]"The first reported, 'Sir, your mina was well invested. There are now ten minas instead of just one.'

[17]"The king was well pleased of course and replied, 'Well done, my friend. Because of your success in a small investment like this, I will ask you to be city manager for ten towns.'

[18]"The second steward then reported, 'Sir, your mina has grown to five.'

[19]"You have done well, my friend. I want you to be manager over five towns.'

[20]"But another steward reported, by bringing the pound all tightly wrapped up in cloth, and said, [21]'I was afraid of you, sir. I know that you are a demanding person and interested in only one thing, money. So here is your money.'

[22]"The noble retorted, 'Sir, I will deal with you just as you have spoken. You knew that I expected an increase. Why did you do what you did? [23]Wouldn't a wise person at least have placed the money in a savings account so that there would be some interest accruing all this time? [24]Come here, guards, take this man into custody. Take the money he has returned and give it to the man who has ten minas.'"

[25]The listeners had trouble with this illustration and asked Jesus about the justice of giving still more to the one who already had the most. [26]So Jesus explained, "Everyone who is wise and prudent will continue to gain more wisdom, but the one who is slovenly will find that even what he has will be taken from him. [27]As for my enemies who do not want Me for their king, their fate will be death, sadly enough."

[28]This was the final illustration He gave before going up into the high country around Jerusalem. [29]After reaching the summit near the villages of Bethphage and Bethany, Jesus called two of His disciples and sent them on an errand. [30]"Go into the next village, and just as you have entered the gate, you will see a young colt tied, one that has never been ridden. Untie this colt

and bring it to Me. ³¹In case someone stops you and asks what you are doing, just tell him simply that the Lord needs it."

³²So they went ahead into the village, and sure enough there was a young colt tied up. They proceeded to untie it and were confronted by the owner, ³³"Hey, what do you think you are doing? Why are you untying my colt?"

³⁴"We know that this is a bit unusual, but would you be willing to lend him to the Lord for a little while, He needs him?"

"Why, yes, of course, use him as long as the Lord needs him."

³⁵So they brought the colt to Jesus. They laid their coats on the colt. Jesus then mounted the little beast and started toward Jerusalem. ³⁶At once people began spreading their coats on the road ahead of Jesus. ³⁷Soon the followers of Jesus began to shout and praise God as they realized that they were witnessing the fulfillment of prophecy. ³⁸"Blessed is the king who is coming in the name of the Lord. Let heaven's peace and glory prevail!"

³⁹In the crowd were a number of Pharisees, as usual, trying to find something by which to condemn Jesus. "Teacher, why don't you tell these emotional zealots to calm down?"

⁴⁰His answer shocked them. "Let Me tell you the truth about this. If they would stop what they are doing and keep quiet, the stones along this road would begin to shout."

⁴¹Coming in view was Jerusalem, and Jesus was plunged into a sorrowful melancholy. His followers must have been perplexed. But He knew the future of that city, which had been blessed by so many favors and which was at this very time rejecting their Savior. ⁴²He uttered these sad words,

"Oh, if only you had known the things that you might have known, things which are the foundation of any future peace and prosperity. ⁴³But you have refused to learn. You have closed your eyes and ears, and the day is coming when your enemies shall surround you completely in a dreadful siege. ⁴⁴They will utterly destroy this city and its citizens and will not leave one stone on another, and only because you would not accept your opportunities, repent, and completely return to God and obey Him."

⁴⁵He went into the city and straight to the temple. There He found merchants profiteering from the sacred services. ⁴⁶He drove them out, quoting Isaiah 56:7, "My house shall be called a house of prayer for all people, but you have made it a den of thieves." ⁴⁷For the next few days He entered the temple in spite of the hatred of the chief priests and scribes who were trying to destroy Him. ⁴⁸They seemed baffled in their plots due to the huge audiences that came to listen to His messages.

Chapter 20

¹One day while He was teaching the people in the temple, He was approached by the chief priests, scribes, and elders. ²"Tell us," they demanded. "Who gave You the authority to come into this temple and to brainwash people as You have been doing?"

³Instead of giving a direct answer, He promised to tell them if they would answer His question to them, ⁴"About John the Baptist, was he giving a message from God or was his teaching just some human ideas?"

⁵Instantly they recognized that they were in a dilemma. ⁶"If we say he spoke God's message, He will ask why we did not

support Him and believe, but if we say he only gave human ideas, we know that the people won't believe us for most of them believe he was a prophet from God."

[7]So they gave up and told Him that they really were not sure of the source of John's teaching. [8]"Neither will I tell you who gave Me authority to teach here," He said. [9]Next Jesus gave them a significant parable as to what had happened to their nation and why it had happened. "There was a landowner who planted a large vineyard and leased it to some tenants while he was away in a distant country. [10]At harvest time he sent one of his employees back to collect the proceeds and evaluate the management of the vineyard. But the tenants turned on him and gave him a vicious beating and sent him back to where he came from. [11]So the owner sent another employee, but the tenants were even more rough with him than with the first one. He was beaten worse than the other man and had to leave empty handed. [12]A third man was sent, but the tenants were so vicious in their treatment of him that he was permanently disabled. Then they dragged him out of the vineyard and left him helpless. [13]Finally, in desperation, the owner decided to send his son. He thought surely they would respect his authority. [14]But no. As soon as the tenants saw the son, they got together and concluded that if this fellow were killed they might be able to seize the whole vineyard without any opposition. [15]So they ganged up on him, captured him, carried him out of the vineyard, and murdered him. Now what do you think would be the right punishment for such tenants? [16]The answer is obvious. The owner will return, try them, and have them executed for their crimes. Then he will lease his vineyard out to new tenants."

The listeners were strong in expressing themselves, "Let not such a thing happen."

[17]Jesus had been watching them and then reminded them of the scripture, "The stone that had been rejected by the builders was found to be the main keystone. [18]Whoever puts their trust in that stone and will fall on it will be broken-hearted, but if it falls on someone, it will grind him to powder."

[19]The priests and scribes failed to see that this parable was aimed at them. Instead of accepting their true condition in repentance, they began to plan how to capture Jesus without stirring up a riot among His many followers. [20]So they hired private detectives to watch Him and record His statements so that they could have something that could be used in court to destroy Him. [21]One of these men came up with this question, and others thought it was a great idea. It would be asked of Him in public, "Master, we know that Your teaching is correct and that You show no partiality, [22]so would you tell us if it is within the law to pay taxes to Caesar or not?"

[23]He sensed their purpose, "You are testing Me, are you not? [24]So show Me a coin, please." Someone pulled a coin out of his pocket and showed it to Jesus. "Now tell me, who is that person represented on the coin? And whose name is it?" They answered "Caesar's." [25]"There, you have the answer to your question. Always pay to Caesar the things that belong to him and to God the things that belong to Him." [26]This left them stunned and speechless. Their little strategy had fallen flat.

[27]The next ones to confront Him were some Sadducees who taught that there will be no resurrection. Their question was a hypothetical one. [28]"Master, suppose that

a man died without having any children, and according to Moses, his brother married the widow. ²⁹There were seven brothers. The oldest was married but died without any children. ³⁰So the second brother married her, but he also died childless. ³¹So the next brother married her. As did all seven, none of which had any children. ³²And finally the woman died. ³³Now in the resurrection whose wife will she be? Which one of the seven?"

³⁴Jesus' answer was gentle. "In this world men marry and women are given in marriage, ³⁵but when those who are counted worthy are resurrected, they will not marry, neither men or women. ³⁶Both marriage and death will be absent in that land. Those who are there will resemble the angels who are not married and who never die. They will be immortal children of God. ³⁷Do you remember the account of Moses at the burning bush? Jehovah was called the God of Abraham, Isaac, and Jacob. Wouldn't it be absurd to call Him the God of those patriarchs if they were dead forever? ³⁸Yes, God is the God of living beings, not dead ones, and all will one day live again."

³⁹A few scribes had to admit to Him, "You have given us good answers." ⁴⁰After that they were convinced that other questions might be ineffective for their purposes. ⁴¹However, Jesus then asked them a question, "How do you explain David's statement that the Messiah is his son? ⁴²Jehovah said to my Lord, 'Sit on My right hand until I make Your enemies Your footstool.' ⁴³David here calls Him Lord. How can he do so if he is a direct descendent? Impossible! For David is calling a descendent superior to himself."

⁴⁵Here Jesus looked at His disciples and warned them, ⁴⁶"Be on guard in dealing with the scribes, and do not follow their example. You know their lifestyle. They wear long robes and like to be greeted reverently in the marketplace. They always like to be elected to the highest positions in the synagogue, and they always expect to be honored guests at the festivals. ⁴⁷In actual practice they are selfish and would foreclose on a widow's home and evict her into the street, all while calling people to prayer services. Their outcome can be nothing less than condemnation."

Chapter 21

¹ While Jesus was speaking, several rich men came to the temple to make their contributions. ²And Jesus was watching them just as a poor widow came up to give her contribution, a mere two pennies. ³"Did you notice this gift by that poor widow?" He asked. "She gave only two pennies, and yet ⁴it was a greater gift than the others because it was all she had, and they gave only a small fraction of their riches."

⁵There were some present at that time who called the attention of Jesus to the temple and its elaborate embellishments, with precious stones and artistic work. ⁶"Yes, they are beautiful, of course, but alas, friends, I must clue you in on something. A time will come when this temple will be totally demolished and not one stone will be left on another."

⁷As you can imagine, His listeners were half unbelieving when they heard this, so they began questioning Him about it. "When will this happen, and what will be the sign as to when it is about to happen?"

⁸"First, I must warn you against deception, for there will be many who will pretend to be Christ. There will be more of these as the time approaches. Do not make

the mistake of following such people. [9]Also, you must realize that there will be wars and upheavals of all kinds as time goes by. These events will be frightening to most people, but they should not terrify you. The end is not necessarily near when wars are everywhere. They are the result of pride and selfishness and will be considered a way of life in this world. [10]There will be wars between small tribes, larger ones, and between huge nations, and they will be very devastating. [11]There will be earthquakes in many places, terrible famines, fearful epidemics of all kinds, terrifying events, and scary things in the sky. [12]Long before these things take place, you, My followers, will be arrested, persecuted in various ways, tried in synagogues and in secular courts, imprisoned, and compelled to face kings because of My name. [13]The court will demand from you a statement of your belief, publicly. [14]You may as well know now that no well-prepared speech will be adequate at that time. [15]But I promise to give you words of wisdom, logic, and conviction that will be persuasive, even to your enemies.

[16]"Sadly enough your own family members—parents, brothers, sisters, and friends—will betray you and will bring about martyrdom to some. [17]And hatred will prevail everywhere, just because you are following Me. [18]But always remember this: Whatever may happen to you cannot cause you to be eternally lost. [19]So endure whatever might be your experience.

[20]"Now for some specifics. Jerusalem will be captured and destroyed. You may know that its destruction is near when an army surrounds it. [21]But this is the very time for you to escape from the city and from all Judea and head for the mountains. [22]These events will be the natural result of rebellion against God and ignoring His advice, just as it is foretold in Deuteronomy. [23]Mothers of nursing babies will have an especially difficult time, and so will those in advanced pregnancy. Everyone will have plenty of trials, trouble, and distress. [24]There will be the loss of many lives due to the wars; others will be taken captive and eventually will be scattered throughout the whole world. Jerusalem will be totally overrun by Gentiles and will never regain prominence. The Gentiles will conquer and harass until the end of time.

[25]"Now here are some signs that will warn the world that the final days are near. Heavenly signs involving the sun, the moon, and the stars will be seen. Signs on the earth also will happen, along with great distress among the nations, as the sea roars in a violent storm. [26]Terror in the hearts of men everywhere will be common as they sense the condition of the world, for even the heavenly powers will be shaken up. [27]After this they will be able to see the Son of man coming in the clouds with power and unbelievable glory. [28]My advice to you is this: When you see these things fulfilling, take heart and be encouraged because your redemption is very near."

[29]To illustrate His advice, He told another parable. "Think of a fig tree and other trees. [30]When the buds begin to grow, when leaves appear, you can reasonably conclude, and actually be certain, that summer will follow soon. [31]So, when you experience these events I have mentioned, you may be certain that God's kingdom is about to be established. [32]Truly I tell you that this generation will live to see the fulfillment of many of these predictions. And the generation that witnesses the heavenly signs, the shaking, will live until the final fulfillment.

³³My word is more reliable than the earth and sky, both of which might be demolished. ³⁴But all of you need to be on your guard against such things as feasting to excess, intoxicants against temporal cares to the place that you will be surprised by that day, ³⁵for it will indeed be a surprise to the whole earth. ³⁶So be alert, pray always for discernment and for a readiness to see these things transpire, so that you may be counted worthy to escape destruction and to stand before the Son of man."

³⁷For several days He taught in the temple during the day and spent much time at night out on the Mount of Olives. ³⁸People kept coming early in the morning to hear Him at the temple.

Chapter 22

¹The feast of unleavened bread called the Passover was very near, ²but the chief priests and scribes, instead of celebrating the great deliverance from Egypt, were planning the death of Jesus. Their plan must be kept undercover because so many of the people were followers of Jesus and would react strongly against the leaders if their intention was known. ³The Great Adversary was not idle during this time and had found access to the mind of Judas Iscariot. ⁴A plot had developed in his mind in which he might betray Jesus into the hands of those who were seeking His life. (The result might be that Jesus would stage a miraculous escape, in which case the cash supply of the twelve would be significantly greater, which would be very desirable in Judas' mind, the treasurer.) ⁵The leaders were jubilant to learn of Judas' plan and were willing to promise a fat sum to the traitor in order to carry out their nefarious scheme. ⁶The deal was made, and Judas

began to plan the best time to betray Jesus. It must be at night after the large crowds had returned to their homes.

⁷Passover day arrived, and ⁸Jesus sent Peter and John to prepare for the ceremony and the meal that accompanies the celebration. ⁹"Where do You want to have our Passover meal?" they asked Jesus.

¹⁰"As you enter the city, you will see an unusual sight. It will be a man carrying a water pitcher. ¹¹Follow him into the house, introduce yourselves to the owner, and ask this favor of him, 'The Master needs your guest room to celebrate Passover with His disciples.' ¹²He will then show you a large room on the second floor, all furnished. This will be the place."

¹³They went, and it was exactly as Jesus had predicted, so they prepared the Passover meal. ¹⁴At the appointed time, Jesus and the other ten disciples arrived and were all seated at the table. ¹⁵Jesus addressed them first with this remark, "I have been anticipating this meal with you men, the last Passover before I go through My great ordeal. ¹⁶I assure you that this is My last Passover until we are together again in the kingdom of God."

¹⁷Then He picked up the mug and gave thanks to God before passing it to His disciples with this advice: "I want each of you to drink a little of this juice, ¹⁸as for Myself, I am not drinking any, and I will not drink any until we share some together in the kingdom of God."

¹⁹He took some unleavened bread also, gave thanks to God, then broke it into pieces for each of the disciples, explaining to them the significance of this bread. "This broken bread will remind you of My broken body, which will be broken for you. From now on do this regularly to

help remember Me. [20]And drink some of this juice to remind you of My blood and the covenant to you, sealed with blood. [21]I must tell you, however painful it is, that one of you at this very table will betray Me to My bitter enemies. [22]I, the Son of man, will indeed go through with My painful experience as planned, but alas for the person by whom I am betrayed."

[23]Shocked, the disciples enquired among themselves who it could possibly be that would do such a thing. [24]They also debated the old issue as to who would be the greatest in the kingdom. [25]Then Jesus spoke, "As you know, Gentile kings are dictators over their subjects and consider this a mark of greatness, [26]but with you, I want to tell you a better way. Whoever wants to be the greatest should act as the youngest, and if one of you wants to be the most important, try serving the others. [27]A question, Who is the greatest, the one sitting at the table or the one serving the person at the table? The answer is obvious—the one at the table. And yet I am like the one doing the serving. [28]Now you are the ones who have stayed with Me through My trials. [29]And I am appointing you as overseers of My kingdom, as My Father appointed Me as overseer of His kingdom. [30]Being overseers you will of course have the privilege of feasting with Me at My table and also have seats of authority over the twelve tribes, each of you over a tribe."

[31]Now Jesus turned to Simon Peter. "Are you aware that Satan wants to put you through his mill, brainwashing you so that you will be what he wants you to be? [32]But I have prayed sincerely for you, asking that your faith will never fail and that you will be a tower of strength to your brothers after you are truly converted."

[33]Peter answered Jesus, "Lord, I am ready to go with You to prison or death if necessary."

[34]"Oh yes, Peter, I realize that you are intending to be strong in My defense, but the truth is that before this night is over, before the rooster crows, you will declare three times that you do not even know Me."

[35]Then He asked this question, speaking to all of the disciples, "When I sent you out with nothing, no extra shoes, no money, or extra clothing, did any of you lack that which was vital to your success?"

"Oh no," they all answered.

[36]"From now on you will need to plan well. Carry a pouch, money, and even a sword. If you have none, you had better sell extra clothing and buy one. [37]I assure you that soon you will see the fulfillment of Isaiah's prophecy, 'He was numbered with the transgressors.'" [38]The disciples now produced two swords. "OK," He said, "that will be adequate."

[39]They then left the upper room and started toward the Mount of Olives. Judas was not among them, for he had left the group some time before. [40]Arriving at the secluded spot where He had often gone, Jesus begged them to pray that they would be equal to the trials so soon to come upon them. [41]Then staggering on a few more steps into the garden, He knelt down and prayed these agonizing words: [42]"My Father, if You are willing, please relieve Me of this agony. This cup is bitter. But if You see that it is best for Me to drink it, I'll do it."

[43]At this point an angel appeared to give Jesus strength to endure but did not remove the trial. [44]In fact, His distress increased in spite of His most earnest prayer. His agony was so intense that blood escaped from His skin and fell like drops of

sweat to the ground. ⁴⁵Finally He believed that His prayer had been heard and that the Father would not remove the trial, for this would threaten the entire universe forever and none of the lost ones on this planet could be rescued. So He returned to the disciples and found them asleep. He had been passing through the keenest suffering for them, but they did not seem to be concerned at all. ⁴⁶He awakened them, "How could you sleep? You need to be alert, praying, on guard, in order to endure trials."

⁴⁷As the disciples awakened, sounds of a mob approaching were heard and presently here came Judas leading them. In the dim light of torches, he quickly spotted Jesus, walked up to Him, and kissed Him. ⁴⁸"Judas, how can you stand to betray Me with a kiss?"

⁴⁹The disciples could see the danger Jesus was in and asked, "Is it time to use the swords?" ⁵⁰Before He answered, one of the disciples swung his sword and lopped off the right ear of the high priest' slave, no doubt intending to kill him. ⁵¹"No more of that," Jesus said. Then He touched the bleeding man and healed him instantly.

⁵²Then Jesus spoke to the chief priests, the temple guards, and the elders. "Can I believe this? You intend to treat Me as a common criminal with clubs and swords. ⁵³Even though you know very well that I have been with you every day in the temple and am no lawbreaker. Had I been a lawless person you would have arrested Me in broad daylight. Evidently you prefer to do your dirty work in the dark, right?"

⁵⁴So they arrested Him and led Him into the city to the home of the high priest. The crowd followed, along with one disciple who wanted to know what would happen. It was Peter. ⁵⁵He followed them into the hall and sat near the fire burning in the courtyard. ⁵⁶Not long afterward a young girl began to stare at him, then turned and said to another, "I saw this fellow out in the garden where the arrest took place."

⁵⁷"I beg your pardon! You are wrong. I don't know this man," Peter shouted.

⁵⁸Not long after this a man noticed Peter and went right over and confronted him, "You are one of those who was with this character, aren't you?"

"Man, how wrong you are. I most certainly am not," declared Peter.

⁵⁹About an hour later someone else spoke up. "I am almost positive that this fellow was with Jesus, because he is a Galilean."

⁶⁰And once again, Peter denied it. "Man, I don't even know what you are saying."

At just that moment a nearby rooster crowed. ⁶¹At this the Lord looked at Peter, who suddenly remembered the prediction Jesus had made, "Before the rooster crows, you will deny knowing Me three times." ⁶²Peter was stunned. He staggered out of the hall, overwhelmed with remorse, wondering how he could have said such things. He then recognized that Jesus knew him better than he knew himself. And then he broke down and wept uncontrollably.

⁶³Meanwhile the guards who held Jesus began to abuse Him physically and verbally. ⁶⁴First they blindfolded Him, then slapped His face and taunted Him, "Who slapped You?" ⁶⁵Then they abused and tortured Him. ⁶⁶But as soon as daylight arrived, they led Him to the council for questioning, hoping to hear an incriminating statement. ⁶⁷First question: "Are you the Messiah? Tell us."

His answer, "If I tell you the truth, you will not believe Me. [68]And if I ask you a question, you will not answer Me as you have done in the past, and furthermore, you will not release Me even in My innocence. [69]But one day, in the future you will see this Son of man enthroned and with infinite power, the power of God."

[70]They suddenly had the same idea, "Then are you the Son of God?"

To this question, He answered, "You are correct."

[71]"Aha! We need no other witnesses. We have heard it from His own mouth."

Chapter 23

[1]The authorities could do no more at this time, so they took Him to Pilate for condemnation and sentencing. [2]They presented their case. "Sir, we found this man attempting to disrupt the nation by telling us that we should not pay taxes to Rome and that He is the Messiah, a king."

[3]Pilate then questioned Him, "Are You the king of the Jews?"

To which Jesus responded, "Yes, what you have said it true."

[4]Pilate then reminded the priests and elders that this claim was not a crime, for there is no law against such a claim. [5]"But sir, He has been stirring up excitement all over the country, beginning in Galilee and going to every city."

[6]"Hold it a moment," Pilate said. "Did you say Galilee? Is He a Galilean?" He was trying to "pass the buck." [7]When he was convinced that Jesus was from Galilee, he ordered Him sent to Herod who was in Jerusalem at the time.

[8]Herod was delighted, for he had heard many stories about this miracle worker and had long hoped to witness some of those alleged miracles. [9]But his curiosity was not to be satisfied, for Jesus refused to answer any of his questions. [10]Then the chief priests and scribes began to shout accusations about Jesus. Herod was frustrated because Jesus would not answer any questions, so Herod let his military men torment Jesus with sarcasm and torture. [11]They put a gorgeous robe on Jesus as if He were a king or other VIP and sent Him back to Pilate. [12]Oddly enough, Herod and Pilate, who had never been friends, were able to agree on one thing and became friends over this trial.

[13]Now Pilate called the chief priests and rulers together again and spoke to them. [14]"You have brought this man, claiming that He has been involved in treasonous activity, but so far you have failed to convince me by your testimony. I then questioned Him and could find no reason to believe that He is such a person. [15]So I sent Him to Herod, and he too failed to find evidence of such activity. [16]I have decided to have Him flogged and released."

[17]This was a custom at the time. Passover was a time when a political prisoner was released from custody, just to appease the Jews. [18]The uproar was instantaneous, "NO, NO, NO Don't release this character! Release Barabbas!" [19]Barabbas was a criminal who in the process of stirring up a riot had committed murder. [20]But Pilate still wanted to release Jesus and began again to tell them why. [21]Their cries drowned out his words. They began to chant in unison, "Crucify, Crucify."

[22]For the third time Pilate tried to reason with these unreasonable priests. "Why, what has He done to deserve death? You haven't convinced me. I will have Him flogged and let Him go."

[23]The roar of the people was even more insistent, "Crucify! Crucify! Crucify!"

Pilate caved in. He couldn't stand the pressure. [24]An order for crucifixion was issued. [25]Then another order—release Barabbas, the criminal who had led a rebellion against Rome. Jesus was turned over to soldiers just as the Jews had asked.

[26]On the way out of the city, seeing that Jesus was unable to physically carry the cross, a stranger named Simon from Cyrene was arrested and ordered to carry it. [27]A large number of people had gathered and were following the procession, among whom were several weeping women, some of whom were likely the ones who had been healed or had children healed of disease. [28]Jesus spoke to the nearest ones. "Daughters of Jerusalem, don't mourn because of Me, but rather because of you and your children. [29]For in the near future, childless women will be looked upon with special favor—infertility will be envied. [30]People will pray, 'Mountains, bury us,' or 'Hills, cover us.' [31]Yes, if they can do this in a time of prosperity, what can they do in difficult times?"

[32]In the same procession on the way to their death were two criminals carrying their crosses. [33]Not far from the city wall was a place known as "The Skull." It was here that the victims were nailed to the crosses, then lifted up, and the crosses placed into the holes dug for them. Jesus was placed between the two criminals. [34]However, Jesus showed no anger. Instead He looked up to heaven and prayed, "Father, forgive them, for they are ignorant of the significance of their act." The soldiers then stripped Jesus' clothing from Him and divided it among themselves.

[35]The crowd commented, "He was able to save other people, I wonder why He couldn't save Himself if He is the Messiah as He claims."

[36]The soldiers jeered but came at times to offer Him some vinegar. [37]They challenged Him, "Save yourself if you really are king of the Jews."

[38]A notice was attached to the cross above Jesus' head. It had been written in Hebrew, Latin, and Greek: "This is the king of the Jews."

[39]One of the criminals began to yell at Jesus, "If You are Christ as You claim, save Yourself, then save us."

[40]But the other one reminded him, "Don't you believe in God? We are all dying together, [41]and we deserve this punishment, but this man has never done anything wrong." [42]Then he turned to Jesus and implored Him, "Lord, when You receive Your kingdom, remember me."

[43]The answer Jesus gave him was clear and positive. "My friend, it seems utterly impossible today. Here we are, both doomed to die soon, and in spite of this grim outlook, I can promise you that we shall be together in paradise."

[44]At noon a mysterious darkness crept over the land, adding fear to the scene. The watchers quieted down and many left the area in deep thought, wondering about the significance of this phenomenon. For about three hours it continued with even the sun becoming invisible. [45]And this was not the only supernatural event to take place. Over in the temple it was time for the evening sacrifice. The priest was ready to kill the sacrificial lamb when suddenly a loud sound of tearing cloth shook the scene as the heavy veil of the temple, the one dividing the holy from the Most Holy Place, was torn apart starting at the upper

margin and continuing down to the floor. No visible cause was present, and just as at Belshazzar's feast, when that hand wrote on the wall of the palace, terror filled the heart of the priest, and he trembled so violently that the knife slipped from his hand and fell to the pavement, while the lamb, intended for sacrifice, escaped.

⁴⁶It must have been at the same moment when Jesus cried out. "Father, I'm dying. I trust You." He was gone. ⁴⁷The Roman centurion who was watching and listening recognized that this was no criminal. He had seen many of them die. He was forced to exclaim, "This man was the Son of God." ⁴⁸All who had been lingering at the scene beat their breasts and fled in fear and awe.

⁴⁹Among Jesus' closest friends were several women from Galilee. They knew that Jesus was now dead. ⁵⁰They were somewhat amazed to see Joseph of Arimathea, a member of the Sanhedrin, leave the crucifixion site, enter the city, and return shortly with some helpers. ⁵¹He had voted against condemning Jesus the day before. ⁵²With Pilate's permission he removed the body of Jesus from the cross. His own sepulcher was nearby, ⁵³and after wrapping the body in a large linen cloth, he and his helpers carried it to his sepulcher, laid it on the stone ledge, rolled the massive stone back over the entrance, and left.

⁵⁴It was getting late in the afternoon and the Sabbath was approaching before they finished and left. ⁵⁵Those friends of Jesus had noted where the body had been placed and went into the city, intending to obtain spices and ointment which they would bring back Sunday morning for a final anointing.

Chapter 24

¹Very early Sunday morning the women brought spices and ointments to anoint the body as planned. ²Consternation seized them as they came in sight of the tomb, for the huge stone had been rolled away from the entrance. ³*Who could have done such a thing?* they thought, as they peered into the tomb only to find it empty. *Someone has stolen His body!* ⁴*Now what do we do?* In perplexity they hesitated, their spices still in containers on their shoulders. Sorrow, fear, and anger were all mingled together when suddenly two beings in brilliant white garments materialized before their eyes. ⁵Now they were really afraid and bowed to the ground before these celestial beings, but their fears began to evaporate as they listened to the message brought by the kind angels.

⁶"Friends, why are you looking for a living person in a tomb? As you have discovered, He is no longer here. He is alive! He has arisen some time ago. Perhaps you remember that He assured you of this very thing in words that could not be misunderstood. ⁷Here is what He said, 'The Son of man is to be handed over to wicked men, to be crucified, to die, and then to rise from the grave on the third day.' You all must have heard that a number of times."

⁸Yes, they began to recall those statements and were chagrined to realize how little impression it had made on them. ⁹This was all they needed in order to give wings to their feet as they quickly returned to the city, found the eleven disciples and some others with them, and related their incredible experience. ¹⁰In spite of the testimony of these three witnesses, Mary Magdalene, Joanna, and Mary the mother of James, plus several other women, all of

whom were reliable and trustworthy, [11]the disciples did not believe the women at first. The tale seemed like fiction created by wishful thinking.

[12]Peter, however, wanted to find out for himself, so he grabbed his sandals and made for the door. He ran out of the city to the tomb and stooped over and looked in. He saw the linen cloth, but there was no body in the tomb. He left with a mixture of hope, consternation, and perplexity. [13]The day had begun for the disciples with no solution to the big question that was on all their minds. Two of Jesus' followers finally decided to return to their home village of Emmaus, a few miles from Jerusalem, and left the other believers in the afternoon. [14]Both of them wore an expression of utter dejection, disillusionment, and despair as they talked together on the way. [15]Some distance from the city a third man joined them. It was Jesus Himself, but in His resurrected form. [16]He disguised himself so that they would not recognize Him.

[17]"Friends, I noticed your sadness as I approached you. Whatever has happened?" He asked.

[18]Cleopas answered, "I suppose that You are a stranger and do not know what has occurred here recently, some really terrible things."

[19]"Really? Tell Me about them, if you don't mind."

So Cleopas opened up. "Well, it's all about a Man known as Jesus of Nazareth, who was a prophet if there ever was one. He performed miracles of all kinds; He was a marvelous teacher and a friend to many of us. [20]But our priests and rulers condemned Him and turned Him over to the Romans who crucified Him. [21]We were fully convinced until last Friday that

He was the promised Messiah of prophecy who would lead us to conquer Rome and establish Israel as the world's ruling kingdom. And now another thing has happened. [22]This is the third day and this morning several women in our group were at the tomb intending to anoint His body, but there was no body to be found, [23]And not only that, but they also reported that they saw angels at the tomb who spoke to them, telling them that Jesus had been resurrected. [24]So some of our group went over to check it out and found things exactly as the women had reported, but they did not see Jesus."

[25]At this the stranger gave them something to think about: "Friends, let Me give you a few thoughts that may help you understand the meaning of what you have just told Me. Let us remember some of the prophecies concerning the Messiah, for I feel sure you have not properly understood what you have been reading. [26]Let us first look at Isaiah's prophecy and remember that the Messiah was willing to be mistreated as Jesus was, and that it was because of our sins that He was willing to go through that torture. But following this He will be exalted to heaven's glory."

[27]Then, beginning in the books of Moses, He showed them throughout Scripture how the prophecies had been fulfilled in the life of Jesus of Nazareth. [28]By the time He was through, the three of them were nearing Emmaus, and this stranger acted as though He was headed for the next village. [29]They both urged Him to stay, "Look, we have plenty of room. Couldn't You stay with us? We are tired and hungry, and we have food. Please."

The invitation was accepted, and He followed them into their home. [30]Suppertime found them sitting at the table together when the stranger picked up a loaf of bread, gave thanks to God, broke it into pieces, and passed the pieces to his hosts. [31]The sudden realization hit them. This was no stranger. It was the resurrected Lord. They were speechless, and then the stranger disappeared before their eyes. [32]Soon they regained a bit of composure and compared their feelings. "You know, there was a familiar warmth about Him and a convincing way with scripture that was fascinating."

[33]Fatigue was abruptly forgotten. They had to let their friends in Jerusalem hear the story. They headed back to the city even though it was getting dark. But the moon would soon rise, and they could see their way. When they reached the city, they rushed to the upper room where the believers were assembled. "It's true! Jesus is alive! [34]He has appeared to Peter." [35]Then the two from Emmaus spoke. The story of their experience came tumbling out. The sad walk home, the stranger who joined them, the explanation of Scripture, the invitation to stay, the meal, the breaking of the bread, their sudden recognition of the resurrected Lord, and His sudden disappearance. All was vividly described.

[36]Right in the middle of their talking, Jesus entered the room. "Let peace be with you!" [37]Fear gripped them again. Was this a spirit being? [38]"Why are you all so frightened?" He asked. [39]"Please come and look at Me. See My hands. It is really I. A spirit being does not have flesh and bones, as you know."

[40]Then He showed them His hands and feet, scarred by the crucifixion. [41]This was too good to be true, surely. Then Jesus asked, "Is there something to eat around here? I'm hungry." [42]Someone still had the presence of mind to bring a piece of broiled fish. [43]He gratefully accepted the food and ate. [44]After He had finished eating, He explained again what He had tried to show them from Scripture even before the crucifixion. "These things in the writings of Moses, the psalms, and the prophets were fulfilled in My life and work." [45]Then, one by one He quoted text after text and explained the fulfillment of every one.

[46]Summarizing, He continued, "You have heard what was written, you have seen with your own eyes the fulfillment of these prophecies, and that they were all fulfilled in Me, even to the torture and death I went through, then the resurrection on the third day. [47]Now that the Messiah has arrived, it is time to begin publicizing the need for repentance so that sins will be forsaken and forgiven. Begin right here in Jerusalem, preaching in My name. [48]Witnesses are needed, and you are my witnesses. [49]And you won't have to depend on human strength, for I promise you that the strength of God will be in your work for Me. Do not leave Jerusalem until it is clear that you possess this supernatural strength."

[50]One day He invited them to follow Him to Bethany where He paused, faced them, raised His hands, and blessed them. [51]Then in the very act of blessing them He slowly began to rise from the earth, and as they watched, He disappeared into the sky. [52]His stunned followers worshipped Him, and gradually the joy that filled their hearts began to be seen in everything they did. Then obedient to Him they returned to Jerusalem. [53]Day after day they were seen meeting at the temple where they were continually praising God.

John

Chapter 1

¹Back to the beginning of things as we know them. I'll use a term that will become meaningful as we go along. That term is "The Word." The Word has always been. The Word was with God. The Word was God. The Word was always God. ²Once again: The Word has always existed, has always been with God. ³The Word is a person. He is the One who created everything. There is not a single thing in existence that was not created by Him. ⁴Life began because of His life. His life was the source of light for human beings. ⁵The light from Him has eliminated darkness, physical and spiritual, but unfortunately not all who were in spiritual darkness have understood that important point.

⁶Just at the right time a man named John was called by God for a special work. ⁷He came to help others to know the Light, to believe in the Light. He wanted everyone to know the Light. ⁸He himself was not the light, but he preached about the One who was the Light. ⁹Yes, he pointed to the true, genuine Light, which has lightened every person on this planet. ¹⁰The Light and the Word are the same person. He was in the world for a while, and although He created the world, He was not accepted for who He was. ¹¹He came to His own nation, but they rejected Him ¹²However, those who were willing to accept and receive him were given the right to be God's children. ¹³God's children are those who have experienced not only physical birth but also a kind of rebirth, a birth into a new life brought about by God's will in our lives. ¹⁴The Word actually became human just as we are, and He lived as a man among us. Some of us were privileged to see Him in full splendor and glory, the very essence of grace and reality.

¹⁵The man John, whom I mentioned, began directing his listeners to the Word. "The man I have been talking about seems to be younger than I, but He is not only superior to me, but He existed a long time before I did. ¹⁶And friends, all of us have received grace from Him. ¹⁷Moses was apparently the one who gave the law to us as a nation, but in reality Jesus Christ is the origin of the law as well as the origin of grace and truth. ¹⁸Now of course, no one has ever seen God, but His unique human Son has made God very well known, being the human form of Deity."

¹⁹During John's ministry a delegation of priests and Levites was sent from Jerusalem to interview him and bring back a report. "Just who are you?" they asked.

²⁰"First, let me assure you that I am not

the Messiah." (Apparently there were some who believed him to be Christ.)

21"Well then, are you Elijah?"

"No," was his reply.

"Then are you the prophet foretold by Moses?"

"No, again"

22"Well then, would you be willing to tell us who you really are. You see, we have been sent from Jerusalem to find out who you are and to bring back a report."

23"If you really want to know who I am, read Isaiah. 40For it says, 'The voice of one preaching in the wilderness, clear the way of the Lord, straighten out a highway for Jehovah.' That is what I have been commissioned to do."

24"Look, if you are not the Messiah, Elijah, or 'that prophet,' why do you have the audacity to be baptizing?"

25John responded that water baptism is indeed significant, 26but not as important as what was expected to happen soon. "Yes, I am baptizing with water, but there is another who is already among you, not known as yet, 27who is far more important than I. In fact, I am wholly unworthy to lace or unlace His sandals."

28This encounter took place at Bethabara on the east side of the Jordan River where John had been preaching and baptizing. 29The very next day, who should appear but Jesus. He approached John, and the Holy Spirit impressed upon John that He was the Messiah. John then announced to all around him, "Look, everyone! Here comes the Lamb of God who will remove the sins of the whole world. 30He is the One I have been talking about, a Man who is far superior to me. In fact, He preceded me. 31I didn't know Him myself, but I knew that He would make Himself known to Israel.

This is why I have been preaching and baptizing, all because of Him."

32Then John described his experience at Jesus' baptism. "I saw the Holy Spirit of God descending and hovering over Him like a dove. 33To me, He would have been just another man, but the commission to baptize came from God who said, 'When you see a Man on whom the Holy Spirit alights and remains, you will know that it is He who will baptize with the Holy Spirit.' 34I witnessed it, and I now proclaim Him to be the Son of God."

35On the following day, John and two of his disciples were standing together when 36Jesus was walking a short distance away. John pointing to Jesus again and said, "Look, the Lamb of God." 37The two who heard John identify Jesus as the Lamb of God decided then and there to become followers of Jesus.

38Jesus turned around and saw them approaching. "Are you looking for someone?" He asked.

"Yes, we are. Where are You staying?"

39"Come along," He invited. "I am going that way now." So they went with Him and saw where He was staying and did not leave for several hours.

40One of these was Andrew. Now Andrew had a brother named Simon, later called Peter. 41Andrew's first task was to find his brother and to announce, "Guess what! We have seen the Messiah. Are you listening? We have seen the Messiah!" 42Simon wanted to see for himself so he went along with Andrew.

When Jesus saw him, the greeting was significant, demonstrating Jesus' divine capabilities. "Your name is Simon, and your father's name is John. I am going to call you by a nickname, 'Peter' (a name meaning a stone).”

⁴³The next day Jesus headed to Galilee where he met a man named Philip. “Would you come with Me, please?” He invited. ⁴⁴Philip lived in Bethsaida, the same town where Andrew and Peter lived.

⁴⁵Philip went looking for his friend named Nathanael. “Hey,” he called when he spotted him, “we have found the One Moses wrote about, the One the prophets predicted. He is Jesus of Nazareth, son of Joseph.”

⁴⁶“Huh?” muttered Nathanael. “Can you really believe that anything good could come from Nazareth?”

“Just come and see for yourself,” said Philip.

⁴⁷Jesus saw Nathanael coming and greeted him. “Look, here comes an Israelite who is completely honest.”

⁴⁸Rather taken aback, Nathanael asked, “Just what do You know about me?”

“As a matter of fact, I saw you when you were under that fig tree before Philip called you.”

⁴⁹Now Nathanael was really impressed. “You must be the Son of God. You must be the king we have been waiting for.”

⁵⁰ “Well,” Jesus replied, “you are convinced because I said I saw you under the fig tree; be assured you will see many things much more convincing. ⁵¹I guarantee that you will see heavenly angels, going to and from the earth, and all because of this Son of man.”

Chapter 2

¹ Three days later a wedding was scheduled at Cana, a nearby village. Jesus’ mother was related to the bride and, of course, was invited. ²Fortunately, Jesus was also invited and was encouraged to bring His disciples.

³As the festivities progressed, the supply of wine rapidly dwindled, and panic was about to overtake the host. Mary decided to speak to Jesus about the problem. So she whispered to Him, asking for advice.

⁴“My dear mother, are you expecting Me to take over and make up for the poor planning that has led to this crisis? Really, you are not responsible to correct such matters either, but when the proper time arrives, I shall follow My Father’s will.”

⁵This encouraged her so greatly that she went to the caterer and slipped this word to him, “If you will do just as my Son tells you, things will be OK.”

⁶So the head waiter came to Jesus with the need.

“You see these six stone water jugs?” Jesus began.

⁷“Yes, sir.”

“Have them filled with water now.”

“Yes, sir, I will follow Your orders.” Shortly they were filled to the brim.

⁸“Now start with the father of the bride, and serve him from one of the jugs.”

“Yes, sir.”

⁹When the host tasted the wine, he was unaware that there had been a shortage and that this cupful had been miraculously provided. (But the slaves who had filled the jugs with water knew the story.) ¹⁰So he called the bridegroom over and spoke to him, “Say, ordinarily we are served the best wine first, and then when all have had plenty they bring in the poorer stuff. But you have saved the best until now.”

¹¹This was the first of many miracles that Jesus performed to help people recognize who He was and so His disciples would have complete faith in Him. ¹²Soon after the wedding, Jesus, His mother, His brothers, and His disciples went down to

Capernaum for a few days. [13]They were there only a few days for the Passover was approaching, and Jesus went up to Jerusalem. [14]After arriving in the city, Jesus went to the temple where He encountered bedlam of a marketplace: cattle, sheep, doves, etc. Besides the animals and their owners, there were a number of money-changers, all trying to attract the worshippers with offers of better exchange rates in temple currency. This scene was foreign to the purpose of the temple, and Jesus could not remain indifferent. [15]He fashioned a whip out of cords and drove all the misguided people out of the temple, along with the animals. He then upended the tables of the moneychangers, spilling money on the pavement. [16]As He went about this strange behavior, He began to explain it, "This place is a center for worship, not a place to buy, sell, and make profits." [17]The disciples were reminded of a verse in the psalms (Ps. 69:9): "My whole being is being consumed because of your house."

[18]But the Jews in authority confronted him. "Look, who do You think You are? You had better think fast and come up with some kind of evidence that You have authority to act like this."

[19]Quickly came His answer: "This temple will be destroyed, and in three days I will restore it."

[20]"How absurd," they replied. "You should realize that it took forty-six years to build this temple, and who are You to claim the ability to rebuild it in three days?"

[21]Now of course we know what He meant—not the stone structure that was before Him, but His body—a body temple—was to be the sign of His authority. [22]It was obvious after He was raised from the dead that He had foretold His own resurrection on the third day. And this fact fortified the faith of His disciples.

[23]The Passover time was accompanied by a number of miracles, and they were effective in establishing faith in the hearts of many people. [24]However, Jesus did not have to tell everything at this time, for He knew their hearts and that was enough for now. [25]There was no need to demand expression of their faith at this time, for He knew them like an open book.

Chapter 3

[1]One of the Pharisees at this time was a man by the name of Nicodemus. [2]He was deeply impressed by Jesus and wanted to have an interview with Him, but among his peers it would have been embarrassing to acknowledge his interest. What to do? He determined to see and talk with Jesus even if it meant a clandestine meeting under cover of darkness. Once that decision was made, he learned where Jesus would be on a certain night. Nicodemus met Him with no one around, not even the disciples. He first affirmed Jesus, "Teacher, we are convinced that God has sent You, for we are aware of the large number of genuine miracles You have performed—miracles far beyond human capacity."

[3]Before he could proceed further, Jesus spoke up, "Truly, sir, very solemnly I assure you that unless a man born again he will not be fit to enter the kingdom of God."

[4]"What do You mean, 'born again'? How can a grown man enter again into his mother's womb and be born?"

[5]This outburst did not trouble Jesus, but He went on to describe the figure of speech He had just coined. "Truly, I tell you this. To enter God's kingdom, a person must have a birth that can be brought

about by the Holy Spirit in a rite known as baptism in water. [6]A material body is the product of another material body, and a spiritual being is one produced by the Holy Spirit. [7]It should come as no surprise when I tell you this, that all of you need this new birth I am talking about. [8]The wind blows this way and that, producing sound and causing real tangible effects, and yet wind is entirely invisible. It is something like this with the 'new birth.' The process is not visible, but the results in a person's life are very easily seen."

[9]Here, Nicodemus asked, "How can this all be understood? Are we not all members of God's kingdom?"

[10]So Jesus explained, "You are one of Israel's accepted leaders and teachers, and you must be prepared to teach others about such truths. [11]So I am giving you knowledge that is absolutely essential. I can speak authoritatively of things I know about, and so can you, but I can see that you are having a hard time believing what I have just told you. [12]If you find it difficult to believe these simple things, how can you expect to believe really mysterious things such as heaven? [13]You see, no one has ever gone to heaven and then come back to report on it. Only the Son of man can accurately testify of heavenly things, for He left heaven and has come to this earth.

[14]"Do you remember the account of the wilderness wanderings and of the deadly snakes that bit so many of the people? Moses was directed to make a snake of brass and fasten it to a pole so that people who had been bitten might look at the snake and escape death. Everyone who looked at that symbol recovered. This is an illustration of what the Son of man will do. He will be lifted up for all to see [15]so

that everyone who accepts His offer will be given eternal life. [16]For God loved the world so much that He gave His special, unique Son, who would be hated like that serpent, to be lifted up on a cross in order that eternal life could be given to all who believe in Him. [17]God did not send this Son of His into the world to condemn the world but so that the world might be saved through this plan. [18]Whoever believes in God's Son is acquitted, but if a person refuses to believe, he or she, being already guilty, is beyond rescue.

[19]"Condemnation is pronounced, not as an arbitrary sentence, but as a result of choosing to reject the light—a free choice of the individual who prefers darkness because evil is more pleasant to him. [20]Everyone who chooses evil rejects the light and does so hoping that his evil deeds will remain hidden. [21]But if a person chooses truth it is like entering into a lighted place where his behavior can readily be seen by others and it is apparent that he is in harmony with God."

[22]Some time after this interview Jesus and His disciples made their way into the countryside of Judea where they baptized those who believed the messages presented. [23]John was still baptizing at Aenon, a place close to Salim, where there was an abundant supply of water for baptisms. [24]John's imprisonment was soon to stop his work completely. [25]A question was at that time being discussed by John's disciples and the Jewish leaders regarding ceremonial purification. [26]During this ongoing discussion, there were some who brought news to John about Jesus' growing popularity.

[27]John's reaction was expressed candidly: "Whatever success anyone has is a

gift from heaven. [28]Now you know very well that I assured them that I am not the Messiah but am sent ahead of Him to call attention to Him. [29]He can be compared to the bridegroom; I am only a friend of the groom, a friend who is very happy over His success. [30]Eventually He will increase in influence, and I will decrease. [31]He comes from above, that is, from heaven and, of course, is superior to all of us. We are only earthlings and can comprehend only earthly matters, while He, being from heaven, has infinite knowledge. [32]And from that infinite supply He is telling us truth, but how few are ready to accept it. [33]Those who do accept it are convinced that our God is a God of truth. [34]We can be certain that God's messenger is speaking God's words because the infinite power of the Holy Spirit is available to Him. [35]Our Father loves His Son and has commissioned Him to carry forward in this world the work that is essential to salvation. [36]To believe in God's Son is to have everlasting life. To refuse Him is to reject life and to accept separation from God."

Chapter 4

[1]The popularity of Jesus was rapidly growing, and eventually the Pharisees were made aware that Jesus was baptizing more people than was John. [2](Although the actual act of baptism was not performed by Jesus but by the disciples.) [3]This fact caused real apprehension among the Pharisees, and of course Jesus knew their hearts and plans, so rather than aggravating them more, He left Judea for Galilee. [4]En route to Galilee He passed through Samaria.

[5]In one of the cities called Sychar, an interesting event occurred. It was very close to the acreage given to Joseph by his father Jacob. [6]They reached the well outside the city at about noon and sat down to rest a little while. [7]Soon a woman from the town came out to the well to get a pitcher of water. "Would you mind giving Me a drink of water?" Jesus asked. [8](The disciples had entered the town to buy food.)

[9]The woman was rather taken aback, "How is it that you, a Jew, would ever ask a favor from a Samaritan?" (It was unheard of that a Jew would ever ask a favor from or even talk to a Samaritan.)

[10]Jesus began this way. "If you knew all that God wants to give you and if you knew who has asked for a drink, you would have asked Him for water, life-giving water."

[11]"Sir, You don't even have a container, and this well is deep, so how could you get this life-giving water? [12]Just who are You anyway? Are You, by chance, greater than our father Jacob who dug this well, drew water from it, and watered his cattle from it?"

[13]Now Jesus shared with her a spiritual truth. "Anyone and everyone who drinks water from this well will get thirsty again in a short while. [14]But the one who drinks the 'water' that I have to offer will always be satisfied, and this will then begin to pour from him to help others and to give life to them—eternal life!"

[15]"Please, please, may I have some of this water so that I won't need to keep coming here for more," she begged.

[16]"I shall tell you all about it if you will go get your husband and bring him here so that I can share the news with him also."

[17]"Oh, sir, I do not have a husband," she said.

[18]"You are quite right," Jesus assured her. "For even though you have had five

husbands, the man with whom you are now living is not your husband."

¹⁹Astonished at His knowledge of her past, she was forced to confess, "Sir, You have to be a prophet. And would You then settle an issue for me? ²⁰Traditionally, we Samaritans have been taught to worship God on this mountain, but you Jews claim that Jerusalem is the proper place to worship."

²¹He answered her question this way: "Woman, some day all ideas of where to worship will be of minor consequence; worship, real worship can be anywhere and everywhere. ²²You Samaritans worship, that is true, but your worship is not based on truth. Now we Jews have truth, and salvation will come through the Jews. ²³However, in the future, and even at the present time, sincere worshippers are worshipping the Father in their inmost being. This is the true worship the Father desires. ²⁴God is a spiritual being, that is, a being with unseen, vital qualities, and those who worship Him must worship Him in their inmost beings, their unseen but real selves."

²⁵The Samaritan woman then spoke up. "I know that the Messiah is coming, the One to be known as Christ, and when He appears He will clear up all these problems for us. Right?"

²⁶She was then astonished to hear Jesus' next statement. "I am He; I who am speaking to you right now!"

²⁷The disciples returned from their shopping trip just in time to hear the last of this conversation. They were a bit amazed that Jesus was talking to a woman, and a Samaritan at that. This was almost too much for them. Yet none of them had the boldness to confront Him over the issue.

²⁸As for the woman, she forgot about her water pot, hurried back into the village, and began sharing with the city fathers the things she had just experienced. ²⁹She urged them, "Come with me, and see for yourselves. This Man told me everything about my whole life story in accurate detail. Is it possible this is the Messiah?"

³⁰It was an impressive thing, and they did go with her to see Jesus. ³¹In the meantime the disciples offered Jesus some food, but He seemed uninterested, so caught up was He in the joy that someone had believed His message. ³²"Thank you, but I've been having food of a different sort."

³³"Oh, has someone brought food to Him?" they wondered among themselves.

³⁴Jesus read their minds as usual and answered them, "My food, My very life, is to do the will of the One who sent Me and to carry on His work to its completion. ³⁵You might be thinking that there are about four months until harvest time, but listen, look, and notice what is going on. Harvest time is here already. ³⁶He who reaps now will be certain of his wages, for he is gathering food from the one who sowed the seed. And now both of them will share in the joy. ³⁷You know the saying, 'One person sows the seed, and another reaps the harvest.' ³⁸Here is an example: You were sent to reap without having first sown any seed, for someone else had already done this. You were actually joining them in a grand effort."

³⁹As a result of this meeting with one woman, a large number of Samaritans believed on Jesus. The key statement seemed to be this one: "He told me everything I had done." ⁴⁰Still they were not satisfied until they had gone out to talk to Jesus themselves, begging Him to come and stay with them for a while, which He

did for two days. [41]So, many more became convinced that Jesus was the Messiah. [42]They were profoundly grateful that this woman had met Jesus, expressing themselves with statements such as this, "Your testimony was indeed impressive, but now that we have heard Him ourselves, we are completely convinced that He is the Messiah, the Savior of the world."

[43]Leaving Sychar, Jesus and the disciples traveled to Galilee, [44]even though He warned them that a prophet is seldom accepted in his own country. [45]Happily a rather large number of Galileans believed Him. They had been to Jerusalem at the time of the feast, had seen Him there, and had heard several of His talks.

[46]Once again in Cana where He had performed the miracle of turning water to wine, He was approached by a royal official from Capernaum [47]who had heard that Jesus was again in the area. He was trying to find Jesus, hoping that He could be persuaded to come and heal his son who was about to die. [48]But Jesus' response to his request did not give him much hope. "You seem to believe in Me only when you see some spectacular miracle performed."

[49]The poor man then earnestly begged Jesus, "Please come before my child dies."

[50]Imagine the joy he felt when he heard these words from Jesus, "You may return home; your son has been restored to health." He started on His way at once. [51]Before reaching home, the royal official was met by his slaves who told him the good news. "Sir, your son has recovered."

[52]"Let me ask you, about what time of day did he begin to get well?"

They answered, "Yesterday at about one o'clock in the afternoon the fever subsided." [53]That was the very time that Jesus

had told the father that the boy would get well. The grateful man, his family, and his slaves all became believers in Jesus. [54]This was the second miracle that Jesus performed in Galilee.

Chapter 5

[1]Later on Jesus went again to Jerusalem to attend one of the annual feasts. While there, He passed by the sheep gate. [2]Nearby, there was a pool known as "Bethesda," which was surrounded by five covered hallways. [3]In the shelter of these porch-like structures could be found a large number of disabled folk—blind, crippled, deformed, and sick—watching the water to detect the first stirring of the surface. [4]It was believed that an angel would occasionally descend from heaven, causing a rippling of the water. Then the first person who was able to get into the water after this mysterious rippling would be miraculously cured of whatever disability he had. [5]Among the ones waiting was a particularly pitiful case—a man who had been crippled for thirty-eight years, unable to walk.

[6]Jesus went up to him and began talking, learning of his plight, and then He abruptly asked, "Would you like to be cured and be normal again?" It seemed to be a superfluous question. Of course he would.

[7]But he answered Jesus sadly, "Sir, I have no one who will stay with me and rush me into the water when the agitation occurs, and someone else always gets in before I can get in."

[8]Try to realize how he must have felt when Jesus, in an authoritative voice, commanded him to get up and walk, "And take your bed roll with you." [9]At once, he attempted to obey that command and

discovered that he was fully restored to normal.

[10]Now it was the Sabbath, and presently one of the religious leaders caught sight of him carrying his bed roll. "Hey you! Don't you remember what day this is? You're breaking the Sabbath. Remember? No burdens on the Sabbath!"

[11]"Sir, I was only obeying the One who was able to heal me after thirty-eight years of disability. He told me to carry my pallet."

[12]"Well, who was it that told you such a thing as to pick up your bed and carry it on the Sabbath? I want to find Him."

[13]But the poor fellow did not know who it was, and Jesus was already lost in the crowd. The religious leader was frustrated and angry. [14]Later Jesus met the healed man in the temple. "Look at you, you are completely healed, so do not go on sinning, or you may find yourself worse off than you were before."

[15]While leaving the temple the exultant man found a Jewish leader and gladly reported that it was Jesus who had miraculously healed him. [16]This, then, was another episode that angered the Jews who stepped up their opposition to Jesus and increased their persecution of Him to the extent that they began to study ways to kill Him.

[17]When He was confronted, Jesus replied by reminding them, "My Father works on the Sabbath, and so do I. The work We do is helping others and blessing those in need."

[18]Now these leader were really angry. Not just because He had violated the Sabbath, but also because He had claimed to be the Son of God, making Himself equal with God. [19]In His attempt to help them understand His relationship to His Father, since accepting human nature, He explained, "Here are the facts. The Son can do nothing on His own. He must do as the Father does. In everything He must look to the Father and implicitly follow Him. [20]The Father loves His Son and is willing to communicate everything needed for His ministry, showing Him exactly what He should do at every moment. He will continue to reveal to His Son greater things than what you have seen in order that all may be adequately impressed. [21]The Father even raises the dead, and so will His Son raise up the ones assigned to Him. [22]The Father has given the Son the responsibility of making judgments in all these matters also, so that [23]the Son might be honored and respected as the Father is honored and respected. And whoever does not respect the Son does not respect the Father who sent Him here. [24]Positively and truly I am telling you. If you believe what I say, believing in the One who sent Me, you have everlasting life. You cannot be condemned but are the possessors of life, everlasting life.

[25]"It is an absolute truth that soon the time will come, indeed it is even right now the case, that the dead will hear the voice of God's Son and will live again. [26]Just as the Father has original life, so also does His Son have original life. [27]And moreover, the Father has given His Son the authority to make judgments regarding these matters. That is the purpose of His becoming a human being. [28]It is astonishing to believe that a dead body can be restored to life, and to believe that every dead person will one day be brought back to life is still more astonishing, and yet it is true. [29]They will indeed. Those who have chosen rightly will be resurrected to eternal life, and those who have rejected truth will be resurrected only to be condemned to eternal death.

[30]"As I was saying, I will not do these things on my own. I listen to My Father and judge accordingly. It must be correct because I choose the Father's will rather than My own. [31]If I should claim to do these things in My own name, I would not be telling the truth. [32]But there is one who witnesses My acts and sees to it that I am telling the truth. [33]Remember John? Of course you do. He was telling the truth about Me. [34]But I would not believe just because one person says it. I am telling you these things so that you all may be saved [35]John indeed was a bright light and was received as such by most of you, and you were right in accepting him. [36]But you have more evidence to believe Me than you had to believe John's message, for My teachings are accompanied by many bona fide miracles. These should convince you that the Father has sent Me.

[37]"Moreover the Father has given good evidence as to My mission, but you apparently have not heard His evidence. No, you have not heard His audible voice nor seen His visible form. [38]But neither have you allowed His word to take root in your minds, for if you had done so, you would now believe in the One He sent. [39]You have searched Scripture, that is true, and you expect to have eternal life by so doing, but Scripture tells of Me, pointing to Me as its main focus. [40]And sadly, you have not come to Me for life.

[41]"I have not received much acceptance from human beings, [42]even though I can read your minds and know your very thoughts. Face it, friends. You do not have God's love in your hearts. [43]I have come in My Father's name, and you have not accepted Me, but if someone comes along in his own name, you will likely accept

him. [44]I often wonder how you can believe at all when you are willing to believe mere humans and refuse to believe God's word and the real honor that He would like to heap upon you. [45]Now don't think that I am about to accuse you before God. You have other accusers, for instance Moses in whom you have placed your confidence. [46]But in fact, Moses' writings are about Me, and if you had really believed Moses, you would believe Me. [47]And if you do not believe him, you can't be expected to believe Me, of whom he wrote."

Chapter 6

[1]After this discourse, Jesus led His disciples to the Sea of Galilee, also known as the Sea of Tiberias, followed by a large number of people. [2]His miracles had become well known and were perhaps the chief reason for attracting so many watchers. They wanted to see more, especially healings. [3]On a hillside above the lake, He invited His disciples to sit down. [4]It was nearly time for Passover; thus, it was springtime and the natural world was beautiful. [5]The day passed with an immense congregation listening, but Jesus became concerned about them, for they had not eaten for so long.

"Philip, do you think it will be possible to find a place to buy food for all these hungry people?" He asked. [6]Actually He was just testing Philip, for He already knew what He was about to do.

[7]Philip made some estimates in his mind and calculated what this would require. "It would take more than a thousand dollars worth of bread to feed all these people, and even that much would hardly give them more than a morsel," he reported.

⁸Right then Andrew came up with this bit of information. ⁹"Here is a little fellow who has five barley rolls and two small fishes, but this would not even start to feed this many."

¹⁰"Great," Jesus answered, "have everyone sit down." There were about five thousand men present where this took place, and the grass was new and clean—a nice place for a picnic lunch. ¹¹Then Jesus took those five rolls and those two fishes, gave thanks to God, and passed them to the disciples who in turn distributed some to all present. The food multiplied in His hands until all were satisfied. ¹²When all were filled, Jesus had the disciples collect the surplus food so none would be wasted. ¹³Remarkably there were twelve basketfuls of perfectly good food left over! ¹⁴Those five thousand people were in awe at this display of miraculous power. This must be the prophet they had long expected! ¹⁵Jesus was able to sense the excitement prevailing and knew that a movement was planned to force Him to be king, so He quietly left for a lonely spot in the hills.

¹⁶After the crowd had dispersed the disciples also left for the lake, ¹⁷boarding the boat and starting for Capernaum. By that time it was dark. ¹⁸A strong wind began to blow before they had gone far, and soon the waves were dangerously high. ¹⁹They had rowed perhaps a mile or a mile and a half when out on the sea they spotted the form of a man walking on the water toward their boat. Fear seized them. ²⁰But it was Jesus. He called out to them, "It is I, don't be afraid." ²¹So they helped Him into the boat, greatly relieved. The next thing they knew they were home.

²²Back at the place where the picnic meal had been provided, some noticed that the disciples did not have Jesus with them and He was nowhere to be seen. ²³There were a few other boats there, and these owners also began to return home, ²⁴but their chief concern was Jesus. Where was He? They searched for Him but to no avail. ²⁵Of course, He was safe in Capernaum when they arrived. Many asked Him, "How did You get here?"

²⁶Jesus replied, "You are searching for Me for the wrong reason. You enjoyed the meal, but I want to give you something of far greater value. ²⁷May I give you some good advice? Don't spend all your energy just to supply yourselves with ordinary food, but rather let those efforts be spent in trying to get food that is eternal—food that the Son of man is ready to give you. God our Father has certified Him as His representative on earth."

²⁸Someone then asked, "What shall we do in order to be sure of doing God's will?"

²⁹Quickly came the answer, "God's will is for you to believe in the One God has sent to you."

³⁰Next question: "What sign can You give us that will show that You and Your work can be completely trustworthy? ³¹Our fathers were given manna out in the wilderness. The scripture immortalizes that experience in these words, 'He gave them bread from heaven to eat.'"

³²Jesus responded in this way: "Truly I tell you, Moses was not the one who gave you the bread from heaven. He did show our forefathers some miraculous signs, but it was God working. And now God is giving you the real heavenly bread. ³³You see, God's real bread is the One sent from heaven to give life to the world."

³⁴They spoke up, "Lord give us this bread forever."

[35]Jesus said, "I am the bread of life. Whoever comes to Me will never go hungry; whoever believes in Me will not be thirsty." [36]As I said before, "You here who have seen Me do not yet believe. [37]As many as My Father gives Me will come to Me in search of life, and be assured, those who come to Me will never be turned down. [38]For I left heaven and came to this world for one reason—it was My Father's will. [39]And His will is to save all who come to Me and to resurrect them at the last day. [40]Yes, this is God's will. Everyone who believes in His Son shall have everlasting life. I will resurrect him at the last day."

[41]There was a murmur of dissent among the listening Jews as they heard these things, especially His statement that He had come down from heaven. [42]"Hey, is not this Jesus, son of Joseph? Don't we know His father and mother? How can He say, 'I came down from heaven?'"

[43]The answer came, "Please do not reject what I am telling you. [44]No one will come to Me for salvation unless My Father impresses him to come, and if he comes, I will raise him from death at the last day. [45]You are acquainted with the scripture, 'God shall teach everyone' (Isaiah 54:13). When God teaches them they will come to Me for salvation. [46]Of course, no one has actually seen the Father except the One who was with the Father. [47]I am telling you positively and truthfully an astonishing fact. Please listen carefully. Anyone and everyone who puts their trust in Me has everlasting life! [48]I am that 'bread of life' that I was talking about. [49]The bread from heaven that was given by God to your ancestors was temporal food and, of course, could not give them eternal life. Now they are all dead. [50]But this 'bread' from heaven

has the power to give you eternal life. [51]Get this please, for it is important. I am living 'bread,' and if you 'eat' Me, you will live forever. I am giving My flesh so that humans may have eternal life."

[52]This statement stirred up a flurry of questions among the Jews. They took these statements literally rather than figuratively. "How can this Man give us His flesh to eat?"

[53]But Jesus emphasized it again, "Unless you eat the flesh and drink the blood of this Son of man, you have no life. [54]But if you do this, you possess eternal life, and I will resurrect you at the last day. [55]My flesh is unique food; My blood is a unique beverage. [56]Anyone who 'eats' My flesh and 'drinks' My blood will live through Me. He in Me; I in him. [57]Just as I live through the Father who sent Me, whoever 'eats' Me will live through Me. [58]This body is the real 'bread' that came down from heaven. It can be compared to the manna that was given and sustained temporal life, but as I said, everyone who ate it has died. This 'bread' will give eternal life to the one who eats it."

[59]This was the message that He presented to the people in the Capernaum synagogue. [60]A number of His followers wrestled with these ideas. "He has given us something I can hardly believe. How about you?"

[61]Jesus was aware of their questionings, so He asked them, "Do these ideas seem offensive to you? [62]What will you say if this Son of man returns to heaven where He came from? [63]Let me be more specific. It is not My physical flesh that is important. Rather, My words are vital to your eternal life—your breath of life. [64]I am aware that some of you do not accept this and do not believe what I have just told you."

Remember, Jesus knew all along who believed Him and trusted Him and who did not believe or trust Him. He even knew at this time who would betray Him. [65]He added this, "Any of you who believe Me and trusts in Me has been impressed to do so by My Father."

[66]Sadly, a significant number of His followers decided to give up on Him at this time. [67]So Jesus asked the twelve, "Are you also planning to leave Me?"

[68]But Peter promptly answered, "Oh no, Lord. If we left You where could we go. You have words of eternal life. [69]Yes, we are completely convinced that You are the Messiah, the anointed Son of the living God."

[70]In Jesus' reply he uttered a prophetic statement, "Yes, I have chosen you twelve, all of you, but one of you is a devil."

[71]This was shocking to say the least, and the twelve failed to grasp His meaning until after the betrayal by Judas Iscariot.

Chapter 7

[1]After this episode Jesus returned to Galilee, shunning Judea because the leaders there were plotting to kill Him. [2]The Feast of Tabernacles was approaching, but He lingered in Galilee. [3]Just before the beginning of the feast, His brothers came to Him and urged that He go back to Judea to the feast to demonstrate His power there as He had been doing in Galilee.

[4]"You have made some large claims, so expand Your influence so the whole world will know if You are indeed what You profess to be." [5]Unfortunately, these brothers had no confidence in Him at that time.

[6]"I must do everything at just the right time," He replied. "You may choose to do anything at any time, [7]but the world does not hate you as I am hated. They hate Me because I have exposed their sins. [8]Naturally I suppose you wish to attend the feast, but until I am told by My Father to go, I dare not go." [9]So He stayed in Galilee for a little time. [10]After His brothers had left, God indicated to Jesus that He should go but to remain as much out of the public eye as possible.

[11]The Jewish leaders looked for Him at the feast. [12]He was the topic of private conversation everywhere. Some claimed that He was a good man. Others declared the opposite, "No, He is deceiving our people." [13]Out in public very few said anything about Him because of the hostility of the leading Jews. [14]About halfway through the feast, Jesus went to the temple where He taught those who were willing to listen. [15]Some leading men were there too and were amazed, "How can this uneducated man have so much knowledge and wisdom?" they asked.

[16]Jesus heard their question and answered, "My teaching is not something I have thought out for Myself—it is what the One who sent Me directs Me to teach. [17]Whoever is willing to obey Him will know whether My teaching harmonizes with God's will or whether I am only teaching My own ideas. [18]A person who teaches his own ideas is one who only wants to make a big name for himself, but the person who teaches what the One who sent Him directs can be depended on to teach truth. [19]All of you revere Moses, who gave us the law, but think this through now. You are definitely breaking that law. How? By planning to kill Me."

[20]"Oh come now, You must be demon-possessed. Who is planning to kill You?"

[21]Jesus did not answer their question, but He reminded them of a recent miracle that triggered their anger. "You

were amazed at that time," He told them. [22]"Remember that the rite of circumcision was given to us by the nation's fathers and supported by Moses, and it should be done on the eighth day, even if that day fell on the Sabbath. [23]Now, if a person believes that it is appropriate to circumcise on the Sabbath in order to follow the law, are you ready to be angry with Me because I healed a cripple on the Sabbath? [24]Be honest now, and decide this issue correctly."

[25]Some citizens of Jerusalem were listening to all that had been going on and asked, "Is not this the Man that the leaders are planning to kill? [26]But look, He is very open, and they don't do anything about it. Do you suppose that they believe He is the Messiah? [27]It surely is significant that we know where this Man comes from, and when the Messiah arrives, it is unthinkable that any will know where He came from."

[28]Jesus had to answer that idea. "It is indeed true that you know where I came from and that you know Me this well. However, I have not come just because it was My idea. I was sent by One who was true, and you do not seem to know Him at all. [29]I know Him well. He is the One who sent Me here."

[30]At this statement a great urge to seize Jesus came over the leaders, but they decided to wait. And the real reason was that God wanted Him to be free for a time to keep teaching the ones who would listen to truth. [31]He had a large following at the time, most of whom accepted Him as the Messiah. Their position was this: When the Messiah comes, could we expect more from Him than we have seen done by this Man? [32]The Pharisees were aware of His popularity, but in spite of this they sent police to arrest Him.

[33]Jesus spoke kindly to them, "Friends, I am going to be with you for only a short time longer, then I shall return to Him who sent Me. [34]Then, even if you search for Me, you will be unable to find Me or follow Me to where I go."

[35]This statement confused them. Where could He possibly go and never be found? Will He go to our scattered people all over the world, or will He go to the Gentiles and begin teaching them? [36]A real puzzling statement: "You will look for Me but will be unable to find Me."

[37]The last day of the feast arrived. Jesus once again boldly invited the people, "If you are still thirsting for more, keep coming for this water I am offering. It is the water of life. [38]For if you believe in Me, the scripture will be fulfilled which states, 'Out of Him will gush living water, like a river.'"

[39]This was a symbolic statement and applied to the Holy Spirit whom His believers would receive after Christ was glorified. [40]A large number of people became convinced that He must be "that Prophet," the one who had been anticipated since Moses' time. [41]Others said, "This is the Messiah," but others expressed doubt that the Messiah could come from Galilee. [42]They remembered Micah 5:2, which prophesied that Christ should come from Bethlehem, David's city. [43]So there was disagreement as to who Jesus really was.

[44]Some were ready to arrest Him then and there but were reluctant to do so, and nothing was done. [45]The priests and leading rulers and Pharisees summoned the police who had been sent to arrest Jesus and demanded, "Why haven't you arrested Him as you were ordered to do?"

[46]They quickly explained the reason, "Sirs, we have never heard anyone give

such profound, beautiful teachings as this Man is doing."

[47]"Oh, then," the Pharisees sneered, "you are gullible enough to be deceived by Him? [48]Look, have any of our rulers or any Pharisees believed Him? [49]It is only those who are not well acquainted with the law who have believed on Him, and of course, these are all doomed to receive God's curse."

[50]Just then Nicodemus stood up and asked for the floor. Remember, he was the one who had interviewed Jesus during the night, and he was one of the highest among the rulers. [51]He began with a question that shook them up. "Does our law allow a person to be condemned before He has opportunity to defend Himself and before His doings have been thoroughly reviewed?"

[52]"Oh," they retorted, "you must also be from Galilee. You had better check the prophecies, for in none of them will you find that a prophet is to come from Galilee." [53]This was the last thing said before the group broke up and went home.

Chapter 8

[1]Jesus left the temple and went to the Mount of Olives, [2]but early the next morning He was back at the temple surrounded by large numbers of people. So He sat down and began teaching them. [3]In the meantime, the scribes and Pharisees had been plotting again. They had caught a woman in the act of adultery and figured that this might be a case in which they could trap Jesus. So they brought the woman to Him.

[4]"Sorry to interrupt you, sir, but we have a problem. We have here a woman who was caught in adultery, in the very act. [5]According to Moses she should be stoned. (They neglected to say that her lover should also be stoned.) But what is Your advice in this case?" They felt certain that they could accuse Him regardless of His answer. If He said, "Yes, go ahead and stone her," they would report Him to the Romans who would arrest Him for taking a capital offense into His own hands. On the other hand, if He should say, "No, do not stone her," they could accuse Him of rebellion against the law of Moses. [6]*Surely we have got Him at last*, they thought.

But as they waited for His answer, He stooped down and began to write in the dust of the pavement. [7]They kept needling Him for His answer, but He was silent until He finished writing. Then He stood up, faced them, and said, "Let the first stone be thrown by the one who is sinless." [8]He then stooped down and wrote some more. [9]The oldest of them silently walked away after reading what had been written, then the next oldest, then the next, until all had gone away. Now only the accused woman was left. She was still standing there in fear. [10]"Ma'am, where are your accusers? Has no one stayed to condemn you?"

[11]"No, my Lord."

Jesus spoke kindly, "Listen, my dear, I am not condemning you either. You may go, but do not keep on sinning." [12]She left with a new resolve.

Then Jesus resumed His teaching of the people. "I am the light of this world. If you will only follow Me, you will not be in darkness but in life-giving light."

[13]Another interruption by a Pharisee took place, "Wait a minute there. You are only trying to exalt Yourself, and You are lying."

[14]"No, gentlemen, I am telling you the truth even though I am telling of Myself.

For I know where I came from and where I am going. You do not happen to know those facts. [15]You are making decisions according to what things appear to be. I am not in the business of judging but, [16]even if I should act as judge, My decision would be true because I am not doing anything on My own. I have the Father as witness, and He sent Me. [17]You are aware, I am sure, that the scripture requires the testimony of two in order to establish truth. [18]Well, my Father has been testifying of Me, and I have been testifying on My own behalf."

[19]"But," they countered, "where is Your Father? We haven't seen Him around here."

"Actually," Jesus replied, "you really don't know My Father, nor do you really know Me. If you had known Me, you would have known My Father also."

[20]Jesus was speaking right in the treasury area where people were coming to give their donations to the temple service. In spite of their bitter hatred toward Him, they could not bring themselves to capture Him. It just did not seem to be the right time.

[21]He continued, "I am going forward doing My job, and you leaders will look for Me one day and will not be able to find Me. You will die as a result of your sins. And you will never be able to follow Me where I am going."

[22]"Wait a minute," they said, "do you suppose He may commit suicide? That might explain why He says we cannot follow Him."

[23]"You people are thinking only of low, worldly things. I am absorbed in heavenly goals. I don't really belong to this world at all. [24]This is why I assured you that you must die in your sins, because if you do not believe in Me, believe that I AM, there is no hope for you."

[25]"Who on earth do You think You are?" they cried out.

"I am who I have always been. [26]I could go on and on telling you many things, but I must speak only the very things that I am told to speak by the One who sent Me. He is altogether true, and what I have told you, I received first from Him."

[27]They could not grasp the fact that He was speaking of God the Father. [28]He continued, "After you have lifted Me up, you will know that I AM, and that I am in perfect agreement with My Father in My words and in My lifestyle. [29]Yes, and He is always with Me. I am not alone in this world, and therefore, I always act in harmony with His will."

[30]Jesus' words were so persuasive that many even in the upper class of Jews believed Him. [31]"Now you dear people who believe what I am telling you, I want you to continue to learn and believe, for if you do the world will have just the ones that are needed, [32]and furthermore, you will be learning and understanding more and more truth. Truth that will set you free. [33]They then wanted to know just what He meant by being "free."

"You know that we are all descendants of Abraham and have never been controlled by any foreign nation. What are you freeing us from?"

[34]" I am referring to the fact that a person who sins is a slave of sin. This is far more important than a national consideration. I am able to free you from sin's slavery. [35]Now a slave has no legal rights in any home, but the son has preeminence in the home. [36]And if the Son makes you free from sin, you will indeed be free. [37]Of course, I am aware that you are Abraham's descendants, but your nation, through

its leaders is bent on killing Me and all because of their rejection of My messages to you. [38]I am giving you the things that I have in common with My Father, and you are doing things that you learned from your father."

[39]"Just a minute there! We are children of Abraham, and don't forget it!"

But Jesus contradicted them. "No, you are not truly Abraham's children in its true sense, for if you were, you would act like Abraham and do the things Abraham did. [40]And Abraham would never plot a murder. And not only murder, but murder of a Man who is sincerely trying to bring truth to you—truth that is direct from God. Never would Abraham have been guilty of such a thing."

[41]Here they retorted, "Look, we are not illegitimate children. God is our father."

[42]"I'm sorry, but no you are not. If God were your father you would love others; you would even love Me, for I came directly from God. He sent Me. [43]Let Me ask you a question, Why is it that you do not seem to understand what I am telling you? It's because you do not want to believe it. [44]You, I am sorry to have to admit, are children of the devil. He was the original murderer, because he rejected truth, for there is no truth whatsoever in him. When he tells lies, he is speaking out of his own heart, for he is a liar and the father of all liars. [45]Now the reason I am not believed is that I am telling you the truth. [46]Can any of you point out sin in Me? When I speak truth, why is it so hard to believe? [47]God's children listen to and obey God. This is perhaps why you do not seem to be listening. You are not God's family after all."

[48]They came right back with sarcasm. "Were we not amazingly accurate in our evaluation of You when we announced that You have been possessed by a demon and are a Samaritan?"

[49]"No, folks, I am not demon-possessed; I am honoring My Father, and you are trying to discredit Me. [50]I am not even trying to boast of My own greatness, but be assured that there is One who right now is passing judgment on all of us. [51]Truly, I say to you, if anyone accepts and follows My teaching that person will avoid the second death."

[52]This really blew their minds. "Now we are even more certain that you are demon-possessed. Abraham is dead, the prophets are dead, and here You are trying to tell us that if we believe Your teachings we will not die. [53]Are You so great that You can boast of being greater than Abraham who is now dead, greater than the prophets who are all dead? Just who do You claim to be?"

[54]His reply was soft and kind. "If I were trying to promote My own honor, it would be utterly meaningless but My Father has honored Me and you claim Him as your God. [55]But honestly, you do not know Him, and the fact is that I know Him. I dare not deny that I know Him, for that would make Me a liar. Yes, I truly do obey Him. [56]Your revered father Abraham was permitted to see Me and rejoiced in the privilege."

[57]"Wait a minute," they interrupted. "You are not even fifty years old, and you have the audacity to say that you saw Abraham and that he saw You?"

[58]Very earnestly Jesus now got to the real issue, trying to persuade them who He really was. "Truthfully, I say—please believe Me—before Abraham lived, I existed. Remember the name. I AM? That

is who I am." [59]At this point they became so angry that they picked up stones and threatened to kill Him on the spot. But He was nowhere to be seen. He had slipped right through the crowd and disappeared.

Chapter 9

[1]One day while Jesus was mingling with the general public, He met a man who was born blind. [2]*Here's a chance*, thought the disciples, *to get an answer to a troubling theological question*. "Teacher," they asked, "here is a man who is blind, and it must have been because of some sin. Who is the sinner, the man himself or his parent?"

[3]"Wrong in both ideas," Jesus answered. "It was not because of any specific sin of his or of his parents that he was born blind. In this case his blindness can be helpful in learning how God deals with such unfortunate people. [4]I shall demonstrate how My Father, who sent Me here, wants Me to act. And now is the opportune time, for not long from now such opportunities will no longer be available. [5]As long as I am in this world, I shall continue to bring enlightenment."

[6]He then did a strange thing. He mixed a little of his own saliva with a little common soil until it was pliable, and then He put some of this clay on the eyelids of the blind man. [7]After that He told the man, "Go wash this clay off in the pool that is called Siloam (a name that means "sent"). The man obeyed. He felt his way to the pool and washed off the clay. From that moment his vision was normal.

[8]His neighbors and others who had known him to be blind were half unbelieving when they first saw him. "Can this be the man who used to sit here and beg every day?" they asked.

[9]One person strongly believed it was the same man, but another differed. "Yes, he may look a lot like that man, but it can't be the same man."

The one who had just received his eyesight settled the matter, "I am the one."

[10]Naturally they wanted to know how his sight had been restored. "What happened? What did you do? This is hard to believe."

[11]"Well, it was like this. A man known as Jesus walked over to me and stopped. He made a little clay from saliva and dirt and put it on my eyes. He then told me to go and wash it off in the pool of Siloam. I did so and came back with good eyesight!"

[12]"Where, oh where, is this man?" they asked.

"Sorry, but I myself don't know," he had to reply.

[13]They then persuaded him to present himself to the Pharisees. Such a miracle needed to be documented. [14]And by the way, the miracle had been performed on the Sabbath. [15]The Pharisees decided to question the man, "How is it that you are now able to see? You were blind from birth, we understand."

[16]Some of those Pharisees were even critical. "The person who did this to you obviously was not using God's power to perform a miracle on you," they assured him. "He must be a sinner. Had He been a worshipper of God He would have never performed this thing on the Sabbath!"

But others pointed out, "How on earth could a sinner do such a miracle as this?" Thus there was disagreement among them.

[17]They then questioned the man himself again. "What do you think about Him?"

"Easy, sirs, He is a prophet."

[18]Yet these leaders would not believe that the man had ever been blind and then had received this miracle until they had interviewed his parents. [19]So they went to them and questioned them as well. "Is this man your son, and do you say that he was born blind? If so, how is it that he can see now?"

[20]They would only answer two of the questions. "Yes, he is our son, and yes, he was blind from birth. [21]As to how he gained his eyesight, or who performed the miracle, we have no idea. Our son is an adult. Ask him."

[22]They were guarded in their answers, for they had learned that anyone who believed in Jesus would be disfellowshipped from the synagogue. [23]That is why they suggested that he answer their questions himself. [24]So they interviewed him again, "Look, you need to thank God for your miracle. This Man who claimed to have done it is a sinner. Of that you may be certain."

[25]"Well, sinner or not, I do not know. But I do know one important fact. I was blind all my life, and now I can see."

[26]"Tell us," they asked again, "what did He do to give you normal sight?"

[27]"You must have forgotten to listen when I told you about that. Or maybe your hearing is poor. Or maybe you want to hear the wonderful story again so you can become His disciples?"

[28]"Perish the thought, fellow," they sneered. "You perhaps are one of His disciples, but we are disciples of Moses. [29]We know certainly that God spoke through Moses, but as for this Man, we don't know where He came from nor where He is going."

[30]"Really now?" he answered them with perhaps a touch of sarcasm. "You are the spiritual leaders and know the prophecies well, and yet here is a Man who had the miracle-working power to give sight to a man who was born blind, and yet you have no idea who He is? [31]We are all taught that a rebellious sinner is not likely to have his prayers answered, while a sincere worshipper of God, one who obeys God, can have his prayers answered. [32]In all human history, since the day of creation, there has never been a person who received sight after being born blind. [33]The evidence is overwhelming. If this Man is not from God, He could have done absolutely nothing about my vision."

[34]"Look, fella, don't think that you are qualified to become our teachers! The very idea! You obviously were suffering the results of your parents' sins and are in no way qualified to make any assessment in this case! As of this moment, you are excommunicated. Do you understand?"

[35]The news of his excommunication reached Jesus, and right away He found him and asked this vital question, "Do you still believe in the Son of God?"

[36]"Sir, who is the Son of God? I truly want to believe in Him."

Gently Jesus spoke, "Now you are able to see, and you are seeing Him at this moment and are listening to His voice."

[38]Falling on his knees, the grateful man confessed, "Lord, I do believe."

Then Jesus declared, [39]"I have come to this world in order to give sight to those unable to see and to expose the blindness of those who profess to see but do not really see clearly."

[40]Some of the Pharisees heard Jesus making this statement and asked Him, "Then are You saying that we are blind?"

[41]"If you were blind, that would not be a sin, but when you profess to be able to

see and understand everything, when in fact you are blind to the kingdom of God, you are then sinning."

Chapter 10

¹"I am telling you the truth. If a person gets into a sheepfold by some way other than the door, he is a thief or a robber. ²But the one who goes in at the door is the shepherd. ³He calls the porter, then the porter opens the door. He then calls his own sheep. His sheep know his voice and come out, and straight to the pasture they go, following the shepherd. ⁴After leaving the fold, he will continue to lead them through the day, wherever it is best for them to go. They will follow him, for they know him so well that they recognize his voice and trust him completely. ⁵If anyone but the owner attempts to lead them, they will refuse to go. They may even run away from him because that voice is not the one they trust."

⁶As Jesus was presenting this parable, He perceived that they were not getting the point, ⁷so He explained it further. "I am telling you something vital, so please believe Me. I am the door in the parable. ⁸Everyone who has preceded Me is a thief or a robber in the parable. The sheep refused to follow them, ⁹but those who have followed Me will all be saved. They will be like the sheep, freely going in and out to the pasture. ¹⁰A thief comes for only one purpose: to steal, to kill, or to destroy. I have come to bring life, everlasting life. ¹¹I am the good shepherd, the shepherd who risks and actually sacrifices His life for His sheep. ¹²This is in contrast to the hired man who does not own the sheep. If he saw a wolf coming, he would think first about his own safety and run away, leaving the sheep to be scattered and killed. ¹³It is

apparent that his first interest is his own security and not the safety of the sheep. ¹⁴But I really care for My sheep. I know them and they know Me, ¹⁵just as My Father and I know each other. And I have come to give My life for My sheep. ¹⁶I have other sheep than those in this fold. And I want to bring them all together into one eternal fold where there will be only one shepherd. ¹⁷My Father loves Me so much that He will restore My life after I have sacrificed it. ¹⁸Please do not blame anyone for My losing My life; I do it freely. I had the choice and that choice is to give My life and accomplish My goal, the saving of My sheep. I also have the authority from My Father to restore My life again. It is His will that I do so."

¹⁹The leaders who heard these things were divided in their interpretation of His statements. ²⁰Many of them said, "He is possessed by a demon! Why listen to Him?"

²¹Others felt this way, "No, these cannot be the teachings of a devil. Can a devil make blind eyes have good vision?"

²²The following winter at the time of the Feast of Dedication in Jerusalem, ²³Jesus was again in the temple teaching on Solomon's porch. ²⁴Many leading Jews surrounded Him and began another interrogation. "Please answer a few questions for us. We need to know the truth. If you are the Messiah, tell us plainly."

²⁵"Do you remember that I have already answered this question? You did not believe Me then, even though the things I did were strong evidences that I was doing them in the name of My Father. ²⁶I already know that you will not believe, and it is as I said, you are not 'sheep' of mine. You belong to another shepherd.

27My sheep respond to My voice; they follow Me and I know them. 28I have a gift of eternal life for them. They will never perish, and no one can ever take them from Me. 29My Father, who is greater than I, has given them to Me, and no one can take them from My Father. 30Can you grasp it? My Father and I are one unit."

31As He spoke these words, some of the leaders picked up stones as if to stone Him. 32But He still spoke calmly to them. "I have done many good things for our people in My Father's name. For which of these are you threatening to stone Me?"

33"You do not seem to understand. We would not think of stoning You because of good things You have done, but because You have been guilty of blasphemy. You have actually claimed to be God!"

34Jesus replied, "Do you remember reading in the Psalms, 'I have said, "You are gods"?' (Psalm 82:6). 35If he could call them gods he who proclaimed God's will, and the scripture is infallible, 36then beware of a tendency to charge with blasphemy One whom the Father has sanctified when He sent Him into the world, One who simply states truth when He says, 'I am the Son of God.' 37If My life and My deeds are not those of My Father, I would not ask you to believe in Me whatever claims I might have made. 38But if My works are those of My Father, then you should accept them as evidence and become believers, accepting the truth that My Father and I are one."

39Again they moved to capture Him, but He evaded them and left Jerusalem, 40travelling to a place beyond Jordan, where John had been baptizing. Here He stayed for some time. 41Many people came to Him there, and their impression of Him was this: "Even John did not perform miracles, but he certainly told us the truth about this Man." 42A large following was constantly there with Him.

Chapter 11

1It was here that Jesus first received a message asking Him to come to Bethany for a personal friend, Lazarus, was seriously ill. He was the brother of Mary and Martha. 2This Mary was the one who anointed Jesus with the costly ointment and wiped His feet with her hair. 3The sisters had sent a messenger to Jesus and were desperately hoping for a miracle in his behalf. But the message only said, "The one You love is very ill." 4The news was shared with His disciples, then He added, "This sickness is one that will bring glory to God and His Son."

5It must be reported here that Mary, Martha, and Lazarus were personal friends of Jesus and very much like a family to Him. 6Yet it was two days later that He announced to His disciples that they would go to Bethany. 7"Let us go back to Judea," He said.

8His disciples were really concerned about the plan. "Lord, the Jews there wanted to kill You. Are You sure You want to go back?"

9"It's like this," replied Jesus, "there are only twelve hours of the day in which to work, and if a person does his duty while the opportunity is open, he is not likely to make a mistake, 10but if he tries to work in the dark, he is almost certain to stumble and fall due to the darkness. 11Now, our friend Lazarus is sleeping, but I need to go there and wake him from his sleep."

12"Oh, good," they answered. "If he is asleep, he is likely on the way to recovery."

13But when Jesus talked of sleep, he meant that Lazarus was dead, and the disciples thought he had been speaking of the rest in sleep. [14]He was sad as He corrected their idea. "Lazarus is dead, [15]and I am thankful that I was not there at the time, for as things are now, you will have further evidence to strengthen your faith in Me. So let us be on our way."

[16]Thomas spoke up, "Let us go with Jesus, even though it is likely that we will have to die with Him."

[17]So they made their way back to Bethany. Jesus had been right. Lazarus was dead and had been dead for four days already. [18]Lazarus had a lot of friends in Jerusalem, which was only a couple miles away, [19]and these were already at the home to help in comforting Mary and Martha. [20]The word got to Martha that Jesus was nearly there, so she left the house and went to meet Him. [21]She poured out her heart, "Oh, if only You could have been here, my brother would not have died. [22]And even now I know that whatever You ask of God will be done. He always answers Your prayers."

[23]"Martha, your brother will live again," Jesus assured her.

[24]"Yes, I know that he will live again at the resurrection day, but I need him now."

[25]"Remember, Martha, I am the resurrection and the life. Everyone who believes in Me need not fear death, because they will live again. [26]And those who live at the resurrection day will never die. You do believe this, don't you, Martha?"

[27]"Oh, yes, I believe that You are the Son of God, the One we have been expecting for so long." [28]She left to tell Mary, "Mary, the Teacher is here and wants to see you."

[29]Now it was Mary's turn to go and meet Jesus. [30]Jesus had not yet reached the town and was right where Martha had met Him.

[31]At the house were a number of family friends, and they all supposed that she had left to weep at Lazarus' grave. But she only wanted to see Jesus. [32]She fell at Jesus' feet with the sorrowful wail, "If only You had been here, my brother would not have died."

[33]Recognizing her grief and the sorrow of all who were there, He Himself experienced intense sorrow and dismay. [34]"Where is his tomb?" He asked.

"Follow us."

[35]Jesus wept. [36]Their friends were moved to see Jesus crying. "Look there, He must have loved Lazarus a great deal."

[37]Some of the cynics expressed doubt, saying, "Couldn't He who brought sight to the blind prevent the death of His friend if He really is who He claims to be?"

[38]When they reached the tomb, Jesus, still weeping, ordered that the large stone covering the entrance be rolled away. "Remove that stone."

[39]Martha immediately protested, "Lord, please! He has been dead four days now and is already decomposing and putrid."

[40]"But did I not assure you, Martha, that if you believe you will see the glory of God?"

[41]Then volunteers went ahead and rolled back the huge stone. When this had been done, Jesus paused and faced upward to heaven and prayed. "Father, I thank You for hearing My prayer today. [42]Of course, You always hear Me, but today is a special occasion for those who are here with Me, and they need to know that You have sent Me. They will soon have convincing evidence." [43]As soon as His prayer was finished, Jesus ordered in a loud, authoritative voice, "Lazarus, come out of that tomb!" [44]He came out walking but still wrapped

in grave clothes. Even his face was covered with a cloth. "Now unwrap the poor man!" His command was obeyed at once. ⁴⁵Everyone present was stunned and silent. It was a tremendous experience. Many of those friends who had come to mourn with Mary and Martha believed in Jesus from that time onward.

⁴⁶But others, sadly enough, went right to the Jewish leaders, those who opposed Jesus, and reported to them what had happened. ⁴⁷A meeting was called at once to deal with this new development. The chief priests and Pharisees were in a crisis. "What can we do, gentlemen? What must we do? This man is truly a miracle worker. ⁴⁸If we just sit here and do nothing, everyone will soon believe in Him and who knows what the Romans will decide to do in such a critical circumstance? Those Romans could completely destroy this whole nation."

⁴⁹One of them, the high priest for that year, by the name of Caiaphas, spoke up. "You don't know the half of what may happen. ⁵⁰It is obvious what we must do. Far better that one life be destroyed than to have the whole nation perish!"

⁵¹This was actually a prophetic statement though not intended to be such. This priest had just predicted that Jesus would die for the nation. ⁵²And not only for that nation, but for the whole human race, scattered out over the whole earth. ⁵³Beginning with that meeting they made definite plans to have Jesus executed. ⁵⁴Knowing their plans, Jesus took His disciples and left the area, going to a place in Ephraim near the wilderness where they stayed for some time. ⁵⁵As Passover time neared, people began wending their way to Jerusalem to engage in purification rites before the actual Passover. ⁵⁶It seemed that all were interested in Jesus, and their conversations were mainly about Him. "What do you think? Will He come to Passover?" This was the topic on everyone's mind. ⁵⁷The chief priests and Pharisees had issued a public plea asking that if anyone saw Jesus to report to them at once. They wanted to capture Him if possible at the Passover celebration time.

Chapter 12

¹It was now just six days before Passover, and Jesus returned to Bethany and went to the home of Lazarus who had been raised from the dead. ²A supper in honor of Jesus was prepared, and Lazarus sat next to Jesus while Martha, as usual, was serving. ³While the meal was in progress, Mary brought in a container of pure nard, very costly, and anointed Jesus' feet then wiped them with her hair. The whole house was filled with the fragrance. ⁴This act stirred up the ire of Judas Iscariot, who was already contemplating betraying Jesus.

⁵"Well, why on earth such extravagance? Just think! It could have been sold for a year's wages and the money given to the poor!" ⁶Now Judas didn't really have that much compassion for the poor, but remember, he was the treasurer for the group and would have had access to the money if it had been sold. (He was really an embezzler.)

⁷Very gently Jesus replied to Judas, "Please do not scold her for this. She has kept this for a long time, knowing that she would soon need it at the time of My burial. ⁸You will always have poor people to help, but you will not always have Me."

⁹The word was spreading rapidly among the Jewish authorities that Jesus was

at Bethany, and a rather large number of visitors began going there to see Him and, of course, Lazarus who had been raised from the dead. [10]But the leaders among them, priests for the most part, caucused in an attempt to come up with some plan to have Lazarus executed! [11]This became an urgent priority with them because of the great increase in people who now believed in Jesus.

[12]The very next day a large number of people who had come for the celebration of Passover heard that Jesus was on His way to the city. [13]They went out to meet Him carrying palm branches and chanting, "Hosanna! Blessed is the king of Israel who is coming in the name of the Lord." [14]When Jesus had found a young donkey, He mounted it and rode toward the city. [15]This was in fulfillment of a prophecy written hundreds of years before by Zechariah: "Daughters of Jerusalem, forget your fears, for your king is coming, riding on an unbroken donkey colt" (Zechariah 9:9). [16]The disciples failed to recognize these fulfilling prophecies until after the resurrection of Jesus. Then they began to apply them to Jesus.

[17]Travelling with Jesus were witnesses of the resurrection of Lazarus. [18]These had influenced many others to join them as Jesus proceeded toward Jerusalem. [19]In dismay the Pharisees began to comment among themselves how ineffective their tactics had been up to this time. "Look how greatly we have failed. It looks as if the whole world has gone out to endorse Him!"

[20]There were even a number of Greeks who had come to celebrate the Jewish feast. [21]These must have heard good things about Jesus and were eager to see Him, so they went up to Philip and begged, "Sir, we would like very much to see Jesus. Do you think that this could be arranged?"

[22]"Let me see what I can do," he answered. He went to Andrew first, presented the request, and both agreed that it was possible. So they went to Jesus about these Gentiles who wanted to see Him. [23]To their surprise, Jesus brightened up with joy. He declared, "At last the Son of Man will be glorified. [24]Truly, I tell you, if a kernel of wheat is not buried in the ground, it never grows, but if it is buried, it dies and then grows and produces many kernels. [25]Whoever tries to cling to life will die, but whoever is willing to give up his life in this world will eventually have everlasting life. [26]If you want to help Me, come and never leave Me, then you may be sure that My Father will one day honor you. [27]But as of now I am facing serious trouble, and I am deeply anxious over what is going on. Should I pray to the Father to rescue Me? No, for I came to this world for this very purpose."

[28]Then He uttered a short prayer in the hearing of all around him, "Father, glorify Your name."

A voice was heard from heaven, "I have just answered Your prayer. My name has been glorified, and it will again be glorified."

[29]Those around Him thought that they had heard thunder, but others decided that it must have been an angel who had just spoken. [30]Jesus spoke up and explained things. "This voice that you heard was not for Me but for you, and it is proclaiming that [31]the prince of this world is now judged guilty— he is being rejected by the whole universe. [32]And as for Me, if I am lifted up I will draw all to Me." [33]In this statement He predicted the manner of His execution.

[34]Next, the listeners had a question, "We have heard it read in the law that the

Messiah will never die. If so, how can You say that You are the Messiah, then go on to say that You will be lifted up as a criminal on a cross? Just what Son of man are You referring to?"

[35]His answer was not direct, yet it was given in such a way that they must be convinced when His prediction proved to be accurate. "Only a short time is left in which to enjoy the light. Behave responsibly now while light is available to you; otherwise darkness, real darkness, will be your lot. A person in darkness cannot see where he is going. [36]Yes, while light is shining, believe it, trust it so that you may rightly be called children of light." Having said this Jesus withdrew and could not be found.

[37]Sadly, in spite of many miracles, those people would not believe in Him. [38]But here also prophecy was fulfilled; the prophecy of Isaiah 53:1: "Who has believed our report? Even among those who have seen God's strong arm at work?" [39]Their unbelief was also predicted in another of Isaiah's prophecies, Isaiah 6:9: [40]"Their eyes were blinded, their hearts were hardened, so much so that they failed to see and understand, thus refusing to be converted and preventing me from healing them." [41]Isaiah said these things when he wrote about God and was shown His glory.

[42]By now we know, however, that a fair number of influential people had become believers, but because of their fear of being disfellowshipped by the Pharisees, they were unwilling to publicly admit their convictions. [43]They were more influenced by what people thought about them than by what God thought about them.

[44]Once again Jesus was willing to continue His explanations of His mission. "Whoever believes in Me is really believing in Him who sent Me. [45]And if you see Me, you are seeing Him who sent Me. [46]I have come to this world to be a light so that you need not continue in darkness. [47]Remember though that if you hear Me and still do not believe I will not condemn you, because My mission is not to condemn but to save the world. [48]Those who reject Me and My teaching will eventually be condemned, but not by Me. No, the very words I have spoken will condemn them on judgment day. [49]For these things I am telling you are directly from My Father. He is the One who gives My orders. [50]And His orders bring about eternal life, and that is why I bring you His messages."

Chapter 13

[1]It was Passover week, and Jesus was shown that His hour was at hand. He would soon complete His task, return to His Father, and leave His followers. It was clear by now that He was committed to them and would carry out His mission to the world, regardless of what might happen to Him. [2]The supper with the disciples was over. Judas had made arrangements to betray Jesus. [3]Jesus knew that His Father had finalized the plan and that the moment of truth had arrived. He would soon return to the Father. [4]So He left the table, removed His robe, picked up a towel, and attached it to His waist. [5]He then filled a basin with water and began washing the disciples' feet and wiping them with the towel. [6]When He reached Simon Peter, the impulsive disciple spoke up, "Lord, are You really seriously planning to wash my feet?"

[7]"I realize, Peter, that you cannot understand right now what I am about to do, but a little while from now it will be made clear to you."

[8]"Well, here is one thing I know. You will never wash this man's feet!"

Jesus replied, "But Peter, if I do not wash your feet, you and I can no longer work together."

[9]Just as quickly, Peter now reversed himself, "In that case, please wash my hands and my head, as well as my feet."

[10]"That will not be necessary, Peter. One who is bathed needs no further washing except his feet. Now, all of you are clean except one." [11]You see, He knew already who was going to betray Him. That person could not be described as clean. [12]When He had finished, He put His robe back on and sat down. "Friends, do you realize the significance of what I have just done? [13]You have been calling Me 'Lord' and 'Master,' and rightly so, for I am. [14]If I your Lord and Master have washed your feet, let this be an example of what I want you to continue doing for one another. [15]Yes, wash each other's feet just as I have done for you. [16]It is a fact that the servant is not greater than his master, and the one who is sent is less important than the one who sends him. [17]Now that you know these things, you will be happy and blessed by doing them. [18]Now I want to speak plainly. I am not able to include all of you in this blessing. I of course know the ones I have chosen, but here is a scripture that is about to be fulfilled: 'He who eats bread with Me has turned against Me and is plotting violence' (Psalm 41:9).[19]The reason I am telling you things before they happen is that after they happen you will be more than ever convinced that I AM. [20]Truly, I tell you, whoever accepts the person I send is accepting Me, and if that person accepts Me, he is also accepting the One who sent Me."

[21]Jesus abruptly became emotional and serious. "I am sorry to have to share this with you, gentlemen, but the fact is that one of you here will betray Me." [22]The disciples were stunned. They began looking at each other suspiciously, hardly believing what He had just announced.

[23]Sitting next to Jesus was the disciple that Jesus never ceased to love. [24]Simon Peter beckoned to him, suggesting that he ask Jesus who it might be. [25]So he did, "Lord, who is it?"

[26]Jesus sadly made this reply, "It is the one to whom I will give a piece of bread after dipping it." So that disciple kept watching, and finally Jesus dipped a piece of bread and handed it to Judas Iscariot, son of Simon. [27]Judas accepted the morsel, then allowed Satan to take control of him. Jesus then made a strange statement, "Please do what you are planning to do and the sooner the better." [28]No one at the table knew the meaning of this statement at the time. [29]Some supposed that Judas, being the treasurer, had planned to buy needed supplies for the Passover or that he intended to give some money to the poor fund. [30]But Judas left the group abruptly and went out into the night.

[31]After Judas had gone, Jesus spoke up, "Now it is the time for the Son of man to be glorified, and God the Father is also to be glorified in the Son. [32]And because God is to be glorified in His Son, He will also be glorified in Himself, and this will occur very soon. [33]My children, I will be with you only a short time. You may search for Me, but it will be as I told the authorities: I am going where you cannot follow. [34]And now I want to give you a new commandment. Here it is: Love each other just as I have loved you. [35]It will be because of your love for each other that people will recognize you as My disciples."

³⁶Here Simon Peter was perplexed. "Just why can't I follow You? You know that I would die for You."

³⁷"Oh, really? Yes, you think so alright, but it is a sad truth that before another rooster crows, you will declare three times that you do not even know Me."

Chapter 14
¹"Please do not let my predictions give you anxiety, for you believe in God and are learning to believe in Me also. ²In my Father's house are plenty of vacancies, all first class. When I go away, these are to be prepared especially for you, My believers. ³Just as surely as I go away, I will return to you again, and then I will take you with Me. I would have told you otherwise if this were not true. But I will take you to where I am going. ⁴And you already know where I am going, and you know the way."

⁵Now Thomas spoke up, "Lord, please pardon me, but we really don't know where You are going, and thus we cannot know the way."

⁶"OK, let Me try to explain. I am the way, I am the truth, and I am the light, and to go to the Father, you must go with Me. There is no other way. ⁷To know Me well is to know My Father also, and as of now you know My Father and have seen Him."

⁸Philip next asked, "Won't you now show us the Father, for this must be what we need?"

⁹"Let Me speak plainly, Philip. You have been with Me for some time now, and yet you have not realized that seeing Me is the same as seeing My Father, so it is actually unnecessary to ask to see the Father. ¹⁰Do you believe Me when I say that I am in the Father and that the Father is in Me? My words are the identical words that the Father is speaking, and the deeds I do are identical to the Father's deeds. ¹¹So please accept the fact that We are in each other or because of what you have seen Me do you should at least believe in Me. ¹²I give you My word that anyone who believes in Me and trusts Me will do the very things I do and even greater things because I go back to My Father. ¹³Furthermore, you are now invited to ask for every blessing in My name. This applies to your personal lives and to your work for My cause. These requests will all be granted, and the Father will be glorified in His Son through this means. ¹⁴Can you try to grasp the reality of this promise? Once again, you may ask for any blessing and I will give it.

¹⁵"Another thing, if your love for Me is genuine, you will observe My commandments faithfully. ¹⁶And I will ask the Father in your behalf to send another Helper who will be with you from now on and forever. ¹⁷This Helper is the Holy Spirit of truth, and He will not be bestowed on the world because they are materialistic and would not receive Him, for they only want to believe in those things that are tangible. You, however, will accept Him because He will enter your very souls and stay there. ¹⁸I hope you understand that I am not leaving you as orphans. It will be just as if I were with you in person. ¹⁹In just a short time the world will get its last glimpse of Me, but you will perceive Me, and because of My life you will be given life also. ²⁰Then you will be fully convinced that these relationships are true: I in the Father, you in Me, and I in you. ²¹Let's talk about a person who knows My commandments and lives by them. This is a person who truly loves Me, and of course, he or she will be loved by My Father. I, too, will love that person and be close to him."

²²Here the other Judas asked Jesus, "Why is it that You will be well-known by us but not by those of the world? Are you not liable to be considered partial?"

²³"It's because those who love Me cherish My words and obey them. My Father and I will come to that person and live in him. ²⁴Those who do not love Me will not follow My instruction, and by the way, My words are actually the Father's. ²⁵All this is good, but you must realize that My physical presence limits the good that you should enjoy. ²⁶And the Helper whom I promised to you, none other than the Holy Spirit, who will be sent by the Father as My representative will fully teach you and help you to remember the things I have told you.

²⁷"I am giving you peace, genuine peace, the peace I have in My own soul. This is not a gift such as you might receive from the world, so try to forget your anxiety and fears. ²⁸As I said before, I am going to leave you and then later return. And if you love Me, you will be glad to hear this, for My Father is greater than I. ²⁹I am telling you this before it happens so that after it happens you will have even greater trust in Me. ³⁰There isn't much more for Me to tell you. My time with you is running out, for the prince of this world is coming, but he has failed to turn Me from My goal in any way, nor has he caused Me to fail any of the tests I have gone through. ³¹And My mission is to let the world know that I love the Father and am completely submissive to His plan. Well, it's time to leave, so let's go."

Chapter 15

¹"I am the true, genuine vine. My Father is the owner and master of the vineyard. ²The branches of the vine are either valuable, fruit-growing branches or are worthless ones. Those who are bearing fruit will be pruned and cared for to help them produce more fruit, but the worthless ones will be cut off. ³You are somewhat like branches. You have been pruned as it were, trimmed and cared for by the words I have been speaking to you. ⁴Continue to stay with Me and in Me. Just as a branch cannot bear fruit unless it stays attached to the vine, so you will not be fruitful unless you stay attached to Me. ⁵Once again. I am the vine, you are the branches, and the branch that stays attached to Me will produce a rich harvest. On the other hand, without Me you will not be able to accomplish anything. ⁶Anyone who does not stay connected to Me will be thrown out like a dead branch that is then stacked up with other worthless trash and burned. ⁷But if you continue on, attached to Me, and if My words are treasured and kept by you, your requests will all be answered. ⁸Let me tell you what will bring happiness to My Father and what will demonstrate that you really are My disciples. It is simply this: bear much good fruit.

⁹"My love for you has been and always will be the same as My Father's love for Me. I want you to never forget this. ¹⁰Keeping My commandments is a sure way to stay in My love. I kept My Father's commandments and thus have stayed in His love. ¹¹Now why is it, do you suppose, that I have told you all these things? It is only for your future happiness, the same sort of happiness that I have, happiness to the full. ¹²Would you like to know My one commandment, the one that will include all the others? Just this: Love each other to the same extent that I have loved you. ¹³The greatest love there is will lead a person to lay down his life, if need be, for his friends.

[14]And speaking of friends, you and all who are willing to keep My commandments are My friends. [15]From now on I will call you friends rather than servants, for the word 'friend' describes the relationship of one who shares everything with another. The servant is never told things that a friend is told. And I have shared with you everything that My Father has told Me.

[16]"I chose you. It was not that you chose Me. I picked you out so that I could consecrate you to your tasks, the chief of which is to bear fruit that will be permanent, and in order for this to happen, I have assured you that whatever you request from the Father will be given. [17]All My instruction centers on this one concept: Love one another. [18]Don't be surprised if you are hated in the world. The world hated Me before it hated you. [19]If you were ordinary people of the world, you would be loved by them, you would be 'one of them.' It is because you are different from the world, because I have called you out of the world, that you will be hated. [20]Please remember this. A slave is not greater than his owner. So if I am persecuted, you may be pretty sure to be persecuted also. If they believe Me, they will also believe you. [21]Their main problem, the problem that underlies all others is this: they do not know the One who sent Me. [22]If I had never come and spoken so plainly to them, their behavior would not be sinful, but now they have no excuse for their sinning.

[23]"The person who hates Me also hates My Father. [24]If I had never come and done so many wonderful things in their presence, their behavior would not be sinful, but as things are, they have hated both Me and My Father. [25]These things are a fulfillment of Psalm 35:19 and of Psalm 69:40.

(They hate Me for no reason). [26]However, when your new Helper arrives from the Father, the Holy Spirit of truth, He will endorse My statements, My life, and My mission. [27]You too will be able to testify to the truth of these matters, and all because you have been with Me this long."

Chapter 16

[1]"I have told you these things to warn you so that when it happens you will not become discouraged. [2]You will be cast out of your synagogues and, yes, some of you will be killed by the very people who claim to be doing service for God. [3]The problem with them is that they really don't know My Father or Me. [4]Knowing such things ahead of time should increase your faith in Me. I didn't tell you everything before this because I knew I would be with you for a while. [5]But now it is nearly time to return to the One who sent Me. You still don't seem to grasp the reality of this; at least, I don't hear any questions as to where I am going. [6]However, I can detect a sadness in your faces since I first mentioned My plan. [7]Please believe Me though. It is to your advantage that I leave you. Surprised? Yes, and here is the reason. If I were to stay here, the Helper I promised would not come because you would feel no need for Him. But if I go away, then He will be needed and will come as you need Him.

[8]"After He comes, this is His mission. He will convince the world of three important matters. Number one, sin. Number two, righteousness. Number three, judgment. [9]Sin needs to be pointed out, and those who need salvation need to be told of Me. [10]Righteousness will be better understood after I have gone to My Father. [11]Judgment will be pronounced

because the world needs to be free from the prince of this world, and he will face the final judgment. [12]There are many other things I'd like to tell you at this time, but they would be too much for you to handle right now.

[13]"However, when the Spirit of truth comes, He will guide your minds into all truth. He doesn't waste His time on unimportant matters, but He will relay to you the words that He hears God speak. Also He will give you insight into future events. [14]He will honor Me and will uphold the work I have done and will make it plain to you. [15]You see, I own everything My Father owns; therefore, when He takes My ideas, it is equal to taking the Father's ideas. [16]In a short time I shall not be seen by you. But then in a short time I will be seen because of going to My Father."

[17]The disciples were baffled when they heard these words, and they questioned, "What does He mean when He says that in a short time we won't see Him, then in a short time we will see Him because He is going to His Father?"

[18]So they decided that it must be impossible to understand. [19]Jesus, however, perceived their perplexity and spoke to them, "Did you wonder about the meaning of this statement regarding going to the Father and then being seen again? [20]Truly I tell you that you will weep and mourn, but the world will rejoice, and your sorrow will melt away and will be replaced by marvelous joy. [21]You know that a woman in labor hates to endure the pain, but as soon as that child is born, she tends to forget the pain she went through and experiences great joy, knowing that a new person is born into the world. [22]So it is now. You will be sad, but remember, I will see you

again and then you will have true, eternal joy. [23]When this day arrives, you will not need to ask anything from Me, for you will have access to every needed blessing by just praying to the Father in My name. [24]Up to this time you have not requested anything in My name, but I now invite you to begin doing so. You will enjoy that sort of relationship to the full.

[25]"So far I have taught you in parables about the Father, but the time will come when I will teach you directly. [26]And when that time comes you will be asking the Father in My name. I won't need to ask the Father for your blessings [27]because He loves you just as I do, and all because you love Me and believe that I have been sent by God. [28]I left the Father to come into this world, and I will soon leave this world and return to the Father."

[29]To this, the disciples responded, "You are now indeed speaking plainly and not in parables. [30]We are fully convinced that You have unlimited wisdom and knowledge and that You need no help from any human being and that You have come from God."

[31]Then Jesus asked, "Do you truly have faith? The hour is right upon you when you will be scattered. [32]Each of you will go his own way and will abandon Me, but I won't be alone even then, for the Father will be with Me. [33]I have told you these things so that you can have internal peace. Tribulation will come to the world, but cheer up! I have conquered the world."

Chapter 17

[1]Right after this, Jesus began to pray with His eyes raised toward heaven, and this was His prayer: "Father, the time has come, the decisive event. Vindicate Your

Son so that Your Son may vindicate You [2]as You have given Him authority over all humanity, to bestow eternal life on all who have received Him. [3]Eternal life? It is simply this: To know You, the only true God, and Your Son whom You have sent into the world. [4]I have glorified You in My life and now My work here is finished. [5]So glorify, exalt, and honor Me according to Our plan with the same splendor I had with You before this world was ever created. [6]I have demonstrated Your character accurately before these men who responded to My call to leave worldly pursuits, its sin and rebellion. You actually gave them to Me, so they are really mine, and they have kept Your word. [7]They are fully convinced that whatever I have is a gift from you. [8]Your very words that they heard were given to Me. They accepted them and believed them. They are persuaded that I have been sent here by You.

[9]"My prayer now is for them, not for the world, no, but for these you have given Me, these who are Mine. [10]And of course, being Mine, they are also Yours and Yours are Mine. I am honored by being in them. [11]Now I am leaving this world in a very short time, but these will be left in the world. So, Father, keep those whom You have given to Me in unity as You and I are in unity. It can be accomplished through Your name. [12]All this time while they have been with Me they have kept true to Your name. They were given to Me, and I have kept them, all except one, the child of death, as was foretold in scripture. [13]Now I am coming home to You, but I want them to experience the joy I have in You. That is why I have been saying these things today. [14]I have spoken only Your words to them, and they are not worldly anymore, but

they are hated by the world as I have been. [15]I am not asking that You take them out of the world, only that they may be protected from the evil and the wickedness in the world. [16]They would never be comfortable in the world any more than I would be. [17]So let Your truth consecrate them. Your word is always truth. [18]I am sending them out into the world, just as You sent Me into the world. [19]And in their behalf I now consecrate Myself to them, so that they too, will be completely committed to truth.

[20]"My prayer today is also for more than just these few here, but also for everyone, everywhere, who will believe on Me through their preaching of Your word. [21]They, too, must be united just as You and I, Father, are in unity. They need to be one with Us so that the world may believe that You sent Me, [22]and that the honor You have shown Me may be given to them; but more importantly, that they may be as one—[23]I in them, You in me—so that they may be completely united with each other and thus convince the world that You have sent Me and have loved them just as You have loved Me.

[24]"Another prayer, Father: My great desire for them is that they whom You have given Me may come to be with Me wherever I am so that they can experience the honor You have shown Me through the ages, since before We created this world. [25]Oh My righteous Father, the world surely has never truly known You, but I have and these disciples have known that You sent Me. [26]And I have faithfully made Your name and Your character known to these men, and I will continue to do so in order that Your love for Me shall be seen in their lives and that I may be in their lives."

Chapter 18

[1]After His prayer Jesus led His disciples across the stream called Kidron and into a garden. [2]This was a place where they had been many times so, of course, Judas knew where they were. [3]It was in this garden that Judas now led a mob of men and their leaders under the authority of the priests and Pharisees. They were well equipped with lamps, torches, and weapons. [4]Even though Jesus knew what would soon be done, He went to meet them and asked calmly, "For whom are you looking?"

[5]The reply was, "Jesus of Nazareth."

"I am He," He replied. Judas was right there with the mob. [6]As Jesus spoke, "I am he," the mob stopped as if shot, reeled, and fell backward to the ground. [7]So Jesus asked them again, "For whom are you looking?"

Again the reply was, "Jesus of Nazareth."

[8]"I assured you that I am He, so if you are looking for Me, let these my friends leave." [9]Thus was fulfilled the statement, "Of all that You gave Me, I have lost none." (The implication here is that Judas was not actually given by God but that he joined the group for ulterior motives.)

[10]Simon Peter decided that things had gone too far, so he felt it his duty to defend Jesus. He had a sword with him, and with this weapon he attacked a fellow named Malchus who was a servant to the high priest. His aim in the darkness was imperfect, and Malchus was not killed, but his right ear was severed. [11]Peter must have felt somewhat put down when Jesus spoke to him, "Better put your sword away, Peter. My Father has given Me a bitter cup to drink, and you probably agree with Me that I should drink it, right?"

[12]The mob then tied Jesus securely with no resistance on His part. [13]They led Him out of the garden and into the city to the home of Annas, the father-in-law of the acting high priest, Caiaphas. [14]Caiaphas was the one who had declared emphatically that it would be better for one person to die than lose the nation. [15]Peter and another disciple followed the mob. The other disciple went into the high priest's house, for he was acquainted with him. But Peter stayed out. [16]The other disciple then asked if Peter might come in. [17]A woman asked Peter, "Are you not one of this Man's disciples?"

He declared, "I certainly am not." [18]A number of officials and slaves were there warming themselves by a fire that had been started, and Peter was mingling with them rather nonchalantly.

[19]The high priest began interrogating Jesus as to His disciples and about His teaching. [20]"Let Me answer your question this way," He replied. "Everything that I have taught has been open to the public or in synagogues. There has been no secret agenda. And all who wished to listen were always welcome, [21]so feel free to ask anyone who listened to Me. They would all give you an accurate idea of what I have been teaching. That also would be a more logical thing to do right now than to listen to Me under these conditions."

[22]As Jesus finished His answer, one of the officers nearby reprimanded Jesus and struck Him with the palm of His hand. "How dare you answer the high priest like that?"

[23]"If I have said something wicked, let Me know what it was. If it was not wicked, why did you strike Me?"

[24]Annas after hearing the case for a time decided to send Jesus to Caiaphas, the

acting high priest. ²⁵Peter again followed the procession. And again was warming himself by a fire when another person asked him, "Are you not one of Jesus' disciples?"

"No way!" Peter replied.

²⁶Then one of the helpers of the high priest, a relative of the one whose ear Peter had cut off in the garden, spoke up, "Didn't I see you with Him in the garden?"

²⁷But Peter the third time flatly denied it, and just then a rooster crowed.

²⁸After the hearing before Caiaphas, they led Jesus away to Pilate's court. It was still early in the morning, and the Jewish leaders refused to enter a Gentile's domain for they would become ceremonially unclean, and besides, this was Passover. ²⁹So Pilate obligingly went out to talk to them. "Why have you brought this Man to me? What crime has He done?"

³⁰"You may be sure, sir, that we would never have brought Him to you if He were not a vicious criminal and deserving of death."

³¹"Why did you not try Him in your own court?" was Pilate's question.

³²They explained, "We are not allowed to try a capital case, sir." This then began to fulfill the manner of Jesus' death that He had predicted.

³³So Pilate called Jesus inside to question Him, "Are You the king of the Jews?"

³⁴"Are you asking for your own information or are you asking because someone demanded that you ask?" Jesus responded.

³⁵"It's like this," Pilate began, "Your own people have accused You and believe You to be guilty of a crime deserving death. So what have You done?"

³⁶So Jesus explained, "Yes, I am a king of sorts, but My kingdom is not in this world but a spiritual kingdom. If it were of this world, My loyal followers would now be fighting to prevent My being captured by the Jews, but as you can see, they also understand that My kingdom is not temporal."

³⁷"Then You really are a king?" Pilate asked.

"Yes, I am," was His reply. "This is why I was born and why I came to this world: to testify the truth about God. Those who want to know the truth will listen to Me," Jesus explained.

³⁸"Just what is truth?" Pilate asked, expecting no reply. He then went out to the waiting crowd. "Look, I can find no crime of any sort in this Man. ³⁹But according to a long-followed custom, I will release one prisoner at Passover time. Shall it be the king of the Jews?"

⁴⁰"NO, NO! Absolutely not. Release Barabbas instead." Barabbas was incarcerated after armed robbery.

Chapter 19

¹In spite of his own statement that Jesus was not guilty of any crime, Jesus was turned over for scourging. ²The soldiers added insult to injury by fashioning a crown of thorns that they pressed down on Jesus' head. Then they brought an old threadbare purple robe that they put on Him ³and began insulting Him. "Hail, king of the Jews!" all the while slapping Him with their hands. ⁴Again Pilate went out, taking Jesus with Him. "I am saying it again, here He is. I cannot find anything wrong with Him." ⁵As Jesus came out wearing the old purple robe, Pilate added these words, "Just take a look at a remarkable Man!"

⁶As soon as the chief priests and rulers saw Him, they began to chant, "Crucify Him! Crucify Him!"

But Pilate said, "If He is crucified, it will be your responsibility. I declare Him innocent."

[7]"Never! He is guilty! By our laws He deserves to die because He claims to be the Son of God."

[8]Now Pilate was really worried. [9]So he drew Jesus back into the courtroom and asked, "Tell me, who are You anyway?" But Jesus did not answer this question. [10]"How dare You refuse to answer me. Don't You know that I have the authority to crucify You and also the authority to set You free?"

[11]"As to your authority," Jesus replied, "all of it is given to you by a higher power. So your guilt in this matter is not as great as that of the high priest who turned Me over to you."

[12]Pilate was thinking to himself, *How can I release this Man?* The Jews, sensing his desire, kept yelling, "If you free this Man, you are no friend of Caesar. Anyone who claims to be a king is automatically an enemy of Caesar." [13]This last idea struck Pilate forcefully. But still he felt impelled to free Jesus, so he brought Him out again to the Jews and assumed the role of judge on an elevated platform called Gabbatha or Pavement.

[14]This was preparation day of the Passover and about six o'clock in the morning. He called for silence, then announced, "Here is a Man who is your king."

[15]But they screamed louder than before, "Away with Him! Crucify Him!"

He then asked, "Seriously, do you want me to crucify Him just because He claims to be king and is not guilty of any crime?"

The chief priests shouted, "We have no king except Caesar!"

[16]In total exasperation, Pilate caved in and gave the order for Jesus to be crucified.

His soldiers took Jesus into custody and led Him away. [17]A cross was laid on Jesus' shoulder, and He was led out of the city to a place known as "the skull," the Hebrew word is Golgotha. [18]This was the common site of crucifixions, and two others were crucified the same day, one on each side of Jesus. [19]Pilate had ordered a small sign to be written and placed on the cross above Jesus, which read "Jesus of Nazareth, the king of the Jews." [20]Many onlookers approached the cross to read the message that had been put there. The site was very close to the gate of the city, which provided easy access to all. The message was in three languages: Hebrew, Greek, and Latin.

[21]The chief priests went to Pilate in protest to the message on the cross, "Don't say, 'the king of the Jews,' but rather, 'He claims to be king of the Jews.'"

[22]But Pilate was fed up with their arrogance and sullenly answered them, "What I have written, I have written."

[23]Then the soldiers took Jesus' clothing and cut it into four parts, one part for each soldier. But his robe was without a seam, a one-piece garment, and [24]it seemed a shame to cut it up, so they decided to cast lots for it and give it to the winner. In this, they inadvertently fulfilled Psalm 22:18, which reads, "They divided up My clothing and cast lots for My coat."

[25]Four women were close to the cross: his mother, his mother's sister, Mary the wife of Cleophas, and Mary Magdalene. [26]Looking at His mother and at His disciple John who was also there, Jesus said, "Mother, here is another son for you." [27]Then addressing John He said, "Look, you now have another mother." John accepted her from that time on and cared for her. [28]Having said this, Jesus knew that His duty

was done, His work accomplished. He was terribly dehydrated and spoke, "I am so very thirsty." ²⁹Nearby was a jug of vinegar, and someone soaked a sponge with vinegar and offered it to Jesus. When He had just tasted it, ³⁰He spoke His last words, "It is FINISHED!" His head dropped to His chest as He died.

³¹The Jewish leaders were concerned about the ones on crosses because the coming Sabbath was a festival Sabbath, and it was considered a violation of the Sabbath to leave a criminal on the cross during such a Sabbath. So they sent a delegation to Pilate asking permission to have the convicts' legs broken before removing them from the crosses. ³²Pilate gave the order, and presently soldiers came to the crosses with clubs and broke the legs of the two criminals who were crucified next to Jesus. ³³When they reached Jesus' cross, they found that He was already dead so there was no need to break His legs. ³⁴But one soldier had a spear, and just to be certain, he thrust the spear into Jesus' chest. Blood and clear fluid poured out. ³⁵This writer was present and can testify to the truth of this statement, knowing that the truth can strengthen the belief of the readers. ³⁶This was a fulfillment of the prophecy of Psalm 34:20: "He keeps all His bones; not one of them is broken." ³⁷And also of Psalm 22:16 and Zechariah 12:10: "They shall look on Him who has been pierced."

³⁸Shortly after Jesus died, a man from Arimathea by the name of Joseph, who believed in Jesus but had not publicly announced his belief, being afraid of the Jewish leaders, went to Pilate and requested the body of Jesus. Permission was given, and he removed the body from the cross. ³⁹Then Nicodemus came up with a huge supply of herbs, perhaps seventy-five pounds of myrrh and aloes. ⁴⁰The two of them then wrapped the body in linen cloth containing the herbs, a customary thing in Jewish burials. ⁴¹There was a garden close to the place of crucifixion where there was a tomb never used before. ⁴²They laid the body in this new tomb. They did all of this hastily because it was preparation day. Fortunately, the tomb was near to the city, and they were able to complete the burial process before the Sabbath began.

Chapter 20

¹Sunday morning before daylight, Mary Magdalene made her way to the tomb and was shocked to find that the huge stone had been removed from the entrance. ²First she decided to tell Peter and John, so she hurried to where they were staying and reported what she had found. "They must have taken away the Lord's body. Who has done it and where is it?"

³Peter and John left as soon as possible and ran to the tomb to see for themselves. ⁴John was the first to reach the place, ⁵so he stooped down and peered in. There were the linen wrappings and the head cloth in a separate place. ⁶But Peter, when he arrived, was not satisfied to look in. He crouched and went right in and found the linen wrappings ⁷and the head cloth over in a separate place by itself. ⁸Then John went in. Both were convinced that Jesus was no longer there, and they began to believe that it was just possible that Jesus had been raised to life! Up to that time the meaning of Psalm 16:10 had not been impressed on their minds: "You will not leave Me in the grave so that My body will decay." ¹⁰Greatly perplexed they returned to their lodging place.

[11]But Mary didn't leave the tomb. She was sobbing there in silence. Then she stooped down to look into the tomb [12]and was startled to see two persons (actually they were angels) in pure white sitting where the body of Jesus had lain, one at the head, the other at the foot. [13]One of them asked her, "Woman, why are you weeping?"

"It's because someone has removed the body of my Lord, and I don't know where they have put Him."

[14]She turned away in tears and confronted a man standing there close by. She did not recognize that it was Jesus Himself. [15]He asked kindly, "Woman, why are you crying? Are you looking for someone?"

This must be the caretaker, she thought to herself. "Sir, if you have removed His body please tell me so that I can give Him a decent burial."

[16]He spoke just one word, "Mary."

Then the truth struck her! "Rabboni!" (which means Teacher). She cried as she fell to her knees and hugged His ankles.

[17]"Please stop clinging to Me here because I must go at once to My Father, but go instead and tell them that I am on My way to My Father and your Father, to My God and your God."

[18]So off she went to the disciples and told them her story and gave them His message.

[19]That very day the disciples were all in hiding behind locked doors, fearing for their lives, when suddenly Jesus was among them. "Peace to all of you," He said. [20]They were stunned. "Come now and look at Me," He invited, showing them His hands and side. This was enough to convince them. Their joy was indescribable! [21]Again He blessed them, "Peace be

to you. My Father has sent Me, and now I am sending you into the world." [22]He then exhaled and said, "Receive the Holy Spirit. [23]If you forgive others their sins, they are indeed forgiven, and if you do not forgive them, they are not forgiven."

[24]At this meeting, Thomas, called the twin, was not with the others. [25]But later the other ten announced to him the wonderful news. "We have seen the Lord!"

Cynic that he was, he responded, "Huh, when I see the scars in His hands and then touch them with my fingers, then when I see the scar on His side and touch it, then and only then will I be convinced."

[26]About a week later, they were together again. This time Thomas was present. And although the door was shut and locked, Jesus abruptly entered and greeted them, "Peace be with you." [27]Going directly to Thomas, He invited, "Come, Thomas, put your fingers on these scars on my hands and on this scar on my side. This will help you to have faith." [28]The effect on Thomas was instant. Humbly he bowed down, confessing, "My Lord and my God!"

[29]"Thomas, you were persuaded only when you could see and touch Me, but a greater blessing I promise to those who believe, even if they never have the privilege you have had."

[30]This book contains only a few of the experiences of Jesus and His relationship with His disciples. [31]The purpose of writing these down is to foster belief in Jesus as the Messiah, the Son of God, for eternal life is dependent upon this belief.

Chapter 21

[1]The disciples were not with Jesus continuously after His resurrection. He did appear to them several times, however.

On one such occasion, they were on the shore of the Sea of Tiberias, also called the Sea of Galilee. ²Simon Peter, Thomas the twin, Nathanael, James and John, and two other disciples were together when Simon Peter announced, ³"I am going fishing, gentlemen."

"In that case we are going with you," they all agreed. So they got into a boat and soon were out in the deep waters of the lake. All night long they worked, and in the morning they had caught zero fish.

⁴But Jesus had come there to the shore, and they did not recognize Him from the distance. ⁵"Friends, do you perhaps have a little food?" He called out.

"No," they answered.

⁶"If you will just put your net out on the right side of the boat, you will have more success," He advised.

"We can't lose," they reasoned, so they proceeded to do just that. Right away the net filled with fish, so many in fact that they had a hard time pulling it in. ⁷John was suddenly aware that it was Jesus. "It's the Lord, Peter!" ⁸Peter agreed at once, then grabbed a coat (he had stripped down to work), and jumped into the water to swim ashore. The other disciples followed in the boat with the big load of fish. ⁹On the beach they discovered a little fire with fish broiling over it and some bread, all ready to eat.

¹⁰Jesus next invited Peter to bring a few of the fish they had caught. ¹¹They counted the haul and it totaled 153 large fish, and yet the net did not break! ¹²"Let's eat," Jesus invited. Although they knew it was Jesus, He did not seem quite the same, but no one asked Him about the change. ¹³So Jesus began serving them bread and fish. ¹⁴That experience was the third time He met with the disciples after His resurrection.

¹⁵After breakfast Jesus asked Peter this question, "Simon, son of John, do you love Me more than these? (The implication in the question may have been, Is your love the divine *agapao* kind of love?)

"Yes, Lord. You know that I love You." (Peter's response shows a humility—old boastfulness gone—he used *phileo*, the Greek word for friend. He doesn't boast that he is greater than others.)

"OK, then feed My lambs." ¹⁶Jesus then repeated the question, "Simon, son of John, do truly love Me with pure, unselfish love?" (*agapao*)

"Yes, Lord, and You know that I am telling the truth." (Again Peter uses *phileo*, perhaps reflecting a self-distrust to claim a divine type of love.)

"OK, feed My sheep." ¹⁷For the third time, Jesus asked Peter, "Simon, son of John, do you love Me as a friend or brother?" (*phileo*).

Now Peter felt hurt. Twice before Peter had affirmed his sincere affection (*phileo*) for Jesus. In self-distrust he humbly answered, "Lord, You know me better than I know myself, and You know that I love You as a brother."

Then Jesus repeated His commission, "OK, then feed My sheep. ¹⁸And now I will tell you something, Peter. When you were young, you would dress yourself and go wherever you wanted to go. But some day, when you are old, you will be forced to stretch out your hands, and another will decide what you must wear, then force you to go where you don't want to go." ¹⁹This was a prophecy suggesting even the manner of Peter's death—crucifixion—a death that would show the depth of Peter's devotion to God's glory. ²⁰Then Jesus added

simply, "Just keep right on following Me."
Peter then looked at John. It was he who
had leaned on Jesus during the last supper,
asking who would betray Jesus.

[21]"And what about this man, Lord?"

[22]The response was not what Peter had
expected. "Just suppose I want him to live
until I return. That decision should make
no difference to you—keep on following
Me."

[23]This remark may have started a
rumor that Jesus said He would return
before John died, but what Jesus was gently saying was, "You have your assignment,
Peter. What My plans are for John does not
concern you. Just keep following Me."

[24]This John is the one writing these
words, telling of the events he witnessed
personally. [25]And there are many other
things Jesus did, so many, in fact, that if
they were all written down, I doubt that
the world itself could hold all the books.

Acts

Chapter 1

¹Dear friend, Theophilus, my first letter to you contained the story of Jesus and His life and teachings. ²It told of His ascension to heaven after having given full instructions to His followers, the disciples He had chosen. ³He spent forty days after His resurrection telling them the things they needed to know about God and giving them added evidence of His divinity. ⁴It was while they were gathered together that He advised them to remain in Jerusalem until they experienced the fulfillment of the Father's promise of power. Here are His words to them, ⁵"Remember what I have told you. John baptized with water, but you will be baptized by the Holy Spirit within a few days."

⁶It was at this meeting that they again brought up the question that was always uppermost in their minds: "Are you ready now to liberate Israel so that we can be an independent nation?"

Following is His explanation: ⁷"God does not reveal to you everything about His future plans, for these things need not concern you, ⁸but here is what should concern you, what is really important. You will be given power, all the power you will ever need. It will be from the Holy Spirit, and it will enable you and motivate you to be My witnesses in Jerusalem, in Judea, then into Samaria, and from there to the entire world."

⁹Just as He finished speaking, right while they were looking at Him, He suddenly was lifted up from the earth and disappeared into a cloud. ¹⁰Astonished, they watched the sky and could not stop gazing upwards even though He was out of sight. Then two strangers in pure white clothing suddenly appeared and stood beside them. ¹¹"Why are you Galileans standing here looking up into the sky? This very same Jesus who has left you will one day return in this same manner from the clouds as He descends toward the earth."

¹²They quickly made their way back to Jerusalem from Olivet, about two miles. ¹³They got together in the upper room, the room where they actually lived at the time. I have recorded their names here for your benefit: Peter, James, John, Andrew, Philip, Thomas, Bartholomew, Matthew, James the son of Alphaeus, Simon the Zealot, and Judas, brother of James. ¹⁴They began a regular series of prayer seasons and sharing meetings and were joined by a number of women including Mary, mother of Jesus, and Jesus' step-brothers.

¹⁵It was during these days following Jesus' ascension that Peter asked to have the privilege of bringing up an important

matter. At the meeting there were about 120 present. [16]"Fellow believers, prophecy has been fulfilled. The one that goes like this: 'My close friend, one in whom I trusted, you have turned against Me.' This was spoken to describe the act of Judas when he led the mob that captured Jesus. [17]He was indeed one of our group and over many months a close friend to all of us, ministering just as we did. [18]Perhaps you already know what happened to him, but if not here is the truth. The money he was given for betraying Jesus, and which he threw back to the leaders, was used to purchase a field. As for him, he committed suicide because of his despair over what he had done. He chose to hang himself, but his body plunged down an embankment. At impact it burst open, eviscerating him. [19]Most of the citizens of Jerusalem knew about it and understand why the field is now known as 'the field of blood.'

[20]"Do you happen to know Psalm 69:25? 'Let his habitation be desolate,' and Psalm 109:8? 'Let another person take his office.' [21]Let us follow this instruction and choose among those who have believed in Jesus from the time of John's preaching, until now. [22]He must be a man who should be ordained to testify of the resurrection."

[23]Two names were nominated: Joseph (Barsabbas) Justus and Matthias. [24]They then prayed over the outcome, "Lord, you know the hearts of all people. Show us which of these two would be your choice, [25]a person to join us in ministry as apostles, a person to take the place of Judas who has failed and fallen, going his own way." [26]They then cast lots to determine whom to accept as one of the twelve, and the lot fell on Matthias. From then on he was officially one of the twelve apostles.

Chapter 2

[1]The day of Pentecost arrived. The believers were all together and were spiritually united in their faith. [2]Suddenly a sound resembling a violent windstorm descended from heaven to the city, enveloping the house where they were gathered. [3]All were aware of fiery flames that split and settled on the heads of those present. [4]The Holy Spirit began to speak through them, giving them a miraculous manifestation of communication.

[5]In Jerusalem at the feast time there were hundreds of Jews who had come from every country, and all were searching for God's will. [6]When this awesome sound started, these devout people made their way to the believers' house and began to realize that a great miracle was in progress. The visitors spoke many languages, but the apostles spoke in a language understood by all. [7]It was amazing! They began comparing notes, and the comments went like this:

"Are not all these people Galileans?"

[8]"If so, how is it that each of us hears them in our native language? [9]Whether Parthian, Mede, Elamite, Mesopotamia, Judea, Cappadocia, Pontus, [10]Asia, Phrygia, Pamphylia, Egypt, Libya, Cyprus, Rome or whether we are Jews by birth or proselytes, [11]it doesn't matter if we are Cretes, or Arabs, we hear them speaking in our own language telling us the wonderful things of God."

[12]Amazed and perplexed, they kept on asking, "What is the significance of all this?"

[13]But there were some who were cynical about the whole thing. They spoke up, "Don't be so excited. These fellows are just drunk, that's all."

[14]Peter stood up with the other eleven by his side and called for quiet. "Ladies and gentlemen of Judea and Jerusalem, may I have your attention please? Listen carefully to what I am about to say. [15]It has been suggested that what you are witnessing today is the result of too much intoxicating wine. Really now, could this be possible? It is only the third hour of the day. Have you ever heard of too much wine improving clarity of speech? No, my friends, what you are seeing is the fulfillment of Joel's prophecy, [16]'It will come to pass in the last days that [17]I will pour out My spirit on human beings; your sons and your daughters shall prophesy, your young men shall see visions, and your old men shall be given prophetic dreams. [18]Even on slaves and housemaids shall be given an outpouring of My spirit and they will prophesy. [19]Then I will produce impressive miracles in the heavens, and on the earth, blood, fire, and smoke. [20]The sun shall fail to produce light, the moon will turn to a blood red before the momentous day of the Lord arrives. [21]And all who call on the name of the Lord will be saved.' (Joel 2:28–32)

[22]"My fellow Israelites, please listen now to what I am about to say. Jesus of Nazareth, a Man who received God's approval by His miracles and signs which were done in many places, were acknowledged and verified by most of you. [23]It was God's will that He was arrested by you and with the help of evil men you, His own nation, crucified. [24]God, however, saw fit to raise Him from the dead because He was divine, and it was impossible for Him to be held in death. [25]Let me tell you this: His resurrection is a fulfillment of Psalm 16:8–10, which reads as follows: 'I was given a preview of God. He was at My side to support and sustain Me. [26]And of course this gave Me great joy and courage. Even my tongue was happy. My body shall rest in death, but My body will live in hope [27]because You will not leave Me in the grave; You will not allow Your Holy One to decompose. [28]You will show Me the way to real life. In Your presence is pure joy. By Your side everyone will find genuine pleasures that shall never end.'

[29]"Ladies and gentlemen, let me be perfectly honest with you. The writer of these words, David our patriarch, our king, our poet and prophet is still dead, still in his tomb, which we still have with us. [30]Being a prophet, David had received a solemn oath from God that a descendant of his would be the promised Anointed One, the Messiah, the Christ and that Christ would be king over David's realm. [31]He foresaw the resurrection of Christ when he wrote these words about not being left in the grave nor subject to decomposition. [32]My dear people, Jesus Christ has been raised from the dead by God. We twelve are here to testify that He is alive again! [33]He has been exalted by God and is now at God's right hand and has received from the Father a sure promise to send the Holy Spirit who has brought about what you have seen and heard today.

[34]"David has not been raised up and taken to heaven. No, No. Remember that he prophesied, [35]'Jehovah has said to my lord: Sit here on My right side until I make your enemies nothing but a footstool.' [36]Now let everyone of us in this whole nation know that God has declared this Jesus, whom you crucified, to be the Anointed One."

[37]Conscience began to awaken in the hearts of many. They began asking the twelve apostles, "Men, brothers, what can we do?"

[38]"Here is what to do," came the answer. "Repent of your errors, turn away from them. Be baptized, every one of you so that your sins may be forgiven. If you do this in the name of Jesus Christ, you too will receive the gift of the Holy Spirit. [39]The promise of the Holy Spirit is for all! God is calling all." [40]Peter continued for some time to renounce the society that was so perverse and in error as to crucify Jesus Christ. [41]His plea was effective to a vast number of people. About three thousand accepted his message that day and were baptized into the newly formed church.

[42]These were not fickle folks. They never turned back. The news that the apostles had taught was true, and they knew it. A wonderful bond developed from their common beliefs. Unselfishness prevailed as they absorbed the apostles' teachings and prayed together. [43]Those new believers were awed by their new faith with its miracles and supernatural signs. [44]It finally led to their sharing all their property with each other. [45]Many sold all they had and used the proceeds to help other believers. [46]Every day they were together, either at the temple or at a home, or sharing a meal. [47]They praised the Lord and won new friends all around them. The Lord saved new believers in large numbers, and the church grew by leaps and bounds.

Chapter 3

[1]One day at about 9:00 a.m., the traditional hour of prayer, Peter and John went up to the temple. [2]Every day a man who was crippled from birth was carried to the temple entrance known as the "Gate Beautiful." He was left there to beg from those entering the temple complex. [3]As Peter and John approached, he asked them for money. [4]They looked him in the eye, and Peter spoke up, "Sir, please look at us." [5]The beggar looked up, expecting to receive a substantial gift. [6]But Peter said, "I'm sorry, we have any money; nevertheless, we will give you a greater gift." Then he said, "In the name of Jesus of Nazareth, I invite you to get up and walk!"

[7]Then taking the cripple by the hand, Peter lifted him up. Amazingly, he at once stood on strong feet and ankles. [8]Exulting in his new strength, he began to jump up and down while shouting praise to God as he went with the two disciples into the temple. [9]Naturally he made quite a stir among the people who saw him, [10]for they knew him well, having seen him regularly begging at the Gate Beautiful. Their astonishment was equal to his. [11]In the delight of that moment, he clung to Peter and John while a crowd gathered, filling Solomon's porch completely. [12]Peter sensed that all eyes were on him and John, hoping to hear from him an explanation of how he did it. Of course, they were not disappointed. Peter was eager to share with anyone who would listen, so he called for silence and addressed the listeners.

"You people of Israel, why do you seem so amazed? You are looking at us as if we are the ones who possessed the power to heal this man so he can walk. [13]Let's keep the record straight. The God of Abraham, of Isaac, and of Jacob has glorified His Son Jesus—the Jesus whom you rejected, abandoned, and turned over to Pilate for crucifixion, even when Pilate wanted to release Him. [14]Yes, you denied the One who was ultimate holiness and justice and chose rather to release from prison a notorious murderer, [15]electing to kill the Prince of life, the One whom God has resurrected from the grave. We can testify to the truth of this. [16]It was the name of Jesus, invoked by faith, that made this man strong. This man who is well known by most of you has been restored to perfect health and strength through the name of Jesus. [17]Now let me say this, brothers and sisters. I believe it was ignorance that led you to do what you did, just as it was ignorance that led your rulers to do as they did. [18]And it was a fulfillment of prophecy, for all the prophets foretold of a Messiah who would suffer. [19]So I ask you now, please repent and be converted so that your sins may be forgiven when the life-giving time arrives.

[20]"God will send Jesus Christ again a second time, the very One who has been preached today among you, [21]the One who will stay in heaven until the time comes for the restoration of all the earth to its original state as has been foretold by the prophets. [22]It was Moses who said this to our ancestors, 'A prophet will be raised up by the Lord, resembling me. He will be the One you must hear and believe. [23]Everyone who will not heed that prophet's message will be separated from God's people. [24]Yes, and Samuel and the prophets who followed him have spoken about these very times that we are now experiencing. [25]You, dear people, are descendants of the prophets, people of the covenant with Abraham, saying, 'In your family the whole world will be blessed' [26]Now after God raised up His Son He sent Him first to you to be blessed that by His goodness you might be persuaded to turn from your wicked ways."

Chapter 4

[1]During this speech priests, temple officials, and several Sadducees gathered around them. [2]They were all upset and irate because Peter and John were telling the people about Jesus and His resurrection. [3]At a signal guards arrested the disciples and took them into custody. The day ended with Peter and John in prison. [4]By this time the number of believers had increased dramatically to about five thousand men.

[5]The following day temple officials, elders, scribes, the high priest, Caiaphas, John and Alexander, plus other relatives of the high priest got together [6]and voted unanimously to summon Peter and John to a hearing. [7]Putting them in the center of the room, they began interrogating them. "Tell us where you received your authority to do what you have done here, and whose power do you claim to have?"

[8]This was the perfect opportunity for Peter. The Holy Spirit took charge of him, and he began to speak to them. "My fellow Israelites, you who are our rulers, [9]if you want to know the answer to your question, listen carefully, for I shall tell you. You have asked about the restoration of the cripple and how he is now in perfect health, and here is the answer. [10]You and this whole nation need to be informed of this fact: it was in the name of Jesus Christ of Nazareth whom you crucified and whom God resurrected. Yes, it was through Him and by His authority and power that this man now stands in perfect health, completely normal. [11]Jesus is the one rejected by the nation, true enough, but as in the building of the temple, one of the stones was first rejected by the builders, but later found to be the keystone. Jesus Christ was rejected but is vital to our nation. [12]And He is the only source of salvation. Let me emphasize this. There is no name on planet earth aside from Him that is able to bring salvation."

[13]Peter's eloquence and courage impressed the listeners. They could sense that these disciples, unschooled as they were, had been with Jesus and had learned from Him. [14]And standing right there with them was the man who had been miraculously cured. No one could refute the facts. [15]So they dismissed Peter and John so that they might privately create a strategy to deal with the problem they were facing.

[16]"Gentlemen, we are here to decide what to do with these men. There has obviously been a remarkable miracle performed. That cannot be denied. And it is now common knowledge throughout the city. [17]Let us prevent any further spreading of their teaching by ordering them to never speak this name again in public."

[18]This approach was agreed on by the group. They then ordered Peter and John back into the room. In no uncertain terms, Peter and John were told to cease and desist from ever mentioning the name of Jesus or from teaching His doctrines.

[19]Their response was unexpected. "We invite you to decide whether we should obey you or obey God. [20]For we have no choice but to continue speaking of the things that we have seen and heard."

[21]The meeting broke up, but again they were threatened with dire punishment if they should go on teaching as they had been. No law had been violated, so nothing could be legally done to them. And besides, the popular opinion was on their side. A vast majority accepted the idea that God had given them the power to perform such miracles. [22]It was indeed a miracle. The man who had been restored was over forty years of age at the time, and this was common knowledge. [23]Peter and John returned to their companions and gave a report of all that the priests and elders had done and said. [24]The whole company rejoiced and gave thanks in these words: "Lord, You are God. You made heaven, earth, the sea and everything in them. [25]Your prophet David wrote it down like this: 'Why do the heathen rant and rave, and why did Your people ponder over such meaningless thoughts? [26]Kings stood up and rulers united themselves against the Lord and against His Anointed One.' [27]We have seen this prophetic psalm fulfilled in the action of Herod, Pontius Pilate, the Gentiles and the Israelites. [28]They have fulfilled it to the letter. [29]Now, Lord, You have heard their threats. Give to Your servants the courage and the boldness to speak Your words. [30]And send Your healing power, Your miracle-working power when we need it, in the name of Your holy Son Jesus."

[31]After they had prayed, their meeting place was shaken and they were again filled with the Holy Spirit and given the power to teach God's word with effectiveness. [32]Every believer was in harmony with every other believer, and they shared together all their temporal possessions. [33]Their message of the resurrection was given with mighty power due to the grace of God. [34]And none of them lacked the necessities of life because those who were landowners and property owners sold what they had and brought the money [35]to the apostles, who then distributed the funds to those in need. [36]One believer Joses was given the name Barnabas, which means, "son of consolation." He was a Levite from the island of Cyprus. [37]He had owned considerable acreage but had sold it and brought the proceeds to the disciples for distribution.

Chapter 5

¹Sadly enough one couple, Ananias and Sapphira, sold some of their property in order to contribute to the cause. ²But having sold it they brought only a part of the proceeds while giving the impression that they were donating the entire selling price. ³Ananias gave the money to Peter when the Holy Spirit told Peter of the deception being practiced.

"Ananias, why have you allowed Satan to control your mind?" Peter asked. "You have attempted to lie to the Holy Spirit and keep some of the money for yourself. ⁴The land was yours, was it not? At least until it was sold, and then the money was yours to do as you chose with it. You did not have to promise any of it to God, but having promised it, then it was God's, not yours. Why have you done this? You have lied first to God, then to men."

⁵As soon as he heard this, Ananias fell over dead. And all those present were filled with awe, mightily impressed at what had happened. ⁶They then did what must be done. They wrapped his body in a sheet, carried it out, and buried it.

⁷About three hours later, Sapphira came in, not knowing as yet what had happened. ⁸Peter confronted her at once. "Sapphira, tell me the truth. Did you sell your land for this amount?"

"Oh yes," she answered.

⁹"Well, how is it possible that you two have conspired together to lie to the Holy Spirit? Look, at the door right now are the feet of the young men who have just buried you husband, and they will have to carry you out shortly."

¹⁰At that, she also fell down dead. The young men picked her body up, carried it out, and buried it beside her husband.

¹¹The new church was deeply affected by this incident as one would expect. So also were all who knew about it.

¹²Many miracles and supernatural signs were performed by the apostles while they were in Jerusalem ministering to the people at Solomon's porch. ¹³And yet many were fearful of joining the believers in Christ in spite of the strong evidence that God was leading them in so many ways. ¹⁴Nevertheless, a large number of men and women were so impressed by the evidence that they were willing to follow the Lord. ¹⁵Some of the evidence was a bit unusual. For instance, sick people were brought to the street on litters so that Peter's shadow might fall on them, resulting in an instant cure. ¹⁶Then there was a substantial flow of people from other towns and villages, sick or demon-possessed, and everyone was healed! ¹⁷All this was too much for the high priest and those in authority, especially the Sadducees. They became envious over the stir being generated.

¹⁸They had the apostles arrested and jailed. ¹⁹But during the night, an angel opened the jail door and led them out, freeing them with this instruction, "Keep right on what you are doing at the temple. ²⁰Go back there and tell all you know to those willing to listen about the life and works of Jesus."

²¹This encouraged them greatly, so early in the morning they were back teaching again although the officials were unaware of it. So the high priest called the Sanhedrin together and ordered the prisoners brought in. ²²The officers went straight to the prison, but no such prisoners could be found. They were compelled to return empty-handed. They reported, ²³"The prison had been well guarded,

locked, and intact, and the guards were at the door on duty, but when they opened it for us no prisoners were there!"

²⁴This account made the officials apprehensive. They could not comprehend what more might have taken place. ²⁵Just then a messenger arrived. "Listen, I have just come from the temple. The men who were arrested yesterday are back there today preaching to a large crowd." ²⁶More officers were sent to the temple, and sure enough, there they were. No resistance was offered when the arrest was made, and the officers were fearful of their own safety if they had made any threats, for the listeners were all sympathetic to the disciples. ²⁷Hustling them off to the Sanhedrin, they were presented to the high priest who stood them up in front of the council to interrogate them again.

²⁸"Didn't you understand the order you were given? You are not to teach your doctrines in Jerusalem, or anywhere else. Yet the whole city is being propagandized, and you are brainwashing the listeners, trying to turn them against us, blaming us for the death of Jesus Christ."

²⁹Peter acted as the spokesman, "We must obey God rather than human authority. ³⁰The God of our ancestors has resurrected Jesus, the Jesus you condemned to death, turning Him over to the Romans for crucifixion. ³¹This Jesus has now been honored as Prince and Savior by our God, and He is offering the gift of repentance to our nation and the forgiveness of our sins, including yours. ³²We stand here today, all of us, as witnesses to the truth of what we are telling you. So also the Holy Spirit is a witness to this truth. He has been given to any and all who will obey God."

³³The members of the Sanhedrin reacted to this speech by starting to implement a plan to have the disciples executed. They were that angry. ³⁴Fortunately, there was one member, a Pharisee, a doctor of the law, by the name of Gamaliel, a person who had an excellent reputation and sound judgment who obtained the floor, then asked that the disciples be excused from the room for little time. ³⁵When this was done, he said, "Gentlemen of Israel, my appeal to you today is this. Be very cautious in deciding what to do with these men. ³⁶As many of you know, a man by the name of Theudas several years ago considered himself to be a real leader. He actually persuaded about four hundred people to follow him in his movement, but he was killed and those who had joined him were soon scattered. And the whole movement fell apart. ³⁷Then later a fellow named Judas, a Galilean, started another offshoot movement that attracted a large following. But he too died and his henchmen were divided and scattered in total failure. ³⁸Friends, take my advice. Leave these people alone. If this message they are teaching is only human, it will finally amount to nothing, ³⁹but if it should be from God, you people cannot possibly stop it, for you would be found fighting against God Himself."

⁴⁰This reasoning made sense to the whole group, so they called the disciples back in and had them flogged, then released, warning them again not to speak further in the name of Jesus. ⁴¹Unjust as this treatment was, they rejoiced as they left, for they had suffered because of their belief in Christ, and this they considered to be an honor. ⁴²So back to the temple and into the homes they went, always preaching about Christ.

Chapter 6

[1]The church grew rapidly and problems arose. For instance, those of Greek origin perceived that their widows were not being given as much help as the Hebrew widows, so their complaint was brought to the apostles. [2]A public meeting was called, and all were invited to attend so that the matter could be discussed and an answer found. When the meeting came to order a spokesman began, "Ladies and gentlemen, we are aware of a number of issues that need to be addressed and that would soon take all of our time if we allow them to do so. This hardly seems to be what Jesus commissioned us to do. No, we must go ahead preaching the words of truth rather than just being 'waiters' at tables. [3]Here is our suggestion. Bring to us the names of seven men, Spirit-filled men, honest, capable men who can take charge of these matters. [4]This will give us time to pray and to preach."

[5]The idea seemed to be workable so nominations were brought. Here is the list of seven: Stephen, a man of great faith, a Spirit-directed man; Philip; Procorus; Nicanor; Timon; Parmenas; and Nicolas. [6]The apostles agreed to these nominations so an ordination service was held where the nominees were prayed for while the apostles laid their hands on them. [7]God's word began to be scattered widely after this, and the believers multiplied in numbers throughout Jerusalem, including even a large number of priests.

[8]Stephen, in particular, received a great endowment of power because of his strong faith, so much so that his miracles were wonderful evidences of his commitment to God. [9]But some men from what is called the Synagogue of the Freedmen, including both Cyrenians and Alexandrians, along with others from Cilicia and Asia, took issue with Stephen in a debate. [10]The outcome was rather unexpected, for he defeated them soundly, single-handedly through the wisdom given him by the Holy Spirit. [11]After their defeat, his opponents conspired together and bribed some witnesses to spread rumors that he was heard to speak blasphemy against Moses and against God. [12]This false report soon came to the attention of the people, including priests, elders, and scribes, who promptly ordered that he be arrested and brought to the Sanhedrin on charges of blasphemy.

[13]The false witnesses were first to testify under oath that Stephen was continuing to speak against the temple and the law. [14]"We heard him say these very words, 'Jesus of Nazareth will destroy this place and will abolish the teachings and customs that Moses gave us.'" [15]During this whole process, Stephen was so calm and confident that the council members could not keep their eyes off him. It was as if they were gazing into the face of an angel.

Chapter 7

[1]The high priest then spoke, "Is it true what we have just heard?" And then he allowed Stephen to defend himself.

[2]"Brothers and fathers, kindly listen to what I have to say. The glorious God communicated directly to father Abraham while he was still in Mesopotamia—even before he moved to Haran. [3]The instruction to Abraham was this, 'Move away from your ancestral home and your family. I will show you the land where I want you to live, so just trust me.' [4]Father Abraham believed God so fully that he packed up and left, first moving to Haran where he

stayed until his father died, after which he moved on into the country where you are now living. [5]But during his entire lifetime he did not realize the fulfillment of God's promise that this whole country would belong to his descendants. In fact, when the promise was made, he had no children. And God did not give him even one foot of land. [6]Still God's promise was that his descendants would one day own and occupy it all. Before that, however, his descendent would live in a foreign land for four hundred years, would be mistreated, and would become slaves there. [7]Following the years of bondage, the nation enslaving them was judged and punished by God, and Abraham's family left and came again to this land where they could serve God.

[8]"God's covenant with Abraham required the sign of circumcision so his son Isaac was circumcised on the eighth day. Isaac grew up, married, and became the father of Jacob. And Jacob became the father of the twelve patriarchs. [9]The patriarchs were jealous of Joseph and sold him to a slave trader who then sold him to an Egyptian government official. But God was with Joseph all through that ordeal. [10]Miraculously he was made known to Pharaoh who recognized his outstanding ability and appointed him as manager of his entire household and finally of the whole land of Egypt. [11]A dreadful famine prevailed for seven years, and our forefathers faced starvation. [12]So when Jacob heard that there was food for sale in Egypt, he sent his sons there to buy food for his family. The food ran out, and they had to return to Egypt for more. [13]This time when they arrived in Egypt Joseph told his brothers who he was, much to their dismay, but he was gracious to them and even

introduced them to Pharaoh. [14]Pharaoh was so dependent on Joseph and admired him so greatly that he invited him to send for his brothers and their families to come to Egypt to live until the famine was over. In all, seventy-five people moved to Egypt. [15]Eventually Jacob died in Egypt as did his whole family. [16]Jacob's body was carried back to Shechem where it was buried in the cave that had been purchased by Abraham from Hamor.

[17]"Time went by and finally the predicted sojourn in Egypt drew toward its close. Abraham's descendants had multiplied many times over. [18]Egypt had forgotten about Joseph and his family and their role in saving the country during the long famine. Pharaoh himself had little knowledge of history that far back. [19]He was a hateful person, bent on advancing himself whatever the results to others. Those Israelites were a threat to him, and he determined to make them slaves and stop their growth. The way to do this was to exterminate all the male babies born to them.

[20]"It was during this fearful time that Moses was born. He was a beautiful child, and his mother refused to drown him as ordered. Instead, she hid him for three months from any Egyptians. [21]They realized that if he were to be spared some other plan must be put into operation. They put him into the river as commanded, but alive in a small basket boat, so that when Pharaoh's daughter came to the river nearby, she would find him and perhaps save his life. The little plan worked. She found him and knew instinctively why he was there, so she rescued him and eventually adopted him as her own son. [22]He was given the best education in Egypt

and became a powerful, influential man. [23]He was fully aware of the slavery of his own people, and at age forty he decided to do something to help them. [24]One of the slave masters was abusing an Israelite one day when Moses was close by. There was his chance. He attacked the Egyptian and killed him, [25]hoping that this might trigger a rebellion that would result in the freeing of his people. But they did not get the point.

[26]"The next day he found two Israelites in a fight and attempted to separate them, reminding them, 'Remember that you are brothers. So why hurt each other?' [27]However the perpetrator of the fight totally rejected the advice of Moses, 'Who do you think you are any way? A king? A judge? [28]Are you wanting to kill me as you did the Egyptian yesterday?'

[29]"Now Moses was in deep trouble and he knew it. Someone had seen him kill and bury the Egyptian and would certainly report to Pharaoh. So Moses fled the country as quickly as possible, fleeing eastward into the land of Midian. Here he found a friendly family and stayed there, finally marrying and fathering two sons. [30]Moses stayed in that country, never planning to return to Egypt, but God had other plans. After forty years he had a rare experience. In the wilderness one day near Mount Sinai, a messenger from God met him, disguised as a bush that seemed to be burning but was not being burned up. [31]This was astonishing to Moses of course, and he approached to see what was going on.

"Then a voice came out of the bush, [32]'I am the God of Abraham, Isaac, and Jacob.' Moses shook with fear and tried to hide his face. [33]God's voice went on, 'Take off those shoes, for the place where you are standing is sacred ground. [34]I am not blind to the condition of My people in Egypt. I see it all. I hear their cries for help and I am on my way to rescue them. And I want you to go back to Egypt to do the job.'

[35]"Remember that this was the same person who had been scoffed at years before, 'Who do you think you are? A king? A judge? A boss over us, God's people?' Yes, indeed this same man was now chosen by God Himself to be a ruler and a deliverer, giving him his authority there at the burning bush. [36]And God did go right ahead and rescue His people from Egyptian slavery through Moses after a number of miraculous signs had been performed, including the parting of the Red Sea and forty years in the wilderness.

[37]"This man Moses is the one who wrote a well-known prophecy, and I quote, 'The Lord your God will raise up a prophet as He raised me. You must listen to Him.' [38]This 'prophet' is the one who was with the church as it wandered in the wilderness, the messenger angel at Mount Sinai, and indeed with all our ancestors who received the life-giving word. [39]He is the one whom our ancestors refused to obey and wanted to return to Egypt. [40]They even demanded of Aaron, 'Here, you make us gods to lead us, for we don't have any idea what has happened to Moses.' [41]Believe it or not, Aaron cooperated with them and a golden calf was fashioned. It was mounted on a pedestal, and they worshipped it even though it was only the product of their own workmanship.

[42]"Later God finally gave up on them for a while as they started worshipping the heavenly bodies. Amos wrote this, 'Have you deluded yourselves into thinking that your sacrifices were dedicated to me?

Those offerings over forty years, you nation of Israel? [43]Yes, you have even worshipped Moloch and the star you call Rephan and images you made to help in your worship of them, and as a consequence you will be carried away from your land to Babylon and beyond.'

[44]"Our ancestors had access to true worship after the tabernacle was built in Moses' time, and according to God's instruction, for he made it in the pattern of the one he had seen. [45]This tabernacle was brought with them to this land of promise, a country formerly inhabited by Gentiles. Joshua led them as they drove out the heathen tribes, and finally David's reign began and the entire country was theirs. [46]David had harbored a dream, and God approved of it, a beautiful house for our God. It was built, not by David, but by his son Solomon. [48]Yet in spite of the presence of such a magnificent structure, it is well to recognize that God does not limit Himself by dwelling in such a building. The prophet Isaiah expressed it this way, [49]"Heaven is My throne, the earth might represent My footstool; so just what could you possibly build for Me? How or where could you expect to build a place for Me to call My home? [50]Remember that I made everything to start with.'

[51]"The fathers of our nation were described as stiff-necked and undisciplined in heart and even in their ears for resisting the Holy Spirit, and sadly enough you, their descendants, have also failed. [52]Can you think of a single prophet who was not persecuted by our fathers? They even murdered some of them. The very prophets who foretold the coming of the Messiah were not treated any better. Now, finally the Messiah has been betrayed and executed by you, their descendants. [53]Yes, you who have custody of God's holy law, a law delivered by angels but which you have not honored by carefully observing it."

[54]This speech infuriated them so greatly that they gnashed their teeth in rage, leading them to murder him. [55]But he raised his eyes toward heaven and, being inspired by the Holy Spirit, spoke out, "I see heaven, I see the glory of God. [56]I see Jesus standing at the right hand of God. Think! The Son of man is at God's right hand!"

[57]Refusing to listen any longer, they screamed out, then overpowered him by sheer numbers. [58]They dragged him out of the city and began to stone him. A young man by the name of Saul was present watching everything. At his feet the mob laid their coats while they hurled the stones. [59]All during the dreadful ordeal Stephen called out to God and committed himself to God. He finally cried out, "Lord Jesus, receive my spirit." [60]He then crumpled to his knees and with his last breath prayed, "Lord, do not condemn them for this sin, please."

Chapter 8

[1]The young man Saul gloated over the death of Stephen as did most of the leaders of the nation who now started a vigorous persecution of the newly formed church at Jerusalem. So the members began to scatter widely through Judea and into Samaria, with the exception of the apostles who continued on in Jerusalem. [2]As for Stephen, a number of his devoted friends arranged a burial for him and a time of mourning was observed. [3]And Saul? He was commissioned to search for believers in Jesus, both men and women, and arrest

them and throw them into prison. This devastated the church, ⁴but the ones who had scattered began to share their faith wherever they went.

⁵At Samaria Philip began preaching to the city, ⁶and he experienced tremendous success. Almost all who listened were convinced by the preaching as well as by miracles performed. ⁷Exorcism of many demons was common, accompanied by loud protests as they were forced to release their captives. Restoration of many who had become paralyzed and many cripples occurred as the work spread. ⁸It is hard to describe the joy that swept over that city as the result of these experiences.

⁹Then there was Simon. He was a spirit medium, and the Samaritans had fallen for his incantations in large numbers. Simon became very proud of his capabilities. ¹⁰Indeed, the large following he had accumulated was completely convinced that he was a great messenger of God Himself. ¹¹So much so that they sought out Simon's advice in many other matters. ¹²However, when these same people heard Philip preach about the kingdom of God, an entirely different faith developed, and many were baptized in the name of Jesus Christ, both men and women. ¹³ Simon himself listened to Philip, then went with Philip to listen more. He was deeply impressed by the miracles that Philip performed.

¹⁴Of course, the news from Samaria reached Jerusalem, creating quite a stir among the believers who had managed to stay there. The church thought it wise to send Peter and John to Samaria in order to help Philip. ¹⁵On arriving in Samaria, they began to pray for the believers and to lay their hands on them as they received the Holy Spirit. ¹⁶Up to that time the new converts had been baptized in water but had not yet received the baptism of the Holy Spirit as had happened in Jerusalem at Pentecost. ¹⁷So now as Peter and John prayed, the Holy Spirit took possession of the new converts, and this was witnessed by Simon. ¹⁸He concluded that the secret was in placing hands on the believers. This is just what he wanted. Going to Peter and John, he offered them a handsome amount of money if they would only give him this power. ¹⁹Oh how he longed for the power to lay hands on people and bring about such manifestations.

²⁰But Peter was quick to reject the offer, "No, Simon, money will disappear, and you may disappear with it if you think that God's gift can be purchased with money. ²¹There is no way by which you will be able to share in this experience until you recognize that your heart is not right with God. ²²So repent and pray sincerely that you may be forgiven for even harboring such thoughts. ²³I fear, Simon, that you are jealous and bitter and that you are covetous and motivated by selfishness."

²⁴Simon responded, "Then please pray for me that God will not permit such a fate to overtake me."

²⁵Following their mission to Samaria, Peter and John returned to Jerusalem but planned for more outreach missions to other cities of Samaria. ²⁶Philip one day heard the Lord's messenger speak to him, "Philip, I need you to move from here at once and proceed south. You will take the main route from Jerusalem to Gaza in a wilderness area."

²⁷He was quick to respond. Mile after mile passed, and then he came to the road described. On that thoroughfare was a

chariot drawn by fine horses belonging to Queen Candace of Ethiopia. She had dispatched her treasurer to travel to Jerusalem for the feast, and this man was now on his way home. [28]As he traveled along, he was reading the book of Isaiah.

[29]The Holy Spirit spoke to Philip, "Go to the chariot and introduce yourself." [30]Philip had to run to catch the chariot, but he reached it. He could hear the words that the man was reading.

Philip spoke first, "Sir, I have heard what you have been reading. Are you able to understand the meaning of this prophecy?"

[31]"Frankly, no; it doesn't make sense to me. I need someone to explain it. Come up here with me. Maybe you can give me some insights."

[32]Yes, Philip could help! The passage referred to was Isaiah 53, and he was perplexed over the meaning of this prophecy, "He was led like a sheep to the slaughter, and as a lamb at shearing time makes no protest, so He did not utter a word. [33]In such humiliation as this He was deprived of every right and left no descendants for His life was sacrificed."

[34]The Ethiopian asked, "Now what is your opinion, was the prophet writing of his own fate or was he predicting the fate of another person?"

[35]Philip had a ready answer. Beginning at this scripture, he told the story of Jesus, showing how prophecy had been fulfilled here and in many other statements of Scripture. [36]The Holy Spirit was bringing conviction to the man. Philip was telling him the truth. He already had heard that baptism was the symbol of Jesus' teaching, so he begged Philip to baptize him as soon as possible. They were approaching a lake, and this was the appropriate time. "Is there

any good reason that I could not be baptized right here?"

[37]"My friend, if you sincerely believe, you may."

Then came his personal confession of faith, "Yes, I believe that Jesus Christ is the Son of God."

[38]The chariot was halted by the shore. They both stepped out, went down into the water, and Philip baptized him. [39]As they were coming up out of the water, Philip suddenly disappeared. The Holy Spirit had snatched him away, but the Ethiopian went on his way with profound joy. [40]The next we heard of Philip was that he was preaching in Azotus (Ashdod). And from there he traveled northward, preaching in every town until he finally reached Caesarea.

Chapter 9

[1]Now about the young man Saul. At this time he violently opposed every disciple of Jesus that he could find. He spoke out publicly against them and threatened them in every way possible, all the time searching for legal grounds by which they could be executed. He even went to the high priest, [2]and obtained authority to go to Damascus and search out these dissidents in the synagogues. He carried warrants for their arrest and planned to bring them to Jerusalem for trial and execution. His plan was just what the high priest wanted. [3]Saul and his companions were nearing Damascus when a dazzling light flashed about Saul from the sky. [4]The effect of this was so strong that Saul fell to the ground, and while lying there helpless, he heard a voice calling his name, "Saul, Saul, Why are you persecuting Me?"

[5]"Who are You Lord?" he managed to ask.

"I am Jesus, and you are persecuting Me. It is hard for you to keep on fighting against conscience as you are doing."

⁶Shaking with fear and amazement, Saul asked, "My Lord, what is it that You want me to do?"

The answer from heaven, "Get up, go on into Damascus, and someone there will tell you what you must do."

⁷Those who were traveling with Saul were speechless and afraid. They, too, had heard a voice but were unable to see anyone. ⁸Saul staggered to his feet and opened his eyes but found that he was blind, so his companions led him into the city. ⁹For three days he was blind and unable to eat or drink. ¹⁰In this city lived one of Jesus' believers, a man named Ananias. He had a vision in which the Lord spoke, saying, "Ananias."

"Yes, Lord."

¹¹"I have a job for you. I want you to go over to Straight Street and ask for a person by the name of Judas. At that house is a man, Saul of Tarsus, who is praying. ¹²He, too, has seen a vision in which a man called Ananias came to him, laid his hands on him, and his sight was restored."

¹³Here Ananias protested. "Lord, is this a trap? You know that I have heard many a story about this Saul and what a wicked person he is, how he has arrested Your saints in Jerusalem and is continuing to do these things. ¹⁴We are aware of his plan to come here with authority from the chief priests to arrest everyone he can find who believes in You and calls on You."

¹⁵But the Lord only replied, "Please trust Me and go anyway, for Saul is a person I have chosen to proclaim My name to the Gentiles, to kings, and to the nation of Israel, ¹⁶but I must also show him what he must endure for My sake."

¹⁷This was enough for Ananias. He went and found the house, knocked on the door, and was invited in. Judas introduced him to Saul. "Brother Saul, the Lord Jesus who appeared to you on your way has spoken to me, telling me to come and place my hands on you in order that your vision may be restored and that you can receive the Holy Spirit."

¹⁸Immediately after praying for him something like scales fell from Saul's eyes and his vision returned. Ecstatic with joy he asked to be baptized at once, and it was gladly done. ¹⁹Then his appetite returned, and he was able to eat and gain strength. He was invited to meet with the Damascus church and was warmly accepted. He stayed for several days with these dear people. ²⁰He was also permitted to meet in the synagogue and to speak to those Jews. They did not refuse him the privilege, so he began presenting his message that Jesus Christ is the Son of God. ²¹The listeners were astonished, "Isn't this the man who had people put to death for calling on the name of Jesus?" they asked. "Isn't this the man who was authorized by the chief priests to come here, capture the believers in Jesus, and take them back to the priests in Jerusalem?"

²²Saul soon gained quite a following in Damascus, becoming more eloquent as time went by, proving that Jesus was the long-expected Messiah. ²³Considerable time passed during which the unbelieving Jews living there began to plot against Saul, intending to assassinate him. ²⁴But the Lord revealed to Saul their murderous plot. The conspiracy had progressed until every gate of the city had a guard to prevent his escape. ²⁵So his friends made a

large basket in which he was lowered from the wall and thus escaped.

²⁶When he returned to Jerusalem, he tried to associate with the disciples of Jesus, but they would not accept him. They were afraid that he was still their enemy. It was hard to believe that this man had actually been converted. ²⁷Barnabas, however, was aware of Saul's conversion story and of his bold preaching of Jesus while in Damascus. It was he who introduced Saul to the leaders, telling them the facts known to him. ²⁸After being thus informed, the apostles and elders welcomed Saul, allowing him to join in all their activities. ²⁹He was a great help to those leaders in their preaching, but not too long after joining them, he was confronted by some Greeks over the messages that he had preached to them. They disagreed violently and were so upset that they plotted to kill him. ³⁰The brethren heard of the plot and whisked Saul away to Caesarea where they found a ship leaving for Tarsus, so he went aboard and was safe.

³¹From that time on the churches were relatively free from persecution in Judea, Samaria, and Galilee. They thrived, in numbers and in influence, through the power of the Holy Spirit. ³²It was during this time that Peter paid a visit to the believers at Lydda, ³³where he was introduced to a man named Aeneas who had been bedfast for eight years due to a stroke. ³⁴"Aeneas, Jesus Christ is making you perfectly well and strong again. Get up out of bed," Peter instructed. The patient did just that at once. ³⁵This incident was followed by a turning to the Lord of the whole town plus those in Sharon.

³⁶One of the believers in Lydda was a woman named Tabitha (in Greek her name was "Dorcas," which means "gazelle"). She was one of those people who was constantly doing good for others. ³⁷Unexpectedly she became seriously ill and soon died. Her friends prepared her body for burial in a second floor room. ³⁸Two men were sent to Lydda to bring the sad news to Peter, asking him to come if at all possible. ³⁹He was soon on his way with the messengers. When he reached Joppa, he was taken to the house where Tabitha's body had been placed and found widows sobbing in grief. They showed Peter the coats, dresses, and other garments that she had made for them. ⁴⁰Peter sent them all out of the room, then knelt down and prayed. Then speaking directly to the body, he commanded, "Tabitha, rise up!" She opened her eyes, looked at Peter, and sat up. ⁴¹He offered his hand, lifted her to her feet, then presented her alive to her friends. ⁴²This caused a tremendous excitement throughout the whole city of Joppa. ⁴²Peter decided that Joppa was a good place to stay for a time, so he found a boarding house owned by a tanner named Simon.

Chapter 10

¹While there in Joppa Peter had an experience that changed the course of the church. North of Joppa in Caesarea, lived a Roman Centurion named Cornelius, an officer in the army unit known as the Italian band. ²Cornelius was a worshipper of the true God, a sincere man of prayer, a generous person, especially helpful to poor people. ³One afternoon, about 3:00 p.m., he saw an angel clearly. The angel called him by name, "Cornelius." ⁴This call frightened him considerably, "What is this all about, Lord?"

The angel reassured him as he spoke. "Your prayers and your generosity to the poor are accepted by God. He has not forgotten your kind deeds. [5]Here is what God wants you to do: dispatch messengers to Joppa at once and call for a man named Simon Peter. [6]He is boarding at the home of a tanner named Simon who lives right on the beach. Simon Peter will tell you what your duties are."

[7]As soon as the angel left him, Cornelius called two of his most trustworthy slaves and his personal soldier guard who was also a believer and had been trusted for a long time. [8]These three were told the whole story of his vision that had frightened him but which he now knew was from God. [9]The journey was thirty-five to forty miles and required two days. On the second day they approached Joppa about noontime. Just before noon, Peter had gone to the solarium for his midday prayers. [10]He was already very hungry, but the meal was not yet prepared, and at that moment a vision was given him. [11]In the vision the sky seemed to open up and an enormous sheet, tied at the four corners, began descending from the sky. [12]In this sheet were many different animals, birds, and reptiles.

[13]A voice spoke to him from the sky, "Get up, Peter, kill one of these and prepare a meal for yourself."

[14]But Peter protested, "Oh, no, Lord, these creatures are unclean, and You know that I have never violated the law given to us regarding clean versus unclean meat."

[15]The voice spoke again, "When God calls something clean, do not call it unclean." [16]This experience was repeated three times, and then the sheet was drawn back into the sky and disappeared. [17]Peter was in great perplexity as to the meaning of this vision, but he did not have to wait long to discover the significance of it all, for at that very moment the messengers who had been sent by Cornelius were at the gate inquiring about Peter.

[18]"Does a man called Simon Peter live here?"

[19]Peter was now out of the vision and the Holy Spirit impressed him, *Peter, there are three men searching for you,* [20]*go down now and greet them, then go with them without misgivings, for I have sent them to you.* [21]Peter obeyed and met the three. "I am the man you are looking for; tell me, what is your mission?"

[22]"We have been sent here by the centurion Cornelius of Caesarea. He is a God-fearing man, an honest man, and one who has the respect and admiration of the Jews. An angel has appeared to him and told him that you have a message for him and his household."

[23]The three were then invited to come in for food and lodging until the next day. [24]They reached the home of Cornelius on the second day of travel. He had been waiting for them and had invited a number of friends, neighbors, and relatives who were eager to listen to the message from God. [25]As Peter entered, Cornelius was so impressed that he fell on his knees in worship. [26]Naturally, Peter gently helped him to realize that he could not accept worship. "Please do not worship me, friend, for I am just a human being." He then helped Cornelius to his feet.

[27]Together they entered the living room where a large group was assembled. [28]After an introduction Peter began, "As you know, I am a Jew and that Jewish laws would not allow me to do what I am doing right now. I am in the home of a Gentile! We were taught that Gentiles are unclean

and unfit to socialize with, but God told me two days ago that I must never again consider another human being unclean regardless of his race or religion. ²⁹As soon as I was shown this, I prepared to come with your messengers. So now let us share experiences with each other."

³⁰Cornelius spoke up. "Four days ago I was fasting and praying when about this time of day a person appeared to me in brilliant white garments. ³¹'Cornelius,' he said, 'your prayers have been heard, and God has recognized your generosity to the poor. ³²I want you to send messengers to Joppa and find a man called Simon Peter who is currently staying at the home of a tanner by the name of Simon who lives in a beachfront home.' ³³I lost no time in getting my servants ready and on their way, and you all should know how happy we are that you have been willing to come. We are here in God's presence waiting to hear what God obviously wants us to know."

³⁴ Peter then rose to speak, "Friends, I am astonished at God's ways. He shows no partiality, contrary to what I have believed all my life. ³⁵No, indeed, God accepts those of every nationality who are willing to obey Him. ³⁴He has sent a message to Israel as a nation, a message of peace, through a person named Jesus Christ, who is actually the Lord of creation. This message was first proclaimed far and wide in Judea and in Galilee, and was begun by the preaching of John. ³²It was about the anointing of Jesus of Nazareth by the Holy Spirit, giving Him power to go about doing good, rescuing all who were oppressed by the devil by the power of God which He exercised. ³⁹I am one of the witnesses of these things that He did in Judea and especially in Jerusalem, but also, I hate to say this, He was rejected

by our nation, then crucified. ⁴⁰Now comes the good news. On the third day He was raised up to life by the power of God and was seen on several occasions by a large number of people. ⁴¹We who had been selected to be His witnesses actually ate and drank with Him after He was raised to life. ⁴²We were given our mission: Preach to others that He will one day be the judge of both the dead and the living. ⁴³All the prophets have written about Him, telling us that through Him all our sins can be forgiven."

⁴⁴Even while Peter was still speaking the Holy Spirit came upon all the listeners. ⁴⁵Those who had come with Peter were totally surprised, for they were of the opinion that none but circumcised believers such as themselves would ever be baptized by the Holy Spirit. ⁴⁶And now here was a large gathering of Gentiles upon whom the gift of the Holy Spirit was bestowed in the same manner as on Jews at Pentecost. And they all rejoiced and glorified God. ⁴⁷Peter's reaction was to suggest that they be baptized in water at once. After all, they seemed equal to the Jewish believers. ⁴⁸So he proposed the idea to them. They were willing and even eager to do so. They then urged him to stay for a time with them, which he gladly did.

Chapter 11

¹News of this experience soon reached Jerusalem and strangely enough it stirred up considerable opposition. ²When Peter finally returned to Jerusalem, he was confronted by a delegation of believers who demanded that he give account of himself for going into a Gentile's home and eating with them. ⁴So he calmly started at the beginning and told them the whole story.

[5]"Let me explain just why I was willing to engage in such forbidden activities. It was while I was working at Joppa that one day I was praying and was given a vision in which a large sheet tied together at the four corners came down from the sky to me. [6]This sheet was packed with all kinds of wild and domestic animals, birds, and reptiles. [7]I was hungry at the time, and a voice was heard coming from the sky, 'Get up, Peter, kill and eat.' That sounded wonderful, but try as I might I could not spot even one clean animal. So my response was, 'Sorry, but there isn't one clean beast available here. [8]And I have never eaten any flesh that was not permitted by the Mosaic law.' [9]Then that same voice spoke from the sky again, 'Just a minute, Peter, I have advice for you. When God says He has cleansed something, you had better not call it common or unclean.' [10]Three times, this whole scenario was repeated, then the sheet was drawn back up into the sky and out of sight.

[11]"At that very moment, three men reached the house where I was boarding— three Gentiles from Caesarea—looking for me. [12]They had been sent by another Gentile who had been told by the Holy Spirit in a dream to come and bring me with them with neither fear nor guilt in so doing. I did not go alone either. Six other believers went with me, and we all went into this Gentile's home. [13]He related to us the experience he had been through, and the command to send messengers to Joppa and find a man called Peter who [14]would be able to give information as to how he and his whole family could be saved. [15]So I spoke to that whole household and some neighbors, telling about Jesus Christ and His message to the whole world. I was astonished to realize that the Holy Spirit was poured out on them just as He had been given to us at Pentecost.

[16]"This then was the fulfillment of the Lord's statement telling that John had baptized with water but that we would be baptized by the Holy Spirit. [17]When I recalled that statement and saw what was going on, that they had been baptized by the Holy Spirit just as we had been, who was I to even consider opposing God?"

[18]The brethren listened, amazed and speechless. Then, praising God, they proclaimed, "Yes, indeed, God has intended that Gentiles hear the truth and repent and be saved."

[19]Persecution kept increasing after the martyrdom of Stephen, scattering the believers far and wide. Some went to Phoenicia, some to Cyprus, and some to Antioch where they preached to the Jews about Jesus. No active attempts to reach the Gentiles had yet begun. [20]A few believers from Cyprus and Cyrene had moved to Antioch where they began to share their faith with the Greeks, teaching them about the Lord Jesus.

[21]God's hand was in this and a large number were convinced and turned to the Lord. [22]News of the outreach was carried to Jerusalem, where the church decided to send Barnabas to further teach the new believers. [23]As soon as he arrived in Antioch, he was cheered by their efforts, then added his own testimony, encouraging them all to be faithful to God. [24]Barnabas was an outstanding person, filled with the Holy Spirit and with great faith. His efforts brought many more people to the Lord. [25]From Antioch, Barnabas made a trip to Tarsus, hoping to find Saul. [26]He was successful and even persuaded

Saul to return with him to Antioch. Here they both worked for a full year in the church teaching people by the hundreds, and it was here that the believers in Jesus were first called "Christians."

²⁷During that year some prophets arrived from Jerusalem among whom was Agabus, ²⁸who received a vision concerning a coming drought and famine. His prophecy was fulfilled in the reign of Claudius Caesar. ²⁹Jerusalem was hard hit by the famine, so the believers in Antioch decided to send a supply of food in order to help out. ³⁰Barnabas and Saul were appointed to go and oversee the distribution of the food gathered.

Chapter 12

¹During this time of famine, Herod the king began to actively persecute Christians. ²James was the first of the apostles to give his life for Christ. Herod's soldiers carried out the order to execute this apostle. ³Most of the Jews were happy about this act by Herod, so he proceeded to go further. He arrested Peter during the Feast of Unleavened Bread. ⁴Peter was imprisoned with four squads of soldiers to guard him so that after the feast he could be brought out and publicly executed. ⁵Several days passed while the church held a twenty-four hour prayer service for him.

⁶The night before Herod planned to carry out his nefarious scheme Peter was sleeping, chained to two soldiers. More guards were at the door. ⁷Suddenly an angel from heaven came, lighting up the prison with a brilliant display of white light. He tapped Peter on the shoulder, awakening him, then commanded, "Get up at once." The chains fell from his hands. ⁸Then another command, "Put on your

sandals and belt." Peter did so. Then, "Now put on your robe and follow me."

⁹Out of the prison he went following the angel, thinking that he must be having a vision of some kind, for it seemed so impossible. ¹⁰They passed the first block of cells, then the second, and then to the main gate. It opened silently by itself, and they were out in the city. The angel stayed with Peter for a block or two, then disappeared. ¹¹When Peter began to comprehend the magnitude of the miracle, he said to himself, "Now I am positive that God sent this angel to rescue me from the king and from the unbelieving Jews."

¹²His first impulse led him to the home of John Mark's mother where a large number of believers were assembled praying for him. ¹³At the gate he knocked until someone heard him, then a young girl named Rhoda came out and recognized Peter by his voice. ¹⁴She was so overcome with joy and gratitude that she forgot to open the gate but ran back in to tell the others that Peter stood out at the gate.

¹⁵"Wait a minute, you must be hallucinating," someone said.

But she insisted, "No! It is really a fact, honestly."

"No, it must be his guardian angel."

¹⁶Peter kept on patiently knocking until someone went out and unlocked the gate to let him in. The whole group gave thanks and expressed their joy. ¹⁷Peter told them his account of how the Lord had wonderfully worked in his behalf, freeing him from prison and death. He then asked them if they would report to James and the leading brethren as he left through the dark streets to a safe hideout. ¹⁸Daylight came, and with it a perplexing problem confronted the guards: "Where was Peter?"

[19]Herod ordered a search, and a thorough questioning was carried out. But none of the guards could tell him what had become of Peter. So Herod, in his cruel manner, ordered the execution of the guards who were on duty that night. This, of course, was Roman policy, but the episode shook Herod to the point that he moved from Jerusalem to Caesarea, hoping to have more respect from those than he could command in Jerusalem.

[20]But his troubles were far from over. It seems that the people of Tyre and Sidon had done something that angered him greatly. They recognized the danger that they were in and made friends with Blastus, Herod's valet, and then through him made overtures of friendship with Herod himself, hoping that their cities might be spared the results of his fury. [21]One day Herod made a speech to his subjects dressed in royal robes. He seemed to be enjoying the pomp. [22]At a given cue, the listeners gave a great shout, "Surely we have heard the voice of a god, not the voice of a mere human being."

[23]Naturally this flattery pleased him, but his pride was his undoing, for he suffered a fatal stroke, permitted by God to demonstrate the folly of such egotism. He died right there before their eyes, and his corpse decayed as they watched.

[24]In contrast, God's word multiplied in that area and became well known and accepted. [25]Barnabas and Saul returned from Jerusalem after they had achieved their goals, bringing with them young John Mark.

Chapter 13

[1]In the church at Antioch there were several outstanding persons, even prophets and skilled teachers. To name a few: Barnabas, Simeon (black) Lucius from Cyrene, and Manaen, Herod's foster brother, and Saul. [2]These were among the members of the Antioch church as it fasted one day and heard the voice of the Holy Spirit say, "I have chosen Barnabas and Saul to do a special work for God. You should ordain them before they begin their assignment."

[3]The church promptly carried out this order. They were ordained at a ceremony of placing hands on them while praying. They were then free to follow God's leading. [4]First they were impressed to journey to Seleucia, then they sailed to Cyprus. [5]In the city of Salamis they began preaching in Jewish synagogues. John Mark was assisting in all these endeavors and beyond.

[6]They were at Paphos when they encountered a sorcerer named Bar-Jesus, a Jew who claimed to be a prophet. [7]He was influential in the life of the island's chief administrator, Sergius Paulus. This Paulus was always looking for more spiritual light, and when he heard of Barnabas and Saul, he was ready to investigate their claims to be God's messengers. [8]There was a problem however, for Bar-Jesus protested and threatened Barnabas and Saul in order to prevent Paulus from hearing the truth.

[9]Then Saul (who later came to be called Paul) was inspired by the Holy Spirit to confront this sorcerer bluntly. He said, [10]"Oh you subtle mischief-maker, you child of the devil, you enemy of right, you must stop trying to distort God's truth. [11]As of now, the Lord's hand is on you and will bring blindness upon you so that even sunlight will not be perceived for a while." Instantly, haziness spread over him, then darkness. He had to have someone lead him around. [12]After witnessing this event firsthand, the official became a believer at

once. The evidence was that persuasive.

¹³The work in Cyprus seemed to be well established by this time, so Paul and his company boarded a ship for Perga in Pamphylia. Unfortunately, John Mark had had enough of this type of life and decided to return to Jerusalem. ¹⁴In Pamphylia the work that had begun in Perga spread to Antioch of Pisidian. Here the group found a synagogue, went in, and sat down. ¹⁵The officers were leading out in the worship service as usual, reading from the Pentateuch, then prophetic scripture. When the scripture reading was completed, the newcomers were recognized and were asked, "Brothers, if you have words of admonition for this congregation, we would like to hear from you at this time."

¹⁶It did not take long for Paul to respond. He stood up and gestured a friendly greeting and began. "Dear brothers and sisters, descendants of Israel, I hope you will be willing to listen to what I have to say in the next few minutes. ¹⁷The God of our father Israel chose this race and gave special favor to him and to his family, beginning as far back in history while they were still in Egypt. His first favor was to provide miracles through which they escaped from Egypt. ¹⁸During the next forty years, God had to endure their rebellious nature as they wandered in the wilderness. ¹⁹Eventually He helped them drive out seven nations from Canaan, and He gave them that entire land, dividing it by lot to all the tribes. ²⁰For about four hundred years He guided them through judges, and then by Samuel the prophet. ²¹But a majority of the people wanted to have a king, and God permitted it, choosing Saul, son of Kish, as their first king. He was from the tribe of Benjamin and reigned for forty years.

²²"Finally Saul had to be replaced, and God found a man named David to be the next king. God said of David, 'I have found a man after My own heart, and he will go along with My plans for the nation.' ²³But finally God has fulfilled His promise to provide a Savior, a man by the name of Jesus of Nazareth, a descendant of David. ²⁴You remember the preaching of John the Baptist, don't you? He urged people to repent all through his ministry. ²⁵When asked if he were the Messiah, he responded, 'Who am I? No, I am not the Messiah, but soon a person will come, one so important that I am unworthy to untie His shoes.'

²⁶"My brothers, my countrymen, descendants of Abraham and all who are God-fearing people, I am sharing with you the good news of salvation. ²⁷As for the citizens of Jerusalem and their officials, they did not recognize him as the Messiah even though they had the prophetic words read to them every Sabbath. They were actually fulfilling prophecy when they condemned Him. ²⁸The accusations and the evidence presented were not such as to deserve death, but in spite of this, they pressured Pilate to execute Him. ²⁹Prophecy having been fulfilled by His death, He was placed in a tomb where He lay until the third day. ³⁰Then God raised Him to life again! ³¹He appeared to His followers for many days after His resurrection. They have testified to this.

³²"And now we can further testify that God's promises made to our ancestors have been fulfilled to us their descendants. ³³Remember Psalm 2:7? 'You are My Son. This day I became Your Father.' ³⁴And another prophetic psalm (16:10), a prophecy of resurrection, ³⁵'You will not

leave Me in the grave, nor will you allow Me to decay.' David wrote these words as a prophecy, trusting in God to eventually fulfill them. ³⁶And they obviously did not apply to David, for he died after a lifetime of service to his people, and his body has long since decayed. ³⁷So the fulfillment of this is found in Jesus whose body did not decay but was brought to life again on the third day.

³⁸"You, my brothers and sisters, need to know that your sins are forgiven through this Man. ³⁹Whatever your past sins are, they can be forgiven through His death for you. The law given by Moses could not forgive sins; it could only identify sin. ⁴⁰So put this down as fact; you will be able to avoid those things that prophets foretold would come upon rebels. ⁴¹Here are the words of the prophet: 'You haters, you will first be amazed, then you will perish, for I will do things that cannot be believed even though you hear them with your own ears form reliable sources'" (Habakkuk 1:5).

⁴²After the service was over, the Gentiles surrounded Paul, urging him to repeat that sermon for them the next Sabbath. ⁴³Finally the synagogue was empty, leaving Paul and Barnabas with a large following of Jews and proselytes. They were admonished to live in harmony with God's wonderful grace. ⁴⁴The following Sabbath the majority of the city's population gathered to listen to God's word. ⁴⁵Sadly, there were some Jews who became jealous of Paul and Barnabas and began to share their hatred with their fellow citizens.

⁴⁶It became apparent that relatively few Jews would truly believe in Jesus, so Paul and Barnabas confronted their leaders, "Gentlemen, we are convinced that we did the right thing in sharing the word

with you first, but now that you refuse to accept it, considering yourselves unworthy of eternal life, there is nothing more we can do for you. From now on we will preach to the Gentiles. ⁴⁷And actually the Lord has commanded us to do this in Isaiah 49:6, 'I have placed you here in order that you may be a light to the Gentiles, a light that will result in salvation everywhere in the world.'"

⁴⁸The Gentiles heard these quotations and were delighted and thanked God for them. Many became believers then and there and received eternal life as God had foretold. ⁴⁹This was only the beginning, for God's message quickly spread throughout the whole area. ⁵⁰It was a disappointment that the bulk of the Jews rejected the work of Paul and Barnabas and then aroused many dependable leaders and some women to persecute them, forcing them to leave. ⁵¹As they left they carried out Jesus' advice and shook the dust off their feet as they started for Iconium. ⁵² Yet they were filled with joy in spite of the persecution—a joy that was supplied by the Holy Spirit.

Chapter 14

¹Arriving in Iconium, they looked up the local synagogue and obtained permission to speak to the members. And the Gentiles were not neglected. Gentiles were part of their mission. In this city their preaching was really persuasive, so much so that a large company of people became Christians, both Jews and Greeks. ²It was not all light and happiness, for here too there was opposition. Unbelieving Jews went to work to undermine their credibility, thus turning many Gentiles against them. ³Undaunted, they determined to

stay for a long time in Iconium, continually telling others about the Lord, and the Lord supported their efforts as He granted them the power to perform miracles.

⁴At length the city was a divided city, some siding with the unbelieving Jews and some with the apostles. ⁵The opposition grew in influence and finally led to a plan to force these preachers out of town and stone them. ⁶The plot was discovered by their friends, but before the date set for the attack, they escaped and went on to Lystra and Derbe. ⁷Here they resumed their mission of preaching the good news.

⁸One incident at Lystra was particularly impressive. A man who had been crippled since birth and was helpless and unable to walk ⁹listened to Paul's preaching. His obviously sincere manner was noticed by Paul. He perceived that his faith was deep and sound, faith that is rewarded by miracles. ¹⁰So Paul spoke directly to him, "Sir, stand to your feet." Instantly he was healed. He not only stood but began jumping up and down with happiness.

¹¹This miracle had a tremendous effect on those who witnessed it. They concluded that Paul must be one of the gods. In their language they voiced this idea around town, "A god has been transformed into an apparition of a human. ¹²So they began calling Barnabas Jupiter, and Paul they considered to be Mercury, for he was the main spokesman. ¹³In the worship of Jupiter was a man acting as priest for their town. He rounded up cattle and garlands of flowers to make a great sacrificial celebration in their honor. ¹⁴Naturally Paul and Barnabas were horrified when they realized what was going on. Quickly they made their way through the clusters of worshippers and began to protest.

¹⁵"Friends, friends, why are you doing this? We are only human beings, not gods! In fact, our message is to abandon all such gods completely and begin to worship the God who created the earth and everything in it. ¹⁶In the past He has allowed all to make their own choices, and still does, ¹⁷and yet He has given evidence of His presence, such as sending rain from the sky, seasons for growing food, and giving joy to His creatures."

¹⁸Finally the sincere proclamation of truth helped to shut down the offering of sacrifices. ¹⁹But into Lystra came a lot of Jews from Antioch and Iconium who were able to influence enough people against the apostles so that they seized Paul, stoned him, and dragged him out of town, believing he was dead. ²⁰His converts were appalled, and in sorrow they stood around his body, wondering what to do. Then Paul suddenly revived, stood to his feet, and led the way back into town. By the next day he was ready to travel, so off to Derbe they went.

²¹Here they preached the gospel with no direct interference, and having succeeded in seeing many new converts join them in the Christian faith, they decided to return to visit the believers in Lystra, Iconium, and Antioch of Pisidia. ²²They intended to encourage them, bolster their faith, and help to strengthen their witness in spite of difficulties that they were encountering on their way to the kingdom of God. ²³In these congregations they ordained new elders, by prayer and fasting, and committed these loyal believers to God.

²⁴Finally having completed the tour of Pisidia, they reentered Pamphylia, ²⁵where they preached God's word for a time, then

on to Attalia, [26]from which port they sailed back to Antioch, their starting point and their home church that had sent them on this successful mission trip. [27]The Antioch church had a great meeting so that they could hear the stories of their missionary work, told by these apostles, how they had worked among the Gentiles. [28]For several months the Antioch believers were blessed by their personal ministry.

Chapter 15

[1]While Paul and Barnabas were at Antioch, some well-meaning but misguided people came from Judea and began to teach that a person could not be saved unless he was circumcised as it was commanded in the books of Moses. [2]This development began to produce a division in the church. Paul and Barnabas held the opposite view and challenged them to an intense series of debates about the matter. The church finally met and appointed a delegation to travel to Jerusalem and meet with the apostles. Both sides of the issue would be represented, and it was hoped that a resolution could be brought about. Paul and Barnabas were among the delegates.

[3]On the way they stopped at Phoenicia and Samaria, met with the believers there, and cheered them with their stories of their mission trip and how the gospel was being accepted by the Gentiles. [4]At Jerusalem they again were invited to relate to the church the wonderful result of their missionary experiences, teaching the gospel to heathen people. [5]When the mission stories ended, those who contended for circumcision had their case brought before the apostles and elders. Most of them were Christians who had been Pharisees and were convinced of the things they had been

teaching. Then the opposing views were presented. The dispute went on and on. [6]The apostles and elders listened patiently to all that was presented.

[7]Peter finally asked for the floor and was given permission to speak. "Brothers, gentlemen, you are all aware, I am sure, that God long ago commissioned me to give the good news to the Gentiles so that they too might believe. [8]Yes, and God even confirmed this move by giving the Holy Spirit to them just as he had done for us on the day of Pentecost. [9]You see, He considers Gentiles and Jews equal in value to Him. Faith is the essential feature in all of us. [10]So now why are you attempting to test God and His new believers by placing a yoke on them that our forefathers were unable to carry and which we are unable to carry? [11]Our faith rests on this point: Salvation is by the grace of God, grace offered to us and grace offered to them."

[12]After Peter's summary, Paul and Barnabas reported their experiences to the whole church about their sharing of the gospel among the Gentiles. They told of the miracles and the supernatural events that they had witnessed while on their mission.

[13]Now it was time for a decision to be made. The chairman, James, stood and said, "Gentlemen, brothers, kindly listen as I speak. [14]Peter has just recounted how God began to send His message to the Gentiles so that He could include them among His chosen people. [15]This was in perfect harmony with the writings of the prophets where the restoration of Israel and the calling of the Gentiles is foretold, [16]'I will return and once more build the tabernacle of David, which has been destroyed. I will rebuild it completely and re-establish it

[17]in order that other people may be able to seek and find the Lord, even the Gentiles.' This is what the Lord says, the Lord who always tells the truth. [18]Of course, you are aware that God knows the future and has known it since it was created. [19]Now, therefore, here is the decision about your question: We shall not burden the Gentiles who are turning to the true God, [20]but we shall put in writing the things that are important, and here they are: 1) Avoid all types of idolatry; 2) Do not engage in illicit sexual relationships; and 3) Refuse to eat meat or blood from strangled animals. [21]You see, we do not need to add anything to the writings of Moses, and his writings are being read in every synagogue."

[22]A motion was made, and a vote was taken. The motion passed that the apostles and elders with the endorsement of the whole church should send representatives to Antioch along with Paul and Barnabas. The two chosen were Judas Barsabbas and Silas both of whom were considered entirely trustworthy. [23]The letters sent contained these instructions: "The apostles, the elders, and the whole church hereby send our greetings to the church in Antioch of Syria and Cilicia. [24]This letter is in response to reports reaching us that some sincere but misguided folk have been among you and have urged you to be circumcised and follow the ceremonial law. Please be assured that we have never sent anyone out with any such message. [25]But having completed the council business here at headquarters, we all agreed to send some representatives to you along with Paul and Barnabas our beloved missionaries. [26]All have risked their lives for the name of our Lord Jesus Christ. [27]So this will introduce Judas Barsabbas and Silas who will explain more in detail the actions we have taken.

[28]"The consensus here is as follows (and the Holy Spirit agrees with our decision). We will not burden you with any unnecessary requirements. [29]But these few principles are important: 1) Avoid food that has been offered to idols; 2) Avoid the eating of blood and the flesh from strangled animals; and 3) Avoid all sexual sins. These principles, if followed, will always be for your own good. May God bless you."

[30]The meeting adjourned and the emissaries set out for Antioch. After their successful trip, they called the church together in special session [31]and read the letter from Jerusalem. This brought real joy and confidence to all the members. [32]Judas Barsabbas and Silas, who were prophets in their own right, stayed on for a time with the Antioch church, teaching and helping the members. [33]But the church knew that it would be best to allow them to return to their homes and released them. [34]However, Silas thought it best to stay for a time, giving counsel to the members. [35]So also did Paul and Barnabas and a number of other teachers who continued to teach the members and also a number of unbelievers.

[36]Eventually Paul became concerned about the status of the churches that had been established. These concerns were voiced to Barnabas, suggesting that they make a tour of all the known churches to encourage them and to receive encouragement from them. [37]Barnabas agreed and added that he wanted John Mark to go along again. [38]But Paul, remembering how John Mark had abandoned them during their first journey, rejected the idea completely. [39]The disagreement was so sharp that they decided not to attempt working

together again. So Barnabas went ahead and invited John Mark to go with him, and the two of them sailed for Cyprus. ⁴⁰Paul invited Silas to join him and was pleased when Silas liked the idea. They left shortly, taking with them the blessing of the church. ⁴¹Through Cilicia and Syria they traveled, encouraging and strengthening the churches.

Chapter 16

¹When they reached Derbe and Lystra, they met a young convert by the name of Timothy whose mother was Jewish but his father was Greek. ²Everyone in the Lystra church and the congregation of Iconium was well acquainted with the young man and thought highly of him. ³Paul felt strongly that Timothy should join their evangelistic team, but before he should do that it seemed wise to have him circumcised because of the possibility that Jewish listeners would be more likely to accept him, knowing that his father was a Greek.

⁴So the three of them traveled and worked together, meeting with the churches in the various cities. They carried copies of the Jerusalem council decision and shared these with every organized church. ⁵It was gratifying to find that the churches were alive and stable, growing in numbers and influence. ⁶Throughout Phrygia and Galatia it was the same—growing churches and enthusiastic Christians. Now having visited them, they considered entering new territory, expanding into the province of Asia. However, the Holy Spirit impressed them to not enter Asia, ⁷but to travel west through Mysia to Troas, rather than northward into Bithynia, for the Holy Spirit had indicated that it would not be best to go into that area either.

⁸They arrived at Troas, and one night Paul received a dream in which a man living in Macedonia was calling out to him, "Come over here to Macedonia and help us." ⁹In the morning he shared the dream with us, and we all agreed that the Lord must want us to preach the gospel there. ¹⁰So we began looking for a ship to take us across the sea to Macedonia. ¹¹Very soon after this decision, we found a ship that was leaving Troas for Macedonia by way of Samothrace and Neapolis, the seaport nearest to Philippi. We all went aboard. ¹²At Neapolis we enquired and found that there was an active Jewish community at Philippi, so we went there. Philippi was the major city in that part of the country and a Roman colony. Once in the city we found that the Jewish community had a meeting place along the river where they observed the Sabbath.

¹³The next Sabbath found us there joining the group in prayer and praise. Most of them were women and very friendly, willing to listen to what we had to say. ¹⁴Among them was a woman by the name of Lydia, who was a retailer of purple cloth. She was a devout worshipper of God, and she listened intently to all that Paul said and quickly grasped the significance of the Christian message. ¹⁵She wanted baptism and so did her whole family. That baptism was a real joy to us. More than that, she graciously invited us to be guests at her home while in Philippi. "If you have confidence that I am faithful to God, please grace my house as your home," she urged, and we accepted the invitation.

¹⁶One day not long after beginning our work there, we were on our way to a prayer meeting when a young girl possessed by a demon met us. She was a slave girl, but

her connection to the spirits was used by her owners to make a fat profit. [17]When we came along, she began shouting to everyone, "These men are servants of the greatest of all gods and will show us the way of salvation." [18]Day after day this went on until Paul faced her and challenged the evil spirit with this command, "I command you in the name of Jesus Christ to come out of her!" He came out. [19]When her owners learned about this and realized the change that had come over her, they were furious.

[20]Paul and Silas were arrested and brought before the city magistrates in the public market with this accusation, "These men are Jews and are bringing great trouble to our city. [21]They are teaching our citizens things that we Romans don't want and things which are illegal."

[22]Soon a large crowd assembled with most agreeing that something must be done. The magistrates believed these accusers and ordered Paul and Silas to be stripped and flogged. [23]After the beating they were taken to the jail and confined there with orders to keep them in maximum security. [24]The jailer complied, taking them to the most secure cell where their feet were fastened in stocks. [25]During the midnight hours the other prisoners were shocked to hear them praying and singing praise songs to God. [26]Suddenly a violent earthquake shook the city, breaking the prison's very foundation and opening all the locked cell doors. [27]Knowing that his own life was at stake if any prisoners escaped, the jailer quickly checked the prison. With the doors all open, he felt certain that the prisoners would all be fleeing for their lives, so rather than being executed he was ready to commit suicide. [28]Out came his sword, but before he could

use it, he heard Paul shouting, "Sir, don't harm yourself, for we are all here."

[29]Greatly relieved he called for a light then made his way to the cell where Paul and Silas were. There he fell on his face trembling before the two prisoners. [30]He unlocked their stocks and led them out of the prison. "My dear sirs," he pleaded, "what must I do to be saved?"

[31]"Simple," they told him, "believe in the Lord Jesus Christ and you will be saved as will your whole family." [32]Then at his invitation they presented to him the message of God. [33]His heart was touched, and he believed what had been told him right then. His first action as a Christian was to help the prisoners. Bringing fresh water, he gently washed their wounds, then anointed the areas to ease the pain. After this was done, he was baptized along with his family before morning. [34]Then Paul and Silas were invited to his home, served a meal, and the jailer was overcome with joy from learning of God. That house was home to a transformed group.

[35]When morning came the jailer received a message from the city officials, delivered by local deputies. It read, "Release these men at once."

[36]Paul was notified of the order, but his response puzzled the jailer. [37]"These officials have broken the law. We were jailed without a hearing or a trial of any kind, even though we are Roman citizens. So now they want to have us released as quietly as possible so as to avoid trouble. No. They must come themselves openly."

[38]The deputies returned to the city officials and gave them Paul's message. Fear seized them when they realized that they had violated Roman law. [39]So they speedily came and urged the wronged preachers to

consider themselves free men and to leave the city as soon as possible. [40]They accepted the offer and went to Lydia's home where the believers had gathered. Here they tried to encourage the little group before leaving town.

Chapter 17

[1]Traveling west they passed through Amphipolis and Apalonia, not stopping in either of these cities. They were looking for a Jewish group and found one in Thessalonica. [2]Here they introduced themselves to the members of the local synagogue and worshipped with them for three Sabbaths, with Paul giving them his message from Scripture. [3]He used the prophecy found in Isaiah concerning the sufferings of the Messiah and His death and resurrection. "Jesus of Nazareth has fulfilled this prophecy fully, and He is the Messiah." [4]Some accepted Paul's message and became believers, happy to learn about Jesus and happy to have fellowship with Paul and Silas. Also there were a number of prominent Greeks and women who became Christians.

[5]But alas, here again troubles faced them. The Jews who rejected Christ mounted a campaign against them, angry over their success. They gathered a bunch of hoodlums and started a citywide riot. They came to Jason's home and tried to break in and capture the believers who were hiding there. [6]But none were found, so they seized Jason and a few Christians and then forced them to appear before the city officials, accusing them of harboring those people "who have turned the world upside down."

[7]"This Jason has protected them, and of course, this is illegal, for they teach that there is another king, Jesus by name, in place of Caesar." [8]The leaders of the mob went on and on, urging the authorities to "do something." [9]At length Jason and the others posted bail and were released, [10]but not before urging Paul and Silas to leave town for their own safety. That very night they made their escape and went on to Berea where there was another Jewish congregation.

[11]In Berea an entirely different attitude was shown. The people drank in the truths they were taught, and then went home and closely searched the scriptures to see if what had been taught was true. [12]As a result of this, a good number of influential Greek women, as well as Greek men who were community leaders, became Christians. [13]News of the Berean effort soon reached Thessalonica, enraging the Jews. They quickly organized a campaign to stir up trouble in Berea, which became so fierce that the Berean church leaders advised Paul to leave for his own safety. [14]They personally escorted him to the nearest seaport so that he could proceed on to Athens. Silas and Timothy stayed in Berea and awaited a message from Paul advising them of his plans.

[15]Not long after his arrival in Athens, Paul sent an urgent message to his colleagues, asking them to come as soon as possible. [16]Paul did not wait in idleness, for as he observed the city and its widespread idolatry, he was deeply stirred. [17]He began by meeting with the local Jewish congregation and by starting discussion groups in the marketplaces. [18]Some of the Athenian intelligentsia—Epicurean philosophers, Stoics—noticed him, and their immediate reaction was to turn up their noses in disdain, "Well, what do you suppose this

guy will say next? He apparently is trying to promote the idea of even more gods than we already have. (They had heard him report the resurrection of Jesus.) [19]They invited him to speak about his beliefs on Mars Hill where he would be assured of an audience. [20] "You, sir are really saying some fantastic things, and we would like to hear you through."

[21]Now Athens was a place where one of the chief activities centered on delving into new ideas and philosophies. [22]Paul's approach to the subject was this: "Gentlemen of Athens, I have been deeply impressed by your learning and your devotion to your religions. You obviously are sincere in your commitment to your beliefs and are willing to admit that you just possibly are missing an important truth. What do I mean? Simply this. [23]As I was exploring your city, I came upon an altar with these words carved into it, 'To the unknown god.' It occurred to me that you might be willing or perhaps even eager to hear bout this God who is unknown to you. I know Him and will here and now tell you about Him. [24]To begin with, He does not live in an altar, a shrine, or even a temple, for He is the cause, the Creator of the earth and everything in it. And not only the earth but of the entire universe. [25]We human beings cannot contribute to His life or comfort. No, just the opposite is true. He is the source of our life; our very breathing is evidence of His continual ministry to us His creatures. [26]We have all descended from Him by a direct creation. Every race of people on this planet came from one original pair whom He created. He planned everything for us, even to our homes, our land, and the limits we should observe. [27]For these reasons everyone

would be well advised to learn of Him and know Him, to grope, search, and enquire about Him. We would all discover that He is near us, very near indeed.

[28]"Yes, let me repeat this. It is in Him that we even exist, that we are what we are. Your own poets have expressed it this way: 'We are His children, His offspring.' [29]Now think this through: Here we are, marvelous mechanisms, incomparably complex creatures. An image made of stone or gold or silver cannot begin to represent a human being accurately. How much less are they able to represent the Infinite Being who designed us in the first place! [30]For ages our ignorance has allowed this God to overlook our behavior, but now He is showing us our true condition and is asking us to change our ways, our practices of the past, and conform to His plan for us.

[31]"Why do this? Here's the reason. A day of judgment is coming, a day of final accounting when every person will be dealt with personally. This judgment will be, fortunately for us, carried out by a person who has already been selected and authorized for this office. He is a person uniquely qualified, who bears Godlike credentials. He demonstrates Godlike power. The evidence is convincing, for He has been resurrected from death and is now living."

[32]Paul's listeners now began to express their opinions of such teaching. In general, they separated into two categories, the scoffers who pooh-poohed the whole idea, and the ones who wanted to hear more before making a decision. [33]So Paul left the group, [34]and some listeners who believed him followed him and became Christians, among whom were Dionysius a judge of the Areopagus and a woman by the name of Damaris.

Chapter 18

[1]Following his Athens experience, Paul went on to Corinth, [2]where he met a Jew by the name of Aquila, a native of Pontus who had recently arrived from Rome. He and his wife Priscilla had been driven out of Rome by the decree of Claudius, which ordered all Jews out of that city. [3]He quickly made friends with them at their home, for they were tentmakers, the same trade that Paul had learned. Now he joined them in their enterprise. [4]Every Sabbath he met with the Jews in their synagogue, giving eloquent discourses to the members. The results were wonderful. Many Jews and Greeks were convinced by the truth he presented.

[5]This continued until Silas and Timothy arrived from Macedonia. By that time he had persuaded many that Jesus is the Messiah. [6]But here also, bitter opposition arose against him. They went so far as to curse him publicly and upbraid him severely. Paul at length responded to their hateful behavior by removing his coat and giving it a vigorous shake, "Gentlemen, I have given you the truth. Your decision is naturally yours alone. Your destiny is your own choice, and my conscience is clear. From now on I will go to the Gentiles."

[7]So he left them and returned to the home of Justus, a God-fearing citizen who lived next to the synagogue. [8]This synagogue had as its chief officer a man named Crispus who with his family had heartily accepted God's message. It was partly because of his influence that a substantial number of his fellow Corinthians became Christians and were baptized.

[9]During the night Paul had a dream in which God spoke to him, "Do not be afraid, Paul. Go on preaching and teaching, [10]for I am with you and will protect you. I have a large number of people in this city who will yet receive salvation."

[11]So for the next eighteen months he stayed and taught the word of God. [12]During this time Gallio was the Roman minister of Achaia, and there was a Jewish conspiracy against Paul. [13]They went to Gallio with their complaints, then brought Paul to Gallio. "This fellow is teaching that one must worship in a way that violates the law."

[14]Paul was allowed to speak in his own defense, but before he began Gallio looked at the Jews and addressed them, "If your charge contained any semblance of evidence of crime or of immorality, it would be proper for me to hear you out, [15]but if it is only a matter of names, words, and Jewish customs take care of that in your own way, for I refuse to consider such things."

[16]He then dismissed the charges, and Paul was freed. [17]The Jews found out that their plot was not easily forgotten. A gang of Greeks seized Sosthenes the ruler of the synagogue and thrashed him right in the presence of Gallio who didn't lift a finger to prevent their attack. [18]As for Paul, he remained for some time in Corinth before leaving his faithful believers. He was on his way to Syria and with him were Aquila and Priscilla. For reasons known only to him, Paul had taken a ceremonial vow with its shaved head symbol.

[19]The first stop was at Ephesus where his traveling companions went ashore while Paul stayed only a few days, still trying to persuade the Jews that Jesus is the Messiah. [20]They invited Paul to stay longer, but he refused because of his desire to be in Jerusalem for the feast. After that,

God willing, he would return. [21]A ship was leaving for Caesarea so he boarded it, and the voyage was uneventful. [22]His stay at Caesarea was short, just long enough to greet the church, and then he proceeded to Jerusalem to headquarters and a brief meeting. He could not be comfortable there for the needs of the new churches weighed heavily on his mind, and soon he was off again, first to Antioch, [23]where he spent some time with the believers before going on into Galatia and Phrygia to encourage and strengthen the Christians there.

[24]Here a man named Apollo comes into the story. He was a Jew, born in Alexandria, and a person who knew Scripture well. [25]He was convinced that John the Baptist was God's prophet and was very zealous about sharing his faith with others. [26]At Ephesus he was at the local synagogue sharing his faith when Aquila and Priscilla heard him. They sensed at once that he had never encountered Jesus, so they invited him home and opened to his amazed mind the fulfillment of his hope and faith until he became a committed Christian. [27]His plans then were to travel to Achaia, and as he went he carried with him a letter of introduction from the church leaders. This proved a great help and allowed him to begin teaching wherever he found believers. [28]He proved himself a master at preaching and publicly evangelizing using Scripture to demonstrate that Jesus is the Messiah.

Chapter 19

[1]While Apollos was at Corinth, Paul visited Ephesus and became acquainted with a number of new believers. [2]In questioning them he asked this: "Have you received the Holy Spirit?"

"Frankly," they replied, "we have never heard of this 'Holy Spirit.' Tell us more."

[3]"Well, then, what baptism did you receive?"

"John's baptism," they replied.

[4]"Now brothers and sisters," Paul said, "John indeed baptized with water those who repented, and rightly so, but he always informed them that they should put their faith in another who was yet to come. And he was referring to Jesus Christ."

[5]This persuaded them at once, and they were baptized in the name of the Lord Jesus. [6]And as Paul placed his hands on them at baptism, they too experienced the Holy Spirit and were given the gift of new languages and the gift of prophecy. [7]This was a group of about twelve people. [8]For the next three months Paul was regularly at the synagogue teaching boldly the truth about God's kingdom. [9]Of course, this raised strong opposition in some of the listeners who refused to accept Paul's message. They began spreading rumors against the Christians, so Paul changed his plans. He left the synagogue and invited his listeners to distance themselves from their opponents.

A philosopher by the name of Tyrannus who operated a private school had become acquainted with Paul and opened his facility for further Christian teaching. [10]And from then on, for about two years, the Christian message was given daily until everyone in the province of Asia, Jews and Greeks, had learned about Jesus. [11]Some unusual miracles were performed by Paul during this time. [12]Such as: A handkerchief or an apron that had been in Paul's possession would be carried to the sick or demon-possessed, resulting in cure of the disease and freedom from the demon.

[13]Having seen some of these miracles, a few Jews who traveled around performing exorcism began to use the name of Jesus in their ministry. Their ritual went like this: speaking to the demon they would say, "I command you in the name of Jesus whom Paul preaches be gone." [14]One case was especially interesting. A man named Sceva, a priest, had seven sons. [15]Once after commanding the evil spirit to leave, the demon replied, "Jesus I know, and Paul I know, but who, pray tell, are you?" [16]The victim viciously attacked them with almost superhuman power, beating them up unmercifully so that they were barely able to escape from him, naked and badly bruised. [17]This experience was widely publicized to everyone in that area, Jews and others, resulting in a widespread knowledge of the name of Jesus.

[18]Believers multiplied, some of whom came to Paul, made a confession of their sins and renounced their evil ways. [19]Others who were dabbling in the occult gathered their books together and made a public burning of them, a huge stack of such books worth perhaps fifty thousand silver coins (a value equal to wages for one hundred forty years). [20]So the work progressed and God's word grew in influence and authority.

[21]Later on, Paul visited Macedonia and Achaia. He then decided to return to Jerusalem and try to get to Rome. [22]Before leaving, however, he persuaded Timothy and Erastus to help the cause in Macedonia while he went into the province of Asia to give help to some believers there. [23]Christians began to be known as "the people of the way." They were increasingly in the public-eye, but trouble lay ahead.

[24]It all began because of a silversmith by the name of Demetrius who was in the business of making small silver shrines. He had several employees in order to keep up with the demand. [25]He called a meeting of his craftsmen and others in the city who were involved, "Gentlemen, I have invited you here to present a problem and to ask for your help in trying to find a solution. We have done very well indeed up to now, but as you know our business is in real jeopardy. [26]A certain fellow named Paul has been active here in Ephesus and throughout the whole province telling people who are our customers that these images are not real gods at all. [27]This is threatening our craft, our livelihood, and even more—the very worship of Artemis and the magnificent temple built in her honor. Now even though nearly all of Asia worships her, yes, and even in other provinces, it is clear that if Paul continues here anything can happen."

[28]This speech had the desired effect. The hearers were enraged and began shouting, "Great is Artemis of the Ephesians; Great is Artemis of the Ephesians." [29]The spirit of the meeting quickly spread to the general population, and a riot broke out. Paul's friends Gaius and Aristarchus from Macedonia were captured and rushed into the arena. [30]Paul was ready to go to their defense, but the Christians with him convinced him of the folly of doing so. [31]Also other friends he had made, high up members of society, sent word to him not to enter the arena where the riot was underway. [32]Inside the arena all was confusion. Some were shouting one thing and some shouting another. In fact, a fair percentage did not know why they were there in the first place. [33]The Jews there did not wish

to be thought of as part of Paul's group, so their first goal was to steer the guilt away from themselves. They persuaded Alexander to make a speech before the crowd, ³⁴but enough people knew he was a Jew, and this appearance brought only a huge shout against him. Then the cry, "Great is Artemis of the Ephesians," was repeated again and again. It continued for two hours, drowning out all others.

³⁵Finally the town clerk was able to get the attention of the mob. Standing before them, he began, "Fellow citizens of Ephesus, there is not a person here who does not know that our fair city is the center for the worship of our great god Artemis, a worship that began with the original image that we all believe fell from Zeus in the heavens to this earth. ³⁶No one here disputes the truth of this fact, so we can be calm, assured, and confident. What I see here today convinces me that I should urge you to suppress this move to a mob psychology and avoid demonstrations such as this. ³⁷What you have done today is to illegally seize these men who are not criminals bent on vandalizing churches or cursing our goddess. ³⁸Now let me remind you what would be a proper and fitting course to pursue. If Demetrius and his craftsmen wish to press charges against these men or against anyone else, our laws will cover such matters. There is a legal and orderly way to go about such an action. Let them go through the established legitimate procedures. ³⁹If a matter comes up that is not specifically stated in our laws, this too can be brought to the assembly and dealt with. ⁴⁰My friends, we are very likely to be investigated by higher authorities over what has happened here today inasmuch as there was no emergency whatsoever to

require such a demonstration as you have witnessed." ⁴¹At the close of his speech he told everyone plainly that it was time to break up the meeting and go home, which they did promptly.

Chapter 20

¹When things finally became calm again, Paul called all the Christians together for a praise session; then he left for Macedonia. ²He spent some time with every congregation in the province, urging all to faithfulness and loyalty; then he went to Greece. ³The next three months were spent there, but a Jewish plot to ambush him was discovered as he was planning to sail to Syria, so his plans changed and he returned to Macedonia. ⁴This time several members decided to go with him to Asia, Sopater a Berean, Aristarchus and Secundus who were Thessalonians, Gaius from Derbe, Timothy, and Tychicus and Trophimus from Asia. ⁵So they went on ahead and waited for us at Troas.

⁶We stayed at Philippi until after the Jewish Feast of Unleavened Bread; then we sailed for Troas. The voyage was a five-day trip, and for the next week we were with the church of Troas. ⁷The last day there was a Sabbath and was spent in fellowship and worship. After the Sabbath ended, a potluck and an evening meeting proceeded as planned. This was followed by another sermon by Paul, who was scheduled to leave the next morning. His sermon lasted until midnight. ⁸The meeting place was on the third floor of the building and was lighted by many lamps. ⁹A young man named Eutychus was sitting in an open window. He became so sleepy during Paul's long sermon that he fell out of the window, hitting the hard path three stories below. Strong

arms picked him up, but he was lifeless. Paul rushed down, embraced Eutychus, and then said, "Don't worry friends; he is alive!"

[11]Once again in the upper meeting hall they shared food together and then listened while Paul went on telling them the thrilling stories of his work, stories that kept them spellbound until daylight. His time had run out and he had to leave. [12]By this time Eutychus seemed to have fully recovered, bringing joy to all his friends.

[13]Paul left for Assos on foot while the rest of us boarded a ship for that port. [14]When our ship arrived at Assos, we wondered if Paul could actually be there, for it was about thirty-five miles by road. No need to worry for there he was waiting for the ship, which then proceeded on to Mitylene. [15]The next day we arrived at a point opposite Kios, a day later at Samos, and the next day we arrived at Miletus. [16]Time was short or we would have stopped at Ephesus, but the Passover was approaching, and Paul was intent on being in Jerusalem by then.

[17]He did get a message to the elders at Ephesus telling them where he planned to be so they could meet him at Miletus, which they did. [18]His meeting with them was packed with conversation regarding the church and its needs. He first reminded them, "You are, of course, well acquainted with my lifestyle since I first came to Asia, and it has been the same summer and winter. [19]I have been the willing slave of our Lord, going through sadness, many tears, and many trials because of the bitter opposition of the Jews. [20]But through all of this I was able to give you the guidance you needed, both in public meetings and in house-to-house labor. [21]I met with both

Jews and Greeks, teaching that we all need to repent before God and put our complete trust in Jesus Christ. [22]Now I am on my way to Jerusalem, urged on, I am convinced, by the Holy Spirit, but apprehensive about what may happen there. [23]Judging by past experiences, wherever I have been, I can expect the worst: arrest, imprisonment, persecution. [24]However, these prospects are not able to turn me from my purpose, for my life is not that important. Of real importance is the completion of my calling, and this will bring true joy to me. Just to tell of the wonderful grace of God—this is of eternal value.

[25]"All of you here, I must tell you this: You will never see my face again in this world. [26]But I tell you this in all sincerity; I have faithfully proclaimed the message given to me. Those who have heard the truth through my preaching are now responsible to God for their decisions. I feel that I have fully borne my responsibility to them. [27]I have not hesitated to tell them everything God wanted them to know. [28]Please remember what I am about to say next. It has to do with every church member over which you are the guardians, appointed by the Holy Spirit. Continue to nourish and feed them. Remember, they were purchased by God with His own blood.

[29]"It had been revealed to me that after I leave the flock will be attacked by wolves, vicious enemies who will not hesitate to destroy the church. [30]In addition to this, some of your own members will become enemies and will produce offshoot movements, attempting to lure members away with them. [31]So be on guard constantly, and remember that for three years I have faithfully, day and night, attempted to warn and instruct you.

[32]"Now brothers, I must commit you to the care of our God, to His grace, for He is able to build you up and to make you sure of your inheritance in God's kingdom, along with all who are willing to make a decision to be on His side. [33]I have never been jealous of your wealth, believe me. [34]You are also aware that I have earned enough by my trade to support myself and some who were with me. [35]I have tried to demonstrate in my own life how we should be willing to aid the weak and the poor, remembering the words of the Lord Jesus that 'it is more blessed to give than to receive.'"

[36]When he was through, he invited all to kneel in prayer as he prayed for them. [37]There was sadness and weeping and farewell kisses. [38]The realization that they would never see him again really brought out their emotions. But time had run out. He must return to the ship. They all followed him to the pier.

Chapter 21

[1]The ship sailed away with our party safely on board, stopping first at Coos, then again at Rhodes and at Patara. [2]Here we changed ships, having found one bound for Phoenicia. [3]It sailed south of Cyprus then directly to Tyre where the cargo was to be delivered. [4]Here we found some believers, so we decided to stay for a week, during which time Paul was urged not to go on to Jerusalem as he had planned, assuring him that the Holy Spirit had revealed to them the dangers of so doing. [5]But in spite of the ominous nature of this advice, we continued on our way. The Christian families went with us to the shore, [6]where we all knelt down and prayed together before boarding the ship.

[7]From Tyre we sailed first to Ptolemais where we met with the church leaders for a full day before heading to our [8]next stop at Caesarea. Philip the evangelist, one of the original seven deacons, lived here. [9]His four daughters, all of whom were prophets, had not yet married. [10]We waited for several days there at Caesarea and another warning was given to Paul. This time it was from the prophet Agabus who had recently arrived from Judea. [11]As soon as he met Paul he removed Paul's belt, using it to tie up his own hands and feet. Then he spoke, "The Holy Spirit says that the Jews at Jerusalem will tie up the man who owns this belt and turn him over to the Gentiles."

[12]We listened in amazement to the prophetic words of Agabus and remembered his prophecy years before about the years of drought that had been fulfilled so accurately. All of us in the missionary group and all the church members at Caesarea who were present felt that this was a direct warning from God not to go on to Jerusalem where his enemies were waiting for him. We all expressed our position in an urgent plea.

[13]But Paul was so intent on going that he would not heed anything that was said. "Why are you weeping and breaking my heart. You know that I am willing to be arrested and shackled and even to die if necessary for the name of Jesus Christ."

[14]It was evident that our entreaties had fallen on deaf ears. There was no point in further pleading so we finally said, "The Lord's will be done." [15]So we began to gather our baggage together in preparation for the journey. [16]Several of the church members went along, having arranged with an elderly Christian named Mnason to house us while in Jerusalem.

[17]When we arrived in Jerusalem, the church was delighted to see us, and [18]they called together the elders for a meeting on the next day, with James presiding. [19]Paul was able to tell them story after story of how God had worked through his ministry among the Gentiles. [20]The brethren rejoiced and thanked God, but they reminded Paul, "You are no doubt aware, brother, how many Jewish Christians still believe that we must obey all of the Mosaic laws. [21]They have heard a great deal about you, how you have been teaching Jews everywhere that it is no longer necessary to follow Mosaic customs, especially that they need not circumcise their children. [22]So be frank with us and tell us where you stand on such matters. They will hear that you have come and will demand answers to these questions. [23]Here is what we think you ought to do: There are four young men now who are taking solemn vows. [24]Join them in these vows, even to shaving the head, so that everyone can see plainly that the rumors about you are false and that you continue to observe the Mosaic laws. [25]Do not worry about Gentile believers. We have already notified them that they need not observe Mosaic customs except to avoid food that has been offered to idols, avoid using blood as food and flesh from strangled creatures, and to avoid sexual impurity."

[26]Paul listened to them and was willing to go along with their advice, "purifying" himself ceremonially, then he went with them to the temple to demonstrate his purification ritual, which would last seven days and culminate in a sacrifice on each day. [27]The week was nearly over when some Jews from Asia spotted Paul in the temple and had him arrested while they stirred the crowds to action, yelling, [28]"Help! Help! Loyal patriots, here is that man who is teaching people everywhere he goes to ignore Moses' laws, this temple, and his own race. Furthermore, he has polluted this place by bringing in Gentiles!"

[29]They had seen Trophimus in the city with Paul a few days earlier and had supposed that he was from Ephesus and, of course, thought that he too had entered the temple. [30]It was only a short time until a riot was in full swing during which Paul was seized and dragged out of the temple after which they locked the temple doors. [31]The mob was bent on lynching him. This was apparent, and the word got to the Roman authority in Jerusalem [32]who dispatched several hundred soldiers and their centurions in charge to quell the riot. [33]This move was successful in bringing about some order, and it saved Paul from a severe beating. The captain took Paul into custody and began questioning him while chaining him with two chains for security. "Who, pray tell, are you? And what have you done?"

[34]The mob was milling around, shouting this and that, and the din was so loud that he ordered Paul moved into the castle where adequate order could be maintained. [35]On the way the soldiers actually picked Paul up and carried him to protect him from the mob. [36]Their cries for execution were getting more insistent by the minute. [37]Seeing the captain nearby, Paul asked, "May I have a few words with you, sir?"

"Oh, do you speak Greek? [38]Are you not the Egyptian who stirred up an insurrection a while back and gathered four thousand murderers and organized them in the wilderness intent on overthrowing the government?"

[39]"By no means, sir! You are thinking of an entirely different incident. I am a Jew, born in Tarsus, Cilicia, an important city. I would like to have the privilege of speaking to these people." [4]

[0]The captain consented and allowed Paul to stand on the stair above the crowd. Beckoning with his hands, he finally quieted the noisy crowd as he prepared to address them.

Chapter 22

[1]Speaking in Hebrew he began: "Gentlemen, brothers, fathers, may I have your attention while I speak to you?" [2]When they heard him speaking in their own language, they became silent. [3]"I am a Jew, born in Tarsus, Cilicia, reared and educated right here in Jerusalem. My training was under Gamaliel, an orthodox education if there ever was one, in line with the conservative education of the day, and believe me, I was zealous for our God just as you are today. [4]I would like to share with you what has happened to me if I may. I was violently opposed to these Christians and was appointed chief prosecutor of them, sending a number of them to their death, others to prison, both men and women.

[5]"The high priest and the board of elders can testify to the truth of this. I was duly deputized with full authority in writing to proceed to Damascus where a nucleus of Christians lived. It was my intention to arrest them and bring them to Jerusalem for trial and sentencing. [6]It was nearly noon, and our party was approaching Damascus when a brilliant, dazzling light fell on us from the sky. [7]I fell to the ground, stunned, then an audible voice spoke to me, 'Saul, Saul why are you persecuting Me like this?' [8]I was shaking with fear, but meekly answered, 'My Lord, who are You?' The voice answered, 'I am Jesus of Nazareth. You are persecuting Me.' [9]My companions were terrified as I was. They too were overcome by the light but did not hear the voice. [10]Alright, Lord, please tell me what I must do,' I replied. He then gave me orders, 'Get up and go on into the city. There you will be told what you must do and your future responsibilities.'

[11]"How was I to know how to go on? I had been blinded by the light. Fortunately, my associates did not lose their eyesight, so they led me on into Damascus where I was given a place to stay at the home of a man named Judas on Straight Street. [12]Then two days later a man named Ananias came to the house looking for me. He was a respected citizen, trusted by all the Jews in Damascus, a devout, God-fearing man. [13]He walked right up to me and spoke, 'Brother Saul, receive your sight.' And would you believe it? I could see again. His face was the first thing I saw. [14]Then he continued speaking, 'The God of our fathers has chosen you for a special purpose. He wants you to know His plans. He showed you the Righteous One, and you heard the voice of that Righteous One. [15]Now you are destined to be a witness for Him, telling people everywhere what you have seen and heard. [16]Saul, do not wait, get up now, and be baptized, washing away your sins as you call on the name of the Lord.'

[17]"You may be sure that I did just that. At once. I was baptized. Later, back in Jerusalem, I was praying in the temple and had a vision in which [18]I saw Him again. This time He told me, 'You had best get out of Jerusalem as soon as possible for the

people here will not believe what you say about Me.' ¹⁹'Lord,' I replied, 'they know that I sent many of Your believers to prison and that I ordered many of them beaten, and surely they will consider this as evidence that I was on their side if they hear about me again. ²⁰Also they will surely remember that when Stephen was stoned, I was right there advocating his death and holding their coats while he was dying.' ²¹But the only answer He gave me was this: 'Leave, I am sending you far away. You will be My spokesman to bring My message to the Gentiles.'"

²²The crowd was listening up to that point, but when he spoke the word "Gentile," shouts began to be heard, "Get rid of him, get rid of him! He doesn't deserve to live!" ²³People started throwing their clothes in the air, and some picked up fistfuls of dust and hurled it into the air. ²⁴The captain ordered Paul back into the castle, and he was preparing to have him scourged so that when questioned he would not dare tell anything but the truth. He must find out what all this rioting was all about. ²⁵As he was being tied up for the beating, Paul asked the centurion, "Are you sure you want to go ahead and scourge a Roman citizen who has not even had a lawful trial? You know, of course, that such a thing is illegal."

²⁶Preparations for the scourging were discontinued immediately, and the centurion reported to the captain. "Sir, I would advise that you think twice before you go ahead with this order. He is a Roman citizen."

²⁷Naturally the captain wanted to find out for himself the truth of this statement, so he questioned Paul himself, "Mister, are you a Roman citizen?"

"Yes, sir," came the answer.

²⁸"So am I," said the captain. "It cost me a lot of money to obtain freedom."

Then Paul explained, "Sir, I was born a Roman citizen."

²⁹Suddenly new orders were issued. The soldiers who were about to flog Paul were withdrawn. As for the captain he was downright afraid for his own standing. He had just violated the law himself by having Paul tied up. ³⁰The following day Paul was released and permitted to face the chief priests and the Sanhedrin who had been planning to accuse him in front of Roman officials.

Chapter 23

¹As Paul stood before the Sanhedrin, he was intensely moved. He was facing men he had known in years past while he was persecuting Christians. Solemnly and earnestly he began, "Brothers, gentlemen, I stand before you this day with a clear conscience. God is my witness."

²Ananias, the high priest, gave a command to the guards to slap Paul on the mouth. And this command was obeyed. ³"You white-washed wall," Paul quickly retorted, "God will certainly strike you some day. This was an illegal act. You who presume to sit in judgment over me are yourself a lawbreaker!"

⁴Someone nearby spoke to Paul, "How dare you revile God's high priest?"

⁵"Oh, was that the high priest? I apologize, for we are commanded never to revile a ruler."

⁶Paul had become aware that some members of the Sanhedrin were Sadducees, others were Pharisees, and he realized that he could use this situation to his advantage. So he continued his speech, "Brothers,

gentlemen, I happen to be a Pharisee, in fact I am the son of a Pharisee. I am being questioned about the hope of a resurrection from the dead."

[7]At once a dispute arose between the Pharisees and the Sadducees over this issue. [8]Sadducees deny that there will be a resurrection, that there are any such beings as angels or 'spirit' beings. [9]The tumult became louder and louder with the Pharisees finally gaining the floor. "We move to acquit this man for if indeed an angel or a spirit being has spoken to him we do not want to be found fighting against God." [10]And again a shouting match began, and the atmosphere was so threatening that the captain ordered Paul back into the castle for his protection.

[11]That very night Paul had an experience that encouraged him greatly. The Lord came and stood by him, then spoke to him, "Paul, cheer up. You have given your testimony here in Jerusalem and I promise that someday you will be able to give the same testimony in Rome."

[12]When morning came some Jews got together and came up with a mutual agreement. In it they swore a solemn oath that they would neither eat nor drink until they had killed Paul. [13]This was no small threat for there were more than forty who were involved in the conspiracy. [14]Moreover, they went to the chief priests and elders and proposed to them what they had agreed to do. [15]"Here is what we hope you will do. Go to the captain and tell him that you want to ask Paul more questions about his life and teachings. When Paul is brought out of the castle on his way to the meeting place, we will overpower the guards and kill him."

[16]Fortunately for Paul, his nephew, the son of Paul's sister, had heard the plot being planned, went to the castle, and received permission to talk with the prisoner. He was granted this privilege, and now Paul was able to hear of the deadly plan. [17]A centurion was nearby and responded to Paul's request for a few minutes of his time. "Sir, this young man has an important message for the captain. Could you arrange a meeting as soon as possible?"

[18]He could and did so. The young fellow was escorted to the captain and introduced. "Sir, our prisoner Paul urged me to arrange a meeting with this young man who has an important message for you."

[19]Taking him by the hand, the captain led him into a private office to hear what he had to say. [20]"Sir, a conspiracy of Jews has planned to ask you to bring Paul to the council again as if they want to learn more of his teaching. [21]However, their real purpose is quite different. More than forty of them are ready to kill him as he is being brought to the council. They have vowed a solemn vow that they will neither eat nor drink until they have killed him. So please do not fall for their scheme."

[22]The captain sensed the seriousness of the situation and admonished his young informer, "Don't you dare breathe a word about your meeting with me and what you have learned." [23]He next gave orders to two centurions, "Prepare your men at once for a trip to Caesarea. Along with your men, I will send eighty of our cavalry. [24]Put Paul on a horse and take him directly to Felix, the governor, beginning at midnight tonight."

[25]He then wrote a letter as follows: [26]" I, Claudius Lysias, herewith send my greetings to your excellency, Governor Felix. [27]This letter is to introduce a prisoner to you. He was captured by the Jews

in Jerusalem and would have been killed shortly had I not rescued him by military force, and then I discovered that he is a Roman citizen. ²⁸Under protection by the army, I allowed them to accuse him of the alleged crimes, and after a short time it became apparent ²⁹that he had violated their religious laws, which seemed to me rather insignificant, certainly not a capital offense nor even anything requiring imprisonment. ³⁰Then I learned that an ambush was planned which would have been fatal to him, so I quickly decided to send him to you and allow his accusers to bring to you their case against him."

³¹Off they went that night as far as Antipatris, ³²where the cavalry soldiers were to proceed on to Caesarea with Paul, leaving the infantry guard to return to Jerusalem. ³³When they reached Caesarea, Paul was delivered to the governor and the letter was presented. ³⁴Governor Felix first asked Paul, "What is your home province?"

"Silicia, sir," he answered.

³⁵"Very well, I shall hear your case when your accusers arrive." Until that, Paul was to be kept in Herod's courthouse.

Chapter 24

¹Five days later Ananias, the high priest, arrived with a group of elders and an attorney named Tertullus to present the charge against Paul. ²When brought to the witness stand, Tertullus opened his remarks by a flattering account of the great progress that Felix had brought about. "Because of your wise administration, we are in an era of great peace and prosperity. You have indeed been a great help to our province through the wise laws that have been enacted. ³How grateful we are for these advantages, most noble Felix!

⁴But right now I am grateful for the privilege you have granted me to present before you the concerns that I have on my heart. I shall make this as brief as possible. ⁵This individual who has been brought to you is a most troublesome fellow. Wherever he goes, he stirs up Jews to sedition. You have heard of the cult known as Nazarenes. Well this Paul is one of their ringleaders. ⁶His latest detestable act was to pollute the temple by his presence. We captured him and would have tried him under our own laws, ⁷but Captain Lysias butted in, interfered with justice, and forcefully took him out of our hands, ⁸demanding that we bring him here to you for prosecution."

⁹The Jews nodded their heads, "Yes, yes, exactly!"

¹⁰Felix then turned to Paul and asked for his side of the story. "Your honor," Paul began, "I am most grateful to have the privilege of speaking here today. You have been here in this position long enough to have full knowledge of the events taking place in this province. ¹¹About twelve days ago I traveled to Jerusalem in order to worship God. ¹²While there in the temple, I had no confrontation with anyone, and when in the synagogue, there was no disturbance whatsoever, and when in the city, never did I engage in any seditious acts. ¹³These accusers will be unable to prove any of the charges that they are bringing against me. ¹⁴I will nevertheless make a confession at this time. Although they consider it heresy, I worship the God of our ancestors in full harmony with the writings of our prophets. ¹⁵My hope is similar to the hope that they possess, that there will be a resurrection of the dead, both of the acquitted and the condemned. ¹⁶With this foundation, my faith has led me to live in such a way as

to have a clear conscience before God and before my fellow human beings.

[17]"My visit to Jerusalem came about this way: I was bringing charitable contributions donated from many churches for the relief of needy folks in Jerusalem. [18]After these funds had been turned over to the church leaders, I rededicated my life to my God at the temple in a solemn ceremony well known to us Jews. Present at that time were some worshippers from the province of Asia. [19]They must have had some kind of animosity for me, but instead of bringing their complaints to you, as they should have done legally, they started a riot. [20]The very most that could have legally been done was to present their complaints to the council that met the very next day. [21]At that council meeting I was asked to present my views which were generating such a demonstration, and I complied with this request. I clearly outlined my views concerning the resurrection, and it was this belief that had triggered the riot."

[22]That was enough for Felix to get a picture of what had happened, but he deferred judgment until he would be able to talk to the chief captain, Lysias. [23]For Paul's protection he assigned a centurion as bodyguard and allowed generous freedom to visit with friends and relatives. [24]Several days later, Felix arranged an interview with Paul regarding the Christian faith at which both he and his wife, Drusilla, were present. She, by the way, was a Jewess. [25]Paul eloquently presented fundamental concepts of Christianity such as right versus wrong, self-control, and the final judgment. Felix began to tremble and brought the interview to a close, saying, "That will be enough for now. I shall call you again when it is convenient."

[26]Felix cherished a hope that someone would come up with money to pay for Paul's release. He had a number of further conversations with Paul. [27]This state of things lasted for the next two years with Paul still in custody because of the desire on the part of Felix to please the Jews. Then a new procurator was appointed to replace Felix, a man named Porcius Festus.

Chapter 25

[1]Within three days of his taking office, Festus made a trip to Jerusalem where he met with some Jewish leaders and the high priest. [2]They started at once to persuade him that Paul was a fearful threat and should be brought to Jerusalem for trial. (Their real intention was to ambush him on the way and kill him.) [3]Festus did not fall for their scheme. [4]"No," he said, "I shall keep him in Caesarea, and inasmuch as I am to return shortly, [5]you should prepare a delegation and have them sent to me. Then we can hold a hearing and try to decide what should be done with him."

[6]A few days later Festus was back in Caesarea, and true to his word he scheduled a hearing and presided over it himself while the Jewish leaders presented their case. [7]His courtroom was not large enough to hold all who wanted to be at the hearing. Charge after charge was leveled at Paul, none of which were substantiated by any credible witness. [8]Then Paul was permitted to act as his own defense. "Not one law of the Jews, not one law of the temple, not one law of Caesar have I defied or broken in any way, your honor."

[9]But Festus interrupted him, "Are you willing to be tried in Jerusalem if I preside over the trial?"

[10]"Your honor, I consider that it is here

that I am able to be tried with justice, an official Roman court. I have wronged no Jew nor the Jewish religion, and I believe you know that this is the truth. [11]If I am guilty of any felony or crime, which is punishable by death, I shall not refuse to die, but if I am not guilty of any charge against me, I shall not consent to be turned over to these people for trial. Therefore, I appeal to Caesar."

[12]At this, Festus had a few words with his attorney. Then he spoke. "Have you appealed to Caesar? Unto Caesar you shall go."

[13]Several days later King Agrippa and his wife, Bernice, paid an official visit to Festus. [14]During this visit Festus brought up Paul's case to the king. "I have in custody a man who was arrested in Jerusalem, brought here to Felix, and is still in custody. [15]Recently while I was at Jerusalem, the chief priests and elders clued me in on his case and are very eager to have him condemned and executed. [16]But I told them Roman law will not permit anyone to be executed until there is a full open trial at which he is able to face his accusers and answer the charges against him. [17]A trial date was set, and he was able to face them as required by law. [18]They accused him in open court, but the crimes were quite different from what I had expected. [19]It was all matters concerning their religion as opposed to his religion. He is preaching everywhere he goes about a man called Jesus who had been crucified but who, he claims, was resurrected and is now alive. [20]Then, because I was not adequately informed regarding the beliefs of either side, I proposed that he be tried in Jerusalem. [21]The prisoner refused to be tried in Jerusalem and appealed his case

to Caesar. So I consented and am keeping him in custody until transportation can be arranged."

[22]Agrippa was immediately interested in the case and proposed that Paul be given an opportunity to tell his story. "Very well," Festus said, "you shall hear him tomorrow." [23]So it was that a formal lavish event was planned at which both Agrippa and Bernice were present as well as high government officials, law enforcement personnel, and civic leaders. Paul was then taken to the banquet hall. [24]In his opening remarks, Festus introduced Paul to the assembled dignitaries and went on to explain that a very strong delegation of Jews had urged the execution of the prisoner because of his crimes against Judaism. [25]"But gentlemen, I was never told of any crime that would demand a death penalty, and further, he has appealed to Caesar, so I have decided to send him to Rome. [26]As you might suspect, I have no recommendation one way or the other, and I felt that perhaps after this appearance today I will be better equipped to send along a formal, accurate account and with it a recommendation for action on his case. [27]It hardly seemed right to send him without a statement of the crimes with which he is charged."

Chapter 26

[1]King Agrippa listened to this introduction and brief history of Paul's case, and he wanted to hear it firsthand. "Sir, what do you have to say for yourself?" he asked. "Please be free to speak."

[2]Paul raised his hand and commenced his story. "Let me express my gratitude, King Agrippa, that you have given me this privilege to answer the charges brought

against me by the Jews. [3]I consider it especially fortunate that I am permitted to speak of my case to you, for you are very knowledgeable in regard to Jewish teachings and customs, so if you would hear me out, it would be much appreciated. [4]My early years, which were spent in Jerusalem among those of my own nation, are well known to the Jewish leaders. They could testify to that if they wished. [5]I was a Pharisee, and lived as a Pharisee, rigidly following the teaching of that party. [6]However, here I stand now, accused by these very ones because of my steadfast belief in the hope that our ancestors had received from God and then passed on to their descendants. [7]This promise is one that all of our twelve tribes have been hoping to see fulfilled for generations now. Ironically, it is this very hope that has led me into my present situation, charged as I am with heresy.

"O King, [8]why should it be thought to be an impossibility to believe that God would raise someone from death? [9]And yet I confess that for a time I felt as they do and went about spending my time and energy speaking against Jesus of Nazareth and His followers, all the while believing fervently that I was doing right. [10]Beginning in Jerusalem I began to have a strong influence among our authorities and was able to bring about convictions in a large number of cases—even securing the death penalty for some. [11]I was an aggressive, persistent enemy of these people and was able to prosecute some in every synagogue in that area so successfully that some of them openly blasphemed. I kept getting more vehement against them and was sent to outlying cities in search of my prey.

[12]"And so it was that I was sent to Damascus with full authority from the chief priests to arrest and punish those of this belief. It was about noon, and I was approaching Damascus when a dazzling light from heaven surrounded me and my traveling companions. [13]We all fell to the ground, shielding our eyes from the brilliance, and then a voice spoke to me in the [14]Hebrew language, 'Saul, Saul, why are you persecuting Me?' It must be hard to violate your own conscience. [15]I was only able to respond, 'My Lord, who are You?' and the voice answered, 'I am Jesus; you are actually persecuting Me! [16]But now get to your feet. I have a plan for you. I want you to be a witness in My behalf, telling people what you have experienced already and what you will be taught in the future. [17]You will be protected from your enemies, Jew and Gentile, and yes, I want you to go the Gentiles and teach them. [18]You will open their eyes, then turn them from darkness to light, from the power of Satan to God. They will be led to accept My forgiveness and to accept an inheritance promised to all who are transformed by faith in Me.'

[19]"King Agrippa, I believed and obeyed this command from God. [20]I began at once, in Damascus, later in Jerusalem, then in all of Judea and finally to the Gentile world, telling people everywhere I went that they needed to turn to God in repentance and live a life that demonstrated their change of heart. [21]It was because of this teaching that I was arrested by the Jews who then tried to have me executed. [22]Had it not been for the help of God, they would have succeeded. As things are now, I am still able to proclaim to small and great the message of scripture, how the Messiah came, [23]suffered and died, and was then raised to life in demonstration of God's power, giving hope to all His people, both Jews and Gentiles."

²⁴Festus broke in, "Paul, Paul you seem to be beside yourself. Are you going insane?"

²⁵"Oh no, your honor, I most certainly am not going insane, but I am speaking words of solemn truth. ²⁶Our King Agrippa knows of these matters. He is aware of the prophecies and of their fulfillment in the things that I have related. They were not hidden in secret, but were well publicized." Then speaking directly to Agrippa he said, ²⁷"King Agrippa, do you believe the prophets? I know that you do."

²⁸"Well, just a minute here," the king answered. "Really, do you expect that in this short time, you will persuade me to become a Christian?"

²⁹Paul's sincerity was obvious. "I would to God that whether it takes a short time or a long time that all who are here listening to me today were just as I am except of course for these chains."

³⁰Paul was through. He had made his earnest appeal, and the hearing was over. The king and Bernice, Festus, and the others in the room rose to leave. ³¹When out of Paul's presence, they all agreed that Paul had committed no capital offense. ³²But Agrippa's ruling was that inasmuch as he had appealed to Caesar, he must be tried by the emperor.

Chapter 27

¹The decision had been made. Plans were quickly arranged for our transportation. Paul and a few other prisoners were placed under an officer named Julius who was the local representative of a network of officials known as the Imperial Regiment. ²A ship was soon found whose home port was Adramyttium. It was scheduled to travel to southern Asia. Once aboard we felt safe from attacks by angry Jews. Also we had our friend Aristarchus of Thessalonica on board with us. ³Our first stop was at Sidon where Paul was allowed the privilege of going ashore to visit friends.

⁴As we left Sidon the wind was unfavorable for sailing northward, so we sailed south of Cyprus instead. ⁵Our next stop was at Myra. ⁶The centurion found here a ship of Alexandria bound for Italy, so we were all transferred to it. ⁷It took several days of slow sailing to reach Cnidus, then our ship headed southwest and passed Salmone, the promontory at the northeast corner of Crete. ⁸Again our progress was very slow, but we finally reached Fair Havens on the southern coast of Crete, not far from the city of Lasea.

⁹So much time had passed by now that sailing had become dangerous, a very common condition during winter months. The Day of Atonement came and Paul was led to give some advice. ¹⁰"Sirs," he told them, "you will find that if you sail now the ship and its cargo and all its passengers will be in jeopardy."

¹¹But the centurion was more inclined to believe the captain and owner than to believe Paul. ¹²Also the place where we were anchored was a rather small berth in which to spend the winter, so a decision was made to go on with the voyage, hoping to reach Phoenix, at least. This was a safe harbor on the shore of Crete, sheltered on the west and northwest. ¹³The wind was now blowing gently from the south, which allowed the ship to sail close to Crete. ¹⁴But suddenly a violent tempest from the northeast began to blow, a wind nicknamed by sailors, "Euraquilo" (Northeaster). ¹⁵It was so stormy that we were forced to let the wind drive the ship

wherever it might. [16]We were blown past an island called Clauda. The crew tried to maintain control of the ship and to hoist the small boat aboard to prevent losing it. [17]When this had been successfully done, the sailors encircled the ship with ropes, hoping to tighten it up enough to prevent it from coming apart in the gale. We were driven toward the coast of Africa where shallow water would doom the ship, so the main sails were pulled down to slow the drift southward.

[18]But the wind increased, the waves grew higher, and the ship sprang ominous leaks. The captain ordered all unnecessary cargo to be dumped overboard to lighten the ship. [19]Even some of the ship's gear was dumped into the sea. [20]No relief came for days and days, with the ship now being driven in a northwesterly direction. No sun by day nor stars at night were visible to give us a clue as to our position, and we were all beginning to realize that our hope of surviving was indeed small.

[21]Paul finally spoke to the captain and crew, chiding them gently for not accepting his advice. "Gentlemen, although you failed to heed my warning, I have good news for you. Take heart. None of us on this ship will lose our lives even though the ship will be lost. [23]You may ask, 'How can you be so sure?' I shall tell you. During the night God's angel, who directs my life and to whom I belong, spoke to me. [24]He promised me that I would be able to appear before Caesar and that all who are sailing with me will be spared. [25]We will, however, be shipwrecked on an island where we shall be able to find refuge. [26]Now I believe God doesn't lie and that this will be our fate."

[27]Fourteen days had passed, and the storm continued. The ship was wallowing in the sea. About midnight the sailors detected evidence that we were approaching land. [28]They measured the water depth, and it was only about one hundred twenty feet. A short time later the sound revealed only ninety feet. [29]Rather than drift onto rocks, they put out four anchors from the stern and then waited hours for daybreak. [30]As daylight began to lighten the sky, the crew wanted to escape from the ship in the small boat, so they went about to put it in the water, pretending that they were trying to let down another anchor from the bow. [31]Paul realized what was going on so he went to the centurion about it.

"Sir, you should know that the crew is trying to abandon the ship, and if they succeed the lives of all passengers will be in real jeopardy." [32]The soldiers finally believed Paul and went to investigate. They could see that he was right and quickly cut the ropes of the small boat and let it fall into the raging water. [33]Now Paul offered some more advice: "Men, it has been fourteen days since you have had a decent meal, [34]so please, for your own sake, eat some good solid food this morning. Not one of you will lose even one hair as a result of this storm."

[35]After this little bit of advice, he took a loaf of bread, thanked God for it and then broke off a piece and began eating. [36]This act of confidence seemed to encourage others, and they followed his example. [37]Eventually all two hundred seventy-six people on board ate enough to strengthen themselves. [38]The ship needed to be lighter yet so the surplus grain was dumped into the water. [39]By this time it was daylight, but no one recognized the land ahead. A small stream was running into the sea close by and it was decided to allow the ship to be

driven into this bay, ⁴⁰So the anchors were raised, allowing the wind to drive us in toward the shore. ⁴¹Presently the bow went aground, allowing the waves to raise and lower the stern violently against the rocks. The ship sank rapidly. ⁴²At this time the soldiers recommended that all prisoners be executed, knowing that some might escape by swimming to shore. ⁴³However, to save Paul, the centurion vetoed the idea and gave a command that all who could swim to do so at once. ⁴⁴The others began to pick up loose boards and other floating objects with which to help them float to shore. Incredibly, everyone reached the beach safely.

Chapter 28

¹Upon reaching shore, we encountered some natives who informed us that we were on the island of Malta. ²We considered them to be barbarians until they treated us kindly. They built a large fire for us to help us dry out and warm up. ³All of us were gathering wood for the fire when Paul, who had just unloaded an armful of wood on the flames, was suddenly attacked by a viper. It had apparently been hiding in the wood. It fastened tight to Paul's hand. ⁴The natives expected Paul to drop dead or swell up. They speculated that Paul must be a murderer and was now being punished for his sins. ⁵Imagine their astonishment when nothing happened to him. He tossed the snake into the fire and showed no signs of poisoning, not even swelling. ⁶After some time had passed, those who had felt certain of God's wrath on Paul now changed their minds and speculated that he must be some sort of god.

⁷Not far from where we found ourselves was the residence and property of the most influential man on the island. Publius was his name, and he was a most gracious person, taking us in to his own home for three full days. ⁸During those three days his father became desperately ill with a bloody dysentery. As soon as Paul heard of the situation, he went to pray for the man. When Paul's prayer was over, the man was perfectly normal. ⁹The word got around and soon others came with various complaints, and they, too, were healed. ¹⁰In gratitude they showered us with praise and gifts of items that we urgently needed.

¹¹For three months we stayed there before another ship could be found to take us on our journey. It was a vessel from Alexandria with the twin brothers, Castor and Pollux, as figureheads. ¹²The first stop was at Syracuse where we spent three days. ¹³Then on to Rhegium where we had to wait for favorable winds through the strait of Messina and then northward to Puteoli. ¹⁴Here we found fellow believers who urged us to stay with them for a week, which we gladly did before sailing on to Rome.

¹⁵News of our coming had reached the brothers at Rome, and we were met at the Appius Forum, a large market about forty miles southeast of Rome. More came and greeted us at the Three Taverns, ten miles farther along. This outpouring of good will encouraged us so much that Paul prayed a special prayer of thanksgiving. ¹⁶Finally, at Rome all the prisoners were delivered to the captain of the guard. In Paul's case, however, the captain allowed a special favor. He could be kept in a private quarter and have a personal guard.

¹⁷Three days after reaching Rome, Paul sent word to the Jewish community inviting their leaders to come for a visit. They came and listened as he explained

his situation. "Brothers, here is my story. I have never harmed any of our people, nor have I ever taught anything contrary to our historic beliefs and customs; yet, I was arrested in Jerusalem and turned over to the Roman government for execution. [18]They held a hearing and ruled that I had done nothing in the way of a capital offense. [19]This angered the Jews so greatly that I appealed to Caesar. And yet I have no animosity toward my own country and nation. [20]However, I thought that you should know the circumstances, and that is why I have brought you this report. My chain you see here is because of my undying belief in the great hope of all Israel."

[21]Their spokesman now responded, "You will want to know that no messages have reached us about your life or teachings, spoken or written, bad or good. [22]However, we would very much like to hear what you have to say concerning this new belief." So an appointment was made [23]to meet him at his residence. The attendance at that gathering was very large as they listened to the facts concerning Jesus and how He fulfilled prophecy and the symbols found in the writings of Moses and in all the prophetic scriptures. [24]As expected, some believed but others refused to accept the evidence.

[25]The disagreement, which was rather heated, brought out a comment from Paul. "Isaiah our prophet truly spoke the truth when he wrote to our ancestors, [26]'God has commissioned me to go to my people with this message. They will hear but will not accept the evidence. They will see but then refuse to believe what is very plain. [27]For my people are hard to convince, their ears are not hearing very well, their eyes are essentially closed. Otherwise they would accept the evidence of their ears and eyes and minds, then they could be healed.' [28]Brothers, God's message of salvation is being proclaimed to the Gentiles, and they are listening, learning, and being converted."

[29]Leaving Paul's presence, the Jewish leaders began discussing with great intensity the things they had heard from his lips. [30]For two full years Paul was able to receive callers at this location, and as one can imagine, [31]he was busy preaching to these audiences all that time, telling them all he knew about Jesus Christ with complete freedom and confidence.

Romans

Chapter 1

¹Greetings from Paul, a slave of Jesus Christ, called to go as an apostle, sent as a completely committed person, laden with the good news about God. ²This good news has been promised in the Holy Scriptures, which were written by God's prophets, ³and is all about the Son of God, Jesus Christ our Lord, a descendant of King David. ⁴He has overwhelming evidence to support His claim to be the Son of God, and this evidence is that He was resurrected from death! ⁵It was from Jesus Christ that we apostles have received our commission and have been sent to all nations with the message to have faith in Him and His name.

⁶To Christians in Rome, to you who can properly be called saints, ⁷I pray that God's peace and grace may be given to you. ⁸Let me begin by thanking God for your conversion to Christianity and that all of you already have a reputation everywhere for a strong faith. ⁹God is my witness that I routinely mention you in my prayers. ¹⁰Furthermore, I am praying that the way will open up for me to go to Rome to meet with you in person. ¹¹I am very eager to see you and to share with you some spiritual blessings that I know will strengthen your faith, ¹²then my own faith will receive a boost in strength as we share together the mighty truths from God.

¹³I might as well tell you right now that for some reason, known only to God, I have been prevented from traveling to Rome, much as I have desired to do so. I have hoped and planned to experience the joy of seeing many more Roman Gentiles converted to Christ, just as I have witnessed in other places. ¹⁴I actually feel that I owe much to the Greeks and even to the heathen, to the educated, and to the uneducated. ¹⁵It is this sense of debt that is driving me to preach this good news in Rome. ¹⁶To say that I am happy with the gospel is a great understatement, for it is the power of God that brings salvation to all who believe, and I mean every person equally, Jews and Greeks alike. ¹⁷For the gospel reveals the essential goodness of God to those of a beginner's faith and to those of a mature faith. Remember Habakkuk 2:4? "Those who are right with God may continue in that saving relationship through faith." ¹⁸But what about the unrighteous? They will ultimately experience God's anger, an anger not like human anger, but a heavenly indignation against those who have purposely suppressed truth.

¹⁹Even these deluded ones have known about God, for He has revealed a great

deal about Himself to everyone. [20]God, of course, is invisible, but His works, His creation is visible and these show us a great deal about God, about His eternal nature and power, about His divinity, so that none of us is completely unaware of Him. So we are without excuse. [21]And yet, even knowing so much about God, they did not recognize Him as God, thankful for what had been revealed, but their minds became empty, and darkness enveloped them. [22]It has reached a point where those who consider themselves very wise have actually become fools. [23]All because of their ignorance concerning God's real character. He is pure, perfect, eternal, but they have believed Him to be only like one of His creatures, such as perhaps a man or bird, mammal or reptile. [24]The final result of such choices is that God must finally abandon them to their own choices, letting them sink lower in filthy habits and abnormal lifestyles. This is exactly what He did.

[25]They so totally distorted the truth about God that they worshipped created beings rather than the Creator, who is the only being deserving of worship. [26]This is one more reason why God abandoned them to their own unnatural desires. Indeed, even their women allowed their affections to be perverted into unhealthy and unnatural desires. [27]And the men! Many of them allowed their desires to be perverted into homosexuality and to its inevitable consequences. [28]They went so far as to reject the very idea of God, so He abandoned them to their own ideas, horrible as they were.

Would you like to know what kind of people we are referring to? Listen. [29]They were irrevocably unrighteous, sexually immoral, wicked, covetous, malicious, envious, murderous, argumentative, deceptive, deadly, sneaky, [30]underhanded, God-hating spiteful, proud, boastful, inventors of all kinds of new evils, rebellious against parents, [31]irresponsible, promise breakers, antisocial, stubborn, and unmerciful. [32]And to top it off, they not only know that God condemns such sins, but they continue in them and promoted such behavior in others.

Chapter 2

[1]Let me insert a warning right here. I don't know any of you personally, but I know that there is a human tendency, even among Christians, to criticize and judge others. This is entirely inexcusable, because you are yourselves sinners and are as guilty as the one you are judging. [2]So let God be the judge, not us. His decision will always be fair, just, and based on facts, even in the cases of those I have been referring to. [3]Can you conceive of a situation where you, who just may be as guilty as the one you are judging, could avoid God's condemnation? [4]Whatever you do, don't ever underestimate the value of God's goodness, patience, and forgiveness. These qualities are essential to our salvation. Actually, it is these attributes of God that leads sinners to repent, [5]whereas the human trait of hard-heartedness will certainly be condemned by God, and justly so.

[6]Yes, God will eventually announce a verdict based on the behavior of the person. [7]The ones who have patiently continued in doing right, continually wanting to know God better, wanting to be honorable, wanting nothing but the glory of God, will receive immortality. They will be given eternal life. [8]But His sentence against the

quarrelsome, rebellious ones is fearful. They will be rejected by God [9]and will face trials, anguish, and final abandonment, whether they are Jews or whether they are Greeks. [10]Once again, glory, honor, and peace will be the reward of every person whose works are good, whether Jews or Greeks, [11]for God is totally impartial.

[12]Those who have sinned, not knowing the written law, may perish for having violated the law of conscience, but those who choose to sin, knowing God's written law, will be judged by that law. [13]And remember this: just hearing the law is not enough. One must obey the law. [14]Even the Gentiles who do not have the written law but have obeyed it because of their conscience, [15]they are demonstrating that God's law is written in their hearts and that their motives are right.

[16]Now to the judgment. It will be all-inclusive, down to the secrets unknown to anyone except the person himself, and will be under the jurisdiction of Christ. [17]But my friend, you call yourself a Jew and are smug because you have "the law" and a knowledge of God, [18]and you claim to know His will and are in favor of everything good because you know God's law so thoroughly. [19]You even consider yourself a safe guide for the blind (spiritual blindness, that is) and a source of light for those in darkness, [20]a wise instructor of the ignorant and a nurturer of new Christians, because you know so well what the law says. [21]But be very certain, before you teach others, that you have taught yourself. You who are teaching against theft, practice what you preach. [22]You who deplore adultery, are you an adulterer yourself? You who would not think of worshipping an idol, do you have some "idol" that crowds God out of your life? [23]You who are so proud of the law, do you dishonor God by breaking his law? [24]Thus fulfilling the prophecy of Isaiah 5:25 and Ezekiel 36:20 ("the name of God is blasphemed among the Gentiles.")

[25]Think now of circumcision. If you religiously keep this ceremonial law, it is significant, but if the ceremonial law is ignored, you may as well not be circumcised. [26]And by the same logic, if an uncircumcised person is faithful to keep the law, need he be circumcised? [27]And is it not reasonable that the uncircumcised one who is obedient to the law may rightly condemn the circumcised one who is violating the law? [28]You see, the "real" Jew is not a Jew because he is circumcised, neither is circumcision just an anatomical condition. [29]But a true Jew is such because of an inner condition of his heart, and this is what meets God's approval.

Chapter 3

[1]Well then, does the Jew have any advantage? Do the people who call themselves "the circumcised" actually find themselves benefited? If so, what are the advantages? [2]I will answer my own question. Yes, they have a great advantage, and this is it. They have the original scriptures entrusted to them by God Himself. [3]Oh yes, I know that not all of them are believers, but should this sad fact alter the validity of the believer's faith? [4] Of course not. Remember that all of us have been given the freedom of choice. One can believe and be saved or refuse to believe and be lost. God, however, is always truthful even if every person on earth is a liar. It is written in Psalm 51:4, "You will be found truthful when you are before the court of the universe."

⁵But if we, in our unrighteous condition, can see that God is always right, what can we say about God's qualifications and decisions? Can we pass judgment on Him? The answer is obvious. ⁶A resounding "no." He and He alone can judge the whole world and judge it accurately. ⁷And now an idea for your consideration. If my lies result in publicizing God's truthfulness, should I not be considered a great benefactor? ⁸Actually some have spread a false report that I have literally claimed this. If they receive condemnation for this distortion, the sentence against them will be appropriate. ⁹Please never harbor the thought that I consider myself to be better than they, for you know that in all my writings I have expressed the truth that Jews and Gentiles are both sinners and to a similar degree.

¹⁰Things are exactly as David expressed it in Psalm 14:1-3, "There are no righteous persons, no, not one." ¹¹Yes, it is a fact that there are none who really understand perfect righteousness and who obey God perfectly. ¹²All of us are separated from God and are unprofitable to him. Not one of us can claim that we are "good," no, not one. ¹³As for all human beings, it is all too true. They are like an open burial pit—putrid. Their speech has been deceptive and continues to be. Their words are like snake venom. ¹⁴Their mouths are committed to cursing and hatred. ¹⁵They are quick to kill anyone whom they hate. ¹⁶In their wake is destruction and misery. ¹⁷Never have they known real peace. ¹⁸They have no reverence for God, not even respect.

¹⁹Now we know that these lawbreakers are condemned by the law. ²⁰And we know that a guilty person cannot be cleared by trying to keep the law, for the law has no function, except to show us what sin is. ²¹On the other hand, God's essential goodness and righteousness is evident, even if there were no law with which to compare him, for we have the record of his dealings with human beings in our scriptures. ²²His righteousness is offered to us who have faith in Jesus Christ and will be given to all of us believers, sinners though we may be. ²³For all have sinned and continue to fall short of God's ideal for us. ²⁴Yet, in spite of this, we have been acquitted fully due to His grace, in the redemption, which has been purchased through Christ ²⁵whom God sent to this world to die as an atonement for our sins, thus demonstrating His justice while erasing our sins at the same time. Marvelous forbearance!

²⁶May I restate it this way. This was to demonstrate to the whole universe His justice and at the same time His unbelievable mercy to those who trust in Jesus. ²⁷Whatever happened to human boasting? Away with it! For our behavior has had nothing to do with providing our salvation. Only our faith in Jesus has accomplished such a wonderful result. ²⁸We are made right with God, reconciled to Him, by faith in Christ, not by any good things we might do. ²⁹And because God is the God of both Jews and Gentiles, the way of salvation is the same for both. ³⁰He reconciles all equally, saving those who receive Christ by faith. ³¹You may wonder then. Am I saying that the law has been abolished by our faith? By no means. Actually, we are honoring the law.

Chapter 4

¹Next I want us to consider Abraham, our biological father, and the significance of some of his experiences. ²You can see

plainly that he would have had a great deal to boast about if his behavior was responsible for his standing with God. But no, ³the scripture says only that he believed God and that this was counted as righteousness. ⁴In the employer-employee relationship, a man works and receives his wages because he deserves it. This is something owed to him. ⁵It is not that way with God and sinners. Our salvation is a gift, gladly given and totally free, from our God. But we must believe and trust Him fully so that God may count our faith as righteousness as He did for Abraham.

⁶Remember also David's statement (Psalm 32:1, 2) where he describes the truly blessed sinner. ⁷"Blessed is he whose transgression is forgiven, whose sin is completely hidden and no longer counted against him. ⁸Blessed is the man to whom the Lord will not impute sin." ⁹Can you imagine that this blessing was promised by God and only for Jews? Remember that it was scripture itself that says that his faith was counted as righteousness. ¹⁰And another thing. He had faith before he was circumcised. ¹¹His circumcision was a visible pledge, a reminder of his faith and the righteousness it stands for, faith which he possessed long before he was circumcised, faith that would be a model for all his descendants with similar faith, even those who were uncircumcised, for they too may have righteousness placed to their account through their faith.

¹²He, the original circumcised person, is therefore the great spiritual father of both Jews and Gentiles, and he is such because of his faith which he had before circumcision, and which he continued to exercise afterward. This faith is that which both Jews and Gentiles may exercise. ¹³Consider this promise to Abraham: "You will inherit the world." This promise is to his spiritual descendants, not only the physical ones. ¹⁴For if only physical descent is referred to, then faith is worthless in the rest of the world. ¹⁵You also understand that law only points out wrong and condemns the wrongdoer. No law, no wrong doing. ¹⁶So in order for us to be certain that it applies to both physical and spiritual descendants and others with similar faith, it must necessarily be a gift from God through His grace.

¹⁷God's promise to Abraham that he would be the father of nations was so unbelievable that it compares to raising the dead or to creating something out of nothing. ¹⁸Against all reasonable evidence, Abraham believed God, and thus became the father of many nations, just as had been promised in these words: "So shall your descendants be." ¹⁹His faith was certainly not weak but strong, even though he was about one hundred years of age and hardly more likely to sire children than a dead man, plus the fact that Sarah was long past menopause. ²⁰And yet he did not refuse to believe the promise of God and gave God the credit for the fulfillment. ²¹He had become convinced that whatever God promised He was able to bring about. ²²This complete trust in God was counted as righteousness.

²³And this story is told, not merely that we might marvel at Abraham's faith, but also ²⁴that we who believe in God may as willingly accept God's promise to accept our faith as righteousness. We have even more evidence of God's power, for we know that He raised Jesus from the grave. ²⁵He had been given up by God because of our transgressions then was brought back

to life, and this only because he wanted us to once again be right with God.

Chapter 5

[1]It follows that we who have been made right through faith in Christ are now at peace with God. [2]Furthermore, it is through Jesus Christ that we have access to God's grace, which we now enjoy, grace that produces hope of endless glory in the future. [3]And more! We even see a benefit in our trials and difficulties, for it is these that develop patient endurance. [4]And this endurance develops more experience in God, which in turn develops more and greater hope. [5]Hope never disappoints us because God's love is so abundant and vast that it possesses our whole being, it then flows out to others through the action of the Holy Spirit in our lives.

[6]I must remind you that we, all of us, were totally unable to rescue ourselves, but just at the right time Christ came to die for sinners. [7]Now you and I know that very few would give their lives to rescue the best person on earth, although someone might be willing to do that. [8]But what a contrast we see in God's love! It is so marvelous that Christ was willing to die for the very worst person on earth, even though He knew that many would not accept that gift. [9]How much more then will He rescue us from the death due us, having gone to such lengths to put us right with God? [10]Surely it is impressive that we who were enemies of God have been reconciled to God by the death of His Son and His next step is to enter our being and live His life in ours, freeing us from the bondage of sin.

[11]And still more. This is the source of our joy. Joy in God, and in our Lord Jesus Christ, who provided the reconciliation.

[12]Let me restate this so that it can be better understood. It was through the sin of one man, Adam, that sin entered our world. Death naturally followed. And because all have sinned, all are doomed to die. [13]Even before God spoke His law on Mount Sinai, the death of every person shows conclusively that the law of God was already applicable to human beings, for had there been no law, there could not have been such a thing as sin. [14]Yes, death was the lot of every human being from Adam to Moses, even though Adam was the only one to eat the forbidden fruit. Sin of any sort gives the same result, and as yet the sinless One had not yet come.

[15]But now He has come, and by the grace of God has given us a free gift— life. So just as sin and its consequences came through one man, so life has come through one Man, a person mightier than Adam. [16]God's gift is not comparable to Adam's sin, however, in this respect, His forgiveness is adequate for innumerable sins. [17]Death ruled over the whole human race just because of one man's sin, but by one Man's gift of righteousness, life will one day reign. [18]In other words, it took just one offense to bring condemnation to all, and it took the obedience of One to bring about forgiveness to all and eternal life as a result.

[19]I repeat and re-emphasize it. Just as one man's rebellion resulted in a whole race of sinners, so one person's obedience will eventually result in multitudes becoming righteous. [20]Here is the true value of the law: God revealed it to us so that we can identify sin and the magnitude of the sin problem; yet, however great the sin problem, God's grace is even greater. [21]And even though sin has been on the throne

in this world, bringing death, most certainly grace will reign someday, bringing righteousness and eternal life, and all this through Jesus Christ our Lord.

Chapter 6

¹Let's engage in a little philosophy. If sin results in an outpouring of God's grace, should we therefore continue sinning so that grace will increase? Does this sound sensible? ²Of course not! Our goal is to die to sin, not continue in our sins. ³Remember your baptism, friends. That symbolized death to sin. ⁴Just as Christ died and was literally buried, so we are symbolically buried and dead to sin, and as Christ was raised to life by God's power, we should come up from the baptismal water a new person. ⁵Now isn't that a beautiful symbol! Death—leaving and abandoning sin; burial—forgetting our past life; resurrection—beginning a new life.

⁶It is true then that our "old man" (past life) is crucified (put to death) and we are to go forward in a sin-free life. ⁷A dead person is a slave no longer, and a person dead to sin is no longer the slave of sin. ⁸And as surely as Christ died and was resurrected, we shall be able to live new lives. ⁹But Christ died only once, never again to fall under the power of death, ¹⁰showing that dying to sin should be an irreversible decision, a one-time experience, and just as Christ now lives as God, ¹¹we must completely separate from sin and live God's will, through Jesus Christ our Lord.

¹²My advice then is urgent. Never again permit sin to control your physical body and its desires. ¹³No, let not one organ or body part be surrendered as a slave of sin, but rather, give them all to God, for you are like a person resurrected. Then they will obey God. ¹⁴And sin shall no longer rule you, for you are recipients of God's grace.

¹⁵Let me restate this. Shall we go on in sin because we have been forgiven? Most certainly not! ¹⁶You realize, I am sure, that you will surrender yourself to one or the other. To sin, and the end result of that choice is death; or to obedience, the result of which is obedience, righteousness. ¹⁷Thank God, you who have been slaves of sin now choose to obey the teachings presented to you. ¹⁸So now you have been freed from sin and have become slaves of righteousness.

¹⁹I am trying to express myself on a deep, complex issue in simple human terms. I shall try again. In the past you surrendered yourselves to impurity and other sinful ways, resulting in impurity of course, so now begin to surrender yourselves to righteousness and righteousness will be the result. ²⁰Another thought: As long as you were slaves of sin you most certainly were not enslaved by righteousness. ²¹What would have been the end result had you continued as you were. Likely you are ashamed to think about such things are you not? For it would have been death. ²²But now the reverse is true. You have escaped from the slave-driver, sin, and are God's slaves, leading to holiness and to eventual everlasting life. ²³To put it in yet another way, sin pays its wages faithfully, and what are its wages? Simple. Death. But God has an infinite gift to hand you and it is life. And this gift is only through Jesus Christ our Lord.

Chapter 7

¹I am certain that I am writing to those who love the law and are knowledgeable regarding it. If so, you know that the law

applies to a person while he lives and not after his death. [2]Also the law of marriage applies to a woman while her husband lives and not after his death. After the death of her husband, she is no longer married to him. [3]A married woman is termed an adulteress if she leaves her husband for another man, but after her husband's death she is free to marry another man without being an adulteress.

[4]We may learn a spiritual lesson from this. We can be considered free from the law now and free to "marry" Christ and then produce offspring for God. [5]In the past while we were "in the flesh," that is, in a state of rebellion against God, the desires and inclinations of sin took charge and were producing the natural fruit of such, which is death. [6]But now, what a difference! We are free from slavery to such sin and rebellion. Now we serve God with new life, instead of just trying to live up to a code as we did before. [7]What about this code then? Is it useless or perhaps even sinful? No, of course not. But its values lie in the fact that it is only a definition of sin. To illustrate, I would never have known that covetousness was wrong had not the tenth commandment been written in plain words, "Do not covet anything belonging to someone else."

[8]But sin became plain to me by reading the commandments, which showed me that I had many desires that were contrary to God's will for me. Without this law I would never have realized that these desires were sinful. [9]I actually felt good about myself at the time, but when God's code was impressed on my mind, sin became a powerful factor in my life. I realized that my sinful self must die. [10]And this commandment forbidding covetousness, which was given to lead me to life, was a warning that I was on a course leading to death. [11]This sin, defined so clearly in that commandment, had doomed me to death. [12]Let me make this perfectly clear. The law itself is holy, altogether good and completely just. [13]Was it the law that brought about death? This good perfect law? Decidedly no, but rather it was sin that had been identified by that law and is extremely wrong. [14]Now we are aware that God's law is spiritual, that it applies to our innermost beings, our minds, our thoughts, and our motives. But I was a slave to sin. I was born that way.

[15]For example, even though I know what is right, I have no tendency to do right. Rather, I do the very things that are defined as sin by the law. [16]And this being the way I am, you can accept the fact that I consider the law to be truly good. [17]And that it is my sinful nature that is responsible for my sinful behavior. [18]Yes, in my natural physical being there is nothing good. Even if I choose to do good, I don't have the capability of doing right. [19]It is for this reason that my behavior is so contrary to my deepest desires. [20]Once again, it is my sinful nature that produces my sinful behavior.

[21]Let me express it as a law: For every good impulse from God, there is an evil impulse within me to prevent me from doing good. [22]Intellectually, I am happy that God's law is always right in every respect. [23]But this nature I have inherited is continually in opposition to God's law and produces my sinful behavior. [24]And this is why I cry out, "Oh, wretched man that I am, who can rescue me from this dead, sinful body?" [25]Now the overwhelming, good news! Thank God, it is possible through Jesus Christ our Lord! Is this clear? I may

want to serve God, but my body always has the desire to be sinful.

Chapter 8

¹From what has just been presented, it seems clear that those who can be said to be "in Christ Jesus" are no longer under condemnation. They no longer live the life of human "flesh," but the life directed and empowered by the Holy Spirit. ²Being "in Christ" demonstrates that one need not live in the law of "sin and death." ³ You see, the law by itself could never accomplish this miracle, for the law is only a description of God's will, not the power to change the sinner. The power comes from the Son of God, who became human flesh and then conquered sin. ⁴Not only did Christ conquer sin in His human flesh, but now He is capable of supplying us with adequate power to live righteous lives. This power is conveyed to us by the Holy Spirit.

⁵Let me suggest that in essence there are only two classes of people, those who are in the "flesh" and those who are in "the Spirit." The person himself must decide to which category he chooses to live in. ⁶Those who choose "the flesh" will one day perish eternally, while those who choose "the Spirit" will enjoy an eternity of peace and joy. ⁷To put it plainly, the person who chooses the "flesh" is by that choice an enemy of God. He cannot keep God's law. It is utterly impossible. ⁸It follows logically that he cannot please God. ⁹But you are no longer "in the flesh" if God's spirit lives in you. A person who does not have God's spirit does not belong on the side of Christ. He is no Christian.

¹⁰Now if Christ rules in you, sin is dead, and because of Christ's life you live righteously. ¹¹It was God's spirit that raised Christ from the dead, and that same creative power will raise your bodies some day, the same power that now lives in you. ¹²With this marvelous possibility, brothers and sisters, we owe it to Jesus to live above the inclinations and impulses of our "flesh." ¹³For if you persist in living lives led by our natural inclinations, eternal death will inevitably follow. Whereas if you appropriate the power of the Holy Spirit and with that strength conquer the impulses of humanity, you shall live eternally! ¹⁴And everyone who lets God's spirit lead him is a child of God. ¹⁵And God's children have no fear of slavery again. They are adopted unconditionally into God's family and may justifiably call out, "Daddy," "Papa." ¹⁶It is God's spirit that convinces us that this is true. ¹⁷And being God's children makes us heirs with Christ, perhaps sharing His suffering for a time, but through eternity sharing His glory!

¹⁸Let's try to evaluate our present suffering as compared to the glory in the future. The two are not comparable at all. ¹⁹Believe me, the entire universe is eagerly waiting for God's children to appear. ²⁰God's creation has been dealt a severe blow and is waiting in hope ²¹that soon this slavery to sin will end and God's children will be gloriously freed.

²²It reminds one of childbirth. Pain is the word. This pain has endured throughout the entire history of this planet. ²³Sinless beings everywhere are suffering with us, all waiting for the great delivery, the end of sin and the commencement of eternal, universal righteousness. ²⁴Our salvation is based on hope, a hope that cannot yet see the final outcome, but which is supremely confident, even so. ²⁵In spite of our inability to see the future, we are cultivating patience as we anticipate the future.

²⁶Through all our difficulties, trials, perplexities, and fears, God's spirit is now present to help us. In truth we do not even know what we should pray for, as we ought, so He takes our prayers and intercedes for us with unutterable intensity. ²⁷And God, who knows the heart more fully than we know our own, accepts the Holy Spirit's intercession in our behalf. ²⁸This gives us the assurance that everything works together for our good, and for all who love God, who have responded to God's call. ²⁹God knew us even before we were conceived and provided everyone of us with salvation, in order to transform us into the image of His Son, who is now our brother, a super-brother, the first and pre-eminent brother. ³⁰And having provided adequately for our redemption, He then called us, inviting us to accept salvation, to accept forgiveness and full restoration to His glorious ideal. ³¹Of what significance are these concepts you may ask. Do they affect us? Most certainly! If God is on our side, it matters not who may be against us.

³²If God loved us enough to give us His greatest treasure, His Son, don't you think He will give us any amount of lesser gifts as well? ³³Who can condemn us for our sins when God has forgiven us? When God has cleansed us? ³⁴Tell me, who would dare to condemn us when Christ died for us then rose again and is now at God's right hand, interceding in our behalf? ³⁵And who can separate us from the love of Christ? Is it possible for troubles, perplexities, famines, nakedness, dangers, or human weapons to do so? ³⁶In Psalm 44:22 we find this statement: "We are killed, one by one, all day long for Your sake. We are like sheep at the slaughterhouse."

³⁷No, my brothers and sisters, through all these experiences, and any others, we are more than conquerors through the One who loved us. ³⁸I am completely convinced that neither death nor life, nor angels, nor governments, nor armies, nor all of them put together, and including all future forces, ³⁹nor height, nor depth, nor anything else in all creation shall be able to separate us from the love of God that is manifested in Christ Jesus our Lord.

Chapter 9

¹Now let me share with you my utmost concern. I tell the truth when I say it, and God knows it is true. ²It causes me so much anxious thought and sorrow ³that if it were possible I would choose to be abandoned by Christ if this could result in the conversion of my whole nation, my brothers and sisters the Jews. A few thousand have accepted Jesus as Messiah, but oh, so few compared to those who have rejected Him! ⁴Think of it. Here is the nation God blessed with His covenant, His law, His promises. ⁵Here is the nation to whom He entrusted the sacred scriptures, who are Christ's human ancestors. The forefathers of God in human flesh, eternally blessed.

⁶Don't get me wrong now. I am not saying that God's promises to Israel have failed. God's true "Israel" includes many more than the literal descendants of Abraham. ⁷You understand of course that Ishamel did not inherit any of Abraham's property and blessings. Isaac was the heir. He was the child of promise. ⁸So the true children of God are those who believe the promise and accept the covenant, whether or not they are Isaac's descendants. ⁹So let us review the promise: "At the certain time next year Sarah shall have a son."

¹⁰Later a promise was made to Isaac and Rebekah. They were to have two sons after considering themselves infertile for many years. ¹¹Their children, you remember, were markedly different, but at the time of the promise they were not yet born, and God in His foreknowledge could predict their future because He controls the future. ¹²He stated to Rebekah, "The older shall serve the younger," and so it turned out. ¹³The record says, "I have loved Jacob the younger and have hated Esau the elder." ¹⁴And now let me remind you that God was not showing partiality, but He was expressing disappointment with Esau for his rebellion and carelessness and favoring Jacob because he obeyed.

¹⁵When God told Moses, "I will have mercy on the one I choose and will show compassion to the one I choose," He was showing His sovereignty, knowing ahead of time what the future held. ¹⁶As you see, God's mercy is not like human mercy, but it is an expression of His infinite knowledge and wisdom. ¹⁷Scripture records this about Pharaoh. God speaks, "I have raised you up for a purpose, to show My power through you so that My name might be made known everywhere on earth." ¹⁸And yes, God shows mercy on the ones He chooses, His dealings with others only hardens their hearts. ¹⁹You may likely ask, "Why does God put the blame on sinners when He has power to completely control them?"

²⁰First, let us not be guilty of questioning God's action, whatever we may think at this time. Should an object complain about the maker and the way he produced the object? ²¹It is somewhat like if a lump of clay should say to the potter, "Why did you make me into this sort of vessel? I would have much preferred to be some other kind." Let me suggest that God has risked a lot in making everyone different from everyone else, ²²but He values individuality and individual freedom, even if it means that some may choose rebellion and its result. ²³But the joy of seeing some saved in glory will be infinite. ²⁴And this includes us, not Jews only, but also Gentiles.

²⁵Hosea puts it this way: "I will call them My people even though they were formerly not My people, and I will call her "My beloved" though she was formerly not "My beloved." ²⁶It will indeed take place that the very people to whom it was said, "You are not Mine," will hear this, "You are children of the living God." ²⁷Sadly enough, Isaiah wrote this prophecy, "Although Israel may increase in numbers like the sand of the sea, yet only a small portion of them will be saved." ²⁸For God will finally decide to complete the work on earth in the only right way, and He will do it very quickly.

²⁹And here is another quotation: "Unless the Lord had been able to save this small remnant, all of Israel would have been destroyed just as was Sodom and Gomorrah." ³⁰What conclusions may we draw from these quotations? Here are Gentiles who previously never gave any consideration to living righteous lives, who are now totally changed because of their faith in Christ. ³¹But Israel, who tried to be righteous by obedience to the law, has failed in that attempt. ³²You ask, "Why did they fail?" They lacked faith. Trying only to keep a law rather than putting their faith in Christ. ³³It is just as Isaiah wrote, "He will be a stumbling stone, offensive to them," but be assured that whoever believes in Him shall never regret it.

Chapter 10

[1]Brothers and sisters, I agonize for my nation Israel. I want them to be saved. [2]I have tried to explain to them that their zeal for God is misdirected and unwise, [3]but they seem to be ignorant of real righteousness, the kind that God wants to give them, and instead they are trying to develop their own righteousness, which is not God's at all. [4]Christ has effectively abolished the mistaken idea that righteousness can be attained by human beings who are trying to conform to the law. A person who has faith need no longer rely on trying to be good by keeping a law, but only by trusting in Christ and His righteousness. [5]Let me remind you of Leviticus 18:5: "If you will obey the laws, these statutes, you will live." [6]And next, Deuteronomy 30:12–14: "Never think that you have to ascend to heaven to be righteous. [7]Or think that you can dive into the sea and bring up righteousness."

[8]No, but it is available to us through faith in Jesus just as we have been preaching. [9]Believe me, if you confess Jesus openly, believing that God has raised Him from the dead, you will be saved. [10]It is in one's heart that true faith resides, and this should be expressed in the words we speak. We are then accounted righteous. [11]Another scripture: "Whoever believes in Him will never be ashamed of his belief. It will never let him down." [12]And let me emphasize that word "whoever." It does not say "whatever Jew," but whoever! You see, in God's sight all are loved equally, all are His creatures. He has redeemed them and treats them with equal love. The only qualification is that they call on Him.

[13]And here I want to quote Joel 2:32: "Whoever calls on the name of the Lord will be saved." This means that any person, anywhere, who recognizes a need for salvation and goes to God asking for salvation will receive salvation. Marvelous promise! [14]Now tell me, how can anyone ask God for anything if they do not believe in Him? And how can they believe in Him if they have never heard of Him? And how can they hear of Him without someone preaching to them? [15]And how can a preacher go to them unless He is sent and supported? In Isaiah 52:7 we have this significant passage: "How beautiful are the feet of him that brings good tidings of peace and good things!"

[16]Unfortunately, not all who have heard this good news have obeyed, for Isaiah asks this question, (chapter 53, verse 1) "Who has believed our report?" Can this imply that perhaps only a minority have believed? [17]So, friends, faith is planted by listening to and heeding the word of God. [18]And I ask you, "Have they not heard?" Psalm 19:4 states it this way: "God's word has gone to the ends of the earth." [19]And did not Israel know? I really believe so. Moses declared in Deuteronomy 32:21: "I will stir you up by bringing salvation to those who are not now my people. It will be done by 'foolish nations' and I will put you to shame." [20]And here Isaiah predicts. "I was found by even those who did not search for Me. I became well-known to those who were not even asking about Me" (Isaiah 65:1, 2). [21]And then the prophet continues, "All day long I have been reaching out to a disobedient, obstinate people."

Chapter 11

[1]Having evaluated Israel so low, have I given the impression that God has abandoned His people? Absolutely not! I myself am an Israelite, a descendant of Abraham,

a member of the tribe of Benjamin, and He has not abandoned me! ²No, God has not cast us aside, but His foreknowledge was so accurate that He was able to predict our apostasy. And yet, in spite of this He chose us to be His special people, and for good reasons. Remember the story of Elijah? He had just confronted God with his own idea of what had happened. ³"God," he complained, "they have killed Your prophets, destroyed Your altars, and I am the only one left who is willing to obey You, and they are ready to kill me when they find me." ⁴Now let us give God's answer. "Listen, Elijah, you may not know it, but there are still seven thousand in Israel who have never consented to worship Baal!"

⁵And believe it or not, there are still some, too few of course, who have remained loyal to God by His grace. ⁶And in fact all loyalty to God is only by His grace and not because of our goodness or behavior. No, it is God's grace alone that is responsible for our continuing loyalty. ⁷What am I trying to say? As a nation Israel has failed to achieve what He had hoped they would achieve, but those of us who have believed in Jesus have received this gift. The others are blind to their real need. ⁸Isaiah foretold this: "God has allowed them to be lethargic, to have eyes which do not see, and ears which do not hear" (Isaiah 29:10). ⁹Another scripture, Psalm 69:22, 23, on this topic says, "Let their table be a trap and a snare. Let it be their only reward. It is a stumbling block. ¹⁰Let their eyes be blinded and let them be helpless slaves."

¹¹Now I have a question for you. Was it God's will that forced them to fail in their mission? Most certainly not. Yet their failure has been a factor in His desires to reach the Gentiles, and even this wonderful development was resented by many of Israel's people. ¹²Now, if the failure of Israel resulted in eternal riches for the rest of the world, how much better it might have been had this been achieved by their fulfilling of God's plan for them! ¹³I am writing to you Gentiles as a part of my mission to you as an apostle, and I have determined to give this task my very best efforts. ¹⁴I hope also to encourage my own people, the Jews, to accept salvation. ¹⁵For if rejection by the Jews can result in salvation for the world, what would have been the result had they received Christ? It would have been spectacular, such as resurrection from death.

¹⁶Here is another illustration. If the first fruit is holy, so also is the main harvest, and if the root of a plant is holy, so also are its branches. ¹⁷It is like the grafting of new branches to an olive tree, when one of the original branches breaks off. You were a wild olive branch, but now you are grafted in, growing and receiving nourishment from the roots and the trunk of the original tree. ¹⁸A word of caution here. Avoid the temptation to consider yourselves more important than the original branches, for the tree is nourishing you, not the other way around. ¹⁹It would be easy to say, "Those branches were broken off so that there would be room for me." ²⁰But the facts are that they were broken off because of their unbelief, and you are attached because of your continuing belief. ²¹For if God had to take the drastic step of breaking off the natural branches, He would surely treat you the same way and for the same reason.

²²Notice these characteristics of God. He is both infinitely gracious and kind, as well as infinitely just. Gracious to you,

and just in dealing with unbelief. So realize that you could be cut off. [23]And now another thought. Those who were cut off may be grafted back in if they come to trust God again. He is capable of doing this and wants very much to do so. [24]If you can be grafted back in, having come from a wild olive, then also the natural branch could be grafted back in.

[25]My brothers and sisters, you need to be fully aware of this mysterious attachment, aware that it is not your wisdom or capabilities that make this possible. Israel was plagued by this problem and likely will continue to be until Gentiles in large numbers come to God. [26]Then it can truly be said that "all Israel shall be saved" if we take the position that spiritual Israel is referred to. See Psalm 14:7 and Isaiah 54:20 where we learn that "there shall come out of Zion a Deliverer and shall turn away all rebellion from Jacob. [27]Here is My covenant with them when I take away their sins and declare them guiltless."

[28]You may consider them to be enemies, but God still loves them. [29]And He never changes His mind when He calls someone and promises them gifts. [30]Yes, there was a time when you were disobedient and unbelieving, but now you have been shown mercy following the rejection of Israel, and God is now extending His invitation to all Gentiles everywhere. [31]And there are yet many others who have no faith, but because mercy was shown to you, you will one day experience God's mercy and salvation, [32]for God is able to utilize unbelief, if need be, to accomplish His purposes. [33]O how wise and knowledgeable our God is! How utterly marvelous are His ways and His decisions. We cannot begin to comprehend them.

[34]And let me quote Isaiah 40:13: "Who could possibly know the mind of God, and who could possibly presume to give advice to Him?" [35]Yes, who could possibly have supplied Him with such wisdom? If any have done this, God should richly reward him, I would think. [36]However, let's face it, God is the origin of everything, the designer and creator, the owner and manager of all material and spiritual entities. Amen.

Chapter 12

[1]Now, my brothers and sisters, let me urge you, in view of what God has done for us through His mercy, to offer yourselves as sacrifices, not dead ones, but living, fully committed to God and accepted by Him. If you will do this, your service to Him will be useful and enjoyable. [2]At all costs avoid the temptation to allow worldly society to influence you toward its patterns of behavior, but let God transform you through His influence. In this way you will demonstrate publicly that God's will is perfect and altogether good. [3]Through God's grace I have been given a message for you, and here it is, you are valuable, but avoid the tendency that we all have to place too high an opinion on self. Rather face soberly the truth that every person has been given some faith.

[4]Consider the illustration of the human body. Every organ has its office and function, and in the church every person has an important part to act. [5]And even though no two of us are alike, we make up the "body" of Christ, each member contributing to the good of the whole body. [6]Here is the important thing. Every one of us has a special gift, a gift appropriate to the person, and we need to allow the Holy Spirit to use this gift as He sees best. For instance, the

gift of prophecy should be recognized as vital to the church and should be trusted by the members. [7]As for the gift of ministry, whoever has this gift, he should allow the Holy Spirit to activate it and put it to use, just as the gift of teaching should be faithfully used. [8]And about the gift of counseling; put it to use in the church. The gift of generosity in financial support of the church and its goals should be practiced with no fanfare. The gift of administrative ability is one that needs diligent attention and active work. Those who have been given the gift of compassion for the less fortunate need to maintain a cheerful attitude while they exercise their gift.

[9]True love (agape) will never separate brother from brother, or separate anyone from the church, but will bring us all closer together. Cultivate a hatred for every species of evil, and cling tightly to the good. [10]Real affection for each other is a wonderful result of our faith. It will even lead us to prefer the other person in promotions, recognition, and responsibilities. [11]And let all your business dealings be carried out promptly and accurately. No sloppy work can be considered successful. Another thought: A warm-hearted Christian is God's most effective witness. [12]We must continually demonstrate joy as we look forward hopefully. Yes, even if we are in serious troublesome times. Prayer is our chief help. A constant, daily, hourly prayer.

[13]And please be on the alert for believers who are in want so that none suffer needlessly. We should be the world's most hospitable people, even to total strangers. [14]It was Jesus who admonished us, "Love your enemies, those who are persecuting you. Don't curse them, bless them." [15]Try to empathize with everyone. Rejoice with those who are rejoicing, and don't be ashamed to shed tears with those who are in sorrow. [16]Always treat others with no partiality or prejudice. Do not be reticent about socializing with those in the poorer classes of society, for they are just as precious to God as any others. Once again, keep a healthy attitude about your own weaknesses and failures. [17]If another person injures you in any way, respond as Jesus did. He was willing to do good things for them. It is very important to be one hundred percent honest in dealings.

[18]If it is at all possible live peaceably with neighbors and all others. [19]My dearly beloved brothers and sisters, never take revenge on others, regardless of their treatment of you. Rather, subdue the desire to retaliate, for God has promised to avenge all wrongs some day. [20]So let us treat an enemy like this: Feed him if he is hungry, give him water if he is thirsty, by so doing you may be able to kindle a warm friendship in him. [21]Never allow wickedness to conquer you; rather, you do the conquering by constantly doing good.

Chapter 13

[1]Let us all be subject to legally constituted authority, remembering that all governments are a part of God's plan in a rebellious world. [2]If we resist governmental power, we are resisting God's authority and will finally be condemned. [3]Law enforcement personnel are no threat to us while we are doing good. In fact, they will approve of our behavior. [4]They are on our side as ministers of God, in a sense, for our protection. However, if you are doing wrong, you should indeed fear the lawman, for he uses force when necessary to suppress crime.

[5]Willingness to obey the laws of the land should be a matter of conscience, not just a means of avoiding punishment. [6]Furthermore, we should pay our taxes accurately and conscientiously and on time, for civil authorities are being directed by God for our good. [7]So be sure to honor the ones in authority by your habits of tax-paying, obeying laws and local ordinances, and by respecting them. [8]Avoid debts of all kinds except the debt we owe to love others. If you have true unselfish love for others, you will be keeping the commandments. [9]Yes, think it through. The law against adultery, murder, theft, lying, and coveting is only expressing the broader law found in Leviticus 19:18 to "love your neighbor as yourself." [10]God's type of love will never injure a neighbor or damage his property, and love is the essence of the commandments.

[11]Let us be alert to the times in which we live. Sometimes I fear that we are almost asleep, so wake up, fellow Christian, for our salvation draws nearer every day. [12]Night is almost over, daylight is coming, so let us rid ourselves of dark behavior and shield ourselves with light. [13]Let us live lives that are sensible, reasonable, knowing that we are plainly visible to all; no quarrelling, drunkenness, or violence, and no vandalism. No fighting or jealousy, [14] but rather, we need to clothe ourselves with Jesus our Lord, thus preventing our natural evil desires from controlling us.

Chapter 14

[1]You may have fellow church members who are weak in the faith, but accept them whole-heartedly and avoid disputes with them for this would be a very doubtful way to help them. [2]For instance, some are convinced that they can eat anything without suffering indigestion, while others wouldn't think of such a thing; no, they must limit themselves to certain herbs. [3]We should learn a lesson from this. No two of us are alike, so if you are a person strong in faith, avoid looking down your nose at a weak one. And if you happen to be a "weak" person, you may be tempted to criticize or judge the "strong" one. God loves us all, strong and weak, impartially. [4]Who are you, trying to judge another person's slave? Let his master do this evaluating. Now God is the master of all of us and has the capability of lifting His slaves and strengthening them.

[5]Here's another illustration. One person may wish to consider a certain day to be very special, while another person may choose a totally different day. Each person should have the privilege of making such choices. [6]Whoever celebrates one of the feast days does so because he believes he is honoring God by so doing. And another person who sees no reason to consider that feast day sacred believes that he is honoring God. He who thanks God for his food is no better in God's sight than the one who thanks God for the privilege of refusing the same food.

[7]You realize, I am sure, that each of us has a significant impact on those around us, [8]and whether it is God's will that we live or that we die, we choose His will for we belong to Him and trust Him. [9]Christ's death showed conclusively that he is Lord of the dead, and His resurrection demonstrates that He is Lord of the living. [10]One day all of us shall stand before Christ our judge, so let none of us attempt to judge others or even criticize them. We must first criticize ourselves.

¹¹Here is what I find in scripture: "Every knee shall bow and every tongue shall confess to God." ¹²You and I are included in this statement. We will give an account of ourselves to God! ¹³This is why none of us has any business in attempting to judge others. But let us be diligent to search our own hearts carefully so as not to cause anyone else to stumble and fall.

¹⁴As an example, I am thoroughly convinced that ceremonial cleanness or uncleanness is no longer significant. But it is significant that ¹⁵my choice of food must be with consideration for the convictions of others who may be watching me. They may be lost in the end because of my behavior, even though Christ died for them. ¹⁶So give no occasion for anyone to misinterpret your words or your behavior. ¹⁷You already know this of course, but the kingdom of God is vastly more than food and drink, important as they are. It has to do with genuine goodness, which in essence is unselfishness and consideration for others. It has to do with true peace and joy, the type of joy that Christ gives through the Holy Spirit. ¹⁸Whoever is serving Christ in these essentials is accepted by God and approved by his fellow men. ¹⁹So let us all pursue any objective that will promote this peace and bring blessings to others.

²⁰Let me state my convictions again about foods. Never let food interfere with the work of God. You see, idols cannot curse food, but food can be a curse if it offends another person. ²¹Far better for us to deny ourselves the pleasure of certain food or beverages than to cause a brother or sister to stumble, be offended, or be weakened in faith. ²²Do you have faith? Do not flaunt your faith, but treasure it as a precious gift from God. Happy is that person who does not bring condemnation on himself by some practice, lawful though it may be, that might offend another soul. ²³That person with weak faith feels condemned by eating food offered to idols. In fact any act, habit, or practice not actuated by faith is sinful.

Chapter 15

¹Let us, being strong, mature Christians, accept the responsibility of nurturing the newer members and those who may be weaker or less mature even though it may mean giving up some things that we might truly enjoy. ²Yes, let every one of us Christians be willing to do anything and everything that would edify and encourage a neighbor. ³We ought to follow Christ's example. He most certainly never tried to please Himself, but rather only those things that would benefit others. He even went so far as to fulfill the scripture that says, "The reproach which was directed to others fell on Me." ⁴This passage as well as all others was written to help us learn about God, His character, and patience so that we may have hope.

⁵And now my prayer for you is that God, who is infinitely patient and comforting, will give you these qualities as you deal with others, and thus resemble Christ. ⁶And that you may honor the Father through your relationships. ⁷In fulfilling this prayer you will accept others graciously just as Christ accepted us as He demonstrated God's character. ⁸I am thoroughly convinced that Jesus Christ was a minister to the Jewish people, establishing the truth of the promises made to our ancestors. ⁹And even more, He intended that the Gentiles should share in His ministry of mercy so that they too might glorify God as prophesied in Psalm 18:40.

[10]Notice also Deuteronomy 32:43: "Rejoice you nations with Israel." [11]Would you like yet another? How about Psalm 117:1: "Oh praise the Lord all you nations, praise Him all you peoples." [12]Another? Isaiah 9:6, 7 and Isaiah 11:1: "There shall come forth a rod of authority from Jesse and through Him to Israel for the benefit of the whole world."

[13]Now my prayer for you is this: "May the God of hope fill you with true joy and peace as you learn to trust Him more and more through the work of His Spirit." [14]Brothers and sisters, I am convinced that you have been given God's wisdom and goodness for the purpose of preparing you to teach others. [15]And yet, even with this vast store of wisdom, I have written to you some things that were on my heart, hoping to add a few more ideas to your already abundant store of knowledge. Frankly, this is the only reason that God has revealed these concepts to me. He intends that I share them with others.

[16]Indeed, I consider myself to be divinely called and authorized to be a minister to the Gentiles, with the help of the Holy Spirit, to give them the good news about God in an acceptable manner, guided by the Holy Spirit. [17]And believe me, it has brought intense, satisfying joy, this mission of sharing Christ with others. [18]Right here, let me assure you that nothing I have done for the Gentiles in bringing them to where they want to obey God has been done in my own strength. It has all been done by the power of Christ. [19]Any miracles connected with my ministry were done by the power of Christ through the Holy Spirit. And my preaching, beginning at Jerusalem and extending to Illyricum, has been centered in Christ.

[20]I have purposely gone to places where Jesus Christ has never been heard of, not wishing to duplicate the work of other Christians. [21]This is in fulfillment of Isaiah 52:15: "To whom Christ had not yet been made known, they shall see, and they who have not yet heard shall finally understand." [22]I'm sure you can now realize why I have not yet come to Rome. Just too many calls to share the gospel. [23]But at last it would appear that there are no immediate calls coming to me and that, after so many years, I will really be able to go to Rome.

[24]My current plan is to find a ship to Rome, and after a time getting better acquainted with you, I am hoping to go on to Spain. [25]But first I have a responsibility to go to Jerusalem, for the believers there are poverty-stricken. [26]The funds that have been given are entrusted to me by unselfish, loving Christians here and in Macedonia and Achaia. [27]It has been a real joy for these generous people to help those who are being persecuted. They have received spiritual blessings from these very ones now being persecuted. [28]But after that, I shall be on my way to Rome and then to Spain. [29]And I feel sure that when I arrive I shall be blessed by your fellowship, your love, your friendship, and your joy. [30]Please, brothers and sisters, remember to pray for me and for the progress of the gospel [31]so that I may be saved from the wrath of those who have rejected Jesus and that the believers there will accept me as one of themselves. [32]Then that I may be able to come to you, God willing, and be encouraged by you. [33]May the God of peace be with you all, Amen.

Chapter 16

[1]Let this be a hearty recommendation of our sister Phoebe as a member of your church. She has been faithfully and

loyally serving her church at Cenchreae. [2]Whatever help you can give to her will be deeply appreciated. This dear saint has helped many others, including myself. [3]Please give my regards to Priscilla and Aquila who were such wonderful fellow workers in Christ. [4]They went so far as to risk their lives for me, and by the way, I am not the only one who is thankful to them, for they are well known in all the neighboring churches of the Gentiles as being the sort of people who would give the shirt off their back in order to help others. [5]So give my greetings to them and to the whole church that meets in their home.

Greet my dear friend Epaenetus, my first convert in Achaia, [6]and Mary who was such a help to us. [7]Then there are many relatives, Andronicus and Junia, both of whom have been imprisoned for Christ and who are well known among the apostles and who became Christians before I did. [8]In addition to these, please greet the following believers also: Ampliatus, a beloved fellow Christian; [9]Urbanus, the willing helper; and Stachys, another much loved believer; [10]Appelles, who is accepted as a true believer; Aristobulus, his family and friends; [11]Herodion, my distant cousin; Narcissus and his family, who are in the Lord; [12]Tryphaena and Tryphosa, the twins who have labored so faithfully for God; and Persis, who labored a great deal for our Lord. [13]Don't forget Rufus. God has certainly chosen him as well as his mother (whom I consider as almost my own mother). [14]Greet Asyncritus, Phlegon, Hermes, Patrobas, and the brothers with them, [15]Philologus and Julia, Nereus and his sister, Olympas and the believers with them.

[16]It is perfectly appropriate to greet one another with an holy kiss. The churches here also send their warmest greetings to all. [17]Perhaps right here I need to give you a word of warning. There will likely be those who have a burden to cause divisions among you and will not follow the teachings you have learned. They are troublemakers, so resist their evil influence. [18]They are not really serving Jesus Christ the Lord but are selfish, attempting to promote themselves. Their words may sound right, but God's true followers will draw people together, not divide them. [19]You should know that your lives as Christians are being scrutinized all over the empire, especially you who live in the capital of the empire. I truly feel grateful for your positive witness. And pray that you will continue to uphold good and reject evil. [20]And if you do, the God of peace will surely conquer Satan in your behalf. May the grace of our Lord Jesus Christ be with you, Amen.

[21]Timothy, my fellow worker, sends his greeting; so do my kinfolk Jason and Sosipater, as well as Dr. Luke. [22]Tertius, the secretary, who has written this letter, sends my own greetings in the Lord. [23]Gaius, our most generous host, greets you. Erastus, the city manager, and Quartus, another Christian brother, send their greetings. [24]May the grace of our Lord Jesus Christ be with you all, Amen.

[25]Now in closing, let us all extol and worship Him who is able to establish you in the gospel and in the teachings of Jesus Christ, those truths that have been there since creation, but which are just now being understood, [26]having been proclaimed by prophets who spoke for God, proclaiming to all nations the truth concerning God, leading many to obey. [27]Now to the only wise God, be glory forever, through Jesus Christ, Amen.

1 Corinthians

Chapter 1

¹Greetings from Paul and brother Sosthenes who, as you remember, was ruler of the synagogue many years ago before his conversion. ²Our letter is to the church at Corinth, those who are Christians there. In fact, it is useful and intended for followers of Jesus Christ wherever they may be living. ³May God's grace and His peace, made available through Jesus Christ, be given to you.

⁴I give thanks to God every day for you and for what God has been able to accomplish through you at Corinth, through Jesus Christ. ⁵For through Him you are what you are now: knowledgeable and capable of persuading others expressively. ⁶Yes, through you God has demonstrated what He is able to accomplish through mere human beings. ⁷Actually, Christians may reach the very highest standards, even while they are anticipating and preparing for the return of our Lord Jesus Christ. ⁸He will continue to constantly strengthen you so that at His return you may be counted faultless. ⁹God never fails, and it is He who has called you into Christian fellowship and into fellowship with His Son, Jesus Christ our Lord.

¹⁰My brothers, let me urge you in the name of Jesus Christ that you do not allow differences to come in among you, differences that will eventually separate you from each other. ¹¹I have learned, to my sadness, from a member of Chloe's family that there has been a factional dispute in the church. ¹²It would seem that the differing factions are divided due to the fact that some were brought into the church by me or Apollos or Peter or by Jesus Christ Himself. ¹³But brothers, is Christ divided? Was Paul crucified for you? Were you baptized in the name of Paul? ¹⁴God must have been leading when you were baptized because Crispus and Gaius were the only ones that I baptized personally. ¹⁵So, of course, the church would not be at all likely to claim that they were baptized in my name. ¹⁶Oh, Oh. There was one other, Stephanas and his family, whom I baptized.

¹⁷My whole emphasis in following Christ was to preach the gospel. Baptism is not the goal in itself; no, the cross of Christ is the key message and of supreme importance. ¹⁸Now preaching the cross may be rejected as utter foolishness by some (these will eventually perish in the second death), but whoever accepts and believes this great truth will receive power as needed from God Himself. ¹⁹Remember Isaiah's statement? "I will expose the folly of those who consider themselves wise and

will demonstrate the emptiness of human wisdom." [20]I ask you, where is the wise person, the scribe, or the human debater when dealing with salvation? [21]Let me tell you this, all the wisdom of this world cannot explain how to know God, but preaching the cross brings healing to those who believe the message.

[22]It seems characteristic of the Jews that they are constantly looking for signs to guide them, and the Greeks, well, they are always groping for more "wisdom." [23]We don't give either group exactly what they want, but we proclaim Christ as the Messiah to the Jews (rejected by the nation, true enough) and the crucifixion of Christ to the Greeks who generally consider such a thing total foolishness. [24]But for those who have responded to God's call, whether Jews or Greeks, Christ is God's power and God's wisdom. [25]You see, God's weakest point is stronger than the strength of the mightiest man, and God's foolishness is vastly greater than all the wisdom of mankind.

[26]Brothers, look around among yourselves and realize that although God calls all, very few who are considered wise by the world have responded and not many who are considered noble by the world have believed. [27]And yet in God's plan those things that are foolishness in the eyes of the world are true wisdom. [28]And those things considered by the world to be hardly worthy of notice have been the very things that God chooses as most important. It might seem that some things that do not even exist in the thinking of human beings are powerful enough to overcome material things. [29]All of this demonstrates how foolish it would be for a man to boast about himself while God is able to view

the true reality. [30]But you, my dear believers, are in union with Christ the Messiah through God's wonderful providence, and this union with Christ is union with ultimate wisdom. [31]You are very likely aware of this statement of Jeremiah: 9:23: "If any of you want to glory, let him glory in the Lord."

Chapter 2

[1]Brothers and sisters, when I arrived at Corinth, it was not by any eloquence of mine that I was able to convince you that I was speaking for God, [2]for I had decided to preach nothing other than Jesus Christ and Him crucified. [3]Believe me, I was keenly aware of my own weaknesses and began with fear and trembling. [4]I recognized that my message, manner of delivery, and style of preaching was not like the ordinary orator who was out there trying to persuade crowds, but rather I was dependent on the power of the Holy Spirit [5]so that those who believed would be Christians, not just because of a certain human being and his ministry, but because of their willingness to be persuaded by God. [6]Of course, I'm not saying that we are failing to give wise advice, the wisdom that you Christians have is far above the wisdom of the world and even above the wisdom of the world's intellectuals, for their wisdom will eventually result in nothingness. [7]But we Christians are blessed with God's wisdom, even though it presents mysteries to the human mind, mysteries that were devised before the earth was created and will result in unbelievable good to us.

[8]Unfortunately, those in authority did not understand these things either, for had they understood, they would not have crucified the Lord of the universe. [9]I

am reminded of Isaiah 64:4: "Eyes have not see, ears have not heard, neither has a human mind been able to imagine what God has planned and made ready for those who love Him." [10]However, the Holy Spirit has made known to us some of these things; of course, the Holy Spirit is aware of all of God's plans, including those plans that are totally out of our realm.

[11]Which of you can possibly know anything about my hidden plans? None of you! My mind and my spirit alone can know such things. [12]We Christians are the fortunate recipients, not of the spirit of the world, but of the Spirit of God who allows us to grasp many ideas given to us by God Himself. [13]It is on these matters that we talk and write about. Not just material, temporal things, human concepts and ideas, but things taught to us by the Holy Spirit who explains such things to humans. [14]But without the aid of the Holy Spirit, our minds will not accept these things given by the Spirit. They cannot receive them because they can learn them only through the power of the Holy Spirit. [15]The one who is "spiritual" (directed, aided, and helped by the Holy Spirit) is able to grasp these matters while he himself cannot be understood by the ones who do not have this aid. [16]Oh, who has known the mind of the Lord? No one of course, but we Christians have been given minds like the mind of Christ Himself.

Chapter 3

[1]Let me share with you, brothers, some real concerns that I have. So far I have been unable to tell you things on a very deep spiritual plane, only as to babes in Christ. [2]My spiritual food for you has been only as milk so far and not as solid food. [3] What I am saying is this: We Christians as we grow develop characters that will have no bickering, jealousy, envy, or "cliques" among us. My plea for you is to keep growing and thus eliminate these undesirable traits. [4]I am aware that groups in your church who were converted under my ministry have developed a subculture of their own while those who were converted under the ministry of Apollos have done the same thing, thus dividing the church. I believe that you can see that this is not in God's plan for Christians.

[5]Paul, just who is he? A minister who brought you to Christ. Who is Apollos? Another minister who brought you to Christ. Now all believers are equal in belonging to Christ. [6]I indeed planted the seed, then Apollos watered the soil, but it was only God who caused the crop to grow. [7]So neither Apollos nor Paul can claim to have produced Christians. We are on the same level, just helpers of God. That's all. [8]We can be called one in purpose, even though our work was not identical and yet our reward will be comparable. [9]We are fellow laborers with God. You are the harvest, the completed structure that God is building.

[10]By the grace of God, our wise Master and Architect, I have had the privilege of laying the foundation. And now another builder adds to what I have started. I now plead that whoever adds to the structure will do it with utmost accuracy and detail. [11]There can be no different foundation laid than the one already in place—Jesus Christ. [12]And whatever materials are put in place from here on, whether they are gold or silver gems, [13]wood, hay or stubble, these will be eloquent testimony as to the character of the builders. The day is

coming that will be a real time of testing, just as fire is a test for ores and will display the type of materials put into the building. [14]Whoever builds wisely enough so that his work endures the test, he should consider himself well rewarded. [15]If his efforts turn out to be lost in the fire, he will be losing much, even though he himself endures through the trial.

[16]Now about this temple. You believers are the temple of God. You surely know that the Holy Spirit of God lives in you as believers [17]so that whoever brings disruption on the temple of God shall reap the certain results—He will be cut off from God, for God and His temple is holy. [18]Please do not be deceived by anyone. There may be some who appear to be very wise, but it is far better to be classified as foolish by the world if by so doing he can achieve God's wisdom. [19]For much that is called wisdom by the world is utter folly in the infinite God's view. Remember Job 5:13: "He traps the 'wise' in their own sly plans." [20]Also Psalm 94:11: "The Lord knows that the thoughts of mankind, even the wisest, are mostly vain." [21]So do not take pride in any human being, but try to grasp the great fact that you Christians are possessors of all that is truly worthwhile.

[22]Whether Paul, Apollos, or Peter brought you to Christ, everything of real value in this world, even life itself, hope even in the face of death, everything of future value is already yours. [23]Yes, you are Christ's, and Christ is God's.

Chapter 4

[1]I hope that you will all consider me and my helpers to be ministers of Christ and caretakers for the great mysteries of God. [2]As you know, anyone who is chosen to be steward of another's property is a person who is wholly trustworthy. [3]And even though I am generally considered trustworthy, this does not prove that I am. Human judgment is not always accurate. Even my own opinion of my stewardship may not be accurate. [4]Yet the infallible Judge, the Lord Himself will pass judgment on me. [5]So defer judgment until the return of Christ, for He will make everything plain at that time, even the things that perplex us so very much. He is able to accurately judge motives and thoughts. Then we shall all praise God and will be commended by God.

[6]Brothers and sisters, I have tried to place these burdens on myself and on Apollos so that you will not need to worry over them. We will attempt to shoulder some of your burdens, and in this way you will be free to share the burdens of others. We are all in this thing together. [7]Think of this, none of us is better than any other. Here's another thought, what do you enjoy that was not a gift in the first place? If it is a gift there is no reason to gloat over it just as if you had earned it or had created it yourself. [8]At present you brothers are rich and share wonderful blessings, like kings, and really are in no need of us. And I wish above all that you were indeed kings and that we might all reign together.

[9]Sometimes it seems that we apostles are the last of all in God's sight, and we are only a demonstration before the universe, as well as, to humans of what one must endure in this great controversy with our adversary. [10]We must seem sometimes to be utterly foolish in our zeal to follow Christ while you people seem wise. We feel weak while you seem to be strong. We are often hated while you are honored. [11]We

apostles are often hungry, thirsty, and destitute of adequate clothing, criticized and homeless. [12]We must work to support our own ministry. We face hateful words, but we still try to bless those who speak them. We are persecuted. [13]We are put down, and yet we try to attract those same people. We are considered, by many, to be nothing other than refuse, thrown out for destruction, fit only for burial in a landfill.

[14]Now please, do not think that I am trying to magnify your problems. No, I am only warning you of dangers ahead. [15]And who can be more concerned about a child than his father? You might have ten thousand Sabbath School teachers, but you have only one "spiritual father," yours truly, the one who fathered your faith. [16]So please follow me instead of others. [17]In order to do my very best for you I have sent Timothy, one of my beloved "children" and a very faithful son indeed, who will help to keep you reminded of my constant desire to see you growing in Christ, as I do for all Christians wherever I minister.

[18]However, some are so certain that I will never return to you that they themselves try to take credit for your conversion and present growth. [19]But be sure of this, if the Lord is willing, I will come to you again and will evaluate the conversation and lifestyle of these people and will also receive God's power to energize you. [20]God's kingdom is not mere words but is actual power to really change humanity. [21]What is your choice? Shall I come as a dictator or in a loving, mild manner?

Chapter 5

[1]Now, beloved friends, I have heard from several reliable sources that one of your members is practicing adultery openly with his step-mother and that the sin of which he is obviously guilty is so unspeakable that even Gentiles would not stoop to such things. [2]You church members have not been entirely free of responsibility in this for you have not been mourning over the situation. In fact, some of you have felt pride in the fact that you have felt tolerant of such sin. Actually you should have disfellowshipped him long ago. [3]It doesn't take me long to make a decision in a matter such as this even though I am not there in person to confront the erring one. [4]Here is what you must do in the name of Jesus Christ our Lord. Call a business meeting of the whole church with the authority that Jesus our Lord has demonstrated. [5]Separate him from the church, even though this may result in his giving himself up to Satan. The end result is more likely to help him see his desperate condition and come to Christ for forgiveness and conversion, and finally salvation at the return of Jesus.

[6]Another thing, you who are not guilty of such a sin should never feel proud of that fact, because the influence of one open sinner in the church is subtle and affects everyone to some extent, like yeast in dough. [7]So get rid of this leavening influence; be "unleavened." This is the reason for using unleavened bread at Passover. Christ is the center of the feast and all leavening must be rejected. [8]So let this ceremony mean this to us as Christians that we reject old sin and also all hatred, malice, and wickedness. But we do celebrate deliverance from the leaven of sin and the entrance of sincerity and truth.

[9](Remember that in my previous letter to you I asked you to have no fellowship with a person practicing fornication.) [10]But of course, if you never have had any

association with fornicators, coveters, extortionist, or idolaters, it would be necessary to be on another planet. [11]My idea here is that in the church anyone who claims to be a Christian must have a far different standard of lifestyle than that of the world: no fornication or other sexual sin. There must not be covetousness, idolatry, harshness, drunkenness, or extortion. This is an illustration of what must not be admitted into the church or kept in the church. [12]As for those outside the church. I am in no position to judge them, but should you not make decisions regarding members of the church? Yes, indeed you should. [13]You see, God will judge those outside the church. So let us allow God to be the judge of this person.

Chapter 6

[1]In regard to judging, I recognize the need we all have to avoid judging others, but in trying to avoid that evil you may have fallen into another evil. I refer to taking other church members to civil courts to settle differences. [2]You may not know it, but Christians saved in God's kingdom will be able to review the cases of the whole world and the sentences of all the lost, assuring themselves that God's decisions are absolutely just as well as infinitely merciful, so surely you should be able to make proper judgments concerning small matters here in this life. [3]Yes, my friends, we shall even have the responsibility of judging the cases of the fallen angels who rebelled against God. A church of believers should be able to discern accurately the proper way to settle disputes in this life.

[4]So now please, if you have cases of disputes between members, you might do well to select a panel of believers who are not experts in the law, would be able to come to right decisions, and do it better than the civil court. [5]I deplore, brothers, the tendency to pass by the believers, considering none of them wise enough to settle such disputes. [6]But one member will sue another in a court presided over by an unbeliever. [7]This is a serious mistake. It would be far better to allow yourself to be wronged and then do nothing about it. [8]No, don't go on cheating one another. Of course, this would be the best answer, wouldn't you say?

[9]You surely know, but I will remind you again that unrighteous people will not be members of God's kingdom. Let no one persuade you otherwise. The sexually impure, idol worshippers, philanderers, or homosexuals, [10]thieves, selfish ones, drunkards, hot-headed ones, and extortionist will not be found in God's kingdom. [11]Some of you Corinthians would have been described by those words in the days before you became Christians, but think now of the change: washed, forgiven, and made right with God by the power of Jesus working through the Holy Spirit. [12]Everything that God permits me to do should be appropriate, right? No, this is not the case. I might give a wrong impression by my behavior, even doing legitimate things, so I will not engage in such things for the sake of others, however, appealing to me they are.

[13]For instance, God has provided a vast variety of foods that can be found and eaten which are healthful, but which might be a stumbling block to some people. Also, our bodies, designed by God are to bring glory to our Creator, and certainly not for fornication, [14]and these bodies are to be resurrected just as God resurrected Christ.

¹⁵Now, being Christians, our bodies are a part of Christ's body, the church. Shall I use this body, which is a part of Christ, and make it a member of a prostitute? By no means! ¹⁶Think! A person patronizing a prostitute is making himself joined to that person, for the scripture says, "They two shall be one flesh."

¹⁷But Christians who are joined to God are united in spirit to Him. ¹⁸So totally avoid fornication. Of all the sins of humanity, nearly all are sins not affecting one's own body, but fornication is a sin against one's own self. ¹⁹You see, your body is the place on planet Earth (and I may truthfully add, the only place on planet Earth) where the Holy Spirit resides, so we call it His temple. It is yours, given to you by God the Creator, as a sacred trust, and you do not belong to yourself. ²⁰You were purchased at a fearful cost to God. And for this reason you should glorify God in every act of the body, as well as in all spiritual considerations.

Chapter 7

¹Next I will try to answer the questions about which you wrote to me. First off it is important that a man avoid caressing or fondling a woman. ²This of course does not apply to married couples, for there is no adultery if the principles of marriage are faithfully followed. One man, one woman. ³Let the husband continually demonstrate the utmost tenderness to his wife and the wife to her husband. ⁴The wife does not have total control over her own body, but shares some rights with her husband. And similarly the husband must share his body with his wife. ⁵Do not withhold from each other the privileges of intimacy unless it is by mutual consent in a time of fasting and prayer, but return to normal relationship again to prevent Satan from gaining an advantage over you by lustful temptations.

⁶Now I would like to bring up something that the Holy Spirit has permitted me to say, but was not commanded to say. ⁷Consider the advantages of living a single life as I am currently doing. Yes, I am aware that no two persons are alike, and what is good for one may not be good for everyone. ⁸Nevertheless, you who are unmarried or widowed might well consider remaining single as I have elected to do. ⁹However, if you have unrelenting sexual temptation, it would be better to be married.

¹⁰And you who are married remember that God, not just Paul, has given this command. Wives, do not leave your husbands. ¹¹And if you separate, do not remarry. But if possible be reconciled to your husband. Husbands, do not divorce your wives. ¹²My advice to others is this. Although I have had no direct word from the Lord regarding this specific situation, it would be right for a man who has an unbelieving wife who loves him and wishes to remain with him to remain married to her. Do not get divorced. ¹³And if you are a Christian woman whose husband is an unbeliever and wants to remain with you, do not leave him. ¹⁴The unbelieving husband is especially fortunate to have a true Christian wife, and the unbelieving wife is especially fortunate to have a true Christian husband. The children in such a home are far better off if their parents stay together. ¹⁵You may of course face a situation where the unbelieving spouse leaves you. In such a case it would be best not to demand that he or she stay, or even to pressure him or her to stay. His leaving you will free you to engage in

church activities, to remarry, to rear your children in the Lord, and certainly to live a life more likely to be peaceful. ¹⁶To make no demands in such a case will be a strong influence, you Christian wife, to win your husband to Christ, and you Christian husband will exert a strong influence on your wife to become a Christian.

¹⁷Having said all this, let God guide your conscience then follow your conscience faithfully. ¹⁸If any Jew is called to follow Christ, he, of course, cannot become uncircumcised, and if a Gentile is won to Christ, he certainly does not need to be circumcised. ¹⁹Circumcision is nonessential; uncircumcision is nonessential. What is really important is a life that is in harmony with God's commandments. ²⁰Let everyone continue on in the Lord after he has been called by the Lord. ²¹If you are a slave, don't let this cause you anxiety. Now if you have been freed, accept freedom as a gift from God and become as useful as possible. ²²It's like this, if you are called in the Lord, even though you happen to be a slave, you are free in the Lord, and if a free man is called in the Lord, he becomes Christ's slave. ²³You have all been purchased with a huge price and so naturally you are God's slaves, not slaves of any human being. ²⁴Whatever your status, continue to walk with God.

²⁵Now let me get back to your questions about virgins. I have no direct revelation from God, yet I believe I can give good advice having been following the Lord faithfully. ²⁶Let me say that at present it would seem good for a man to remain unmarried, even though society might expect him to marry. ²⁷If you are a married man, don't let anyone try to persuade you to separate from your wife. If you are

now separated, do not remarry. ²⁸I am not saying that marrying is wrong or sinful. I am not saying that it is wrong for a virgin to marry, but I am attempting to spare you a lot of troubles in this life. ²⁹And speaking of troubles, life is really short whether married or single. Troubles come to everyone. ³⁰Grief and weeping will come to all of us. Some joy and gladness will come to all. Having a lot of property will not be very important.

³¹Those who find their only interest to be in the world will not be well rewarded by the world. And it is the same for those who have little in common with the world. For the world is doomed to perish one day. ³²But I hope you will not have undue anxiety over such things. An unmarried man naturally will likely be more concerned about pleasing the Lord. ³³A married man is more likely to be concerned about temporal matters and how best to please his wife. ³⁴The converse is also true. An unmarried woman is free to spend her energies and interests in the things of the Lord, being completely committed to Him, but a married woman is very likely to have a higher interest in temporal matters, so she will be able to please her husband. ³⁵I am not trying to cause you trouble, but honestly it is for your own good that I advise you this way, in order that you may be completely given to the Lord and serve Him.

³⁶So if any of you has a daughter about whom you are concerned and are convinced that you have been treating her unjustly in refusing to let her marry until she is past marriageable age, you may with clear conscience give her in marriage. There is nothing wrong in such a course. ³⁷However, if you are convinced in your heart that to preserve her from future

trouble, she must not marry. Then stand by your decision, for it is the correct choice. [38]It comes down to a choice between a good decision and a better one, good to choose marriage, better to choose not. [39]You see, the wife is legally the property of her husband as long as he lives. After her husband dies, she is free to marry another man without the consent of her father. But remember, she should marry only within God's will for her. [40]In my judgment she would be happier to remain unmarried, and I believe that the Holy Spirit would agree.

Chapter 8

[1]Your next question was about food offered to idols and is therefore "on sale." We all possess knowledge enough to reason our way through this question, but let us not exhibit spiritual pride in making these choices. Let us rather be charitable with those around us who may differ with our opinions. [2]Remember, all of you, if you consider yourself to have wisdom, then you don't have a fraction of the wisdom you need. [3]So depend on God. If you know God, you know that He has a personal interest in you and will give you the needed guidance, for He knows you very well. [4]So let us think of these foods that have been sacrificed to some idol. We Christians know of a certainty that an idol is essentially nothing but matter, and inanimate matter at that, and the only true God has originated this matter.

[5]Oh yes, I know that there are plenty of objects that are called gods, some on the earth and some out in space. [6]But to us there is but one God, the Father, creator of all things, including us, and one Lord, Jesus Christ through whom creation

came about. [7]Unfortunately, not everyone is aware of this knowledge. These perhaps have no more conscience than an idol has, and thus they are easily led into gross error. [8]But really, friends, food does not change our relationship with God. If we eat a certain food, we are not necessarily better persons, and if we refuse that food, we are not necessarily worse persons. [9]One warning, however, and this is very important, let us not allow this freedom we have to permit us to offend someone who is weak and thus to fall when he sees our example. Let us consider his feelings and his convictions.

[10]It works like this. Suppose that you are so well aware of truth and are observed eating food that has been offered to idols, perhaps even in an idol temple. Now, if you are the only person involved, this makes good sense, knowing that an idol means absolutely nothing to you. Yet an observer might be influenced by your example to revere that idol. [11]Thus, your knowledge of truth could cause the weaker, less knowledgeable brother to stumble, and he is a person for whom Christ died. [12]And don't forget, Christ has assured us that whatever we do for another or against another can be considered to be done for or against Him. [13]As for me, I have decided never to eat any food that in any way could cause any of my Christian brothers or sisters to lose their way.

Chapter 9

[1]Am I not one of the apostles? Am I not free? Have I not seen Jesus Christ our Lord? Are you not good evidence of the truth of these assertions? [2]Even though I may not be an apostle to other people and nations, I certainly have been sent to you,

and your membership in the Christian church is the seal of my apostleship. ³Now there are those who will take issue with me, and I am willing to face their questioning. ⁴But don't we apostles have the right and the authority to be fed? ⁵Don't we also have the authority and the right to take with us a believing wife in our ministry just as the Lord's brothers do, just as Peter does?

⁶And do I not have the right to cease this self-supporting work? ⁷Can you think of any example of a self-supporting soldier? Can you think of a vineyard owner who has no right to eat of the fruit? Can you imagine a herdsman who has no right to use the milk from the herd? ⁸Am I just voicing my own ideas or am I in harmony with a universal code of right and wrong? ⁹For instance, Moses wrote it out like this: "Never muzzle the ox that tramps out the grain." Does God perform miracles for the oxen that they may have enough to eat? ¹⁰Surely Moses must have had in mind something more than just allowing an ox to eat. Surely this principle must apply to us also. The one who plows the soil does so in anticipation of a harvest. The one who threshes also hopes for some return.

¹¹Now we have sown seed of infinite value in your hearts, and it is not unreasonable to expect material blessings from you believers. ¹²If others have benefited from this privilege and right, should not Barnabas and I have the same benefit? However, as you know, we have never demanded or appropriated what we might have rightly claimed in order that our preaching can be seen to be wholly unselfish, wholly Christlike. ¹³You are doubtless aware of the fact that those who tended to the temple service in the pre-Christian era were supported by the offerings to the temple service and that those priests who offered the meat and meal offerings were fed by the offerings. ¹⁴In much the same way the Lord has planned that we who spend our lives preaching the good news should be supported by those who believe and give gifts intended to promote the progress of the preaching. ¹⁵In my case, never have I received support from believers, and I am not writing this to urge anyone to begin supporting me, correct as that would be, and justifiable as it would be. I would prefer to die than to see anyone reject Christ because of a wrong impression in this matter.

¹⁶I really have done nothing worthy of boastfulness in my ministry. I actually feel compelled to preach. More than that, I would feel that a terrible fate awaited me if I were not preaching. ¹⁷I have always preached like I do, voluntarily, and I believe that in so doing I am rewarded. If it were not done voluntarily, then it could be said that I was only carrying out orders. ¹⁸What is my reward? To preach without compensation so I do not feel a desire for material benefits.

¹⁹Although I have complete freedom, I have considered myself to be a slave, obliged to serve others in order to win more souls. ²⁰In dealing with Jews, I was Jewish in order to persuade those who still follow Jewish laws. ²¹In dealing with those outside our law, I try to sense their viewpoint, though it is difficult to imagine their life without God's law as explained by Christ. To gain their souls is my only goal. ²²In dealing with the weak, I take the position of a weak person. Thus I attempt to become one with my listeners, whoever they might be, in order to at least rescue some of them. ²³For the sake of the good

news I suppose I would do any of these things, just as I share with you the marvelous story.

²⁴Just as in a foot race there may be many runners, but only one goes home with the first prize or a gold medal. You should run with the same dedication as that gold medalist. ²⁵All runners in any contest use the utmost in self-discipline—and to think that they do so in their desire for a transient moment of glory. We on the other hand must use the same self-discipline and for a vastly superior reward. ²⁶As for me, I am running for a certain win. I fight as if fighting a certain win in the bout. I can't lose! ²⁷For I discipline my body constantly. If I should ever fail to do this, I would lose the reward even though I have spent so many years preaching to others.

Chapter 10

¹Let's continue with some thoughts I've been having lately. Remember the exodus from Egypt and the crossing of the Red Sea? Remember how the whole nation was immersed in the cloud? And was able to walk through the sea following Moses? ³Remember that they all had the same food—miracle food? ⁴That they all drank of the miracle water that gushed miraculously from a mysterious rock. Friends, that rock was Christ. ⁵Alas, even with such abundant evidence of His providences, they still failed Him, disappointing Him. They were finally allowed to die in the wilderness.

⁶Let us think for a while why this sad story has been preserved in scripture. First, consider that they are examples, horrible examples to be sure, to help us learn some lessons. First lesson: They desired wrong things. ⁷Second lesson: Avoid idol worship such as they tended to do so easily. Remember the calf? Third lesson: Hedonism is not a safe goal in human living. Scripture says that they sat down to eat and drink and rose up to play. ⁸Fourth lesson: Sexual sins are downright dangerous. Remember that after their orgy of sex with the heathen neighbors, twenty-two thousand died in one day. ⁹Fifth lesson: It is never appropriate to presumptuously put God to a test. Some of them did this and were then unprotected from the poisonous snakes of the desert. ¹⁰Sixth lesson: Complaining against God and against His leaders will cut one off from God's protection. Let me remind you that your adversary would destroy you if he had the power. You need God's protection at all times.

¹¹As a reminder, these examples are given to show us what can happen to any of us today. God saw fit to have them recorded in Scripture as a warning to all, a special warning to us who have experienced the fulfillment of so many prophecies. Yes, nearly all of them have been fulfilled, and we face the end of the age. ¹²Just in case you feel confident that you are able to endure, beware! You could fall. ¹³Your trials are many and painful, but remember that none are unusual for us human beings. Furthermore, God watches over you. He knows all about your trials and your character, so He will not allow you to be tempted and tried beyond the point that you can endure them. He will provide help for each trial so that you may endure it.

¹⁴Dear friends, idolatry is rampant. Totally reject it. ¹⁵I consider you wise enough to recognize this as timely advice. ¹⁶Now some thoughts on the communion supper. The benefits we obtain from the

communion cup are only available because of the blood of Christ. The broken bread is of spiritual benefit only because it represents the broken body of our Lord Jesus Christ. [17]And all of us share the blessings. We are members of one body. We all benefit equally from the blood and body of Jesus. [18]Look at the history of Israel and the altar services. Are not the blessings of that service found at the altar of sacrifice? [19]What am I saying? That whatever is offered is valuable? No! For if it is offered to an idol it is worthless because the idol is worthless. [20]In fact, things are worse than that. If it is offered to an idol, it is really being offered to devils, not to God. I fervently hope you will have no fellowship with devils. [21]No, beloved friends, we cannot drink the Lord's cup and Satan's cup at the same time. [22]We are not able to change the Lord, but He is able to change us. He is jealous over us and about His own reputation, and we did not make Him that way. It is His nature.

[23]As for food, no offering to an idol would make the food forbidden to me. However, it would not be best for me for the sake of others who do not yet understand these things. [24]So let us all consider the impact of our actions on the lives of others. [25]Anything that is sold in the market would be legitimate, idol or no idol, so let your conscience be your guide. [26]For everything was created by God and belongs to God. [27]Now suppose you are invited by an unbeliever, let's say an idolater, to share a meal with his family. Don't worry over whether or not the food has been dedicated to an idol, and do not even ask about it. [28]But suppose someone invites you to share a meal and then he specifically consecrates this food to an idol. I would invite you to reject the food for his sake, because he would immediately believe that you are also an idolater if you eat it.

[29]Be very sensitive about others and their feelings, just as you want others to be sensitive to your principles. [30]So if I decide to partake of their food and am thankful for it, why should anyone give me a bad time over that? [31]Here is a good principle to follow. In all food, as well as in all other activities of life, let your motive be to give glory to God. [32]This is why I seriously attempt to please others. I am hoping my actions will benefit them in some way for their salvation.

Chapter 11

[1]Please, all of you, never try to imitate me unless I am imitating Christ. [2]But how thankful I am, brothers and sisters, that you remember me in so many ways and continue to live as you were instructed as Christians. [3]Always remember, however, that I am never your final authority. Christ holds that position somewhat as a wife defers authority to her husband and as Christ recognized God as His final authority.

[4]For a man to pray or prophesy with a hat or cap on would be doing dishonor to his head as well as to Christ. [5]But a woman who prays or prophesies with her head uncovered would be doing dishonor to her head as well as to her husband. It would be about the same as having her head shaved, which is totally unacceptable in our culture. [6]She would be as if she were in public, a very shameful thing. Let her head be properly covered. [7]By contrast, a man should not have his head covered in our culture, for he was created in the image of God and shares in the glory of God. A

woman shares in the glory also for she was taken from man in her creation. [8]Man was not created from a woman, but the woman was created from the man. [9]Neither was the man created for the woman, but the woman for the man.

[10]Ideally this relationship should continue—the woman completes the unit, each is incomplete without the other. Now in a sinful world a woman should be under the care, protection, and authority of her husband, as angels are under the care, protection, and authority of God. [11]In God's plan man is incomplete without woman and woman is incomplete without man. [12]Actually, woman was created from man, and yet every subsequent man was created from woman and all of us were created from God.

[13]Decide for yourself. Would it be wise for a woman to pray without a covering? [14]It seems natural that if a man allows his hair to grow long it is unbecoming and unadvisable. [15]But if a woman has long hair, it is glorious. It seems to be a natural covering for her.

[16]If any of you tend to be quick to enter a dispute with another, you did not learn that from me or from the church. [17]I'm sorry to have to write this, but I cannot commend you in your gathering together for it has not always been for your good. Occasionally it is downright detrimental to you as a church. [18]How could a church be helped if you came together just to dispute with each other? This is the situation at times if I am well informed. [19]It sounds to me as if there are false teachings being promoted by different groups, and every group is trying to impress the whole church with the correctness of their positions. [20]So much so that even your communion services are not effective in bringing about unity. [21]You compete with each other in the communion supper, producing a situation where some leave the group with no communion meal while others eat to gluttony. [22]Think it through. Would it not be better to just eat and drink at home than to allow such a state of things to exist where some believers are "put down" just because they are poor? One thing is sure, I cannot commend you in this behavior.

[23]My advice, beloved, is not based on my own impressions but on the revelation given to me by the Lord. Here is the account of what I received from the Lord about the last supper of Jesus before His betrayal, and it was verified by the account from others of the eleven who were there. So the Lord does reveal matters like this at times. I'll repeat it for your good now. [24]Jesus took bread, thanked God for it, then broke it into small pieces, and gave one to each disciple as He explained the significance of the food. "Take some, eat it, for the bread represents my body, broken for you. This will remind you of me from now on as you repeat the symbolic meal." [25]After they had eaten the bread, He next picked up the mug of juice. After sipping from it, He passed it on to each of the disciples, saying, "This represents My blood, the blood by which My covenant is to be ratified. [26]Do this to keep reminding yourselves of this covenant and continue to do so until I return."

[27]Anyone who participates in this memorial service with known, indulged, presumptuous sin in his life is guilty of the death of the Lord. [28]So really examine yourselves diligently and faithfully before the supper begins. Harbor no sin in your life. [29]Presumptuous sin, sin of defiant

rebellion only brings condemnation in the end. The sinner has not realized the significance of the Lord's body. [30]Without this searching of heart and soul there will be spiritual weakness, illness, and death, spiritual death.

[31]So remember, judge yourself, not someone else. [32]If the Lord examines us and finds us in need of chastening, it is in order that we might not be condemned with the world. [33]In view of these things, be gracious to one another as you come to the Lord's Supper. This is not a meal to satisfy physical hunger. [34]So if one is hungry, it would be better to eat at home before coming together for communion. I may have more to say on this when I see you next.

Chapter 12

[1]Next, brothers and sisters, I should bring you some help on other matters. The first is about spiritual gifts. [2]You were all Gentiles, worshipping various idols, dumb images, not long ago. [3]You understand, I am certain, that God's Spirit never influences anyone to curse Jesus Christ. Moreover, I hope that you realize that if a person testifies that Jesus Christ is Lord he has been influenced by the Holy Spirit.

[4]Let us start with this fact. The Holy Spirit gives many different gifts, one to this person and another to that person. But any spiritual gift is from Him because there is no other source. [5]Also, there are a number of ways in which to manage church affairs, but the same Lord is guiding each church. [6]And as He leads each church, there may be a great variety of programs through which He is able to work, but it will all be brought about by the same agent, the Holy Spirit. [7]Every manifestation of the Holy Spirit, regardless of what it might be and

to whomever given, is for the benefit of the receiver and for the church.

[8]For instance, to one person may be given the gift of wisdom by the Holy Spirit. To another, the gift may be knowledge. [9]To another, the gift may be unusually strong faith. To another, it may be the gift of healing by the same Spirit. [10]Another may have the gift of working miracles, and someone else may have the gift of prophecy. Another may have the gift of sorting out various claims of spiritual manifestations. Another may have the gift of being able to speak in foreign languages. Another may have the gift of being able to understand other languages and correctly translate them. [11]Every one of these gifts has been given by the Holy Spirit, who bestows gifts exactly as He deems wisest and best.

[12]And just as the human body is composed of many organs and structures, yet it is a unit, so also is the body of Christ, His church. [13]And every member, baptized into the church, has been brought in by the same Holy Spirit, whether we are Jews or Gentiles, whether we are slaves or free, and we have partaken of that one Spirit's influence. [14]The body, I say, is not one person but many. [15]Suppose that a foot should say, "I am not a hand, therefore, I do not belong with this body." Is that foot right or wrong? [16]If an ear should say, "I am not an eye, therefore, I don't amount to much in this body," does this mean that the ear is not needed in the body? [17]If one body were one huge eye, how would that body hear? If the whole body were an ear, how would that body sense odors?

[18]You see, God, our Creator, has designed the body, and he has wisely provided every one of its faculties. [19]If the whole body were just one organ, where

would the body be? Obviously there would be no such body. [20]As things are, the body is a unit composed of many parts. [21]The eye cannot say to the hand, "I don't need you." The head cannot say to the feet, "I can get along very well without you." [22]Indeed, an organ that seems almost unnecessary often proves to be more vital than the one we might term "essential." [23]And those organs that we might classify as scarcely worthy of consideration may actually be the more essential ones. The less attractive ones may turn out to be beautiful. [24]Yes, those features that we feel are attractive and need no change are parts of the body that have unattractive features.

[25]So let us not divide the body in order to make it according to our liking, but all cling together, helping one another. [26]Let us especially encourage those who are suffering and rejoice with those who are rejoicing. [27]You, my dear brothers and sisters, are members of Christ's body, and each is special and important to His body. [28]Each and every one of you are important, even though you have not been given the responsibility of an apostle, or prophet, a teacher, a miracle worker, or healer. You may have been given a very simple, but important gift, the position of a helper. You may be a good organizer or manager. You might have the gift of foreign languages.

[29]Are all apostles, prophets or teachers? Of course not, neither have all been given the gift of healing or of miraculously speaking in a foreign language or understanding other languages. [31]You should all ask for and desire the gift best suited to you. Right now let me bring to you the very best gift, one that all should have and one that all of us may possess.

Chapter 13

[1]Of course, the gift of languages is spectacular and important, but let me tell you something. If I could speak in every language on earth and even the language of angels, I would not be worth much if I were a selfish, uncaring person and had no love. I'd just be a noisy gong or a harsh cymbal. [2]Or suppose I had the gift of prophecy or was able to understand all the mysteries of this life and the mysteries of God, and suppose, further, that I possessed infinite knowledge and also had such strong faith that I could move mountains but had no concern or care for others I would still be worth zero. [3]Now imagine that I gave away everything I possess to feed poor people and willed my body to medical research so that I could call attention to my own importance, it would give me no "brownie points" with God.

[4]A truly unselfish person will be like God, patient and long-suffering with others. He will not be envious, proud of his accomplishments, or boastful. [5]He will conduct himself appropriately and will seek to help his family and look out for their benefit. He will be slow to become angry and will reject evil thoughts as they come to mind. [6]He will not enjoy sinful things but will obtain his joy in only those things that are true and good. [7]He will be able to bear any trial, will be a trusting person, will have unfailing hope, and will outlast any adversity.

[8]A totally unselfish person will not fail even though prophecies fail, though all languages on earth cease, even though all knowledge vanishes from the earth. [9]Our present knowledge is at best sketchy and incomplete; likewise, our prophecy is not yet fulfilled. [10]But eventually complete

knowledge will be available; all prophecy will have been fulfilled, eliminating the gap that now perplexes us.

¹¹As a child my speech was childlike and immature. My understanding was poorly developed, and my thoughts were appropriate only for children. But upon reaching manhood these childish characteristics were left behind. ¹²At present we are able to see only distorted, poorly reflected images, but eventually we shall have perfect vision, perfect understanding, and face-to-face communication with each other and with God. We shall know others and shall be known by them. ¹³These three graces are superlative: faith, hope, and agape (Greek for Godlike love). Of these three, agape is the most important.

Chapter 14

¹So make "agape" love your first priority. It is essential that you treasure your spiritual gifts also. Perhaps more than others, your member or members who have the gift of prophecy should be treasured. ²Because you who may have this gift are to be speaking to fellow human beings, whereas the ones who speak in other languages may find that their gift is rarely needed and seldom listened to regardless of their commitment and the spectacular nature of their gift. God naturally hears all and understands all these matters. The one with a prophetic gift is often called on to bring comfort, instruction, and spiritual growth to the church. ⁴Whereas the "tongues" gift may seem to bless only the speaker. ⁵Now I recognize that great good might be accomplished if all of you had this language gift, and yet it would not be so valuable as if all had the gift of prophecy. ⁶Brothers and sisters, if I should speak

to you in other languages, what benefit would you receive? You are all capable of understanding Greek and so there is no need for such a manifestation, but there is a real need for more knowledge, more revelation, and more teaching and more prophesying.

⁷Consider an inanimate object such as a musical instrument. There must be a tune to make this instrument meaningful. ⁸And a military bugle is useless unless the signal is sounded for all to hear, as in the call to battle. ⁹Another item. This gift of tongues or languages is subject to abuse and can be of no more use than to speak to the sky. To be useful, it must be understood by the listeners. ¹⁰There are in the world a great many voices, some of which are valuable and some of which are dangerous; some are genuine gifts of tongues, and some are merely mumbo-jumbo and deceptive. ¹¹You see if a man speaks in a foreign language and I do not understand him I will be to him a total foreigner and he to me will be a total foreigner. ¹²So it is imperative that this language be such that it can be understood. ¹³So I advise any of you who speaks in a foreign language, the gift of the Holy Spirit, to pray that your gift may be interpreted by the listener. ¹⁴For even if I were praying in another language I may be ever-so-much in earnest, but if no one present understands me, it is of no value to any of them.

¹⁵My conclusion: I am determined to pray both with my heart and with my intellect. I will sing both with my heart and with my intellect. ¹⁶Unless this is done, how can you just wish a blessing on one who is ignorant of the gospel? He will not even know to say "Amen" when you are thanking God because he doesn't understand.

¹⁷Your giving of thanks may be entirely sincere and appropriate, but you still have not helped that other person. ¹⁸Yes, in the church I prefer to speak five words and be understood, ¹⁹than ten thousand words in a language unknown to the listeners. By the way, I am thankful to have spoken in more languages than any of you.

²⁰My brothers and sisters, continually keep on maturing as your wisdom and knowledge increases, but remain as little children in your lack of hatred. Mature thinking is vital in this whole matter. ²¹Let me remind you of a passage in Isaiah 28:11, 12: "With stammering voice and in a foreign language, I am compelled to speak to my people, and even then they will not listen." ²²God certainly used the gift of tongues as evidence of His power to those who had never heard the gospel. Believers didn't need that gift, however. Remember that prophesying helps believers. ²³Imagine what would happen if the whole church were assembled and some visitors were also present, those who are attempting to learn more of Jesus Christ. Then all of the members began speaking in foreign languages. Won't your visitors think there must be something wrong?

²⁴Now suppose that instead of speaking in other languages your members are imparting God's word as prophets. Any visitor will be helped, convinced, and persuaded ²⁵because he will hear the very secrets of his own soul spoken and will fall before God, thanking Him for the divine presence in that church. ²⁶Believe me, you can grasp what I am trying to say, brothers and sisters. Every church member has some gift, perhaps a beautiful voice in song, an insight, a language, an ability to interpret scripture, a prophetic revelation. And all these gifts should be used to uplift and help the church. ²⁷Just in case the gift of tongues is needed, God can give that foreigner enough evidence to persuade Him if only three persons exercise the gift and then only one at a time. ²⁸But if no one is there who needs that language spoken, let the members keep silent in the church, praying, of course silently.

²⁹If you have prophets with a message, two or three of them would be willing to add to the service. ³⁰And when one has concluded his message, let another begin. ³¹It just could be possible that all might have a message from God to encourage and comfort the church. ³²A true spirit-filled prophet will always speak in harmony with the words found in Scripture, for they are prophetic utterances also. ³³For God does not reveal one message to one prophet that contradicts His message to another prophet. This would surely bring confusion into the church rather than peace.

³⁴Another thing. In our culture women, seem to have no rights as speakers, evangelists, and pastors, and this they must accept as they accepted God's will in Genesis 3:16. ³⁵A question that arises in the church over any of various matters may be freely discussed at home with their husbands and family. This will protect them from a bad reputation in the community. ³⁶Stop and think. Did God's word originate with you? Did God's word come only to you? The answer is obvious. ³⁷If any of you have the prophetic gift, or any gift of the Spirit, you will recognize that I am writing to you only that which is in harmony with God's law. ³⁸However, if any cannot or will not accept my advice, there is no point in trying to compel you. ³⁹Finally, brothers and sisters, please desire

earnestly the prophetic gift, but do not try to stop the gift of tongues. [40]And whatever is done, make it orderly and acceptable to a rational mind.

Chapter 15

[1]Now I wish to go on to other matters. My message to you is the good news. You have accepted it, and you are on a solid platform. [2]This is the message by which you are saved, if you stay saved. My good news is in vain if you abandon the message. [3]Let us review the fundamentals together. I received them from the Lord through revelation, then shared them with you. I shall start with this: Christ died for our sins. This was in fulfillment of prophetic scripture in Isaiah 53. [4]He was buried, but He was resurrected on the third day. This too was in fulfillment of scripture in Palms 16:10. [5]He was met by Peter, then by the other apostles. [6]Later on He was seen by more than five hundred people, most of whom are still living, but some have died. [7]He was seen by His brother James, then by the apostles again.

[8]And finally He was seen by me also. Why me? I am no better than an aborted fetus. [9]Yes, truly I am the least apostle of all, really not fit to be called an apostle seeing how I persecuted God's church. [10]It is only by God's grace that I find myself an apostle, and let me say that His grace bestowed on me was not in vain, for I have labored more than any of them. Please understand that my labor has been altogether by the grace of God, not by my own efforts. [11]If I have preached, or the other apostles have preached, we have preached the same message that you now believe—[12]about Christ's resurrection. How is it that some of you honestly doubt that resurrection is a reality? That resurrection has been widely publicized for years.

[13]If resurrection is impossible with God, then of course Christ is not resurrected. [14]If Christ is not risen from the dead, our whole message is totally worthless. And so is your faith. [15]Indeed, we preachers could be accused of lying, preaching Christ was raised to life and if the facts are otherwise and God did not raise Him. [16]I repeat, if it is impossible for the dead to be resurrected, Christ has not been resurrected. [17]And if He is not resurrected, your faith is groundless and you are hopelessly lost in sin. [18]So also are all who have died in Christ. They have perished—permanently. [19]If this present life is all we have, then the hope we have in Christ is really a false hope and we are worse off than those who have never had this hope.

[20]Now for the good news, friends. Christ has been resurrected. He is alive. The most important person in our universe has been resurrected, assuring us that others too may be resurrected. [21]Death was introduced into the universe by the first man, Adam, and resurrection was made possible by another man, Jesus Christ. [22]Yes, all descendants of Adam die, but all who are in Christ shall be given life—eternal life.

[23]Let's keep in mind this important fact: Christ is the one who makes eternal life possible. He was the preeminent, the number one resurrected person. Later the ones who belong to Him, who are "in Christ" will be resurrected at His return. [24]When the end comes, He shall have completed His task of purchasing the kingdom back from Satan and will have presented it back to the Father. He will then have total authority and power. [25]When He shall have finally conquered all enemies, [26]we shall understand that the last

enemy to be destroyed is death. [27]When this occurs everything will be in harmony under the authority of God. Let me be clear on one point. When Christ shall have conquered His last enemy and the universe is under His authority, God the father is still God the Father and not subordinate to the Son. [28]Rather, when this is accomplished Christ will take His rightful place with the Father, willing to have God be supreme in authority.

[29]Now that we are clear regarding the eventual victory over death and that the dead will rise again, it seems irrelevant to take the position that a prayer for the dead is appropriate. If there will be no resurrection, the whole idea is absurd. If there is to be a resurrection, no one needs to be baptized for the dead. [30]And further, if there is no resurrection, why would we risk so much to preach the good news? [31]I proclaim again that I take great joy in your conversion, but Christ the Lord knows that my joy has been brought about by my risking my life daily. [32]Let me liken my experience at Ephesus to fighting against wild beasts. I would never have been in such a perilous situation if there is to be no resurrection. I would long ago have taken the attitude: "Let's all eat, drink, and be merry, for tomorrow we die." In other words, "Let's live it up today, for this is the only life we will have."

[33]So don't be deceived, beloved. Even the smallest wickedness harbored in the mind, cultivated, then shared with others will result in a death-producing lifestyle. [34]So wake up. Begin to really know what right doing is all about. I am sorry to have to say it, but there are some among us who do not know God. [35]The whole idea of resurrection often brings up the question, "How are the dead resurrected?" and "What sort of body will they have?" [36]Remember the seeds that you bury in the soil. If that seed is never buried, it will never sprout up and produce a new plant. [37]The new plant is like the seed that was buried. Every seed—wheat, barley, oats, or corn—is changed into a new plant as it sprouts and grows. [38]And just as God has designed the seed and the new plant [39]so human beings, animals, and other creatures have their individual characteristics while growing as a seed. [40]So also the heavenly bodies are different from the earthly, not all alike—[41]as the sun is vastly different from the moon and the stars and as all stars show difference in brightness.

[42]This may illustrate in a crude way the resurrection. A body dies, is buried, and decays, but in the resurrection it is different. No more decay, no more putrefaction. [43]It dies in obscurity but is raised in splendor. It dies in weakness but is raised in immortal strength. [44]It dies as a material being, but in the resurrection it will have the qualities of a spiritual being. [45]In Genesis 2:7 we find that the first man, Adam, was made into a living being. The last "Adam" is a life-giving spirit. [46]First the material, temporal being; later the spiritual being. [47]The first man was made from earthly elements and was therefore material. The second is heavenly; yes, the Lord Himself. [48]Just as earth elements appear in these beings on earth, so heavenly elements are in the heavenly beings.

[49]Next the climax of what I am trying to say. We on this earth have been earthly, material beings. But in the resurrection we shall have heavenly elements as heavenly beings possess. [50]Remember, brothers and sisters, that our earthly ancestry gives us

no inheritance in the kingdom of God, for we are corrupt and of sinful nature and as such cannot claim any inheritance in an incorruptible perfect kingdom. [51]Then how is it that we can even hope for an inheritance in God's kingdom? I will share with you a fabulous mystery, a secret insight that all should learn about. There will be some who will never die, but even these will have the same change in nature as those who die and are resurrected. [52]It will take place in an instant, in the twinkling of an eye, at the time of the great blast from God's trumpet, and at that moment the dead will rise to new immortal selves, and we living ones will be as instantly changed into the same bodies as they.

[53]We human beings are now subject to death and decay. But this change must be given to us. Immortality is a gift from God at that time. [54]So when this degenerating, decaying being shall have been changed into an incorruptible, immortal being, this mortal being shall have been changed into an immortal being, then we shall experience the fulfillment of Isaiah 25:8, "Death is swallowed up in victory," and Hosea 13:14, "Oh death, where now is your sting? Oh grave, where now is your victory?" [55]Sin stings us to death. And the law defines sin and gives it authority. [56]But let us thank God! In Jesus Christ we may have complete victory. [57]In view of this, brothers and sisters, go on from here, solid, committed Christians, always attempting more efficient work for our God, knowing that whatever you do for Him cannot be considered unimportant.

Chapter 16

[1]And now to another topic. As you are already aware, there are many Christian believers who are in need. I shall outline for you what I told the churches of Galatia regarding my plan to bring help to them. [2]I hope that every Sunday morning you take an inventory of your material assets and profits and then choose a systematic way of giving, such as a certain percentage. Then place it in a special fund so that when I come through Corinth I won't have to wait for it to be gathered up. [3]Also get together and choose a trustworthy, strong person who will be able to carry your gift to Jerusalem. [4]It just may be that the person you choose may be able to travel with me. [5]I plan to go through Macedonia on my way.

[6]I may decide to spend the winter with you so that I may be encouraged by you people. [7]Do not expect me very soon, but hopefully when I come I will be able to stay for a time, God willing. [8]Also I expect to stay at Ephesus for a while, probably until Pentecost. [9]I have information that there is a good opportunity opening up there to advance the cause, even in spite of the fierce opponents who are there. [10]I am hoping that Timothy will be moving to Corinth, and if he is, I know he will be welcomed, cared for, and made comfortable, for he is one of the Lord's dedicated workers, equal in every way to me. [11]Let there be no sudden decisions made by any of you that would tend to diminish his usefulness, but do your best to cooperate with him, and I expect to join him there.

[12]About Apollos, it was my idea, and I thought an excellent one, that he should go to Corinth to be with you. He did not think it best to go there, at least for now. Later on he may visit you. [13]Be watchful, brothers and sisters, stand unmoved in the faith, conduct yourselves like heroes, be

strong. [14]In all of your activities, with all your strength, remember that we all need God's "agape" love. [15]I urge you to take note of Stephanas and his family, the first believers in Achaia, a family always willing to help others. [16]Notice how they have been helping us, the apostles, and if they have new ideas, I hope you give them your support. [17]How thankful I am for their presence, also for Fortunatas and Achaiicus. They seem to know just what to do in supplying the needs of the church. [18]They have encouraged me as well as your members, and they need to know how much they are appreciated.

[19]All the churches in Asia are sending their greetings. Aquila and Priscilla send their greetings and wish you God's blessing. The church that meets in their home sends their greetings. [20]All fellow Christians greet you, and I like the idea of a warm Christian hug and a kiss. [21]Here is my own handwriting: Paul. [22]I hate to say this, but anyone who does not love Jesus Christ is anathema. Maranatha! [23] May the grace of God be with you. I love you all in Christ, Amen.

2 Corinthians

Chapter 1

¹From Paul, one of Christ's apostles, God willing, and from Timothy our brother, to the church at Corinth and to the other believers in Achaia. ²May God's grace be with you, may His peace be yours, the peace promised by the Lord Jesus Christ. ³Thank you God, the Father of our Lord Jesus Christ, Father of mercies and the originator of all comfort. ⁴He brings comfort to our hearts, even when we are going through trials, and our comfort can help others who are enduring their own brand of trials. ⁵It seems that as we suffer, being Christians, we are consoled to the same degree by Christ. ⁶Another thought. Our afflictions and sufferings as ministers can be a help to you as you face similar experiences. And when we have found relief, this may also help you.

⁷We ministers have great hope for you, for we know that when you are called on to endure persecution you also will be consoled and given grace to endure. ⁸Right here I should clue you in on our experiences while in Asia. We were in deep trouble to the point that we nearly lost our lives. ⁹But we learned something from that episode: never trust self; only trust in God who is able to raise the dead. ¹⁰It was almost like being raised from the dead when God delivered us. Now He is still protecting us, and we have full confidence that He will continue to do so in the future. ¹¹Your prayers for us helped. Many prayers were answered in our behalf, and we are very grateful. ¹²What makes us very happy is that we have had the simple trust to obey through trials, not in our own wisdom, but by God's grace, and that our lifestyle has been so well accepted by you, brothers and sisters.

¹³I hope you will continue to accept the ideas we write about as you have done thus far. ¹⁴We sense that you have been accepting us as we have been happy and pleased with you. All of us will rejoice together at the return of Jesus. ¹⁵I am truly anticipating my next visit with you. We both will be blessed I'm sure. ¹⁶This will occur on my way from Macedonia to Jerusalem. ¹⁷As I was planning my itinerary, did you think that I was being undependable? Telling you one thing, then doing something else? Be assured that my intentions are always for your good. ¹⁸As God lives, my word can be depended on. ¹⁹And as Jesus Christ, God's Son—the One Silas, Timothy, and I have been preaching about—is dependable, ²⁰God's promises are likewise dependable and enhance the glory of our God. ²¹Of course, He is the driving force, urging us

onward and establishing us soundly in the truth of Christ. [22]He has given us His solemn word, a seal if you please, and backed it by the Holy Spirit working in our hearts.

[23]In addition, God is my witness that the delay in coming to Corinth was so that I could spare you some words of rebuke. [24]Words that do not indicate a dictatorial spirit, but words which, if heeded, will increase your joy and stabilize your faith.

Chapter 2

[1]I have decided to come to you not in a sorrowful mood. [2]For if I am sorrowful, then you will also sorrow and then who can cheer any of us up? [3]I wrote this way so that when I arrive I may be cheered by you dear people and that all of us can be cheerful together. [4]In my previous letter I had done some real soul-searching and personal agony, not to cause distress to you, but that you might know how much I love you. [5]As to grieving, if any of you has been causing grief it is not you who has caused my grief. Oh perhaps a small fraction of it, but I truly cannot blame you for the sadness I have been having. [6]I believe that by now the one causing my grief has suffered enough. [7]So instead of censoring him, please forgive him, comfort him so that he will not be discouraged and yield to depression. [8]It is better to reassure him that he is still loved.

[9]This is another reason I have written to you, testing you whether you can follow my sincere advice, [10]especially in forgiveness. I myself need this same advice, and if forgiveness comes about at all, it comes through the grace of Christ. [11]Satan would like to take advantage of our human weakness, but he cannot conquer us as long as we persist in communing with Jesus. This

is our secret in defeating him. [12]You should know that when I reached Troas the Lord took charge of my plans to preach the gospel, and I could not stay there, [13]because of an unexplainable urge to look for Titus, my fellow evangelist whom I expected to find there. So I left for Macedonia. [14]Looking back I can say, "Thank you, God, for urging me on," for by moving to Macedonia, Christ was made known everywhere I went. [15]Unfortunately, there were some who would not receive salvation.

[16]What a responsibility we have! We must accept the idea that some people will choose death when they hear the gospel just as others receive life by hearing the same words. This thought is overwhelming at times. [17]But we are not ordinary messengers who are prone to distort God's word, but in sincerity we speak as if God were speaking audibly as Christ did.

Chapter 3

[1]Do we ministers need to boast of our work to you? Do we need some letter of commendation to you? Or do we need a letter of commendation from you to others? [2]A much more effective "letter of commendation" than any written note would be you yourselves. For you are good evidence to others of what we have been able to do in your behalf. Everyone can see the results. [3]You are persuasive open recommendations of the Christian religion—a "letter" not written with ink, but by the Holy Spirit; not written on stone, but on the living pages of the human heart. [4]Christ has brought all this about, and of course we have increased trust and faith in God as a result of what He has done. [5]It has not come about by our wit or wisdom, but only by the strength and convicting power of God.

[6]We apostles have only been ministers of the new covenant, not in a legalistic way, but through spiritual influences, for legalism can only condemn and kill, but the Spirit brings life—eternal life. [7]Now there is nothing wrong with the commandments. It was a glorious experience when God wrote them in stone for Moses and the people, so glorious that Moses' face became radiant enough to dazzle the onlookers. And he was just a human being. [8]If a mortal human face was glorious, the Holy Spirit is able to bring radiance perhaps even greater than at that time. [9]If a law, which can only condemn, can bring on such splendor, surely the righteousness produced by the Spirit may bring greater splendor.

[10]As glorious as was the giving of the law, it would appear rather drab when compared with the true glory that will ultimately be witnessed. [11]And if the keeping of the law was thought to be the way to immortality (and it was glorious), how much more the true source of immortality. [12]With such a hope as we have, our attitude is one of great confidence as we speak in literal terms and not in figures of speech. [13]We need no veil as Moses needed one when his people could not look on his face due to the glory he had just witnessed. [14]Unfortunately, the minds of the people were blinded and actually are still remaining blinded whenever the Old Testament is read to them. But they need not go on in misunderstanding, for Christ has made everything so clear. [15]Yes, even now when the books of Moses are read, a veil seems to be on their minds. [16]But when the nation shall turn to the Lord that veil will no longer be present.

[17]The Lord is the Holy Spirit, and where He is there is true liberty. [18]And all of us who center our attention on the glory of God are being slowly but surely transformed more and more into His image through the influence of the Spirit.

Chapter 4

[1]Now because of this continuous process, for it is indeed a progressive phenomenon worked in us by the Holy Spirit, through the grace of God, we need not falter in the journey. In fact, we are all progressing. [2]We have been given victory over all underhanded, sneaky, deceitful methods that human minds have used, sometimes, alas, even in trying to preach the gospel. We are now entirely open in our methods, a fact that brings us into favor with many people, as well as in the sight of God. [3]I think I can truthfully say that the gospel is now so widely known that the only areas of darkness are in the minds of those who refuse to believe. [4]Their minds are blinded by worldly gods, Satan himself being the chief source of blindness. He has been able to prevent them from responding to the glorious news of Christ, God's human manifestation, who longs to enlighten them.

[5]Once again, Jesus is the object of all our preaching, the focus and reason for being what we are. [6]The same Creator who created light in the beginning has enlightened our minds, giving us a perfect manifestation of Himself in the person of Jesus Christ. [7]What a fortune we possess, even though it is now seen only in these poor, earthly containers. [8]Humanly speaking, we are always in trouble of some kind, yet not seriously distressed, we are perplexed, but this does not cause us to despair. [9]We are persecuted, yet God has not forsaken us; we have been put down but not destroyed. [10]We seem to always be right on the verge

of dying, and Jesus Christ actually did die so that His life could be lived in us. ¹¹And we who are alive are always ready, prepared to die for Jesus' sake so that we will be like He was. His life now lives on in our mortal bodies. ¹²In other words, we ministers are facing death so that you may face everlasting life.

¹³Our faith has compelled us to speak and remember the scripture: "I believed and consequently spoke out my belief" (Psalm 116:10). We believe so strongly that we speak out our faith. ¹⁴Our knowledge of God, who resurrected Jesus, gives us assurance that we too will be resurrected and will join you on resurrection day. ¹⁵Everything centers in our interest in you so that God's abundant grace, which results in so much thanksgiving, may bring out more of God's glory. ¹⁶It is because of this that we continue to have hope, a never-weakening hope; though in body we may have to suffer and die, yet our real selves are revived daily. ¹⁷We consider our present persecution to be trivial and transient, enduring it, realizing that the contrast one day will be without comparison. Glory yes, eternal glory. ¹⁸At present we have our attention focused on unseen realities, for we consider them to be eternal and all-important while visible material things are only temporary.

Chapter 5

¹Yes, and we are aware that if our material bodies, tents if you will, disintegrate and die that is not the end, for God has a place for us to live again in immortal "tents." ²At the present we long earnestly to be transformed and made immortal, to be given this new, permanent home rather than this perishable "tent." ³Then we never again face the danger of being unclothed,

helpless, and mortal. ⁴Don't get me wrong, we are not eager to die so that we may have immortal bodies, yet the longing for that ultimate transformation goes on and on. ⁵I am convinced that God who created us has that same longing desire and has demonstrated His concern by having the Holy Spirit place that longing in our minds.

⁶We Christians are the most optimistic people on earth with confidence in God. A confidence in spite of our mortality is in that immortal future with God. ⁷I, of course, know that all this is a result of faith, not demonstration. ⁸And yet faith is so strong that we are willing to die, knowing that our future is secure with God. ⁹And so we are willing, to the best of our ability, whether we live or die, to place ourselves in God's hands, ¹⁰knowing that every human being will eventually appear before God's court to receive sentence for what we have done, whether good or bad. ¹¹Consequently, we are doing our very best to convince everyone of their peril when facing God, for God knows everything about us. I trust that you all grasp the reality of this assertion. It is indeed a fact.

¹²Truly friends, we are not just patting ourselves on the back, even though we have your support in our activities and are ready to sustain us against those who are interested only in appearances. ¹³If we appear to be fanatics, it is because we are so committed to God. If and when we seem calm and sober, it is so that we can best help you. ¹⁴Please be assured that whatever we do it is urged on by the love of Christ who died for all in order to rescue us from eternal death. ¹⁵Now that He has died for all, we should never insist on living selfish lives, but rather live for that magnanimous Person who died, then rose again.

[16]Moreover, we can scarcely recognize the person who has become a Christian. He is so drastically changed, somewhat in the same order that Christ was changed from God to man and is now again God. [17]Indeed anyone who is "in Christ" is a new creation. His former self is in the past, he is a different person, a new one. [18]This transformation has been God's work, the result of being reconciled to God through Jesus Christ, a reconciliation that we have been commissioned to preach. [19]In other words, God was in Christ, working to accomplish the reconciliation, not to condemn us for our sins, and we Christians are His messengers to spread the wonderful news. [20]We are all ambassadors for Christ. We are carrying God's urgent message: "Be reconciled to God. It is all there waiting to be bestowed on you." [21]Consider this important fact. Jesus was made to accept the penalty of being a sinner (although He was totally free from sin) just so we can become the righteousness of God Himself.

Chapter 6

[1]We who are working for God continue to plead with you to make God's grace effective in your lives. [2]You may need to be reminded of the scripture in Isaiah 49:8 that reads: I have heard you at the time most likely to bring you help. Guess when that time is? Right now, yes, when you are calling on God, this is the most likely time to be helped, to be saved. [3]We workers for God sincerely and intensely want our ministry to be above reproach, completely free of anything that will offend souls. [4]And everything we do needs to be approved by God, even when we are afflicted, sick or poverty stricken, [5]even if we are being flogged, jailed, or attacked by mobs, worn out with hours of work, perplexed over the state of our churches, or during times of fasting.

[6]By severely disciplining our lives, by continual learning, by learning more and more about patience, about kindness and through the Holy Spirit, to experience more and more of God's "agape" love, [7]by God's truthful word, and by the strength given to us, by the armor of righteousness wherever we may be, [8]by being honored (occasionally), by gossip, or by helpful words, sometimes being condemned as deceivers while telling the truth, [9]by being mostly unknown, by being strangers, or perhaps by being "best friends," by being thought dead, and then being restored to health, by being beaten and yet not killed. [10]In great sorrow and in great joy, in poverty while dealing with infinite wealth, in bankruptcy, while in possession of eternal riches. [11]Oh you dear Corinthians, how can I express more effectively how my heart goes out to you every day? [12]In our view you occupy no tiny spot. [13]But it is always possible that you feel rather small in your own eyes.

[14]Please avoid any close associations with unbelievers, for there can be no true fellowship between righteousness and unrighteousness, or how, pray tell, can light and darkness be reconciled to each other? [15]How can Christ and Satan work together, and what does a believer have in common with an atheist? [16]And can you see any similarity between God's temple and heathen temples? Remember that you are God's dwelling place on earth, expressed in scriptures such as Jeremiah 31:33, 32:38; Ezekiel 36:28, 37:26; Zechariah 8:8, and 13:9: "I will live in them, walk and work in them; I will be their God, and they shall be My people";

[17]"So be entirely different from them; have nothing to do with their filthy dirty lives, and I will accept you"; [18]"And I will be your Father and you will be My sons and daughters," says Jehovah God.

Chapter 7

[1]With such wonderful promises as these, my beloved friends, let us cleanse ourselves from all kinds of sin, both of mind and body so that we may be fully committed people, obedient to God. [2]Accept and receive us, for we have hurt none of you nor have we led any of you in wrong directions, nor have we deceived any of you. [3]I am not trying to say that you have treated us poorly, not at all. But I will only repeat what I have said before, that you are in our hearts throughout our lifetime and even to death if that should take place. [4]I feel perfectly comfortable in your presence. I rejoice always because of you and am happy even in trials because of you.

[5]How well I remember coming to Macedonia. We certainly had no reason to relax and take it easy for on every side were serious troubles. We had to contend with conflicts and with our own anxiety. [6]But God knew just what would help us most. He sent Titus. What a blessing! But who could expect less from such a God as we have? [7]And it wasn't just the presence of Titus that helped us. It was also his wonderful relationship with you folks and how you had encouraged him and assured him of your support of our work. This brought me real joy. [8]I know one thing, I was deeply concerned about your feelings toward me after reading my other letter to you. I was almost wishing I had never sent it. Yet I knew it was timely and had to be said, painful or not.

[9]Eventually I recovered my contentment, for you received my message and were willing to repent. [10]You see, there are two types of sorrow: godly sorrow that brings about a change for the good and worldly sorrow that brings about despair and loss. [11]Your sorrow should be remembered for it was what I would call "godly sorrow," and it resulted in these wonderful changes in you: more caring for others, self-examination, earnestness, concern for truth, sincere longing, zeal, and a desire to correct wrongs. In all these matters you have shown that you have truly been converted.

[12]Please understand that my writing to you was not just to point out a wrong done by one of you, but that you might be more firmly persuaded that God was at work among you through our ministry. [13]Eventually we were benefited as well as you were, and this pleasant fact was enhanced by the fact that Titus was so greatly encouraged by your responses. [14]Let me confess that I may have been a bit boastful about you when I communicated with Titus about you and your piety. I was sincere, however, and still am. [15]Now Titus has a deep affection for you as he recalls the commitment to God that you possess and the warmth with which you accepted him in spite of some apprehension. [16]It gives me satisfaction just to be able to express my confidence in you as I am doing.

Chapter 8

[1]I want to bring you up to date as to the great progress seen in the Macedonian churches. [2]They were going through real trials and troubles, yet in spite of this they were cheerful, and although poor they were generous in sharing what they had

for the benefit of other Christians. ³I felt they gave to the very limit of their ability, and maybe beyond that, and they needed no persuasion. ⁴They went so far as to urge us to accept their gifts for those in greater need. ⁵Their actions were abundant proof that their first and most important gift was their own selves as they gave them to God.

⁶And now we are hoping that Titus will continue to minister to you, developing in you this same generous attitude. ⁷You already possess abundant faith, effective witnessing, thorough understanding of God and His plan, plenty of zeal, and unselfish love, and we hope that your willingness to share will be one of your gifts. ⁸This is no command on my part, but only a report of the blessings that others have received after being transformed by the gospel. ⁹You know how totally gracious Jesus is in leaving His riches and becoming poor so that He could make us all rich. ¹⁰Try to accept some advice at this time, advice that will be of great help to you and which you have already begun to follow.

¹¹Please, continue in the good work, your willingness, and then the carrying out of those impulses. ¹²This is the correct order, I'm sure you would agree. First, a choice of the mind; then as blessings come your gifts seem to naturally follow. Yet no giving needs to be above what one is able to do. ¹³And I would never suggest that you do more than others. ¹⁴Here is the principle to follow: Those in want now need help from your abundance and possibly someday you might be in want and will need help from others who by then may have abundance again. ¹⁵It reminds us of the scripture in Exodus 16:18: "Those who gathered a lot of manna had none left over and those who gathered less always had

enough to satisfy their hunger."

¹⁶Thank God that He put into the heart of Titus a real interest in you. ¹⁷As you can see, he has accepted the challenge and has exceeded it since his coming to Corinth. ¹⁸And not only Titus, but the brother who accompanied him, a brother who loves the gospel and who is appreciated by all the churches. ¹⁹More than this, he was selected by the churches to associate with us, for which we thank God. ²⁰Of this I can be "confident"; no one can complain that the help available is one of our failings. ²¹We can see that what we planned has been adequate, both in the eyes of God and in the eyes of humanity. ²²This brother who has been sent has been proven many times before and now once again in his diligence. ²³Whether Titus or other brothers, they are all messengers to the churches, messengers from Christ. ²⁴So keep going forward. Show them and show all the churches that our confidence in you was justified.

Chapter 9

¹No doubt the things I have just written were not really needed at all ²because I know the way you have been in the past. That's why I used you as examples when I was in Macedonia and Achaia about a year ago, and already your example has been a good stimulus to others. ³Even so, it seemed wise to send these brothers ahead to plan with you, just in case some Macedonian believers come with me ⁴and find that your plans were not fully implemented, leaving you and me feeling a bit sheepish over the outcome. ⁵This is why I was careful to instruct these brothers to go on ahead, help you with your plans, and have your generous gifts all collected and ready.

⁶Another reminder: He who plants but few seeds will have only a small harvest, and he who plants plenty of seeds will have an abundant harvest. ⁷Let each of you make his own plan for giving then carry out his plans being under no pressure whatsoever from others, and you already know that God loves cheerful givers. ⁸Furthermore, God is able to provide everything you need, and with His blessing you will be able to accomplish all the good things He wants you to do. ⁹In scripture we find this statement: "God has scattered His blessings everywhere. He has supplied the poor, and His righteousness will live forever."

¹⁰My prayer for you is that God who provides seed for the sower and bread for the eater will greatly bless your "sowing," rewarding your generosity ¹¹in both material things and in spiritual blessings. And this will bring out expressions of thanksgiving to God. ¹²It is in God's plan that those who share with needy ones are themselves recipients of blessings so that prayers of thanksgiving ascend from both the giver and the receiver. ¹³The receivers praise God for this result of the gospel, then you praise God as your blessing is received. ¹⁴Those who are blessed by gifts will long keep you in their prayers, I assure you. ¹⁵Let's all give thanks to God for His infinite gift to all of us.

Chapter 10

¹I want you to know that I plead with my whole being, more than I could if present with you, ²for if I were there I might lack the courage to say the things that need to be said to some of you. It concerns the notion that all of us are just human beings and that we have no special message for the world. ³We are, of course, just human beings, but we are in a battle, and this battle is not physical, ⁴nor are our weapons physical weapons, but with God on our side they are effective in breaking down the defenses of our adversary. ⁵They have the ability to conquer evil thoughts and every other tendency that is contrary to God's will, capturing the mind and making it willing to obey Christ in all details. ⁶Also, our weapons are able to rectify and correct the results of rebellion when one is fully committed to God.

⁷Do any of you take a superficial view of things? I had better be specific. You believe that you belong to Christ, right? Now if you consider yourself to be His, others may have that same commitment as you have. Give them the recognition that they deserve. They may be as thoroughly surrendered to Him as you are. ⁸I could go on upholding our authority, given to us by the Lord, but the point is that we are ordained to promote your growth, not your destruction. ⁹This growth is the key to the whole message I carry to the believers. I believe that is concise enough.

¹⁰I've heard things "through the grapevine" like this: "His letters are truly something, very impressive, but in person he seems small, weak, and not very persuasive." ¹¹Let those who have repeated such sayings be aware that I probably am about the same, by letter or in person. ¹²We apostles don't have a chance with those who consider themselves "elite," but in fact they are not very wise in setting up criteria by which to judge us. It may just be that they wish to promote their own image.

¹³We shall not boast, but go ahead in our efforts to accomplish God's purpose in sending us to you. ¹⁴We are not attempting to do anything beyond God's ability to

accomplish through our labor, which is the preaching of Christ. ¹⁵I cannot boast beyond this simple statement: God has worked in and through us in establishing your faith. This is enough to make us humbly grateful. ¹⁶And looking forward beyond the present we hope to see continuing results through whatever means God might use. ¹⁷With this in mind let all praise by given to God, not to any of us. ¹⁸When the Lord commends a person, that means something. When one commends himself, forget it.

Chapter 11

¹ My dear people, let me go on. I may seem foolish, but you are very precious to me, so try to be patient as I continue. ²I actually have a very jealous feeling over you as a man might have for his daughter. I have given you to Christ as His bride. ³But alas, I greatly fear for you that you may have been deceived as Eve was deceived by the serpent and that you may have been drawn from the simple gospel truth in Christ. ⁴Remember that anyone who preaches any other Christ than we have preached, or if you have been tempted to follow another spirit than the Holy Spirit, you may be tempted to listen to him.

⁵Although I am not one of the twelve apostles, I believe that my ministry compares favorably with theirs. ⁶And I may not be as eloquent in speech as they are, yet I have given you facts upon which you can be very confident. ⁷Sometimes I wonder if I have erred in my attitude toward you, for in my attempt to preach the full gospel to you I may have given you the impression that I have little confidence in my presentations. The truth of the matter is that I have complete confidence in the message I have given if not in myself as its teacher.

⁸While I was with you, I was being supported by the other churches. ⁹If I lacked anything necessary to my well-being, the brothers in Macedonia would have come to my aid and would have supplied such a need. Thus I was no burden on you financially. And this is the way I hope it will continue to be. ¹⁰I assure you again that no one can persuade me to cease from this sort of self-confidence. ¹¹Why? Because God knows how much you mean to me. ¹²My purpose has been and will continue to be to remove any excuse in the minds of those looking for excuses so that those who are proud of their own position may be able to recognize their own condition.

¹³Some of these are called apostles, but they are impostors, trying to be perceived as apostles. ¹⁴It is like Satan attempting to be perceived as an angel of light. ¹⁵Surely it is not surprising then that his agents are able to deceive listeners into believing that they are ministers of righteousness. ¹⁶I hope you will accept the fact that I am no ordinary fool, so be tolerant toward me as if I were handicapped. ¹⁷This may not have much importance in the sight of God, for it could be a form of boasting. ¹⁸Most folks want to take credit for their accomplishments, and I admit to the same tendency. ¹⁹So try to treat me as you might treat any other person with imperfect wisdom, and it seems evident that you have done this.

²⁰You have the grace to allow others to enslave you, to steal from you, and to take advantage of you, to lord it over you and slap your face. ²¹Think of such things as evidence of God's grace rather than evidence of weakness. Whoever might come across as "bold" or "daring" will understand me, for I do the same things. ²²Are they entitled to a confident outlook because they

happen to be Hebrew, Israelite's descendants of Abraham? Well, so am I. ²³Perhaps they are Christ's; I am too. I have endured for Him such things as incessant labor, lashings (Who knows how many?), imprisonments, and attempts on my life. ²⁴Four times I received the thirty-nine lashes by Jews. ²⁵Three times I was beaten with canes, once I was stoned. I have been shipwrecked three times and was once afloat in the sea for a day and a night.

²⁶After innumerable miles of travel, I have experienced dangers on the rivers, dangers by terrorists, dangers from my own countrymen, as well as dangers from heathens, dangers in cities, dangers in the wilderness, dangers at sea, and even dangers from other Christians. These I have experienced for Christ. ²⁷I have been fatigued to the point of exhaustion; I have been in pain; I have had to remain awake for hours to protect myself. I have been hungry, thirsty. I have willingly fasted several times; I have been cold; I have been stripped of clothing. ²⁸And besides all these things, I have been constantly concerned about the churches.

²⁹Who could claim to be weaker than I? Who could claim to be insulted more than I? ³⁰So now there is no glory due to me, but in spite of all these experiences and through my infirmities, let God be glorified. ³¹He knows I have told the truth. ³²It might interest you to know that when I became a Christian in Damascus, the mayor, under orders from the king, had intended to arrest and capture me by a garrison of soldiers. ³³But miraculously the effort was thwarted by having my friends let me down in a large basket held by ropes from a window in the city wall, and thus I was able to make my escape.

Chapter 12

¹Again I want you to know that I take no special credit for being an agent for God in what I am about to say, but the fact is that, unworthy as I am, the Lord has given me a number of prophetic visions and revelations. ²Let's say that a certain man I know, a Christian, somewhat more than fourteen years ago was given a prophetic vision in which he seemed to be snatched from the earth and transported to the third heaven. ³Believe me, I know him well. He was actually in vision, perhaps not physically, but in his vision, ⁴and it could be that God who knows all bodily transported him to the third heaven, also known as paradise, where he heard things that human beings find impossible to express or even to describe.

⁵I could legitimately glory in such an experience, but I shall not do so because of a strong feeling that this would not be appropriate. You know that I have some infirmities that God has allowed me to endure. ⁶Now if these infirmities would be miraculously removed I would be greatly tempted to become a bit "cocky." People would quickly suppose that I was greater than I really am. ⁷So I accept my infirmities as a means of giving me the proper perspective on life. Even though Satan is at the bottom of such goings on, God does not overrule them, and all for my eventual good of course. ⁸Three times I asked God to remove this "thorn in the flesh." ⁹But he calmly said to me, "No, Paul, I'd love to do it, but for your good I am not answering your prayer as you might hope because I need to demonstrate that I am able to supply you with grace enough to get along regardless of circumstances. When a man senses his own weakness, he then is able

to trust in My unlimited strength." After God's kind reply and explanation, I now look at infirmities differently for they result in Christ's power being given to men.

[10]Shall I say it? Infirmities, needs, criticisms, persecutions, and distresses now give pleasure when they come as a result of my labor for Christ because I become strong with His strength. [11]It must seem like foolishness to take pleasure in such things, but you have had some responsibility in it yourselves when you doubted my apostleship instead of affirming it. And yet we apostles are really nothing and therefore on the same level, all of us. [12]Apostles do not have the power to perform miracles, wonders, and mighty deeds that you may have witnessed. This occurs only when the person is totally submissive to God.

[13]I can think of only one way in which you are inferior to other churches, and this is it, I was never a financial burden to you, and this may have been an error on my part. Please forgive. [14]And when I return for the third time, I don't intend to be a financial burden, because my purpose in coming is not to get what you have but to "get" you. It is somewhat like a parent who leaves his estate to his children. The children do not give to the parent, it's the other way around. [15]I shall gladly give to you, even my life if necessary; although in practice, rather often the more one loves the less love is received. [16]But this is my choice, and I never have wanted to be a burden to you. As it was, you were aware of my concern for you, perhaps not expressed in words, but yet clearly understood. [17]Was I benefited in any other way when I sent others to help you? No, of course not. [18]I chose Titus and sent a brother with him. Did either of them profit financially from their visit? Indeed not. We were both of the same mind and conducted our work in similar ways.

[19]As God is my witness I can say that I have nothing to cover up and neither does Titus. Everything we have done is in your behalf—to build up, to strengthen, to fit you to serve God more effectively. [20]Frankly I fear that when I come I will find you less effective than I am hoping for and that you will find me less than you are hoping for. Surely there should be no big debates, jealousy, anger, battles, gossiping, backbiting, or uproars when I get there. [21]My worst fear is that my ministry has been less than effective in your behalf, that I shall find those who have not yet renounced their sins, especially those sins of sexual immorality.

Chapter 13

[1]My next visit will be the third, and you know the scripture: "In the mouth of two or three witnesses every word shall be established." [2]It has always been my intention, whether speaking or writing, to call sin by its right name, never "pussyfooting" with evil. [3]This will satisfy your need to prove that I was called by Christ, a ministry that has been strong through His strength. [4]Even Christ may have been considered weak at His crucifixion, but He demonstrated infinite power three days later at His resurrection. We are naturally weak in comparison with Him and yet with His strength we shall be adequate for fulfilling His purpose. [5]So do this: Thoroughly examine yourselves and honestly evaluate your faith. Christ is certainly in you, with a possible exception of those who at heart are still rebels. [6]How I hope that we Christians will not be classified as rebels!

[7]My prayer continually is that you be kept from sin, not just to make us apostles look good, but for your own sakes if we apostles should turn against Christ. [8]Remember, truth cannot be overcome by anyone, even by rebellious apostles. [9]We apostles are always happy to find you strong, always growing stronger toward complete maturity. [10]This is my reason for having written this letter. If I were present in person I might have been too sharp with my words (you know me!), but by writing I want to be contributing to your growth, not your destruction.

[11]And now, my brothers, farewell. Continue to grow, be of good cheer. Be in unity. Be peaceful, and the God of love and peace will be with you. [12]Greet everyone with a holy hug and kiss. [13]The believers here in Philippi send their greetings. [14]And may the grace of our Lord Jesus Christ, the love of God, and the communion of the Holy Spirit be with you all. Amen.

Galatians

Chapter 1

¹Greetings from Paul, an apostle sent not by my own decision nor by the decision of some committee but by Jesus Christ and God the Father who raised Him from the dead. ²The Christians who are with me send their greetings and this goes for all the believers in Galatia. ³May God's grace and peace be with you, grace that comes only from God the Father and from Jesus Christ our Lord, ⁴who yielded up His life because of our sins so that we might be delivered from this present evil world, thus fulfilling the will of God the Father. ⁵Let's give Him the praise and thanksgiving forever. Amen.

⁶I feel reluctant to write what comes next, but it must be done for your sakes with God's help. I am greatly distressed over the fact that you have abandoned me and my instruction. (Remember that I am the one who first invited you to come to Christ.) You seem to have taken up another teaching, but not the gospel. ⁷It is definitely a perverted message in spite of the fact that it has been advocated by some who claim to follow Christ. ⁸My first thought is this: If we or an angel from heaven ever preach a "gospel" that is not the one we preached before, condemnation is the sure result. ⁹I shall repeat that for emphasis. If any being, heavenly or earthly, ever preach what is claimed to be the gospel and it is different from what we preached first to you, let them be cursed. ¹⁰Am I trying to have God change His mind? No, but I am trying diligently to change the mind of men. Do I just want to say something pleasing and flattering? If this were the case I could not be a messenger for Christ.

¹¹My brothers and sisters, I assure you that the gospel I preached to you was not mere human philosophy. ¹²I did not get it from human beings, but by direct revelation from Jesus Christ. ¹³I know you have heard of my lifestyle in the past, how I upheld Judaism and persecuted God's true church, even contributing to the death of some of them. ¹⁴I advanced the religion of the Jews more than did any of my colleagues. I was that zealous over it. ¹⁵But at the time of God's choosing, the God who gave me life from the time of conception to this very day, I was given a call, graciously, to be His messenger. ¹⁶He asked me to reveal His Son throughout my life to the Gentiles. After my conversion I had no human teachers, ¹⁷not even the great apostles at Jerusalem, but I went into Arabia to be alone with God for a time, then returned to Damascus. ¹⁸It was not until three years later that I went to Jerusalem to

see Peter with whom I conferred for about two weeks. [19]The only other apostle I saw was James, the brother of our Lord Jesus.

[20]I solemnly declare that what I am telling you is the truth. God is my witness. [21]Later on I went to Syria and Cilicia and was still unacquainted with the Christians at Judea. [22]All that they knew about me was this: [23]The persecutor of Christians has himself become a Christian. [24]They praised God for this transformation, naturally.

Chapter 2

[1]It was not until fourteen years later that I again visited Jerusalem, this time with Barnabas and Titus. [2]The Holy Spirit had sent me there to consult with our brothers regarding the message I had been preaching to the Gentiles. I needed to be confident that my message was the truth. [3]You remember that Titus is a Greek and, of course, had not been circumcised when he was converted to Christianity and the leaders at Jerusalem agreed that this was entirely proper.

[4]However, there were some there who differed with the leaders, acting as spies, trying to convince us that we should compel converts to follow the Jewish rites and customs, all of which were only symbols of Christ and are now meaningless. [5]We did not for a moment agree with them, but we upheld the freedom that is in Christ. [6]The leaders who seemed to be in charge of things in Jerusalem—although in truth God is the ultimate leader—never once attempted to add to my message or to subtract from it. [7]They were certain that God had chosen me to preach to the Gentiles and that Peter's primary responsibility was for the Jews. [8]And of course it was God who made Peter's ministry effective and also made my ministry fruitful.

[9]Furthermore, when James, Peter, and John, the obvious pillars of the church, were convinced that I had been called, they welcomed Barnabas and me into their fellowship and agreed that we should expand our work with the Gentiles while they tried to reach Jews everywhere. [10]They encouraged us to continue our efforts to relieve the poor as well. [11]However, a rather sad note, even Peter made a mistake in judgment, a serious mistake. For when he came to Antioch I felt I had to confront him face to face because of this error. [12]It happened like this. He was freely socializing and eating with Gentiles there at Antioch until James our president sent a number of church leaders to us. Then Peter feared to disregard Jewish laws in the presence of these brothers and so withdrew from the Gentiles and refused to eat with them. [13]And Peter wasn't the only one. Several others, including Barnabas, reverted to their old ways.

[14]This aroused my indignation until I challenged them all, addressing my words to Peter: "If you men have chosen to ignore Jewish customs because of your faith in Christ, and rightly so, how can you now put pressure on Gentile Christians to live as Jews lived, depending for salvation on customs, rites, and exclusiveness?"

[15]Let me direct my words to us Jews for a little while here. [16]We have learned that a person is not now and never will be saved by obeying a law, but by completely trusting Christ. Not even we Jews can be saved by obedience, for obedience is unable to save a single human being. [17]Now, after committing ourselves to Christ for salvation, what if we make mistakes, what if we sin? Was this sin because of our connection with Christ? Naturally not. [18]My dear brothers and sisters, I would not dare

revert to Judaism. It would be a fearful mistake.

[19]No, I am virtually dead if my salvation depends on my keeping the law, for I have given up on that possibility and have put my life fully in God's hands. [20]In a sense I have been crucified with Christ and though I have life now it is not my own life but His, which is being lived out in me. My faith in the Son of God who loved me and gave Himself for me is the only way that this is possible. [21]The grace of God is everything. If righteousness is possible by following the law faithfully, then Christ need not have died.

Chapter 3

[1]My poor dear friends in Galatia, who, pray tell, has been deceiving you? Surely there must have been a devilish influence at work, for it has confused your minds so greatly as to cause you to abandon your trust in the crucifixion of Jesus Christ, which at one time you relied on completely. [2]Please tell me, did you receive the gift of the Holy Spirit by obeying the law? Or by faith? The answer is obvious. [3]Then having begun your lives as Christians through the influence of the Holy Spirit, can you expect to develop mature characters through ceremonies and rites?

[4]Yes, I am aware that you have suffered by becoming Christians. Is all that suffering now in vain? [5]Now consider this question. The person who was instrumental in bringing you the message of Christ by the power of the Holy Spirit, was it because he was practicing ceremonies or rites? Or was it because he trusted in the Lord? [6]It reminds me of Abraham. In Genesis 15:16 we read this statement, "Abraham believed God, and it was counted as righteousness."

[7]Now the true descendants of Abraham are the ones who exercise the same trust and faith—faith enough to obey God.

[8]According to Scripture even the heathen may be forgiven and saved. Refer to Genesis 12:3 and Psalm 72:17. This is what God had in mind when He promised Abraham: "In you all the families on earth will be blessed." [9]Then Abraham was not the only one to be blessed by Abraham's faith. In fact, all who have faith as he did will be blessed as he was. [10]But if we rely on good deeds we shall find ourselves cursed, for it is written, "Cursed is everyone who fails to live up consistently to whatever is written in the law." [11]Also, consider this text as more evidence, "Those who fight with God are in that state because of their faith." Notice that it is not because of their behavior (Habakkuk 2:4).

[12]And law keeping is not the same as faith. It is just an attempt to save oneself. [13]All of us have broken the law, many times. And as lawbreakers we should be forever cursed. But Christ has accepted that curse Himself and in so doing has rescued us from that curse. Remember the statement in Deuteronomy 21:23, "Whoever is hanged on a tree is cursed by God"? [14]Friends, it is because of the curse that fell on Jesus that the blessings given to Abraham may also be given to Gentiles. And by faith these blessings are ours.

[15]Brothers and sisters, a simple human illustration may help us understand. A human contract cannot be changed. Right? [16]Just so, the contract made with Abraham was to his descendant (singular), who would bless the whole world, a clear reference to his most illustrious descendant, Jesus Christ. [17]This contract was made long before the Mosaic law was written, in fact

four hundred thirty years before. So, of course, the law could not alter the contract to bless the whole earth. [18]You see, if the inheritance of this blessing was a function of law, then the promise was meaningless. But the fact is that the promise was God's own and is one hundred percent valid.

[19]Then of what value is a law? Just this, it was given because of sin and rebellion and is meaningful until the coming of the One who fulfills the promise. It was so important that it was entrusted to angels, then brought to us by the One who mediates between man and God. [20]Now a mediator is one who is capable of representing God to a large number of people, mediating between these people and the one God.

[21]Another thought about the law. Is law contrary to God's promises or is it in harmony with them? I shall answer that question. It is emphatically in harmony with the promises. And yet God's law is not able to produce righteousness and eternal life. [22]The Scriptures clearly teach that all of us are sinners and that Christ's promises are for those who have faith. [23]Before Christ came, bringing with Him faith, we as a people had to depend largely on the law as we anticipated the coming of the Messiah. [24]So you see that the law was sort of a schoolmaster to lead us to Christ, who would make us right with God. [25]And after faith in Christ is established, we don't need the schoolmaster any longer.

[26]All of you are children of God by faith in Christ. [27]Yes, all who have been baptized into Christ have put on His character—perfection. [28]This means that everyone—Jews, Greeks, freemen and slaves, men and women—are equal before God through faith in Christ. [29]And being in Christ you belong to Him; you are the true

children of Abraham and have the right to inherit everything promised to him and his descendants.

Chapter 4

[1]Let me explain this idea of being an heir. A child who is an heir has no authority as yet. In fact, he is little different from a slave, except as he matures he becomes owner and lord. [2]During the maturation process, he is under tutors, governesses, and parents, until the time decided on by his father. [3]And like this child we were enslaved, as it were, to the influences of this world. [4]But finally, at just the right time, God sent His Son into the world, conceived in a woman's body, nourished there until birth, then delivered as any other baby is delivered, subject to the law [5]in order that we who are under law could be adopted into His family. [6]And because you are now children of God, you may consider yourselves as equal to His Son who calls out, "Father, Daddy." [7]Yes, you are no longer slaves but sons and daughters, heirs, and all because of Christ.

[8]Friends, before you knew God, you were slaves, owned by beings who are certainly not God. [9]And now that you know God, or should I say now that God knows you, how can you go back to senseless, bankrupt rites, hoping to be saved by them? [10]You have returned to observing ceremonial days, ceremonial months, times and years, which have no valid significance. [11]I am fearful, dear friends, that I have wasted my time, bestowing on you so much labor. [12]Brothers and sisters, I implore you, take my word for it, to follow my example, my teachings, for I never will be persuaded to abandon the truth.

[13]You may remember that while I was with you I was troubled by serious physical

disability, [14]yet this did not cause you to reject my message. No, you received me as you would have received an angel or even Christ Himself. [15]So where has this assurance gone? You were so concerned about me that I felt your willingness to give me your own eyes if that had been possible. [16]Now have I become your enemy because of being so frank in telling you the truth? [17]Believe me when I say that these people who have had such an influence on you, sincere as they are and zealous as they are, have attempted to alienate you from me. [18]Zeal is wonderful, but only when focused on a good goal, so whether I am with you or not, do not lose your zeal.

[19]Oh, my dear children, I am agonizing over you, constantly praying that Christ's character is fully developed in you. [20]My great desire now is to be with you and to change my tone of voice, for truly I am anxious over you. [21]Please tell me, you who prefer to save yourselves through keeping of ceremonies and rites, what is written in God's word? [22]Here is what I find. Abraham had two sons, one by a slave girl and one by a free woman. [23]The child born by Hagar was the product of an attempt to solve a problem by human methods; the child born to Sarah was a miracle from God, a child of promise.

[24]These events are illustrations of the two covenants, one at Mount Sinai, represented by Ishmael, child of the slave girl Hagar. [25]And yes, Hagar is an appropriate symbol of the law at Mount Sinai, a law of types and ceremonies such as we find now at Jerusalem. [26]But the heavenly Jerusalem is our real mother. [27]Let me remind you of Isaiah 54:1: "Rejoice you childless women, shout and cry out for joy you who have never had a baby, for one day you will have more children than the married wife." [28]We Christians are a fulfillment of that promise, just as Isaac was the fulfillment of a promise. [29]And as it was then—the one born in fulfillment of a promise was persecuted by the one born as a result of human planning—so it is now—we are persecuted by those who want to depend on behavior. [30]Do you remember the scripture? "Banish the slave girl and her son, for he cannot be an heir; the child of the free woman is the heir." [31]We, brothers and sisters, are children of the free woman, not the slave girl.

Chapter 5

[1]Having established the fact that we are children of the free woman, let us never again yield this freedom in Christ. [2]I take the position unequivocally that you who think that circumcision is necessary for salvation have missed the whole point that Christ came to make. [3]Logic demands that if a person proceeds with circumcision he must also observe all the other rites and ceremonies of the sacrificial system. [4]No, Christ cannot save you in such legalism. You have rejected His grace. [5]The Holy Spirit teaches that righteousness is achieved only when we accept Christ's righteousness by faith. [6]When you are "in Christ," circumcision means nothing, uncircumcision means nothing; faith, however, means everything, faith that produces "agape" love.

[7]My dear people, you were doing so well. Who could have possibly turned you away from the truth? [8]Whoever it was does not follow Christ and does not follow the one who first preached Christ to you. [9]As a small amount of leavening affects a large amount of dough, a small error has come in and has affected a whole body of believers.

[10]But I feel confident that the Lord will now persuade you to change your minds and that the one who has misled you will receive appropriate punishment, whoever he is.

[11]As for me, brothers, I might well avoid some persecution if I should start advocating circumcision and quit emphasizing the cross of Christ. [12]Oh how I wish that whoever he is that is troubling you would leave you and never return. [13]My brothers and sisters, your calling is to wonderful liberty, not a license to fall back into sin but freedom from sin and freedom to help others. [14]The law can be summed up in this way: "Love your neighbor as you love yourself." [15]But if you snap at each other, biting and eating each other, you are in grave danger of being devoured and annihilated. [16]The prevention and cure of this wretched condition is as follows: Live as the Holy Spirit teaches and refuse to yield to the desires of human nature. [17]For human nature is contrary to the Holy Spirit, and the Holy Spirit is contrary to human nature, so it is humanly impossible to do the things that should be done. [18]But if you are willing to let God's Spirit lead you, there is no need to fear the law.

[19]Here are some characteristics of one who is unchanged by the Holy Spirit: adultery, other sexual abnormalities, filthiness, lustful practices, [20]idolatry, witchcraft, hatred, misunderstandings, outbursts of temper, anger, quarrels, treason, heresies, [21]jealousy, murder, drunkenness, wild parties, and similar things—none of which will be in the kingdom of God. [22]In contrast, let me now tell you what the fruit of the Holy Spirit is: love, joy, peace, patience, gentleness, goodness, faith, [23]meekness, and self-control. No law ever condemns these. [24]Those who belong to Christ have been willing to have their natural human tendencies killed, painful though it may be. [25]If we profess to obey God's Spirit, let us live our lives guided by His Spirit. [26]Let us not crave human glory, for it leads to jealousy and envy.

Chapter 6

[1]My friends, there may be some among you who at times might be overcome by temptations. If this should happen, please do not abandon them. Rather, let some of your most loving members visit them in a meek spirit, doing everything possible to restore them, all the while remembering that we are all subject to temptations. [2]In this way we will be sharing one another's burdens as Jesus instructed us.

[3]And remember also that he who has an exalted opinion of himself when he is actually nothing is truly self-deceived. [4]So let's all examine ourselves carefully. This is necessary on a continuing basis so that eventually we shall find true joy. [5]In the last analysis each one of us is responsible for his own salvation. [6]So let all who have been taught God's word be willing to share it with others and acknowledge the worth of the ones who teach. [7] Never be deceived about this; God cannot be tricked. Whatever you sow, you will always reap.

[8]To illustrate: If a man puts carnal matters into his life, he shall harvest death. But if he sows spirit-directed habits, he shall harvest everlasting life. [9]And now my friends, let us never tire of doing good for eventually we shall all harvest the results if we never give up. [10]We should use every opportunity to help others, especially those in God's family of faith.

[11]Finally, notice this letter. It has been handwritten by me, not by a secretary. This

explains the large letters. ¹²Now to reiterate a few points before I close. Those who rely on works are urging you to be circumcised because they can't seem to rely on anything except visible evidence, and should they trust only in the cross of Christ they should face persecution. ¹³If the facts were known, these very ones who are promoting circumcision do not actually keep the whole ceremonial law themselves. Their desire is to draw you Gentiles into their own group.

¹⁴Never let it be said that I take joy in anything but the cross of Christ, for this separates me from the world and separates the world from me. ¹⁵Really, friends, in Christ circumcision is insignificant. What is significant is the new creature that Christ creates. ¹⁶Those who accept this truth and live lives with this as their constant ideal are the true Israel of God, blessed by Him with peace and mercy. ¹⁷And from now on, dear friends, I hope never again to be troubled by reports about you. My commitment to Jesus Christ has resulted in permanent scars, but I have no regrets. ¹⁸May the grace of our Lord Jesus Christ be with you. Amen

Ephesians

Chapter 1

¹From Paul, one of the apostles of Jesus Christ, in obedience to the will of God in my calling. ²May grace and peace be yours, both of which originate in God our Father and the Lord Jesus Christ. ³Let us praise the God and Father of our Lord Jesus Christ who has blessed us with every possible spiritual blessing, each of which is the result of our being "in Christ." ⁴And being "in Christ" we accept the fact that God chose us before the world was ever formed, chose us to be entirely his, to be above reproach in our love-directed lives. ⁵His goal was to adopt us back into his family through Christ ⁶so that His grace may be praised more and more, grace that was willing to accept us into His beloved family.

⁷It was through Christ and His death that we are objects of redemption, having been completely forgiven. His grace is more than adequate to accomplish such a task. ⁸And also it is through His abundant grace that He has bestowed wisdom and good judgment on us ⁹as He opened to our understanding the mysteries of His will, His purposes, and His desires for us. ¹⁰Here is His goal: To restore us to one family, those in heaven and those on earth, through the ministry of Jesus Christ, ¹¹through whom we have become heirs, just as He planned things from the beginning, perfect planning, ¹²for all who completely trust in Christ.

¹³And to think of it: You are among those who trust in Him ever since you heard the message of truth, the good news of salvation. You have believed in Christ, and by so doing you have been assured, activated, and sealed by the Holy Spirit— promised to us. ¹⁴We may compare the Holy Spirit to earnest money. It is the promise of future possession, already purchased for us. Praise be to God.

¹⁵I want you to know that since I heard about your faith in the Lord Jesus Christ and your love for others that ¹⁶I have never ceased to thank God in my prayers. ¹⁷I keep asking God, the Father of our Lord Jesus Christ, to give you the necessary wisdom as He has given you the knowledge. ¹⁸And that your minds can grasp the magnitude of your hope, the inestimable riches of your inheritance, ¹⁹plus the miraculous power that we may receive from Him. ²⁰It's the very same power that raised Christ up from death and restored Him to the throne in heaven, ²¹where His name is now above every other name in God's universe, now or ever in the future. ²²Let me emphasize it. Everything is under His command,

certainly the church also is, [23]for the church is His body, the full complete creation of Christ.

Chapter 2

[1]Now about you, dear people. All of you were in total darkness and as nearly dead spiritually as anyone could be. [2]You were no different from the rest of the world, in perfect agreement with the prince of the world, and you had the same attitude as disobedient children. [3]Yes, all of us lived a lifestyle of selfishness, sinful desires, sensual behavior, and evil thoughts and, therefore, were accurately described as "children of wrath" just as other people were. [4]But God, who is so marvelously merciful, so full of love for us, [5]even when we were lost in sin and dead spiritually, has brought us back to life, just as He brought Christ back to life. (This was entirely through grace.)

[6]He has restored us and has now placed us together in a heavenly relationship with Christ [7]so that for eternity He may demonstrate His amazing grace that was shown in us through Jesus Christ. [8]Let's get this straight. You are healed and saved only by grace and through faith. And grace is a gift from God, as is faith itself. [9]Human behavior has had and will always have nothing to do in obtaining salvation. If it could, there would be many proud Christians around. [10]We are products of his activity, a creative process that produced good works. Of course, it was God's plan that we would demonstrate good works. [11]So please remember that you Gentiles, rudely referred to by Jews as "those uncircumcised fellows," [12]were once outside of Christ. You were not in Israel either. You were not included in the covenants God gave. You had no hope in your pagan religion; you did not know God, [13]but now you have been brought close to Him, having accepted the blood of Christ in your behalf.

[14]He has produced peace between us, having destroyed that wall that separated us. [15]Further, He has, by coming to this earth as a human being, abolished the hatred between us through that willingness to die on a cross. This brought an end to the rules and regulations of the sacrificial system that were so repulsive to Gentiles. [16]So now, both Gentiles and Jews are reconciled to God and to each other through the death of His human body. It is as if He killed the hostility while He Himself was dying. [17]Now this beautiful reality has reached you through preaching, having spread rapidly from the place where it all happened.

[18]All of us have access to God the Father because of Him and through the agency of the Holy Spirit. [19]Believe it, you are no longer aliens, but fellow citizens with all believers, members of God's one large household. [20]This household is built on the foundation of prophets and apostles with Jesus Christ being the chief cornerstone. [21]In Him the entire building continues to grow into a holy temple. [22]Think of it, you are a vital part of that structure where God, the Holy Spirit lives.

Chapter 3

[1]It is because of this calling, a calling to preach to you, dear Gentiles, that I am now a prisoner. [2]You know about God's grace, and it is His grace that has brought about these things. [3]It was by a direct revelation that I learned of the wonderful, mysterious message of reconciliation that I have written about above. [4]Please read again

that portion of my letter so that you will understand it clearly. [5]In past ages the plan was not nearly so well understood as it is today with prophets and apostles preaching a message through the power of the Holy Spirit, [6]showing plainly that Gentiles are fellow-heirs, a part of the same body, claiming the same promises in Christ. [7]These promises are a part of the message I have been given, by God's grace, and empowered to preach to others.

[8]I am humbled just to think that I am less than the least of all believers, and yet it is truly amazing that I was entrusted with such a challenge. And to think that I should be sent to the Gentiles with this rich blessing from Christ is equally awesome. [9]Included in my commission is the privilege of explaining to everyone wherever I go the mysterious things of God, hidden in God's mind since creation, which He did through Jesus Christ. [10]To know these things gives the church an explanation of the wisdom of God as He organized the universe. [11]For it is a fact that God's purpose has always and ever been just what it is now, to have our Lord come to this earth [12]and build up complete trust in God.

[13]So please do not deplore the fact that I am in trouble as I carry out my mission, for it is in your behalf. [14]As for me, I thank God on my knees daily for His Son Jesus Christ, [15]the head of the family of heaven as well as on the earth, asking [16]that He will give you riches comparable to His own riches, the riches found in the power of the Holy Spirit, [17]and that through your faith He will possess your beings, anchoring you securely in God's love. [18]May you be able to comprehend as much as a human being can comprehend, the immensity, the width, the length, the depth, the height of God's love, [19]then not only to comprehend it but to experience it, a love that is beyond these human minds and then be filled with God's attributes.

[20]Let me try to extol Him who is able to accomplish vastly more than we can ever ask for or even think about. He has that power and wants to use it in us. [21]To Him all praise must be given for His accomplishments in the church, and to Him shall praise be given through eternal ages, world without end. Amen.

Chapter 4

[1]Now, although I am a prisoner for God, I want to urge you to live lives in harmony with your exalted calling, [2]lives characterized by meekness, humility, endurance, tolerance, and love. [3]Continue to stay in unity with each other, working together in peace. [4]There is just one body of believers, one Spirit, one fabulous hope for us all. [5]Here is one Lord, one faith, one baptism, [6]one God, Father of all who is above all, throughout all and in you all. [7]And most important is this point: Grace is offered to us in an amount necessary, just as one might expect from such a generous Savior.

[8]Listen to what He promised when He returned to heaven—gifts to us human beings. He demonstrated His power by leading to freedom a multitude of Satan's captives. [9]His ascension was a wonderful ascent after living in the lowest depths imaginable. [10]For now He is in the highest position known to our universe where He is able to fulfill those promises. [11]But He promised gifts, and this promise was fulfilled as follows: Some were made apostles, some were made prophets, some evangelists, some pastors, some teachers. [12]All gifts were for the goal to make the believers

able to grow into mature Christians, to develop effective ministers, to build up the entire body of believers [13]into a unified church, all fully trusting in the Son of God, completely mature in faith, comparable to the perfect pattern, Jesus Christ.

[14]So that we no longer will be like children, first being influenced one way then another by every teaching that happens along, teachings that originate with our crafty enemy as he leads men who are ready to jump in and deceive people. [15]Rather, we may be able to give words of truth, may keep growing into the likeness of Christ our head [16]who directed the body in all its parts and functions, finally completing the process of producing a church that loves each other. [17]So, dear people, God has instructed me to admonish you and to urge you not to live as other Gentiles live. Their lives are largely lived in vain, [18]being unable to understand the real issues, separated from God as they are, sadly enough, content to remain in that condition. [19]In fact, many have fully committed themselves to sexual immorality, impurity, and greed.

[20]But you have learned from Christ just the opposite. [21]Everything you learned from Christ is superior to that which you knew before. So completely renounce your former lifestyle. Let the "old man" die, for he was controlled by corruption and deceitful desires. [23]But you have accepted a new way of life and a complete change of heart. [24]It is like a new person, recreated by God to be righteous and holy. [25]As an example, cease to falsify and misrepresent things. Say only those things that are one hundred percent true, all the time, for we are part of a large body and depend on each other.

[26]Are you angry? Don't let that lead you into sin. Do not harbor that anger for even one day. [27]And never allow the devil to have access to your mind for a moment. [28]Those of you who used to steal, never go back to that wicked act. Rather, go to work, manual labor if necessary, to support yourself and have enough beside to help those in greater need. [29]Concerning your conversation, never let it degenerate into filthy, corrupt talk such as you hear all around you, but let it always be uplifting and beneficial to the listeners. [30]Please do not grieve the Holy Spirit, for He is the one who seals you for eternal life.

[31]A little more advice: Get rid of all bitterness, rancor, anger, and squabbling, all wicked speech, and all hatred. [32]But always be kind to each other, tenderhearted, willing to forgive each other just as God for Christ's sake has forgiven you.

Chapter 5

[1]Because of following these admonitions, you will be true children of God, gladly obeying Him. [2]Your lives will resemble that of Jesus who loved enough to give Himself as an offering to God, a voluntary sacrifice, a fragrant offering. [3]Now this kind of love will not lead to sexual immorality. Far from it. Rather, it will reject all impurity and covetousness. These should never be a problem among you believers. [4]And neither should any filthiness or useless foolish talking or ribaldry, for these are not a part of the Christian life. A Christian should be known as one who is habitually thankful.

[5]You already know, I am sure, that no dealer in prostitution, no "dirty old men," no greedy ones, no idolaters will have an inheritance in the kingdom of God. [6]In spite of what people may try to tell you,

do not believe them for it is on account of these very things that God's judgment will fall on unbelieving sinners. [7]Have nothing to do with such things.

[8]Remember, you were in darkness but now are in God's light, so live as a child of light is to live. [9]In everything good and righteous, you can discern the work of the Holy Spirit, [10]showing you what is acceptable to God. [11]Please, never parley with the activities promoted by spiritualistic agencies. Reprove them instead. [12]Their secret behavior is altogether shameful. [13]Bringing in light will help to identify wrong. [14]Do you recall the words of Isaiah 6:1? (Rise from the dead and shine.) Christ will supply the needed light, [15]so let your behavior be always prudent, wise rather than foolish.

[16]Make the very best use of the time available to you in spite of the prevailing evil around us. [17]In all things, seek to know the will of God, the way of wisdom. [18]Totally avoid intoxicating wine, but be filled with the Holy Spirit. [19]Sing together the songs of praise, gospel songs and songs of joy and thanksgiving. [20]God has given everything that is good in His giving Christ our Lord. [21]In your reverence for God, defer to each other.

[22]Wives, be submissive to your husbands as you are to the Lord. [23]The husband is the head of the wife, just as Christ is head of the church and Savior of the entire body. [24]The church looks to Christ for its leadership, and it is thus that a wife should look to her husband. [25]You husbands, cherish your wives unselfishly in the same way that Christ cherishes the church and has given Himself for it. [26]By so doing He cleanses it and makes it holy, washing it from all impurity in the cleansing water of the word of God. [27]He then presents the church as a supreme achievement, glorious, spotless, wrinkle-free, no blemishes of any kind.

[28]Yes, Jesus is an example of what a husband should be, loving his wife as he loves himself. And if he loves his wife, he will also love himself. [29]A man who hates himself has not yet been born. No, a man nourishes, guards, protects, and takes care of his body just as the Lord looks out for the church. [30]And because we are the church, we must consider ourselves to be His body, His flesh, His bone. [31]Remember the words of Genesis 2:23, 24: "A man will leave his father and his mother and will unite with his wife and they will be a single unit"? [32] Yes, these things are a bit mysterious, but so it is mysterious how Christ loves the church and is united to it. [33]In conclusion, men, love your wives with the same passion that you love yourselves, and wives, return this love to him with utmost respect.

Chapter 6

[1]Now I have a message for the children. Be obedient to Christian parents for this is the right thing to do. I quote: [2]"Honor your father and your mother." This is the first commandment with a promise, and here is the promise: [3]"It will be well with you and your life will be good on planet earth." [4]Fathers, avoid exasperating your children. This will only make them angry. But rear them with the Lord always in mind and you will be successful.

[5]Slaves, your duty is to be the most obedient slaves in the nation, totally obedient to your human owner, just as you are to Christ. [6]Work efficiently as if for Christ Himself. [7]In all your toil be cheerful and

helpful, for you are serving God as well as man. [8]And realize that every good deed will get its reward from God whether you are slave or free.

[9]Slave owners, please take note, you must treat your slaves with honest consideration for their good, never arrogant, because you too are a slave of Jesus Christ who is now in heaven dealing with us humans in real impartiality.

[10]In conclusion, brothers and sisters, grow stronger and stronger, not in yourselves but in the strength given by God. [11]Use the whole armor of God to protect you from every weapon of the devil. [12]God's armor is not something material, for our enemy is not an ordinary foe. He is in the spiritual realm, the realm of evil spirits, wicked ideas, and unseen influences. [13]So it is vital that we put God's armor on, and His armor is our only protection in the wicked age. With this protection we can continue to stand until final triumph.

[14]Let me liken our protection to the physical. The first is truth, which may be compared to your belt. Next is righteousness, such as a chest protector. [15]Third is a thorough work of preparation, such as the knowledge of the gospel. [16]Fourth is faith, well symbolized by a shield, which is able to deflect every dart of your enemy. [17]Salvation is number five. Compare it to a protective helmet. And number six is your offensive weapon, the sword of the Holy Spirit and the word of God. [18]Of vital importance in your victory is to remain in an attitude of prayer for the strength you will need.

[19]And speaking of prayer, don't forget to pray for me as I try to teach the whole truth of the gospel. [20]As you know I have landed in prison because of my willingness to follow my calling. And yet I am permitted to keep on speaking my message to those who will listen here. [21]It will be of interest to you that when Tychicus reaches Ephesus he will give you the details of what I am able to do. He is such a precious servant of God. [22]When I proposed that he go, he willingly agreed to set forth soon in order to keep you informed and to prevent unnecessary anxiety. [23]May peace be given to all of you. May mutual love and faith, gifts from God and Jesus Christ, be yours. [24]And may God's grace be given to all who have committed their lives to our Lord Jesus Christ.

Philippians

Chapter 1

¹We, Paul and Timothy, slaves of Jesus Christ, send our greetings and our love to the Christian believers in Philippi. ²We are praying for God's grace and peace to be with you, grace that is provided through Jesus Christ. ³Oh, how often I thank God for you, actually it comes to several times every day. ⁴And always as I give thanks, I ask for God's blessings to be on all of you, especially the blessing of joy. ⁵You are fellow believers, of course, and just that fact gives me joy. My joy began when you became Christians. ⁶And my confidence is great that the God who started such a good work in you will continue to develop your faith until the day of Jesus' return.

⁷It is natural for me to think constantly about you, for I am simple enough to believe that you are thinking of me as I go about preaching, and even when I am in prison. ⁸God knows how intensely I miss you and long to see you again. ⁹This is my prayer for you. May your love deepen and grow, may your knowledge and wisdom increase, and may you be given good judgment. ¹⁰May you constantly explore different ways to do good to others, using sincerity and tact in all your dealings with others and continuing until Jesus returns. ¹¹May you be satisfied and blessed by the fruit of righteousness, all of which comes from Christ and results in glory and praise to God.

¹²Now, brothers and sisters, please do not feel sorry for me here in prison, for as you know, everything that has happened to me in the past has happened for a definite purpose, to speed the proclamation of the gospel. And I have faith that this is another instance with a similar purpose. ¹³And actually, (you will be delighted to hear this), my imprisonment has already made it possible for the gospel to be introduced into the emperor's palace. ¹⁴Moreover, a number of other Christians have been given more courage as they learn of my experience and are now witnessing with greater effectiveness. ¹⁵It seems paradoxical, but those who quarrel with me, as well as those who love and assist me, are both being used to preach Christ, ¹⁶even though my enemies are zealously trying to persecute me. ¹⁷But oh how I appreciate the work of my loyal supporters as I attempt to defend the gospel.

¹⁸So you can see that Christ is still being preached, and this brings joy to my heart, and more joy can be anticipated. ¹⁹As a matter of fact, I sense that my own salvation is being made more secure in answer to your prayers for the presence

of the Holy Spirit. [20]At present my earnest hope is that I may never be ashamed of my message, but will continue to preach and exalt Jesus with greater and greater confidence, whether it be through living or through dying. [21]When I speak of life, I intend to say "life in Christ" and to die in Christ is ultimate gain. [22]And if my life is allowed to go on for a time, I shall consider this to be the result of my working in a way that brings real satisfaction. But I will not share the details of my deepest longing. [23]You see, I face life or death, neither of which is nice to contemplate as you can understand. No, I have in mind a third option far better than either of these: to be with Christ. [24]Yet if I must continue as I am for a time, I can be of more benefit to you. [25]So I shall be truthful and confess that I expect to go on for a while, and if so, I want to keep on encouraging your joy and faith.

[26]A spirit of joy is characteristic of Christians, and of course, my joy would be unspeakable if I should be able to come and see you again. [27]Friends, be diligent to have your conduct in perfect harmony with the gospel of Christ so that in the event that I am permitted to come to Philippi, or even if I cannot come, I will be permitted to hear that your faith is constantly growing. [28]This will protect you from undue fear of persecution by your enemies, while your faith in God may cause them to do even worse things to you, while you will increase in faith of ultimate salvation through God's mercy. [29]It is altogether possible that you will endure some suffering and persecution, [30]for I was persecuted in Philippi, altogether unjustly, and I have been again persecuted while here in Rome.

Chapter 2

[1]Now if you really want to comfort me, live at peace, loving each other, enjoying fellowship with God, and blessing each other with a forgiving spirit. [2]I hope that you will have the same true inward joy that I possess, the same love and unity that I feel toward you. [3]In all that you do, aim first for complete freedom from strife and misunderstandings among you. Selfishness is the root of pride, feelings of superiority. So learn that others may be better than you are. [4]Take an interest in others' property, then your own; their welfare, then your own welfare.

[5]Pray for the attitude of Jesus, our example, [6]who, although He was God and could claim divinity, left His position as God, risked everything, [7]became a human being, and then became a servant to His fellow humans whom He had created. [8]And if that was not enough, He humbled Himself much more by accepting death, and not just an ordinary death but death on a Roman cross. [9]Because of His willingness to step down, God the Father has exalted Him above every other being, and now His name is honored more than any other name in the universe. [10]One day everyone will kneel at the mention of His name, not only those of us on erath, but all created beings everywhere. [11]Then every voice will proclaim that Jesus Christ is their Lord and by so doing will bring honor to God the Father.

[12]My beloved people, in view of these things, continue in your willing obedient ways, not only while I was with you but even more so in my absence. Make sure of your salvation with awe and amazement. [13]The good news is that God is working in you to make salvation a reality, first

to convince your mind, then strengthen your will, so that you will carry out your choice. [14]Whatever else you do, please do not descend to vain argumentation and complaining, [15]But let us all be blameless, sincere children of God, living such lives that the wicked society in which we find ourselves will be unable to find anything about which to rebuke us. We should be like lights in the darkness. [16]Our behavior will be such that others may learn of our God by just noticing us.

How happy I will be in the day when Jesus returns to realize that my life has not been spent in vain, my efforts were not wasted. [17]Even if I myself should become a sacrifice as a result of bringing the message to you, I still will rejoice right along with you. [18]And I know that you, dear people, are happy because of our faith. [19]You may confidently expect Timothy to be with you soon, and I am eager to hear from his lips how you are faring. [20]And as you know, there is no one more dependable than Timothy. He is a person who will really watch out for you.

[21]There is always a tendency to become interested in our own needs and to neglect the needs of God's work and His people. [22]But you know as well as I that His attitude is one of complete dedication to God and to me, his spiritual father. [23]So as soon as I find out how things here will turn out, I will send him, [24]trusting that God will see fit to have me released so that I will be able to come shortly.

[25]But whatever the outcome I feel confident in sending this message with Epaphroditus, a real brother to me, a fellow laborer and soldier, as my messenger, for he has helped me in very many ways. [26]He too has a great interest in you and was deeply concerned about you, knowing that you were aware of his serious illness and wanted to know as soon as possible as to his condition. [27]The fact is that he was near death at one time, but God had mercy on him and strengthened him so that he was able to recover. In God's wisdom I too was strengthened, for in saving that dear man, God spared me from an almost overwhelming sorrow. [28]So, with a recent life-threatening illness and the weakness that followed it, to send him on such a long trip would have been rather risky. You will be very happy to see him I know and I am rejoicing. [29]So welcome him with joy in the Lord, and show him the honor that he deserves. [30]It was for the cause of Christ that he nearly lost his life, being willing to give me the help I needed and which you could not supply.

Chapter 3

[1]Brothers, the ultimate source of joy is being "in the Lord." I have no reluctance to reach you with this letter, for it will bring you real help. [2]First, let me share some thoughts that will be important in your church. I want you to avoid men with loose morals. Beware of those who persist in wickedness, and do not believe those who insist on circumcision in order to be saved. [3]We who worship God, happy in Christ, not trusting in humanity, are the spiritually circumcised ones.

[4]If any person could claim confidence in humanity, I would be that one. Now hear me out: [5]I was circumcised when one week old, a full-blooded Israelite, tribe of Benjamin, a genuine Hebrew, and even a Pharisee. [6]Zeal? I had it. I regret to say that my zeal was terribly misguided, and I persecuted the Christians, but judging by Old

Testament standards, I was right up there with the best of them. [7]But those qualities that seemed so important then now seem a total loss compared to the knowledge of Christ. [8]Again, everything I considered valuable then seems utterly worthless in comparison with Christ my Lord for whom I have suffered the loss of every material possession. Actually, they are nothing but refuse. I made a good trade.

[9]Now to be objective, the only valuable consideration is to be "in Him," secure in His righteousness, rather than relying on my own. And you are now certain that His righteousness is a gift received by faith. [10]Friends, to know Him and the tremendous facts of His resurrection, even to share in His suffering, to die if need be for others, [11]these are the only true values in this world, values that will result in my resurrection one day. [12]And yet, I am still only a growing Christian and will continue to grow if I fulfill God's purpose for me, which is full maturity.

[13]Please let me emphasize that I cannot claim perfection of character or maturity as a Christian, but believe me when I say that the number one goal of my life is to forget the past and press on toward the ultimate goal—[14]to achieve the place to which God has called me in Christ. [15]So let us all keep on growing and reaching forward to this ideal, allowing Christ to direct our growth. [16]And as we advance let us all continue to do so in unity.

[17]Brothers and sisters, I am committed to keep on providing leadership and to provide a reliable role model. [18]Unfortunately, there are many I know, and I weep as I say it, who are enemies of Christ and His cross. [19]Their aim in life is only for material things such as food, recognition, and other earthly interests. Alas, the result of this will be annihilation. [20]By contrast, our lifestyle is directed toward heaven from where we await the return of our Savior, the Lord Jesus Christ [21]who at His coming will change our degenerate sinful bodies into bodies like His, glorious, perfect, immortal, by the power He uses to recreate us.

Chapter 4

[1]So dear friends, precious people, my source of joy, be faithful in the Lord. [2]Let me give a special plea to Euodia and Syntyche: Do not let your differences separate you from the Lord. [3]And fellow workers, I urge you to help those women who worked so faithfully in the gospel with me while I was there. Their names are in the book of life. [4]And be joyful Christians. Let me repeat it. Be joyful. [5]Let your forgiving spirit be experienced by everyone around you for the Lord is here and observes all you do. [6]Never let the cares of life overwhelm you, but in every situation pray for the help you need, then thank God for it. [7]When you do this, peace beyond comprehension will possess you through the power of Jesus Christ.

[8]Finally, brothers and sisters, whatever is true, whatever is honest, whatever is just, whatever is pure, whatever is lovely, whatever is good, if there is virtue, if there is praise, let your minds dwell on these things. [9]And if you may have seen these qualities in me, if you have learned them from me, practice them and the God of peace will be with you. [10]You should know that I am rejoicing in the Lord for now in my declining years you have taken such good care of me. You have always been caring people but I have not always been near enough to enjoy your care. [11]In fact,

I have never been in genuine want and have learned a wonderful lesson: Be content with any level of material blessings. [12]I know what it is to be put down. I know what it is to be really popular. Sometimes I am destined to eat heartily, at other times to feel hunger, and either poverty or affluence is always present.

[13]Actually I can do anything necessary through Christ who has strengthened me. [14]Now in all these experiences you have been most helpful for which I thank God. [15]You may as well be told that when I left Macedonia there was only one church that continued to send me any financial support and that church was yours. [16]You even sent gifts of food as far as Thessalonica more than once, and it always seemed to come at just the right time to save me from hunger. [17]And yet my greatest desire was not for my own self but that you should demonstrate a loving spirit of generosity like that of Jesus.

[18]As of now I have all that I need since you sent Epaphroditus with your sacrificial gift, a beautiful, loving demonstration of generosity that must have pleased God. [19]And I know that God will supply all of your needs for He owns the world and everything in it. [20]We all need to thank God our Father forever and ever. [21]Greet every believer for me. The church members here in Rome send their love. [22]All the believers in the household of the emperor are especially glad to greet you with their love. [23]May the grace of our Lord Jesus Christ be with you all. Amen.

Colossians

Chapter 1

¹From Paul, one of the apostles of Jesus Christ, and brother Timothy. ²To the Christians, faithful brothers and sisters in Christ living at Colosse. May grace and peace from God the Father and from our Lord Jesus Christ be with you. ³Our constant prayers for you always include thanksgiving that we know you. ⁴For we have good reports of your faith in Christ and of your love for fellow Christians everywhere, ⁵and of your hope of heaven through the truth of the gospel that ⁶has reached you as it has reached the rest of the world, and which has produced fruit in your lives, beginning as soon as you heard it.

⁷From Epaphras, beloved, faithful minister, ⁸it was he who was able to report to me of your conversion. ⁹Ever since this wonderful news, we have never ceased to pray for you that God's will be done in your lives and that your growth may be continuous, always gaining knowledge and wisdom, ¹⁰your lives always witnessing to your faith, in harmony with God, and blessing your fellow men, doing good wherever you are, learning to know God better every day, ¹¹getting stronger spiritually every day as Jesus did, developing patience, endurance, and through it all continuing to be cheerful and happy. ¹²These gifts are from God who has transformed us into people prepared to inherit the heavenly world that He has prepared for those who are saved.

¹³God has rescued us from the devil's power and has placed us in the kingdom of His dear Son Jesus Christ, ¹⁴through whom we have forgiveness of our sins and redemption through His death. ¹⁵Jesus is the perfect representation of the invisible God, superior in every way to any of His creatures. ¹⁶For it was Jesus who created everything in the universe as well as in this world, including human society, its kingdoms, its authorities, and its civil organizations. Yes, even these were devised by Him, and they continue to exist for His purposes. ¹⁷He existed before things existed, and it is by His power that things hold together.

¹⁸And logically, He is also the head of the church, which can be compared to His body. He is the one person who stands out above every other who shall be raised from the dead and is above every other created being. ¹⁹This preeminence was in God's plan. In Christ every good quality is found. ²⁰In His death on the cross He has reconciled every sinner to God, and not only sinners, but every being in God's universe. ²¹Friends, He has reconciled you, His former enemies, aliens in fact. Not

only are you reconciled, but you are now His friends. [22] And it was through His death that this was made possible. He is now able to display you as holy, spotless beings who cannot be charged with any sin! [23] At least, while you continue faithful, well grounded in truth of the gospel, the same gospel that has been preached everywhere, and which I am still preaching.

[24] I am still happy although I have suffered a great deal for you and for the whole body of Christ's church. [25] But it was the church that gave me authorization to go out and preach the word of God. This is my calling. [26] His word has been less than clear in former ages but is now abundantly understandable to us believers. [27] What am I trying to say? Just this: God wants people everywhere, Jews and Gentiles, to understand all that is possible and to grasp the gospel, which boils down to the fact that Christ is in you and among you and with Him comes the certain hope of a glorious eternity. [28] Once more, Christ is the center of our preaching, trying as we are to teach every person on earth, with all the wisdom and tact possible, so that all may mature completely as Christians. [29] This, friends, is my goal, my work, but a work that I can accomplish only as He works in me, providing the strength.

Chapter 2

[1] I want you to know that I have first of all an intense interest in your spiritual condition, not only for you at Colosse, but also for those in Laodicea and all the Christians who have never seen me personally. [2] My earnest desire is that your hearts may be bound together in brotherly love so that all of you may share the rich blessing that can be yours when you understand the mystery of God the Father and of His Son Jesus Christ. [3] In Him may be found infinite knowledge and wisdom. [4] This is important, for there will always be those who will attempt to turn believers away from Jesus, and what enticing words they use!

[5] Although I cannot be bodily present with you, I am constantly thinking of you, as in my mind's eye I attend your meetings and try to bring to you the encouragement found in your faith in Christ. [6] Oh, keep on walking with Him just as you have received Him by faith, [7] daily building your lives in Him, rooting down into Him, strengthening your faith in Him, and ever gaining a spirit of thankfulness for Him. [8] Also, beware, for there are those who desire to ruin you through worldly philosophy and empty human reasoning that is contrary to the teachings of Christ, [9] who is the perfect exemplification of God.

[10] And as you remain "in Him," you are complete, you are mature, for He is the source of all power in this universe. [11] He is the fundamental reason for the adoption of circumcision, for it is in Him that your sins may be cut off. [12] Another illustration: When you were baptized, you were buried, then raised up again, just as Christ was buried and then raised up by the Father. [13] Before receiving Christ you could be described as being dead, dead in sins that is, but now it is as if you had been resurrected just as Jesus was, your past sins all forgiven [14] and with that condemning document nailed as it were to the cross, obliterated completely.

[15] Furthermore, all evil agencies in heaven and on earth are now defeated by Christ. [16] Let no one give you a guilt trip when you fail to offer food and drink offerings, keep ceremonial days, holy days,

or Sabbath days. [17]These ceremonial acts were symbolic of Christ and of His mission on earth. [18]So don't allow anyone to rob you of your reward through faked humility and angel worship, delving into things about which he knows nothing, yet feeling important in his own eyes. [19]He is not attached to Jesus our head from whom come unity, nourishment, and growth in God.

[20]Therefore, if you are dead to the world, as Christ was dead, [21]why should you be subject to "nitpicking" rules such as "touch not, taste not, handle not"? [22]These manmade regulations will finally be seen for what they are and will be abandoned. [23]They may appear to be based on good principles, such as human will, humility, and subjection of the body to the mind, all of which are valid of course.

Chapter 3

[1]My brothers and sisters, if you are "born again," and I trust that you are, I urge you to center your attention on eternal realities, heavenly things, where Christ is now seated at God's side, [2]and not just your attention but also your affection as well. Heavenly matters are infinitely more valuable than earthly things. [3]Christians can accurately be described as dead to the world and its lifestyle and so completely submerged in Christ that you are in a sense invisible to the world. [4]But at Christ's return you will all be very noticeable, glorious just as He is glorious. [5]So let us each put to death our earthly tendencies, vices, and habits such as sexual immorality, filthy minds, illicit infatuations, and covetousness, which is basically idolatry. [6]It is because of just such evils that God's judgments come upon disobedient ones.

[7]Before you became Christians, you were involved in such wickedness. [8]But now you have rid yourselves of such things, including hot tempers, hatred, wicked plotting, blasphemy, and dirty language. [9]Now that you have discarded your old selves, [10]let truth be your pattern of speech, for you are to be like the One who created you. [11]There should be no racial discrimination whatsoever, no partiality toward Jew or Gentile, slaves or masters, for Christ is in all of you. [12]So clothe yourselves with genuine compassion, humility, kindness, and patience, [13]being charitable to all, forgiving each other as readily as Christ has forgiven you. [14]Above all else is "agape" (love), a love that resembles God's love, a true unselfish interest in the other person and his needs. This is the pinnacle of character development.

[15]You should daily invite God's peace, His truth, His contentment into your very beings, bringing all of you to a blessed unity, thankful to God for His care over you. [16]Open your minds to the words of Christ, allowing them to dwell in you, motivate you, and strengthen you, giving you His wisdom, then sharing that wisdom in psalms, gospel songs, and all other forms of sacred music. [17]And remember, everything you say or do must be done with Jesus as your central focus, always thanking God for His sacrifice.

[18]You wives, yield yourselves and your judgment to your husbands as long as it is consistent with God's will. [19]And you husbands let God's love direct you in your relationships with your wives, and do not permit bitterness to come into your hearts. [20]And children, be obedient to your parents, for all too soon you will be grown and independent of them, and God knows that

you will be happier this way than in rebellion and hostility. ²¹You who are fathers, be careful not to provoke or anger your children, for they will become discouraged if you do so.

²²Slaves, do not defy your owners or rebel against their orders. Your service to them must be genuine, not just a visible sham, for your service is to God as well as to your human owners. ²³Every activity should be done diligently and efficiently, for you are dealing with God Himself. ²⁴And faithfulness in serving Him will be rewarded by an eternal inheritance. All your labor is in reality a service for your Lord Jesus Christ. ²⁵But if you sink into wrong doing, your reward for that will be certain also, for we live in an orderly universe.

Chapter 4

¹Slave owners, treat your slaves with respect and justice, for your Master in heaven treats you this way. ²Prayer is important and should be practiced regularly, but make sure that your prayers are mostly prayers of thanksgiving. ³And please remember us in your prayers, asking that once more we will have opportunities to preach the gospel, for I much prefer preaching rather than being in prison. ⁴And I always need your prayers that my preaching will be easily understood.

⁵In dealing with non-Christians always exercise the greatest tact and wisdom, for your time is short and needs to be used efficiently. ⁶Every word you speak must be gracious with just the right amount of seasoning, just as food needs the right amount of salt. Then your answers to their questions will be loving, attractive, and gracious.

⁷My beloved brother Tychicus will bring you an update on my situation. ⁸And he will naturally learn how all of you are faring as he brings encouragement to you. ⁹Accompanying him will be Onesimus, a faithful member of your congregation and slave of Philemon. They will inform you of all the events now going on here in Rome. ¹⁰Aristarchus, my fellow prisoner, sends his greetings and so does Marcus, nephew of Barnabas. You have already been urged to receive him warmly when he reaches you. ¹¹My other fellow worker is Justus, a Jewish Christian, and a wonderful help to me.

¹²Epaphras, a former member of your congregation, sends his greetings. He is a true follower of Christ, praying and working for you, hoping that God's will is done in your lives. ¹³I should add that his interest in you is truly impressive, and likewise his interest in Laodicea and Hierapolis. ¹⁴Our beloved physician Luke and Demas also send their warm greetings. ¹⁵Please, if you will, send our greetings to the church at Laodicea, and to the church that meets at the home of Nympha. ¹⁶After you have read this letter you may want to share it with the church at Laodicea or maybe read it to them. ¹⁷Now a special word to Archippus: Be diligent in the ministry given to you by God so that you may fully reach His expectations for you. ¹⁸My final greetings to you, my dear friends. Signed, Paul.

1 Thessalonians

Chapter 1

¹Greetings to the church at Thessalonica from Paul, Silas, and Timothy. You are indeed blessed by being "in God the Father" and "in the Lord Jesus Christ." May grace and peace from the Father and Son be yours. ²As for us, we are constantly thanking God for you dear people. Yes, you are still on our prayer list, but mostly in praise. ³Praise God for your faith which works, for it is the result of your love, and praise be to God for your hope, so patiently maintained, founded as it is in the Lord Jesus Christ and in the Father. ⁴You know of a certainty that God has chosen you. ⁵And this certainty was brought to you not only in words but also in divine power in your lives by the Holy Spirit working in you to bring about complete assurance. This is the very result we were diligently working for while we were with you.

⁶You placed great confidence in us, even to imitating us and teaching others about us, though it meant a great deal of persecution, but the Holy Spirit has kept you cheerful through it all. ⁷You will be happy to know that your example has been a great inspiration to all Christians in Macedonia and Achaia. ⁸Your widespread proclamation of God's message has been so effective that we might just go ahead and let you do all the preaching and teaching. Those whom you have influenced have told us what a blessing we were to you and what a blessing you must have been to them, leading them to turn away from their idols to worship the only living God, then to anticipate the return of Jesus from heaven, the One who was raised to life, thus rescuing us from the sure consequences of sin.

Chapter 2

¹I really don't need to tell you all this, for you yourselves know it as well as I and are very deeply happy that we came to your city and that it was so wonderfully worthwhile. ²You remember that we had been shamefully treated at Phillipi just before we had been sent to you, but this did not cause us to hesitate in proclaiming God's truth in the face of bitter opposition. ³I know that our success was because of the fact that we were telling truth rather than lies, pure doctrine rather than some deceptive philosophy, something clean and uplifting rather than something low and degrading, dragging the listeners down to the gutter. ⁴Just to think that God entrusted us with such good news gave us the strength to publish it. That in itself thrills our hearts even though we know that some would not be pleased. We were learning that God was testing us to

show what kind of people we were.

[5]Never in our ministry have we stooped to flattery in order to influence people, nor did we work with a selfish motive of enriching ourselves. (God knows we did not do that!) [6]Nor did we try to glorify self in your sight or in the sight of those outside the church. In fact, if the truth be known, we could have exercised considerable authority being apostles of Christ. But we acted more like a nurse with her children, gently supplying their needs. [8]We were so moved with brotherly love toward you that we wanted you to share the gospel and not only that but also to claim us as friends and family. [9]You, of course, remember our days, weeks, and months of work, often far into the night in order that we might make clear to you the whole gospel of God.

[10]You are witnesses, and so is God, that our lifestyle was entirely above reproach and committed to God. [11]Also, you are aware of our willingness to nurture, admonish, and challenge you, much as a faithful father would teach his children, [12]with this goal in mind: to walk with God, giving an accurate example of His goodness, and remembering that He has called us to His glorious kingdom. [13]Another thing for which we are thankful. When you heard us proclaiming God's word, you accepted the truth that we were actually giving you God's word and not just some of our own ideas. God's word then had a great influence on you as it always does on those who believe.

[14]You, brothers and sisters, have experienced the same things that were faced by Christians in Judea—persecution by your own countrymen—which is hard to accept. [15]The Jews who initiated the persecution in Judea are the same group who killed the Lord Jesus, the same type of people who killed God's prophets, the same who drove us out of their land, all the time believing that they were pleasing God, though fearfully mistaken. They seem to be against everything and against everyone. [16]They did their best to prevent us from giving the message of salvation to the Gentiles, adding to their long list of sinful behavior. Furthermore, adding to the wrath that comes finally on the enemies of God.

[17]We are now separated from you, but our hearts are with you. Oh how we long to see you again. [18]And believe me, we would have come again. I, Paul, would have would come already, but the old devil prevented it. [19]I hope you all realize that our hope, our joy, our whole reason for living is centered in you believers who will meet Jesus at His return. [20]Yes, you are our joy, our very lives.

Chapter 3

[1]Our concern finally became so great that we decided to do something even though it meant being left in Athens alone. [2]So we sent Timothy, our beloved brother, minister, and fellow worker in the gospel of Christ, to encourage you, fortify you, and build you up in the faith. [3]We hoped that this would prevent any of you from being shaken in his faith by the persecutions you have endured. I'm sure you know that we too have been through similar experiences.

[4]Furthermore, remember that while we were with you we warned about the impending tribulation that has been the lot of all of us. [5]A compelling reason to my mind was the dreadful thought that the tempter might have tried you so severely that you had given up, and that thought was too painful to think about. Were all the efforts in your behalf wasted? [6]But

now that Timothy has returned from his trip, bringing us good news of your faith and unselfish ministry and bringing us the assurance that you have not forgotten us, perhaps as eager to see us as we are to see you, [7]we are greatly relieved and happy, our distress and anxiety having melted away.

[8]It is like this. To really live, we must know that you are all steadfast in God. [9]How can we praise God adequately for bringing us this joy? [10]We have spent days and nights praying for you, hoping to see you and to build you up more fully in your faith. [11]I still have a great desire to come to Thessalonica and am praying that God and the Lord Jesus Christ will guide me in that direction. [12]And may God keep on increasing your love for each other as well as for non-Christians everywhere just as He has increased our love for you. [13]His goal is to solidify your faith and to eradicate from your hearts every hereditary and cultivated tendency toward evil so that you and all of His saints will be fully prepared and ready for the return of our Lord Jesus Christ.

Chapter 4

[1]Let me say a few more things, brothers and sisters. I urge you in the name of the Lord Jesus that having been taught by us what you need in order to please God, go forward, constantly learning more. [2]Our instruction to you was fundamental and directly from our Lord Jesus.

[3]And let me reiterate that your sanctification will lead you to avoid illicit sex of every form. [4]It will teach you how to manage your bodies in full commitment to God, for His honor. [5]It will make a clear distinction between you and the Gentiles who do not know God, for every lustful desire is considered normal by them.

[6]Another thing: Gentiles have a habit of overreaching in trade, but you Christians must avoid all such temptations. Better to give special deals and perhaps more so to fellow Christians. Remember that the Lord takes notice of all our dealings and will take all these things into account some day.

[7]He has not called you out of the world to live a life just like your neighbors but to a life of complete commitment to God. [8]Anyone who rejects these bits of advice is not rejecting a mere man but actually rejecting God who bestows the Holy Spirit.

[9]There is one quality that perhaps I need not mention, but I shall do so to commend you. This is the matter of brotherly love. God has already done a wonderful job along that line. [10]You not only love your fellow church members but all other citizens of Macedonia as well. Just keep on expanding your circle of love more and more. [11]Continue to practice meekness, diligence, and industrious habits of labor in your vocations. [12]Be one hundred percent honest in your dealings with everyone. In this way you may expect to lack no essential material blessings.

[13]Now I know that all of you have lost loved ones, but these sleeping ones are resting in hope. Your sorrow is not the despair that the pagans experience. They have no such certain hope as we do in times of bereavement. [14]We who believe that Jesus died and rose again accept the teaching that those who sleep in Him will be brought from their graves as Jesus was. [15]I am telling you God's truth when I say that we who are alive at the return of Jesus will not be with Jesus one moment sooner than those who have fallen asleep. [16]Here is how it will be. The Lord will descend from heaven with a thunderous shout of victory, the voice of

the archangel and with the blasting of God's trumpet. At the sound of that blast, the dead in Christ will be restored to life. ¹⁷As soon as that happens, we who are still living will be snatched up from the earth to join them in the clouds of glory as we meet the Lord in the sky, never again to be separated from Jesus our Lord. ¹⁸Sharing this hope will bring comfort to many.

Chapter 5

¹But as to just when all this will take place, you already know some facts. ²It will be unexpected, just as the approach of a thief is not expected. ³Here's a clue, however. The impression will be widespread that peace, prosperity, and safety can be anticipated and will endure. What a delusion! The day of the Lord will arrive. Sudden destruction will come, much as labor pains come on a woman at term. There will be no escape for anyone.

⁴You, my brothers and sisters, are enlightened. You are aware of what is to happen, and therefore, you will not be overwhelmed by the events taking place so suddenly. ⁵You are all children of light, children of day, not in some dark night. ⁶So let us not go to sleep as others do, but keep on watching, expecting and seriously living for that moment.

⁷Night is a time for sleeping and, for a large number of folks, a time to get drunk. ⁸But let us stay sober, well armed with the body armor of faith and love, and having on the helmet of salvation, then charge forward into the battle. ⁹We should be completely confident of victory, for God has not called us out to inflict His wrath upon us but to save us through our Lord Jesus Christ. ¹⁰He died in our place so that whether we live or die here we shall

eventually have eternal life. ¹¹Once again, encourage and comfort each other in the way you have already been doing so well.

¹²In closing, I want to give you a few more words of advice, possibly not in proper order but still important. Get acquainted with your pastors. They are special people, so listen to them and to their exhortations. ¹³Hold them in high esteem because of their diligent work. Keep peaceful relationships among you all. ¹⁴I urge you to sound warnings for those who tend toward disorderly conduct. Do not neglect the weak ones among you. There are mentally handicapped ones who need special attention, patient kindness. ¹⁵Avoid the present tendency to retaliate against wrong doers, rather follow the habit of doing good to your fellow members as well as to those outside of your church family. ¹⁶Cultivate happiness always. ¹⁷Be always in an attitude of prayer. ¹⁸Be thankful under all circumstances, for this is God's will for you who are in Christ.

¹⁹Never ignore the Holy Spirit as He nudges you and convicts you of a wrong course. ²⁰Do not just brush off prophetic statements, but be sure to ²¹test all such things and then hang on to those that are good. ²²And even if some pursuit may be morally sound and legitimate, avoid it if there is a chance that it might give a wrong impression to another.

²³And now a final prayer in your behalf. May our God continue to mold your characters into His image, committed to Him, body and spirit, faultless until the return of Jesus Christ our Lord. ²⁴Please don't forget to pray for us. ²⁵Give the believers a hug and a kiss for us. ²⁶And please arrange it so that this letter may be read to all your church members. ²⁷And may the grace of God and our Lord Jesus Christ be with you. Amen.

2 Thessalonians

Chapter 1

¹From Paul, Silas, and Timothy, to the Christian church in Thessalonica, you who are "in God" and in the Lord Jesus Christ. ²May God's grace be with you, and may peace be your lot, the peace that comes from God the Father and the Lord Jesus Christ. ³We cannot refrain from thanking God for you. This thanksgiving is entirely appropriate because your faith has been growing and strengthening greatly in recent months. So also is your concern for each other. ⁴So much so that we ourselves are blessed as we share with other churches how you are progressing during persecution and difficulties. ⁵God's justice in all this is seen, for in your trials you are counted worthy of entering God's kingdom. ⁶And furthermore, God's justice will be seen some day when He permits troubles and trials to come on those who are giving you such persecution.

⁷Now you who are being persecuted, continue to be longsuffering and patient; rest your cases with God until the return of Jesus when He comes with His mighty angels. ⁸He will then mete out justice in the cases of those who refuse to know God and reject the gospel of the Lord Jesus Christ. ⁹Sadly enough these will die an eternal death, separated from God and His glory.

¹⁰At the very same time the saved will be glorified and welcomed by God, the God they love and admire, and I refer to you dear members who believe our teaching. ¹¹Be assured that we pray constantly for you that God will count you worthy of this infinitely valuable calling, accomplishing in you everything He desires to see in you: goodness, faith, and power. ¹²By so doing He will advance the cause of our Lord Jesus Christ who is in you and in whom you are, to the limits of His grace.

Chapter 2

¹Next, I wish to let you in on a matter of importance. I am frank and earnest about it, brothers and sisters. And I refer to the return of our Lord Jesus Christ and the final triumphant gathering together of the saved. ²I am doing this to prevent disappointment, disillusionment, and a loss of confidence, whatever impressions you may have had regarding this, through words, letters, or something else leading you to believe that the day of the Lord is near at hand. This is an erroneous idea.

³Be on your guard against deceptions of all kinds, for there will first come a dreadful falling away, a terrible apostasy, and the development of a monstrous system of falsehood, sin, and error, all

intended by our adversary to lead us to trust in a sinful man who himself is a sinner and doomed to perish. ⁴His true goal is to oppose God and to elevate himself to God's level or higher if possible. He may sit in God's temple; he may consider himself to be God on earth, but he is self-deceived. ⁵You probably remember that I mentioned these things while I was with you. ⁶At present he is being restrained, and he will continue to be restrained until God sees fit to expose him. ⁷This mysterious evil is already developing and will be hindered only by God who is now hindering him somewhat. ⁸Finally, it will be made very clear just how wicked he is and why the Lord must abolish him and his evil influence, an event that will not take place until the return of the Lord in brightness and splendor.

⁹Satan is behind all this, giving strength to it by apparent miracles and outright lies, ¹⁰and by an unbelievable array of deceptive devices designed to cause the loss of souls. In the last analysis, people will be lost because they reject the truth that could save them. ¹¹After refusing to accept truth, God will permit powerful delusions to influence their minds until falsehood will seem like truth. ¹²All such will be condemned, having refused to believe truth and having taken pleasure in sin. ¹³But how thankful we are that you, our brothers and sisters in the faith, beloved by God, have been chosen to receive salvation through the work of the Holy Spirit and by believing truth, ¹⁴which truth He brought to you through our preaching of the gospel, and which assures you of eventual glory in Jesus Christ.

¹⁵So, brothers and sisters, stand firm and unmoved, cling to the teaching of God's word and our letters. ¹⁶Now may God the Father who loved us, and the Lord Jesus Christ who has given us so much hope and comfort ¹⁷continue to encourage your hearts and strengthen you in word and action.

Chapter 3

¹Before ending this letter, I want to ask you to continue praying for us so that the word of the Lord may be accepted freely by others as it has been with you. ²Pray also that we may not be hindered by unreasonable, evil men, for as you know there are many who have no faith whatsoever. ³But God is dependable; trust Him and He will protect you from all evil. ⁴We have complete confidence that God will direct you in your present and future activity for Him, ⁵that your love for Him will grow, and that your patience in waiting for Christ's return will not falter.

⁶As much as I am reluctant to say this, nevertheless, it must be said. Do not retain in your fellowship any member who continues to resist order and organization that has been established. ⁷I'm sure you know how important it is to go ahead with good planning such as we demonstrated while we were with you. ⁸We would not even accept gifts of food from you but worked to earn our keep so that we would not owe any of you a thing, ⁹not that we didn't have a right to accept it but because we wanted to give you a proper example. ¹⁰We followed our own teaching; we practiced what we preached, which is that if anyone refused to work he should not eat.

¹¹It has come to our attention that there are among you some who are against law and order, who resist the necessity for working, who somehow do little else than

gossip. [12]I have a message from the Lord for these members: go to work, earn your own living, and cease your gossiping. [13]Do not consider the possibility of quitting to do what you know is right just because you get tired. [14]And if you notice any who refuse to accept this advice it will be for your good to disfellowship that person, even if he feels abused by your doing so. [15]But even then remember that you are to consider him not as an enemy but as a brother who is in need of help.

[16]Now may the Lord of peace give you peace in every phase of your lives. May He be with you in everything you do. [17]Here is my signature so that you will know that this letter is genuine as were all of my letters. PAUL. [18]May the grace of our Lord Jesus Christ be with you all.

1 Timothy

Chapter 1

¹From Paul, an apostle sent by order of Jesus Christ our Lord, our Savior, our hope. ²To Timothy, my precious son in the faith. May grace, mercy, and peace be with you from God our Father and from Jesus Christ our Lord. ³You remember my counsel as I left for Macedonia and you stayed at Ephesus: Be sure that no one is permitted to teach false doctrine ⁴or pay any attention to useless myths and genealogy, for such things only cause big questions instead of nurturing real faith. Please continue the good work. ⁵The purpose of this was to cultivate true unselfish concern in the hearts of all, to quicken conscience, and to help faith thrive.

⁶As you know, some have veered away from the true faith and have gone into useless nitpicking. ⁷They somehow desire to be teachers of the law, but they actually do not know what they are trying to teach. They have nothing to offer. ⁸This is not because the law is at fault, not at all. It must be presented in the right way, however. ⁹The law is of no value to beings that are in harmony with God. It is only for rebels who disobey, for the worldly, for secular people, for murderers of fathers and mothers or of anyone else, ¹⁰for those who profit from prostitution, for homosexuals, for kidnapers, for liars even under oath, and for anyone who is against the truth of God's gospel, ¹¹which has been so wonderfully revealed to me for sharing.

¹²How thankful I am for Jesus our Lord! He has given me this ability and has counted me worthy of such a calling as the ministry. ¹³Before He called me, I was a blasphemer, a persecutor, a negative influence in the world. Yes, I did it in ignorance, but that is no excuse. God had mercy on me. ¹⁴His grace was abundant, monumental, providing faith and love such as that which is in Jesus Christ. ¹⁵I am not exaggerating when I say that of all the sinners on this earth whom Jesus came to save I was number one. ¹⁶And because I am the chief sinner, He extended mercy to me, demonstrating that He can and will extend mercy to every other sinner, assuring them of everlasting life. ¹⁷What a God! He is the eternal King, the immortal One, invisible to be sure, but the only God who has wisdom. He deserves honor and worship forever and ever.

¹⁸I charge you my son Timothy to fulfill the prophecies that you know and believe, to lead the warfare on to victory, ¹⁹holding firmly to your faith and being true to your conscience, not as some have done who ran from faith and were shipwrecked as it

were, [20]such as Hymenaeus and Alexander, whom I must admit are following Satan. Oh how I hope they cease their blasphemy.

Chapter 2

[1]So let me urge you that your number one priority should be to pray intercessory prayers for humanity, giving thanks while you are in prayer. [2]Kings need these prayers, and all law enforcement officers need them in order that they may live in peace and safety in this world as God intended, altogether honest in our dealings with one another. [3]God truly wants society to live up to this standard and so does our Savior. [4]He will not be fully satisfied unless every human being is rescued by coming to a knowledge of the truth. [5]There is a God and only One who mediates between God and humanity, the man Christ Jesus, [6]who surrendered His mortal body as a ransom for all humanity, as a witness to God's love at just the right time.

[7]I have been set apart; I have been charged with the responsibility and sent with no other purpose in life than to proclaim this truth (I am not lying) to the Gentiles. [8]My desire, my only desire, is that wherever human beings live they will come to the place where they pray to this true God, hands lifted up to Him, with perfect confidence and without anger toward any other person.

[9]May this advice be a guide to women: Shun elaborate, expensive hair-dos; dress modestly please; and be unobtrusive. There is a need to avoid gold, pearls, and other jewelry so prevalent among heathen women. [10]Your most effective adornment as Christians who profess godliness is your behavior and lifestyle. [11]In our society it is good to be diligent learners but always

with meekness and quietness, [12]never with the idea of trying to take over the role of an authority figure over men. [13]Adam was created first, then Eve. [14]Adam was not the first sinner; no, Eve was. [15]I am not implying that women cannot be saved; their salvation, like that of men, has come through the Messiah who was born by a human mother and provides faith, love, and holy living.

Chapter 3

[1]Now please believe me. It is a good thing when a man is willing to serve in the office of elder. [2]An elder should be a man who has never been divorced and remarried; a man who is diligent, hard-working, and serious-minded and whose deportment is above reproach. He should be a hospitable person, willing to learn. [3]He should be a person who drinks no intoxicating beverages or who tends to lose his temper and strike at others. He should not be obsessed with gaining wealth nor ruled by covetousness. He should not be quarrelsome but forbearing and patient with the faults of others. [4]He should have an orderly home, whose children have learned to submit to authority. [5]For if he is incapable of managing his own home, how could he expect to manage the church?

[6]Avoid choosing as elder a man who has just recently been converted and baptized. This would tend to develop pride and arrogance in his heart and put him in a vulnerable position where the devil could manipulate him. [7]He should be respected by non-Christians as a good citizen. You surely do not want it ever said that a Christian has broken civil laws, although the devil would love to have him do so.

[8]It is very much the same in the choosing of deacons. They should be

serious-minded, truthful men, non-drinkers, not obsessed with money-getting, [9]men who cherish our faith and live up to their conscientious convictions. [10]Here again, do not rush new converts into office, but give them time to prove themselves, after which they may serve faithfully. [11]Just as the men should measure up to these standards, so also should their wives. They, too, should be serious-minded women who refuse to spread rumors and are completely trustworthy. [12]Let your deacons be once-married men with well-ordered homes. [13]A man who has served as a deacon and has served faithfully has accomplished much for God in his ministry for the church of Jesus Christ.

[14]These instructions have been written down, and yet I truly hope to come and speak face to face in a short time. [15]If I find it impossible to come soon, you will still have good instructions on how to conduct the affairs of the church, which is the very foundation of truth. [16]No one will dispute my statement that godliness is indeed a great mystery. Try to grasp this: God was actually seen as a human being. He was made complete in the Holy Spirit. He was seen by angels. He was proclaimed to the Gentiles and was accepted by human beings. He was taken up into heaven.

Chapter 4

[1]The Holy Spirit has revealed to me some things regarding the final events on earth. There will be some Christians who apostatize through the influence of evil spirits and their teachings. [2]They will stoop to lying and hypocrisy and in such condition will fool themselves into thinking that their consciences are clear. [3]They will be so far from God's plan that they will promote celibacy as a necessity. They will say that certain foods must not be eaten, even though those very foods have been created by God for our use and for which we should give thanks. [4]Remember that everything God created is "good"; in fact, it was declared to be "very good." So we cannot rightly say that anything is evil, but accept with gratitude whatever God has made and has given to us as food.

[5]His word has been given to us so let us accept it as our standard of holiness and let us pray that his will is done in our lives. [6]Keep on teaching your brothers and sisters these things, for it will be the work of a good minister of Jesus Christ. Keep them well-nourished in doctrine and everything needed for their faith just as you are continually nourished. [7]But refuse to be drawn into secular concerns and philosophies, superstitions and the like, instead concentrate on godliness. [8]Physical activity is not your main concern either, while godliness is important now as well as in the life to come. [9]All of us should believe in that fundamental truth. [10]It is for this reason that we work and that we are persecuted, because we trust in the living God and in the Savior. [11]So continue teaching and advising your people.

[12]Don't let anyone make light of your leadership just because you are young. Continue as a proper role model in your words, your lifestyle, your unselfish concern for others, your outlook on life, your faith, and your purity. [13]Keep on reading, teaching truth, and preaching faithfully until I am able to come. [14]Your spiritual gift should be constantly operative. It was, after all, given to you as a miracle and confirmed by the laying on of the hands of your church leaders. [15]Think about this

often, commit yourself to your duties so that it will be completely evident to all what your calling is. [16]Continuously be on your guard for your own sake as well as for your influence on others. The salvation of them as well as yourself depends on this.

Chapter 5

[1]Avoid the tendency to rebuke one of your local elders. It would be preferable to merely point out a better course, as one might treat his own father. Treat the younger men in the church as you would your own brother. [2]The older women should be treated as if they were mothers. The younger women as if they were your sisters, free of any possible suggestion of over-familiarity. [3]Be especially gracious to widows. [4]Ideally, if a widow has children or perhaps a nephew, one of these should assume the responsibility for her care. God prefers it that way. [5]A woman who has lost her husband has become totally dependent on God, and she is praying that you will be aware of that. [6]But a woman who does just as she pleases must be living a very shallow existence.

[7]Always include this concept in your teaching so that none will fall into error. [8]If a person will not provide the necessities of life for his own relatives, especially his immediate family, he is certainly not a Christian and is in greater need than an infidel. [9]A practical plan to follow would be like this: A widow of sixty years of age would be a person who could be supported by the whole church if she has no other support, providing she has been the wife of only one man, [10]if she has an unsullied reputation, if she has reared children without help from others, if she is hospitable, if she has ministered to church members,

helping those who are in trouble, and if she has untiringly lived a good life.

[11]The younger widows often must be treated differently. They are prone to abuse the privilege if granted a church subsidy, thus denying Christ. Besides, they are very likely to remarry and no longer be in need. [12]They will of course be condemned if they abandon their faith [13]and turn in to gossipers, telling tales here and there, idling away their time. [14]My advice is for younger widows to remarry, have children, manage their households, and live lives above reproach.

[15]Sadly enough some have already backslidden and are in Satan's camp. [16]Here is my advice for all church members. If you have among your relatives a widow, go about relieving them privately if at all possible so that the resources of the church will be available to help those with no means of support.

[17]It would be advisable if you would take special notice of your elders who are doing a good job. Encourage them. And if they are also teaching God's word, they need double encouragement. [18]Remember the instruction in Deuteronomy 25:4: "Never muzzle the ox that is threshing your grain for you"?

[19]If you hear an accusation against one of your elders, take no action unless it is supported by two or three witnesses. [20]Those found in open sin should be rebuked publicly so that others will be warned away from the same errors. [21]I urge you as if God Himself were speaking to you personally to follow these instructions with total impartiality. [22]Do not be too ready to ordain men, and you yourself must completely avoid those sins you see in others. Keep yourself pure.

²³You need not limit yourself to water but some grape juice would be beneficial for your health if you are having aches and pains. ²⁴You realize that some people's sins are forsaken and accounted for on judgment day, while others' sins catch up with them on that occasion. ²⁵Also, the good that some do is apparent at the time, while in others their evil deeds are obvious to everyone.

Chapter 6

¹You who are slaves should respect your owners, and for this reason, you have taken on the name of God and His name must be kept above reproach in any way. ²If your owner is a Christian, all the more reason to respect him. He is a brother, so give him your very best service, for God loves him as he does you. These principles should be kept before your people. ³Just in case you encounter those who like to teach against this advice, refusing to accept the words of our Lord Jesus Christ and His doctrines, all of which promote godliness, ⁴remember that pride is the basis of his lifestyle and that his philosophy of life will not bring any wisdom, but rather useless arguments over words, then envy, then outright feuds, ⁵angry confrontations between those who are corrupt and at odds with the truth, all the while supposing that getting rich is almost identical to godliness. Please do not condone such things, have nothing to do with such teachers.

⁶True godliness and a contented mind is a goal of inestimable value. ⁷Remember that we brought nothing into this world and we shall certainly take nothing with us. ⁸Perhaps we ought to be content with food and clothing and little else. ⁹Those that make riches their goal in life are prone to yield to temptations of various kinds, which will eventually lead downward to destruction and oblivion.

¹⁰Love of money is the very root of all sorts of evil. This has led some Christians to apostatize and will ultimately lead to remorse and sorrow. ¹¹But you, God's man, center your desires on righteousness, godliness, faith, love, endurance, and meekness. ¹²Let your warfare be the warfare of faith, seize eternal life; this is your calling, you have proclaimed this widely. ¹³I am urging you, God knows I am, to remember that God is the one who gives life to all, who gave life to Jesus Christ, who witnessed the Godlike confession when He was before Pilate, ¹⁴who wants you to follow this advice precisely and fully until the return of Christ. ¹⁵At that time He shall demonstrate fully that Jehovah God is the only Monarch, the King of kings, the Lord of lords, ¹⁶the only being with immortality, the One who lives a life in dazzling light so bright that no human being has seen it or can see it. He is the one who deserves honor, who has unlimited power forever.

¹⁷Teach your wealthy members to be humble, not trusting in material riches that are so easily lost, but trusting rather in the living God who gives us so many things to enjoy. ¹⁸Teach them to be benevolent, to be rich in good deeds, ready to share with others, willing to associate with poorer brothers, ¹⁹so that they will have a solid foundation for their faith; then they may confidently expect eternal life. ²⁰ Oh Timothy, treasure highly the responsibility that you have accepted. Just ignore completely the philosophy that controls most human behavior, even though it is supported by our brainiest scientists. They are wrong! ²¹Sadly enough, a few Christians have been deceived by these ideas. May God's grace be with you.

2 Timothy

Chapter 1

¹From Paul, an apostle of Jesus Christ, God willing, and because of the promise of eternal life in Jesus Christ. ²To Timothy, my precious son. May grace, mercy, and peace be yours, a gift from God the Father and from the Lord Jesus Christ. ³I am thankful to God whom I have served so consistently for these many years. I pray faithfully, day and night, for you. ⁴Oh how I long to see you, knowing that you have had a great sadness in your life. But seeing you will bring some joy to both of us.

⁵Whenever I meditate on your unbounded faith, a faith that was guiding your grandmother, Lois, and your mother, Eunice, and now is guiding you, ⁶I must again let you know how important it is to keep that faith alive. It has been alive ever since your ordination when I laid my hands on your head in that solemn ceremony. ⁷God has not assigned your work, and then allowed you to be afraid of going forward in it. No, He has given enough strength, love, and intelligence needed for your tasks. ⁸So never be apologetic about your calling as a witness for our Lord, or about your being a friend of mine, even though I am in prison now and considered to be a criminal. Be willing, if need be, to accept persecution yourself for the sake of the gospel. God will give you that strength should it be necessary.

⁹God has rescued us and invited us into a holy calling, not because of our wisdom but because He, in His wisdom has chosen to bestow on us His grace. This grace is now ours, due to our acceptance of Jesus Christ, and was in existence before the world was. ¹⁰It is of course now widely known by the coming of our Savior Jesus Christ to the world. Through Him death has been defeated. Life, even immortal life, has been assured through the gospel. ¹¹This gospel is my commission, my motivation, my whole purpose in living. I have been sent to share it with the Gentiles. ¹²And now I am in prison because of my sharing the gospel, but I would not have it otherwise seeing the joy I have experienced through the years. You understand the reason, don't you? I know well the One in whom I believe. I know that He is able to manage things best, even better than I could do for myself, not just now but for the future until He returns.

¹³So treasure and cling to the solid truths I have given you, based as they are on the faith and love that Christ taught. ¹⁵I am sure that two of those who have turned from me are Phygellus and Hermogenes. ¹⁶In beautiful contrast is the case of

Onesiphorus. My God bless his whole family. He has frequently provided refreshment for me and was never embarrassed to help me, though I am a prisoner. [17]When he came to Rome, he spent a lot of time and effort to look me up. [18]Just as he helped in Ephesus, he has helped here, and you well remember his dedication there. May God be merciful to him on that great day!

Chapter 2

[1]Now, my son, be strong. The grace of Christ Jesus is available to strengthen you. [2]Everything you have learned from me, directly or through others, should be taught to your best leaders who will in turn teach their listeners. [3]You are like a general who demonstrates fortitude, for you are a role model as a soldier for Christ. [4]And as a soldier, nothing of a worldly nature gets serious attention. Your only concern is to be exactly what your commander wants you to be. [5]Everyone in your position, while striving for victory, will never receive the coveted crown unless he maintains strict integrity.

[6]The owner of an orchard or of a vineyard is entitled to the first fruit. [7]Seriously consider this principle, and may the Lord give you wise judgment in every decision. [8]Fundamental to everything is this: Jesus Christ, a descendent of David, was raised from the dead. This is the essence of the gospel. [9]And this gospel has led me into serious trouble, for now I am in prison because of it. But thank God, His word is not imprisoned. [10]I am willing to endure this for the sake of my fellow believers, for it is through the gospel that they have the hope of salvation and eternal glory.

[11]Think of this: Even if we die as He did, we shall be resurrected as He was. [12]If we suffer with Him, we shall also share His throne one day. But if we deny Him, He will deny us. [13]If we give up our belief, He will not change, but remain loyal to us. He cannot deny Himself. [14]Keep these principles constantly before your people so that they will not quarrel about words. Such quarrels do no good and often bring about the loss of souls.

[15]Always make God's approval your number one goal so that your work as a minister cannot be criticized as you explain and apply God's word. [16]And shun worldly, useless banter about this, for such things only tend to degrade rather than to uplift. [17]Eventually such words will only produce necrosis and death, as it has to Hymenaeus and Philetus. [18]They have strayed away from truth, proclaiming that the great resurrection day has already occurred, and they have been successful in destroying the faith of a few others. [19]However, God's foundation is immovable and solid; He knows well who are on His side. So let everyone who has taken the name of Christ completely avoid all iniquity. [20]Yet in spite of all we humans can do, there will be in every large institution not only precious gold and silver vessels, but also a few of wood or clay, some honorable ones, some dishonorable. [21]If only those negative influences could be removed, then the loyal, faithful vessels would be suitable for use by the Master, always ready to do all necessary duties for him.

[22]Continue to resist the desires that most young people have, but pursue righteousness, faith, charity, and peace, as do those who call on the Lord sincerely. [23]Try to avoid arguments over unimportant matters, for they so often produce bitterness. [24]God's slave must not spend his

time fighting, but be gentle at all times, quick to learn, and very patient with others. ²⁵He must be a meek person as he gives instruction to people who are opposing the very ideas that would actually help themselves. May God inspire them to repent and acknowledge truth ²⁶so that they may escape from the devil's trap in which they have been willingly caught.

Chapter 3

¹Before the history of this world is ended, you should be aware that there will be some really dangerous times, and it will be in the very final times. ²Following are some of the causes for the perils. People will be selfish to an extreme measure; they will be covetous, boastful, proud, foul-mouthed, rebellious against their parents, lacking in appreciation of what their parents have done for them, vulgar, ³without affection, contract breakers, false witnesses, uncontrolled, vicious, haters of the few righteous ones on the earth, ⁴double-crossers, willful, headstrong, and lovers of physical pleasure more than lovers of God.

⁵Even those who make a profession of belief in God will not acknowledge Him and His power in their lives. From such people and from such sins, turn away. ⁶These types of sins have led to terrible acts of violence, such as kidnapping of girls as prostitutes. ⁷They also lead to a situation where people cannot find a solid basis for belief, even though they spend time in various philosophical meditations as it was in Egypt ⁸when Jannes and Jambres contended with Moses about the plagues, resisting the evidence to the bitter end. ⁹Stubborn, unbelieving men will finally reach their limit, and the folly of their position will be plain to see.

¹⁰You believers know me well enough. You know my teachings, my goals, my faith, my long-suffering, my love, my endurance, ¹¹my many persecutions, and my trials that I faced at Antioch, Iconium, and Lystra. In spite of these persecutions, the Lord delivered me from all of them. ¹²I believe that everyone who decides to live a godly life as a Christian will suffer persecution. ¹³Wicked people will increase in number and in hatefulness as time goes by, deceiving others as they themselves are being deceived.

¹⁴As for you, continue in the way you are going. You have learned truth, it has been verified thoroughly, and you know well the One from whom you learned. ¹⁵From the days of your childhood you were taught the Holy Scriptures, that source of wisdom which is able to show you the truth of salvation in Jesus Christ. ¹⁶The Scriptures are inspired by God. They are effective in teaching true doctrine, in correcting wrong ideas and habits, as well as in supplying true ideas and habits; ¹⁷thus God's man may grow continually toward a fully mature person whose lifestyle is filled with good works.

Chapter 4

¹Let me challenge you now in God's name and for the sake of Jesus Christ who will one day judge both the living and the dead when His kingdom is established. ²Preach nothing but the word of God, in season and out of season, at every opportunity. When necessary, don't hesitate to reprove wrong and rebuke those who are teaching error, always patiently of course and with truth as your weapon, ³for the time is coming when people will reject sound doctrine, choosing to allow their own desires

to dictate their acceptance or rejection of every teaching, regardless of who teaches it. ⁴They will refuse to hear truth, preferring fairy tales instead.

⁵So you need to be watchful continually. You need to be able to endure trouble, to continue your work as an evangelist and be fully committed to the ministry, ⁶for I shall not live much longer. My time is running out, but I am prepared. ⁷I have fought a good fight. I have completed my task; I have kept my faith. ⁸So someday the Lord will give me the crown of righteousness that He promised and not to me only but to all who long for His return.

⁹If at all possible, come, for I need you ¹⁰because Demas abandoned me finally because of his love for the world. He left for Thessalonica. Crescens has returned to Galatia, and Titus to Dalmatia. ¹¹Luke is the only friend I have left. When you come bring Mark, for he would be a great help in the ministry. ¹²Oh yes, I sent Tychicus to Ephesus. ¹³My warm coat, which I left at Troas, would be a great help to me. Could you bring it? And try to find place for the books and more important, the parchments.

¹⁴You will be disappointed to know that our friend Alexander the coppersmith has done a lot of harm to my cause. May God reward him with complete justice. ¹⁵Beware of him, for he has resolutely refused to accept our message.

¹⁶At my first hearing no one would testify in my behalf; they all left. May God forgive them. ¹⁷But the Lord was with me and gave strength so that my message might be more widely heard among the Gentiles. Also, I was acquitted; it was as though I had been rescued from the mouth of a lion. ¹⁸He will rescue me eventually from every wicked plot and bring me into His eternal kingdom someday. Let Him be praised now and forever!

¹⁹Please give my greetings to Priscilla and Aquila and to the family of Onesiphorus. ²⁰Erastus stayed at Corinth, but Trophimus became ill and had to stay at Miletus. ²¹Oh I hope you can come before winter. My brothers, Eubulus, Pudens, Linus, and Claudia, send their greetings as do all the believers. ²²Now may the Lord Jesus Christ be with your spirit. May God's grace be with you. Amen.

Titus

Chapter 1

¹From Paul, one of God's slaves, one of His apostles, sent by Jesus Christ in harmony with the faith of God's chosen ones who acknowledge truth, which produces godliness. ²From one who has hope of eternal life, a hope founded on the promise of God Himself, who cannot lie, who planned this whole thing before the world was created ³and has at the proper time made His word known through preaching, a preaching committed to me as my responsibility, by God the Father and our Savior. ⁴To Titus, my spiritual son in the faith. May grace, mercy, and peace from God our Father and our Lord Jesus Christ, our Savior, be yours.

⁵My purpose in sending you to Crete was two-fold. First, that you would be able to confront the errors that had crept into the churches, errors that had not yet been challenged. And second, to ordain elders in every city on the island. ⁶Here are the qualifications of an elder (bishop). His conduct must be above reproach, he must have a stable, monogamous relationship, and his children must be well behaved, not always getting into trouble. ⁷As God's steward he must be above criticism, he must be teachable, slow to anger, a person who refuses intoxicating wine, who will not retaliate when injured, and one who considers money-getting a minor goal in his life. ⁸He must be a hospitable person, one who appreciates the good qualities in others, a discreet prudent man, a man who insists on justice, a man committed to God, temperate in all things. ⁹He must hold strictly to God's word, having himself been blessed by learning the word. He must be able to teach others who are wanting to learn and be able to meet and defeat those who contradict truth. ¹⁰There are many such persons with which to contend, men who are rebellious, talkative, deceptive, most of whom are Jews who still claim that circumcision is necessary. ¹¹These dangerous minds must be defeated or otherwise they will lead whole families astray just for the money.

¹²One of the Cretans, a self-proclaimed prophet, has put it this way: "Face it, fellow countrymen, we are prone to be liars, vicious beasts, and lazy gluttons." ¹³He was telling the truth. So they need to be very directly rebuked as you uphold the true faith. ¹⁴Never listen to Jewish fables or Jewish regulations that are only man-made and only turn minds away from truth. ¹⁵Pure-minded people center their thoughts on pure things while the minds of unbelievers run every which way— his very thoughts are polluted, his mind

untrustworthy. [16]Some may profess to know God, but if one studies their behavior one finds that they deny God. They practice abominations and boldly disobey Him.

Chapter 2

[1]Your responsibility is to preach only truth, unchanging doctrine as illustrated by some ideas that follow. [2]Teach elderly men to be serious, discrete, self-disciplined, faithful, unselfish, and willing to endure hardship. [3]The older ladies should be the same. Their behavior should be above reproach, not always stirring up arguments or quarrels. They should avoid alcoholic drinks; they should be able to teach others, [4]especially the younger women, to be sober, to unselfishly love their husbands and children, [5]to be tactful, pure, modest, good homemakers, supportive of their husbands, so that God's word will be held in high esteem. [6]As for younger men, they too should be serious-minded.

[7]Whatever you do, remember that you are a role model and need to be exemplary, your teachings unassailable, your lifestyle always serious, always sincere. [8]Your sermons as well as your ordinary conversation should be thoroughly truthful so that anyone who wants to oppose you would be unable to find a single error. [9]In talking to slaves, tell them to serve their owners well in everything they do, diligent in work, never talking back, [10]never pilfering, but always perfectly honest, thereby to enhance the teachings of God our Savior by their behavior. [11]For God's grace that brings salvation to us has been clearly demonstrated and shown to us.

[12]Reject ungodliness and all worldly pleasures, living lives that are sober, serious, and righteous in this present world.

[13]All the while eagerly hoping and anticipating the return in splendor of Jesus Christ our Lord and Savior. What a blessed hope we have! [14]He gave His very life for us in order to redeem us from all kinds of sin, then to purify for His use a special people who are filled with zeal for doing good. [15]These are the very things that need to be taught, rebuking sin with full authority. Let no one look down on you or on your position.

Chapter 3

[1]Be sure to remind your believers of their obligation to be subject to the civil authorities, local and state. Be quick to respond to calls for help in times of need and to [2]resist the temptation to criticize or to engage in "rabble-rousing," but to be truly meek citizens. [3]We should remember that in the past we may have done some rather foolish things ourselves, deceived as we were, rebellious, satisfying every sort of desires and forbidden pleasures, ready to give way to malice, jealousy, and hatred. [4]But once our Savior's kindness and love is shown us, we are entirely changed. [5]Not that we are saved by our behavior but only by His mercy and His work in washing us thoroughly, regenerating our natures by the power of the Holy Spirit, [6]all of which is the result of what Jesus Christ has done. [7]This marvelous grace has put us right with Him and assures us that we are heirs of eternal life.

[8]What I have just written is sound, true, and important, so continue teaching them along these lines so that they will keep right on doing good works, because what I have just written is for mankind's greatest need. [9]Please avoid if possible the tendency to become involved in trivial

questions, genealogy, and unsolvable disputes over theological puzzles, for they waste a lot of good time. [10]If a person persists in going on believing and practicing error after a counseling session or perhaps two such sessions, do not let him remain a formal member of your congregation. [11]Such a one is bound to be a negative influence in your church by his behavior. [1]

[2]After Artemas and Tychicus have arrived, do your very best to come and meet with me. I have decided to stay at Nicopolis all winter and will so much enjoy having you there with me for a time. [13]And if you find it at all possible, bring your lawyer friends, Zenas and Apollos, so we can complete their needed education. [14]Continue teaching our believers how to grow into effective workers for God, fruitful in evangelizing as well as in developing their own characters. [15]All the believers here send their greetings. Please greet the believers there, those who love us as brothers in the faith. May God's grace be with you all. Amen.

Philemon

¹From Paul, Christ's prisoner, and from Timothy our brother. ²To Philemon our beloved friend and fellow Christian. ³May grace and peace from the Father and from our Lord Jesus Christ be with you. ⁴Every day I thank God for you, naming you in my prayers. ⁵Don't think I haven't heard about your love for Jesus and your faith in Him, plus your love for fellow believers. ⁶You may be encouraged to know that your expressions of faith and your acknowledgements of the good things you enjoy as a Christian are effective witnesses. ⁷So we are overjoyed as we receive reports of your love, which is very important in the encouragement of the believers.

⁸Right now I feel justified in being rather bold in presenting my request, a very reasonable one too. ⁹But because of my love for you and your love for me, I will only suggest that you consider what I have to say. After all, I am called "old Paul" and am now in prison. ¹⁰My request is for my child Onesimus, who has been "born again" through my imprisonment. ¹¹Yes, I know he was wrong in escaping, having given you poor service indeed, but he has now become valuable to you as well as to me.

¹²I am sending him back to you and asking that you receive him as kindly as if I were to personally come with him.

¹³You understand that I could have kept him here to help me during my imprisonment, and he was willing to do this, just as you might have been. ¹⁴But I just couldn't bring myself to do this not knowing your thoughts as yet, for that would have been pressing him to benefit me instead of what I knew to be the right thing—send him back to you for your benefit. ¹⁵Might it not be that his leaving you has resulted in a situation that will result in his return to you for the rest of his life? ¹⁶But perhaps not as much as a slave but as a brother, loved by me and more so by you as a fellow human being and a Christian believer.

¹⁷So if you will be so good as to consider us partners, accept him as readily as you would accept me. ¹⁸If you feel that he owes you money, make out a statement and send it to me. ¹⁹My signature will be security enough I am sure, but remember that you owe your very life and your hope to the fact that I brought you the gospel.

²⁰My brother, cheer me up with your response; this will refresh my whole being. ²¹ Frankly, I have so much confidence in you that I expect you to do a lot more than I am asking. ²²And I am so assured of seeing you again one of these days that I ask you to save a bed for me when I arrive. You have been so good to keep me in your prayers.

[23]Please give my regards to Epaphras who I understand is also in prison because of his faith in Jesus. [24]And of course, greet Mark, Aristarchus, Demas, and Luke, my associates in labor. [25]May the grace of our Lord Jesus Christ be with you. Amen.

Hebrews

Chapter 1

¹Our Creator God, the God who communicated His will and His knowledge to our ancestors by inspiring prophets to speak and write for Him, ²has in this modern time revealed His will and His knowledge to us, their descendants, through His Son. This Son is heir of the whole universe, and in fact, He was the creator of it. ³It is He who is the very essence, the splendor of God's person, and who is the sustaining, supporting power over everything, and who has now pruned off our sins, then returned to take His rightful place as the authority over all creation. ⁴Let's not even try to compare Him with angels, for He is infinitely greater than they, being their Creator and the One who truly owns them. Thus, His name is far greater and better than theirs.

⁵Think of this. Did God ever say to any angel, "You are My son. You are the offspring of My very person"? Or did God ever say, "I will be his Father and he shall be My son," while addressing any angel? No indeed. ⁶Here's another thought, when God reproduced Himself in human flesh He proclaimed: "Let all the angels of God worship Him." ⁷He says this of angels (Psalm 104:4), "Who makes His angels spirits, His ministers a flaming fire."

⁸But to His Son He says (Psalm 45:6, 7), "Your throne, Oh God, is eternal. Your kingdom is founded on truth and perfect righteousness. ⁹You have loved righteousness, and You have hated sin and because of this, the true, the only God, Your God has anointed You with the oil of gladness far exceeding that of Your earthly fellow humans." ¹⁰And another statement to His Son. "You, Lord, in the beginning laid the foundation of the earth; You created the heavens. They are Your handiwork. ¹¹They, the earth and the heavens, shall disappear. You will continue on while they disintegrate as clothing does with time. ¹²Just as a person changes clothing, folding it up and putting it away, so these will finally be changed, but You will never change."

¹³Did any angel ever hear these words spoken to him? "Sit here at My right hand (the position of authority) until your enemies are totally defeated and are nothing more than a footstool." ¹⁴Think of the angels like this: Every angel is a spirit being and is commissioned to go to the aid of a human being who will receive the gift of eternal life.

Chapter 2

¹So why have I brought up these matters? It is that we might be more earnest, more

sincere in our acceptance of truth, and obedient to the things that we have heard, for unless we follow them we shall lose them. [2]God's word delivered to us through His messengers the angels can be counted on, can be trusted. We really are doomed to reap a fully justified consequence of rebellion. [3]There can be no escaping that fact. Then let us not neglect salvation. God initiated it, and His disciples heard it from Jesus. They in turn have repeated it to us. [4]And further, the proclamation of God's message has been substantiated by miracles, signs, and wonderful evidences of its authenticity, then by gifts of the Spirit as He saw best to bestow them.

[5]No, God has not made the angels to be rulers over the world now nor at any future time. [6]Remember Psalm 8? "What is man that You take notice of him, what is any child of humanity that You have seen fit to do anything for him. [7]For You have created him only a little lower than angels. You have given him authority, honor, and glory as administrators over the earth and all that there is in it. [8]You have put everything into subjection to human beings," but now it is hard to believe that mankind ever had such authority. [9]For we see Jesus becoming a mere human being, lower than angels in order that He would be subject to death, and this infinite condescension terminated in His death, not merely the sleep of death but the "second death," separated from God the Father for the sake of us humans.

[10]Just think of it! He who created all things and wanted to have all of us rescued was willing to endure such suffering in order to complete His mission. [11]And not only that but this infinite captain who has brought rescue to sinners has become a brother to those whom He saved. [12]This was foretold in Psalm 22:22 as follows: "I will announce My name among My brothers and sisters; in the church I will sing praises." [13]And another, "I will trust Him completely." And yet another, "Here I am and the children whom God has given Me." [14]The children mentioned here are real flesh and blood people, and He took the very same flesh and blood as they are, became one of them, so that through death He could eradicate death and the originator of it—the devil—[15]then deliver everyone who feared death all their lives.

[16]Once again try to grasp this. He did not assume the nature of angels, those sinless spirit beings with such great capabilities. No, He assumed human nature, not just ordinary human nature, such as Adam and Eve possessed, but the nature of Abraham, a sinner, and the nature of Abraham's descendants. [17]And in fact, this was the only way to save us. He had to become a person such as we are so that His priesthood would be effective and so that His sacrifice might be effective in reconciling us to God. [18]It is because He was willing to go through His agonizing death that He is able to save us in our testing times.

Chapter 3

[1]Now, in view of these facts, my committed brothers, we need to consider more deeply our High Priest sent by God. He is the founder of our faith. [2]He carried out faithfully His assignments from God, just as Moses had done so many years ago. [3]But Moses' household was the result of the influence of this man Jesus, so Moses does not deserve the glory that Jesus deserves. A building does not deserve the honor that is bestowed on the architect. [4]A house of

course is built by someone, but God is the builder of everything. ⁵Now I have nothing against Moses. He really was faithful in his responsibilities and is an example to all who want to follow him. ⁶But Christ was the Son and heir in His household, a household that includes us as long as we remain confident to the end.

⁷Please refresh your minds with words inspired by the Holy Spirit in Psalm 95:11: "Today, if you will only pay attention to His voice, ⁸quit being as stubborn and rebellious as My people were back there in the wilderness. ⁹Your ancestors tested Me presumptuously for forty years, ¹⁰and I grieved over them as I moaned, 'This whole nation is prone to err; they just don't want to know My way.' ¹¹So all I could do was to solemnly conclude that they would never enter with Me into the true rest."

¹²My dear brothers, search your hearts and discover if there is even the slightest tendency to unbelief or to abandon the living God. ¹³Rather, encourage each other every day while it is still possible to do so lest you become hard-hearted through sin's fearful, deceptive nature. ¹⁴If we cling in confidence to our hope, and cling to the very end, we shall be given the same victory that Jesus gained. ¹⁵Today is the only day we have, so let us listen and heed His voice, avoiding stubborn rebellion such as was seen back there in the wilderness. ¹⁶Some of those who escaped miraculously from Egypt and heard God's voice still persisted in rebelling, ¹⁷and did they not cause God untold grief during those forty years as they died, one by one, out in the desert? ¹⁸These were the ones to whom He addressed the words, "You will never enter into My rest." ¹⁹And we know that they could not enter God's rest because of one reason—unbelief.

Chapter 4

¹Let us take warning from their experience, for if we fail to believe, we too will fall short of God's rest. ²Those people had the good news spoken to them just as we now have the good news given to us, but without faith and trust in it, they could not be blessed by it. ³But trust in God, real belief, has given us the intended rest as He promised just as He completed His object in creation at the beginning of the world's history. ⁴The Sabbath was evidence, and still is, that His creation is complete. ⁵So we may be confident that He will fulfill His promise of rest, especially spiritual rest. ⁶And God will have people who truly enter into the rest He has promised, even though unbelief has shut some out.

⁷A specific day is mentioned in Psalm 95:7, "Today open your hearts if you will." ⁸Joshua indeed led them into the Promised Land, but this was not the true rest God had in mind or He would not have mentioned the entering of rest again. ⁹So God's Sabbath, the symbol of His ultimate rest, continues on for God's people. ¹⁰And as we cease from our secular labor, we also have ceased our efforts to save ourselves, just as the Creator terminated His creation on the seventh day. ¹¹Let us decide right now that come what may we will not make the same mistake as our ancestors did—refusing to believe God. ¹²His word is living and powerful, sharper than any double-edged sword, even to separating the soul and the spirit, cutting through hard bone into the marrow, into the joints, and actually is able to read the motives and thoughts.

¹³Nothing in this world can be hidden from Him, but everything is completely exposed to His vision. That is the sort of being with which we are dealing. ¹⁴Since

we are not dealing with Jesus our High Priest in heaven's sanctuary, let us cling to our faith in every situation. [15]For we have a High Priest who is sympathizing with us at all times, who went through our pain Himself, our weakness, our temptations and trials just as we must do, yet overcame the trials completely, never sinning once. [16]Now He invites us to present ourselves, by prayer, to His throne of grace, confident that He will be merciful to us and provide grace and help in our times of need.

Chapter 5

[1]Let us speak now of the high priest. In earthly things the high priest is one set apart for his office by God Himself and entrusted with the responsibility of presenting gifts and sacrifices to God. [2]He is a person who will take pity on the ignorant and the erring, for He Himself is a human being tempted and troubled by human weaknesses and disabilities. [3]Therefore, he needs to offer sacrifices for himself as well as for the people. [4]No high priest became such due to his own choice, but was named high priest by God himself, for instance Aaron. [5]Christ also has been named to this holy office by God. He did not assume this position by His own choice (see Psalm 2:7); "You are my son, today I fathered you." [6]See also Psalm 110:4, which reads, "You are a priest forever, after the order of Melchizedek." [7]Yet while on the earth He was often praying, begging God to save Him, often weeping as He prayed, knowing that God had the authority to rescue Him. God always heard Him as He does for all who revere Him.

[8]And even though Christ was a Son, He went through intense suffering in His commitment to obey the Father. [9]Finally, He completed His mission and became the basis of eternal salvation for all who are obedient. [10]Thus, He was ordained by God as a priest, forever resembling the priest Melchizedek. [11]There is a great deal more that could be said about him, but it would be difficult for you to accept at this time. [12]For as yet you who should be teaching others by now are in need of instruction yourselves. You are still beginners in the knowledge of God's word. You still need milk, as it were, rather than solid food. [13]Those who are not yet weaned in God's word need to be treated as a baby. [14]But with growth and maturity comes the ability to use solid food and the ability to clearly distinguish between right and wrong.

Chapter 6

[1]So I invite you to advance from the basics of Christianity, from depending on behavior, to the place where you depend wholly by faith in God, [2]then on to true doctrines about baptism, ordination, resurrection, and the great judgment. [3]We shall proceed to do this, God willing. [4]First though, a fearsome warning. All those who have been given light and have received it have received the Holy Spirit [5]and have been nourished by God's word with its powerful message about the world to come. [6]They are in a nearly hopeless situation if they backslide. Repentance is almost impossible for such souls who have wounded the Son of God and publicly shamed Him.

[7]An illustration would be helpful. The rains come and water the soil for the farmer who is growing vegetables, and of course, this is God's way of blessing him. [8]But if that soil produces noxious weeds such as thorns and briars that are doomed to be burned, it will not at the same time

produce vegetables. ⁹However, I believe that you will not fall into that error. You surely are committed to salvation but are in some danger, so I have spoken freely and plainly. ¹⁰Never doubt that God is just and will not overlook your deeds of kindness that you have done and are still doing.

¹¹We hope that every one of you will continue to demonstrate the same diligence in the future, encouraged by our hope in the future, ¹²that you will not drift into apostasy, but rather imitate those who endured through every vicissitude in order to inherit God's promises. ¹³Remember those promises to Abraham? Every one was more than a promise; it was a judicial oath, sworn by God Himself who could swear by no greater, so swore by Himself with these words: ¹⁴"I promise that I will bless you while I am blessing, and I will multiply you while I am multiplying." ¹⁵Abraham kept on patiently believing, and eventually he began to see the fulfillment of the promise beginning to take shape. ¹⁶It is a fact that human beings when taking an oath to tell the truth will swear by a greater being than themselves. Then when they testify it settles all arguments. ¹⁷When God wanted to demonstrate the reliability of His promise He took an oath, ¹⁸which reinforced His promise. Because God cannot lie, these two give us unassailable hope for the future, ¹⁹a hope that might be compared to a ship's anchor that prevents us from being carried away by the wind, kept in the Holy Place with Jesus who has already entered into heaven as our High Priest, a priest of the order of Melchizedek.

Chapter 7

¹Why do I mention Melchizedek? You know of course that he was king of Salem, that he was one of God's priests, that he met Abraham after the victory over the heathen kings, and that he bestowed on Abraham a divine blessing. ²Think of this. Abraham gave tithes to Melchizedek, whose name means "king of righteousness"; he was also a priest. ³His qualifications for the priesthood were not based on his ancestry, for we have no record of his father, his mother, or even of his birthdate or age. In these ways he represents God's Son who is a priest forever.

⁴Abraham, great as he was, considered Melchizedek even greater and gave tithes of all the profits from the spoils of the battle. ⁵But we generally recognize as priests only men from the tribe of Levi. They are the ones who can lawfully receive tithes from you Hebrews. ⁶However, here is a person who is most certainly not a Levite, who lawfully accepted tithes from a Hebrew, indeed the father of Hebrews, the one to whom God's promises were made. ⁷We all agree that a lesser person receives blessing from the greater one. ⁸Among human beings, men who are mortal receive tithes, but Levites gave tithes to a priest, who represents a still greater one, an immortal one. ⁹For Levi, a descendant of Abraham, was in essence giving tithes to Melchizedek ¹⁰when Abraham did so, for he was a direct descendant of Abraham.

¹¹Now if the Levitical priesthood was the reality, instead of merely a type, there would be no need for a priest to come along similar to Melchizedek, not a descendant of Aaron. ¹²But the priesthood has changed, from Aaron to Melchizedek, and the law recognizes this change. ¹³He who fulfilled the prophecies came from a different tribe. ¹⁴Our Lord came from the tribe of Judah, and Moses said absolutely

nothing about the tribe of Judah in relation to the priesthood. [15]But Jesus Christ is "in the order of Melchizedek." [16]He does not qualify as priest by His ancestry, but by the power of an eternal life. [17]Once again recall Psalm 110:4: "A priest *forever* after the order of Melchizedek." [18]Thus, the law of the priesthood had to be bypassed, for it depended on humanity and, therefore, was limited and weak.

[19]The law was unable to complete God's plan, but the bringing in of a better hope was able and did so. And this hope draws us to God. [20]Christ, our hope, was ordained as priest by an oath, [21]but the Levitical priests were not so ordained. Christ was made a priest by an oath, not just a human oath, but by the oath of Him who declares, "The Lord swears and will never reverse His decision. You are a priest forever after the order of Melchizedek." [22]And just as God's oath is more dependable, so also can Jesus be fully depended on.

[23]Also, those priests of old were necessarily many, for they were mortal and died. [24]But Jesus, who is immortal, will be priest forever, never surrendering His office to another. [25]Thus, Jesus is able to save everyone who comes to God through Him. His salvation is one hundred percent final and irrevocable, for He will live forever as He continues to intercede for them. [26]It is just such a priest that we need, one who is holy, completely sinless, and thus different from us sinners, and is now installed into an office that is higher than any other being. [27]He doesn't need to keep offering sacrifices every day as the Aaronic priests did, for they had to offer sacrifices for their daily sins, then for the sins of their people. But Jesus needed only one offering, and He did that when He offered Himself.

[28]According to the law of Moses, the high priest was a man subject to infirmity, sickness, and death, but God's oath, which was sworn long after Moses, has named God's Son as High Priest who shall never perish.

Chapter 8

[1]Now let me summarize what I have been trying to establish. We really do have a High Priest seated in the position of authority at God's right hand. [2]This High Priest is the minister of sacred things in the original, eternal tabernacle that was built by God, not by humanity. [3]Every high priest is consecrated to his office before he is qualified to offer gifts and sacrifices, and this Man, too, has an offering to present. [4]If He were on earth, He could not be a priest because the law specifies only certain ones as priests. [5]They serve their purpose, which is to represent the heavenly ministry. Remember that Moses was commanded to make the earthly sanctuary like the great heavenly pattern shown him while on Mount Sinai.

[6]But now Jesus our High Priest has assumed a more significant office than any earthly priest, for He is the administrator of a vastly better covenant based on better promises. [7]The old covenant had a serious flaw, and therefore, a new one is in order. [8]God knew all along that this was inadequate, and in Jeremiah 31:31–33 He spells out His new covenant based solely on His promise, not on human promises. [9]"That covenant that I made with them when I took them by the hand to lead them out of Egypt was based on their promise to Me, and as you know they broke their promise within days, so I could not fulfill My promise to them. [10]Here is the covenant that I will make with the nation of Israel

one day: 'I will imbed My laws into their minds and will write them on their hearts, and I will be a God to them and they will be My people. [11]They will never again need to teach a brother or a neighbor about Me, for everyone will know Me, from the very least of them to the greatest of them. [12]Further, I will show mercy in dealing with them and their sins, and I will forget those sins completely and forever. [13]Once this covenant is made, the old one is obsolete and insignificant.'"

Chapter 9

[1]That first covenant was associated with certain ceremonies and with an earthly tabernacle. [2]As you know, housed in the first room of the tabernacle was the candle holder and the table for the bread, which symbolized God's presence. This first room was called the Holy Place, or just "Holy." [3]It was separated from the second portion of the tabernacle by a heavy curtain, and the second room of the tabernacle was known as the Most Holy Place, or the "Holiest." [4]Adjacent to the Holiest was the golden altar, and within the Holiest was the ark of the covenant covered with gold and containing the pot of manna, Aaron's rod that budded, and the stone tablets on which were written God's Ten Commandments. [5]Above the ark was its cover called "The Place of Mercy" or "The Sin Hider"; I shall not comment on this at present.

[6]When the tabernacle service began, the directions were to have the priest enter the Holy or first apartment every day in his ministry. [7]Only once a year did anyone enter the Holiest, and it was only the high priest. On that occasion he always brought blood because of his own sins and the sins of his people. [8]The Holy Spirit intended

this as a lesson; namely, that the true holy sanctuary in heaven was to be understood only after the services of the earthly sanctuary had fulfilled their purpose.

[9]These services were typical but could not by themselves do the work of cleansing, which sinners need to have done. [10]They had a real purpose of course but were symbolic: to constantly observe various ceremonies, such as foods, drinks, washings, and other material measures, which were of themselves ineffective but which were all pointing forward to the time of reformation and real effectiveness in Christ.

[11]He has become the High Priest in a perfect tabernacle not made by human hands. [12]This tabernacle of which I now write has nothing to do with the blood of goats or calves but only with the blood of our High Priest Himself, by which He has obtained eternal redemption for us. [13]Now if the blood of bulls and goats and the ashes of a heifer were capable of representing the cleansing of the human being, [14]how much more effective is the blood of Christ to rid us from evil and to purify our conscience so that we may obey the living God. [15]It is because of His willingness to die that He is now our mediator of the new covenant. Yes, through death He can effectively cancel out our transgressions and bestow on us an eternal inheritance.

[16]Here is an illustration that may help. If a person makes a will and this will is officially written and witnessed, it is effective only after the death of the person; [17]then it becomes law, before this it has no value whatever. [18]That first covenant was ratified with blood. [19]When Moses had finished giving the law to the people, he took blood from calves and goats, water and hyssop and a sponge of purple wool, and then he

sprinkled the written document and also the people while declaring, [20]"This is the blood of the testament to which you have agreed." [21]He even went so far as to sprinkle blood on the tabernacle and the utensils of the tabernacle.

[22]Almost without exception, it takes blood in the law of Moses to rid anything of sin. Without blood no remission of sin can take place. [23]This explains the symbolic sanctuary services where the ceremonies showed what actually, and in reality, takes place in the heavenly sanctuary. There the better sacrifice (of Christ) really purifies. [24]For Christ did not enter the manmade sanctuary when He ascended; it was only a symbolic representation of the true sanctuary. No, He entered the true sanctuary in heaven to represent us before God.

[25]Another significant thought. He does not offer Himself every year as the high priest did here on earth. He offers His own blood, and only once! [26]If His sacrifice had been yearly, think how many times He would have suffered agony since the earth began. This was not necessary at all. One sacrifice was all that was needed to do away with our sins. [27]Just as human beings die only once, then face judgment, [28]so Christ offered Himself once as He accepted the sins of everyone. One day He will reappear, not to deal with sin this time, but to rescue those who are looking for Him.

Chapter 10

[1]Now some more about sacrifices. In the law of Moses, these things were only shadows of the real effective sacrifice; they could never provide eternal security to those who offered them. [2]Had they been capable of this, once would have been enough, for the worshipper would have been fully cleansed and would not require a yearly sacrifice. [3]But as you know they were repeated year after year as a reminder. [4]You can easily grasp the fact that the blood of a bull or goat is inadequate to remove sin. [5]Therefore, something better must be offered, and in this case it was the sacrifice of Jesus. The following scriptures show us the futility of other offerings: Psalm 50:8; Psalm 40:6; Isaiah 1:11; Jeremiah 6:20; and Amos 5:21. [6]Jesus' sacrifice was adequate, thankfully, for He had intrinsic value to God.

[7]Going on in Psalm 40 we find this prophecy: "Look, I am coming just as the whole book predicts, to demonstrate true obedience to Your will, O My God." [8]He plainly states that our offerings and sacrifices are not the reality, not what is truly effective. He is not pleased by such things even though He initiated them Himself and it is written into the law. [9]His statement, "Look, I am coming to carry out Your purpose," is the clue to understanding these things. Animal sacrifices are to be terminated; the sacrifice of Jesus is to take their place. [10]And it is this and only through this that we can be sanctified, made pure, and clean, and fit for the presence of God.

[11]Our priests went about their rituals, but these could never abolish sin. [12]But this man with one, and only one, sacrifice for sin is enthroned with God. [13]His enemies are finally all subdued. [14]Yes, only one offering is necessary and capable of transforming those who accept it for themselves. [15]The Holy Spirit has given further light on the subject in Jeremiah 31:33 and onward: [16]"Here is my promise, a solemn covenant that I make; I will put My laws into their hearts, I will install them into their minds [17]and will completely abolish

and forget all their sins forever." [18]Once this has taken place there is no need for further sacrifices.

[19]In view of this, brothers and sisters, we may be confident as we enter into the Holiest through the blood of Jesus [20]in the new and living way that He has established by His body. [21]Furthermore, knowing that we have a High Priest over God's household, [22]I invite you to come with a sincere heart, complete trust, with hearts sprinkled as it were from their wickedness and with bodies washed with pure water. [23]I invite you to cling to your faith unwaveringly, for He who promised is completely dependable.

[24]Let us constantly be aware of one another as to how we may be a help, doing loving services for them. [25]We should never neglect our meeting together (some tend to do this), but rather encourage each other regularly and with even more diligence as we see the time for Jesus' return drawing near. [26]If we deliberately reject our faith after once accepting Jesus, there is no sacrifice that can rescue us from our sins, [27]only a dark future ahead, final judgment, and annihilation with all of God's other enemies. [28]Consider this, in Moses' time the law stated that two or three witnesses could testify and pass a death sentence on a criminal. [29]How much more deserving of death, do you think, is a person who has trampled on the Son of God, completely scorning the blood shed for him, the blood that might have cleansed him, actually insulting Him and rejecting the plea of the Holy Spirit.

[30]We are all aware, I am sure, of the statement: "Vengeance is mine to mete out as I see fit," (God's statement). He also says, "God will judge the people." [31]Here is an awesome thought. The living God is the one to whom we shall finally give an account. [32]Think back a few years to when you received your present light and became the target of your enemies who persecuted you, [33]holding you up to public scorn. Or perhaps you were not persecuted but your friends were. [34]You then sympathized with me when I was put in prison and joyfully submitted to the confiscation of your property, for you knew that these material goods are of far less value than the eternal riches you owned through Jesus.

[35]Cling to your confidence; there is a wonderful reward awaiting you. [36]Patience needs to be cultivated, endurance needs to be cultivated, so that having believed you may continue until God's promise is fulfilled. [37]It will not be fulfilled right away. He will come someday, and the waiting will be over. [38]The secret to such endurance is faith, and those who are right with God will all be people who live each day having perfect trust in God. If a person gives up his faith, he is not much of a role model in my opinion. [39]We surely are not the kind of people who are likely to surrender our faith, but will continue to trust and in this way receive complete salvation.

Chapter 11

[1]I now want to share with you some thoughts on faith, belief, and trust. First let me define faith. It is complete confidence in what we are hoping for; it is the evidence of the reality of things as yet unseen. [2]It was through faith that the elders of old received the approval of God. [3]It is through faith that we can understand that the universe was created by the word of God, that matter itself was not created from pre-existing matter but from nothing. [4]It

was because of his faith that Abel offered to God a better sacrifice than did Cain. And it was in this obedience to God's will that he was declared to be righteous, and God accepted his offering so that after his death, his testimony still continues.

⁵By faith Enoch was translated, never having to experience death. He just disappeared from the earth, for God translated him, having pleased God while on this earth. ⁶Without faith no one can please God, for a human being who comes to God must believe that God exists and that God acts in response to a prayer that is prayed with sincerity. ⁷It was by faith, complete trust in God and His word, that Noah, when he was warned of the coming flood, a thing that had never happened up to that time, believed God meant what He said and built the ark, spending one hundred twenty years building a boat in which to save his family. It was this ark that showed who believed God and who did not. Unfortunately, those who refused to have faith in God were lost.

⁸Abraham's faith motivated him to obey God's call, leaving home and friends to travel hundreds of miles to a country he had been promised for his descendants. He had never seen it and did not even know of its existence until God led him there. ⁹His faith continued to guide him as he camped in tents year after year in that land. Here his son Isaac was born and then his grandson Jacob; they were the recipients of the very same promise. ¹⁰He sensed that God's promise included far more than an earthly land and led to a heavenly city built by God.

¹¹It was by faith that Sarah, who was well past menopause, conceived Isaac. She took God at His word, and He kept His promise. ¹²So it was that from this one couple, both of whom were already old, came a race of people that resembles the stars in number, or almost like the grains of sand at the seashore. ¹³But they finally died, having never realized the complete fulfillment of the promise. However, they were convinced that the promise would eventually be fulfilled and that they themselves were only short time dwellers on this earth.

¹⁴People like these I have mentioned made a statement by their lives, as well as by their words, and that statement is that there is a future country to anticipate, vastly more desirable than the world we now live in. ¹⁵If this present world was their goal, they had ample opportunity to retrace their steps and live solely for it. ¹⁶But no, they believed in something better, far better, a heavenly country. It was because of their faith that God is happy to claim them as His, eventually giving them the city He is preparing for them.

¹⁷One of the greatest examples of faith we have is another episode in Abraham's life. This time he was really put to the test with the command to offer Isaac as a sacrifice. Here Abraham acted only because of his trust in God, carrying out the order to the letter, ¹⁸in spite of the fact that God had promised Isaac as the fulfillment of a previous promise. ¹⁹Abraham's faith was so great that he expected God to bring Isaac back to life. It was like a resurrection when at the last second God spoke to him, letting him drop the knife and spare Isaac. ²⁰Isaac himself had a superb faith years later when he pronounced blessings on Jacob and Esau, for these had to do with events far in the future. ²¹By faith Jacob, when he was near death, unable to balance without a cane, pronounced a blessing on Joseph's

two sons. ²²And by faith Joseph, just before he died, declared that the Israelites would one day leave Egypt and told them to carry his bones with them when they did so.

²³The parents of Moses acted by faith when they hid this baby for three months, knowing him to be a special person and willing to defy the order of the pharaoh. ²⁴Moses' faith led him to turn down the offer of being the king of Egypt, a position he was expected to accept, being an adopted son of Pharaoh's daughter. ²⁵He elected to stay with his people, regardless of the trouble it would cause him, rather than to enjoy the honor and prestige that would have been his as king, for a while. ²⁶He rightly decided that unpopularity was to be preferred over power if it would result in being with Christ. So he rejected Egypt and its treasures, and now has already received the reward that goes with his wise choice. ²⁷His faith was so firmly founded that he left Egypt, knowing that the king would be furiously angry, but he stuck to his purpose as if God were right there with him.

²⁸The Passover was another act of faith. He obediently sprinkled the blood as directed so that the destroyer would not be able to touch the firstborns. ²⁹It took faith to go forward at the Red Sea, but in doing so they went through on dry ground. After reaching the opposite shore, they were able to see the Egyptian army drowned in the waters of the Red Sea.

³⁰Only by faith could the walls of Jericho fall flat after the priests and the army marched around the city for seven days. ³¹And because of her faith, the prostitute Rahab was spared at the destruction of Jericho. She demonstrated her faith by shielding the spies from the searching soldiers.

³²It is hard to stop this recital of people with faith, but it must be done. Yet here are a few more names to consider: Gideon, Barak, Samson, Jephthah, David, Samuel, and many prophets, ³³who because of their willingness to trust God were able to conquer nations, overcome evil and do right, realize the fulfillment of promises, escape from lions, ³⁴live through fire, avoid death by the sword, receive strength when weak, and become brave in war, routing their enemies. ³⁵Women saw their dead children raised to life. Others, however, were not that fortunate, for rather than yield their faith, they were tortured, enduring it because of their belief in a future joyful resurrection.

³⁶Still others went through severe trials such as being made a public disgrace, whipped, incarcerated, chained, ³⁷stoned, cut in pieces, fearfully tried in other ways, killed by the sword, made a fugitive, camouflaged in sheepskins or goatskins, and completely destitute with no one to help them in their trials. ³⁸The world was not worthy to associate with these heroes of faith who fled to the desert or hid in animal dens or caves. ³⁹Every one of them through faith is now honored by God, even though they have not lived to see the fulfillment of the promises made to them. ⁴⁰Yet we, who may not have to endure such trials, will receive equal honor by God when He restores us.

Chapter 12

¹Now, in view of the fact that we too are surrounded by celestial, as well as human witnesses, let us remove these weights that impede our progress and continue to run with endurance and determination this race in which we find ourselves ²with

Jesus as our constant model and source of strength. He is the One in whom our faith is centered and in whom we will complete our course. He looked forward to the joys of eternity even while enduring the cross and the shame of it, and He is now seated at the right hand of God on the throne.

³When you are tempted to think you have things rather difficult and are about to give up, consider how He must have felt and how He refused to yield to His desires, the urge to abandon those sinners who were mistreating Him so grossly. ⁴You will then realize that your endurance has not yet been tested nearly as much as was His, to the point where death was His only option.

⁵Perhaps you have forgotten the admonition in Job 5:17: "My son, don't lightly regard God's corrections or give up when He rebukes you ⁶for He corrects everyone He loves, and sometimes this requires a spanking." ⁷If you accept His corrections, you will realize that He is dealing with you as you might deal with a son of yours, for where is the son who doesn't need a spanking occasionally. ⁸But if you have experienced no corrections from God, you just might conclude that you are an illegitimate child of His.

⁹All of us have received correction from our earthly fathers; far from causing us to rebel, these corrections have caused us to have more respect and better obedience. Then is it not more likely that we will respect and obey our Creator who occasionally corrects us? ¹⁰You see, our earthly fathers corrected us for only a few days, as it seemed necessary, and God always corrects us for our own benefit because He wants us to become like Him. ¹¹It is natural to feel that punishment is an unhappy event in our lives, and rather painful, yet later it produces righteousness in us and then peace. ¹²So take heart. Raise your hands in thanksgiving and kneel before Him. ¹³Go on, straightforward, so that you will not lead a limping, lame one astray, but rather heal them.

¹⁴Let your goal be peace with everyone, and holiness, without which no one will ever see God. ¹⁵All the time be searching your own hearts lest you fail to experience God's grace and lest any bitterness be allowed to enter your souls, then through your influence others might be dragged down. ¹⁶We certainly don't want any to become fornicators, or worldly, like Esau who sold his birthright for just one meal. ¹⁷You remember that he expected to obtain the blessing later in spite of this but found that it was too late. He had made his choice, and the blessing was no longer available, which brought him to tears.

¹⁸You people have never had the privilege of approaching Mount Sinai, seeing the fire, the blackness and the storm over it, ¹⁹or of hearing the sound of God's trumpet blast and the actual voice of God, words so loud that the people begged Moses to have them stopped. ²⁰It must have been indeed a fearful thing that they went through, knowing that if even an animal touched the mountain it would have to be stoned or impaled just as a human would have died. ²¹Moses himself was forced to confess, "I am dreadfully afraid; I shake with fright."

²²You dear people have never come to a burning mountain, but to Mount Zion, city of the living God, the heavenly city, New Jerusalem, into the presence of a numberless assemblage of angels, ²³to the congregation, the church of chosen ones, firstborn, whose names are written in heaven and to God Himself, the ultimate

judge, and to mature, committed persons, spiritual champions, [24]and to Jesus our Savior and mediator, the executor of the new covenant and to His blood, which is vastly more significant than the blood of the martyr Abel.

[25]I plead with you to never reject the One who now invites you. For if those in ancient times who rejected the invitation could not escape the consequences of their choice, it is sure that we in this time shall not fare any better if we reject the One who speaks from heaven. [26]His voice then shook the earth, but the warning now comes to us: "Once more, I will shake the earth and this time even the heavens will shake." [27]This shaking, He tells us, will remove everything that is not securely anchored. [28]We shall receive the unshakable kingdom, so let us accept God's grace, for it is effective in leading us to serve God acceptably with awe and reverence, [29]for our God is a consuming fire.

Chapter 13

[1]You have brotherly love. Let's hope that this continues. [2]With this kind of love, remember to show the same love and concern for strangers. Be hospitable, for they too are important, and besides, you might actually be entertaining an angel in human form, for they have been known to appear as strangers. [3]Please pray for and help those who are in prison. You would appreciate the visit of a friend if you were incarcerated, I am sure. The same caring attitude should be to those who are suffering adversity of any kind.

[4]About marriage: This is the ideal for everyone. Complete commitment and loyalty to your spouse, and total refusal to engage in "affairs." God will judge fairly every case of adultery and prostitution. [5]Your lives should be free of covetousness, and you should cultivate contentment with your lot in life. "Things" are not that important.

If you remember God's promise (I will never leave you nor forsake you), true happiness can be expected. [6]We can be confident in declaring, "The Lord is my helper, I shall not be afraid of anything humans can do to me." [7]Please remember your spiritual guides who have proclaimed the word of God to you. Their faith is worth imitating, and their goals are lofty ones. [8]Consider this for it is true. Jesus Christ is the same now as He always has been and He will always be the same forever. [9]Don't be carried away by "new light." You will be safe if you are first established solidly in the grace of God rather than in various ceremonial things such as foods; these ceremonial rites are only symbols and not reality.

[10]Our altar is one that is vastly superior to the earthly altar, for it involves the bread of life. [11]In ancient times the carcasses of the sacrificial animals whose blood was carried into the sanctuary was burned outside the camp. [12]This was symbolic of Jesus who, in order to sanctify the people through His blood, agonized outside of the city. [13]So let us follow Him outside of the camp if necessary, sharing the reproach that He suffered. [14]These temporal matters are really not so important; yes, it would be pleasant to have a permanent city in which to live, but we must be content to look forward in God's eternity to such a city. [15]As of now, our part is to continually offer our sacrifices of praise, as expressed by our lips, while we give thanks to His name.

[16]And as we express ourselves in words, let us not forget or neglect to do

well to others, for God wants us to be people who not only speak but also act out their religion. [17]Take very seriously the advice of your spiritual leaders, for they are watching out for your good at all times and want nothing more than your happiness. [18]Please continue to pray for us while we trust that our consciences will lead us aright, always living in openness and fairness. [19]Also please pray that I will be able to see you again soon.

[20]Now here is my prayer for you: May the God of true peace, the God who brought our Lord Jesus up from death, the Good Shepherd who fulfilled the covenant by dying for us, [21]may He mature you in every activity of your lives until everything you do will be carrying out God's will. This will be pleasing to Him and will be possible through Christ who deserves honor and praise forever and ever. Amen.

[22]Please, brothers and sisters, permit me to give you these words of admonition. My previous letter was altogether too brief; this should help. [23]I hope you are aware that our brother Timothy has been released and together we hope to see you soon. [24]Greet your leaders for me and all the believers too. Your fellow believers in Italy send their greetings. [25]Grace be with you. Amen.

James

Chapter 1

¹From James, servant of God and of our Lord Jesus Christ, to the twelve tribes who are scattered everywhere: my greetings to all. ²Brothers and sisters, some of you are suffering through real trials, but try not to surrender your courage. May I say it? Trials might possibly be for your good. Believing this will keep you joyful through all your difficulties. ³For as trials are encountered, we endure, patience and fortitude increase, ⁴and as patience and fortitude develop and mature, you finally reach the place in your spiritual growth where God wants you to be.

⁵Just in case any of you do not seem to have the wisdom you need, (and who does?) here is the most effective thing you can do—pray to God earnestly for the needed wisdom. He is the one who supplies wisdom enough for all situations and does so without scolding you. ⁶Your petition can be placed before Him in complete faith, faith that is willing to obey Him implicitly. If you are wishy-washy in your faith, however, you will be like a wave on the sea, driven by the wind first one way then another. ⁷Such faith is of no value, and a person such as this need not expect to receive the answer to his prayer.

⁸If your loyalty to God is not complete, your life will reveal this in constant instability. ⁹You poorer brothers, rejoice, for you have been called to a high, exalted status. ¹⁰And you wealthy ones, remain humble and be thankful, for all of us will die in the end, like grass. ¹¹When the hot sun comes up, grass wilts and dies, then turns into brown rubbish. This illustrates the fate of all, even the wealthy among us. ¹²The happiest people are those who have been through trials and have endured them. Their reward will be a crown, not a thing to wear on the head but a crown of life, the ultimate gift. ¹³If you have trials, please don't blame God. He is not the cause of trials and is never inclined to do anything wicked as we are. ¹⁴Our trials and temptations come when we surrender to our sinful desires. ¹⁵When those sinful desires are allowed to grow, sin is the product. When sin matures, it results in death—¹⁶make no mistake about that, brothers and sisters.

¹⁷Every good thing that we have received has been a gift from God, the source of light, our Creator, who is always unchangeable. ¹⁸He is the one who gave us existence by His word, and we are the most important of His creatures. ¹⁹So let us all be quick to listen, slow to speak, and resistant to anger. ²⁰Human anger does not fit in with God's perfect righteousness. ²¹So

do this: put aside all dirty, filthy behavior and allow God's word to grow in your being and finally mature and heal you.

²²Don't stop at just hearing His word, but put that word into practice; otherwise you will be deceiving yourselves. ²³Here is an illustration. If one just hears the word and refuses to act on it, he is like a man who looks in the mirror. ²⁴He studies his face, noticing any soiling or blemishes, then promptly goes away and does nothing about it. Rather stupid wouldn't you say? ²⁵But those who look into God's law, the law of freedom, with willingness to do something about themselves, will be truly blessed in so doing.

²⁶Being "religious" is not necessarily good for one. It is like a charade to go through all the motions of being a Christian and still talk like a heathen at times; the tongue must be included in one's religion or that religion is phony. ²⁷Genuine Christianity, the kind that comes from God our Father, will cause its followers to take note of the needs of others, especially orphans and widows, doing whatever is needed to help them while resisting the urge to go along with the evils in this world.

Chapter 2

¹My dear brothers and sisters, the Christian faith, based on Jesus Christ the Lord of glory, will eliminate favoritism among its followers. ²Suppose for instance, on Sabbath, a man wearing expensive clothing and a signet ring, showing that he has official authority, walks into your meeting place and about the same time a fellow from the "other side of the tracks," a transient with grubby clothing, dirty and unkempt, comes in. ³If you show favoritism by ushering the one in fine clothing to the best seat, while you brush off the transient, suggesting that he sit in the rear or perhaps on the floor, ⁴are you not showing partiality? Are you not acting the part of a judge? A role forbidden by Christ Himself.

⁵Listen, beloved, don't you think that God has called poor people as well as the rich? It is faith that counts. His kingdom is promised to all who love Him. ⁶And you have just shown contempt for the poor man. Is it not true that most cases of legal actions against us Christians are initiated by wealthy persons? ⁷And do they not commit blasphemy in their contempt for the name of Jesus Christ? ⁸If you are truly in harmony with the royal law, in harmony with the scriptures, which teach us to love our neighbors as ourselves, you will be doing right. ⁹But if you show partiality, you will be acting contrary to the law and will be sinning.

¹⁰Failure to keep even one of the commandments is breaking the entire law. ¹¹The very same law that forbids adultery also forbids murder. Now if you do not commit adultery but do commit murder, you are guilty of breaking the law. ¹²In all your words and all your behavior, remember that you will be judged by the great law of liberty. ¹³A person who shows no mercy will in the judgment be shown no mercy, and mercy is certainly what you and I must have on judgment day. ¹⁴Now let me ask you this question. Of what benefit is a person's faith? One may say, "I believe; I have faith," but if his actions are no different than they were before becoming a Christian, can his "faith" save him?

¹⁵Consider the case of a brother or a sister who is in abject poverty, who has nothing but rags to wear and is starving

for lack of good food. ¹⁶If you say to them, "I wish you well; I do hope you will keep warm and have plenty to eat," but do not raise a finger to supply clothing or food, of what value is your so-called "faith"? ¹⁷I believe you see my point. If faith does not impel a person to godly action and unselfish deeds, it is dead, it is a sham. ¹⁸Someone may proclaim, "I have faith; I believe." Show me your faith, if possible, with no corresponding good deeds, and I will show you my faith by my good deeds. ¹⁹Oh yes, I know you believe. You believe in only one true God, and this is of course true, but devils believe exactly the same truth and tremble for their future.

²⁰So once again, believe me, I am telling the truth. Faith without corresponding works is dead and without any value whatsoever. ²¹Consider the life of our patriarch Abraham. Was he not commended by God when he demonstrated his total trust in God by sacrificing his son Isaac on that altar? ²²You see, his works were the result of his faith and declared eloquently that his faith was the genuine article. ²³The scripture in Genesis 15:6 says, "And he believed God, and God accepted that faith as righteousness." His faith was fully demonstrated by his actions. That is why he was known as "the friend of God."

²⁴I think by now that it is clear to you that faith is a quality which justifies a person only if it is powerful enough to produce good works. ²⁵Another example might be the Jericho prostitute Rahab. Her faith was real enough so that she was willing to risk her life by harboring the spies and providing an escape route for them, and she was saved when Jericho fell. ²⁶Just as a human body without breath is dead, so faith with no corresponding works is dead.

Chapter 3

¹And now I want to give some advice: Not many of you should aspire to be teachers, for they have a responsibility that is more demanding than others. ²We are all prone to error and the danger of erring in our conversation is very great. In fact, if you can speak without hurting others, you are able to control every other behavior. ³We put a bit in a horse's mouth, and with this small object we are able to control this animal. ⁴And think of a ship. A rudder that is very small in comparison to the ship is able to control the ship and make it go wherever the captain wants it to go, even in contrary winds. ⁵So the human tongue, small as it is, becomes very significant in the life of a human being. Remember, one tiny flame can start a forest fire. ⁶In a way the tongue is like a fire, a destructive fire at that, for it is capable of turning the whole being into a killing machine, destroying itself as it destroys others.

⁷There is hardly an animal that cannot be tamed. Bird, reptile, mammal, or sea creature, they all have been tamed by someone. ⁸But the tongue, it seems, cannot be tamed even by its owner. It is loaded with poison at times. ⁹We use it to praise God our Father, and then in the next breath we curse our fellow men who are created in God's image. ¹⁰Out of the same mouth come both blessing and cursing. My brothers, this is a situation that should not exist.

¹¹Can a spring produce both sweet water and bitter water? ¹²Can a fig tree produce olives? Can a grape vine produce figs? So no fountain or spring can produce both sweet water and bitter water. ¹³Do you happen to have among you a person who is especially wise and blessed with

knowledge? If so, he will demonstrate his character by his actions, and in so doing he will still be meek about it. ¹⁴On the other hand, if your hearts are filled with jealousy, hatred, and contention, you need to be concerned and to recognize and acknowledge the truth about your condition. ¹⁵The so-called wisdom that produces this in a person is not from God, you may be sure, but it is from the world and is the natural result of the devil's principles. ¹⁶He always incites envy, jealousy, and strife when he directs human beings in his ways, and the end result is violence, tumult, and every other kind of evil.

¹⁷But God's wisdom has these qualities: purity, peace, a willingness to be taught, mercy, good deeds, fairness, and freedom from hypocrisy. ¹⁸A person who has real peace is one who will see peace growing in the lives of others.

Chapter 4

¹My next question: where do your squabbles and arguments come from? Let me answer my own question. They come from the desires of the heart, the covetousness and selfishness within. ²You even covet things that are not yours to the point that murder is no worse. That which you really need is not received because you don't ask for it. ³Your asking is self-centered, and God does not answer those requests, for they are not in your eternal interest.

⁴This attachment to worldly things is in reality a form of adultery. It is an abandonment of God and a transfer of loyalty to this world. Any who love the world are enemies of God. ⁵Do you for a moment think that scripture is lying when it says, "The spirit of mankind craves intensely, until it is defined as envy." ⁶But God will give you enough grace, yes, more than enough, just as is promised in Psalm 138:6: "God gives grace to those who are humble but not to the proud, haughty ones."

⁷So what is the solution? Be willing to submit yourselves and your desires to God. As for the devil, resist him, and he will give up and run from you. ⁸Draw near to God, and He will respond by drawing near to you. Thoroughly cleanse your hands, you sinners (we are all in this category). You have a divided loyalty. You must purify your hearts by committing them solely to God. ⁹It may require affliction, mourning, and weeping. Your laughter may have to be silenced and be replaced by mourning and your present joy by sorrow for a time.

¹⁰As you humble yourselves and submit to God, He will lift you up into a world of true joy. ¹¹You must resist the temptation to talk about the faults you see in one another. If we talk over the evils in someone else, this puts us in the position of judge, not only a judge of that other person but of the law itself, and we are to be doers, not judges, of the law. ¹²For we have but one lawgiver and He is omnipotent, able to save and able to destroy, so just who do you think you are, you who presume to judge another person?

¹³Here's another thought. You who say, "Here is what I shall do; I shall go to a certain city today or perhaps tomorrow, set up my business so that in a year or so I shall be wealthy." ¹⁴Unfortunately, you do not know about tomorrow, much less a year or more. Life is very transient indeed, like the morning mist that evaporates in the sunshine. ¹⁵So let us all remember to say, "If the Lord is willing, I shall do such and such." ¹⁶As things are now, much of our joy and happiness is boasting of what we are

and what we can do, but such joy is not at all necessarily God's will for us. [17]Now if you know what is good and acceptable to God, yet fail to do it that is sin.

Chapter 5

[1]I have a message for you men who are wealthy. You will not always live in luxury, quite the opposite. The time will come when you will be miserable and will cry out in distress. [2]Your wealth at that time will be worthless, even a liability, and your clothing will be moth-eaten. [3]Your gold and silver will be tarnished and of no value at that time. In fact, it will be used against you and will cause pain such as fire might cause. Your stacks of treasure will not help you, for we are speaking of the last days. [4]Your riches have been obtained by dishonesty. You have refused to pay a living wage to those who have harvested your fields, and the Lord of the universe has heard their prayers for help. [5]You have lived only for pleasure; you have been reckless, downright hateful, and spiteful while spending large sums of money on self. [6]You have taken righteous people to court, and they have been condemned and sent to their death with no chance of appeal.

[7]My brothers and sisters, endure patiently until the Lord returns. Our farmers know what it is to be patient and wait for the harvest. They do this every year; they wait for the former rains, and later on they wait for the latter rain. [8]You too must be patient. Your hearts must be fully committed, for every day is one day nearer to the coming of the Lord. [9]Do not hold grudges against one another, for this will result in guilt in your own lives. Our judge is just outside the door waiting to pass sentence.

[10]If you need an example of patient endurance under trial and persecution, remember the prophets who proclaimed God's message. [11]We naturally admire those who endure trials, do we not? Take for instance Job. Now we can see the purpose in permitting him to be so terribly tested. All along through Job's ordeal God was merciful and filled with true pity for the poor sufferer.

[12]Another bit of counsel, and this is important. Let us not be swearing by heaven or by the earth or by any of the other entities. It is much better to just say, "Yes, Yes," or "No, No," for oath taking can get us into trouble.

[13]Do you have any church members who are depressed? Prayer can and will help them. They should sing about the troubles. [14]Do you have a member who is sick? He should call for the church elders, asking them to come and pray for his recovery as they anoint him with oil in the name of the Lord. [15]The prayer offered in faith will save that sick person. God will raise him up and will forgive his sins as well. [16]It is important that you confess your faults to one another then pray for one another. This will result in healing of body as well as healing of soul. A fervent sincere prayer of a righteous man is immensely effective. [17]Elijah was a man who had some of our weaknesses, and through his prayer the rains stopped for three and a half years. [18]And when he finally prayed for rain, God answered, and the rains began again and once more food would be grown. [19]If any of you should wander from the truth and one of you take enough interest in him to restore his faith, [20]that act will rescue a sinner from death and will result in the blotting out of innumerable sins.

1 Peter

Chapter 1

¹From Peter, one of the apostles of Jesus Christ. To my fellow believers scattered out there in Pontus, Galatia, Cappadocia, Asia, and Bithynia. ²You are God's chosen. He knew all about you before you knew Him. His Spirit has set you apart for special holy service, for obedience to His will, all because of the blood of Jesus Christ. May God's grace be abundant; may His peace possess you completely.

³How I praise and thank God the Father of our Lord Jesus Christ, whose mercy has been extended to us, for creating us anew in the marvelous hope of the resurrection. This hope is certain because of the resurrection of Jesus from death. ⁴The resurrection to which we look forward is not just another life such as we live here and now, but to a life free from aging, illness, or death, free from every form of sin—and endless! A place is already reserved in heaven for you. ⁵And it is God's power within us that has kept us in the faith and will continue to keep us until the very end—the return of Jesus Christ.

⁶I am confident that you are all joyful over these prospects, even though you may now be enduring trials of many different kinds, real life and death trials. ⁷But remember that the testing of your faith is a very valuable thing, far more precious than gold, yes, even the refined gold, for gold will eventually disintegrate. Your faith will be found to be of infinite value, leading to honor and glory at the return of Jesus Christ. ⁸Now you, at least the majority of you believers, have never seen Him, but you love Him and believe in Him. This belief brings unspeakable joy that can be described as glorious. ⁹This faith will certainly bring eternal life, complete salvation.

¹⁰This salvation has been of monumental concern, even to the prophets of old. They foretold God's grace that was promised, but although they searched for its true meaning, they failed to completely grasp it. ¹¹The Holy Spirit spoke through them, and through their writings, we learned before it ever took place about the sufferings of Christ and about the ultimate glorious outcome. ¹²These prophets received their messages from God, and their messages had to do with not just themselves but with us who are now living and have seen the fulfillment of those prophecies and are spreading the good news. This good news is so wonderful that angels are fascinated by it.

¹³You might ask, "What must I do now?" Just this: Discipline your minds,

be sober and sincere, and never give up hope of the ultimate outcome when Christ returns. [14]As obedient children obey their parents, you should obey God so that your former desires have all been abandoned. [15]Then you will respond to this admonition in Exodus 19:6: "As God is holy in every phase of life, so you are to be holy. [16]For it is written, 'Be holy for I am holy.'"

[17]If you ask the Father, who is utterly fair and impartial, you may spend your time here on earth in awe. [18]Marveling that He was willing to redeem you from the corrupt and futile lifestyle of former days and not with money, which can rust and tarnish, [19]but with the precious blood of Christ, the Lamb of God, spotless and pure in every detail. [20]He committed Himself to the task before the world was ever inhabitable and now has carried out His plan during these last few years. [21]It is through Him that you are able to believe in God who raised Him from death and restored Him to glory. It is also through Him that your hope is centered in God.

[22]Now that you have committed yourselves to God and to obeying Him through the power of the Holy Spirit, and to loving your fellow Christians unselfishly, continue on with that decision wholeheartedly. [23]Your present status is that new birth of which Christ instructed us—the work of God's word, not of human beings in any sense of the word. [24]Human beings are transient, here today, gone tomorrow, [25]but God's word is eternal and is the basis for all that we have been preaching.

Chapter 2

[1]Now because we humans are so transient, so vulnerable, we are commanded to cast off and lay aside every suggestion of malice, deceit, hypocrisy, and jealousy, then with them out of the way we want to refrain from all evil gossip too. [2]And just as a newborn cries out for milk, we newborn Christians should cry out for God's word daily so that we can grow. [3]When this has been done, we shall have sound spiritual growth, for God is gracious. [4]He can be represented by a living stone, one which men rejected as they were building the temple but the very one needed at that spot and one that God was choosing, a very precious, indispensable one. [5]You too are living stones, placed solidly in the spiritual building, and further, you are also like priests, those who offered sacrifices, for you offer, not animals to be sure, but spiritual offerings accepted by God because of Jesus Christ. [6]This is the meaning of the scripture in Isaiah 28:16: "Look, I am laying a keystone in Zion, the most valuable of all; whoever believes in Him shall never feel insecure." [7]You who believe in Him know that He is that precious. Those who do not believe and rejected Him finally discovered Him to be the chief keystone. [8]And as predicted in Isaiah 8:14, He is a stumbling block, just a troublesome old stone.

[9]You are a unique generation of people. You are royal priests, a holy nation. You are different; you are here to display before the world the value of Him who called you from darkness into the brilliant light of the gospel. [10]You are the fulfillment of Hosea 2:3 where we find this: "Who at one time were not even recognized as a people, but now are God's own; who had not obtained mercy, but now have been mercifully saved."

[11]My dear beloved people, take my advice. Reject those earthly desires that

will threaten your spiritual growth. [12]Keep your behavior on a high, honest, truthful plane in your dealings with non-Christians. Who knows but that these very ones who speak so vehemently against you may see how much good you do and may turn to God in the end and glorify Him on the Great Day. [13]As for the laws of the land, obey them. God would want it this way, from Caesar's laws [14]to the governor's laws and local laws, for they are necessary in order to punish wickedness and justify the upright. [15]Once again, it is God's will that we Christians show by our behavior that we have a valuable lifestyle, so desirable that these foolish, ignorant adversaries will be silenced.

[16]Thank God that we are a free people, but you should not take advantage of this freedom and engage in political manipulations. No, just continue to be God's humble, obedient servants. [17]Honor everyone. Show true love to fellow believers, hold God in reverence and awe, and again, honor your king. [18]Slaves, do your duty, submit to your owners, and not just to those owners who are kind and gentle, but also to owners who are hateful, arrogant, and unjust.

[19]Here is good advice: To suffer for following conscience even though the punishment is completely unjust and undeserved is the way to go. [20]There is not a bit of merit in suffering for a wrong you have done, however patiently you may have acted, but when you have done only good and are then unjustly punished, your patience pleases God. [21]In fact, God's call includes a willingness to suffer injustice, just as Christ did for us. [22]He never once yielded to the temptations he faced. He never stooped to deceit of any kind.

[23]When He was ridiculed and castigated, He did not retaliate or reply in the same manner. He did not threaten to repay His tormentors, but He left any revenge entirely in "God's hands," knowing that in the end God's decision would be the right one. [24]He accepted our sins and experienced the inevitable result of such sins when He died on the cross in order that we might die to sin and live righteously. Remember Isaiah 53:5, "By His wounds we are healed." [25]In the past you were going astray like a lost sheep, but now you have returned to your owner, the hope of your entire future.

Chapter 3

[1]Wives, you should give complete loyalty to your husband so that if those around you go astray from God's word they may still have you as an example and be won back by observing your behavior and loyalty. [2]They will sense that your lives are strictly upright and that you reverence God. [3]Let your ornamentation be different from the heathen around you (elaborate hair styling, gold jewelry, luxurious clothing). [4] Rather, let your adornment be just a meek, quiet behavior, an inner experience that in God's sight is priceless. [5]It was this lifestyle that was so evident in holy women of old who trusted in God while loyal to their husbands. [6]Sarah was a wonderful example. She referred to Abraham as "my lord," and you are daughters of Sarah as you decide to do right, refusing to be afraid of threats.

[7]You husbands, your lives should be filled with deep respect for your wives, remembering that she is a more dependent person than you. However, you are both heirs of eternal life through God's grace. Your prayers for this Christlike virtue will

be answered. [8]Ultimately your goal should be oneness and unity, all of you taking a real interest in each other. If you are brothers in Christ, your love for each other will be obvious. Your sympathy and your courtesy will show. [9]There will be no retaliation or revenge for wrongs, no sharp verbal thrusts against any who may scold you. But you will be blessing them, for you are called to just such a ministry and will as a result be blessed yourselves.

[10]Let me quote Psalm 34 right here; I will begin with verse 12: "Anyone who desires real life will shun evil speaking and will never stoop to deceit. [11]He will overcome the tendency to sin; he will cultivate every good trait. He will try to live in peace and will actively promote peace in others. [12]For the eyes of the Lord are on the righteous, and His ears are open to hear their prayers, but the Lord finally turns His face away from evildoers."

[13]Who can possibly inflict harm on you if you persist in doing like Jesus did? [14]However, if you are persecuted for doing good, be thankful, do not fear assaults or doubt that eventually good will prevail. [15]Make the Lord God supreme in your hearts, and be prepared at all times to answer those who want to know about your hope, with utmost meekness and gracious speaking. [16]Follow your conscience closely, for even if they accuse you as being wicked, your accusers may be shown to be utterly mistaken. [17]Actually, it is much better to suffer for doing right than for doing wrong. God may permit such things at times.

[18]Keep in mind that Christ suffered for sins that were not His so that He could bring us to God. He allowed Himself to be put to death but was raised from death by the Holy Spirit of God. [19]It was by the Spirit of God in His preaching that gave Him so much power to release those who were bound by Satan. [20]Back in the time of Noah, God demonstrated His patience in dealing with disobedient spirits for all those years while the ark was under construction. After attempting that long to save them, He finally was only able to persuade eight to believe and be saved from the water. [21]But now, water in the rite of baptism symbolizes salvation, not just physical cleansing but the cleansing of our consciences, reminding us of the resurrection of Christ. [22]This Christ has now returned to heaven and is reinstated at the position of authority at God's right hand, being the commander-in-chief of all the angelic host.

Chapter 4

[1]Considering how Christ suffered for us, fortify yourselves with His mind, remembering that the one who suffered as He did was totally free from any sin [2]and that He will continue as a human, a sin-free human, in perfect harmony with God's will. [3]In the past we were in dreadful error as were all Gentiles. We were sexually sinful; we had other evil desires—drunkenness, wild parties, overeating, and unbelievable idolatry. [4]Now you are no longer joining with them, and they wonder what happened to you. Also, some are criticizing you because of this change. [5]Eventually these will have to give account to God for their behavior, for He is the one who will judge the living and the dead. [6]As for the dead, they will be judged fairly, even those who never had the gospel preached to them, and the living will be judged in accordance with light received.

[7]The world is coming to an end, so it behooves you to be serious and consistently prayerful. [8]The most important trait of all is to have "agape" love among you, for this love will never expose the sins of others. [9]Be hospitable to one another, and there is no need to begrudge the cost of so doing, for God is able to make it up to you and more.

[10]Every one of you has received a gift of the Spirit, enabling you to be Christ's witnesses, so let that gift operate freely among you. After all, we are indebted to God for the gift, and it is His. We are just stewards. [11]If your gift is preaching, do so as if God Himself were speaking. If your gift is helping others, do so to the best of your ability so that God will be glorified through Jesus Christ who deserves praise and authority forever. Amen!

[12]My beloved Christian brothers and sisters, you may expect fierce trials in this world. It will be all too common, and you won't be alone in being persecuted. [13]Actually, it is a great honor and should bring joy if we are called on to suffer as Christ suffered, for when His glory is revealed, you will be supremely happy beyond any imagination. [14]Especially happy will be those whose only crime is being a Christian, for during the trial of your faith, God's glory will rest on you. Your persecutors may revile Him, but you will glorify Him. [15]See to it that no follower of Jesus is convicted of murder, thievery, or other wickedness. Never be willing to poke your nose into another's business. [16]But if you are called to suffer for being a Christian, this is nothing to be embarrassed about. Rather thank God for the privilege. [17]Eventually the judgment will come, and it will begin with those who claim to follow God. Later it will end when the fate of those who reject God has been decided. [18]And if in the judgment the righteous are barely saved, what chance do the ungodly and open sinners have? [19]So if you find yourself persecuted for being a Christian, commit your case to God, determining to do the right thing regardless of the outcome.

Chapter 5

[1]Now you local elders, I entreat you earnestly (remember that I too am an elder) as one who was an eyewitness to the sufferings of Christ and as one who eagerly looks forward to the sharing of future glory with Him to [2]continue to give spiritual nourishment to your flocks, for this is your responsibility, not because you are compelled, but because of your free choice, and certainly not for money. [3]You most assuredly are not rulers over God's people but only role models. [4]One day when the Chief Shepherd appears, you will be given a crown of life in the glory land, a crown that will never lose its splendor.

[5]As for you younger ones, accept the leadership of your elders. Yes, all of you should consider yourselves to be subjects of the others, humbly helping them, for God hates pride but gives grace to those who are humble. [6]So humble yourselves under God's mighty hand, and then He will be able some day to exalt you. [7]When you are burdened with cares and perplexities, always give them to Jesus, for He is concerned about you and will bring solutions to your problems.

[8]And don't forget this: Your enemy the devil is stalking you constantly, ready to devour you, so be vigilant and aware of his devices. [9]He should be resolutely repulsed

continually by all who are in the faith, for throughout the whole world we can expect to have trials. [10]But God, who has an infinite supply of grace, the God who has called us to share His glory through Jesus Christ, after suffering is forever ended, He is able to and will finish the job of completing His work in you. He will solidify, strengthen, and settle you into His truth. [11]To Him belongs all glory and dominion forever and ever. Amen!

[12]This letter is being sent by Silas, a faithful brother. I may have written briefly, too, trying to teach, exhort, and strengthen you in the grace of God where you now find yourselves. [13]The entire church at Rome sends greetings, as does my son Mark. [14]Greet each other with a kiss of love, and may peace be with you all who are in Christ Jesus. Amen.

2 Peter

Chapter 1

¹From Simon Peter, a slave and apostle of Jesus Christ, to you who have come to share the faith that we possess through the utter goodness of God and our Savior Jesus Christ. ²May grace and peace be multiplied to you through the knowledge of God and Jesus Christ our Lord ³through whom divine power has given us every possible thing needed for eternal life and for godly living in this world. This blessed gift is the knowledge of Himself, who has called us to accept virtue and eternal glory. ⁴Furthermore, it is this gift that contains so many incredible, valuable promises that instill in us the very nature of God, after having rescued us from the corruption in the world, corruption expressed in all kinds of selfish desires.

⁵But even with all this we must be diligent, constantly adding these following graces to our characters: faith, purity, knowledge, self-control, ⁶patience, godliness, ⁷more and more real kindness, and "agape" love. ⁸These characteristics, if found in abundance in our lives, will bring about not only activity but real tangible results in the proclamation to the world the knowledge of Jesus Christ. ⁹On the other hand, if these qualities are not found, blindness or at least myopia is the result, and one forgets that he is a sinner cleansed from his past sins. ¹⁰Let us not be among this class, but be in dead earnest in searching our souls to discover our real needs. If you do this you will never fall. ¹¹You will be welcomed into the eternal kingdom of God and His son Jesus Christ.

¹²Let this letter be a reminder that I want you to regard present truth to be the most important knowledge on earth. I am aware that you know these things already, ¹³but as long as I live it will always be appropriate for me to nudge your memory. ¹⁴Knowing that my life is precarious at best and that probably soon I will no longer be able to communicate with you, you may not be aware of it but the Lord Jesus Christ prophesied my death. ¹⁵So it will be important to have these things in permanent written form as a continual reminder, even though I may not be able to go on with my mission.

¹⁶You see, we have not been fabricating fancy stories when we told you about the coming of our Lord Jesus Christ, but were eyewitnesses of His majesty. ¹⁷We actually saw Him honored, covered with splendor from God the Father when that voice was heard from the glory of that cloud saying, "This is My beloved Son in whom I am well pleased." ¹⁸Our ears heard (there were

three of us as witnesses) that mighty voice from heaven while we were with Him on the mountain that night. [19]But even more persuasive than our personal testimony is the prophetic word contained in scripture, prophecies that you need to listen to and to heed, for those prophecies are like a brilliant light suddenly illuminating a dark place, getting more brilliant as time passes, finally reaching the brightness of the morning sun. [20]Most important is the fact that all prophecy is so plain that it does not need some wise professor to interpret it for you. [21]For it was given centuries ago by the power of God moving on the minds of holy prophets, and not by some so-called seer. No, the Holy Spirit was the source of their inspiration.

Chapter 2

[1]It is sad to say but there were false prophets then as there are now. Beware of them. They will bring in heresies, denying that Jesus came and purchased them. Their teachings will result in certain destruction. [2]Yet however great their errors, there will be many who will follow them in their evil ways, and because of them God's truth will be ridiculed. [3]The motivation for these movements is covetousness, for by manipulation of you believers, through deception, they will reap temporal prosperity. The eventual decision by our divine Judge, although deferred so long, will be given and the verdict will be condemnation.

[4]Think of it this way. If God could not save those heavenly angels who rebelled but had to consign them to this world where they must remain until the verdict has been recognized as just and right by the whole universe; [5]and if God could not persuade the antediluvians to be obedient through those one hundred twenty years of Noah's preaching truth, finally permitting them to be destroyed in the flood; [6]and if God had to reduce the cities of Sodom and Gomorrah to ashes, destroying everyone there, showing clearly to all generations who would live later His hatred for their vile wickedness, [7]saving only Lot, a man who was constantly offended by their filthy lifestyle [8]as they insulted him visibly and audibly while he lived among them; [9]and let me repeat, if God must deal with sinful rebellion, yet is able to rescue the godly from temptation while He defers the final judgment of the wicked until all can see His justice and goodness in annihilating rebellion, then be assured that He is able to deliver you.

[10]God is especially against those who live for the lusts of the flesh, those who hate to have anyone tell them what to do and what not to do. They presume to believe that they are a law unto themselves and don't hesitate to criticize anyone in authority. [11]Angels who are vastly superior beings do not dare bring accusations before God. [12]But these rebels, very little better than beasts who live only to be slaughtered, will loudly criticize and condemn things that they know little about; their fate will be to perish with the corruption they have chosen. [13]This then is the final reward of unrighteousness, just as those who incite bold riots will perish. They piously attend your meetings, pretending to be Christians, but are far from God's ideal of spotless unblemished characters—here is what they actually are.

[14]Adultery is a constant goal, and sin is a persistent habit pattern. They not only live sinful lives but influence weaker persons to fall into the same sins. They have

practiced covetousness religiously and they have subjected children to verbal curses. [15]They are in apostasy in the pattern of Balaam the son of Beor who was willing to defy God himself in order to gain wealth and honor promised him. [16]You will recall that he was soundly rebuked by the angel after the donkey spoke to him, trying to get his attention and persuade him to turn from his stupid, rebellious mission.

[17]These people are like a promising well in a dry country, but there is no water in it. They are like clouds that are blown around by a storm without a mind of their own and with their fate fixed; darkness and oblivion. [18]Their manner is to speak great alluring speeches, pander to immoral desires, and if possible recapture for Satan those who had given their lives to God. [19]These poor victims have been promised complete freedom by people who themselves are enslaved by corruption. As you know, if you are conquered by an enemy you become his slave. [20]And if a person who has at one time been a Christian, freed from the corruption of the world through our Lord Jesus Christ, slips back into his former life, he is in worse condition than when he was ignorant of Christ. [21]Yes, it is better to have never known the right way than to have known it and then turned from it. [22]This situation is exactly as is described in Proverbs 26:11, "The dog goes back and eats his own vomit; the sow who has just been washed, heads for the nearest mud puddle."

Chapter 3

[1]The purpose of this second letter, dear people, is to get you thinking seriously, reminding you [2]of the words of holy prophets of old as well as our teachings as apostles of our Lord and Savior. [3]First, be aware that in the last days of the world there will be plenty of those who will ridicule the very idea of Christianity. Most of these are chiefly concerned about their own desires. [4]Here is the approach they will use: "Where do you see any evidence of this so-called 'second coming,' for history keeps going on just as it always has while the earth has evolved?" [5]You see, they don't want to accept the evidence we have about creation and the fitting up of this planet to be a place where human beings can live. They will not believe the story about the great flood [6]even though the evidence for a universal flood is abundant.

[7]God is still in command and is still controlling the planet on which we live, keeping everything in order, just preparing for the final annihilation of everything sinful. This will be done by fire and will be permanent. [8]But please be aware that with God a thousand years may be represented as just a day, or conversely, one day is like a thousand years. [9]You see, when God makes a promise, He keeps His promise and keeps it on time. He is not like us humans, and yet it might appear that He delays these promises because He wants everyone to be saved and thus exhibits ultimate compassion and patience with us.

[10]The day of the Lord will come, and it will be on time, but it will come as a thief and surprise everyone. When it arrives, the sky will seem to be on fire while the elements from which the earth is made will melt with extreme heat. Every human structure will be destroyed. [11]Now think seriously about your future in view of this scenario. Godliness is what we need. [12]Let us continue to expect, work for, pray for, and hasten that day. Even with the fire we

shall be safe if we are on God's side. [13]For He has given us a solemn promise of new heavens and a new earth where everything will be done right.

[14]So, dear people, knowing that you anticipate this day with eager longing, never fail to be diligent in your decision to be at peace with God, victorious over every temptation by His strength. [15]You understand, I am sure, that God's longsuffering is centered in His salvation. Things are just as our beloved brother Paul has described in all of his letters, having been given wisdom from God. [16]He has written many of you, accurately explaining matters. Yes, I realize that in some of his messages there are concepts rather deep and hard to grasp. But this should not be an excuse to twist and distort his clear explanations. Whoever does so is threatening their own salvation, just as they do when they distort other passages of scripture.

[17]Now that you are well informed don't feel "holier than thou" and lose your way because of pride. This is an ever-present danger, even for Christians, as it is with rebels against God. [18]Here is what is needed: Continually grow in grace and in the knowledge of Christ. Let us give glory to Him for He deserves it now and will continue to deserve our adoration throughout eternity.

1 John

Chapter 1

[1]In this letter I want to share with you some eternal truths that were demonstrated so forcefully in the life and ministry of Him who is rightly called, "the Word of life." He is eternal, and we apostles have seen Him with our own eyes. We have touched Him. [2]Let me put it another way. The Father is eternal. His life was shown to us, and we want to tell everyone about Him. [3]For what purpose do we share these marvelous things? Simply this: That you too may have the blessing of companionship with us, with the Father, and with His Son Jesus Christ. [4]We want you to share in the joy that we have, the true joy, the unutterable joy that comes when one knows Christ.

[5]We have received from Him this joyful message and are now sharing it with you, that God is a God of light and joy. In Him is no darkness whatsoever. [6]Anyone who claims to be a friend of Christ but continues to walk in darkness and gloom is bearing a false witness. [7]But if we walk in light coming from Him, we shall have fellowship with His followers also, and the blood of Christ will cleanse us from sin and continue to do so. [8]Face it. We are sinners. Let's not deceive ourselves by claiming to be otherwise. I am telling you solemn truth. [9]Yet if we confess our sins, He is dependable and will forgive our sins, and not only will He forgive us, but He will clean us up so that we can resist sin. [10]We have it on good authority that we are sinners. He has not lied about this. So let's believe it.

Chapter 2

[1]But listen. Although we are sinners by nature, I appeal to you, claim victory over sin. If we sin there is a person who will represent us at God's throne. He is on our side. He is Jesus Christ the only righteous person who has ever lived. [2]He is the atonement for our sins and for the sins of all who live on this world. [3]Here is how you can tell if you know Him. You will be keeping His commandments. [4]If a person says, "Oh, yes, I know Jesus," but refuses to keep His commandments, he isn't telling the truth. [5]And if a person obeys God's word, God's love has indeed done its work in that life. And now here is the way to know whether or not a person is in Christ. [6]One who is in Christ will be living the same sort of life that Christ lived. It's that simple.

[7]My dear brothers and sisters, as you can easily see I am not giving you any new orders, only the very same that you have had from the first—the very same instructions that are so very familiar to you already.

[8]But in a way it is new, for darkness has ended and light glows everywhere. [9]Here is something to think about: Anyone who claims to have light but still hates a brother is still in darkness. [10]A person who has the true "agape" love for his brother will always be in the light and will not stumble or fall. [11]But if a person hates his brother, darkness surrounds him, and he cannot see where he is headed. It is that serious.

[12]Children, I am writing this to you in order to remind you that your sins are forgiven for Christ's sake. [13]I am writing to you fathers because you have known Christ for many years. And you young men, I include you, for you have defeated our wicked adversary. Young children, young like you are, have learned to know our heavenly Father. [14]You fathers, I remind you again that you have known Him for many years, and you young men have demonstrated strength of character, and God's word is cherished continually in your very beings. [15]All of you, do not become attached to this world or any material things, for if you do your love for God will diminish. [16]The plain truth is that nothing in this world that we might desire, physical desires, beauty of all kinds, and our satisfaction in such things, not one of them, is necessary for our salvation. [17]Everything worldly will be annihilated in the end, and we will then realize the truth of what I am saying. Only those who choose God's will can be trusted with eternal life.

[18]My dear children, the present is vital, for you may have no further chance. Jesus may return or your lives may end, so right now be aware that anything usurping the place of Christ in your life—let's call it the "antichrist." There are many "antichrists," and this is another reason to recognize when we are in the time of the end. [19]Many who were with us in the faith have left for one or more antichrists, thus demonstrating that the love of Christ was not uppermost in their lives. Had Christ been uppermost they would have remained with us. [20]But you have been anointed by the Holy Spirit and know all about such things already.

[21]I am not telling you these things just to inform you but to encourage you in the truth that you already know and to help you avoid falsehoods. [22]The greatest lie of all is the denial that Jesus is the Messiah. This is the greatest antichrist, for he is opposed to both Father and Son. [23]All who deny the Son in actuality deny the Father also. Remember when He said, [24]"He who has seen Me has seen My Father." So let the truth that you heard in the beginning remain firm in you minds. Stay with the Father and with the Son. [25]It will be vastly more than just worthwhile, for His promise is that it means *eternal life*.

[26]Let my letter be a shield against the deceptions that surround you, some of which may originate in those who may be close or dear to you. [27]As of now the spiritual anointing given to you by Jesus continues to transform you and to produce growth, so right now you don't need to be taught by me or by others, and yet you need to continue in Christ and to keep on learning from Him. [28]So my children stay in Him. As you do this His return will be anticipated with confidence and great joy. [29]He is altogether righteous, and those who are righteous have had this born-again experience.

Chapter 3

[1]Now I want to challenge your thinking. Look at what God has done in showering

us with His love. His love has enveloped us, encircling us and making us children of God. But because we are God's children, the world cannot understand us, just as it could not understand Jesus. ²Yes, we are God's children and have only a poor conception of what this will eventually mean to us. But we know that when He returns, we shall resemble Him closely in our pure characters. We shall be at ease in His presence. ³Everyone who has this wonderful hope is committed to surrendering their sinful natures to Him so that He can transform us into His perfection. ⁴All are sinners and lawbreakers by nature for that is exactly what sin is: lawlessness.

⁵Now you are at a great advantage, for you know that Jesus came to this earth to obliterate our sins. He Himself was sinless. ⁶If you or anyone else is in Christ, you will conquer sin through Him. A person who continues sinning does not know Him or see Him. ⁷A person who is righteous does the right things, just as Jesus did. ⁸A person who continues in sin is associated with the devil. It was for just this sort of person that Jesus came here. He was accomplishing His purpose when He came to destroy the work of the devil, and the devil was the first sinner.

⁹But what can we do to conquer sin? A sinner who experiences the new birth receives power to resist and overcome sin. That power is a gift from his Creator when he receives Christ. ¹⁰And this is an accurate way to know who are God's children and who are the devil's. If a person is not doing the right things, he is not God's, for a righteous person will love his brothers and sisters. ¹¹Jesus Himself told us this: "I give you a new commandment to love your fellow humans." ¹²We have the dreadful example of Cain, the first person to have hated then killed; his victim was his own younger brother. He was a child of the devil, and his actions prove it. The only explanation for such an atrocity is that his brother was righteous while he was evil. ¹³When we think about Cain and Abel, we are aware of the fact that we Christians can be expected to anger some people in this world and for the same reason.

¹⁴So how can we know when we have been born again? Try this for an answer— when we have shown true "agape" love such as God demonstrated. If we do not have that we may as well consider ourselves to be on death row. ¹⁵Make no mistake about it. If a person hates a brother, he is a murderer. And we know that no murderer will have everlasting life; nothing could be more plain. ¹⁶Just as we are made aware of God's love by His willingness to die for us, we should be willing to die for another.

¹⁷Now think of a wealthy person. He has plenty of property, money, luxurious home, comforts of life, food, clothing, and whatever the human heart might desire. But if he sees a fellow human in want— needing food, shelter, warmth—and does nothing to help that man, can you believe for a moment that God's love is in him? ¹⁸Dear children, let us love others. Love enough to do something about it, not just to mouth the words. ¹⁹It is this very quality that will show how thoroughly God's truth has captured us, how real our faith is.

²⁰Let the conscience convict us of our true condition, for God is greater than our weakness and is able to bring about the needed change. ²¹If the conscience is clear, we are in right relationship with God. ²²This person is entitled to ask God for any of the promised blessings, with full

assurance that it will be given. ²³These two commandments come to mind: "believe in the Lord Jesus Christ" and "love one another as I have loved you." ²⁴If we keep these commandments, we shall live in Christ and He will live in us. Others can tell whether or not Christ in us by the spirit that directs us.

Chapter 4

¹My dear brothers and sisters, we need to be on guard against false spirits, for there are plenty of them, and they must be tested carefully. ²Here is how to identify the Spirit of God: If one preaches and teaches that Jesus came as a human being, he is teaching God's message. ³Every spirit that tries to tell you that Jesus just appeared to be human is not telling God's message but is teaching the message of the antichrist who is already in the world. ⁴Dear children, you have already won the battle with these false prophets. What is the secret of victory? Only by the power of God can you overcome—He is in you and is greater than any worldly influence. ⁵These false prophets are interested chiefly in the world; therefore, they speak things of interest to the world, and the world loves what they say. ⁶But we Christians belong to God, and anyone who knows God will listen to us. Conversely, those who don't know God will reject us. This is another way by which we can differentiate between truth and error.

⁷Dear people, let us love each other, for love is from God, and everyone who loves with "agape" love has experienced the new birth and really knows God. ⁸A person who has no "agape" love does not know God, for God is the essence of "agape" love. ⁹How do we know that God loves us? Just this, He sent His only Son to this world to bring life to us, for we had lost our right to life. ¹⁰Yes, here is real "agape" love, not that we loved God but that He loved us and sent His Son to atone for our sins. ¹¹So if God demonstrated that much love for us, we should show the same love to others. ¹²Of course, no human being has seen God. But nevertheless, if we love each other with Godlike love, we shall be able to see what God can do as He dwells in us. He will transform us so that we will be like Him. ¹³If God has truly captured us as He wants to do, it will be evident by our lifestyle and by the spirit we exhibit toward others.

¹⁴Another evidence that God dwells in us is that we will be witnesses that God has sent His Son into the world to be our Savior. ¹⁵Those who testify to this truth show that God dwells in them and they in God. ¹⁶We apostles and Christians have believed in God's love for us. Let me repeat. God is love, and everyone who is dominated by Godlike love can be said to be "in God" and that God is in him. ¹⁷And it is only "in Him" that our love is truly complete, for this love is of the same order as God's love. Now if we have this measure of love, we can be confident on judgment day that we will have the same status as Jesus has.

¹⁸Once we have Godlike love, we shall be free from all kinds of fear, because love drives out fear. Fear produces torture in one's soul, so if a person is fearful of the judgment, it is because he has not yet really had Godlike love. ¹⁹This love is ours because He first loved us. ²⁰Beware of the person who says, "I love God," but hates a brother. He cannot love God while hating a brother. Love requires a close relationship, and loving God is dependent on this

relationship, just as loving another person requires a close relationship such as touching, seeing, hearing, and talking to that person. ²¹Christ's command to love includes loving God and loving others.

Chapter 5

¹Everyone who believes that Jesus is the Messiah has been born again, and everyone who loves the Father loves His Son also. ²Now let me tell you how you can be certain to love God's children. Your love is enough to obey God's commandments. ³Keeping His commandments is loving, and His commandments are not in the least painful. ⁴The new birth experience gives us overcoming power so that each and every worldly influence can be resisted; our Christian faith is that strong. ⁵Can you think of anyone on earth who has the power to be an overcomer except those who believe that Jesus is the Son of God? ⁶He came to us by baptism (water) and through human substance (blood), and it is obvious that I am referring to Jesus Christ and the Holy Spirit who give more evidence of this fact.

⁷In heaven there are three witnesses—the Spirit, the Father, and the Word (Jesus)—and they all testify to the same thing. ⁸And on earth there are three witnesses—the Spirit, the water, and the blood—and these three testify alike. ⁹If we are willing to accept the testimony of human beings, we surely ought to be willing to accept the testimony of God who is so much greater, and right here let me give you what God testifies regarding His Son: ¹⁰"A person who believes in the Son of God can testify to His own experience." If one does not believe in God, it is equivalent to saying God is a liar; one is really saying that God cannot be trusted when he tells us of His Son. ¹¹And he tells us this: "We have been given eternal life, and this life is received by receiving His Son who is life."

¹²If you have Jesus, the Son of God, you have eternal life. Without Jesus you have no life. ¹³I have written to you who believe in Christ to assure you that you are already in possession of eternal life and to encourage you in your faith that Jesus Christ is indeed the Son of God. ¹⁴Here now is the confidence we may have in Him. Of all things that He has promised, we may merely ask and we know that He hears our prayers. ¹⁵And then we can thank Him for giving us what we have requested. ¹⁶For instance, if one of us sees a brother fall into some temptation that is not defiant rebellion, a sin which is forgivable, he may ask for forgiveness and restoration to God's favor, for that brother and that petition will be granted. Yes, I know that there is a sin that is unpardonable, just as Jesus explained—the rejection of the Holy Spirit. I do not claim that this sin can be forgiven.

¹⁷Everything that is unrighteous is sin, but there are sins that can be forgiven, ¹⁸of this we may be confident. A born-again Christian is not continuing in sin but is continually on guard against Satan so that he cannot be led into sin by temptation. ¹⁹Another thing of which we may be certain: We are on God's side in a world that is almost entirely wicked. ²⁰And most important of all, we know that the Son of God has come and has given us understanding in matters of eternal life and that this involves being "in Him" who is truth and that this person is Jesus Christ in whom is eternal life. ²¹Dear ones, be constantly on guard against idolatry. Amen.

2 John

¹From Elder John ²to a special chosen lady. My dear madam and family, let me first tell you how much I love all of you who are "in the truth." I am certainly not the only one who holds you in such high regard, for all of us who have accepted the truth of God feel the same way. Truth has a way of getting into us and becoming such a part of us that we will never separate from it. ³May God's grace be with you. May His mercy and His peace envelope you, sent as it is from the Father and from His Son Jesus Christ because of His love and in perfect harmony with truth.

⁴You can scarcely believe the joy I felt when I learned that your children are walking with Jesus just as He walked with His father and was obedient to him. ⁵You won't feel that I am being "preachy" or demanding will you when I urge you, my dear woman, to cultivate continual love to one another, as we have been told to do by none other than Jesus Himself. ⁶For He is the one who said, "Love is keeping God's commandments." Of course you already know this and have known it ever since you became a Christian. ⁷Let us all be on guard against the many deceivers in this world. These people may properly be included in the term "antichrist," for they deny that Jesus Christ was a real flesh-and-blood person.

⁸It behooves you to carefully examine yourselves, to realistically take inventory of your spirituality on a regular basis so that you will never lose this close relationship with Jesus. It is through this relationship that the great reward will come. ⁹Anyone who abandons the teachings that Christ gave us can be accurately described as one who is contrary to God's will, but those who continue in those teachings has both the Father and the Son. ¹⁰Doctrines then are important, whatever you may hear to the contrary, so have nothing to do with people who teach otherwise. Do not shelter them when they are in your vicinity or bid them Godspeed when they leave. ¹¹You would be in the same error if you encouraged them in this wickedness. ¹²There are many things that I would like to write about but shall not do at present, hoping to see you face to face in the near future; then I shall share them. ¹³The children of your sister send their warm greetings to you. Amen.

3 John

¹From John the elder to my beloved friend Gaius, a pillar of truth. ²My first and most important prayer for you is that your health and prosperity will be equal to your spiritual growth. ³Oh how happy I felt when I was visited by some of your fellow believers who assured me that you are loyal and effective in your Christian life, "walking in the truth" as we put it. ⁴In fact, there is no joy that can compare with the joy which comes when I learn that my children are "walking in the truth."

⁵My dear brother, I am convinced that your life is a faithful witness in your home, your church, and in the world. ⁶Yes, even unbelievers are persuaded that you are a loving, caring person and have commended you for this in the presence of your church members. These will continue to be blessed as you lead them along the way, and you yourself will have the assurance that you are doing the right thing ⁷as you encourage them to proclaim the name of Jesus in your community of Gentiles, asking nothing from them in return. ⁸We Christians are obliged to receive these dear people, for they need all the help they can get, and we have just the help they need most.

⁹I was deeply disappointed after I wrote a letter to the church to learn that Diotrephes has turned against us and has been trying to take over the leadership there. ¹⁰If at all possible, I will come. If I do, his actions will be remembered, especially his malicious, hateful, words, his aloofness, and his highhanded attitude, even disfellowshipping some believers with no other authority than his own decision.

¹¹Dear brother, please do not fall into such wickedness, but be diligent in doing good. Those who actually do good are God's children, but evildoers most surely have not caught the vision of God's plan. ¹²Demetrius has a good reputation among everyone in the area, including the church members, and we too want to commend him and testify that he is doing a good work, for that is indeed the truth. ¹³I had planned to write much more, but I must wait until later or better still, ¹⁴I plan to visit you soon so that we can have a face-to-face meeting. May peace be with you. Our mutual friends greet you. Please greet all my friends for me.

Jude

¹From Jude, the slave of Jesus Christ and brother of James. To all who are set apart by God and have remained faithful to His cause through Jesus Christ, to all who have been called. ²May God's mercies, His peace, and His love increase rapidly. ³My goal in writing to you can be briefly stated, to remind you of the salvation we share and to encourage you as you stand firmly in defense of our faith.

⁴As you probably know, there are a few men who have entered in among us, of which we were unaware at the time (but God knew all about them), ungodly fellows who have so perverted God's grace that it promotes lustful behavior. Moreover, they reject both God the Father and Jesus Christ our Lord. ⁵So I have an urge to remind you of an important fact in our history as a people. This is the truth. Although the Lord rescued His people from Egypt, this did not give them permanent status with God, for they later rebelled and were destroyed. ⁶Another reminder. Even angels who were inhabitants of heaven made a decision to rebel against God and left His presence. They have not died but are on "death row," awaiting execution. ⁷Likewise we have the example of Sodom and Gomorrah and the neighboring villages whose inhabitants freely practiced fornication and homosexuality. What was their fate? Eternal fire. ⁸So now these perverts are among us. They dishonor humanity. They rebel against any authority and speak out boldly against honor, dignity, and glory.

⁹How careful we should be in our evaluation of others, even though they may be utterly wrong. Remember Moses. When Michael, the highest of all archangels, found Himself in conflict with the devil as He was on His mission to resurrect Moses, He refused to upbraid the adversary; instead He referred all such responsibilities to God, saying, "The Lord rebuke you." ¹⁰But we now have these characters among us who are carrying evil reports of others, true or not, they do not care. They have descended to the level of brute beasts, thus defiling themselves. ¹¹Woe to them, for this is just the way Cain acted and is similar to the behavior of Balaam when he arrogantly tried to enrich himself. It also resembles the horrible mistake of Korah while he was in rebellion.

¹²Unfortunately, these very people come to your communion feasts and take part with you unashamedly. They are deceptive, like a cloud that produces no rain, and like a tree with dead fruit on it after having been uprooted. ¹³Or like

the foamy, wind-whipped waves of the sea, demonstrating their destructiveness openly, or like the planets that in their orbits disappear from view out in space at times. [14]Judgment on them was predicted as far back as Enoch, the seventh generation patriarch, when he prophesied the following, "Look, the Lord will return with ten thousands of His saints to execute judgment." [15]This will include all, both the righteous and the wicked, and as for the ungodly, they will be convinced that their ways are wrong in speaking against God. [16]These include complainers and dissatisfied ones who are content to just do their own thing, whose utterances demonstrate their great pride and their favoritism.

[17]So my dear brothers and sisters, keep ever in mind the admonition given by the apostles of our Lord Jesus, [18]where they warned us against scoffers and mockers in the last days who would be intent on only one thing, satisfying their own desires. [19]They constantly consider themselves to be in a better class than others, but they are really only bent on doing what feels good at the time, regardless of the impressions of the Holy Spirit. [20]You, however, should be constantly building up your faith, a faith that is pure and given by God Himself, always in an attitude of prayer and willing to be led by the Holy Spirit. [21]Always stay in God's love, blessed by the mercy of our Lord Jesus Christ who offers eternal life.

[22]Do take pity on those who are wandering, for you know that no two people are alike. [23]Some can be dealt with dramatically, snatching them out of the fire, as it were. But never allow your own garments to be contaminated by "the flesh," the desires we all possess as sinners. [24]Finally, remember that there is one who is able to keep you from falling, able to present you as if you had never sinned, into the glory of God's presence and will be elated as He does so. [25]Let us all recognize Him as the only God, who has infinite wisdom, who is our Savior, who has glory, true majesty, infinite power, now and forever. Amen.

Revelation

Chapter 1

[1]What you are about to read is the account of a remarkable experience that was revealed to me by Jesus Christ and authorized by God the Father. It was given for the purpose of establishing faith in all of His servants who read it or hear it read, for it tells of events yet future, events that will begin in the not distant future. An angel brought it, certified its authenticity, and entrusted it to Christ's servant John. [2]It is John who has written it out, this the words of God Himself and the testimony of Jesus, and it describes everything he saw. [3]It will be a great blessing to everyone who reads it and to all who listen as it is read, then heeds the advice here recorded for the fulfillment will soon begin.

[4]From John to seven churches in the province of Asia. May grace and peace be yours. They will be given by the One who was, who is now, and who always will be, through the agency of the seven spirits who are always at the throne—[5]Jesus Christ the true accurate witness of whom I am writing. He is the preeminent One, raised from the dead, and the Prince over all the kings on earth. It is He, the One who loved us and washed our sins from us in His own blood, [6]who has declared us to be kings and priests for God His Father.

It is to Him that all glory and dominion belongs forever and ever. Amen.

[7]Listen, this Jesus is coming again in a cloud. He will be seen by every person on this earth, not only by the living, but also by a few who will be resurrected to see Him return, and I refer to the soldiers who drove the nails through Him and the one who drove the spear into His side there on the cross. All on our world will cry out when He comes, some with terrible despair, and others with unspeakable joy. So be it.

[8]Here are His words: "I am the Alpha and Omega, the Beginning and the End. I am the One who has always been, the One who now is, and the One who always shall be, the infinite God." [9]Let me now state that I am John, your brother who shares your persecution and trials. I also share the kingdom of Christ and to some extent the patience of Jesus. As you may have heard, I was banished to the island that is called Patmos because of my faith in God's word, in Jesus Christ, and in His testimony.

[10]One Sabbath I was given a vision by the Holy Spirit. In my vision a thundering voice, loud as a trumpet blast, startled me with this message: [11]"I am Alpha and Omega, the First and the Last. What I am about to tell you must be written

down for the benefit of the seven churches in Asia. They will then share it with the other churches everywhere. Begin with Ephesus, then these to follow: Smyrna, Pergamos, Thyatira, Sardis, Philadelphia, and Laodicea."

¹²I turned around to see who it was with such a message, and the first thing that appeared was a seven-branched golden candlestick like the one in the temple. ¹³Then, moving about among the candles was a person like the Son of man. He wore a long beautiful robe reaching to His feet and a gold colored garment around His torso. ¹⁴His head and hair were dazzling white, and His eyes glowed like fire. ¹⁵His feet were visible and reminded me of polished brass, or brass melting in a crucible. His voice was soothing like the sound of running water. ¹⁶He carried in his right hand seven stars. His mouth was odd to say the least. Out from it came a razor-sharp two-edged sword. The whole impression of His face was that of a midday sun, too bright to look at.

¹⁷In my vision I fell at His feet ready to die there, but He gently reached down and touched me, saying, "Don't be afraid, I am the first and the last, ¹⁸I am the One who is alive but had been dead, and now I shall live forever, can you hear Me? *Forever!* I have the keys to the grave and death. ¹⁹Now I want you to begin at once to write out the things that you shall see, some of which are yet in the future. ²⁰Let me explain the symbols of the seven stars in My hand and the seven candlesticks. The stars are the messengers, angels, sent one each to the seven churches. The seven candlesticks are the seven churches I named for you."

Chapter 2

¹"Write this message to the angel of the Ephesus church: 'Listen, and heed the words from the one who holds the seven stars in His right hand and walks among the seven candlesticks. ²I am aware of your actions, your toil, your endurance, and that you can't stand wicked people. You have tested those who claim to be apostles and have discovered that they were liars. ³You have carried heavy loads, you have been patient, and you have worked for my cause untiringly. ⁴Now a negative item: I am not fully content with you for how your first love has been waning. ⁵Try once more to remember your experience when you first became Christians. Relive that time and live as you did then, or I will have to come and remove your candlestick. Please repent. ⁶You and I have one thing in common, we both hate the behavior of the Nicolaitans. ⁷Let everyone with ears listen to this message, a message from the Holy Spirit to the churches. The one who overcomes, who defeats selfishness, will be given fruit from the tree of life, the tree in God's paradise.'

⁸"Next a message for the Smyrna church leader: 'The one who is the First and the Last, who was dead and is now alive, has this message for you. ⁹I know all about you, your persecutions, and your poverty (but you should consider yourself wealthy). I know about the deception that has been perpetrated against you; people stoutly claiming to be Jesus when they can rightly be described as in Satan's camp. ¹⁰Never fear even though you may go through difficult times. The devil may see to it that some of you will be imprisoned, and your tribulation will last ten days, but if you are faithful through it all, even to the

loss of your lives, you will be given eternal life as a crowning gift. ¹¹If you have ears, listen and take heed to the message of the Holy Spirit. Whoever is triumphant will not die the second death.'

¹²"And now a message for the leader of the Pergamos church: 'The one whom you saw with the sharp sword speaks. ¹³I am aware of your deeds; I know where you live, right at Satan's headquarters. I commend you for upholding My name, for your steadfast faith, even when My steadfast believer Antipas was martyred in your city because of his faith. ¹⁴I must tell you also that some problems exist in Pergamos. You have in your church some members who are following that ancient prophet Balaam who advised Balak to trip the children of Israel by leading them into fornication and idolatry. ¹⁵Furthermore, there are in Pergamos some members who are astray, believing and teaching the very same as the Nicolaitans, teachings that are false and which I hate. ¹⁶This is what you in Pergamos must do: Repent and turn from these evils at once, or I will have to come and fight the evildoers with My sword. (Remember the sword that you saw coming out of My mouth?) ¹⁷If you have ears that hear, heed this message from the Holy Spirit. Those who triumph will receive from Me a plentiful supply of manna, and in addition, I will write a new, meaningful name on a white gemstone and give it to each one personally.'

¹⁸"My next message is to the leader of the church at Thyatira: 'I am the one with the eyes like fire and the feet like polished brass. ¹⁹I am fully acquainted with everything you do, with your unselfish love, your willingness to serve others, your faith, and your increasingly significant works.

²⁰But let me point out a few things that need to be changed, things in which you are in error. You are allowing that wicked woman Jezebel to come into your church, telling everyone that she is a prophetess, then influencing them to commit adultery and to engage in idolatry. ²¹I urged her to repent, but she flatly refused. ²²Here is what I shall do: I will dump her and her lovers into a bed of troubles unless they are willing to repent. ²³I also will kill her children. Then all the churches will know that I am the one who reads minds and am able to read your inmost thoughts and will treat you as your actions deserve. ²⁴You and the other members of the Thyatira church who have never followed these abominable teachings from Satan will not be given any more burdens. ²⁵So cling in faith to your confidence until I return. ²⁶Whoever wins out in the struggle, doing right as I have done, shall one day have authority over nations. ²⁷He shall have them in complete subjection, with power to shatter them into pieces, just as I received such power from My Father. ²⁸Then I will give him the morning star. ²⁹Whoever can hear must now take heed to what the Holy Spirit is saying to the churches.'"

Chapter 3
¹"The next message is for the church leader at Sardis: 'The One who gives orders to the Holy Spirit and to all the stars sends you this message: I know enough about you to recognize that you are essentially dead even though your name might indicate life. ²You must become more alert. You must cultivate the good qualities that you still possess, for some of these are ready to die. Your behavior has been anything but upright in God's sight. ³Remember that

you have received every needed blessing. Never let them be forgotten, but repent. If you fail to be watchful, you will miss Me, for I will come unexpectedly. ⁴You should be thankful that there are still in Sardis some who have not wandered from God. These shall one day walk with Me, clothed in beautiful white garments. Yes, they are that near to my ideal for them. ⁵Encourage them to believe that only those who are conquerors will be dressed in perfectly white garments and will be assured that their names will be permanently recorded in the book of life, and that their names will be recommended by Me in the judgment, where angels will be listening and where God the Father makes the final favorable decision. ⁶Here, also, tell the church leader that everyone who can hear must heed the message from the Holy Spirit.'

⁷"Next a message to the church leader of the church of Philadelphia: 'Here is instruction from One who is holy, true, and has David's key, the One who has authority to open and shut doors, regardless of human wishes. ⁸I know all of your behavior intimately. You cannot deceive Me. I have opened a door for you that no human being can close. You are fundamentally weak, but you have obeyed Me and have faithfully proclaimed My name. ⁹Look, here is what I promise: I will someday compel those who worship Satan while claiming to be Jews to worship at your feet and to admit that I have loved you. ¹⁰You have taken my word seriously; you have exhibited patience through trials; therefore, I promise to keep you in times when trials will put everyone on earth to the test. ¹¹Remember, I will come unexpectedly, so never yield your faith, for should that happen someone else will take your crown.

¹²Those who are overcomers will become pillars in My Father's temple and will forever be with God, having God's name and His address—the New Jerusalem, the city coming down from heaven to earth—plus, My own new name. ¹³If you can hear, listen and heed these words.'

¹⁴"And finally a message for the leader of the church at Laodicea: 'It is directly from the Amen, the Faithful and True Witness who can be trusted to tell the truth, the whole truth, and nothing but the truth, the One who created the whole universe. ¹⁵I am fully aware of your attitude. You are neither cold nor hot. It would be better for you if you were cold or hot ¹⁶rather than lukewarm as you are, for you are nauseating and about to be vomited out of my mouth. ¹⁷You keep boasting of your great wealth, thinking that you lack nothing, when the facts are quite the opposite. You are unaware of your true condition: poverty, wretchedness, misery, blindness, and nakedness. ¹⁸Here is My advice: Waste no time but go at once and buy some purified gold so that you will be truly rich, some white garments so that you may be adequately clothed and unashamed, then some eye ointment to cure your blindness. ¹⁹Please realize that if I sound harsh it is because I love you and I know that this is your only hope. Be serious, my dear people, and repent. ²⁰Look, I am standing at your door, knocking for admittance. Anyone who opens the door will have the privilege of sharing a meal with Me. ²¹The overcomer will be given the privilege to sit with Me on My throne, just as I triumphed and have been seated next to My Father on His throne. ²²If you have ears listen to what the Holy Spirit is telling the churches.'"

Chapter 4

[1]After the messages to the church leaders were completed, I looked up, and there in heaven was a door swinging open. As it slowly turned, I heard a voice speaking to me in tones like the blasting of a trumpet: "Come up here, and I will show you some things that are yet future." [2]I was in a vision at once and saw a throne in heaven. On this throne was One with authority and power. [3]His color was that of jasper, and another stone with a red hue. Around the throne was a gorgeous rainbow with a beautiful emerald band in it. [4]Beyond the rainbow and encircling the throne were twenty-four seats occupied by twenty-four elders, all dressed in perfect white and wearing golden crowns. [5]The throne flashed with lightning, thunders, and loud voices, and in front of it were seven burning flames that represent the complete Spirits of God.

[6]In the foreground was a lake of crystal-clear glass that seemed to blend into the throne itself. In addition to the seated elders were four living beings that had eyes everywhere. [7]The first resembled a lion, the second a calf, the third had an almost human face, and the fourth reminded me of a flying eagle. [8]Each of these odd creatures had six wings, had many eyes, and was continually worshipping God: "Holy, Holy, Holy, Omnipotent God who has always been and who always shall be." [9]When those beings recognize and worship the Eternal One who is on the throne [10]the twenty-four elders do the same, falling prostrate at His feet, then laying their crowns before Him as they sing these words: "You, Lord, are worthy to receive our worship, our honor, as well as our best efforts, for You have created the universe and everything in it. Only You could have done this, and it was through Your choice that creation took place and that Your creation continues to exist."

Chapter 5

[1]Next my attention was called to the throne and to the One who occupied it. In His right hand He held a scroll that was filled with writing on both sides, but it was sealed with seven seals. [2]Nearby I saw a mighty angel who began loudly asking, "Who is able to remove these seals and open the scroll?" [3]Not one person claimed to have that right or authority. No one in heaven, on earth, or anywhere else would venture to try or even to examine the scroll. [4]I was in despair and sobbed bitterly because no one could break those seals, read the book, or even to examine it.

[5]While I was thus weeping, one of the twenty-four elders said quietly to me, "Don't despair, stop crying, for there is One who has the authority to break the seals and open the scroll. You ask who this might be. It is none other than the Lion of the tribe of Judah, the descendant of David." [6]Then to my surprise, not a lion but a Lamb appeared among the elders and the four living creatures. It was a Lamb who had been killed but now was alive again and was equipped with seven horns and seven eyes, which I recognized as the seven Spirits of God in the world. [7]This awesome, odd-looking Lamb came up to the throne and took the scroll out of the hand of the One on the throne. [8]Just as He took the scroll, the four living creatures and the twenty-four elders prostrated themselves before Him in worship. Each of them was carrying a harp and a vial of fragrant perfume, which I knew represented the prayers of believers.

⁹Then the believers sang a new song that went like this: "You have the right and the authority to take the scroll, to break the seals, and to read it. You were killed in order to redeem us who were rescued from every nation, language, and family. ¹⁰You made us capable of being kings and priests for God and giving us authority to reign over the earth." ¹¹I kept on watching and listening. Presently, I began to hear angel voices, a vast host, joining the living creatures, the elders, and the saints. Then the number of angels was given to me: ten thousand times ten thousand plus thousands of thousands. ¹²Their song joined the song of the redeemed ones and contained these words: "This Lamb deserves to be given power, wealth, wisdom, strength, honor, glory, and blessing." ¹³Then every created being in the universe joined in the song, repeating this refrain: "Praises, honor, glory, and power belong to the One on the throne and to the Lamb forever, for eternity." ¹⁴At the conclusion of the song, the four living creatures responded with a loud "Amen" while the twenty-four elders prostrated themselves in worship before the One who is eternal.

Chapter 6

¹Now back to that scroll with the seven seals. The Lamb opened one of the seals, and I heard thunder, then I heard one of those living creatures speaking to me: ²"Come and see something." So I went and right before me was a white horse with a rider in the saddle, armed with a bow. He was apparently a king, for there was a crown on his head, and he charged straight ahead, conquering as he went.

³Then the Lamb opened the second seal, and the second living creature spoke:

"Come and see something." ⁴This time there was a red horse and its rider. This man had the power to abolish peace in the world and incite people to kill each other. He himself was armed with an enormous sword.

⁵Then the third seal was opened by the Lamb, and the third living creature said, "Come and see." So of course I went and before me was a black horse with a rider in the saddle. This rider held in his hand a pair of balances. ⁶Now a voice seemed to be coming from among the four living creatures. The words were mysterious: "A measure of wheat for one day's wages, three measures of barley for a day's wages, and be sure not to damage the oil and the wine."

⁷When the fourth seal was opened, the fourth living creature said, "Come and see something." ⁸So I went and looked. There before me was a gray horse. The rider on this horse was named "death." The grave followed him everywhere he went. He had the power to kill one fourth of the earth's inhabitants with the sword, with starvation, with a fatal illness, or by predatory animals.

⁹Then the fifth seal was opened and under the altar I saw people who had been martyred for their faith. ¹⁰They were appealing their cases to God. "Oh Lord, how long will it be before You avenge our blood on those who live on the earth?" ¹¹As I watched, white robes were put on them, but they were told that they must rest yet a little longer until their colleagues and brothers should suffer the same fate.

¹²When the sixth seal was opened, there was an earthquake of monumental proportions, the sun turned black as midnight, and the moon became blood-red.

[13]And there was a shower of meteors that reminded me of a fig tree that was being shaken by a hurricane and its unripe figs were being blown off in every direction. [14]Then there was a scene in which the sky above seemed to roll away as a scroll is rolled, the islands were all being moved from their places, and the mountains were moved away. [15]Then the kings of the world, the famous, the powerful, the wealthy, the military leaders, the industrialists, the slaves, and the slave owners were seen trying to hide themselves in the mountains, the caves, and among the rocks. [16] They said, "Fall on us so that we will be hidden from the one on the throne and from the wrath of the Lamb, [17]for this is the day of His anger and who will be able to endure?"

Chapter 7

[1]After this scene faded, another was presented in which there were four angels standing at four corners, preventing the wind from blowing over the land, over the sea, or on any tree. [2]Then coming up over the eastern horizon was another angel who carried God's seal. He called out loudly to the four angels who had authority over the wind with this instruction: [3]"Do not let the wind harm the earth, the sea, or the trees until we have sealed the servants of our God in their foreheads." [4]Then a significant number was heard, indicating the number of those who should be sealed. The total was one hundred forty-four thousand from the tribes of Israel. [5]From the tribe of Judah were sealed twelve thousand, from the tribe of Reuben there were twelve thousand, from the tribe of Gad there were twelve thousand, [6] from the tribe of Asher there were twelve thousand, from the tribe of Naphtali were twelve thousand,

from the tribe of Manasseh were twelve thousand, [7]from the tribe of Simeon were twelve thousand, from the tribe of Levi were twelve thousand, from the tribe of Issachar were twelve thousand, [8]from the tribe of Zebulon were twelve thousand, from the tribe of Joseph were twelve thousand, and from the tribe of Benjamin were twelve thousand.

[9]Then I looked beyond the children of Israel and saw a mighty multitude of people that was not counted from every nation on earth, every family, every tribe, and every language. They were standing before God's throne clothed in white and holding palm branches of victory. [10]They were singing at the top of their voices, "Salvation is God's gift; He is on the throne, and the Lamb has saved us." [11]Then the angels surrounded the throne, the elders, and the four living creatures and prostrated themselves in adoration before God while they sang this song. [12]"Amen: All praise, all glory, all wisdom, all thanks, all honor, all strength, and all capabilities we owe to God; they are His forever."

[13]One of the elders asked me, "Do you know who these white-robed ones are? Do you know where they are from?"

[14]"Sorry, I don't," I replied. "But I am sure that you know, sir."

"Indeed I do," he responded. "And I will tell you about them. These are people who have been through severe trials, people who have washed their robes, thoroughly whitening them, in the blood of the Lamb. [15]Having been through so much, they are given the privilege of being before God's throne, the privilege of serving as honored helpers in His temple day and night. [16]Never will they be permitted to starve; never will the devil be permitted to torture them again with thirst, nor with fire, [17]for the Lamb who shares the throne of the universe will supply their food and will lead them to beautiful fountains and more; their tears will all be wiped away by God Himself."

Chapter 8

[1]Finally He opened the seventh seal, and heaven became silent for about half an hour. [2]Standing before God were seven angels who were given seven trumpets. [3]Then another angel came carrying a golden censor to the altar of incense. A good supply of incense was given him for burning at the altar while the prayers of the saints were coming up to God. [4]Then I noticed smoke coming up from the censor in the angel's hand while the saints were praying. [5]When the incense was completely burned, the angel threw the censor down, following which I heard voices, then thunder and lightning, then an earthquake.

[6]At this point the angels began to prepare to play their trumpets. [7]The first one blew his trumpet, and immediately hail began to fall, then fire followed, then bloodshed, covering the surface of the earth. One third of the trees were burned and all of the green grass. [8]When the second trumpet sounded, I saw what appeared to be a burning mountain falling into the ocean. This turned a third of the ocean into blood. [9]And a third of all sea life died and a third of all ships were lost. [10]Then the third angel blew his trumpet and a large star plummeted to earth, blazing as it fell. It seemed to land in the rivers and springs, damaging a third of them. [11]The water was made bitter by this star that was called "wormwood." Many human beings died because of the bitter water. [12]The fourth angel then blew his trumpet, resulting in dimming the sunlight, the moonlight, and the starlight for about eight hours.

[13]Before the last three trumpets were blown, I saw an angel flying through the sky proclaiming, "Three fearful woes are coming on the earth and its inhabitants because of the next three trumpets."

Chapter 9

[1]Just then the fifth angel sounded his trumpet, and I saw a star that had fallen to earth. He had the key to the bottomless pit [2]and proceeded to unlock it, releasing smoke like a furnace. The smoke was dense enough to obscure the light from the sun. [3]This smoke seemed to be producing locusts that swarmed over the earth and had the sting of a scorpion. [4]They were under strict orders to spare the grass, the trees, and every other green plant. However, they were allowed to hurt the people who did not have God's seal on their foreheads. [5]They were not permitted to kill them, but only to hurt them by the sting, and the pain was to last for five months, typical of a scorpion sting. [6]Conditions at that time will be very bad, so bad in fact that many will choose death but will not die.

[7]The locusts resembled horses ready for battle, with gold crowns on their heads and faces like human faces. [8]They had long flowing hair like women; they had huge sharp teeth like lion's teeth. [9]They had breastplates strong as iron. Their wings made a roar like that of chariots and horses charging into battle. [10]They had tails, not like locust tails but like scorpion tails, armed with stingers with which they could torment human beings for five months. [11]The king of the locusts was the angel who

dictated the policies of the bottomless pit. His name in Hebrew is Abaddon and in Greek, Apollyon. [12]So much for the first woe, but two more are to follow.

[13]The sixth angel then blew his trumpet, and I heard a voice from the four horns of the golden altar [14]telling him to release those four angels who were assigned to the great river Euphrates. [15]Those four angels were ready to kill one third of the human life on this earth during the next year plus one month plus one day plus one hour. [16]The cavalry numbered two hundred million. Yes, that is exactly what I heard. [17]The soldiers themselves had breastplates of fire, of hyacinth, and of brimstone. [18]And it was through these agents that one third of humanity died: the fire, the smoke, the brimstone, and their deadly effect. [19]The smoke and fire was coming from their mouths and tails, tails that resembled snakes. [20]But notwithstanding the fearful slaughter of one third of humanity, the remaining people refused to repent of their worship of devils or their idolizing of gold, silver, and wood—images that cannot see, hear, or walk. [21]Nor did they quit murdering their fellowmen; quit their sorcery, their sexual sins, and their thievery.

Chapter 10

[1]Next I saw a very powerful angel surrounded by a cloud as he descended to the earth. Over his head was a rainbow, his face shone like the sun itself. Even his feet were brilliant, like columns of flame. [2]In his hand was a little book that he had just opened. He was standing on the earth with his right foot on the sea and his left foot on the land. [3]He began shouting loudly, like the roaring of a lion. As if in answer to his shout, seven thunders began talking.

[4]I was sitting there, pen in hand, ready to write down what the thunders were saying when out of heaven I heard these words of instructions: "Do NOT write down what the thunders are saying."

[5]Naturally I obeyed, but then the angel who was standing on the land and sea raised his right arm toward heaven in a solemn vow in the name of the Eternal One [6]who created heaven and everything there, earth and everything here, and the sea with everything in it, that time was running out. The fulfillment of the last time prophecy had arrived. [7]The seventh angel began his trumpet blast, and during the first part of his performance God's message, a mystery to men, will be completed as predicted by his prophets. [8]At this the angel whose voice I had heard from heaven instructed me, "Go and take the little book from the hand of the angel standing on earth and sea, the book that he opened up."

[9]So I went to the angel and requested the book in his hand. "OK," he said. "Take it and eat it up. It will taste sweet in your mouth but will give you a sour stomach." [10]I did just that, and sure enough, it was sweet as honey but after swallowing it I developed a sour stomach. [11]Then he said, "You must give God's message again to kings, nations, tribes, and languages.

Chapter 11

[1]The angel then handed me a measuring rod with these instructions: "Take this rod and measure the temple of God, the altar, and the worshippers. [2]Don't spend time measuring the court because it will be occupied by the Gentiles who will enter and eventually occupy the whole city for the next forty-two months. [3]However, I will have two witnesses who will have the

gift of prophecy for all that time, one thousand two hundred sixty days in all, disguised and camouflaged in sackcloth for their own safety."

⁴These witnesses will be identified with the two olive trees that furnish oil for the candlesticks that light up the people in God's presence. ⁵They shall be protected from wicked men who would harm them, and if such an attempt is made the two witnesses will destroy them with fire blowing out of their mouths. ⁶They have incredible capabilities, such as to bring drought on the earth while they are prophesying, power to change water to blood, and to bring plagues on the earth when they choose. ⁷They will complete their testimony in spite of hardships, but then the beast from the bottomless pit will confront them, fight against them, and kill them. ⁸Their dead bodies shall lie in the street of the large city that is known as spiritual Sodom and Egypt where our Lord was crucified. ⁹People of many languages, races, and nations will see their dead bodies lying there for three and a half days. No one will be permitted to bury them. ¹⁰But poor wicked human beings will take joy over their fate, actually celebrating with a gift-giving party; all because these witnesses made them uncomfortable by the messages they carried.

¹¹When three and a half days passed I saw that God's Spirit entered into these lifeless bodies. They leaped to their feet, astonishing the onlookers. ¹²Then a voice from heaven was heard, "Come up here," and they ascended in a cloud while their enemies watched. ¹³As this took place a tremendous earthquake occurred, destroying one tenth of the city and killing seven thousand people. Everyone else was terribly frightened and recognized that the God of heaven was trying to help them.

¹⁴Now for the third woe that will come shortly. ¹⁵The seventh angel blasted his trumpet, and there were loud proclamations in heaven: "All earthly kingdoms have become God's and belong to his anointed One, and He will be king forever, even forever and ever. ¹⁶Then the twenty-four elders seated before God fell to their knees, faces toward the ground in worship as they prayed: ¹⁷"We are thankful, Almighty God, You who have always been, are now, and who will always be, for You have once again assumed Your rightful place and from now on will rule forever." ¹⁸Then angry nations came into view while the elders continued: "Your wrath can now be seen, Your work in judging the dead has begun, Your justice in rewarding the prophets, the saints and all who reverence Your name, and in destroying those who were destroying the earth, is now plainly seen." ¹⁹The heavenly temple opened to view and in it could be seen the ark of the covenant while around the temple a fearful storm raged, with lightning, thunder, and voices crying out.

Chapter 12

¹Next I witnessed a wonderful scene in heaven. Here was a woman clothed with the sun. Her footstool is the moon, and her crown is embellished with twelve stars. ²She is pregnant and about to give birth. She goes into labor. ³But then a fearful scene comes to view. Here comes a huge red dragon with seven heads, ten horns, and a crown for each head. ⁴His tail whipped around and captured one third of heaven's stars. Then the dragon and his captured prey were expelled from heaven and landed on planet earth. This wicked

beast came over to where the woman was about to deliver her child and waited for the moment of delivery so that he could seize her child and devour it. ⁵She delivered a little boy, who was destined to rule all the nations with an iron rod of authority, so her baby was snatched from the grasp of the dragon and carried safely to God's throne. ⁶The woman? She escaped and ran off into the wilderness to a shelter that God had prepared for her there. Here she was sustained, protected, and fed for one thousand two hundred sixty days.

⁷Here I will describe the war that took place in heaven. It was Michael and His loyal angels fighting against the dragon and his angels. ⁸The war was decisive. The dragon and his angels were defeated and banished from heaven. God permitted them to stay for a time on this earth. ⁹This dragon is the one who has deceived the whole earth and is also known as the devil and Satan. ¹⁰In heaven a victory celebration was held and I heard a loud shout: "Salvation is made certain, strength is available. God's kingdom is secure. His Anointed One has gained the victory. Now this enemy who was constantly accusing our brothers before God has been defeated. No longer will he have any influence in heaven. ¹¹The brothers on earth defeated him through the strength found in the blood of God's Lamb, and by their courageous testimony, willing to face death if necessary. ¹²Now you who live in heaven be happy indeed, and you who are loyal to God through the whole universe, rejoice! But for you on earth, things will be difficult because of the devil who is there on your planet. He is raging with anger, for he knows that his days are numbered and that his life is destined to be terminated."

¹³Back to the story. When the dragon was cast out of heaven and found himself on this planet, he determined to torment the woman who had given birth to the baby boy who had been snatched up to heaven out of the reach of the dragon. ¹⁴To help her, God gave her powerful wings so that she could escape from the dragon, and like an eagle she flew away into the wilderness where she was sustained for three and a half years. ¹⁵And even though the serpent was able to send a flood of water from his mouth to try to drown her, ¹⁶God intervened and opened up a large crevice in the earth that swallowed the flood. ¹⁷But now the dragon is frustrated and furiously angry at the woman who has been saved from all his plots, so he has turned his attention to her descendants who are still on planet earth, declaring war on them and vowing vengeance, for they are obeying God's commandments and possess the testimony of Jesus.

Chapter 13

¹What a scene came before me next! I was standing on the beach when right there in front of me was a strange, weird animal of some kind crawling up out of the ocean. It had seven heads and ten horns, each horn wore a crown. Every head was named, and every name was blasphemous. ²This creature was spotted like a leopard, had feet that resembled the feet of bears, and had a mouth that was about like a lion's mouth. He was supported, sponsored, and authorized by the great dragon. ³I was watching when one of his heads was dealt what was obviously a mortal blow, but surprisingly, the injury healed. The whole world knew about it and expressed awe and admiration.

⁴They began to actually worship the dragon who had given that miracle of

healing and the beast himself, saying these words, "Who is able to compare with this creature, and who could defeat him in war?" ⁵Then it was given a mouth that was able to speak human language. It began to speak like a person and began to speak blasphemy. Its power continued for forty-two months. ⁶Its mouth blasphemed God, His name, His temple, and the heavenly beings. ⁷He was allowed to fight against God's saints and to kill them, and his dominance spread to every nation, tribe, and language. ⁸Finally every person on the earth worshipped him except for those whose names were in the Lamb's book of life. This was the Lamb whose murder was predicted before the world was founded. ⁹If you can hear, take heed.

¹⁰A person who kidnaps and imprisons another will himself be captured and imprisoned. One who kills with the sword shall die by the sword. Now let me show you the patience of the saints. ¹¹Just then another creature appeared. He came up out of the earth like a plant. It was docile like a lamb and apparently harmless, it had two horns like a lamb, but eventually it resembled the dragon in its proclamations. ¹²It began to resemble that first beast, persuading all on the earth to worship and admire the first beast whose wound had been healed. ¹³It was a marvelous creature, able to do miracles such as to bring fire down from the sky in plain sight of everyone. ¹⁴His influence was dreadfully deceptive through those miracles, and he began to order earth's inhabitants around, commanding them to make an image resembling the first beast, the one whose wound had healed.

¹⁵Once this image had been produced this beast had the ability to give it life and the ability to give it speech, and finally it had the authority to force that other beast on pain of death. ¹⁶To enforce this he assigned to everyone, rich and poor, large and small, free or slave, a mark that was located on the right hand or on the forehead. ¹⁷No one could buy or sell unless this mark was placed properly, or as an alternative, the name or the number of the beast was visible. ¹⁸Here is wise counsel: If you want to know what I am writing about, add up the number of this beast's name, a human number that comes to six hundred sixty-six.

Chapter 14

¹Another scene: I was looking at Mount Zion, and there on the summit was a Lamb. Grouped around Him was a multitude of people, one hundred forty-four thousand in all, each of whom had on his forehead the name of God the Father. ²Then a sound came from heaven resembling the roar of the surf or the crash of thunder; then soft music began as harpists played. ³These one hundred forty-four thousand were then heard singing a new song before the throne of God, before the four living creatures and the elders. No others could have learned that song, only those who had been redeemed from the earth. ⁴They are people who have maintained their purity, having refused to commit sexual sins. They follow the Lamb wherever He goes. They have been purchased and set free, the first of such ones to have been redeemed by the Lamb and God the Father. ⁵There was absolutely no deception in them; they are without fault.

⁶The next scene: I watched as another angel flew through the sky, proclaiming the everlasting gospel to everyone

on the earth. [7]He was preaching loudly and announced: "Everyone, reverence and obey God, recognize Him and worship Him because the judgment hour has arrived. Worship Him for He is the creator of the entire universe, the earth, the seas, and the springs of water." [8]After that angel preached, another angel joined him with this message: "Babylon has completely fallen and cannot be trusted. It has tried to coerce all the nations to drink her wine, which is her beverage, as she commits fornication."

[9]Then a third angel began to proclaim his message: "Everyone who worships that seven-headed, ten-horned beast, or even his image, and accepts his mark on the forehead or on the right hand [10]shall drink the wine of God's anger, undiluted. He shall be tormented with fire and brimstone, and observed by the Lamb and the holy angels as witnesses. [11]The smoke from this fire goes up and up forever; they will never be rescued from their plight. That is the fate of those who worship that beast and his image and receive the mark of his name."

[12]And now let me show you God's saints. Here they are. They have unlimited endurance, and they continue to keep God's commandments and maintain their faith in Jesus. [13]A voice was heard! It came from heaven to me and gave me this instruction: "Write this: The ones who die while they have faith in the Lord are truly blessed. The Holy Spirit assures us that they will be able to rest from all their trials and that their good deeds will be remembered."

[14]Just then I witnessed a pure white cloud with a person seated on it resembling Jesus. He wore a golden crown and carried a sharp sickle in His hand. [15]Then came a command from an angel in God's temple to the one seated on the cloud. "It is time to reap. Earth's harvest is ripe so begin at once." [16]The one on the cloud began wielding His sickle and the harvest was quickly accomplished. [17]Then another angel left God's temple. He too was carrying a sharp sickle. [18]His superior emerged from the altar with full authority over fire and issued orders to the one with the sickle: "It is now time to begin gathering the clusters of grapes, so proceed." [19]The sickle was wielded and the task was soon completed. The grapes were being dumped into the winepress of God's wrath. [20]The winepress was located outside the city and went into action with blood pouring out of it deep enough to reach up to a horse's bridle and flowing for two hundred miles.

Chapter 15

[1]Let me tell you of another scene. It was in heaven, and here were seven angels, each of which had control of a plague. These seven plagues are the last ones that this world will experience, and they will be permitted by God as He abandons this world to its rebellious fate. [2]But then I saw another scene from heaven; a huge sea with a glassy appearance, brilliant with light like fire. The people who are victorious over the wicked beast, his image, his mark, and his number are standing on this glassy sea playing harps given to them by God Himself. [3]They are singing with harp accompaniment the song of Moses, a song of deliverance.

Here are some of the words: "How great Thou art, how marvelous are all Your doings, Lord God Almighty. You are perfectly just, perfectly true in everything You do, O King of saints. ⁴Who in the entire universe should not loyally reverence You? Who should not exalt Your name? For only You are completely holy. Every nation shall come and bow down in worship, for all of Your decisions have proven to be totally just and fair."

⁵Then I watched as the heavenly temple was opened. ⁶From it came seven angels, the angels with the seven last plagues. Each was clothed in pure white linen and had a gold sash around the waist. ⁷As they emerged, one of the four living creatures handed each angel a vial containing the wrath of God. ⁸The temple was now filled with smoke because of God's glory and power. So dense was the smoke that no one could enter the temple until the seven plagues were over.

Chapter 16

¹From the temple came a loud, author-itative command to those seven angels dressed in white. "Go to the earth now and empty the vials of God's wrath upon the earth." ²The first angel went and emptied his vial, resulting in dreadful skin lesions on the ones who had the mark of the beast and who worshipped the image of the beast. ³The second angel emptied his vial into the ocean, which turned red, thick, and foul like blood from a corpse. Every living creature died in that poisonous liq-uid. ⁴The third angel emptied his vial into the rivers and springs, and they turned into bloodlike liquid. ⁵The angel who was in charge of the water was heard speaking to God: "You, Lord, have done right. You always have done right and always will. Your decision regarding the water was right, ⁶because they have shed the blood of Your saints and prophets. You did right in

making them drink blood. They deserved nothing better." ⁷Then another voice from the altar was heard saying essentially the same thing, "Omnipotent God, Your deci-sions are correct, just, and appropriate."

⁸Then the fourth angel emptied his vial on the sun, and a burst of heat scorched the earth and its inhabitants. ⁹Even this heat wave did not result in repentance; instead, they cursed the very name of God, the God with authority over all the plagues. ¹⁰The fifth angel emptied his vial on the headquarters of the beast, which resulted in darkness over all the territory that he controlled. The beast and his subjects were already in pain due to the sores and were chewing their tongues in anguish. ¹¹This added plague of darkness only brought on more curses on God who had treated them this way. But still there was no repentance for their sinful lives.

¹²The sixth angel emptied his vial on the great river Euphrates, drying it up completely. This opened the way for the kings from the East. ¹³Then I watched the beast, the dragon, and the false prophet while wicked spirits resembling frogs came out of their mouths. ¹⁴These were demonic spirits who went to the earthly rulers and to all others who would listen. They had the ability to perform miracles and thus were able to persuade their victims to enter the battle against God. ¹⁵"Remember, I am to return as unexpectedly as a thief comes. Happy are those who stay alert, clothed, and ready when I appear." ¹⁶They mustered their forces together at a place called Armageddon.

¹⁷Then the seventh angel emptied his vial into the atmosphere, at which time I heard a mighty voice coming from heav-en's temple announcing, "It is done."

[18]Lightning and thunder followed, then an earthquake the likes of which the earth had never seen. [19]The city was split into three parts as major cities of the earth fell in ruins while Babylon was brought to account before God who passed sentence on it in consequence of its history through the years. [20]Islands seemed to run away out of sight and mountains disappeared, [21]and a humungous hailstorm hit the earth with hailstones weighing about sixty-five pounds each. Men cursed God because of the hailstorm, for it was indeed a fearful thing.

Chapter 17

[1]When that scene had passed, one of the angels with a vial came to talk with me. "Come with me please, and I will show you the fate of the world's greatest prostitute, the one whose clientele was scattered over many oceans. [2]She is the one with whom the rulers of the nations have committed fornication and offered her wine to earth's people in such amounts that they are dead drunk." [3]So I consented to go. He did not just invite me. He carried me off to a desolate place and here appeared a woman sitting on a scarlet-colored beast, a creature with seven heads and ten horns and covered with blasphemous names written all over it. [4]The woman was robed in purple and scarlet and decorated with gold, precious gems, and pearls, while in her hand was a gold cup filled with fornicating wine. [5]She wore a headband with this name: "Mystery, Babylon, the great mother of prostitutes and other worldly abominations."

[6]I watched this woman in a drunken stupor. She had become inebriated by drinking the blood of many of God's saints, martyred for their faith. Needless to say I was awed by the sight of this debased woman. [7]Then the angel guide spoke, "Why are you in awe and perplexity? I shall tell you the significance of these symbols of the woman and the scarlet-colored beast with seven heads and ten horns. [8]The beast was once a great power but now is weak, and one day it will come up out of the bottomless pit and then be annihilated. Earth's inhabitants will be deeply impressed when they see this creature that was strong, then seemed to die but later revived. Yet those whose names are written in the Lamb's book of life will not be deceived. [9]Here is wisdom. The seven heads are the seven hills over which she sits as queen. [10]There are seven kings to consider. Five of these have already come and gone. One is reigning at the present. The other has not yet arrived, and when he comes he will be in power for only a short time. [11]That animal which was, but is no longer significant, he is number eight but belongs with the seven. He will be annihilated as I mentioned. [12]The ten horns represent ten kings that are yet to come but in the future will receive power for an hour with the beast. [13]These kings are all agreeing to surrender their sovereignty to the beast. [14]They will declare war against the Lamb but will be defeated because He is Lord of lords and King of kings, and those who are on His side are called, chosen, and faithful."

[15]Then he explained, "The water where the prostitute is seated represents many people, many languages, and many nations. [16]Finally the ten horns will hate the prostitute and will strip her naked and leave her without a friend. They will then cannibalize her and burn the remains. [17]They will eventually do God's will, fulfilling every

prophecy. [18]The prostitute is the great city that dominates the nations of the world."

Chapter 18

[1]My next scene was of a mighty angel coming down from heaven, so gloriously bright that the whole earth was illuminated by his approach. [2]He had a powerful message to proclaim, very similar to that of the second angel of chapter 14: "Babylon the great has fallen. It has become the dwelling place for demons, the refuge for every foul spirit, and the cage for all scavenging birds. [3]Her influence has polluted every nation on earth. They have drunk the wine of fornication with her; the merchants of the earth have become wealthy because of the popularity of her products."

[4]Then a voice was heard from heaven with this urgent appeal: "Come out of her my people; separate yourselves from her sins so that you won't be infected by her plagues. [5]Her sins have been accumulating until they reach up to heaven, and now God is calling her to account because of them. [6]This is the sentence: The punishment shall be double what she has been guilty of. And as she has filled the cup, give her two cups. [7]Oh how she has glorified self, has enjoyed the life of abundance, but now she must have an equivalent amount of pain and sorrow. Now, instead of being enthroned as a queen, free from worries, free from losses and abandonment, [8] she must endure plagues, famine, sorrow, eventually death, and then cremation. God will be just and able to carry out this sentence. [9]As for the nations who have committed fornication with her, reveling in her lustful practices, they will regret, lament, and bewail her fate as they watch the smoke of her funeral pyre. [10]From a respectful distance, they will repeat these words: 'Alas, alas, that great city Babylon, that powerful city, for her fate has been sealed, and destruction has taken place in just one hour.'

[11]"Also the businesses and corporations who have profited from her wickedness will be in trouble, for she can no longer buy their merchandise. [12]This merchandise consists of gold, silver, precious stones, pearls, fabrics of purple, scarlet, silk goods, aromatic wood, ivory, carvings of beautiful hardwoods, brass objects, ironwork, marble, [13]cinnamon, fragrant ointments, frankincense, wine, flour, oil, wheat, cattle, sheep, horses and vehicles, human beings, and even human bodies. [14]And those goals you had had have all been placed out of reach. Every desirable object has entirely disappeared, and you will never be able to find them. [15]The entrepreneurs who profited in the sale of such things will not dare to get too close to the fire but will be wailing and weeping as they cry out, [16]'Alas, alas, oh for that rich city that was always so richly clothed in purple, gold, gems, and pearls. [17]What a pity that all of this wealth has been wasted all in one hour.'

"Also the shipping companies, the captains of ships, and even the sailors backed away from her, [18]crying out as they watched the funeral pyre, 'What other city could ever compare to this one?' [19]Then they scattered dust on their heads as they wept and wailed out these words, 'Alas, alas, the great city that contributed so much to the shipping industry, for within one hour, everything is gone.' [20]Now, heaven, holy apostles and prophets, you should rejoice, for God has finally avenged your enemy's wrongs."

²¹Then a mighty angel picked up a huge stone, like a millstone, and hurled it into the ocean as he proclaimed, "This illustrates how Babylon shall be defeated, destroyed, and never again found. ²²Never shall harpists or other musicians, trumpeters, or other brass music ever be heard in you again, neither the sound of a millstone as it grinds away. ²³Neither shall the candles ever be lighted in you again, nor the vows of bride and groom ever be heard in you again. Yes, your dealers were considered great in the earth, having been able to deceive all nations. ²⁴It was found that in Babylon was the responsibility for the blood of prophets and saints and of all who had been killed."

Chapter 19

¹My next vision was a view of heaven where a vast number of people were singing, "Alleluia, praise God. Salvation, glory, honor, and power are His and originate with Him. ²His decisions are just and correct in every case. For example, He correctly decided the case of the great prostitute who corrupted the earth with her sexual immorality, avenging the blood of His saints, blood shed by her." ³Again the shout arose, "Alleluia," as the smoke kept rising until the destruction of the prostitute was complete. ⁴When that was over the twenty-four elders and the four living creatures bowed down before God on His throne in worship, shouting, "Alleluia."

⁵Then a voice came from the throne, "Praise our God, all you His servants and everyone who fears Him, both great and small." ⁶Then in unison came this shout from the vast multitude, reminding one of the roar of water and thunder combined, "Alleluia, for God the omnipotent is King.

⁷Let us all rejoice with joy and gladness and honor our God; the time for the wedding of the Lamb has arrived, and His wife has completed her preparation. ⁸She has been provided with a pure white wedding gown, representing the righteousness of God's saints."

⁹I was then commanded to write these words: "Blessed are those who have been invited as guests to the marriage supper of the Lamb. God Himself cannot lie or deceive." ¹⁰At this I fell on my knees at his feet in worship, but he protested, saying, "No, do not worship me. I am only a fellow servant and a brother who is telling the testimony of Jesus. Worship God alone, and by the way, the testimony of Jesus is the spirit of prophecy."

¹¹Then heaven opened and I saw a white horse with a rider named Faithful and True. He is the judge, and He wages war against all evil in a perfectly right manner. ¹²His eyes resembled a flame of fire, His head was crowned with many crowns, and he had a special name, unknown to humanity but known only by Him. ¹³His robe had been dipped in blood, and one of His names is The Word of God. ¹⁴Heaven's armies followed Him, all of them on white horses and all wearing pure, white linen. ¹⁵Out of His mouth came a sharp sword with which He could defeat all earthly nations. He shall dominate them completely with His iron rod, and He will tread God's winepress of wrath. ¹⁶On His royal robe and on His thigh is written, "King of kings and Lord of lords."

¹⁷Then I saw an angel standing in the sunlight who announced, "Attention all you flying birds, come and surround the table of the great God. ¹⁸He will let you feast on the flesh of kings, captains, great

men, horses, riders, and all people, free or slave, small or great." [19]Then appeared before me the beast and earthly kings and their armies, all ready for war against the One on the white horse and against His army. [20]The battle was won by the One on the white horse. His army captured the beast and the false prophet who had deceived through miracles the ones who had worshipped the beast and the false prophet. The beast and the false prophet were then thrown alive into the lake of fire. [21]The others were killed by the sword of the victor, that sword which came out of His mouth; so the birds began feasting on the flesh.

Chapter 20

[1]And now another scene. I saw another angel descending to the earth. He held a key to the abyss in one hand and in the other a huge chain. [2]With the chain he securely shackled the old dragon, also known as the serpent, the devil and Satan. Here the criminal was to stay chained for the next one thousand years. [3]Within this abyss, there was no possibility of deceiving the nations until the millennium had passed. The plan was to once again have access to them for a short time following the one thousand years. [4]During the millennium, I saw thrones and people sitting on them, passing judgment. Here were those who had been beheaded because of their belief in Jesus. Here were those whose faith in God's word was consistent and immovable. They had refused to worship the beast or his image, nor did they receive the mark of the beast on their foreheads or on their hands. They had been restored to life and will reign with Christ for the duration of the millennium.

[5]I have described the first resurrection and its result; now for the second resurrection, that of the wicked dead. It will occur after the one thousand years have passed. [6]Those who received life at the first resurrection are indeed blessed. They are also holy. They will be spared the fate of the second death but will be acting as God's priests and will share kingship with Christ during the millennium. [7]When the millennium is finally ended, Satan will be unchained and released from his prison. [8]He will at once begin again his work of deception, attempting to deceive even Gog and Magog, and then drawing them together into a vast army whose number is like the sand of the seashore. [9]He leads them from everywhere on earth and surrounds the camp of the saints and the Holy City, expecting to capture it quickly. Just at that time their fate is sealed, for a fireball falls from heaven and instantly devours the entire army.

[10]The devil who deceived them met his fate in that lake of fire, where also are the beast and the false prophet. This marks the end forever of God's enemies. [11]Then a huge white throne came into view on which was seated the Creator. Before His majesty, heaven and earth seemed to be reduced to nothingness, totally insignificant. [12]Next I witnessed the resurrection of all who have ever lived on earth. All must stand before God and face the great judgment day. The books were opened, last of all the book of life. All were judged by what was recorded in the books, the account of their deeds. [13]Even those who had drowned in the ocean were brought to life along with those in graves and crypts. They were all judged by the record of their deeds. [14]Then death and the grave were ended forever in

the lake of fire. This is the second death. [15]All whose names were not in the book of life perished in the lake of fire.

Chapter 21

[1]Then in vision I saw a new heaven and a new earth. The first heaven and the first earth had vanished, and there were no great oceans. [2]Next I, John, saw the Holy City coming down to earth from heaven, all prepared as a bride for her wedding. [3]Then the announcement from heaven came in thunderous tones, "Look, God's temple is now with humanity. They will be his people from now on and God Himself will be with them and be their God. [4]Furthermore, God will wipe away the tears from every eye, and there will be no more death, sorrow, crying, or pain. Those things are forever in the past."

[5]Then the One on heaven's throne made this pronouncement, "Look, I am creating everything new, write it down for these are true words and can be trusted." [6]Then He said, "This is it. I am Alpha and Omega, the Beginning and the End. I will give water of life to everyone who is thirsty, and there will be no more thirst. [7]Whoever overcomes will inherit the infinite blessings I have described. I will be his God and he shall be My son. [8]But those who are afraid to trust Me and those who are rebellious, who are murderers, who promote prostitution, who are sorcerers, idolaters, and who are liars will perish in the lake of fire, which is the second death."

[9]Then one of the angels who brought the seven final plagues came and talked with me, inviting me to come and see the Lamb's new bride. [10]He picked me up and carried me to the summit of a high mountain and showed me the Holy City, the New Jerusalem, coming slowly down from the sky to the earth. [11]It had the splendor of God in it, brilliant like polished stones such as jasper and clear as crystal. [12]Around the city was a very high wall with twelve gates, each one of which had an angel greeter and the name of one of the twelve tribes of Israel. [13]On the east wall were three gates, on the north wall were three gates, on the south wall were three gates, and on the west wall were three gates.

[14]The wall had twelve foundations, each one with the name of one of Christ's apostles. [15]The one who was showing me the city had a gold measuring rod with which he measured the city, the wall, and the foundations. [16]The city is a perfect square, measuring 1,378.4 miles (the original is 12,000 "stadia." The Roman stadia of John's day was 606.5 feet, which would be 1,378.4 miles) in perimeter. It is also perfectly proportioned, measuring 344.6 miles in height. (The original contains the idea of a perfect cube with equal dimensions for length, width, and height.)

[17]The wall is two hundred sixteen feet in thickness [18]and is of jasper. The remainder of the city is pure gold but gives the appearance of clear glass. [19]The foundations are adorned with different gemstones, the first being jasper, the second sapphire, the third quartz, the fourth emerald, the fifth sardonyx, [20]the sixth sardius, the seventh chrysolite, the eighth beryl, the ninth topaz, the tenth a green quartz, the eleventh jacinth, and the twelfth a blue quartz. [21]The gates are pearl, each one being one solid massive pearl. The streets are paved with pure gold resembling clear glass.

[22]In the city I was surprised to find no temple for the Almighty God and the Lamb are its temple. [23]And there is no need

of light from the sun or the moon because the glory of God and the Lamb floods the city with light. [24]All the saved from every country on earth have free access to the city and its light, and the kings from earth are able to bring their glory into it. [25]The gates of pearl will never be closed, for there will be no night there. [26]The splendor of all nations shall be brought into the city. [27]Into that city there will never come anyone who defiles, who practices abominations, or who is deceptive. Its inhabitants are those whose names are in the Lamb's book of life.

Chapter 22

[1]Next he showed me a pure, clear, sparkling river, the water of life. It was springing from the throne of God and the Lamb. [2]Right in the middle of the main street on each side of the river stood the tree of life. It is a remarkable tree, for it produces a different fruit every month; even the leaves are of value in helping the differing nationalities and cultures to understand each other better. [3]Never again will a curse be pronounced on the inhabitants. Instead the dwellers there will serve the Almighty God and the Lamb whose throne is in the city. [4]They shall be able to look directly at God's face, and His name will be built into their very being. [5]In that city no darkness will ever come. With no artificial lights and without the light from the sun, it will never darken there for the presence of God will be more than enough light for it. His saved ones will live like kings forever.

[6]My informing angel went on: "Everything I have told you is true. You can depend on it." The God of the true prophets has dispatched His angel to tell His people what will be taking place, beginning very soon. [7]"Yes, I am returning, and My return will be sudden. Oh how blessed and happy are those who accept, believe, and act on the words of this prophecy."

[8]I, John, repeat what I said before: I saw all these things and heard them all. When I saw the final scene, I fell in worship at the feet of the angel who had guided me. [9]But he gently protested: "Please do not worship me, for I am only a fellow created being, just as are the prophets and the ones who obey and keep the instruction in this book. Worship is appropriate of course but only as directed at our Creator. [10]Another thing, do not let the book be closed up, sealed, and unknown for the time of fulfillment is about to begin. [11]The person who is unjust shall make his decision and stay unjust, the filthy person will remain so; the righteous person will forever be righteous, and the holy person will always be holy."

[12]"Look, I will come suddenly, and when I come I will bring rewards with Me, rewards appropriate to the deeds of every person. [13]Once again I must tell you that I am Alpha and Omega, the Beginning and the End, the First and the Last."

[14]Oh how happy are those who keep God's commandments, for they are entitled to eat the fruit from the tree of life, and to enter the pearly gates into the city of God. [15]Outside the city are promiscuous ones, dealers in prostitution, murderers, idolaters, and all who practice lying and deceit. [16]"I, Jesus, have dispatched My angel to inform you in the churches about these important matters. I am the Root, the stock of David, as well as the descendant of David; I am the Bright and Morning Star."

[17]The Holy Spirit and the bride of the Lamb invite you to come. And everyone who receives the invitation should invite

others. Let every thirsting person come, for the water of life is free and abundant.

[18]Now for a warning: Whoever hears the words of this book of prophecy and adds anything to it will be affected by the plagues I've written about. [19]Furthermore, whoever hears the words of this prophecy and deletes any of it shall be denied access to the Holy City. God will erase his name from the book of life, and he shall never enjoy the blessings promised in this book.

[20]The one who certifies to the authenticity of this book says: "Truly I will come suddenly." Amen. Please, Lord Jesus, come soon. [21]Now may the grace of our Lord Jesus Christ be with you all. Amen.

We invite you to view the complete
selection of titles we publish at:

www.TEACHServices.com

Scan with your mobile
device to go directly
to our website.

Please write or email us your praises, reactions, or
thoughts about this or any other book we publish at:

P.O. Box 954
Ringgold, GA 30736

info@TEACHServices.com

TEACH Services, Inc., titles may be purchased in bulk for
educational, business, fund-raising, or sales promotional use.
For information, please e-mail:

BulkSales@TEACHServices.com

Finally, if you are interested in seeing
your own book in print, please contact us at

publishing@TEACHServices.com

We would be happy to review your manuscript for free.